THE NEW
AMERICAN
COMMENTARY

An Exegetical and Theological
Exposition of Holy Scripture

THE NEW
AMERICAN
COMMENTARY

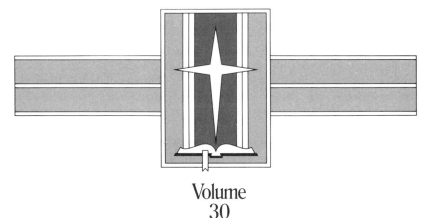

Volume
30

GALATIANS

Timothy George

BROADMAN
& HOLMAN
PUBLISHERS

© Copyright 1994 • Broadman & Holman Publishers
All rights reserved
ISBN: 978-08054-0130-1
Dewey Decimal Classification: 227.4
Subject Heading: Bible. N.T. Galatians
Library of Congress Catalog Number: 94-12544
Printed in the United States of America
15 14 13 12 11 10 09 08   15 14 13 12 11 10 9 8 7

Library of Congress Cataloging-in-Publication Data

George, Timothy.
   Galatians / Timothy George.
      p.   cm. — (The New American commentary ; v. 30)
   Includes indexes.
   ISBN 0-8054-0130-X
   1. Bible. N.T. Galatians—Commentaries.   I. Bible. N.T.
Galatians. English. New International. 1994. II. Title.
III. Series.
BS2685.3.G46   1994
227' .4077—dc20

For
Charles T. Carter,
my beloved pastor and faithful friend,
on the forty-sixth anniversary of his divine
calling to preach the Word of God, and the
twenty-third anniversary of his pastoral
ministry at Shades Mountain Baptist Church,
Birmingham, Alabama

Editors' Preface

God's Word does not change. God's world, however, changes in every generation. These changes, in addition to new findings by scholars and a new variety of challenges to the gospel message, call for the church in each generation to interpret and apply God's Word for God's people. Thus, THE NEW AMERICAN COMMENTARY is introduced to bridge the twentieth and twenty-first centuries. This new series has been designed primarily to enable pastors, teachers, and students to read the Bible with clarity and proclaim it with power.

In one sense THE NEW AMERICAN COMMENTARY is not new, for it represents the continuation of a heritage rich in biblical and theological exposition. The title of this forty-volume set points to the continuity of this series with an important commentary project published at the end of the nineteenth century called AN AMERICAN COMMENTARY, edited by Alvah Hovey. The older series included, among other significant contributions, the outstanding volume on Matthew by John A. Broadus, from whom the publisher of the new series, Broadman Press, partly derives its name. The former series was authored and edited by scholars committed to the infallibility of Scripture, making it a solid foundation for the present project. In line with this heritage, all NAC authors affirm the divine inspiration, inerrancy, complete truthfulness, and full authority of the Bible. The perspective of the NAC is unapologetically confessional and rooted in the evangelical tradition.

Since a commentary is a fundamental tool for the expositor or teacher who seeks to interpret and apply Scripture in the church or classroom, the NAC focuses on communicating the theological structure and content of each biblical book. The writers seek to illuminate both the historical meaning and contemporary significance of Holy Scripture.

In its attempt to make a unique contribution to the Christian community, the NAC focuses on two concerns. First, the commentary emphasizes how each section of a book fits together so that the reader becomes aware of the theological unity of each book and of Scripture as a whole. The writers, however, remain aware of the Bible's inherently rich variety. Second, the NAC is produced with the conviction that the Bible primarily belongs to the church. We believe that scholarship and the academy provide an indispensable foundation for biblical understanding and the service of Christ, but the editors and authors of this series have attempted to communicate the findings of their research in a manner that will build up the whole body of Christ. Thus, the commentary concentrates on theological exegesis while providing practical, applicable exposition.

THE NEW AMERICAN COMMENTARY's theological focus enables the reader to see the parts as well as the whole of Scripture. The biblical books vary in content, context, literary type, and style. In addition to this rich variety, the editors and authors recognize that the doctrinal emphasis and use of the biblical books differs in various places, contexts, and cultures among God's people. These factors, as well as other concerns, have led the editors to give freedom to the writers to wrestle with the issues raised by the scholarly community surrounding each book and to determine the appropriate shape and length of the introductory materials. Moreover, each writer has developed the structure of the commentary in a way best suited for expounding the basic structure and the meaning of the biblical books for our day. Generally, discussions relating to contemporary scholarship and technical points of grammar and syntax appear in the footnotes and not in the text of the commentary. This format allows pastors and interested laypersons, scholars and teachers, and serious college and seminary students to profit from the commentary at various levels. This approach has been employed because we believe that all Christians have the privilege and responsibility to read and seek to understand the Bible for themselves.

Consistent with the desire to produce a readable, up-to-date commentary, the editors selected the *New International Version* as the standard translation for the commentary series. The selection was made primarily because of the NIV's faithfulness to the original languages and its beautiful and readable style. The authors, however, have been given the liberty to differ at places from the NIV as they develop their own translations from the Greek and Hebrew texts.

The NAC reflects the vision and leadership of those who provide oversight for Broadman Press, who in 1987 called for a new commentary series that would evidence a commitment to the inerrancy of Scripture and a faithfulness to the classic Christian tradition. While the commentary adopts an "American" name, it should be noted some writers represent countries outside the United States, giving the commentary an international perspective. The diverse group of writers includes scholars, teachers, and administrators from almost twenty different colleges and seminaries, as well as pastors, missionaries, and a layperson.

The editors and writers hope that THE NEW AMERICAN COMMEN-

TARY will be helpful and instructive for pastors and teachers, scholars and students, for men and women in the churches who study and teach God's Word in various settings. We trust that for editors, authors, and readers alike, the commentary will be used to build up the church, encourage obedience, and bring renewal to God's people. Above all, we pray that the NAC will bring glory and honor to our Lord who has graciously redeemed us and faithfully revealed himself to us in his Holy Word.

SOLI DEO GLORIA
The Editors

Author's Preface

Much of the Christianity that I know and still believe in I learned from an old-fashioned, godly grandmother who could hardly read or write but who taught me to revere and love the Holy Scriptures as the infallible Word of the living God. I remember the long summers spent at her country home in rural north Georgia. When the day's chores were done and the shadows of evening had lengthened, she would take down her large-lettered Bible and, with trembling hands and stammering lips, try to read several pages from that precious book. Although "Aunt Bessie," as everyone called my grandmother, was a real Baptist through and through—duly dunked and camp-meeting certified—she would have agreed heartily with the words of the great Methodist patriarch John Wesley: "The Scriptures, therefore, of the Old and New Testament are a most solid and precious system of divine truth. Every part is worthy of God and altogether are one entire body, wherein is no defect, no excess. It is the fountain of heavenly wisdom, which they which are able to taste prefer to all writings of men, however wise or learned or holy."[1]

John Wesley and my grandmother shared a presupposition about the Bible that is sadly lacking in much contemporary discussion today: the Bible is the very Word of God and as such it deserves not only to be studied with utmost diligence but also cherished, obeyed, and proclaimed as the living oracle of a holy God. Much of the so-called historical-critical study of the Bible assumes that the Scriptures are a fortuitous collection of obscure texts from the ancient world which, if they have any value to us at all, must be interpreted solely in terms of our contemporary concerns and values. True enough, the Bible is not a lazy man's book, and warm-hearted piety is no substitute for the hard work of linguistic, exegetical, and historical analysis which any serious study of the Scriptures demands. However, the true purpose of biblical scholarship is not to show how "relevant" the Bible is to the modern world, but rather how irrelevant the modern world—and we ourselves as persons enmeshed in it—have become in our self-centered preoccupations and sinful rebellion

---

[1] John Wesley, *Wesley's Notes on the Bible* (Grand Rapids: Francis Asbury, 1987), 403.

against the God who spoke and still speaks through his chosen prophets and apostles.

We do not come to the study of the Bible alone but in the company of the whole people of God, the Body of Christ scattered throughout time as well as space. Thus, in approaching a document such as Paul's Letter to the Galatians, it will not suffice merely to have our New Testament in one hand and the latest word from Bultmann, Käsemann, or Conzelmann in the other. In this commentary we have tried to give more than cursory attention to the important task of "reading alongside" the church fathers, schoolmen, reformers, and theologians of ages past. None of their interpretations is inerrant, and we must subject them all—including, *a fortiori,* our own—to the divine touchstone of God's perfect revelation in Holy Scripture. But the Holy Spirit did not abandon the church with the death of the apostles. As we listen for what the Spirit is saying to the churches today, we will do well also to heed what He has been saying all along to the people of God throughout the history of the church.

To those acquainted with my previous work, it will come as no surprise that this commentary is in some ways little more than a footnote to the magisterial studies of this Pauline letter by Martin Luther and John Calvin in the sixteenth century. It is not that the reformers were more learned or more holy than others who came before or after them, but rather that the decisive theological conflict of their age so closely paralleled that of the apostle Paul that they were able to interpret his writings with penetrating insight and extraordinary power.

In recent years scholars committed to what is called "the new perspective on Paul" have challenged the Reformation paradigm as essentially misdirected and wrong-headed. In light of these revisionist studies, we cannot simply deracinate the reformers from the sixteenth century and bring them without remainder into our own. In any event, that kind of repristination would only be of antiquarian interest and would not serve the reformers' overriding concern that the living voice of the gospel— *viva vox evangelii*—be heard afresh in every generation. However, when the writings of the reformers are compared with the attenuated, transcendence-starved theologies which dominate the current scene, they yet speak with surprising vitality and spiritual depth. Hans Dieter Betz is on target when he observes that Luther spoke as Paul would have spoken had he lived at the time when Luther gave his lectures. From first to last Galatians is a book about God—God's grace, God's sovereignty, God's purpose, God's gospel, that is, His good news of justification by faith in a crucified Savior. There is no better perch on which to stand to hear this God-intoxicated message than the broad shoulders of the great reformers whose legacy we can hardly celebrate in any better way than to listen to them again, for we still need desperately to hear what they have to say.

This commentary aims to be a work of theological exposition the primary purpose of which is to bring the dual disciplines of exegesis and dogmatics into the closest possible relationship. For too long biblical scholars have isolated themselves into their chosen cocoons of specialization leaving systematic exposition of the faith to "those theologians." For their part, theologians have developed their own often quite fanciful interpretations of Christian doctrine with only minimal reference to the primary documents of the believing community for whom they should be writing. Throughout this commentary I have dared to ask the question, "What was at stake theologically for Paul in his Letter to the Galatians?" Not everyone will agree with the answers I have proposed, but I trust that in some small measure I have helped others to see the legitimacy of the question. Theology must not be left to the theologians, nor biblical studies to the guilded scholars. True biblical theology is the task of every pastor and indeed every believer. God's truth-telling Word is the treasure of the church, and to this audience the present work is especially directed.

Many people have encouraged me in the writing of this commentary, and to them all I owe a debt of gratitude. Luther referred to Galatians as "My own epistle, to which I have plighted my troth; my Katie von Bora," a measure of the high esteem in which he held his wife Katherine. My "Katie" is Denise, whose love and support has not languished since we plighted our own troth twenty-five years ago in the little town of Chickamauga, Georgia. My son, Christian, and my daughter, Alyce Elizabeth, two wonderfully active preteens, have a way of bringing the most sublime theological thoughts down to earth. On more than one occasion they have asked, "Dad, aren't you finished with Galatians yet?" President Thomas E. Corts of Samford University has given strong encouragement to my efforts to combine administrative and scholarly labors. The faculty and staff of Beeson Divinity School, my colaborers in Kingdom work, embody the fruit of the Spirit in numerous ways that serve the upbuilding of Christ's church. To one of them, especially, I owe much more than a prefatory acknowledgment can express. Mrs. Cecile Glausier, my wonderful administrative secretary, has worked long hours under stressful conditions to prepare this manuscript for press while also fulfilling her other demanding responsibilities at Beeson Divinity School with remarkable proficiency, poise, and grace.

It is my prayer that the Lord may see fit to use this commentary to encourage a renewal of sound doctrinal preaching and systematic expository study of the Scriptures within congregations of faithful believers throughout the evangelical community. Concerning my interpretation of Galatians, I ask no one to follow me any further than I have followed Christ, and I invite everyone to join me in earnestly seeking the wisdom of the Holy Spirit for a better understanding of this great book. In commending what I have written, I can do no better than to echo the sentiments of William Tyndale in the preface to his 1525 translation of the New Testament in English:

> As concerning all I have translated or otherwise written, I beseech all men to read it for that purpose I wrote it: even to bring them to the knowledge of the Scripture. As far as the Scripture approveth it, so far to allow it, and if in any place the Word of God disallow it, there to refuse it, as I do before our Savior Christ and his congregation. And where they find faults, let them show it me, if they be nigh, or write to me, if they be far off: or write openly against it and improve it, and I promise them, if I shall perceive that their reasons conclude, I will confess mine ignorance openly.[2]

Timothy George
Beeson Divinity School
Samford University

Ascension Sunday, 1994

---

[2] William Tyndale, "Yet Once More to the Christian Reader," *Tyndale's New Testament,* ed. D. Daniell (New Haven: Yale University Press, 1989), 16.

Abbreviations

Bible Books

Gen	Isa	Luke
Exod	Jer	John
Lev	Lam	Acts
Num	Ezek	Rom
Deut	Dan	1,2 Cor
Josh	Hos	Gal
Judg	Joel	Eph
Ruth	Amos	Phil
1,2 Sam	Obad	Col
1,2 Kgs	Jonah	1,2 Thess
1,2 Chr	Mic	1,2 Tim
Ezra	Nah	Titus
Neh	Hab	Phlm
Esth	Zeph	Heb
Job	Hag	Jas
Ps (pl. Pss)	Zech	1,2, Pet
Prov	Mal	1,2,3 John
Eccl	Matt	Jude
Song	Mark	Rev

Commonly Used Sources

AB	Anchor Bible
ACNT	Augsburg Commentary on the New Testament
AJT	*American Journal of Theology*
AJTh	*Asia Journal of Theology*
ANF	Ante-Nicene Fathers
ATR	*Anglican Theological Review*
ATRSup	*Anglican Theological Review Supplemental Series*
AusBR	*Australian Biblical Review*
AUSS	*Andrews University Seminary Studies*
BAGD	W. Bauer, W. F. Arndt, F. W. Gingrich, and F. Danker, *Greek-English Lexicon of the New Testament*
BARev	*Biblical Archaeology Review*

BDF	F. Blass, A. Debrunner, R. W. Funk, *A Greek Grammar of the New Testament*
Bib	*Biblica*
BJRL	*Bulletin of the John Rylands Library*
BK	*Bibel und Kirche*
BR	*Biblical Research*
BSac	*Bibliotheca Sacra*
BT	*The Bible Translator*
BTB	*Biblical Theology Bulletin*
BZ	*Biblische Zeitschrift*
CBQ	*Catholic Biblical Quarterly*
CNTC	Calvin's New Testament Commentaries
CO	W. Baur, E. Cuntiz, and E. Reuss, *Ioannis Calvini opera quae supereunt omnia,* ed.
CJT	*Canadian Journal of Theology*
CSR	*Christian Scholars' Review*
CTM	*Concordia Theologial Monthly*
CTQ	*Concordia Theological Quarterly*
CTR	*Criswell Theological Review*
Did.	*Didache*
DNTT	*Dictionary of New Testament Theology*
DownRev	*Downside Review*
DSB	Daily Study Bible
EBC	Expositor's Bible Commentary
ETC	English Translation and Commentary
ETL	*Ephemerides theologicae lovanienses*
EvT	*Evangelische Theologie*
EvQ	*Evangelical Quarterly*
ETR	*Etudes théologiques et religieuses*
ETS	Evangelical Theological Society
Exp	*Expositor*
ExpTim	*Expository Times*
FNT	*Filologia Neotestamentaria*
GAGNT	M. Zerwick and M. Grosvenor, *A Grammatical Analysis of the Greek New Testament*
GNBC	Good News Bible Commentary
GTJ	*Grace Theological Journal*
HBD	*Holman Bible Dictionary*
Her	Hermeneia
HeyJ	*Heythrop Journal*
HTKNT	Herders theologischer Kommentar zum Neuen Testament
HTR	*Harvard Theological Review*
HUCA	*Hebrew Union College Annual*
IB	*The Interpreter's Bible*
IBS	*Irish Biblical Studies*

ICC	International Critical Commentary
IDB	*Interpreter's Dictionary of the Bible*
Int	*Interpretation*
INT	Interpretation: A Bible Commentary for Preaching and Teaching
ISBE	*International Standard Bible Encyclopedia, Revised*
JAAR	*Journal of the American Academy of Religion*
JANES	*Journal of Ancient Near Eastern Studies*
JAOS	*Journal of the American Oriental Society*
JBL	*Journal of Biblical Literature*
JES	*Journal of Ecumenical Studies*
JETS	*Journal of the Evangelical Theological Society*
JJS	*Journal of Jewish Studies*
JR	*Journal of Religion*
JRS	*Journal of Roman Studies*
JRH	*Journal of Religious History*
JSNT	*Journal for the Study of the New Testament*
JSOT	*Journal for the Study of the Old Testament*
JSS	*Journal of Semitic Studies*
JTS	*Journal of Theological Studies*
LouvSt	*Louvain Studies*
LTQ	*Lexington Theological Quarterly*
LW	Luther's Works
LXX	Septuagint
MCNT	Meyer's Commentary on the New Testament
MDB	*Mercer Dictionary of the Bible*
MNTC	Moffatt NT Commentary
MQR	*Mennonite Quarterly Review*
MT	Masoretic Text
NAC	New American Commentary
NBD	*New Bible Dictionary*
NCB	New Century Bible
NIC	New International Commentary
NPNF	Nicene and Post-Nicene Fathers
Neot	*Neotestamentica*
NovT	*Novum Testamentum*
NRT	*La nouvelle revue théologique*
NTS	*New Testament Studies*
NTD	Das Neue Testament Deutsch
NTI	*New Testament Introduction*, D. Guthrie
NTM	*The New Testament Message*
NTS	*New Testament Studies*
PC	Proclamation Commentaries
PEQ	*Palestine Exploration Quarterly*
PRS	*Perspectives in Religious Studies*

RB	*Revue biblique*
RelSRev	*Religious Studies Review*
RevExp	*Review and Expositor*
RevQ	*Revue de Qumran*
RevThom	*Revue thomiste*
RHPR	*Revue d'histoire et de philosophie religieuses*
RSPT	*Revue des sciences philosophiques et théologiques*
RSR	*Recherches de science religieuse*
RTP	*Revue de théologie et de philosophie*
RTR	*Reformed Theological Review*
SBLMS	Society of Biblical Literature Monograph Series
SEAJT	*Southeast Asia Journal of Theology*
SPCK	Society for the Promotion of Christian Knowledge
SJT	*Scottish Journal of Theology*
SNTU	*Studien zum Neuen Testament und seiner Umwelt*
ST	*Studia theologica*
SWJT	*Southwestern Journal of Theology*
TB	*Tyndale Bulletin*
TBT	*The Bible Today*
TDNT	G. Kittel and G. Friedrich, eds., *Theological Dictionary of the New Testament*
Theol	*Theology*
ThT	*Theology Today*
TLZ	*Theologische Literaturzeitung*
TNTC	Tyndale New Testament Commentaries
TrinJ	*Trinity Journal*
TRu	*Theologische Rundschau*
TS	*Theological Studies*
TSK	*Theologische Studien und Kritiken*
TynBul	*Tyndale Bulletin*
TZ	*Theologische Zeitschrift*
UBS	United Bible Societies
UBSGNT	*United Bible Societies' Greek New Testament*
USQR	*Union Seminary Quarterly Review*
VE	*Vox Evangelica*
WBC	Word Biblical Commentary
WTJ	*Westminster Theological Journal*
WUNT	Wissenschaftliche Untersuchungen zum Neuen Testament
ZDPV	*Zeitschrift des deutschen Palästina-Vereins*
ZNW	*Zeitschrift für die neutestamentliche Wissenschaft*
ZRGG	*Zeitschrift für Religions- und Geistesgeschichte*
ZTK	*Zeitschrift für Theologie und Kirche*

Contents

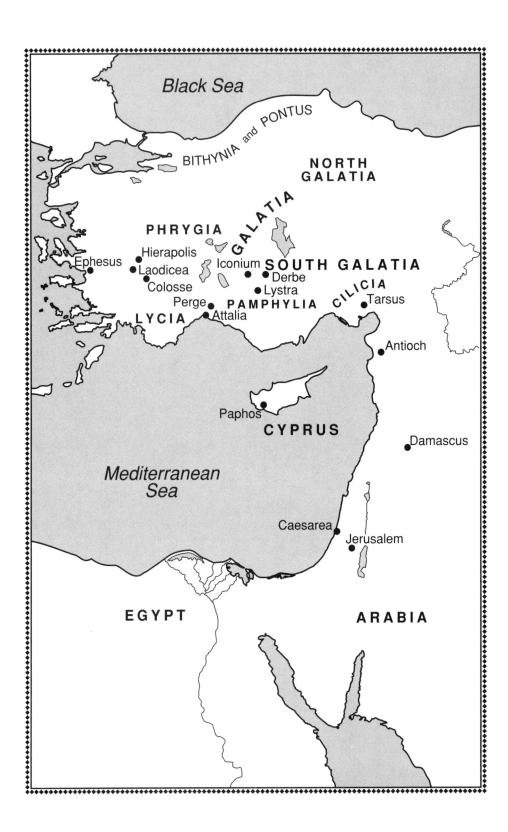

Black Sea

BITHYNIA and PONTUS

NORTH
GALATIA

PHRYGIA

GALATIA

Hierapolis
Ephesus
Laodicea
Iconium
SOUTH GALATIA
Colosse
Derbe
CILICIA
Lystra
Perge
PAMPHYLIA
Tarsus
LYCIA
Attalia

Antioch

Paphos

CYPRUS

Damascus

Mediterranean
Sea

Caesarea
Jerusalem

EGYPT

ARABIA

Galatians

──────── **INTRODUCTION** ────────

Jerome once said that when he read the letters of the apostle Paul he could hear thunder. Nowhere in the Pauline corpus is such stormy dissonance more evident than in the Epistle to the Galatians. Though written

21

from prison, Philippians is a love letter on the theme of joy. Romans reflects the considered objectivity of a master theologian reveling in the doctrines of grace. Ephesians is an uplifting commentary on the body of Christ. Even the Corinthian correspondence, though obviously written out of great personal anguish and pain, revolves around the great triad of faith, hope, and love, with Paul's hardships and concerns set over against his greater confidence in the God of all comfort who causes his children to triumph. In 2 Cor 13:12 Paul could admonish the believers in Corinth to greet one another with a holy kiss.

But Galatians is different. From beginning to end its six chapters of 149 verses bristle with passion, sarcasm, and anger. True, there is a touch of tenderness as well; once in the midst of the letter Paul referred to the Galatians as his "dear children" (4:19). As the context reveals, though, this was the tearing tenderness of a distraught mother who must endure all over again the pains of childbirth because her children, who should have known better, were in danger of committing spiritual suicide. Paul was astonished and "perplexed" by their departure from the truth of the gospel. He feared that they had been "bewitched" and deceived. In frustration he dubbed them, as J. B. Phillips translates it, "my dear idiots" (3:1).

What was so decisively at stake for Paul in Galatians? Why does this letter strike us "like a lion turned loose in the arena of Christianity"?[1] Who were the opponents against whom he complained with such vehemence? How did the Christians in Galatia react to Paul's letter? How is it related to his other writings and to the account of his life and ministry that Luke gives us in Acts? How has Galatians fared through the ages in the history of Christian interpretation from Paul to the present? What is its message for us believers today who, no less than the Galatians long ago, have been called to salvation in "this present age of wickedness" (1:4, NEB)? We will attempt to answer these questions throughout the commentary. First, though, by way of introduction we will focus on the author, the churches, the occasion, the genre, and the history of interpretation.

1. The Author: Paul and His World

Few facts related to the history and interpretation of Galatians have virtual unanimity among all scholars everywhere. But here is one: Galatians was indeed written by Paul the apostle as its opening verse attests. In the nineteenth century F. C. Baur and his disciples in the "Tübingen School" pushed many New Testament writings, including most of Paul's letters, into

---

[1] R. Longenecker, *Galatians*, WBC (Dallas: Word, 1990), lvii.

the mid-second century, thereby calling into question their genuine apostolicity and historical trustworthiness. This radical criticism was based on a hypothetical reconstruction of early church history that denied to the apostolic age the kind of highly developed Christology found, for example, in Colossians and the Pastoral Epistles. For all this, even Baur himself recognized the genuineness and integrity of Galatians and included it, along with Romans and the two letters to the Corinthians, among what he called the *Hauptbriefe,* "the four great Epistles of the Apostle which take precedence over the rest in every respect."[2]

Who was Paul? What were the influences that shaped his life and worldview prior to his writing Galatians?

(1) Hebrew Religion

Galatians contains one of the most important autobiographical reflections anywhere in the writings of Paul. Here he spoke of his "previous way of life in Judaism," his ardor for the "traditions of [his] fathers," and his surpassing zeal as a persecutor of the Christians (1:13-14). These statements are borne out in his other writings as well. He told the Philippians (3:5-6) that he belonged to the tribe of Benjamin (as had King Saul, his biblical namesake), that he had been properly circumcised on the eighth day, and that he held to a strict Pharisaic position on the law.

In none of his extant letters did Paul refer to the city of his birth. However, on five occasions in Acts (9:11,30; 11:25; 21:39; 22:3) he is identified as a native son of Tarsus, the chief metropolis of the Roman province of Cilicia. Once Paul referred to his hometown as "no ordinary city." In fact, Tarsus was a major center of commerce, culture, and education with a university so renowned that it could be spoken of, so the geographer Strabo tells us, in the same breath with that of Athens.[3]

Paul was thus brought up in a Jewish family of the diaspora. An estimated 4.5 million Jews were scattered throughout the Roman Empire at this time. There may well have been more Jews in Rome than in Jerusalem. It would be a mistake, however, to imagine that all diaspora Jews were as far removed from the strict traditions of Judaism as they were from its cultic

---

[2] F. C. Baur, *Paul: His Life and Works* (London: Williams & Norgate, 1875), 1:246. One of the few scholars to deny the genuineness of Galatians was B. Bauer, who carried to their logical extreme the theories of his mentor, F. C. Baur. For discussion of various positions on the Pauline authorship of Galatians, see E. deW. Burton, *Spirit, Soul and Flesh* (Chicago: University of Chicago Press, 1918), lxv-lxxi.

[3] Strabo, *Geography*, XIV, 673. Cf. the extensive study of Tarsus by W. M. Ramsay, *The Cities of St. Paul: Their Influence on His Life and Thought* (Grand Rapids: Baker, 1960).

center and official headquarters, so to speak, in Judea. Indeed, it is likely that Paul's family maintained strong personal ties with Palestinian Judaism. Writing from Bethlehem in 492, Jerome recorded an ancient tradition claiming that Paul's hometown was the Palestinian village of Giscalis.[4] While no historical credence can be given to this tradition, it may well be that Paul's father was originally associated with this village and then migrated to Tarsus sometime after the capture of Jerusalem by Pompey in 63 B.C.[5] This would help explain the fact that Paul apparently had relatives, including a nephew and (presumably an older) sister, who were residents of Jerusalem during the episode of the Jewish conspiracy against his life there (Acts 23:12-22). In any event, Paul clearly identified himself with the Aramaic-speaking Jews of Palestine, as his self-description, "a Hebrew of the Hebrews," evidently means.[6]

After he had learned the trade of tentmaking and completed his basic education at the local synagogue in Tarsus, Paul was sent to Jerusalem, where he became the prize pupil in the Pharisaic school of Rabbi Gamaliel. Gamaliel, whose surname was "the Glory of the Law," was a renowned teacher and grandson of the even more famous Hillel. From Gamaliel, Paul learned that subtle and intricate manner of biblical interpretation he was to put to such good use in Galatians and elsewhere.

Prior to his conversion, however, Paul was not merely a scholar; he was also an activist. One of the primary reasons Judaism had spread so extensively throughout the Roman Empire was the ardent missionary spirit that guided its zealous adherents at this time. The Pharisaic Judaism of Palestine, to which Paul was committed heart and soul, was especially known for its aggressive proselytism. Jesus himself referred to this policy in his rebuke of the Pharisees: "You hypocrites! You travel over land and sea to win a single convert, and when he becomes one, you make him twice as much a son of hell as you are" (Matt 23:15). There is reason to believe that Paul, in his desire to advance in Judaism "beyond many Jews of my own age" (Gal 1:14), already had committed himself as a full-time missionary, perhaps even with a special orientation to the Gentile world, prior to his encounter with the risen Lord on the Damascus Road. Only then he was a missionary of the Jewish faith intent on winning as many converts as possible to the

---

[4] Jerome, *Lives of Illustrious Men*, 5. NPNF 3.362.

[5] Ramsay argues instead that Paul's family descended from a colony of Jewish settlers transplanted to Tarsus by the Seleucid monarch Antiochus Epiphanes in 171 B.C. (*Cities,* 185).

[6] Cf. Paul's citation of such Aramaic expressions as *Abba* (Rom 8:15) and *Maranatha* (1 Cor 16:22) as well as Paul's address in Aramaic following his arrest in Jerusalem (Acts 21:37–22:2). Even more telling is the fact that the risen Jesus spoke to Paul in Aramaic on the Damascus Road (Acts 26:14).

obedience of the law including, no doubt, the requirement of circumcision.

Paul's opponents in Galatia may in fact have alluded to his preconversion proclamation in their efforts to embarrass him and denigrate his law-free gospel. To this charge Paul replied: "Brothers, if I am *still* [emphasis added] preaching circumcision, why am I *still* [emphasis added] being persecuted? In that case the offense of the cross has been abolished" (Gal 5:11). Bornkamm has given a plausible interpretation of this verse: "This most probably means that had he continued in the kind of missionary preaching that the Judaizers were now propagating, but with which Paul had long also broken, he would have been spared persecution at the hands of the Jews— but at the cost of the gospel of the cross."[7] If this hypothesis is true, then Paul may well have been retracing his earlier missionary itinerary as he persecuted and pursued the followers of Jesus on various journeys even into "foreign cities" (Acts 26:11-12)

(2) Hellenistic Culture

We have seen that while Paul was a diaspora Jew from Asia Minor, he belonged inwardly to Palestine, the primary setting of his rabbinic training and early religious activism. This fact, however, should not obscure the even larger context in which Paul and indeed all of the New Testament writers fulfilled their calling and mission, namely, the reigning culture of Hellenism.

The Hellenistic age refers to that period dating from the death of Alexander the Great in 323 B.C. through the consolidation of the Roman Empire in the early centuries of the Christian era. This age was characterized by a historical transformation that gave to the Mediterranean world a common intellectual culture and eventually political unity. A new form of the Greek language, the *koiné* or common tongue, came into general use. Greek philosophical concepts drawn from the teachings of Plato, the Stoics, the Epicureans, the Neo-Pythagoreans, and others became the common possession of educated people throughout the empire, providing the basis for an interpretation of reality in objective and rational terms.

The impact of Hellenism on the Jewish faith is most clearly seen in developments at Alexandria, a major center of culture and learning at the mouth of the Nile. Here under the sponsorship of the Ptolemaic king of Egypt, the most influential of the Greek versions of the Hebrew Scriptures was produced in the third century B.C. It is called the Septuagint (LXX) because of the tradition that seventy-two scholars had completed the trans-

---

[7] G. Bornkamm, *Paul* (New York: Harper & Row, 1971), 12.

lation process in seventy-two days. Early Christian writers including Paul inherited the Septuagint and commonly quoted the Old Testament passages from it. During the time of Jesus there flourished in Alexandria a Jewish thinker and exegete of great ability, Philo, who produced a remarkable synthesis between Greek philosophy and Hebrew religion through the allegorical interpretation of the Old Testament. Philo has been called "a none too distant cousin of St. Paul," and one certainly can point to a number of parallel passages in their respective writings, due largely to Paul's ability to draw upon the language and thought forms of Hellenistic Judaism. However, the contrasts between the two are equally striking, as seen, for example, in the quite different ways they both employ allegory in the story of Hagar and Sarah.[8]

Paul no doubt was acquainted with the major currents of Greek philosophy and could appeal to its tenets in presenting the gospel to a pagan audience, as he did with great finesse in his famous address before the Areopagus in Athens (Acts 17:16-34). On three occasions Paul incorporated quotations from Greek poets in his speeches and letters (Menander, 1 Cor 15:33; Epimenides, Titus 1:12; Aratus, Acts 27:28). At the same time Paul's appeal to the learning of the Greeks is altogether different from that of such later Christian writers as Clement of Alexandria and Origen, who may rightly be said to have achieved for Christianity what Philo did for Judaism: a synthesis of revealed religion and pagan wisdom. By contrast, Paul warned the Colossians to beware lest they be deceived "through hollow and deceptive philosophy" (Col 2:8). By these words Paul was not completely rejecting the Greek philosophical tradition *en toto,* but he clearly was subordinating it to the "wisdom of God" and the gospel of grace he received "by revelation from Jesus Christ."

When Paul set sail from Selucia on his first missionary journey, he was entering a world marked by a great longing for redemption and filled with many new religious options to supply it. Chief among these were the various mystery religions, originally tribal cults imported into the empire through the Hellenizing of the East. From Syria came the cult of Adonis, from Egypt that of Isis and Osiris, from Phrygia that of Cybele and Attis. Each of these religions offered salvation of the soul and immortality through a secret rite of initiation by which the initiate was mystically united with the savior-god. In these ceremonies the myth of the dying and rising deity was reenacted through baptism and participation in a sacred meal.

---

[8] H. Chadwick, "St. Paul and Philo of Alexandria," *JRLB* 48 (1965): 286-307. Chadwick points out a number of Philonic-Pauline parallels but finally concludes, "St. Paul writes as a man with a prophet's call, Philo as a speculative thinker inclined to mysticism."

Understandably, many of those who heard the first Christian sermons understood the movement as simply another mystery religion from the East. Thus when Paul preached Jesus and the resurrection, some believed that he was introducing a new deity, the god Jesus and his female consort Resurrection (*Anastasis,* a feminine word in Greek). A similar view has prevailed in modern scholarly circles as well. Thus P. Tillich wrote, "These mystery gods greatly influenced the Christian cult and theology."[9] The most substantial scholarly treatment of Paul from this perspective was that of W. Bousset, who argued that Paul's attribution of the title Lord (*Kyrios*) to Jesus reflected his transmutation of the primitive Christian message into the categories of the Hellenistic mystery cults.[10]

However, two crucial aspects of the Christian message Paul proclaimed stood in irreconcilable contrast to the mystery religions: its historicity and its exclusivity. Unlike the gospels of the mystery gods, the death and resurrection of Jesus were not timeless events detached from a specific historical context. As the Apostles' Creed confesses, he was crucified "under Pontius Pilate" and raised from the dead "on the third day." Moreover, unlike the syncretism and pluralism of Hellenistic religion, Christianity required an undivided loyalty to only one *Kyrios;* for just as there is only one God, so also there is only one mediator between God and humankind, the man Christ Jesus (1 Tim 2:5).

(3) Roman Rule

In the year A.D. 410 the Visigothic barbarians invaded and sacked the city of Rome. When news of this disaster reached Jerome, who was living in Bethlehem at the time, he exclaimed, "The lamp of the world is extinguished, and it is the whole world which has perished in the ruins of this one city."[11] In the same year Augustine began his massive *City of God* in which he reviewed the long history of the Roman Empire and placed both its success and its imminent demise in the larger context of God's providential purposes in history. "The cause of the greatness of the Roman Empire," he argued, "was neither chance nor destiny. . . . Without the slightest doubt, the kingdoms of men are established by divine providence."[12] For Jerome, Augustine, and their contemporaries the fall of Rome brought to an end the

---

[9] P. Tillich, *A History of Christian Thought* (New York: Simon & Schuster, 1967), 13.

[10] W. Bossuet, *Kyrios Christos: A History of the Belief in Christ from the Beginnings of Christianity to Irenaeus,* trans. J. E. Steely (Nashville: Abingdon, 1970).

[11] Quoted, H. J. Carroll et al. eds., *The Development of Civilization* (Glenview, Ill.: Scott, Foresman & Co., 1961), 150.

[12] Augustine, *City of God* 5.1 (New York: Penguin, 1972), 1791.

Pax Romana, an epoch of relative peace and stability that had witnessed the appearance of the Messiah and the birth of the Christian church. This way of reading history can be traced back to Paul himself, who told the Galatians that God had sent his Son into the world "when the time had fully come" (4:4).

Under Caesar Augustus and the emperors who succeeded him the Roman Empire was fused into a unified political entity with one common language, a centralized military organization, a shared legal system, a uniform mail and transportation service, a single monetary currency, and an interconnected pattern of trade and commerce. Never before or since have all the shores of the Mediterranean been under one single rule. The earliest heralds of the Christian gospel coursed along the major highways and well-developed sea routes of the Roman Empire as they continuously "gossiped" (cf. Phillips translation of Acts 8:4) the story of Jesus in all of the great urban and commercial centers of the known world. Nearly two hundred years after Paul's death, Origen reflected on the significance of the *Pax Romana* for the expansion and development of Christianity.

> There is abundance of peace which began at the birth of Christ, God preparing the nations for his teaching, that they might be under one prince, the king of the Romans, and that it might not be more difficult, owing to the lack of unity between the nations due to the existence of many kingdoms for Jesus' apostles to accomplish the task laid upon them by their Master, when he said: "Go and teach all nations."[13]

As the Roman Empire assimilated the Hellenistic kingdoms of the East into a new political structure, the right of Roman citizenship was gradually extended to those in the provinces who had distinguished themselves by education, wealth, or some form of extraordinary public service. In one of these ways we may assume that Paul's father acquired the status of *civis Romanus* that he passed on as a hereditary right to his son. This privilege meant two important things in Paul's missionary career. First, it served as a kind of universal passport that gave Paul access to Roman institutions and permitted him to travel with minimal difficulties from one end of the empire to the other. Second, it enabled Paul to appeal to Caesar before being condemned to death for a capital offense. Paul exercised this right in his trial before King Agrippa (Acts 25:23-25), who sent him on to Rome. There, according to ancient tradition, he was beheaded in the first imperial persecution against the Christians, which took place in the tenth year of Nero's reign in A.D. 64.

---

[13] H. Chadwick, ed., *Origen: Contra Celsum* (Cambridge: Cambridge University Press, 1980), 92.

Thus while Paul was a citizen of the Roman Empire and urged obedience to the civil authority, he also knew that the Christian's prior political allegiance (*politeuma,* cf. Phil 3:20) was to that heavenly commonwealth, "the Jerusalem that is above" (Gal 4:26). There is no evidence that Paul ever conceived of Christianity as providing the social and religious basis for imperial consolidation and stability, "the soul which might give life to the body of the empire,"[14] as a historian of an earlier generation put it. The *Pax Romana* was based on violence and oppression, and Paul, despite his legal status, had to endure harsh treatment at the hands of Roman officials as well as Jewish authorities. The peace with God that Paul proclaimed to Jew and Gentile alike was based not on the changing fortunes of political structures but rather on the death and resurrection of Jesus Christ and the expectation of his coming again in judgment and glory.

(4) Conversion and Calling

The conversion of the apostle Paul is one of the most remarkable facts in the history of Christianity. How was it that the brilliant, urbane, and unrelenting persecutor of Christians became, almost overnight, the devoted advocate and protagonist of the very faith he had endeavored with all his might to eradicate? In Galatians, Paul answered that question with tantalizing brevity. God, he said, "was pleased to reveal his Son in me" (1:15-16).

Actually, six passages in the New Testament together present a composite picture of this historic event; three in Paul's letters (1 Cor 9:1-2; 15:3-11; Gal 1:11-16) and three in Acts (9:1-7; 22:6-10; 26:12-16). Luke related the conversion as a sequel to the stoning of Stephen, at which Paul was present and over which he may well have exercised some judicial oversight, indicated by the fact that the "witnesses" who stoned Stephen deposited their garments at his feet (Acts 7:58). The execution of Stephen signaled a new wave of harassment and persecution against the Christians, with Paul pursuing the Jesus-believers "from house to house" (Acts 8:3). So successful was this effort that many Christians were forced to flee from Jerusalem carrying the gospel into Samaria and beyond. With the dispersal of the church in Judea, Paul received permission from the high priest to take his campaign of holy

---

[14] Ramsay, *Cities,* 71. Ramsay's work, originally published in 1907, reflects the cultural and political optimism that prevailed in Western civilization in the decades prior to World War I. For a more sober analysis of Paul's political ethic, see K. Wengst, *Pax Romana and the Peace of Jesus Christ* (Philadelphia: Fortress, 1987), 72-89. W. Stegemann has questioned the traditional assumption, derived from Acts, that Paul was a Roman citizen ("War der Apostel Paulus ein römisches Bürger?" *ZNW* 78 [1987]: 200-229). But see M. Hengel, *The Pre-Christian Paul* (London: SCM, 1991), 101-2.

terror on the road. His new target: Damascus. His aim: to ferret out followers of "the Way" and bring them back to Jerusalem in chains.

Luke said that Paul was approaching the ancient city of Damascus along with his party of fellow travelers—perhaps members of the Levitical temple guard assigned to accompany the persecutor as bloodhounds would a hunter. Suddenly they were beset by a light from heaven, brighter than the Syrian sun at midday, which knocked them all (Acts 26:12-14) to the ground. Jesus of Nazareth, the crucified Messiah, appeared in his risen and ascended glory and spoke to Paul in his native tongue: "*Shaûl, Shaûl,* why do you persecute me?" "Who are you sir?" Paul asked in reply. "I am Jesus, whom you are persecuting. Stand up . . . go into the city. . . . You will be told what to do." Later before King Agrippa, Paul recalled his response, "I was not disobedient to the vision from heaven" (Acts 26:19). Blinded by the dazzling light, Paul stumbled in darkness toward his original destination. The irony is profound: he who had gone to Damascus to take others captive was himself led, helpless and blind, to one of the very disciples he had intended to subdue. After three days of fasting, Paul received a visit from a believer named Ananias. In quick succession he was healed and baptized and, to the astonishment of all who heard him, immediately began to proclaim in the synagogues his first sermon as a Christian: Jesus *is* the Son of God!

Through the centuries various attempts have been made to discredit the authenticity of Paul's conversion.[15] According to the early Christian apologist Epiphanius, an early Jewish Christian sect known as the Ebionites circulated a fantastic slander about Paul that was widely believed in their circles. According to this tale, Paul was not really a Jew by birth but rather the son of Greek parents. Paul's father had come to Jerusalem and had fallen in love with the daughter of the high priest there. In order to obtain the girl, he became a Jewish proselyte and submitted to circumcision. When this ruse fell through, however, he took revenge by attacking circumcision, the Sabbath, and the law itself with all the fury of an unrequited lover.[16] While

---

[15] The literature on Paul's conversion is enormous. In addition to the standard biographies, see especially U. Wilckens, "Die Bekehrung des Paulus als religions geschichtliches Problem," *ZTK* 56 (1959): 273-93; and J. Dupont, "The Conversion of Paul and Its Influence on His Understanding of Salvation by Faith," in *Apostolic History and the Gospel: Biblical and Historical Essays Presented to F. F. Bruce on His Sixtieth Birthday,* ed. W. Gasque and R. P. Martin (Grand Rapids: Eerdmans, 1975), 176-94. Cf. also the recent treatment by A. Segal, who, as a Jew, offers a different perspective altogether (*Paul the Convert: The Apostolate and Apostasy of Saul the Pharisee* [New Haven: Yale University Press, 1988]).

[16] Epiphanius, *Adversus Haereses* 30.16. Longenecker (*Galatians,* 26) attributes the story to the second-century author of the *Ascension of James.*

this story has no historical basis whatsoever, it does show what great pains were taken to manufacture an explanation of the radical change Paul underwent from a zealous proponent of strict Pharasaic Judaism to the premier Christian "apostle to the Gentiles."

In modern times myriads of naturalistic and psychological explanations of Paul's conversion have been set forth by various scholars who refuse to accept what Paul himself asserted, namely, that he had a personal encounter with Jesus Christ and actually heard him speak in words that could be looked up in a dictionary. Some have claimed that what Paul mistook as the voice of Christ was really nothing more than the crash and lightning of a Syrian thunderstorm. Others have attributed the vision to some serious physical ailment, perhaps a burning fever or a fit of epilepsy. Still others have opted for the theory of psychological self-delusion: what Paul thought he saw as Christ was merely a Freudian projection of his own inner conflict and guilt feelings over the death of Stephen. In 1866 the French philosopher and skeptic E. Renan brought together several of these theories in one of the most romantic castings of Paul's conversion ever written:

> Every step to Damascus excited in Paul bitter repentance; the shameful task of the hangman was intolerable to him; he felt as if he was kicking against the goads; the fatigue of travel added to his depression; a malignant fever suddenly seized him; the blood rushed to the head; the mind was filled with a pitcher of midnight darkness broken by lightning flashes. It is probable that one of those sudden storms of Mount Hermon broke out which are unequaled for vehemence, and to the Jew the thunder was the voice of God, the lightning fire of God. Certain it is that by a fearful stroke the persecutor was thrown on the ground and deprived of his senses; in his feverish delirium he mistook the lightning for a heavenly vision, the voice of thunder for a voice from Heaven; inflamed eyes, the beginning of ophthalmia, aided the delusion.[17]

Earlier (*La Vie de Jésus,* 1863) Renan had published an equally fanciful life of Jesus that portrayed him as a charming and amiable Galilean preacher devoid of either a prophetic role or miraculous power. In both cases Renan's reconstruction reflected his own biased repudiation of the supernatural element in the Christian faith rather than a serious engagement with the historical materials.[18]

---

[17] E. Renan, *Les Apôtres* (Paris: Michel Lévy Frères, 1866), 175.

[18] A. Schweitzer places Renan's work in the context of other liberal "lives of Jesus," the most notable of which was by his great German counterpart D. F. Strauss (see *The Quest for the Historical Jesus* [New York: Macmillan, 1968], esp. 180-92). Schweitzer characterized Renan as "one to whom the New Testament was to the lost something foreign . . . , who was not accustomed to breathe freely in its simple and pure world, but [who had to] perfume it with sentimentality in order to feel himself at home in it" (p. 192).

In sharp contrast to Renan and other unbelieving theologians who have followed in his train, Baron George Lyttelton published a thorough character study of Paul in which he concluded that the apostle was neither an imposter nor an enthusiast nor one who had been deceived by the fraud of others. Rather "what he declared to be the cause of his conversion, and to have happened in consequence of it, did all happen, and therefore the Christian religion is a divine revelation."[19] Clearly there is no way to understand Paul's theology or mission apart from the fundamental fact that stands at the center of his life: on the road to Damascus, Saul of Tarsus and Jesus of Nazareth came face-to-face. After that event neither Saul nor the Christian church was ever the same again.

No doubt Paul's conversion is the most famous in the history of Christianity, and for this reason it frequently has been held forth as a classic paradigm for all people who come to Christ. The New Testament, however, does not advance a single stereotype for an authentic conversion experience. For example, just a few pages after reading about Paul's dramatic conversion on the Damascus Road, we learn of a woman named Lydia who was quietly converted while listening to a gospel sermon (Acts 16:11-15). Still other patterns of conversion are prevalent throughout the history of the church. Both Augustine in the fourth century and C. S. Lewis in the twentieth came to faith in Christ only after a protracted period of intellectual struggle and doubt. D. L. Moody was converted through the witness of a shoe salesman. E. Stanley Jones came to Christ at the altar of a Methodist church when his Sunday School teacher, Miss Nellie Logan, knelt beside him and asked him to repeat John 3:16 this way, "God so loved Stanley Jones, that He gave His only begotten Son, that if Stanley Jones will believe on Him he shall not perish, but have everlasting life."[20]

This is not to say that Christ no longer appears to chosen individuals in as decisive and dramatic a fashion as he did to Paul long ago. In India a Hindu of the highest caste, Sundar Singh, became a Christian after undergoing such an experience. Like Saul of Tarsus, he had been endued with a fanatical zeal against the things of Christ. As an act of malice he one day poured kerosene over a Bible and burned it. This act of sacrilege occurred early on the morning of December 18, 1904. He immediately, as he recorded in his diary, "saw. . . . I thought the place was on fire. . . . I saw the form of the Lord Jesus Christ. It had such an appearance of glory and

---

[19] G. Lyttelton, *Observations on the Conversion and Apostleship of Saint Paul* (1769; reprint, Philadelphia: Monarch, 1895).

[20] H. T. Kerr and J. M. Mulder, *Conversions: The Christian Experience* (Grand Rapids: Eerdmans, 1983), 180-83.

love."[21] Following this experience Singh became one of the most widely read Christian writers and evangelists in modern Asia.

Though mediated in different ways, all of these persons shared with Paul a personal encounter with Jesus Christ that resulted in their surrender to him in repentance and faith. In two very important respects, however, Paul's conversion was unique. In the first place, it enabled him to be ranked among the witnesses to the resurrection. Thus in 1 Cor 15, after listing the appearances of the risen Christ to Peter, the Twelve, the more than five hundred, and James, Paul then added, "And last of all he appeared to me also, as to one abnormally born" (1 Cor 15:8). The phrase "last of all" indicates the special role God had chosen for Paul to play in the fulfillment of salvation history. And this fact is closely related to the second unique feature of Paul's encounter with the risen Christ on the Damascus Road: his conversion was also his calling. His special vocation of carrying the gospel to the Gentiles was the burden of the commission he received directly from Christ by divine revelation. This is abundantly clear from all three accounts of Paul's conversion in Acts as well as his own emphatic statements about it. "Am I not an apostle? Have I not seen Jesus our Lord?" (1 Cor 9:1). "For God, who said, 'Let light shine out of darkness,' made his light shine in our hearts to give us the light of the knowledge of the glory of God in the face of Christ" (2 Cor 4:6). "Therefore, . . . we have this ministry" (2 Cor 4:1); "[God] . . . was pleased to reveal his Son in me so that I might preach him among the Gentiles" (Gal 1:16).

We will return to this theme in the commentary itself since it forms the crux of Paul's opening argument in defense of his apostleship against his Galatian opponents. Suffice it to say now that Paul's personal deliverance from the darkness and death of sin into the light and life of Christ was at the same time his special calling to be the Apostle to the Gentiles.[22]

---

[21] Ibid., xvii.

[22] K. Stendahl rightly protests against the modern tendency to interpret Paul's experience through the lenses of Protestant pietism. He goes too far, however, in referring to Paul's encounter with Christ as "call rather than conversion." Clearly it was *both* a conversion and a calling. In his preconversion life Paul indeed possessed "a quite robust conscience," one unplagued by introspection. This simply means that his own "deeds of darkness" were not those of orgies, drunkenness, and debauchery against which he warned the Romans (Rom 13:12-13). For all that, he still saw himself not only as a sinner but as the *worst* of the lot: "a blasphemer and a persecutor, and a violent man . . . dead . . . in transgressions and sins . . . disobedient," following the desires and thoughts of our sinful nature (1 Tim 1:13-15; Eph 2:1-3). Paul, no less than those to whom he preached, needed to be delivered from the bondage of sin and death, a slavery that in his self-righteous zeal he had once believed to be true freedom. See K. Stendahl, *Paul Among Jews and Gentiles* (Philadelphia: Fortress, 1976), 7-23.

(5) Eschatology and Mission

It would be a great mistake for us to interpret Paul's conversion as his switching from one religion to another or, even worse, his abandonment of the faith of Israel in favor of the Hellenistic philosophies of the Greek world. In other words, when Paul became a Christian, he did not cease to be a Jew. What he did receive by revelation from the risen Christ was the true meaning of God's historic dealings with his ancient people. The law, the covenant, the temple, the Old Testament sacrifices, the destiny of Israel, and indeed the fate of the world itself were now all illuminated in light of God's decisive intervention through the life, death, and resurrection of his promised Messiah, Jesus. Paul wrote as a man who had been let in on an incredible secret, a "mystery" that though "hidden for ages and generations" had now been "disclosed to the saints" (Col 1:26). The burden of Paul's life was to make this secret known to all peoples everywhere, that is, to proclaim the word of God in its fullness to Jew and Gentile alike (Col 1:25).

The horizon of Paul's theology is thus defined by his understanding of salvation history with its specific background in Jewish apocalyptic thought. As a Pharasaic Jew, Paul would have accepted as canonical the apocalyptic Books of Ezekiel and Daniel and also would have been acquainted with the two-aeon concept set forth in 4 Ezra: "The most high has not made one aeon, but two" (4 Ezra 7:50).[23] According to this view, the present age of sin and death, which began with Adam, is quickly running its course toward a rendezvous with divine judgment. The new age will be inaugurated by the coming of the Messiah in clouds of glory (Dan 7:13-14), the resurrection of the dead (Dan 12:1-4), the subjection of the demonic powers who now hold sway in the world, and the descent of the universal reign of peace foretold by prophets of old (Isa 11:1-9). It was precisely this hope that constituted "the consolation of Israel" for which the devout Simeon waited with earnest expectation in the temple at Jerusalem (Luke 2:25).

Paul's encounter with the risen Christ led him to modify radically his understanding of salvation history in light of the traditional apocalyptic expectations. Paul now discovered that what the persecuted Christians had said all along was true: the crucified Jesus is indeed God's chosen Messiah. His resurrection from the dead (to which Paul was made a witness, 1 Cor 15:8) already has inaugurated the new age. In this sense Christians are those

---

[23] E. P. Sanders (*Paul and Palestinian Judaism* [Philadelphia: Fortress, 1977], 409-24) argues that 4 Ezra is atypical of Pharisaic Judaism during the time of Paul and his contemporaries. For the contrary view see J. C. Beker, *Paul the Apostle* (Philadelphia: Fortress, 1980), 143-81. Cf. also U. B. Müller, "Apocalyptic Currents," in *Christian Beginnings,* ed. J. Becker (Louisville: Westminster/John Knox, 1993), 281-329.

who live at that critical juncture in history known as the fullness of time (Gal 4:4); they are those "on whom the fulfillment of the ages has come" (1 Cor 10:11). In Jesus Christ the future has invaded the present. "Therefore, if anyone is in Christ, he is a new creation; the old has gone, the new has come!" (2 Cor 5:17).

Yet to make this claim is to invite the question that Jews have asked of Christians for two thousand years. If the Messiah has already come, then why is there still so much suffering, violence, and chaos in the world? Why do people, including Christians, contract cancer and die? Where is the universal reign of peace and the suppression of the forces of evil the prophets said would mark the messianic age? These are not merely modern questions of recent vintage, but they also are endemic to the Christian message and were keenly felt in New Testament times as well. For example, Peter said that the skeptics and scoffers of his day were asking: "Where is this 'coming' he promised? Ever since our fathers died, everything goes on as it has since the beginning of creation" (2 Pet 3:4).

Paul found a solution to his problem in his concept of the overlapping of the two ages and the eschatological tension between the "Already" of Christ's finished work and the "Not Yet" of the consummation of redemption. The whole of Paul's theology revolves around these two foci: the saving significance of Jesus' death and resurrection on the one hand and the hope of his return in glory on the other. Within this structure of thought Paul developed his distinctive understanding of the church and waged a two-pronged battle against those who would deny the decisiveness of the Christ-event on the one hand (legalists) and others who would mitigate the futurity of the resurrection (libertines) on the other. We can illustrate Paul's concerns with the schema on p. 36.

As we shall see, Paul's major struggle in Galatians was with certain Jewish-Christian missionaries who had failed to discern the radical character of Christ's salvific work. They agreed with Paul that Jesus is the Messiah. They, no less than he, were eager to see Gentiles as well as Jews evangelized and brought into the church. They insisted, however, that in order for Gentiles to become Christians they first of all had to become Jews. They must submit themselves to the strictures of the law, especially to circumcision, and thus complete by this act of obedience what Christ had begun through his life and work on earth. For them the meaning of Jesus Christ was deducible from the law. Paul, however, put it the other way around: only in light of Jesus Christ and his finished work on the cross can we begin to understand the true meaning of the law, the covenant, and indeed the whole burden of God's special revelation to Israel.

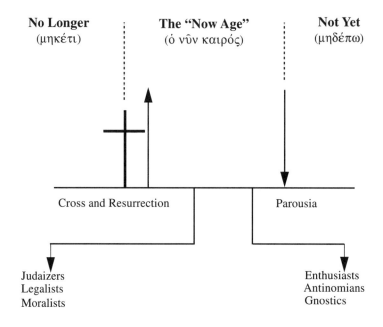

No Longer (μηκέτι)   The "Now Age" (ὁ νῦν καιρός)   Not Yet (μηδέπω)

Cross and Resurrection   Parousia

Judaizers
Legalists
Moralists

Enthusiasts
Antinomians
Gnostics

In the face of the legalists and Judaizers, Paul shouted, *No Longer!* Now that Christ has come, we are no longer under the supervision of the law; we are no longer slaves but rather sons; we are no longer captive to the passions of our sinful nature but liberated to keep in step with the spirit by fulfilling the law of love (Gal 3:25; 4:7; 5:14-26). Paul's doctrine of justification by faith, as set forth in Galatians and more completely in Romans, was forged in the context of a life-and-death struggle with those who would pervert the gospel by minimizing the decisive character of God's grace in the person and work of his Son.

On the other hand, Paul confronted an equally pernicious danger among several of the young churches he had established in the course of his missionary travels. Some believers emphasized the "No Longer" to the exclusion of the "Not Yet." Thus they reasoned: If God justifies us by faith alone no matter how great our sin, should we not then sin all the more in order to enjoy grace more? If indeed we have received the Holy Spirit on the basis of grace and not obedience to the law, then why may we not disregard the law completely? Why must we conform to the norms of sexual morality or be stifled in our worship from the kind of frenzied ecstasy enjoyed by the mystery religions? This kind of thinking led to the abuse of Christian freedom and resulted in the excesses of enthusiasm and antinomianism.

Against this pattern of thinking Paul said sternly, *Not Yet!* The Christian is caught in the tension between the old aeon that is passing away and the new aeon of salvation, a new creation that already has begun and will be consummated at the Parousia; but we are not there yet. Against the over-realized eschatology of the Corinthian Christians, Paul emphasized the futurity of the resurrection when faith will become sight, the perishable transformed into the imperishable, and death swallowed up in victory (1 Cor 15:50-57). In the meantime we are not to opt out of our present responsibilities but rather give ourselves fully to the work of the Lord. It is significant that Paul's great chapter on the resurrection is followed immediately by a word of instruction about taking the offering (1 Cor 16:1-4).

Between the *No Longer* and the *Not Yet* stretches what Paul called in Romans the *Now Age* (*ho nun kairos*).[24] In the Now Age, Christians must live out their vocation as those who have been rescued from "this present evil age" (Gal 1:4). That is, they are to live as those who have been justified, adopted, and sealed with the Holy Spirit while being subjected to persecution, distress, and ferocious attacks from Satan, "the god of this age" (2 Cor 4:4). Living in this kind of eschatological tension produces what Paul called "groaning." We groan with the brokenness of creation around us (Rom 8:22); we groan as we struggle with the power of sin within us (Rom 7); we groan with the longing to be released from our earthly "tent" and to be with Christ, which is "better by far" (2 Cor 2–4; Phil 1:20-23). In the midst of all of this, the Christian does not face life with a stoic apathy but rather with rejoicing and confident hope. We "eagerly await" (Gal 5:5) the return of Christ in glory even when we are hard pressed, perplexed, and persecuted; for we know that we will not be crushed, abandoned, or destroyed. We take comfort from the Holy Spirit who, dwelling with us, also groans alongside us with words too deep to be uttered (Rom 8:26).

Paul clearly understood his own role and apostolic vocation in terms of the unique *kairos* ("age") of salvation history in which he had been saved and called. He saw himself as "the man of the hour whose mission took place in the last hours of world history. He knew himself to be the eschatological apostle who spans the times between the resurrection of Christ and the final resurrection of the dead."[25] Only in light of this kind of apocalyptic expectation can we understand the passion of a Paul, who without blinking an eye was willing to damn false teachers to hell because they were pervert-

---

[24] On this concept in Paul, see the excellent study of P. Stuhlmacher, "Erwägungen zum ontologischen Charakter der KAINE KTISIS bei Paulus," *EvT* (1967): 1-35.

[25] Beker, *Paul the Apostle,* 144-45.

ing the gospel (Gal 1:7-9). In like manner, only a former pharisaic Jew imbued with an extreme zeal for the traditions of his ancestral religion would be willing to damn himself to hell (Rom 9:1-4) in order to bring his fellow Jews to a saving knowledge of the true Messiah. Because "the time is short" (1 Cor 7:29), Paul had no time to waste. His burden was to preach the gospel to the very ends of the earth so that "all nations might believe and obey" (Rom 16:26). It was this burden that prompted Paul to preach the good news of Jesus Christ to the people of Galatia in the first place. This same burden forms the backdrop of his vigorous defense of the gospel in his letter to the Galatian Christians.

2. Who Were the Galatians?

The destination of most of Paul's letters presents no problem to the student of the New Testament. Rome, Corinth, Ephesus, Colosse, Philippi, and Thessalonica are all specific cities precisely situated at strategic points in the Mediterranean basin. Galatians is the only one of Paul's letters addressed neither to an individual nor to Christians in one specific city. In the period of late antiquity "Galatia" was an elastic term reflecting the changing political developments in central Asia Minor. In recent years we have seen how the current of events in Eastern Europe have resulted in the complete redrawing of the maps of such entire areas as the former countries of Yugoslavia and the Soviet Union. A similar development occurred on the war-swept plains of Asia Minor as the geographical boundaries of "Galatia" expanded and contracted with the rise and fall of invading tribes, nation states, and empires. All of this has led to much confusion and controversy concerning the identification of the Galatians to whom Paul addressed his letter. It is not our purpose here to review the extensive literature on this subject but rather to point to several leading theories including the one to be adopted in this commentary.[26]

---

[26] All of the major commentaries deal at length with these issues. Especially worthy of note are J. B. Lightfoot, *Saint Paul's Epistle to the Galatians* (1890; reprint, London: Macmillan, 1986), 1-35; E. deW. Burton, *A Critical and Exegetical Commentary on the Epistle to the Galatians,* ICC (Edinburgh: T & T Clark, 1921), xxi-xliii; F. F. Bruce, *The Epistle to the Galatians,* NIGTC (Grand Rapids: Eerdmans, 1982), 3-18; H. D. Betz, *Galatians,* Her (Philadelphia: Fortress, 1979), 1-11; R. Y. Fung, *The Epistle to the Galatians,* NICNT (Grand Rapids: Eerdmans, 1988), 1-8; Longenecker, *Galatians,* lxii-lxii; D. Lührmann, *Galatians* (Minneapolis: Fortress, 1992), 1-6. The view adopted in this commentary is that set forth classically by Ramsay and, more recently, argued for conclusively by Bruce. On issues of provenance and date, I have also found useful the brief article by C. J. Hemer, "Acts and Galatians Reconsidered," *Themelios* 2 (1976-77): 81-88. Cf. also the helpful summary in P. Feine, J. Behm, W. G. Kümmel, *Introduction to the New Testament* (Nashville: Abingdon, 1965), 190-98.

(1) Galatia before the Time of Paul

In his opening salutation Paul addressed his letter "to the churches in Galatia" (1:2). Later, with a tone of exasperation, he breaks his train of thought and speaks to them directly: "You foolish Galatians!" (3:1). The English word "Galatians" comes from the Latin *Galatae,* which in turn is an exact transliteration from the Greek. The same word is also rendered in both Greek and Latin as *Celts* and *Gauls.*[27] The Celts first appeared in history as a distinct ethnic or people group sometime around 500 B.C. when they occupied the Danube River basin in central Europe. They were known for their bravery in battle and for their restless spirit. From their Germanic base they spread out into the various extremities of the European mainland. Some of them settled in what is today France, giving the name Gaul to that country (cf. Julius Caesar's *Commentaries on the Gallic War*). Others migrated to the British Isles, where their form of life took root in the Celtic culture of Ireland and the Gaelic dialect of the Highland Scots. Other groups of Celts spread southeastward into the Balkan peninsula and from there into Asia Minor. In 278–277 B.C., King Nicomedes of Bithynia invited a group of these Celts to assist him in defending his territory against attackers from the East. Not content to serve as mercenaries, the Celts undertook their own campaign of conquest, eventually gaining control over a vast tract of land in central Asia Minor. Around 230 B.C. they were defeated by Attalus I, king of Pergamum, who restricted them to a defined region on the Anatolian plain around Ancyra, the modern capital of Turkey.

As the Roman Empire expanded eastward, all of the peoples of Asia Minor fell under the sway of the new superpower on the Tiber. By this time the Celts (called Galatians) had organized themselves into an independent kingdom with their own distinctive language and center of government at Ancyra. For a while the Romans allowed the Galatians to maintain their status as a client-kingdom within the empire with their king Amyntas ruling under the tutelage of the Roman overlords much as Herod the Great ruled over Judea. However, when Amyntas fell in battle in 25 B.C., Augustus Caesar reorganized the Galatian kingdom into a Roman province. For administrative purposes the geographical boundaries of this new imperial province were extended to include not only the original Galatian territory around Ancyra ("North Galatia") but also the southern regions of Phrygia and Lycaonia ("South Galatia"). Thus in the days of Paul the Roman province of Galatia technically stretched all the way across the heartland of Asia Minor from Pontus on the Black Sea to Pamphylia on the Mediterranean. In 1 Pet

---

[27] Cf. the Latin forms *Celtae* and *Galli.*

1:1 Galatia is used in this wider geographical sense alongside the other Roman provinces of Pontus, Cappodocia, Asia, and Bithynia.

(2) North or South Galatia?

NORTH GALATIA. Given what we know about the history of Asia Minor in this period, there seems to be three possible ways of interpreting the phrase "the churches of Galatia," those Christian congregations to whom Paul addressed his letter. Theoretically, at least, this phrase could encompass various groups of Christians scattered throughout the enlarged Roman province of Galatia. This sometimes is called the Pan-Galatian theory and in fact was advocated by a number of biblical scholars in the nineteenth century.[28]

It is not surprising that this hypothesis has been generally discounted, for there are obvious difficulties with it. Galatians is one of Paul's most contextually oriented letters. For example, Romans and Ephesians, though addressed to Christian believers in specific places, tell us very little about the development or problems faced by the churches in Rome and Ephesus. On the other hand, Galatians, in this respect very much like Paul's Corinthian correspondence, addresses specific issues and controversies arising at a particular place and time in his missionary activities. In Galatians, Paul wrote about a matter of great urgency to people he knew very well. He also wrote with a kind of specificity that would make it almost inconceivable for him to address the letter to disparate congregations scattered over so large a geographical terrain. We are left then with two major theories of destination, each of which has claimed strong advocates among biblical scholars during the past century.

Until the late nineteenth century it was almost universally held that the Galatians to whom Paul wrote were the descendants of the ancient Celtic peoples who settled in north central Asia Minor. This view was taken for granted by the church fathers who commented on Paul's Letter to the Galatians several centuries after he had written it. In their day the *Provincia Galatia* had again been reduced in size to encompass an area roughly equivalent to the old pre-Augustan kingdom of Galatia, a fact that reflected the shifting circumstances of Roman imperial policy. Moreover, by the fourth and fifth centuries the Christian faith was thriving in this part of northern Asia Minor. For example, in A.D. 314 an important meeting of the church, the Council of Ancyra, convened in the ancient Galatian capital. Very likely the church fathers of this period read back into the New Testament the con-

---

[28] Longenecker (*Galatians,* lxiv) lists as advocates of this hypothesis J. P. Mynster, R. Cornely, E. Jacquier, and T. Zahn.

temporary church setting of their own day.[29] In the sixteenth century Martin Luther, John Calvin, and the other Reformers accepted, although they did not advance new arguments for, the North Galatian tradition.

In modern times the classic statement of the North Galatian view was set forth by J. B. Lightfoot in his magisterial commentary on this epistle (1865). J. Moffatt[30] recapitulated Lightfoot's arguments and added some nuances of his own in favor of the North Galatian hypothesis. These views have been adopted by recent commentators such as Betz, Lührmann, Harrington, and Ebeling. In addition to appealing to the testimony of tradition, those who argue for a North Galatian destination put forth various arguments in support of their position. However, these can largely be grouped under the following three headings:

Galatians as a Term of Ethnicity. Lightfoot, among others, believed that the term "Galatians" referred to those descendants of the Celtic peoples who embodied distinctive ethnic characteristics. Caesar described the Celts he encountered in Western Europe as a fierce and hearty race, impetuous and fickle in their dealings with one another. Should we not expect to find similar traces of the Celtic character among the Galatians of Paul's epistle if indeed they were descended from the same stock? Evidently so, for "beneath the surface the Celtic character remains still the same, whether manifested in the rude and fiery barbarians who were crushed by the arms of Caesar or the impetuous and fickle converts who called down the indignant rebuke of the Apostle of the Gentiles."[31] Thus the fickleness of Paul's Galatians was detected in their turning so quickly away from the true gospel to embrace the corrupt message of the false apostles (Gal 1:6). Likewise their treachery and quarrelsomeness, their superstition and debauchery, are said to be glimpsed in Paul's comments about their obedience to the elemental powers, their drunkenness and revelings, and their bitter disputes (Gal 4:9; 5:19-21; 6:1-5). Today this kind of reasoning carries little weight since there is nothing uniquely Celtic about any of these traits. Indeed, Paul made similar comments in his other letters, all of which obviously were

---

[29] However, a dissenting witness from this period is Asterius, bishop of Amaseia in Pontus (d. 410), who interpreted "the Galatic region and Phrygia" of Acts 18:23 as "Lycaonia and the Cities of Phrygia" (*Homilia VIII in S S. Petrum et Paulum*; Migne PG 40.293 D). Ramsay and Bruce cite Bishop Asterius's comment as a vestigial testimony to a lingering South Galatian tradition.

[30] J. Moffatt, *Introduction to the Literature of the New Testament* (1911).

[31] Lightfoot, *Galatians,* 13. Lightfoot wrote at a time of intense national consciousness in Europe when it was popular to assign specific character traits to national groupings. Thus the English were seen as stuffy, the French effeminate, the Germans strong-willed, the Italians hot tempered, and so forth.

addressed to non-Celtic peoples.

The Development of Paul's Theology.   Some have argued that Galatians should be placed near the end of Paul's apostolic ministry, around the same time as Romans, since both epistles share a literary and theological affinity centered on the doctrine of justification by faith. In response to this argument, it can be said that while Galatians doubtless deals with this major theme of Pauline theology, the differences between the two epistles are quite as striking as the similarities. Moreover, the entire Pauline corpus must have been composed between twelve to fifteen years, a relatively brief span for the kind of theological hiatus presupposed by some New Testament scholars.

Linguistic and Chronological Concerns.   J. Polhill has correctly observed that "one's view of the nature of Acts will tend to influence his view of the Galatian destination."[32] The term "Galatia" occurs twice in Acts (16:6; 18:23), at the beginning of Paul's second and third missionary journeys, respectively. In the former text Paul and Timothy are portrayed as traveling "through the Phrygian and Galatic region, having been forbidden by the Holy Spirit to speak the word in Asia." In the second text Paul is returning from a visit to Palestine en route to begin his missionary work in Ephesus. On this journey he "went from place to place through the Galatic region and Phrygia, strengthening all the disciples." The Greek phrasing in both of these texts is ambiguous and, taken alone, could lend support to either the North or South Galatia theory.[33] These are especially important texts for those who favor a North Galatian destination. If indeed they can be read to mean that on these two missionary journeys Paul visited both Phrygia (in Southern Galatia) and Galatia proper (in the North), they constitute the only evidence, biblical or otherwise, of Paul's evangelization of this region of Asia Minor.[34]

SOUTH GALATIA.   The two scholars who have done more than anyone else to establish the South Galatia hypothesis as the preferred option are W. M. Ramsay and F. F. Bruce, the one an expert in historical geography and the other well trained in classical literature. Their careful research and consideration of all angles of the question are not likely to be superseded in the near future.[35]

---

[32] J. B. Polhill, "Galatia Revisited: The Life-setting of the Epistle," *RevExp* 69 (1972): 441.

[33] The texts in question read thus: Διῆλθον δὲ τὴν φρυγίαν καὶ Γαλατικὴν χώραν (Acts 16:6), and ἐξῆλθεν διερχόμενος καθεξῆς τὴν Γαλατικὴν χώραν καὶ φρυγίαν (Acts 18:23). Cf. Bruce, *Galatians,* 10-13.

[34] Cf. C. J. Hemer's "Acts and Galatians Reconsidered," 84. Cf. also Ramsay's (*Historical Commentary,* 165-74) discussion of the emergence of Christianity in North Galatia.

[35] Cf. W. M. Ramsay, *A Historical Commentary on Saint Paul's Commentary to the Galatians* (Grand Rapids: Baker, 1965), and Bruce, *Galatians.*

The great advantage of the South Galatia hypothesis is that it provides a precise identification of "the churches of Galatia" to whom Paul's letter was addressed: they are the congregations at Derbe, Lystra, Iconium, and Pisidian Antioch, which he founded on his first missionary journey. Acts 13–14 records the missionary activity of Paul and Barnabas in these South Galatia cities, all of which were located some one hundred miles inland from the Mediterranean coast where the two evangelists had landed following their preaching mission on Cyprus.

Paul and Barnabas stopped briefly at the town of Perga, a small city some twelve miles inland from the Mediterranean port of Attalia (Acts 13:13-15). This was an important turning point in their missionary itinerary, for it was at Perga that John Mark decided to leave his companions and return home to Jerusalem. As we know, this defection greatly angered Paul and led to a later break with his partner Barnabas (Acts 15:37-38). Ramsay has suggested that originally Paul had intended to travel as far west as Ephesus on this missionary journey but that he was forced to change his plans due to his contraction of malaria at Perga.[36] In order to secure relief from this ailment, he decided to leave the Pamphylian lowlands and travel northward across the Taurus Mountains to Pisidian Antioch, the chief city of South Galatia, where the Romans had established a strong military presence. Although this theory goes beyond the evidence of the text, it does provide a plausible explanation of Paul's statement that it was because of an illness that he first preached the gospel to them (Gal 4:13).

It is beyond dispute that from 25 B.C. until well after Paul's death the cities of Pisidian Antioch, Iconium, Derbe, and Lystra belonged to the reorganized province of Galatia. Since, as Ramsay observed, "Paul writes as a Roman and a citizen of the empire," it would have been natural for him to use the generic provincial designation, Galatians, in addressing those churches founded in these cities on his first missionary journey. Indeed, it is difficult to know what other name Paul could have devised to include the residents of these different cities since they lay in the separate subdistricts of Pisidia, Lycaonia, and Phrygia. Moreover, in his letters Paul always used the names of Roman provinces when speaking of a wide geographical area within the empire. Thus in 1 Cor 16 he spoke of the churches of *Galatia* alongside his travels through *Macedonia,* his first converts in *Achaia,* and the congregations of *Asia,* in each case using the commonly accepted provincial name for the area in question. On the other hand, Luke, who was not a Roman citizen but a member of the Greek educated elite, often preferred

---

[36] W. M. Ramsay, *St. Paul the Traveller and Roman Citizen* (London: Hodder & Stoughton, 1897), 89-97.

the local geographical or ethnic designations for the regions he described in Acts. Thus in Acts 13–14 he spoke of "Pisidia," "Phrygia," and "Lycaonia."

The cities of Pisidian Antioch, Iconium, Derbe, and Lystra were situated along the Sabastian Way, a major imperial highway linking Ephesus in the west to the provinces of Syria and Cilicia in the east. This highway was not only a major trade route between Rome and the eastern reaches of the empire; it was also an essential artery of communication for the Roman governor, who administered the province from his base in Pisidian Antioch. Along this highway Paul and Barnabas traveled, preaching in the synagogues and marketplaces of these cities, planting churches and appointing elders to lead them, and evangelizing the countryside of the surrounding region.

When we compare the content of Galatians with Luke's account of Paul's evangelization of the South Galatian cities, we find a number of striking parallels that point toward the identification of "the churches of Galatia" with these Christian congregations.

First, the theme of justification by faith constitutes a major theme in the Galatian letter and was at the heart of the missionary message delivered by Paul and Barnabas. For example, in the synagogue at Pisidian Antioch they declared that "through Jesus the forgiveness of sins is proclaimed to you. Through him everyone who believes is justified from everything you could not be justified from by the law of Moses" (Acts 13:38-39). It was precisely the doctrine of justification the false brothers attacked by their insistence that circumcision be added to faith in Christ as a requirement for salvation.

Second, it is clear that Galatians was written to a congregation composed primarily of Gentile believers. This is confirmed by the missionary strategy Paul and Barnabas pursued in the cities of South Galatia. Here, as elsewhere, Paul followed his usual practice of going to the synagogues and proclaiming the gospel to the Jews first. When his message was spurned, however, he then turned to the Gentiles. Thus Paul and Barnabas declared to the Jewish inhabitants of Pisidian Antioch: "We had to speak the Word of God to you first. Since you rejected and do not consider yourselves worthy of eternal life, we now turn to the Gentiles" (Acts 13:46). Luke said that when the Gentiles heard this "they were glad and honored the word of the Lord; and all who were appointed for eternal life believed" (Acts 13:48). A similar pattern of response occurred in the cities of Iconium, Lystra, and Derbe as well.

Third, we know that the initial preaching of the gospel among the churches of Galatia was accompanied by miraculous signs and wonders. Paul referred to the supernatural acts of the Spirit, asking the Galatians whether God had worked miracles among them because of their observance of the law or because of their belief in the gospel of grace (Gal 3:5). Some of these miracles are recorded in Luke's account of the first missionary journey through South Galatia. For example, in Iconium we are told that the Lord confirmed the message of his grace by enabling Paul and Barnabas to do miraculous signs and wonders (Acts 14:3). Likewise, a man crippled from birth was miraculously healed in the city of Lystra (Acts 14:8-10).

Fourth, at one point in his Letter to the Galatians, Paul reminded them of how they had initially welcomed him "as if I were an angel of God, as if I were Christ Jesus himself" (Gal 4:14). Some scholars have found in this statement an echo of the extravagant adulation shown to Paul and Barnabas following the healing of the lame man in Lystra.

Fifth, at several points in the Galatian letter Paul referred to the persecution he had suffered as a preacher of the gospel. At the very end of his epistle Paul reminded his Galatian disciples that he still bore the brand marks of Jesus on his body (Gal 6:17). We know from Acts that Paul and Barnabas were harassed and hounded from city to city as they preached the gospel throughout the region of South Galatia. At Lystra, Paul was stoned, dragged outside the city, and left for dead. Perhaps some of the brand marks he mentioned were scars from this stoning.

After reaching the city of Derbe, Paul and Barnabas did an about-face and retraced their steps through the Galatian cities they had just evangelized. It would have been far easier for them to continue traveling eastward on the Sebastian Way through the Cilician Gates and southward to their home base of Antioch in Syria. The reason for the reversal of their itinerary is clear; they desired to strengthen the new Christians and to confirm them in the true faith. Given the intensity of opposition to their efforts and the short-term duration of their visits, however, it is likely that the missionaries had to leave their new converts before they were thoroughly rooted and grounded in an understanding of the salvation they had received. In any event, some of them obviously fell easy prey to the false doctrine promulgated by Paul's detractors in his absence. To rescue them from this peril and to reestablish them in "the truth of the gospel," Paul wrote his Letter to the Galatians.

Two additional points are in order concerning the destination of the Galatian Epistle. First, while more conservative scholars, following Ramsay and Bruce, accept the South Galatian hypothesis, there is no necessary correlation between one's theological commitments and historical conclusions on this issue. Conservative scholars such as J. G. Machen, E. F. Harrison, and R. H. Stein have argued for a North Galatia view while R. H. Fuller and E. D. W. Burton, both South Galatianists, call into question the historical veracity of Acts.[37] Second, wherever the "churches of Galatia" were, the

---

[37] Cf. Longenecker, *Galatians,* lxviii-lxix.

passion and urgency of Paul's theological concern for them remains the same. On balance, however, the weight of evidence falls strongly in support of the view that Paul addressed his letter to the congregations in South Galatia that he and Barnabas established on their first missionary journey.

(3) The Date of Galatians

When and from where in the course of his apostolic career did Paul write his Letter to the Galatians? It has been said that "the date of Galatians is one of the most knotty problems in Pauline studies."[38] The truth of this statement is borne out by a review of the literature on the subject, which shows a bewildering variety of scholarly opinion related to diverse ways of reckoning the chronology of Paul's life and ministry.[39] For the purposes of this commentary, we will forego an extensive review of this literature, focusing instead on the option that seems to fit best all of the evidence.

How the destination of Galatians is decided will necessarily affect one's judgment about the date. It is beyond doubt that Paul wrote to the Galatians after he had made at least one and perhaps two personal visits among them. If we accept a North Galatian destination, then the earliest possible occasion for the letter will be after Paul's second missionary journey, assuming that Acts 16:6 refers to North Galatia. Most scholars who take this view place the writing of Galatians during Paul's Ephesian ministry, when for some two years Paul carried on extensive evangelistic and missionary work in the province of Asia (Acts 19:10).

Lightfoot argued for an even later date near the end of the third missionary journey when Paul was resident in Corinth. He based this conclusion on his analysis of literary and theological affinities between Galatians and the other Pauline Letters. In particular he found Galatians and 2 Corinthians strikingly similar not only in words and arguments but also in tone and feeling. An even closer resemblance, he felt, could be demonstrated between Galatians and Romans, the former being in some ways a rough draft of the latter. Lightfoot's proposed sequence was 2 Corinthians-Galatians-Romans, with Galatians serving as a kind of connecting link between 2 Corinthians, where the issue was primarily personal, and Romans, where it was almost exclusively doctrinal.

---

[38] Longenecker, *Galatians*, lxxiii.

[39] In addition to the standard commentaries, the following studies are worthy of note: J. A. T. Robinson, *Redating the New Testament* (Philadelphia: Westminster, 1976); C. H. Talbert, "Again: Paul's Visits to Jerusalem," *NovT* 9 (1967): 26-40; J. Knox, *Chapters in a Life of Paul* (New York: Abingdon, 1950); R. Jewett, *A Chronology of Paul's Life* (Philadelphia: Fortress, 1979).

In Galatians both the personal and the doctrinal coalesce as Paul moves from a defense of his apostolic calling to an exegetical and theological apology for the doctrine of justification. Lightfoot has convincingly demonstrated the close thematic parallels between Galatians and Romans. However, he goes too far in claiming that "we should be doing violence to historic probability by separating the Epistles to the Galatians and Romans from each other by an interval of more than a few months."[40] Chronological proximity may not be the best explanation for the close similarity between these two letters. More plausible is the idea that justification by faith was a major concern for Paul throughout the course of his apostolic career. The doctrine Paul set forth in the white-hot polemics of Galatians he developed in a more formal and comprehensive way in Romans.

If, as we have suggested, Paul addressed his Galatian letter to the churches he and Barnabas had founded during their first missionary journey, then it makes good sense to see Galatians as the earliest extant letter in the Pauline corpus. On this view Galatians would have been written sometime after Paul's return to Syrian Antioch and just before the meeting of the Jerusalem Council recorded in Acts 15.

Two passages in Galatians itself bear on the date of the epistle, although both are subject to multiple interpretations. In Gal 1:6, Paul wrote, "I am astonished that you are so quickly [*houtōs tacheōs*] deserting the one who called you by the grace of Christ and are turning to a different gospel." The most natural and most obvious way to read the expression "so quickly" is with reference to a defection that took place shortly after the conversion of the Galatians, that is, almost immediately after Paul's missionary activity among them. True, this expression is a relative one and could conceivably be stretched to cover a period of several years. However, it more likely refers to the eruption of a controversy that followed almost in the wake of Paul's first preaching ministry in Galatia.

Later in Galatians, Paul remarked that "it was because of a bodily ailment that I preached the gospel to you at first" (Gal 4:13, RSV). The phrase "at first" (*to proteron*) is ambiguous in Greek and could well mean, as the NEB has it, "As you know, it was bodily illness that *originally* led to my bringing you the gospel." However, even if we insist on the temporal meaning of this expression, it can well be accounted for by the fact, already noted, of Paul and Barnabas's return visit through the cities of South Galatia on their way back to Antioch. It is not necessary to suppose, as North Galatianists do, that this text presupposes the later visits to Galatia referred to in Acts 16:6 and 18:23.

---

[40] Lightfoot, *Galatians,* 48.

Given the evidence for an early dating, we can construct the following scenario for the writing of Galatians. Although Paul had engaged in evangelistic and missionary work for a number of years following his conversion, he and Barnabas were deliberately set apart and sent forth for a specific missionary undertaking by the church at Antioch. From Seleucia they sailed to Cyprus and from there to the mainland of Asia Minor. Crossing the Taurus Mountains, they came to the provincial capital of Pisidian Antioch, where they preached the gospel to both Jews and Gentiles. Hounded by Jewish persecutors, they made their way along the imperial highway and continued to win new converts in the cities of Iconium, Lystra, and Derbe.

Having briefly confirmed these new believers, Paul and Barnabas returned to Syrian Antioch by the same route they had come. Soon after their departure the new churches of South Galatia were thrown into great confusion by the arrival of another team of Christian missionaries who contradicted much of what Paul and Barnabas had proclaimed concerning the way of salvation. These same men, or at least their partners and allies, also had appeared in Antioch teaching their law-observant gospel: "Unless you are circumcised, according to the custom taught by Moses, you cannot be saved" (Acts 15:1). So great was this disturbance at Antioch that Paul and Barnabas were sent to Jerusalem to discuss the whole matter with Peter and the other apostles there.

In the meantime Paul had received word that these false brothers or their emissaries had spread this perverted gospel among the newly planted churches of Galatia. Unable to visit these foundling congregations in person, he wrote the Letter to the Galatians as a way of restoring order and reestablishing the doctrinal integrity of his dear children in Christ. Thus it is likely that Galatians was written from Antioch on the eve of the Council of Jerusalem, which usually is dated around A.D. 49–50. One scholar has suggested that Galatians might even have been written while Paul was en route from Antioch to Jerusalem or perhaps even from Jerusalem itself "in the whirl of discussion that seems envisaged in Acts 15:7 before the actual Council itself."[41]

Another issue must be mentioned in this introductory discussion of the date of Galatians although we will revisit this question in fuller detail in the commentary proper. Put simply, the problem is how we can square the three visits of Paul to Jerusalem mentioned in Acts (9:26; 11:30; 15:4) with the two visits Paul himself recounted in Galatians (1:18; 2:1-10). How this issue is resolved depends largely on the historical credibility given to Acts.

---

[41] R. A. Cole, *The Epistle of Paul to the Galatians* (Grand Rapids: Eerdmans, 1965), 23.

Several scholars have suggested that Luke, either inadvertently or deliberately, "invented" one or more of the visits or else telescoped several themes from early church history into an apocryphal setting such as the Jerusalem Council described in Acts 15. The position taken in this commentary is that Luke was a credible historian who, under the inspiration of the Holy Spirit, recorded with unerring accuracy, if not always with minute precision, only those events that actually occurred in space and time. There is no contradiction between Luke and Paul, although it must be admitted that both men sometimes described the same event from different perspectives and for diverse purposes.[42]

Traditionally the visit of Paul to Jerusalem recorded in Gal 2:1-10 has been equated with the Jerusalem Council in Acts 15. Clearly there are similarities between the two accounts. Both speak of a meeting in Jerusalem between Paul and Barnabas on the one hand and Peter and James on the other. In both accounts the issue at stake concerned the participation of Gentile Christians in the life of the church with the attendant topic of circumcision high on the agenda. However, there are substantial, we think insuperable, difficulties in regarding these two passages as separate reports of the same event. Chief among these is that nowhere in Galatians does Paul refer to the decision reached at the Jerusalem Council. Yet we know that Paul and Barnabas personally delivered a letter from the council to Gentile believers following the Jerusalem summit. Indeed, "it is difficult to see why in the midst of the Galatian conflict he chose to be silent about the decision reached at Jerusalem—or how, in fact, he could have avoided any mention of it—if he were writing after the Jerusalem Council."[43] If, however, as we suppose, Galatians was written *prior to* the Jerusalem Council, the problem of correlating Paul's account of his visits to Jerusalem with those recorded in Acts is more easily resolved.

On this reckoning, Gal 1 equals Acts 9, and Gal 2 equals Acts 11. The first visit occurred some three years after Paul's conversion following his "silent years" in Arabia. This was a short visit of fifteen days in which he met Peter and James and came into conflict with the Hellenists of Jerusalem who sought to kill him because of his speaking so boldly in the name of Jesus. The second visit occurred some fourteen years later when Paul and

---

[42] F. F. Bruce, *Commentary on the Book of Acts,* NICNT (Grand Rapids: Eerdmans, 1977), 43-56. E. Haenchen reflects the commonly accepted critical consensus on the historical value of Acts (*The Acts of the Apostles* [Philadelphia: Westminster, 1971]), but see the massive counterstudy by C. J. Hemer, *The Book of Acts in the Setting of the Hellenistic History* (Tübingen: Mohr, 1989). On the accuracy of ancient historians generally, see C. W. Fornara, *The Nature of History in Ancient Greece and Rome* (Berkeley: University of California Press, 1983).

[43] Longenecker, *Galatians,* lxxix.

Barnabas were sent by the church at Antioch to Jerusalem to bring famine relief to the Christians in Judea. This visit involved a special meeting with certain "pillars" in the Jerusalem church, namely, James, Peter, and John, who extended the right hand of fellowship with Paul and gave their official blessing to his ministry as an apostle to the Gentiles. Paul attested with an oath (Gal 1:20) that his recollection of his visits and dealings with the Jerusalem apostles was indeed accurate. That Paul nowhere in Galatians made mention of his third visit to Jerusalem, on the occasion of the council of Jerusalem in Acts 15, is best explained by the simple fact that it had not yet occurred when he wrote to the churches of Galatia.

3. The Problem in Galatia

The New Testament has been called "a bad-tempered book" given the amount of space it devotes to explicit attacks and polemical arguments against various opponents who were subverters of the gospel.[44] To sense the force of this statement one has only to think of Peter's likening of certain apostates to dogs who turned back to their own vomit (2 Pet 2:22) or of Jude's designation of false pastors as clouds without rain, trees without fruit, and "wild waves of the sea, foaming up their shame" (Jude 12-13). Nor are such remarks confined to the latter books of the New Testament when the Christian church was engaged in a fight for its very life. No, they are equally present in the Gospels themselves. Witness John the Baptist's blast against "the brood of vipers" or even Jesus' pronouncements of woe against the Pharisees in Matt 23. Still, perhaps no one in the New Testament was more belligerent in his denunciation of opponents than the apostle Paul. And nowhere was he more "bad tempered" than in Galatians. We will have to take up this theme again in the commentary proper, but it is well to note from the outset that from the standpoint of Pauline theology, polemics cannot be divorced from dogmatics. What was at stake was not merely the outbursts of an ill-tempered preacher but rather the truth of the gospel itself.

Who were the opponents against whom Paul defended himself and his gospel in Galatia? The traditional answer to this question has been the Judaizers, those teachers who sought to add certain strictures of the Jewish law, notably circumcision, as a requirement for inclusion in the Christian church. In the early church Marius Victorinus, who produced the first Latin commentary on

---

[44] This expression is attributed to Professor Christopher Evans by J. M. G. Barclay, "Mirror-Reading a Polemical Letter: Galatians as a Test Case," *JSNT* 31 (1987): 73.

Galatians, summed up this received interpretation in the following way:

> The Galatians are going astray because they are adding Judaism to the gospel
> of faith in Christ, observing in a material sense the sabbath and circumcision,
> together with the other works which they received in accordance with the
> law. Disturbed by these tendencies Paul writes this letter, wishing to put them
> right and call them back from Judaism, in order that they may preserve faith
> in Christ alone, and receive from Christ the hope of salvation and of his
> promises, because no one is saved by the works of the law. So, in order to
> show that what they are adding is wrong, he wishes to confirm [the truth of]
> his gospel.[45]

During the Reformation, Luther and Calvin also accepted the traditional
view and passed it along unaltered except that they (especially Luther)
found a direct analogy between Paul's opponents in Galatia and those who
refused to embrace the gospel of grace in their own day. Calvin, for example, referred to them as "the false apostles, who had deceived the Galatians
to advance their own claims, pretending that they had received a commission from the apostles. Their method of infiltration was to convince people
that they represented the apostles and delivered a message from them. But
they took away from Paul the name and authority of apostle . . . in attacking
Paul they were really attacking the truth of the gospel."[46] This view
remained virtually unchallenged until the nineteenth century when F. C.
Baur offered his radical reconstruction of New Testament history. Since
then the identity of the anti-Pauline opposition in Galatia has generated considerable debate and spawned numerous theories, the most important of
which fall into the following five groupings.

(1) The Tübingen School

As early as 1831, F. C. Baur proposed that the history of early Christianity could be read in terms of the polar opposition between two rival factions.
One, led by Paul and Apollos, emphasized the Christian mission to the Gentiles; the other, gathered around Peter and James, stressed the priority of the
Jerusalem church and the continuing validity of the Jewish law for Christian
believers. Baur's theory was cast in terms of the prevailing Hegelian philosophy with its dialectic of thesis-antithesis-synthesis. According to this view,
the Pauline party continued to become more and more radical in its break

---

[45] C. Marius Victorinus Afer, *In Galatas,* Introd.; cited in Bruce, *Galatians,* 21.
[46] J. Calvin, CNTC 11.4.

with Judaism until it was ultimately absorbed into Gnosticism. The Petrine party, on the other hand, became more and more narrow, gradually evolving into such Jewish-Christian sectarian groups as the Ebionites. Eventually a synthesis between the Pauline and Petrine extremes was achieved in the emergence of "early Catholicism" (*frühkatholizimis*).[47] According to the Tübingen critics, the Pastoral Epistles were written in the mid-second century to portray an "orthodox" Paul more palatable to the church leaders of that day than the real, historical Paul with his radical gospel of spiritual freedom and law-free grace. Similarly, the Acts of the Apostles was depicted as historical fiction designed to paper over the irreconcilable differences between Paul on the one hand and Peter and the other apostles on the other.[48]

Galatians, it will be recalled, was one of only four Pauline letters that Baur regarded as authentic. Galatians, in fact, is a major piece of evidence in this theory of the radical bifurcation of early Christianity. Paul's opponents in Galatia were only representatives of the leaders of the Jerusalem church, his true adversaries. The troublemakers in Galatia were the spiritual first cousins, if not the identical twins, of those "men . . . from James" who had earlier disturbed the church at Antioch, leading to Paul's famous confrontation with Peter (Gal 2:11-14). Now they had infiltrated the churches of Galatia preaching this same pernicious message, repudiating Paul's doctrine of grace, and denying his apostolic authority.

(2) The Two-Front Theory

In the early twentieth century two scholars, one a German, W. Lütgert, and the other an American, J. H. Ropes, redirected the discussion of the Galatian problem by arguing that Paul was simultaneously fighting against

---

[47] Baur, *Paul: His Life and Works,* 1:251-53. Cf. also Baur's earlier essay, "Die Christuspartei in der korinthischen Gemeinde," *Tübinger Zeitschrift für Theologie* (1831): 61-206. J. Blevins has given a helpful summary of the continuing influence of the Tübingen School in Galatian studies: "The Problem in Galatia," *RevExp* 69 (1972): 449-58.

[48] Baur's disciple, A. Schwegler, and his son-in-law, E. Zeller, extended the thesis of their mentor even further, claiming that Paul's Galatian opponents carried on their work with the full knowledge and blessing of the Jerusalem authorities, including Peter and James. In this same tradition E. Meyer regarded Peter as the real leader and spiritual hero of Paul's Galatian opponents. See his *Ursprung und Anfänge des Christentums* (Stuttgart: Cotta, 1925), 3:434. The NT historian H. Lietzmann suggested a slight modification of the Baur thesis. James, he argued, was the true pillar of opposition, while Barnabas reconverted to strict Jewish Christian habits after the embarrassing incident at Antioch and was the local source of agitation in Galatia itself. See his *An die Galater* (Tübingen: Mohr, 1923), 38. See also the recent study by R. Bauckham, "Barnabas in Galatians," *JSNT* 2 (1979): 61-70.

two groups rather than one.[49] The title of Lütgert's book, *Gesetz und Geist*, "Law and Spirit," indicates the nature of the two-pronged battle Paul had to wage: on the one hand legalists had infiltrated the churches of Galatia with their message of justification by faith plus circumcision; at the same time certain libertines within the church had misinterpreted Paul's message of freedom by converting Christian liberty into unrestrained license. Thus Paul admonished them not to use their freedom as "an opportunity for the flesh" (Gal 5:13, RSV).

The two-front theory has much to commend it. In the first place, as we have noted already, Paul did have to fight against a dual distortion of his basic message—against a Judaizing group that minimized the all-decisive character of Christ's death and resurrection through their promotion of the law as a means of salvation but also against a pneumatic group of spiritual enthusiasts whose charismatic and antinomian excesses scandalized the church and called into question the efficacy of the gospel. It is also true that Paul sometimes encountered both extremes within the same congregation. Thus in the faction-ridden church at Corinth, Paul opposed both "the spiritual ones" who had abandoned traditional sexual mores in the name of Christian liberty as well as certain law-observant believers who sought to impose kosher regulations as a test of fellowship for the entire church (1 Cor 5:1-5; 8:1-13). Could not a similar situation have prevailed in Galatia?

The two-front theory does provide a ready answer to a problem that must occur to any close reader of Galatians, namely, how do the last two chapters relate to the burden of Paul's argument in the first part of the book? According to this view, Paul was addressing the legalists in chaps. 1–4 with his strong emphasis on justification by faith. In chaps. 5–6, on the other hand, he turned his guns against the libertines whose abuse of Christian liberty was as much a threat to the Galatians as the Judaizers' denial of grace.

Despite the attractiveness of this theory, it flounders on the fact that Paul consistently treated his opponents as a homogeneous group whose subversive maneuvers have proved so successful that they require a strong and unitary response. The two-front theory, if pressed very far, would require Paul to shift his argument with great rapidity, sometimes in midsentence, as he weaves his response toward one and then another group of adversaries. Such mental sleight-of-hand does not square with the overall impression of

---

[49] F. Lütgert, *Gesetz und Geist* (Gütersloh: Bertelsmann, 1919); J. H. Ropes, *The Singular Problem of the Epistle to the Galatians,* HTS 14 (Cambridge, Mass.: Harvard University Press, 1929). See the helpful survey of these and other theories by E. E. Ellis, "Paul and His Opponents: Trends in the Research," in *Christianity, Judaism, and Other Greco-Roman Cults,* ed. J. Neusner (Leiden: Brill, 1975), 1:264-98.

Galatians as a carefully wrought and logically sophisticated piece of rhetoric. For all this, the two-front theory has forced into the open the question of the relationship between the theological foundation we find at the heart of the epistle and the ethical exhortations we encounter in the concluding section.[50]

(3) Gnostics in Galatia?

One of the most creative interpretations of Paul's opponents in Galatia has been set forth by W. Schmithals, who saw them as incipient Gnostics who had broken with their Jewish past in order to find salvation through the cultic rites and secret "knowledge" (*gnōsis*) of an esoteric religious system.[51] While most scholars have identified Paul's argument for a law-free gospel (Gal 2:15–4:31) as the center of gravity in his Letter to the Galatians, Schmithals reverses this balance, claiming that Paul was merely repeating in these chapters the kind of standard sermonizing he would have preached in the synagogues. Only when he began to attack the libertines in chaps. 5–6 did he come close to the real problem about which in fact he had only sketchy information.

Schmithals bolsters his thesis by appealing to several texts, including Paul's reference to the elemental spirits in 4:9 and his charge in 6:13 that those who are pressing circumcision on the Galatians do not themselves obey the law. Similarly, Paul's reference to the observing of "special days and months and seasons and years" (4:10) recalls the later Gnostic practice of following various calendar rituals as a means of finding union with the divine.

Suffice it to say that most scholars have not been persuaded by Schmithals' arguments, preferring to interpret these verses in light of Paul's obvious struggle with some kind of legalistic perversion of his gospel. However, as one of Schmithals' critics has admitted, there are sufficient hints in the letter to justify the hypothesis that the germs of what later developed into a full-scale Gnostic system were "already in the air" in Galatia during Paul's day.[52] Clearly Paul's writings, including Galatians, were later used by sec-

---

[50] S. Westerholm, "Letter and Spirit: The Foundation of Pauline Ethics," *NTS* 30 (1984): 229-48. See also J. M. G. Barclay's helpful monograph, *Obeying the Truth: A Study of Paul's Ethics in Galatians* (Edinburgh: T & T Clark, 1988).

[51] W. Schmithals, *Paul and the Gnostics* (Nashville: Abingdon, 1972). Schmithals restates his argument with some modification in "Judaisten in Galatien?" *ZNW* 74 (1983): 51-57. For a refutation of the Schmithals hypothesis, see R. M. Wilson, "Gnostics: In Galatia?" *Studia Evangelica, Texte und Untersuchungen zur Geschichte der altchristlichen Literatur 4* (1968): 358-67.

[52] Ibid., 367.

ond-century Gnostics to buttress their own deviant interpretation of the Christian faith.[53]

(4) Jewish-Christian Syncretism

In 1945 F. R. Crownfield published an article on "the singular problem of the dual Galatians" in which he argued that the error Paul confronted in Galatia was a kind of Jewish Christian syncretism that involved both a reversion to certain patterns of Jewish legalism but also incorporated more esoteric features associated with various spiritualist and Gnostic groups.[54] Although one scholar has criticized the syncretistic hypothesis as "quite incredible," C. H. Talbert has declared it "the best alternative concerning the identity of the Galatian opponents of Paul."[55] Talbert bases this judgment in part on the similarity between the false teaching in Galatia and that which Paul encountered in Colosse. Both letters include references to elemental spirits, calendrical observances, visions and revelations, the practice of circumcision, and libertine tendencies. The chief advantage of this theory is that it makes sense of Paul's homogenous treatment of his Galatian adversaries while taking into account the diverse elements of his complex argumentation. Clearly Paul presupposed a high level of acquaintance with the Old Testament Scriptures on the part of his Galatian readers, a familiarity that his opponents played on in their appeal to these new believers. Diaspora Judaism was not a monolithic system, and many of Paul's Gentile converts may have been exposed to Jewish syncretistic strands prior to their acceptance of the Christian kerygma.

(5) The Gentile Theory

One of the most influential books in Pauline studies during the latter half of the twentieth century is J. Munck's *Paul and the Salvation of Mankind*.[56] Munck's great contribution was to interpret Paul's mission to the Gentiles in terms of his overall concern for the salvation of Israel. Recent scholars such as K. Stendahl, E. P. Sanders, and N. T. Wright have extended Munck's insights, emphasizing the covenantal character of Paul's theology and his concern for the redemptive-historical work of God rather than (or alongside

---

[53] See the fascinating study by E. Pagels, *The Gnostic Paul: Gnostic Exegesis of the Pauline Letters* (Philadelphia: Fortress, 1975).

[54] F. R. Crownfield, "The Singular Problem of the Dual Galatians," *JBL* 64 (1945): 491-500.

[55] Cf. Barclay, "Mirror Reading," 89; Talbert, "Again: Paul's Visits to Jerusalem," 26-40.

[56] J. Munck, *Paul and the Salvation of Mankind* (Richmond: John Knox, 1959).

of) personal individual salvation. However, on the issue of the anti-Pauline opposition in Galatia, Munck's proposed solution has not been followed by most scholars. Munck believed that the problem Paul confronted in Galatia was uniquely tied to the Gentile context of his mission work there. His opponents had no connection with the Jerusalem apostles but were themselves Gentile converts, perhaps some of Paul's very own, whose reading of the Hebrew Scriptures persuaded them of the need to receive circumcision as a seal of the covenant.

The major argument for the Gentile identity of Paul's opponents is an interpretation of one word found in Gal 6:13: "Not even those who are circumcised obey the law." Here Paul used a present participle in the middle voice, *hoi peritemnomenoi,* which, according to Munck, means not "those who practice circumcision" but rather "those who receive circumcision." Thus Paul's opponents who were agitating for Judaism among the Gentile Christian Galatians were themselves Gentile Christians. Their circumcision was still in the present, so that all "this Judaizing movement is of recent date."[57]

However, as Bruce among others has recognized, the present participle *peripemnomenoi* could well be taken as the middle voice with causative significance meaning something like "causing to be circumcised."[58] Clearly the context supports this reading, for the issue under discussion was the campaign of the Judaizers to impose circumcision on the Galatians, not on themselves. Also worthy of note is that throughout the letter Paul presupposed that the agitators were outsiders who had infiltrated the churches of Galatia rather than former converts within the churches who had lapsed from the true faith. Only thus can we make sense of his pointed question in 3:1: "You foolish Galatians! Who has bewitched you?"[59]

(6) Paul's Characterization

None of these alternative theories has offered sufficient evidence to displace the traditional interpretation of Paul's opponents as Jewish Christian teachers of a legalistic bent who dogged Paul's trail in Galatia just as they or their associates had done earlier in Antioch (Acts 15:1). Although Paul was writing *to the Galatians,* not to his opponents, he did allude to them in every chapter of the book.

---

[57] Ibid.

[58] Ibid., 89.

[59] Bruce, *Galatians,* 270. See also A. T. Robertson, *A Grammar of the Greek New Testament in the Light of Historical Research* (Nashville: Broadman, 1934), 808-9.

At this point it will be helpful to recapitulate Paul's characterization of these theological disturbers of the peace in order to appreciate more fully his stern reply to their teaching. In Gal 1:6-9 he referred to them as "some people" who are sowing confusion and distorting the gospel of Christ. They were preachers of another gospel who deserved to be damned for their subversive activity.

In Gal 2:1-14 Paul recounted two important incidents from his earlier ministry, one at Jerusalem and the other at Antioch. In the former Paul referred to "some false brothers" who had sneaked into the Gentile churches to subvert their Christian liberty. In the latter he referred to "certain men" who "came from James," representatives of "the circumcision group," whose intimidating presence at Antioch precipitated his confrontation with Peter. Paul evidently rehearsed these two incidences in the context of defending his apostolic authority because he believed them to have direct relevance to the situation in Galatia. The mission churches of Galatia were experiencing a problem similar, if not identical, to that which had earlier shaken their mother church at Antioch. In 3:1 Paul assumed that his Galatian converts had succumbed to the demonic enchantments of the false teachers who had "bewitched" them. Whether this expression was meant to be taken in a figurative sense or referred to the actual magical powers of the false teachers, it clearly indicates that a number of the Galatians had fallen under their influence.

In 4:17 the personal rivalry between Paul and his opponents comes into play as he criticizes their strategy to alienate the Galatians "from us" in order to enlist their support "for them." In 5:10-12 Paul picked up on an expression he had used earlier in chap. 1, referring to his adversaries as those who were "throwing you into confusion." This passage contains some of Paul's strongest language against the agitators. He said, "I wish they would go the whole way and emasculate themselves!"—an obvious reference to their emphasis on the necessity of circumcision. In 6:12-13 Paul further characterized the false teachers as those who wanted to make a good outward impression. They were urging circumcision on the Galatians in order to "boast about your flesh" and thus "avoid being persecuted for the cross of Christ." Thus the agitators were a homogenous group of false teachers who were bent on undermining Paul's apostolic authority and denigrating his message in order to win over his recent converts for their own selfish purposes.

(7) Jewett and Martyn

In recent years two important essays have shed new light on the problem in Galatia including the identity of the opposition Paul faced there. The first is an article published by R. Jewett in 1971 on "The Agitators and the Galatian Congregation."[60] Jewett is particularly struck by Paul's charge in Gal 6:12 that his Galatian opponents had mounted their campaign for circumcision in order to avoid being persecuted for the cross of Christ. It would have been more understandable had Paul accused his Galatian converts of submitting to circumcision in order to avoid persecution. On the contrary, however, he assumed that they, just as he and Barnabas, had already suffered (at the hands of the synagogue leaders?) for their acceptance of a gospel based on faith rather than observance of the law (Gal 3:4). His point in Gal 6:12 is rather that the *agitators* had sought to avoid persecution by requiring the *Galatians* to be circumcised. Assuming that the agitators were Jewish Christians attached in some way to the church at Jerusalem, Jewett frames his question thus: "Under what circumstances would a nomistic Christian group in Judea be in danger of anti-Pauline persecution and have an interest in converting the Gentile churches to nomism in order to save itself from such a threat?"[61]

Jewett relates the problem in Galatia to political events in Judea that gave rise to a violent Zealot movement aimed at purging the people Israel of all Gentile accommodation in order to prepare the way for the coming of the Messiah. The Zealot movement had been a part of Palestinian Judaism since the time of the Maccabean revolt; indeed, one of Jesus' disciples, Simon the Zealot, was converted out of this milieu. However, during the period of the late forties until the outbreak of the Jewish War in A.D. 66, the Zealot movement received a new impetus from the mounting pressures imposed by the Roman rulers. For example, the emperor Caligula demanded around A.D. 40 that a statue of himself be erected in the temple at Jerusalem. Several years later the Roman procurator Cuspius Fadus required the vestments of the high priest to be held in custody by the Romans. His successor Cumanus (A.D. 48–52) was confronted with a riot in the streets of Jerusalem resulting in thousands of deaths, according to Josephus.[62]

In this highly charged atmosphere, it is not unlikely that Jewish Christians would have become prime targets for the Zealot brigands (Josephus's

---

[60] R. Jewett, "The Agitators and the Galatian Congregation," *NTS* 17 (1971): 198-212.

[61] Ibid., 204.

[62] On the role of the Zealots during this period of history, see M. Hengel, *Die Zeloten* (Leiden: Brill, 1961). Significantly, Paul described himself as ζηλωτής when describing his preconversion persecution of the Christians (Acts 22:3; Gal 1:14). For the references in Josephus see his *Jewish War* 2.12.1 and *Antiquities* 20.5.3. J. D. G. Dunn has supported Jewett's thesis by placing the Galatian problem in the wider context of Jewish nationalism and the conflict with Rome. See his "Incident at Antioch," *JSNT* 18 (1983): 3-57; reprinted in *Jesus, Paul, and the Law* (Louisville: Westminster/John Knox, 1990), 129-82.

term) who roamed the countryside of Judea and Samaria. Jewett finds a reference to such a persecution in 1 Thess 2:14-15, where Paul spoke of the Christians in Judea suffering at the hands of "the Jews who killed the Lord Jesus and the prophets and also drove us out." Thus, in order to "avert the suspicion that they were in communion with lawless Gentiles," certain Jewish Christians in Judea, under pressure from the Zealots, undertook a "nomistic campaign" aimed particularly at the growing circle of Pauline churches with their preponderant membership of noncircumcised Gentiles. According to Jewett, the agitators did not directly oppose Paul's work but set out rather to complete it by adding circumcision and obedience to the law as prerequisites of salvation. "If they could succeed in circumcising the Gentile Christians," Jewett surmises, "this might effectively thwart any Zealot purification campaign against the Judean church!"[63]

While Jewett's thesis presupposes a specifically anti-Pauline thrust in the motivation of the Galatian agitators, J. L. Martyn offers a rather different reconstruction of the situation. In his essay Martyn challenges the traditional designation of Paul's evangelistic efforts as *the* mission to the Gentiles. Looking backwards from the perspective of the pseudo-Clementine literature of the second century, he imagines that early Jewish Christianity likely sponsored its own law-observant mission to the Gentiles quite apart from Paul's itinerant work. The opponents, then, far from being interlopers who were dogging Paul's trail in deliberate reaction to his mission efforts, were themselves evangelists "embarked on an ecumenical mission under the genuine conviction that, through the law of his Messiah, God is now reaching out for the Gentiles and thus for the whole of humankind."[64] On this reading, it is not the opponents who were reacting to Paul's theology but he who was reacting to theirs. Elsewhere the two groups pursued their own distinctive missionary activity without the kind of intense confrontation we read about in Galatians. Galatia became a battleground because the two groups, with their similar and yet decisively different presentations of the gospel, converged on this unevangelized area at approximately the same time.

While Martyn's essay is highly suggestive and certainly plausible in its basic argument, it must be said that there is very little evidence for the existence of such a widespread Jewish Christian mission apart from the reactionary efforts of those who resisted the Pauline effort. Paul, it seems, was the catalyst both for the expansion of Christianity into the Gentile world and also for what might be called "an evangelism of entrenchment," that is, a

---

[63] Jewett, "The Agitators," 206.

[64] J. L. Martyn, "A Law-observant Mission to Gentiles: The Background of Galatians," *SJT* 38 (1985): 315.

proselytizing mission to domesticate Paul's radical gospel of salvation by grace through faith in Jesus Christ and him alone.

It may be that "the identity of Paul's opponents is more concealed than revealed in Galatians."[65] Part of the difficulty, of course, is that Paul nowhere named his adversaries or even addressed himself directly to them. We are forced to reconstruct the nature of the Galatian opposition by "mirror-reading" their theology through Paul's refutation of it. The varying views of who they were and what they taught stems from the different ways scholars have carried out this precarious exercise. Still, taking into account the various theories we have surveyed, we can set forth the following profile as the working hypothesis for this commentary.

Paul's opponents were Jewish Christians who infiltrated the churches of Galatia that Paul and Barnabas had established soon after the founding missionaries departed for Antioch. Their message included both destructive criticism of Paul and his apostolate and a specific program of legalistic observance they exhorted the Galatians to follow. At the heart of their message was the plea for the Galatian Christians to be circumcised as a means of becoming true children of Abraham. They based their arguments on the Hebrew Scriptures and also claimed to have a close relationship with the church at Jerusalem. They may well have pointed to certain libertine tendencies within the churches of Galatia as evidence that Paul's gospel provided no firm foundation for living the Christian life in the midst of a pagan world. Whatever their precise message, these intruders were successful in their canvassing campaign among the Galatian churches, for many of the new believers there were thrown into confusion by this turn of events.

4. Galatians as a Pastoral Letter

In the preface to his paraphrase and notes on the Epistles of Paul, the philosopher J. Locke lamented that in modern printed versions of the Bible, Paul's letters have been "so chop'd and minc'd" into chapters and verses this device made it more difficult to follow the flow of his argument and grasp the coherence of his thought. Locke recommended reading each epistle through at a single sitting, the better to discern "the Drift and Design" of the apostle's writing. Paul's writings, he believed, should not be regarded as "disjointed, loose, pious, Discourses, full of Warmth and Zeal, and Overflows of Light," but rather as "calm strong coherent Reasonings that [carry] a Thread of Argument and Consistency all through them."[66] In recent years

---

[65] J. J. Gunther, *St. Paul's Opponents and Their Background* (Leiden: Brill, 1973), 298.

[66] J. Locke, *A Paraphrase and Notes on the Epistle of St. Paul*, ed. A. W. Wainwright (Oxford: Clarendon, 1987), 1:105, 110.

scholars have taken seriously Locke's concern by giving increasing attention to the form as well as the content of Paul's letters, not least to Galatians.

(1) Letter or Epistle?

Early in the twentieth century A. Deissmann published a groundbreaking work in the study of early Christianity.[67] For many years scholars had noticed that the Greek of the New Testament was markedly different from that of the classical writers of ancient Greece. Beginning in the 1880s an enormous cache of hitherto unknown documents from the Hellenistic world were discovered in Egypt. Written on a fragile material called papyrus, these documents had been preserved across the centuries in the dry air of the Egyptian desert. Deissmann pioneered in the recovery and publication of these papyri, which included large numbers of private letters written on all sorts of occasions precisely in the kind of Greek we find in the New Testament.

Comparing these papyrus letters to those in the New Testament, Deissmann concluded that Paul's letters, in particular, should not be seen as classical "epistles" or theological tractates but rather as ordinary letters usually written in haste to address some specific situation or problem that had come to Paul's attention. Paul was not a literary man; he wrote for the moment, with no idea that his writings would be preserved and canonized for later generations to scrutinize and dissect. For example, Deissmann described Galatians as "the offspring of passion, a fiery utterance of chastisement and defense, not at all a treatise *'De lege et evangelio';* the reflection rather of genius flashing like summer lightning."[68]

Doubtless Deissmann made a great contribution by emphasizing the authentically personal character of Paul's letters and also by showing their congruity with the language and letters of daily life of ancient times preserved in fascinating detail in the nonliterary papyri of that era. On closer examination, however, it appears that Deissmann may have overstated his case by ignoring other features of Paul's letters that point to their public character as public documents of the church rather than private letters dashed off on impulse. For example, the very fact that Paul wrote as an apostle of Jesus Christ indicates that he spoke with special authority, under the commission of Christ, for the guidance of the church. Paul frequently reminded his readers that what he had written to them was the very commandment or word of the Lord himself (cf. 1 Cor 14:37-38; 1 Thess 4:13).

---

[67] A. Deissmann, *Light from the Ancient East: The New Testament Illustrated by Recently Discovered Texts of the Graeco-Roman World* (London: Hodder & Stoughton, 1909).

[68] Ibid., 237.

Moreover, his letters were always addressed not to private individuals but rather to communities of faith. Even Philemon, which might seem to be an exception to this rule, was addressed "to the church that meets in your home" (Phlm 2). Likewise, Paul's letters to Titus and Timothy, while indeed written to individuals he knew well, were also intended to serve a larger purpose by reinforcing their efforts to refute false teachers and establish order and church discipline in the congregations under their care. Paul obviously intended for his letters to be read aloud to a gathered congregation because he specifically stated at the close of 1 Thess (5:27): "I charge you before the Lord to have this letter read to all the brothers."[69]

It would be going beyond the evidence of Scripture to claim that Paul foresaw the collection of his letters into a discrete corpus of writings that would be preserved and canonized for generations to come. Indeed, there is every reason to believe that Paul expected the imminent return of Christ in his own lifetime rather than anticipating a centuries-long stretch of time before the parousia (see, e.g., Phil 1:18-26). On the other hand, he sometimes did expect that a letter written to one congregation would be shared with other churches in the area. He instructed the Christians at Colosse to pass along the letter he had written to them to their sister church at Laodicea so that it could be read there as well (Col 4:16). Clearly Galatians too was intended not merely for one congregation but for several, all of whom had been infected by the same theological heresy Paul was seeking to counteract. In time the mutual sharing of Paul's letters among the various churches he addressed led to the gathering of his letters into a distinct literary collection. When and how this took place we cannot say for sure, but it obviously was well underway before the death of Peter (A.D. 64), who addressed his second epistle to those who evidently were familiar with all the letters of "our dear brother Paul" (2 Pet 3:15-16).

It is best then to see Paul's epistles, including Galatians, as belonging to the genre of the "pastoral letter." To be sure, these letters are intensely personal and were written to address specific crises or needs that had come to Paul's attention. Yet his letters invariably served a wider purpose, namely, that of rooting and grounding all of his churches in both sound doctrine and holy living. Thus Paul's letters were teaching documents similar in some respects to a papal encyclical in the Roman Catholic tradition or to circular letters local Baptist associations historically used to encourage doctrinal and disciplinary fidelity among the churches within their fellowship.

---

[69] T. D. Lea and H. P. Griffin, Jr., *1, 2 Timothy, Titus,* NAC (Nashville: Broadman, 1992), 41-45. The second person plurals that appear throughout the Pastorals also indicate the communal context of these letters.

(2) Structure and Form

In recent years New Testament scholars have devoted much attention to the structure and form of the Pauline Letters, analyzing their literary features and comparing them with other letters that have survived from the Hellenistic world.[70] By the time of Paul, letter writing in the Roman Empire had developed into a fine art among the professional clientele of the educated elite. The publication of 931 letters by the great Roman statesman Cicero (d. 43 B.C.) set a high standard for others who desired to use the letter form for political, philosophical, or moral exhortation as well as for communicating matters of a more personal nature.[71] Those who wished to perfect the art of letter writing had available various handbooks and manuals of style to guide them in this process. One of these, by Proclus, "lists forty-one epistolary types including letters of friendship, introduction, blame, reproach, consultation, criticism, censure, praise, interrogation, accusation, apology, and gratitude."[72] The questions scholars have been keen to study are exactly how Paul's letters fit into this pattern of literary constructs. Generally Paul's epistles do seem to follow the normal pattern of the Hellenistic letter, the basic form of which consists of five major sections:

1. Opening (sender, addressee, greeting)
2. Thanksgiving or Blessing (often with prayer of intercession, well wishes, or personal greetings)
3. The Burden of the Letter (including citation of classical sources and arguments)
4. Parenesis (ethical instruction, exhortation)
5. Closing (mention of personal plans, mutual friends, benediction)

A quick look at the text of Galatians will show that it fits this pattern rather neatly with one exception: there is no thanksgiving or blessing. Otherwise, using this structure, we could outline Galatians thus:

1. Opening 1:1-5

---

[70] Within the extensive literature on this topic, I have found the following especially helpful: W. G. Doty, *Letters in Primitive Christianity* (Philadelphia: Fortress, 1973); R. N. Longenecker, "On the Form, Function, and Authority of the New Testament Letters," in *Scripture and Truth,* ed. D. A. Carson and J. D. Woodbridge (Grand Rapids: Zondervan, 1983); D. E. Aune, *The New Testament in Its Literary Environment* (Philadelphia: Westminster, 1987); T. R. Schreiner, *Interpreting the Pauline Epistles* (Grand Rapids: Baker, 1990).

[71] Although many of his letters were published after his death, Cicero clearly distinguished letters written for private purposes from those intended as public documents. To his friend Trebonius he observed: "You see, I have one way of writing what I think will be read by those only to whom I address my letter, and another way of writing what I think will be read by many" (*Ad fam.* 15. 21. 4.; quoted, Doty, *Letters,* 2).

[72] Ibid., 9-10.

2. Body 1:6–4:31
3. Parenesis 5:1–6:10
4. Closing 6:11-18

A far more detailed analysis of Galatians from the standpoint of rhetorical criticism has been set forth by H. D. Betz.[73] Betz believes that Galatians best fits the model of a judicial apologetic letter, a genre that presupposes the setting of a law court with arguments carefully mustered to defend oneself against a false accusation. When applied to Galatians, the defendant is Paul, the false teachers are his accusers, and the Galatians themselves are the jury. Paul was seeking to defend himself and his gospel and to win over, or rather win back, his recent converts who had been swayed from the truth by the arguments of the intruders. Betz outlines Galatians as an apologetic letter with the following features:

1. Prescript 1:1-5
2. Body 1:6–6:10

Exordium	1:6-11 (states the basic reason for the letter)
Narratio	1:12–2:14 (autobiographical section with narration of events to counter false accusations)
Propositio	2:15-21 (transition from the previous section to the main body of the letter; sets forth the thesis Paul will argue for in the next section)
Probatio	3:1–4:31 (a series of arguments from experience, Scripture, and theology intended to prove Paul's central thesis: justification by faith)
Paraenesis	5:1–6:10 (moral exhortation and ethical instruction)

3. Postscript 6:11-18 (conclusion and summary of issues discussed in the letter)

The great advantage of Betz's analysis is that it forces us to appreciate the intentionality with which Paul wrote Galatians. However personal and passionate the letter may be, it also was drafted with much care and cunning. At the same time, just as Deissmann overstated his case by placing Paul's letters on a par with private correspondence of the ancient world, so Betz seems to have gone too far in pressing Galatians into the rhetorical structure of apologetic letters.

T. Schreiner has conveniently summarized the major objections to Betz's approach: (1) The genre of apologetic letter fits much better for Gal 1–2

---

[73] Betz, *Galatians,* 14-25 and pass. See also his earlier article, "Literary Composition and Function of Paul's Letter to the Galatians," *NTS* 21 (1975): 353-79. For a helpful critique of Betz see Longenecker, *Galatians,* c-cxix; W. P. Davies, P. W. Meyer, and D. E. Aune, "Review": *Galatians: A Commentary on Paul's Letter to the Churches of Galatia* by H. D. Betz," *Religious Studies Review* 7 (1981): 310-28.

than for the rest of the book, with the thesis really breaking down with the analysis of the parenetical section. (2) The exordium in Greek rhetoric was intended to secure goodwill by making a favorable impression, but Paul's harsh *anathema* in 1:8 is hardly a shining example of how to win friends or influence people. (3) Betz has constructed an attractive theory of a judicial apologetic letter, but despite his numerous citations of parallel literature in classical antiquity, he nowhere adduces an apologetic letter comparable to Galatians. (4) The effort to find a structure for Galatians in Greek rhetoric may not take seriously enough Paul's own background in rabbinic Judaism with its distinctive traditions of exegesis and argument.[74]

In considering Paul's style as well as the structure of Galatians, we would do well to listen again to J. Locke, whose close reading of Paul's letters had convinced him that the Apostle to the Gentiles "was not a man of loose and shattered parts, incapable to argue, and unfit to convince those he had to deal with."[75] On the contrary, he was a "coherent, argumentative, pertinent Writer." But Locke observed:

> Tho I say he has right Aims in his Epistles, which he steadily keeps in his Eye, and drives at in all that he says, yet I do not say that he puts his Discourses into an artificial Method, or leads his Reader into a Distinction of his Arguments, or gives them notice of new matter by Rhetorical or study'd Transitions. He has no Ornaments borrow'd from the Greek Eloquence; no Notions of their Philosophy Mix'd with his Doctrine to set it off.... But tho Politeness of Language, Delicacy of stile, Fineness of Expression, Laboured Periods, artificial Transitions, and a very methodical arranging of the Parts with such other Imbellishments as make a Discourse enter the Mind smoothly, and strike the Phansie at first hearing, have little or no place in his stile, yet Coherence of Discourse, and a direct Tendency of all the Parts of it to the Argument in hand, are most eminently to be found in him. This I take to be his Character and doubt not that he will be found to be so upon diligent examination.[76]

From my perspective Galatians divides quite naturally into three major sections, which can be dubbed, with slight oversimplification, as "History," "Theology," and "Ethics."[77] In the historical section (Gal 1–2) Paul established the foundation of the gospel he had proclaimed and which he now had to defend. In the doctrinal core of the book (Gal 3–4) he unfolded the faith of the gospel in terms of God's promise in the old covenant and its fulfillment in the new. In the final third of the letter (Gal 5–6) Paul appealed to his read-

---

[74] Schreiner, *Interpreting Pauline Epistles.*
[75] Locke, *A Paraphrase,* 1:10-12.
[76] Ibid.
[77] This rubric was suggested by C. K. Barrett, *Freedom and Obligation* (Philadelphia: Westminster, 1985), 3.

ers to live out the freedom of the gospel both in their witness to the world and their relationship with one another. To press this outline into an artificial construct of three airtight divisions would be to miss the overlapping and unitary character of Paul's entire argument in Galatians. Clearly there is history in chap. 4, much theology in chap. 1, and ethics throughout. However, the sequence history-theology-ethics was not chosen fortuitously by Paul. It corresponds well to the pastoral approach he took to the crisis in Galatia. Only after Paul had established the historical basis of the gospel and shown how his own apostolic vocation was related to it could he gain a hearing for the beleaguered message of justification by faith that in turn had crucial implications for how the Galatians lived as well as for what they believed. And, in a broader sense, Paul was merely following the logic of the Christian life: Because of who God is and what he has done (history) we must believe what he has said (theology) in order to live as he commands (ethics).

5. Galatians in the History of Christian Interpretation

Well before the close of the first century the letters of Paul were collected into a distinct corpus and circulated among Christian churches through the Roman Empire. The earliest arrangement of Paul's letters was based apparently on descending order of length. By the mid-second century, however, a new sequence was set forth by Marcion, who placed Galatians first in his proposed canonical arrangement. Marcion published a highly expurgated version of Galatians, along with nine other Pauline Epistles, under the general heading *Apostolikon*. On the basis of his distorted reading of Paul, Marcion posited a radical disjunction between the God of the Old Testament and the Father of Jesus Christ. Paul's arguments against the Judaizers became the pretext for Marcion's dispensing with the Old Testament altogether as Christian Scripture. Paul's clash with Peter at Antioch, reported in Gal 2:11-14, he interpreted as a paradigm of two distinct forms of Christianity: the Jewish-tainted religion of orthodox Christianity on the one hand and pure Paulinism with its radical dualism on the other. Marcion was condemned as a heretic by the church of Rome in A.D. 144, but his radical misreading of Paul has influenced many others, including, in our own century, the great historian of dogma Adolf von Harnack.

Tertullian of Carthage was the first Christian writer to refute Marcion's erroneous interpretation of Galatians. Tertullian agreed with Marcion that of all Paul's letters, Galatians is "the most decisive against Judaism."[78] How-

---

[78] ANF 3.431 *(Adversus Marcionem* 5.2). On Marcion's continuing influence, see A. von Harnack, *Marcion: Das Evangelium von fremden Gott* (Berlin: W. de Gruyter, 1921).

ever, "the supersession of the law" that Galatians describes was precisely the work of the Creator-God, not of some other "alien" deity. Similarly, when Paul declared that he bore in his body "the scars of Christ," he therefore "expressed the truth that the flesh of Christ is not putative, but real and substantial, the scars of which he represents as borne upon his body."[79] Tertullian, like Irenaeus before him, flatly rejected any radically dualistic reading of Paul, whether by Marcion or Gnostics proper. The God who made the world and then revealed himself to the Jews was the same God who redeemed lost humankind through his Son Jesus Christ. While not denying the important distinctions between the old and new covenants, the orthodox fathers of the early church thus rightly interpreted the gospel of Christ, which Paul preached as a fulfillment of the Creator's purpose both in making the world and in revealing himself to the Jewish people through the Old Testament Scriptures.

In the third and fourth centuries two great schools of interpretation developed around the thriving Christian communities at Alexandria and Antioch. Origen was the father of biblical criticism and the pioneer of the Alexandrian approach. In commenting on Gal 5:13, Jerome declared that Origen wrote fifteen books and seven homilies on Galatians, none of which have survived in their original form. Yet Origen had a great influence on those who came after him, most notably Jerome and Cyril of Alexandria. He also was the first commentator to distinguish explicitly the moral and ceremonial aspects of the law, a distinction still debated by Pauline scholars today. Also his use of the Hagar-Sarah allegory of 4:21-31 as a basis for allegorizing and spiritualizing the entire canon of Holy Scripture would have far-reaching consequences throughout the Middle Ages and beyond.

The excessive allegorizing of the Alexandrian exegetes was strongly opposed by the Antiochene school of interpretation. Classic commentaries on Galatians were produced by three leaders of this tradition: John Chrysostom (d. 407), Theodore of Mopsuestia (d. 429) and Theodoret of Cyrrhus (d. 460). These church fathers did not accept Origen's division of the law into ceremonial and moral aspects, nor did they follow the allegorical exegesis of the Alexandrian school. They read Galatians in terms of the history of salvation, interpreting it through the schema of promise and fulfillment.

The Bible was the most studied book in the Middle Ages. Augustine set forth the basic rules of biblical exegesis in his handbook *On Christian Doctrine,* which became the starting point for scriptural interpretation in both the monastic and scholastic traditions. The *lectio divina,* or "divine reading," of the Bible was a traditional part of the monastic routine. In addition to the

---

[79] Ibid., 438.

weekly recitation of the entire Psalter in the daily offices, the Rule of St. Benedict required two hours of private Bible reading each weekday and more on Sundays. From the fifth through the tenth centuries the monastery provided the only place for serious study in Western Europe. The commentaries on Paul's letters that have survived from this time are mostly summations of earlier patristic writers, the most notable being Origen, Jerome, and Ambrosiaster (an otherwise unknown fourth-century commentator on Paul's epistles wrongly identified by medieval writers as Ambrose).[80] The chief representative of the early medieval exegetical tradition was the Venerable Bede. His biblical studies had a lasting impact because he was both a judicious compiler of earlier insights and a creative interpreter of the text itself.[81]

Scholasticism refers to a distinctive kind of theology that first appeared in the cathedral schools and universities of twelfth- and thirteenth-century Europe. In its most developed form it involved a method of study that drew heavily on the recently discovered philosophy of Aristotle in applying the rules of logic to the sacred text. Although he is best known for his *Summa Theologiae,* Thomas Aquinas also produced commentaries on many books of the Bible, including Galatians. It has been said that Steven Langton, an older contemporary of Thomas, "perfected the technique of moralizing Scripture as an aid to preaching."[82] Thomas also interpreted Paul's Letter to the Galatians in terms of its great themes of sin, law, and grace and their role in one's moral movement toward God. Thomas's glosses on the text of Galatians reveal his medieval Catholic context. For example, he interpreted Paul's anathema in Gal 1:6-10 in terms of the contemporary practice of excommunication and baptism in 3:27 in terms of the sacramental theology of the times.

During the Protestant Reformation, Galatians and Romans became the bedrock of a Pauline renaissance as Luther, Calvin, and other Reformers rallied around the doctrine of justification by faith over against a compromised theology of grace in the prevailing Roman Catholic systems of the day. It has been said that "Erasmus laid the egg which Luther hatched." The publication of Erasmus's Greek New Testament in 1516 and his *Paraphrase on Galatians* in 1518 certainly influenced Luther's engagement with this Pauline Epistle. However, Erasmus, for all his brilliance, was never able to free him-

---

[80] See A. Souter, *The Earliest Latin Commentaries on St. Paul* (Oxford: Oxford University Press, 1927).

[81] See B. Smalley, *The Study of the Bible in the Middle Ages* (Notre Dame: University of Notre Dame Press, 1964), 22-36.

[82] Smalley, "Steven Langton," *The Oxford Dictionary of the Christian Church*, ed. F. L. Cross (London: Oxford University Press, 1974), 799.

self from the semi-Pelagian tendencies that are so evident in his great debate with Luther over free will and predestination. The primary achievement of Erasmus's biblical scholarship, along with that of other humanists such as Jacques Lefèvre d'Etaples of France and John Colet of England, was to set aside the tradition of New Testament study developed by medieval scholars who had "increasingly allowed logic and dialectic to dictate the questions they asked and the methods they used to answer them."[83] The Protestant Reformers would build on this humanist legacy, but they would also transform it in ways that Erasmus and his friends could never appreciate.

Martin Luther was not a systematic theologian but a *lectura in Biblia,* that is, a professor of biblical exegesis at the University of Wittenberg, where he had received the doctorate in theology in 1512. During his long career he lectured several times on Paul's Letter to the Galatians. The American edition of *Luther's Works* translates both his short commentary of 1519 and his definitive revision of 1535. Shortly before his death Luther commented on plans to bring out a complete Latin edition of his writings: "If they took my advice, they would print only the books containing doctrine, like Galatians."[84]

H. D. Betz has wisely observed: "Luther speaks as Paul would have spoken had he lived at the time when Luther gave his lectures."[85] Just as Paul confronted the dangers of legalism on the one hand and libertinism on the other, so Luther saw the same dangers in resurgent Roman Catholicism, with its doctrine of works-righteousness and the sectarian extremists with their challenge to traditional rites such as infant baptism and their splitting asunder of Word and Spirit.

Modern New Testament scholars have justly criticized Luther for reading his own situation back into Paul's and for hurling anathemas at his opponents just as the apostle did against his Galatian adversaries. This criticism is well taken. No one can read Luther today without realizing how the reformer's perspective was skewed by the polemical context in which he lived and wrote. These caveats aside, we are prepared to affirm that on the crucial matter of justification by faith alone, Luther was a careful and faithful interpreter of Paul. The words he wrote in the preface to his 1535 commentary still ring true today:

> This doctrine can never be discussed and taught enough. If it is lost and perishes, the whole knowledge of truth, life, and salvation is lost and perishes at the same time. But if it flourishes, everything good flourishes—religion, true

---

[83] J. Bentley, *Humanists and Holy Writ* (Princeton: Princeton University Press, 1983), 218.
[84] Longenecker, *Galatians,* liii.
[85] Betz, *Galatians,* xv.

worship, the glory of God, and the right knowledge of all things and of all social conditions. There is clear and present danger that the devil may take away from us the pure doctrine of faith and may substitute for it the doctrines of works and of human traditions. It is very necessary, therefore, that this doctrine of faith be continually read and heard in public.[86]

It has been well said that the greatest disciple of Martin Luther was John Calvin. Yet Calvin was no mere echo of the great German reformer but rather a creative reshaper and transmitter of the genuine Reformation theology Luther had set forth with such passion and clarity. Drawing on his superb knowledge of Greek and Hebrew and his thorough training in humanist philosophy, Calvin produced commentaries on all of the New Testament books except 2 and 3 John and Revelation. His exegetical work is marked by brevity on the one hand and modesty on the other. His goal was to understand the mind of the biblical author as concisely and clearly as possible, avoiding lavish displays of erudition and digressions into secondary concerns. For this reason J. Arminius, who modified several principles of Calvin's theology, still recommended his commentaries as the greatest religious writings outside the Bible itself, for Calvin "is incomparable in the interpretation of Scripture."[87]

Calvin began writing his commentary on Galatians in 1546 and published it at Geneva in 1548. On two other occasions, in 1558 and 1562, he worked through Galatians in his regular ministry of expository preaching.[88] Throughout his commentary Calvin emphasized that Paul's struggle with his opponents was not merely a matter of personal rivalry but rather a struggle for the truth of the gospel itself. "We must always take care of the main articles of the gospel. He who attacks them is a destroyer of the gospel."[89] Calvin also pointed out that the dispute over circumcision was no mere squabble over ceremonies but rather controversy over how one obtains a right standing before God. Hence Paul "takes his stand on this argument: If ceremonies have no power to justify, then the observance of them is unnecessary. Yet he does not treat only of ceremonies but disputes of works in general; otherwise the whole argument would be weak. . . . The controversy was not concerned with some insignificant trifle but with the most important matter of all, the way we obtain salvation."[90] Calvin was well aware that the

---

[86] *LW* 26.3.

[87] Quoted, A. M. Hunter, *The Teaching of Calvin* (London: James Clarke, 1950), 20.

[88] The first two lectures from the 1562 series have been discovered and edited by R. Peter, *Jean Calvin: Deux Congrégations et Exposition du Catéchisme* (Paris: Presses Universitaires de France, 1964).

[89] CNTC 11.14.

[90] Ibid., 6.

grace of God could be abused by antinomianism as well as by legalism. Thus he stressed more than any other sixteenth-century commentator the relevance of the ethical exhortation of Paul in Gal 5 and 6.

Between the death of Calvin in 1564 and the rise of modern historical critical study of the Bible during the Enlightenment, Galatians continued to be a fertile source for Christian preaching and devotion. Three commentaries from this period are outstanding. William Perkins' *Commentary on Galatians* was first published in 1604, two years after the death of this great Puritan preacher and exegete. His commentary on Galatians was based on his sermons on this Pauline letter at Great St. Andrews Church in Cambridge. Thomas Fuller, one of his listeners, later reported that Perkins "would pronounce the word *damn* with such an emphasis, as left a doleful echo in his auditors' ears a good while after."[91] His *Commentary on Galatians* is marked by his addiction to Ramist logic with numerous subdivisions and practical applications for every verse. Perkins also set forth a robust defense of the Protestant view of justification by faith with due attention to the literal sense of the text. As G. T. Sheppard has noted in his introduction to the recent reprinting of this classic commentary: "Accompanying Perkins' assertion that there is only one literal sense is his repeated assumption that the expression of the Word of God coincides (without error) with the intent of the apostle as found in his letters."[92]

John Locke is best remembered as one of the greatest English philosophers of the early modern period, but he also was a brilliant apologist and careful student of the Scriptures. Locke's *Paraphrases and Notes on the Epistles of Paul* was published during the years 1705–1707. Locke was convinced that it was the Christian's duty to study the Bible, "receiving with steadfast belief, and ready obedience, all those things which the Spirit of Truth has therein revealed."[93] Locke's paraphrase and notes on Galatians are marked by his desire to understand Paul in his original historical context and to emphasize the unity and coherence of his argument throughout the epistle. At the same time, Locke was eclectic in his theology and failed to grasp the significance of Paul's writings on many important points of doctrine.

The Scottish preacher John Brown was pastor of the Broughton Place Church, Edinburgh, for thirty years. He was widely celebrated as an expos-

---

[91] T. Fuller, *The Holy State and Profane State* (London, 1642), 81. See T. George, *John Robinson and the English Separatist Tradition* (Macon: Mercer University Press, 1982), 61.

[92] G. T. Sheppard, "Between Reformation and Modern Commentary: The Perception of the Scope of Biblical Books," in W. Perkins, *A Commentary on Galatians* (New York: Pilgrim, 1989), lxv.

[93] J. Locke, *A Paraphrase and Notes on the Epistles of Paul,* ed. A. W. Wainwright (Oxford: Clarendon, 1987), 1.

itory preacher without parallel in his own day. It was also said of him, "The old Puritan theology, traced to its roots in an inspired and unalterable Bible, contented him the more, the longer he lived." His *Exposition of Galatians* was published in 1858, the year of his death. It is an admirable summary of the Puritan tradition of Pauline exegesis, replete with penetrating insights into the mind of Paul and pastoral applications for devout believers.

Since the time of F. C. Baur in the early nineteenth century, Galatians has been a battleground for modern historical reconstructions of New Testament history and theology. Among the many commentaries published during the modern period, five stand out as classic expositions of this great Pauline letter. J. B. Lightfoot's commentary was first published in 1865. It was a rejoinder to the Tübingen critics and a ground-breaking study of the historical background of the letter. Although some of Lightfoot's theories have been challenged by later scholars such as William Ramsay, it is accurate to state that his work on Galatians "set the standard for all commentary writing from his day to the present.[94] E. deW. Burton, a liberal Baptist who taught at the University of Chicago, published in 1921 a thorough and still useful commentary on Galatians for the International Critical Commentary series. H. D. Betz's magisterial commentary on Galatians appeared in the Hermeneia series in 1979. More than anyone else before or since, Betz focused on the rhetorical structure and literary shape of the Galatian epistle. His commentary is a model of judicious learning and imaginative interaction with the scriptural text. F. F. Bruce, the doyen of evangelical biblical scholars in this century, published in 1982 a commentary on the Greek text of Galatians. In the introduction to this volume, Bruce argued convincingly for the South Galatia theory of destination and for an early dating of Galatians. R. N. Longenecker, building on the work of both Betz and Bruce, published in 1990 a superb study of Galatians for the Word Biblical Commentary series. My indebtedness to Lightfoot, Burton, Betz, Bruce, and Longenecker will be evident to the reader of this commentary.

W. D. Davies' *Paul and Rabbinic Judaism* (1948) and E. P. Sanders, *Paul and Palestinian Judaism* (1977) have spawned a whole "new perspective on Paul," one that challenges many of the traditional assumptions of Pauline scholarship. In the plethora of publications generated by this debate, I have found most helpful the writings of N. T. Wright, S. Westerholm, T. Schreiner, and my colleague at Beeson Divinity School, F. S. Thielman. J. D. G. Dunn's *The Epistle to the Galatians* in Black's New Testament Commentaries appeared too late for me to consult in preparing the present work. However, my indebtedness (and sometimes respectful disagreement) with Dunn are

---

[94] Longenecker, *Galatians,* lvi.

duly noted at appropriate places throughout this study. My perspective on Galatians has been greatly enriched by two other studies, both more suggestive than exhaustive. C. K. Barrett's *Freedom and Obligation* shows clearly the connection between Paul's theology and his ethics. G. Ebeling, a leading interpreter of Luther, has illumined both the Reformation and the New Testament in his masterful study of Galatians, *The Truth of the Gospel*.

I have learned much from all of these scholars, and yet I have felt compelled to state again in my own words the message of Paul's Letter to the Galatians for the church today. The Bible is not a dead document to be once and for all mastered and deposited in the reservoir of academic achievement. The Word of God is alive and powerful, and it must be owned and studied reverently and faithfully in every generation. Theology is a discipline of faith that must be pursued arduously but not dispassionately in the service of the church to the glory of God, its gracious and sovereign Object. From this perspective every act of biblical exposition is once an act of prayer. No one has said this better than the great Baptist theologian J. L. Dagg, who opened his *Manual of Theology* with these words:

> The study of religious truth ought to be undertaken and prosecuted from a sense of duty, and with a view to the improvement of the heart. When learned, it ought not to be laid on the shelf, as an object of speculation; but it should be deposited deep in the heart, where its sanctifying power ought to be felt. To study theology, for the purpose of gratifying curiosity, or preparing for a profession, is an abuse and profanation of what ought to be regarded as most holy. To learn things pertaining to God, merely for the sake of amusement, or secular advantage, or to gratify the mere love of knowledge, is to treat the Most High with contempt.[95]

---

[95] J. L. Dagg, *Manual of Theology and Church Order* (Harrisonburg, Va.: Gano, 1982), 13. See the essay on Dagg by M. E. Dever in *Baptist Theologians,* ed. T. George and D. S. Dockery (Nashville: Broadman, 1990), 165-87.

OUTLINE OF THE BOOK

I. History: No Other Gospel (1:1–2:21)
   1. The Apostolic Salutation (1:1-5)
   2. The Apostolic Curse (1:6-10)
   3. The Apostolic Vocation (1:11-24)
   4. The Apostolic Message—Confirmation and Contradiction (2:1-21)
II. Theology: Justification by Faith (3:1–4:31)
   1. The Argument from Conversion (3:1-5)
   2. The Case of Abraham (3:6-9)
   3. Christ and the Curse (3:10-12)
   4. The Law and the Promise (3:15-22)
   5. Sons and Servants (3:26–4:11)
   6. Paul's Personal Appeal (4:12-20)
   7. The Analogy of Hagar and Sarah (4:21-31)
III. Ethics: Life in the Spirit (5:1–6:18)
   1. Freedom in Christ (5:1-12)
   2. Flesh and Spirit (5:13-26)
   3. Freedom in Service to Others (6:1-10)
   4. The Apostolic Seal (6:11-16)
   5. Benediction (6:18)

I. HISTORY: NO OTHER GOSPEL (1:1–2:21)
1. The Apostolic Salutation (1:1-5)
    (1) The Sender (1:1-2a)
         His Name
         His Office
         The Contrast of Christ and Humans
         The Unity of the Son and the Father
    (2) The Churches (1:2b)
    (3) The Greeting (1:3-5)
2. The Apostolic Curse (1:6-10)
    (1) The Crisis in Galatia (1:6-7)
         Their Desertion from God
         Their Devotion to a False Gospel
    (2) The Counterfeit Gospel: Anathema! (1:8-9)
    (3) The Motive for Ministry (1:10)
         Summary
         Excursus 1: The Nature of Heresy
3. The Apostolic Vocation (1:11-24)
    (1) Called from Above (1:11-12)
    (2) Paul's Life before Christ (1:13-14)
    (3) Conversion and Calling (1:15-17)
    (4) The First Visit to Jerusalem (1:18-24)
4. The Apostolic Message—Confirmation and Challenge (2:1-21)
    (1) The Second Visit to Jerusalem (2:1-10)
         The Occasion of the Visit (2:1-2)
         Titus and the False Brothers (2:3-5)
         Paul and the Pillars (2:6-9)
         Concern for the Poor (2:10)
    (2) The Incident at Antioch (2:11-21)
         The Problem: Table Fellowship (2:11-13)
         The Protest: Two Apostles Collide (2:14)
         Excursus 2: Luther and Calvin on Peter and Paul
         The Principle: Justification by Faith (2:15-21)

──────── I. HISTORY: NO OTHER GOSPEL (1:1–2:21) ────────

1. The Apostolic Salutation (1:1-5)

Letters in the first century, whether Jewish or Greek, usually began with a salutation that included three parts: the name of the sender, that of the recipient, and a formula of greeting, usually just the word *chairein,* a word that literally meant "rejoice" but that had come to represent a standard greeting, such as "welcome" or "hello." Paul followed this same format in all of his letters usually with the addition of a word of blessing or prayer of thanksgiving for the one(s) to whom he was writing. However, Paul by no means followed the same formulaic salutation in all of his letters. For example, rather than merely repeating the everyday word for "greetings," he forged a distinctively Christian expression, "Grace and peace." In addition, he also adapted his salutations to the unique circumstances and conditions of his writing to a particular person or place.

The salutation in Galatians is significant both for the added information it contains and the important feature it lacks. In v. 1 Paul provided an important clarification concerning his apostolic vocation; in v. 4 he included a decisive elaboration on the salvific work of Jesus Christ. From the outset, then, we are confronted with the two major themes that will dominate Paul's Letter to the Galatians: the vindication of his own apostolic authority in the context of salvation history and the divine initiative God has taken to redeem lost men and women through Jesus Christ and him alone. The salutation in Galatians also is remarkable because it does not contain the traditional prayer of thanksgiving with which Paul routinely opened his other letters (cf. Rom 1:8-15; 1 Cor 1:4-9; Phil 3:11; 1 Thess 1:2-3). Just where we would expect to find such a word of blessing and affirmation, Paul lashed out with his statement of astonishment concerning the apostasy of the Galatians, "I am astonished that you are so quickly deserting" (1:6). In this way we are prepared for the tremendous emotional intensity of the letter that follows.

Some commentators have passed over the content of the salutation lightly as though it contained merely formal niceties such as the "Dear Sir" or "Yours truly" of a modern letter. However, this is to ignore the fact that the prescript of a Pauline letter by itself constitutes "an essential part of the letter's content."[1] The salutation reveals not only the mood in which Galatians

---

[1] G. Ebeling, *The Truth of the Gospel: An Exposition of Galatians* (Philadelphia: Fortress, 1984), 8.

was written but also the passion and burden of Paul's heart that prompted him to write it. What is at stake is the content of the gospel Paul proclaimed to the Galatians. This too is restated with force in these opening verses as Paul draws a theological line in the sand against the false teachers who have undermined the gospel by undermining his apostolic authority.

(1) The Sender (1:1-2a)

¹Paul, an apostle—sent not from men nor by man, but by Jesus Christ and God the Father, who raised him from the dead— ²and all the brothers with me,

HIS NAME.   We know from fifteen references in Acts 7–13 that Paul also was called Saul. *Saulos* was the Hellenized form of the Jewish name *Šaʾul*. This was the form of his name Jesus used when addressing Paul on the road to Damascus (Acts 26:14). Saul is first called Paul in Acts 13:9 when in the course of the first missionary journey he proclaimed the gospel to the Roman governor of Cyprus, a man named Sergius Paulus. Some scholars have equated this change of names with a major shift in Paul's preaching career: his transition from a largely Jewish orientation to his new role as Apostle to the Gentiles. It is true that Paul nowhere referred to himself by his Jewish name in his letters. He did speak of the pride he once had taken in stemming from the tribe of Benjamin who had given Israel King Saul, after whom Saul of Tarsus likely was named (Phil 3:5). However, as one whose expressed missionary strategy was to become "a Jew to the Jews" that he might thereby win some to Christ, Paul may very well have continued to introduce himself as *Šaʾul* when working in a largely Jewish setting. It is even more likely that he carried the double name Saul Paul from birth since this was a common practice among Jews of the diaspora. Paul's companion Silas also was called Silvanus, just as Barnabas's nephew John carried a Roman surname, Marcus (cf. Acts 12:25).

1:1a   The word "Paul" in Greek literally means "small," or "little."[2] The earliest physical description we have of Paul comes from *The Acts of Paul and Thecla,* a second-century apocryphal writing that describes the apostle as "a man of small stature, with a bald head and crooked legs, in a good state of body, with eyebrows meeting and nose somewhat hooked, full of friendliness; for now he appeared like a man, and now he had the face of an angel."[3] Although written many years after his death, these words may well

---

[2] *Paulus* is thus used by Terence and other classical writers. See also the related word παυρος in *A Lexicon Abridged from Liddell and Scott's Greek-English Lexicon* (Oxford: Clarendon, 1972), 537.

[3] E. Hennecke and W. Schneemelcher, eds., *New Testament Apocrypha* (Philadelphia: Westminster, 1964), 2:354.

reflect an authentic tradition about Paul's actual likeness.

We know that his opponents in Corinth poked fun at his physical appearance, claiming that while his letters were weighty and bold, he was not much to look at in person. "His bodily presence is weak," they alleged (2 Cor 10:10, RSV). They themselves were "super-apostles" (2 Cor 11:5), as Paul dubbed them, glorying in their eloquent speech, miraculous powers, and impressive platform performance. What were Paul's credentials compared to theirs? What could he possibly brag about, this "little Apostle Little"?

While we cannot be sure that Paul's opponents in Galatia were the same as those he confronted in Corinth, there seems to be a common thread running through his defense against both sets of adversaries. In both Galatians and 2 Corinthians he advanced a theology of the cross in distinction from a theology of glory. In 2 Cor 12 Paul resolved to boast only in his weaknesses, afflictions, and persecutions, "for when I am weak, then I am strong" (12:10). In Gal 2 he identified himself with the crucified Christ and his cross, the only proper standard of boasting for a true follower of Jesus (Gal 6:14).

HIS OFFICE.   Paul called himself "an apostle." This was his favorite term of self-designation and occurs in the salutation of eight of the twelve New Testament letters that bear his name. He also referred to himself as a prisoner (in Philemon) or a slave (Philippians, Romans, Titus) of Jesus Christ. Indeed, he also claimed the title "servant of Christ" in Galatians as well but not until 1:10. The second word in the epistle is *apostolos*—an indication that Paul's apostolic office and his right to bear its name would figure prominently in the Galatian letter.

The word "apostle" had a rich and varied history prior to its assuming a New Testament meaning.[4] As the noun form of the verb *apostellein,* meaning "to send" or "to dispatch," an apostle is literally an envoy or ambassador, one who has been sent in the service of another. In classical Greek the term was actually used of a naval expedition, perhaps deriving from the *apo* prefix, indicating "to send away from," that is, to send off on a long and arduous mission.

Some scholars have derived the immediate background for the Christian office of apostle from the Jewish concept of the *šālîaḥ.* This term, derived from rabbinic sources, referred to a person who acted on behalf of another, particularly in legal or ceremonial matters. A *šālîaḥ* possessed a delegated

---

[4] See the classic discussion in E. deW. Burton, *A Critical and Exegetical Commentary on the Epistle to the Galatians,* ICC (Edinburgh: T & T Clark, 1921), 363-84. Also helpful is J. B. Lightfoot's earlier treatment, "The Name and Office of an Apostle," in his *Saint Paul's Epistle to the Galatians* (1890; reprint, London: Macmillan, 1986), 92-101. Cf. also K. H. Rengstorf, "Ἀπόστολος," *TDNT* 1.407-45.

authority comparable to what we might call the power of attorney. He could, for example, transact business on behalf of his client, carry certain offerings to the temple in his stead, even enter into engagement or divorce proceedings at the behest of another. While these parallels are intriguing, there are also important differences between the Jewish concept of the *šālîaḥ* and the Christian office of the apostle, not least of which is the prophetic notion of a divine commissioning that the New Testament apostolate assumes.[5]

Turning to the New Testament, we find that "apostle" is used in both an exclusive and an inclusive sense. Luke said that out of a larger band of disciples Jesus chose twelve individuals and designated them apostles (Luke 6:12-16). By the end of Jesus' earthly ministry, the concept of the Twelve had become so fixed that it could refer to this special circle of Jesus' followers even after one of the apostles, Judas Iscariot, was no longer a part of it (cf. 1 Cor 15:5). When the early church met to choose a replacement for Judas, it was deemed necessary for his successor to have been a participant both in Jesus' earthly ministry and an eyewitness of his resurrection (Acts 1:21-22). In the exclusive sense, then, the apostles were, as Calvin put it, "the highest order in the church."[6] In this special sense the apostles represent the continuity of salvation history from the old covenant to the new. In John's vision of the New Jerusalem the twelve apostles are linked with the twelve tribes of Israel as representatives of God's redeemed people of all the ages (Rev 21:12-14). In a similar way, the apostles and prophets together form the foundation for the household of God, with Jesus Christ himself as the chief cornerstone (Eph 2:19-22).

To be sure, the word "apostle" is used in a more general sense in the New Testament as well. Once even Jesus himself is referred to as "the apostle and high priest whom we confess" (Heb 3:1). More often the name is applied to early Christian missionaries or emissaries who were sent forth as representatives of a particular congregation. Thus Paul and Barnabas are so described by Luke in his account of their first missionary journey (Acts 14:14). Paul also referred to Andronicus and Junias, two otherwise unknown fellow workers, as "outstanding among the apostles" (Rom 16:7). He also referred to Epaphroditus as the *apostolos* of the Philippians, "whom you sent to take care of my needs" (Phil 2:25). In Galatians, however, Paul nowhere used the word "apostle" in its more general or generic sense.

The source of Paul's apostolic consciousness is evident from his bold

---

[5] On the *šālîaḥ* see the helpful discussion in R. Longenecker, *Galatians,* WBC (Dallas: Word, 1990), 3-4, and also C. K. Barrett, "Shaliah and Apostle," in *Donum Gentilicium,* ed. C. K. Barrett et al. (London: Oxford University Press, 1978), 88-102.

[6] Calvin, CNTC 11.8.

assertion that he had been "sent not from men nor by man, but by Jesus Christ and God the Father, who raised him from the dead" (Gal 1:1). The expressions "not from [apo] men nor by [dia] man" indicate that Paul's apostolic vocation neither originated nor was mediated by human agency. Here in the very first sentence of his letter Paul was countering the allegations of his Galatian opponents who had alleged that he had no divine apostolic appointment at all. To their mind Paul was a latecomer, at best an apostle of the apostles, and not a very faithful one at that!

Paul would have to deal with this charge at greater length as he unfolded the historic basis of his apostolic calling and ministry in chaps. 1–2. Here at the outset it was important for him to assert the divine source of his apostleship: he was called directly by the risen Christ without any human intermediary at all. On the basis of his divine commission Paul claimed nothing less than an apostolic status equal with the Twelve. In later ecclesiastical tradition we find that Paul had displaced Matthias in standard listings of the twelve apostles. However, this interpretation by no means represents the unanimous consensus of the early church. As late as Augustine, we hear an echo of anti-Pauline rhetoric as he depicted how Paul's hearers might have responded to his question, "Do you not know that we will judge angels?" (1 Cor 6:3):

> What do you mean by boasting that you will be the judge? Where will you sit? The Lord appointed twelve seats for the twelve apostles. One fell—Judas. Mathias was ordained to fill his place. So all twelve seats are occupied. First find somewhere to sit; then you can boast that you will be the judge.[7]

Paul surely must have confronted similar jibes in his own day. Unlike his opponents, who brought impressive résumés and letters of recommendation to validate their apostolic claims (2 Cor 3:1-3), Paul appealed to the one unique authority for his distinctive self-awareness and assurance: the living God who "set me apart . . . called me . . . and revealed his Son in me" (Gal 1:15-16).

1:1b Paul was called "by Jesus Christ and God the Father who raised him from the dead." Paul decisively qualified his calling in a negative way: it is neither *from* men, that is, from a human source, nor *by* men, that is, mediated through any particular person whether Peter, James, Ananias, or whomever. Now follows a strong adversative, "but" (*alla*), and a positive ascription of the true source of his life and mission. It would be a serious error to pass over these words lightly as though they were "a kind of pious window dressing intended to furnish evidence of orthodoxy."[8] The entire

---

[7] This is from Augustine's exposition of Ps 118. Quoted, J. Bligh, *Galatians* (London: St. Paul Publications, 1969), 55.

[8] Ebeling, *Truth of the Gospel*, 16.

message of Galatians is contained in these words. True, they are words that belong to the confessional and kerygmatic tradition of earliest Christianity; they are part of the heart of that message that Paul claimed to have "received" and then "passed on" to his converts (1 Cor 15:3). These words were not invented by Paul but rather already were there in the praise and proclamation of the first believers. Still, Paul pressed this confession into service in Galatians at this particular point in order to establish a firm foundation about everything he would say about faith and works, law and gospel, freedom and bondage, circumcision and the cross. Let us examine three aspects of this foundational statement.

THE CONTRAST OF CHRIST AND HUMANS.   Paul said that he had been appointed and commissioned "not . . . by man, but by Jesus Christ." We are struck by the fact that Paul here completely separated Jesus Christ from the category of all other humans and placed him on the side of God. Why did he do this? Clearly he was not denying the true humanity of Jesus. Later in this same letter he reminds his readers that "God sent his son, born of a woman" (Gal 4:4). Elsewhere he could speak of the "one mediator between God and men, the man Christ Jesus" (1 Tim 2:5). In Gal 1:1, however, Paul was concerned to show that Jesus is *much more* than a mere man. He is qualitatively different from every other human being who has ever lived, not only with reference to his sinless life but also in respect to his unique relationship with the Father. This was a critical issue for Paul for this one reason: if Jesus Christ were not fully divine, he could never have redeemed us from the curse of the law or freed us from the power of sin by his death on the cross.

THE UNITY OF THE SON AND THE FATHER.   Paul had been called not by man, but "by Jesus Christ and God the Father." This is an unusual expression in the Greek text, for both Jesus Christ and God are governed by the same preposition (*dia,* "through" or "by"). Moreover, Jesus Christ is placed first, followed by God the Father, which is a reversal of the usual sequence. In this expression Paul was making two points at once: he was claiming that there is no distinction between the calling of Jesus Christ and the calling of God, and, further, he was asserting the essential and eternal unity between the Father and the Son. Clearly Chrysostom understood this text to imply "no distinction of essence" between the Father and the Son over against the Arians, who taught that Jesus Christ was an exalted, godlike creature, not the eternally divine coequal Son of the Father.[9]

---

[9] J. Chrysostom, "Homilies on Galatians," NPNF 13.3. Cf. the following comment quoted by G. Alexander in the translation of Chrysostom's homily: "To urge this use of *dia* in connection with Son and the Father as direct evidence for the *homoousia* of the Father and the Son

Obviously we should not read the Trinitarian disputes of the fourth and fifth centuries back into the texts of the New Testament. But neither should we lose sight of the fact that to a large extent the same great issues were involved in both eras even if they were couched in different words and thought forms. The question then as now is, Who is Jesus Christ? By so directly linking Jesus Christ and God the Father in such an unqualified, absolute, and intimate way, Paul was making a stupendous claim about a specific Jewish teacher who had lived and died in Palestine just a few years before these words were written. His brother James was still alive as were hundreds of other friends who had known and seen him (Gal 1:19; 1 Cor 15:6). Paul was saying that the life and work of this man, Jesus of Nazareth, transcends the bounds of all human categories—rabbi, prophet, guru, miracle worker, religious genius, philosopher, and statesman. When we consider who he was and what he did, we can only say that this one, Jesus, is God, the eternal Son of God, who freely came to earth to accomplish the Father's plan of redemption. He came into the very thick of our humanity, as bone of our bone and flesh of our flesh, but God has vindicated his shameful death on the cross by raising him from the dead and exalting him to his right hand in heaven. He is the Lamb of God slain from the foundation of the world, now worthy to be worshiped and glorified by all who are his.

1:2a   In the southern part of the Roman province of Galatia, such a weighty letter written by Paul and authorized by their mother church in Antioch might well have made a lasting impression on these embryonic congregations. All of this, however, goes beyond the evidence of the text. We do not know who the "brothers" were or how many they numbered or whether the entire church (at Antioch or elsewhere) endorsed the letter. It is significant that Paul did not write as a lone-ranger Christian, however unique his commission and solitary status. He deliberately associated himself with fellow believers who shared with him a burden for the gospel as well as for the Galatians. Thus at the outset the unity of the church was acknowledged in marked contrast to the fractured fellowship within the churches of Galatia (Gal 5:15).

A further word about the term "brothers" is in order. "Christians are brothers as the children of the heavenly father, a status to which they are called and of which they are assured through Jesus Christ. They are not children of the Father by nature but by grace, not by birth but by virtue of rebirth, as belonging to one and the same Lord, they are made each other's equals. None of them is Lord over the others, not even the apostle!"[10] The word

---

may perhaps be rightly deemed precarious. Yet there is something very noticeable in this use of a common preposition with both the first and second persons of the Trinity by a writer so cumulative and yet for the most part so exact in his use of prepositions as St. Paul."

[10] Ebeling, *Truth of the Gospel,* 21.

"brothers" thus anticipates the theme of freedom Paul would expound throughout the epistle. To be a brother or sister in Christ is to be a son or daughter of God, a status in which the categories of one's former existence (Jew/Greek, slave/free, male/female) pose no barrier to union with Christ and fellowship in his body (Gal 3:26-28).

(2) The Churches (1:2b)

To the churches in Galatia:

1:2b The word "church" is used in two senses in the New Testament. Sometimes it refers to the whole company of all the redeemed of all ages and places, the body of Christ extended throughout time as well as space. Thus Paul spoke to the Ephesian elders of "the church of God, which he bought with his own blood" (Acts 20:28). To the same believers Paul wrote this doxology: "To [God] be glory in the church and in Christ Jesus throughout all generations, for ever and ever!" (Eph 3:21). More often, however, the word "church" is used as it is here in Galatians to refer to local congregations of baptized believers who regularly meet for worship and witness.

Just as Paul did not deny the word "brothers" to the recipients of his letter, despite his stern warnings against false brothers in their midst, so here he extended the title "churches" to the communities of believers he and Barnabas had established, though they seem to be at the point of defection. In his other letters Paul lavished compliments on the churches to whom he wrote. It was "the church of God in Corinth . . . sanctified . . . and called to be holy." The Colossians were "holy and faithful brothers in Christ." The Philippians were his partners in the gospel; the Thessalonians, a "model" to all other believers. Even when addressing the church at Rome, which he neither had founded nor visited at the time of his writing, he rejoiced because their faith was being reported all over the world. Not so the Galatians! His terse words betray his tense mood and the gravity of the situation with which he had to deal—"to the churches in Galatia."

There is much about these churches, of course, that we do not know. Apart from the vexed question of whether they were in North or South Galatia, other issues remain hidden from sight. How many churches were there? How did they relate to one another. Evidently they shared a common founding by Paul and a common threat from his adversaries. Who brought the letter to them? Was it read aloud in the common worship service? Most intriguing of all, what was the reaction of the Galatian churches to this letter? The very fact that it was preserved and included among Paul's collected writings and eventually received into the canon of the New Testament may indicate a positive response to Paul's appeal. If, as we have argued, the letter is dated early in Paul's missionary career, then we may have evidence for the letter's positive impact from the report of Paul's second journey through the cities of Southern Galatia. In one of these, Lystra, he recruited Timothy to be his missionary associate. Luke also noted that the churches in that region were strengthened in the faith and "grew daily in numbers" (Acts 16:5). We would like to believe that the reception of Paul's letter jarred the Galatians from their spiritual stupor, leading to repentance and revival. What happened to the agitators with their gospel of legalism? If indeed they were expelled from the churches of Galatia, we can be sure that they continued their anti-Pauline campaign in other places. We hear echoes of their arguments in Paul's letters to the Colossians and the Corinthians.

Galatians is a tornado warning! None of God's elect will ever utterly or finally fall away, and the gates of hell certainly will never prevail against the church of Jesus Christ. But there is no such thing as "eternal security" for a local congregation that has lost its first love (Rev 2:1-7). The fact that today we read Galatians as a bisected conversation, not knowing the outcome or hearing the reaction, means that we should receive and heed its message with the same expectancy as the original recipients. What God said through Paul to the Galatians long ago he wants to say again to us here and now.

(3) The Greeting (1:3-5)

[3]Grace and peace to you from God our Father and the Lord Jesus Christ, [4]who gave himself for our sins to rescue us from the present evil age, according to the will of our God and Father, [5]to whom be glory for ever and ever. Amen.

1:3 Galatians begins and ends with "grace." Verses 3-5, which form the closing part of the long, one-sentence (in Greek) salutation, are no doubt taken from a standard formula of community prayer with its liturgical opening, "Grace and peace," and its concluding affirmation, "Amen!" This introductory blessing corresponds to the final benediction in 6:18, where again Paul invoked the grace of Christ for his Galatian brothers before offering a further and final "Amen." One scholar has suggested, somewhat ingeniously, that Paul deliberately inserted these standard liturgical rubrics into his letter so that when it was read aloud in the churches it would fit with ease into the order of worship.[11] More likely, however, is that Paul wanted to reiterate the basic burden of the letter in the context of prayer and doxology at both the beginning and end of his epistle.

---

[11] Bligh, *Galatians,* 67-68.

Each of Paul's letters begins with a reference to "grace and peace." Chrysostom relates these two words to the special situation in which the Galatians found themselves: "For since they were in danger of falling from grace, he prays that they may recover it again, and since they had become at war with God, he beseeches God to restore them to the same peace."[12]

As a matter of fact, "grace and peace" are a succinct summary of the entire Christian message. Grace (*charis*) is closely related to the common Greek word for "hello" (*chaire*).[13] For Paul, grace was virtually synonymous with Jesus Christ since he nowhere conceived of it as an impersonal force or quantity. Grace is God's unmerited goodwill freely given and decisively effective in the saving work of Jesus Christ. Peace (*eirenē;* cf. Heb. *šālôm*), on the other hand, denotes a state of wholeness and freedom that the grace of God brings. Both concepts are deeply rooted in the Old Testament Scriptures and are beautifully brought together in the Aaronic blessing in Num 6:24-26, "The Lord bless you and keep you; the Lord make his face shine upon you and be gracious to you; the Lord turn his face toward you and give you peace."

This double blessing is attributed to a single source—the one God who knows himself as Father, Son, and Holy Spirit. While Paul's trinitarian thinking would only become explicit in chaps. 3 and 4, the soteriological focus of the greeting already presupposes the regenerating ministry of the Holy Spirit (cf. "God sent the Spirit of his Son into our hearts," 4:6). Here grace and peace are said to be "from God our Father and the Lord Jesus Christ." Just as in 1:1 the Father and Son were linked together by a single preposition (*dia*), so too in 1:3 Paul used another solitary preposition (*apo*) to convey the equality and deity of both divine persons. The true deity of Christ is seen in the fact that he is associated indissolubly with the Father in all the mighty acts of salvation.[14]

Significantly, Paul did not develop an abstract or metaphysical doctrine of God apart from his self-revelation in Jesus Christ. In commenting on this verse, Luther remarked that Paul always associated Jesus Christ with the Father in order to teach us true Christian theology that "does not begin at the top, as all other religions do, but in the utmost depths. . . . Therefore you must put away all speculations . . . and run directly to the manger and the

---

[12] Chrysostom, "Homilies on Galatians," 4.

[13] H. Conzelmann, "Χάρις," *TDNT* 9.393-96.

[14] Cf. Luther's comment: "The true deity of Christ is proved by this conclusion: Paul attributes to him the ability to grant the very same things that the Father does—grace, peace of conscience, the forgiveness of sins, life, and victory over sin, death, the devil, and hell. This would be illegitimate, in fact, sacrilegious, if Christ were not true God. For no one grants peace unless he himself has it in his hands" (*LW* 26.31).

mother's womb, embrace this infant and virgin's child in your arms, and look at him—born, being nursed, growing up, going about in human society, teaching, dying, rising again, ascending above all the heavens, and having authority over all things. In this way you can shake off all terrors and errors, as the sun dispels the clouds."[15] In the following verse Paul made three important affirmations about the saving work of Christ.

1:4a Just as Paul already had referred to the resurrection in v. 1, so here he brought into view the suffering and death of Christ on the cross, "who gave himself for our sins." The NEB translates the expression "who sacrificed himself for our sins." This recalls Jesus' own description of his mission in Mark 10:45, "The Son of Man did not come to be served, but to serve, and to give his life as a ransom for many." Behind this language stands the image of the Suffering Servant in Isa 53 who bore our iniquities and carried our sorrows through being smitten and crushed by God's righteous judgment. Paul here emphasized the voluntary character of Jesus' self-offering, "He gave himself." This theme is further developed in the kenotic hymn in Phil 2:5-11, "He made himself nothing . . . he humbled himself and became obedient to death—even death on a cross!" Jesus' death was not a fortuitous accident. He willingly submitted himself to the divine purpose of his Father, saying "Here I am, I have come to do your will" (Heb 10:9). We confess this truth when we sing:

> Be this my everlasting song,
> He took upon Himself my wrong,
> And cried while facing Calvary,
> "Send me, O Lord, send me."[16]

We also glimpse in these words the radical character of sin, another major theme Paul developed throughout Galatians. So serious is the breach between us and God caused by our sins that nothing less than the substitutionary atoning death of God's Son can reconcile us to the Father. We are not sure which Greek preposition Paul used in the phrase "for our sins." Some manuscripts read *peri*, which means simply "concerning" or "in regard to." Other manuscripts read *hyper*, "on behalf of," "for the benefit of." Paul used the latter word in 1 Cor 15:3, "Christ died for [*hyper*] our sins." This is likely the intended reading here as well since Paul used *hyper* twice again in Galatians (2:20; 3:13) when speaking of Christ's death on our behalf. In either case, however, his meaning is clear: there is an intrinsic connection between

---

[15] Ibid., 30; cf. Ebeling, *Truth of the Gospel,* 32.

[16] Ross Coggins, "Send Me, O Lord, Send Me," © Copyright 1956 Broadman Press. Used by permission.

our sins and Christ's death. The only avenue to a right relationship with God is the path that leads to Calvary.

1:4b Christ "gave himself for our sins," Paul said, "to rescue [or deliver] us from the present evil age." Here Paul described what Jesus' death accomplished not only in terms of our personal salvation but also in regard to God's redemptive purpose in the wider historical and cosmic arenas. Interpreters of Galatians have been divided over whether Paul's concern in this book was strictly for the salvation of individuals through justification by faith alone apart from dependence on human works or whether its focus was more communal and eschatological, that is, concerned with how Gentile believers could be included within the community of Israel's Messiah, an issue with important implications for understanding salvation history and the divine consummation of all things.[17] The former view, that Galatians is about individual salvation and justification by faith, was given classic expression by Martin Luther in the Reformation and has found modern champions in such diverse interpreters as R. Bultmann, H. Hübner, and J. Stott. The latter view, that Galatians is about a first-century problem with corporate and eschatological implications, has been advanced by a host of recent scholars including J. Munck, K. Stendahl, and E. P. Sanders. However, by juxtaposing so closely in Gal 1:4 the personal and historical dimensions of salvation, Paul indicated the inherent unity between these two dimensions of Christ's work. That Christ died for our sins and justifies us by faith should not be reduced to a subjective, existentialist interpretation. As Paul will argue at length in Galatians, what God has done in Christ is directly related to his covenant promises to Israel as well as to the final salvation of all the redeemed.

"The present evil age" is the context in which God's purpose of salvation is now unfolding. The notion of two ages, borrowed from Jewish apocalyptic thought, juxtaposes a present age of sin and decay and a future age of blessing and peace. For Paul, however, the death and resurrection of Jesus has radically punctuated this traditional time line. The Christian now lives in profound tension between the *No Longer* and the *Not Yet*. The coming of Christ has drastically relativized, though not completely obliterated, former distinctions of race, class, and gender. It also has placed in a totally new perspective such former requirements as circumcision, food laws, and feast

---

[17] See the helpful survey of "Galatian debates" by J. M. G. Barclay, *Obeying the Truth: A Study of Paul's Ethics in Galatians* (Edinburgh: T & T Clark, 1988), 1-8. Two other helpful reviews of this voluminous literature are F. Thielman, *From Plight to Solution* (Leiden: Brill, 1989), 1-27, and S. Westerholm, *Israel's Law and the Church's Faith: Paul and His Recent Interpreters* (Grand Rapids: Eerdmans, 1988), 1-101.

days. Christ has rescued us from this present evil age through justifying us by faith and pouring out his Spirit in our lives. This is an accomplished fact, and we must not be drawn back into "a yoke of slavery" (Gal 5:1). But while Christ has rescued us from this evil age, he has not taken us out of it. Thus our liberty must not degenerate into license nor the gift of the Spirit be abused by selfish carnal behavior (Gal 5:16-26).

1:4c Christ has died for our sins and rescued us from the grip of this evil age in accordance with the will, good pleasure, and command of the Father. As R. A. Cole comments, "Here is no possibility of unreal antithesis between a harsh father and a loving son. The action of the Son was the very proof of the Father's love."[18] In other words, God loves us not because Jesus died for us; rather Jesus died for us because of the Father's eternal and unconquerable love for us.[19] Elsewhere in his writings, especially in Eph 1 and Rom 9–11, Paul developed at length the doctrine of divine election, pointing out that in accordance with his eternal decree we were chosen in Christ before the creation of the world. While this doctrine receives no detailed elaboration in Galatians, it forms the very bedrock of doctrine of justification by faith alone.

1:5 Such a great God merits our highest praise, so Paul concluded his long salutation with a doxology, "To whom be glory for ever and ever. Amen." The inclusion of this exclamation of praise is no mere formality. To contemplate who God is and what he has done in Jesus Christ is to fall on our knees in worship, thanksgiving, and praise. We study the Bible and the great doctrines of the Christian faith not out of vain curiosity, nor merely to increase our intellectual acumen and historical knowledge but rather that we might come more fully to love and enjoy the gracious God who delights in our praise. As Calvin put it so well, "So glorious is his redemption that it should ravish us with wonder."[20]

2. The Apostolic Curse (1:6-10)

Paul moved with great abruptness from the salutation into the body of the

---

[18] R. A. Cole, *The Epistle of Paul to the Galatians,* TNTC (Grand Rapids: Eerdmans, 1965), 36.

[19] Thomas Aquinas describes the *ordo salutis* in terms of traditional categories of Aristotelian causation. Thus the formal cause of the plan of salvation is the Father's plan, the efficient cause is the death of Christ, and the final cause is the forgiveness and deliverance wrought but the Spirit. We may accept this schema as a helpful teaching device so long as we remember, as Aquinas did, that the works of the Trinity are inseparable. See Thomas Aquinas, *Commentary on St. Paul's Epistle to the Galatians* (Albany: Magi, 1966), 5-9.

[20] Calvin, CNTC 11.

letter itself. As we have seen, the thanksgiving section that usually comes at this point in his letters is omitted in Galatians. Instead of being able to give thanks for the Galatians' advance in the gospel, Paul expressed astonishment at their apostasy from it.

The transition from doxology in v. 5 to rebuke in v. 6 is especially harsh, almost unparalleled in its jarring dissonance. However, Paul reserved his heaviest fire not for the Galatian defectors but rather their pernicious seducers. They were the real perverters of Christ's gospel. Against them he hurled an uncompromising anathema. Where we would normally expect to find an apostolic blessing, we hear instead an apostolic curse.

Verse 10 serves as a transition from Paul's expression of shock to the vindication of his person and office. If we accept the hypothesis that the structure of Galatians was informed by the forensic rhetoric of the Hellenistic law courts, then we can see 1:6-11 as the *exordium,* or statement of the cause, that prompted Paul to write his "apologetic letter." This is followed in turn by the *narratio* (1:12–2:14), in which his case was demonstrated by statement of the facts; the *propositio* (2:15-21), or definition of the central thesis he wanted to argue; and finally the *probatio* (3:1–4:31), a series of historical and exegetical arguments demonstrating his thesis.[21] While such a formal analysis of the letter may help us appreciate the thrust and flow of Paul's argument, it should not obscure the fact that in Galatians Paul was responding to a real life situation of pressing urgency. His main concern was not winning points in an argument but saving souls from perdition.

(1) The Crisis in Galatia (1:6-7)

⁶I am astonished that you are so quickly deserting the one who called you by the grace of Christ and are turning to a different gospel— ⁷which is really

---

[21] Thus Longenecker (*Galatians,* 11-12), following Betz (*Galatians,* 16-23). Betz extends his rhetorical analysis to chaps. 5 and 6 as well, dividing them into an *exhortatio* (5:1–6:10) and *conclusio* (6:11-18). The magisterial contribution of Betz to a better understanding of the formal structure of Galatians is recognized by all students of the epistle. At the same time, serious questions have been raised concerning the development and application of this method. The critique of W. A. Meeks is pertinent: "The major question which must be put to Betz, then, is whether *apologia* is the most appropriate category to apply to the letter as a whole. . . . Betz's determination to discover a tight, sequential outline in the letter leads in places to a fragmentation of the text and a strangely atomistic interpretation." Review of H. D. Betz, *Galatians: A Commentary on Paul's Letter to the Church in Galatia, JBL* 100 (1981): 304-7. See also the review by C. K. Barrett, "Galatians as 'An Apologetic Letter,'" *Int* 34 (1980): 414-17. For a rather different rhetorical analysis of Galatians, see G. A. Kennedy, *New Testament Interpretation through Rhetorical Criticism* (Chapel Hill: University of North Carolina Press, 1984).

no gospel at all. Evidently some people are throwing you into confusion and are trying to pervert the gospel of Christ.

1:6 The word *thaumazō* has been variously translated as "astonished, marveled, amazed, astounded, surprised" (cf. the French *très étonné*). While the expression "I am astonished that" was a literary device commonly used in Hellenistic letters to express irritation and irony as well as surprise, Paul appears to have been genuinely shocked at the news he received from Galatia. The shock was further deepened because the slippage of his erstwhile disciples had occurred "so quickly." This phrase could refer either to the short duration of time that had elapsed since Paul first preached the gospel in Galatia, or it could mean that the Galatians had immediately lapsed from the true faith as soon as they were confronted with the message of the false teachers. The former interpretation is more natural and supports an early dating for the letter.

It is clear from Acts 13:14 that God had greatly blessed the missionary efforts of Paul and Barnabas in the cities of South Galatia despite the strong opposition they encountered there. Many new believers were won to Christ, churches were planted, elders appointed, and miracles displayed. Now, in the afterglow of this great awakening, the Galatian Christians for whom Paul harbored such great hope were at the very point of abandoning the gospel itself. Doubtless this accounts for the tone of dismay we hear in this verse and throughout the letter. "I am astonished. . . . You foolish Galatians! Who has bewitched you? . . . You were running a good race. Who cut in on you?" (1:6; 3:1; 5:7).

We are reminded here of how fragile young believers are, how susceptible to the blandishments of the Evil One. Nothing delights the devil more than to disrupt and destroy, insofar as he can, a true work of God. Whenever there is a genuine moving of God's Spirit or a major advance in missionary outreach, we can be sure that Satan and his minions will have a vested interest in casting doubts, sowing discord, and wreaking havoc. So it was among the churches of Galatia. Paul responded to the situation there not merely in anger and irritation but with a love and concern that went deep enough to confront. He prayed for them, wrote to them, and later revisited them because he took with utmost seriousness the work of "evangelistic follow-through." We do poor service to Christ and his church when we indiscriminately lead men and women to profess faith in Christ but then leave them vulnerable, like the exposed infants of ancient Rome, to the ravenous wolves that seek their destruction.

Although Paul clearly was frustrated and angry at his "dear idiots" (Gal 3:1, Phillips) in Galatia, he did not give up on them. Indeed, he wrote his letter with the hope of winning them back from the verge of spiritual collapse and ruin. He focused next on the two aspects of their lapse that had caused him so much bewilderment: their desertion from the true God and their devotion to a false gospel.

THEIR DESERTION FROM GOD.   Paul used a strong word to describe the crisis that had befallen the churches of Galatia. The word translated "deserting" in the NIV is *metatithesthai,* which means literally "to bring to another place."[22] The word is used in this literal sense in Heb 11:5 to describe Enoch's translation from earth to heaven. It occurs eighteen times in the Greek Old Testament, where it translates a variety of Hebrew words meaning "to transplant," "to set in another place," "to alter or change." From these meanings it was extended metaphorically to one who had changed allegiance from one country to another, a political traitor, or one who had switched sides in an armed conflict, a military deserter. Paul claimed the Galatians were spiritual turncoats! That he used this verb in the sense of a continuous present, "you are deserting," "you are in the process of leaving," indicates that their apostasy is not yet complete. Obviously the false teachers had made great inroads among them; the situation was desperate, but not beyond hope. Paul was "hard pressed on every side, but not crushed; perplexed, but not in despair" (2 Cor 4:8). Later in the letter he expressed confidence that they could be recovered, and he reminded them that they would "reap a harvest if [they] do not give up" (Gal 5:10; 6:9).

What was stupefying to Paul about the defection of his Galatian friends, the really radical character of their sin, was not simply that they had switched allegiance from him to his rivals but rather that they were becoming renegades of God himself, "deserting the one who called you by the grace of Christ." What is the referent of the expression "the one who called you"? Three answers to this question have been given in the history of interpretation.

It could refer, of course, to Paul himself since he, along with Barnabas, was the human instrument God used to awaken faith in the Galatians. Yet as Paul would make abundantly clear in v. 8, he himself was not the standard by which the situation in Galatia was to be judged. Something far greater than personal prerogative or pastoral loyalty was at stake in this struggle. Another possible interpretation, adopted by Calvin and many scholars since, holds that "the one who called" refers to Jesus Christ. This is certainly a possible reading since many of the earliest and best manuscripts do not contain the qualifying genitive "of Christ," following the word "grace" in the next phrase.[23] It is true that by following the way of the false teachers the Galatians had contradicted the finished work of Christ, making him and his cross

---

[22] See C. Maurer, "Μετατίθημι," *TDNT* 8.161-62.
[23] See B. M. Metzger, *A Textual Commentary on the Greek New Testament* (London: United Bible Societies, 1971), 589-90.

Paul linked it to an even more serious one: the Galatians were guilty of nothing less than deserting God himself. In Paul's writings "he who calls" is synonymous with God, as can be seen in Paul's two other uses of it in Galatians (1:15; 5:8; but see also Rom 4:17; 9:12; 1 Thess 2:12; 5:24). The Galatians were deserting the God who calls—the God who called the world into existence by his creative power, the God who raised Jesus from the dead, the God who wrought the miracle of conversion in the Galatians themselves. True, they also were deserting Christ, Paul, and the gospel he had preached. But these defections could perhaps be explained away through clever manipulation. After all, it could be said, both Paul and his opponents believed in Jesus Christ. Both had a message about being right with God and preached it with apparent sincerity. Among the various churches and sometimes within a single church (e.g., Corinth) are different personalities, various methodologies, and distinct political groupings. Why should Paul have had the final or authoritative word? Doubtless this kind of reasoning must have gone on within the Christian circles where Paul and his entourage moved. Paul, however, adamantly refused to reduce the conflict in Galatia to the level of personality, ideology, or church politics.

By adding additional requirements for salvation to what Jesus Christ has once and for all done, the Galatians had deserted God. This point is made all the more clear by Paul's insertion of the phrase "by grace" into his description of how the Galatians had been called by God. Here grace stands absolutely (not the grace "of Christ" as the variant readings have it) in order to show that this is the only basis on which we can relate to God in any sense. Already we have encountered the word "grace" in the salutation (1:3); it is the operative concept in Galatians and runs like a scarlet thread throughout the epistle from start to finish (1:15; 2:9; 2:21; 3:18; 5:4; 6:18).

There is not a wasted syllable in Galatians; we must not imagine that Paul here threw in one of his favorite words as a kind of theological grace note to soften his otherwise harsh rebuke. No, grace is what Galatians is all about. Both here and in Romans, Paul set grace and faith together over against law and works as the basis of justification (Rom 6:14; 11:6; Gal 2:21; 5:4).[24] At the end of his explication of the doctrine of justification by faith, Paul would summarize his verdict against the Galatians thus: "You who are trying to be justified by law have been alienated by Christ; you have fallen away from grace" (5:4). Here at the beginning of the letter he wanted them to realize that the God who called them out of pagan idolatry to salvation and new life in Jesus Christ did so on no other basis than his own good pleasure and gra-

---

[24] H. Conzelmann, "Χάρις," *TDNT* 9.372-415. Cf. also D. P. Fuller, *Gospel and Law: Contrast or Continuum?* (Grand Rapids: Eerdmans, 1980).

in Jesus Christ did so on no other basis than his own good pleasure and gratuitous favor. To forget this is worse than betraying an army or a country; it is to betray the true and living God.

THEIR DEVOTION TO A FALSE GOSPEL. In addition to the negative movement of the Galatians away from their former allegiance to the true God, Paul noted here a further development, the positive side, so to speak, of their falling away: "They are turning to a different gospel—which is really no gospel at all." This is a difficult expression to translate into English as the awkward wording in most modern versions indicates. The AV reads "another gospel, which is not another." However, Paul used two separate words in Greek for "another." The first is *heteros,* which connotes a difference in kind between one thing and another. For example, Heb 7:11 poses the question of why, if perfection were possible through the Levitical priesthood, there still was need for another (*heteron*) priest to come, that is, a priest of a different class or kind from that of the old order of Aaron. The other word, *allos,* on the other hand, means "another one of the same kind." We are familiar enough with this usage from everyday life; it is used when the waitress asks whether we would like another cup of coffee, meaning a second (or third) installment of our original drink.

So here in Galatians Paul asserted that his fickle followers had embraced a *heteros* gospel, one drastically different in kind from that they had received from him, for there is, in fact, no other (*allos*) genuine gospel to be placed alongside the real thing. Perhaps the NEB comes closest to the original: "I am astonished to find you . . . following a different gospel. Not that it is in fact another gospel."[25]

What is the true gospel Paul was so careful to distinguish from its counterfeit model? The word "gospel" itself was not uniquely Christian, being used in both classical Greek and the Septuagint to refer to good news of various sorts. Bruce has suggested that the specific background for the Christian adaptation of the word in the "glad tidings" of salvation and liberation scattered throughout Isa 40–66 (cf. Isa 40:9; 52:7; 60:6).[26] How-

---

[25] While *heteros* and *allos* carry the distinction referred to above in the Galatian passage under review, they are sometimes used synonymously (cf. Matt 16:14; 1 Cor 12:10). See the discussion in E. deW. Burton, *A Critical and Exegetical Commentary on the Epistle to the Galatians,* ICC (Edinburgh: T & T Clark, 1921), 420-22. See also J. H. Thayer, *Greek-English Lexicon of the New Testament* (Grand Rapids: Associated, 1963), 254. For the adverbial use of *heteros* meaning "otherwise, differently," see Phil 3:15.

[26] F. F. Bruce, *Galatians,* NIGTC (Grand Rapids: Eerdmans, 1982), 81. As Bruce points out, Jesus quoted from Isa 61 in his inaugural sermon in the Nazareth synagogue, announcing that "the Spirit of the Lord is upon me, because he has anointed me to bring good tidings to the poor" (LXX εὐαγγελίσασθαι πτωχηοῖς).

ever, only with the fulfillment of the Old Testament prophecies in the coming of Jesus Christ does "gospel" receive its full and potent meaning. Of all the New Testament writers, Paul used the word most frequently, sixty times to be exact. On occasion he summarized the content of the gospel in a pithy confessional statement, as in 1 Cor 15:3-4 and Rom 1:1-4. Paul offered no such definition in his Letter to the Galatians obviously because he assumed they were quite familiar with it already from his recent preaching campaign in their midst. Clearly it included a recital of God's mighty act of deliverance through the life, death, and resurrection of Jesus Christ, the benefits of which—including forgiveness of sins, a right standing with God, and the gift of the Holy Spirit—are appropriated only by grace through faith.[27]

1:7 Here for the first time in the letter Paul spoke explicitly of the agitators who had caused so much distress to him and to the churches of Galatia. Significantly he did not identify them by name; they simply were "some people." Paul used the plural, for evidently there was a band or at least a team of false teachers disseminating their views among the Galatians. Paul leveled two charges against them: one, with reference to their disturbance of the Galatians; the other, relating to their subversion of the gospel. The Greek verb translated "to throw into confusion" (*tarassō*) means to "shake," "agitate," or "to excite to the point of perplexity and fear." Here again is an indication of how vulnerable the new Christians of Galatia were to evidently impressive presentations of the false teachers. Paul's second charge against them was that they were perverting, or rather, wanted to pervert, the gospel of Christ. As J. Stott has wisely observed: "These two go together. To tamper with the gospel is always to trouble the church. You cannot touch the gospel and leave the church untouched, because the church is created and lives by the gospel. Indeed the church's greatest troublemakers (now as then) are not those outside who oppose, rid-

---

[27] In some circles it is still popular to distinguish sharply the gospel "of Jesus," that is his proclamation of the kingdom of God as recorded in the Synoptic Gospels, from the gospel "about Jesus," the doctrine of his person and work elaborated by the early church, particularly by Paul. Hence the simple piety of the Galilean rabbi is extolled in distinction from harsh doctrinaire theology developed by Paul. This view was dominant among liberal scholars in the early part of the twentieth century, but recent studies have shown it to be untenable. The gospel Jesus preached, no less than Paul, was a gospel about his own person and work. Moreover, his miracles and teachings, especially the parables, demonstrate vividly the reality of divine grace that Paul, inspired by the Holy Spirit, was led to formulate in terms of justification by faith. On the relationship between Jesus and Paul, see J. G. Machen, *The Origin of Paul's Religion* (Grand Rapids: Eerdmans, 1965), 117-69. See also N. A. Dahl, "The Messiaship of Jesus in Paul," in *The Crucified Messiah and Other Essays* (Minneapolis: Augsburg, 1974), 34-47; M. Brisebois, *Saint Paul: Introduction à Saint Paul et seo lettres* (Montreal: Editions Paulines, 1984).

icule and persecute it, but those inside who try to change the gospel."[28]

The Greek verb for "pervert" (*metastrephō*) means "to reverse, to change to the opposite, to twist into something different." In the early church Jerome observed that this word carried the literal meaning of "setting behind what is in front and putting in front what is behind."[29] Applied to Paul's opponents in Galatia, we can say that the gospel they preached implied a reversal of salvation history.

What they failed to realize was the decisive character of who Jesus was and what he had accomplished in his atoning death on the cross, though their Christology may have been formally correct. To Christ's completed work they wanted to add something of their own. But the gospel of Christ is like a chemical compound to which no mixture can be added. It stands on its own. It needs no props or helps. It only asks to be its own free, unhindered, disarming self. For only then can it really be good news to lost men and women imprisoned in the tyranny of sin and self.

Paul was unsparing in his condemnation of these perverters and seducers of God's flock. They doubtless saw things quite differently. If, as seems likely, they had strong connections with those Judean Christians who precipitated a similar crisis in the church at Antioch (Acts 15:1-4), then we might summarize their presumed message in this way:

Dear brothers of Galatia, we greet you in the Name of our Lord Jesus Christ! We have heard how through the ministry of Brother Paul you have been converted from the worship of dumb idols to serve the true and living God of Israel. We are glad you have made such a good beginning, but we are afraid that there are some very important things about the gospel Paul has omitted to tell you. We ourselves come from the church at Jerusalem which is directed by the very apostles Jesus called and ordained. Paul though is an upstart. Why, he never even knew Jesus while he was on earth and was certainly never commissioned by him as an apostle. True, Paul did visit Jerusalem just after he stopped persecuting us, and there he learned the ABCs of the Christian faith from the true apostles. But the message he now preaches bears no resemblance to theirs. I don't imagine he even told you about circumcision! Why, this is the very way God has made it possible for you Gentiles to become a part of the New Israel. Jesus did not come to abolish the law but to fulfill it. Circumcision is just as important as baptism—nay, more important, for it will introduce you to a higher plane of Christian living. If you will observe this holy ordinance of the law, God will be pleased with you. We are just now forming a new association of law-observant churches, and we would love for

---

[28] J. R. W. Stott, *Only One Way: The Message of Galatians* (Downers Grove: InterVarsity, 1968), 23.

[29] Quoted by Luther in his 1519 Galatians commentary (*LW* 27.176).

Galatia to be represented! We are the true Christians. Jesus, our great example, pleased the Father by fulfilling the law and so can you!

But why would such a message be appealing to the Christians of Galatia? Again, there is much about the situation we do not know, but Ebeling probably is correct when he surmises that "the Judaizers can hardly have precipitated a crisis not already in the making."[30] We know that most of the Christians in the churches of Galatia came from a Gentile background, though some were likely Jews and others "God-fearers" attached to the local synagogues. Some may have dabbled in the mystery religions that were well represented in the cities of Southern Galatia, while others perhaps bowed at the shrine of the imperial deity.

In any event, there was likely a deep hunger and thirst for spiritual reality that the religious marketplace of "this present evil age" could not satisfy. To these people Paul and Barnabas preached the good news of salvation through Jesus Christ. The Holy Spirit was poured out in miraculous power, the new believers were baptized, local churches were formed, and the missionaries departed. Soon thereafter, before the first wave of enthusiastic ardor had been dampened, the false teachers arrived with their new message of how the Galatians could perfect the good beginning they made and so move on toward complete salvation.

Christ was still prominent in their preaching, but only as an adjunct to the law. Grace was a word they used as well, but grace for them meant simply one's natural ability to obey the laws and rites required in the Torah. This kind of "gospel" Paul saw as a total perversion. But the Galatian Christians, naive and immature, were intrigued by its promise of an even more elevated spiritual status. What the false teachers offered the Galatians was a way to enhance and elevate their already robust spirituality. Luther masterfully captured the genius of their appeal in his summary of their message: " 'Christ's a fine master. He makes the beginning, but Moses must complete the structure.' The devil's nature shows itself therein: if he cannot ruin people by wronging and persecuting them, he will do it by improving them."[31]

(2) The Counterfeit Gospel: Anathema! (1:8-9)

⁸But even if we or an angel from heaven should preach a gospel other than the one we preached to you, let him be eternally condemned! ⁹As we have already said, so now I say again: If anybody is preaching to you a gospel other than what you accepted, let him be eternally condemned!

---

[30] Ebeling, *Truth of the Gospel,* 54. See J. C. Beker's reconstruction of the arguments of Paul's opponents in his *Paul the Apostle* (Philadelphia: Fortress, 1980), 42-47.

[31] Ibid., 54. cf. *LW* 26.50.

In these verses Paul intensified the antithesis between himself and his Galatian opponents by pronouncing a solemn curse upon anyone who proclaimed a counterfeit gospel. The fact that Paul issued this condemnation in the strongest words possible and then repeated it for emphasis makes this one of the harshest statements in the entire New Testament. It does not set well on modern ears accustomed to tolerance at any price and a doctrine of God devoid of the notions of judgment and wrath. Yet here it stands, stubbornly and ominously, at the forefront of Paul's concern. How are we to understand this anathema?

In the first place, it is important to see that, hypothetically at least, Paul brought himself under his own curse. "But even if we . . . should preach a gospel other than." Here Paul showed once and for all that the issue at stake in Galatia was not the messenger but the message. Later in the history of the church, during the time of Augustine, a great dispute arose concerning the sacraments, such as baptism, the Lord's Supper, and ordination. The question was whether these religious rites were valid and effective when performed by a minister who was morally impure. One party in the dispute, the Donatists, argued that they were not. Their efficacy was tied to the spiritual and moral condition of the presiding minister. Augustine and the majority of others in the church took the opposite view. The sacraments, they said, were *ex opere operato,* that is, they were effective by virtue of the power invested in them by Christ himself and the promise of his Word. At the time of the Reformation, both of these views were subjected to a fresh biblical critique, but the essential point of the Augustinian position was recognized as valid: the true touchstone of doctrinal and spiritual authenticity is God himself, what he has irrevocably done in Christ and infallibly vouchsafed to us in Holy Scripture, and not the qualifications, charisma, or even theology of any human leader.[32]

Of course, how our message is received is directly related to the way we live. Paul elsewhere recognized the importance of high moral standards and a good reputation for those who assume leadership posts in the church (1 Tim 3:1-13). His point in Galatians was that none of these traits, significant as they are, can ever compete with the gospel itself as the ultimate criterion for both sound doctrine and holy living. Paul did not ask the Galatians to be loyal to him but rather to the unchanging message of Christ, Christ alone, that he had preached to them.

In the second place, Paul brought even the angels within the purview of his anathema. As Luther quaintly put it: "Here Paul is breathing fire. His zeal

---

[32] On the significance of the Donatist controversy in the history of Christian thought, see J. Pelikan, *The Emergence of the Catholic Tradition (100-600)* (Chicago: University of Chicago Press, 1971), 307-18.

is so fervent that he almost begins to curse the angels themselves."[33] This is the first of three references to angels in Galatians. In 3:19 Paul referred to the belief that the law was ordained through the mediation of angels, and in 4:14 he reminded the Galatians that they initially welcomed him as an angel of God, perhaps a reference to the incident at Lystra recorded in Acts 14. But why did Paul raise the specter of an angel preaching an apostate gospel? If we identify the Galatian error with what Paul confronted at Colosse, then it may be assumed that the kind of angelic adulation that prevailed in that setting was also a part of the "higher spirituality" brought to Galatia by the anti-Pauline missionaries (cf. Col 2:16-18).[34]

Paul's opponents also may have cited the role of the angels in the deliverance of the law (Gal 3:19) to give a supernatural enhancement to their own proclamation of a law-observant gospel. In that case, Paul wanted to make clear that even if an angel, even such an exalted angel as Gabriel or Michael, were to preach a different gospel, the curse of God would be upon him. Early Christian preaching was aware of just such an angelic apostasy when the angels who rebelled with Satan "abandoned their own home" (Jude 6) for the chains of darkness and eventual condemnation on the day of judgment. Moreover, Paul was aware that Satan himself could masquerade as an angel of light. Indeed, by this cunning he had led astray many sincere believers from their pure devotion to Christ (2 Cor 11:3-15).

What is the fate of one who thus perverts the gospel of Christ, be it Paul, any other human teacher, or even a messenger straight from heaven itself? The answer is given in two words: *anathema estō,* "let him be accursed!" Originally the word *anathema,* which literally means "something that is placed up," referred to any object set aside for divine purposes, whether an offering in the temple set aside for divine blessing or the captured booty of Achan reserved for divine cursing (Josh 7:11-12). In time the negative sense of the word prevailed, and *anathema* became synonymous with anything or anyone under the "ban" (Heb., *ḥerem*) and hence delivered over to God's wrath for final judgment. Later in church history *anathema sit!* became the standard postscript pronounced by the church on a notorious heretic. This is a derivative use of the word since, at best, the church's decision can only be a ratification of the pronouncement of God's own excluding wrath.

To be anathematized then means far more than to be excommunicated.[35]

---

[33] *LW* 26.55.

[34] On the worship of angels in the Colossian heresy, see R. R. Melick, Jr., *Philippians, Colossians, Philemon,* NAC (Nashville: Broadman, 1991), 269-72.

[35] Thus the rendering of the NEB, "Let him be outcast!," is far too weak to do justice to the gravity of Paul's language. As R. Y. K. Fung (*Galatians,* NICNT [Grand Rapids: Eerdmans, 1988], 47) observes: "it thus more likely means being delivered up and devoted to the

It means nothing less than to suffer the eternal retribution and judgment of God. The GNB comes close to capturing the essence of Paul's tone in this passage, "Let him be condemned to hell!" We can gauge something of what this curse must have meant to Paul's readers by looking at a curse in one of the documents found among the Dead Sea Scrolls:

> And the Levites shall curse all the men of the lot of Satan, saying: 'Be cursed because of all your guilty wickedness! May He deliver you up for torture at the hands of the vengeful Avengers! May He visit you with destruction by the hands of all the Wreakers of Revenge! Be cursed without mercy because of the darkness of your deeds! Be damned in the shadowy place of everlasting fire! May God not heed when you call on him, nor pardon you by blotting out your sin! May he raise his angry face toward you for vengeance!'[36]

Paul did not pronounce this tremendous condemnation lightly. But neither did he hesitate to unleash the full fury of his righteous indignation when he was convinced that the integrity of the gospel was at stake.

1:9 Why did Paul repeat the apostolic curse introducing the second version with the words, "As we have already said, so now I say again"? It is possible that Paul was referring here to his utterance of the original anathema during his recent preaching mission in Galatia. Perhaps he anticipated the problems his opponents would bring and tried in this way to forewarn the Galatians against heeding their erroneous teaching (thus Schmithals, Ebeling, Longenecker). Most commentators, however, believe that Paul repeated the anathema in order to emphasize its severity and further impress upon the Galatians the utter folly of their flirtation with false doctrine (thus Bruce, Fung, Lightfoot). There is one important stylistic difference between vv. 8 and 9. Although the expression "Let him be eternally condemned!" is identical in both, the if-clauses are given in two different moods. In v. 8 the if-clause is followed by a subjunctive verb, "should preach," because what is being contemplated is a highly improbable, though not impossible, situation. However, in v. 9, the if-clause is followed by the indicative mood, "is preaching," indicating the ongoing crisis unfolding in Galatia even as Paul wrote. Also in v. 9, Paul reminds the Galatians that they had in fact embraced the true gospel when he had preached it to them. A solid foundation had been laid in the missionary work of Paul and Barnabas. Paul now reminds them, as later he would warn the Corinthians as well, that "no one can lay any foundation other than the one already laid, which is Jesus Christ" (1 Cor 3:11).

---

judicial wrath of God." Cf. C. Jordan's colloquial rending: "Now get this straight: Even if we or an angel fresh out of heaven preaches to you any other message than the one we preached to you—to hell with him!" (Cotton Patch, 94).

[36] 1QS 2.5-17 in G. Vermes, *The Dead Sea Scrolls in English* (New York: Penguin, 1987), 63.

(3) The Motive for Ministry (1:10)

¹⁰Am I now trying to win the approval of men, or of God? Or am I trying to please men? If I were still trying to please men, I would not be a servant of Christ.

1:10 This verse, in which Paul's emotions are seething just beneath the surface of the text, serves as a transitional bridge from the introductory sections (salutation and exordium), which it concludes, to the long autobiographical account that follows (1:11–2:14). Up to this point Paul has mentioned himself only once: his self-introduction as an apostle of Christ in 1:1. Now the spotlight falls squarely on him as he wards off the insinuations and false charges leveled by his opponents. Obviously they have attacked not only Paul's message but also his motivation for ministry. This is evident in the way he responds in the twofold question here.

The first question, "Am I now trying to win the approval of men, or of God?" harks back to the apostolic curse in the two preceding verses. Evidently Paul had been accused of being something of a flatterer, of turning like a weather vane whichever way the wind blows. There is a touch of sarcasm in the way he rebutted this charge: "Come on now, so you think I am the sort of preacher who cajoles a congregation by playing to their vanity? A flatterer who entices others with fancy rhetoric and soothing words? Is that so? Then why have I just consigned the whole lot to perdition in hell for their distortion of the gospel?" The second question, "Or am I trying to please men?" is best explained in terms of the word "still" that Paul introduced in the concluding sentence of the verse. There was a time when in fact Paul did indeed seek to please other human beings. Before his conversion to Christ, he was on a fast track toward the highest echelons of the Jewish rabbinic establishment. His entire career, including his persecution of the Christians, was designed not only to justify himself before God but also to curry the favor of those in power so as better to advance his own ambitions. But this kind of self-serving, time-serving endeavor was forever shattered when Saul of Tarsus and Jesus of Nazareth collided outside Damascus. Serving Christ and pleasing humanity are mutually exclusive alternatives, "If I were . . . I would not be."

The expression "trying to win the approval of . . . God" cannot mean, of course, striving to win God's favor by virtue of our human efforts. It was precisely this doctrine that Paul railed against as a perversion of the gospel of Christ. The entire burden of Galatians is to show that "no one is justified before God by the law" (3:11). The "approval" Paul spoke of in 1:10 is something else.

We might put the question this way: What is the constituency for our ministry? In a market-driven age we are accustomed to think of every church having a special niche, of every visitor as a prospective customer, and every aspect of worship designed to satisfy the consumers. Paul was reminding the Galatians that the gospel was not a product to be peddled on the marketplace of life. It has no need of shrewd salesmen to make it more palatable to modern tastes. The gospel has its own self-generating, dynamic authority and need not be propped up by artificial means, however sophisticated or alluring. One day every person called to the ministry of the word of God must give an account for the stewardship of that office. On that day we will either be "disqualified for the prize" or hear those coveted words, "Well done, faithful servant." God, not any human audience, is our true constituency.

In another sense, of course, Paul was indeed seeking to win the approval and thus the hearts of those to whom he preached. He said so explicitly: "Since, then, we know what it is to fear the Lord, we try to persuade men" (2 Cor 5:11). Within the limits of his calling and convictions, he tried "to please everybody in every way" (1 Cor 10:33). To the Jews he became a Jew, to the Greeks a Greek; he was made all things to all people that he might "by all means save some." In fact, Paul could be remarkably flexible and tolerant about many things.[37] He agreed for Timothy to be circumcised even though he was only half-Jewish by birth; he conveyed the decision of the Council at Jerusalem to the churches he had founded in Asia Minor despite certain reservations he may have harbored concerning the wisdom of that agreement; he submitted to the purification rites for entering the temple at Jerusalem; he even rejoiced when certain rival missionaries preached Christ out of envy and ambition while he sat in chains (Acts 16:2-5; 21:26; Phil 1:15-18). He was willing, if not always happy, to make such adjustments and concessions whenever the missionary situation required that kind of flexibility so long as the foundational principles of the gospel were not being compromised. When that did occur, however, he was adamantine in his resistance—not budging an inch in his dispute with the false brothers, opposing Peter to his face in a painful confrontation (Gal 2:5,11-14).

It would be a great mistake, then, to interpret Paul's two questions of vindication in 1:10 as the angry outburst of an egotistical preacher. What we have instead is a clear rejection of unworthy motivations for ministry. In commenting on this verse, the Puritan William Perkins set forth a standard by which every God-called preacher must be judged:

> He that would be a faithful minister of the gospel must deny the pride of his heart, and be emptied of ambition, and set himself wholly to seek the glory of

---

[37] For an excellent discussion of this principle in Paul's life and ministry, see R. N. Longenecker, *Paul: Apostle of Liberty* (New York: Harper & Row, 1964), 230-44.

God in his calling. And generally, he that would be a faithful servant of Christ, must set God before him as a judge, and consider that he hath to deal with God: and that he must turn his mind and senses from the world, and all things therein, to God; and seek above all things to approve his thoughts, desires, affections, and all his doings unto him.[38]

SUMMARY. In the first ten verses of Galatians, Paul telegraphed in advance the major themes he would deal with throughout the letter. It is a turbulent overture presaging the stormy weather to come. Paul began by asserting his apostolic authority, which evidently had come under attack in Galatia. He anchored his vocation in a confessional affirmation of the person and work of Jesus Christ. His doxology is followed immediately by a statement of astonishment and rebuke. He attributed the confusion to his adversaries, whose agitation among the churches of Galatia amounted to nothing less that the perversion of the gospel of Christ. The state of affairs calls for the strongest condemnation possible, a curse or imprecation to damnation for anyone—Paul, angels, whomever—who preached a false gospel.

In conclusion Paul set forth a vindication of his true motive for ministry: it was God and not any human beings he sought to please. Already in these opening verses the two key concepts in the letter have surfaced—gospel and grace. Against every inclination of disloyalty to the truth, Paul would recall the Galatians to these twin peaks of divine revelation. Paul's concern for the grace of God and the truth of the gospel, not an obsession with peevish self-interest, led him next to recount to the Galatians the story of his conversion, calling, and early ministry.

EXCURSUS 1: THE NATURE OF HERESY. Paul's anathema against the false teachers of Galatia raises the question of the nature of heresy and its persistent presence throughout the long history of the Christian church. The word "heresy" derives from the Greek noun *hairesis,* which means literally an "act of choice." This word is used several times in the New Testament in a neutral sense meaning simply "party" or "distinct group" (cf. Acts 5:17; 15:5; 26:5). Elsewhere, however, it assumes a more negative connotation, referring to a faction or splinter group whose ethical or doctrinal "choices" have resulted in the disruption of the Christian community (cf. 1 Cor 11:19; Gal 5:20). By the second century heretics were identified as those persons whose teachings on fundamental Christian truths deviated so radically from the doctrine of Jesus and the apostles as to undercut the very basis for Christian existence.

Today the word "heresy" frequently is touted as a badge of honor, a mark

---

[38] W. Perkins, *A Commentary on Galatians,* ed. G. T. Sheppard (New York: Pilgrim, 1989), 36-37.

of theological innovation and creativity, while "orthodox" is often a term of disparagement meaning "old-fashioned, unyielding," and, above all, "deadly dull." Thus the late Episcopal bishop J. Pike defended his deviant doctrinal views in a personal manifesto entitled *If This Be Heresy.* About the same time W. Kaufmann, a Princeton philosopher, published his intellectual autobiography which he called *The Faith of a Heretic.* Heresy must be defined in terms of an assumed orthodoxy. Hence Pike was at least correct in identifying his revisionist theology as heretical, while Kaufmann, a self-proclaimed atheist, advocated a system of unbelief very different in both its affirmations and denials from what can properly be called heresy.[39]

As Paul and other Christian heralds carried the message of Jesus Christ into the marketplace of ideas throughout the Hellenistic world, they were forced to define their proclamation over against Judaism on the one hand and paganism on the other. However, the distortions and misrepresentations that arose from within the Christian movement proved far more insidious to the survival of the church than external threats. Thus not only here in Galatians but elsewhere in the New Testament we find repeated warnings against those who are wont to "abandon the faith," giving themselves over to "godless myths and old wives' tales . . . things taught by demons . . . hollow and deceptive philosophy, which depends on human tradition and the basic principles of this world rather than Christ" (1 Tim 4:1,7; Col 2:8). More positively, Paul encouraged Timothy to hold on the pattern of sound doctrine and to "guard the good deposit that was entrusted to you—guard it with the help of the Holy Spirit" (2 Tim 1:14).

In guarding the church against doctrinal corruption, the apostles and church fathers had to be especially alert because inevitably heresy arose not as a frontal assault on Christianity but rather as an alluring, seductive distortion of some valid theological principle. For example, Irenaeus observed: "Error, indeed, is never set forth in its naked deformity, lest, being thus exposed, it should at once be detected. But it is craftily decked out in an attractive dress so as, by its outward form, to make it appear to the inexperienced (ridiculous as the expression may seem) more true than truth itself."[40]

---

[39] See the excellent discussion in H. O. J. Brown, *Heresies: The Image of Christ in the Mirror of Heresy and Orthodoxy from the Apostles to the Present* (Grand Rapids: Baker, 1984), 1-5. Cf. the following definition by K. Barth: "By heresy we understand a form of Christian faith which we cannot deny to be a form of Christian faith from the formal standpoint, i.e., insofar as it, too, relates to Jesus Christ, to his church, to baptism, Holy Scripture and the common Christian creeds, but in respect of which we cannot really understand what we are about when we recognize it as such, since we can understand its content, its interpretation of these common presuppositions, only as a contradiction of faith" (*Church Dogmatics* 1.1 [Edinburgh: T & T Clark, n.d.], 32).

[40] Irenaeus, *Against Heresies* 1.2.

There is an old Latin proverb that says, *Corruptio optimi pessimum est,* "The corruption of the best is the worst."

The heretics of Galatia did not deny that Jesus was the Messiah or that he had died and risen from the grave. Nor did they claim some new and special revelation; rather they based their arguments on the Old Testament Scriptures. They had many valid theological ideas with which Paul himself was in perfect agreement: the oneness of God, the holiness of the law, God's faithfulness to his people Israel, the importance of the Ten Commandments, and so on. So far as we know, they did not openly deny either the deity or humanity of Jesus Christ. Their error was to add to the finished work of Christ a measure of human achievement as the basis of a right standing with God. Yet to do this was to change the nature of the Christian faith so drastically that it could no longer be trusted to be saving faith. Hence it was necessary for Paul to identify and condemn this teaching with all the force of an apostolic anathema. As D. Bloesch has wisely written, "Saving faith cannot be maintained apart from contending faith, the faith that vigorously upholds the integrity of the gospel against all efforts to embellish it with other gospels."[41]

Today in the polite circles of mainline Protestantism, heresy in its historic Christian sense has become a most unfashionable word. In much contemporary theology, biblical miracles are demythologized and classical Christian doctrines devalued in the name of a faith that emphasizes a subjective relationship with Christ, or at least a vague spiritual awareness of him, at the expense of the embarrassing doctrinal accoutrements the church has proclaimed as indispensable ever since Nicea and Chalcedon.

The New Testament, however, nowhere presents a "relation with Christ" apart from a theological affirmation of his person and work. When Paul said to the Philippian jailer, "Believe on the Lord Jesus Christ" (Acts 16:31), he was indeed making a profound doctrinal claim about the One he believed could deliver him from his sins. "Christ" was not Jesus' last name, nor "Lord" his first! These were messianic titles fraught with rich theological meaning. The essence of Christianity is knowing and trusting Jesus Christ, not in the abstract but precisely as Lord, the incarnate Son of God, as Prophet, Priest, and King, as Savior, Redeemer and Victor. Thus the earliest portrayal of the New Testament church depicts a band of committed believers who "continued steadfastly in the apostles' doctrine" (Acts 2:42).

What should be our attitude toward heresy today? First, we must learn to distinguish between evangelical essentials, over which there can be no compromise, and secondary doctrinal matters about which orthodox believers

---

[41] D. Bloesch, *A Theology of Word and Spirit* (Downers Grove: InterVarsity, 1992), 139.

may differ and still maintain the bond of Christian fellowship. Where to draw this line, of course, is not always easy, but failure to do so will lead to theological vacuity on the one hand or sectarian rigidity on the other. Second, we should recognize that in the providence of God, heresy has sometimes served a useful purpose in calling forth a clearer definition of the true faith. For example, Marcion's rejection of the Old Testament as Christian Scripture accelerated the formation of the New Testament canon, while Pelagius's merit-based soteriology prompted Augustine's exposition of the doctrines of grace. Similarly, the rationalistic assault against the authority of the Scriptures during the Enlightenment gave rise to clearer definitions of biblical inspiration and inerrancy that still guide believers today. Third, we must always be careful to distinguish the heresy from the heretic. We are called to speak the truth in love, not to shout the faith in anger. There is no place for censorious personal attacks against anyone made in the image of God, however serious their theological deviations may be.

At the same time, while renouncing cruelty to heretics, we must ever guard against what F. Allison has called "the cruelty of heresy."[42] The church of Jesus Christ must be willing to recognize and to reject gross perversions of the gospel when they crop up in its midst. A church that cannot distinguish heresy from truth or, even worse, that no longer thinks this is worth doing is a church that has lost its right to bear witness to the transforming gospel of Jesus Christ, who declared himself to be not only the Way and the Life, but also the Truth, the only Truth that leads to the Father. The ancient words of Polycarp are relevant still: "Wherefore, forsaking the vanity of many, and their false doctrines, let us return to the Word which has been handed down to us from the beginning."[43]

3. The Apostolic Vocation (1:11-24)

Having set forth the issues and alternatives that would dominate his Letter to the Galatians, Paul now began in earnest to develop the first major section of the epistle, a historical overview of his conversion, call, and ministry prior to his evangelistic work in Galatia. This long autobiographical account runs from 1:11 through 2:21 and is itself divided into three discrete subsections: Paul's early Christian experience and his first encounter with church leaders in Jerusalem (1:11-24), the summit meeting between Paul and the Jerusalem leaders over the scope and sphere of his missionary work (2:1-10), and the confrontation with Peter at Antioch leading to the central pro-

---

[42] C. F. Allison, *The Cruelty of Heresy* (Harrisburg: Morehouse, 1994).

[43] Polycarp, *Epistle* 8.

nouncement of justification by faith (2:11-21).

These verses contain the longest and richest autobiographical material we have from the pen of Paul. They supplement in significant ways what Luke said about Paul's background, conversion, and early missionary activity. This entire section and the prominence it holds in the structure of Galatians, occupying as it does nearly one-fourth of the book, underscore the fact that Christianity is a historical faith. It is based upon certain specific, irreversible, and irreducible historical events. Jesus was born during the imperial reign of Caesar Augustus. He was crucified under Pontius Pilate, he rose again on the third day, and was taken up into heaven forty days later. Christianity is not a philosophy of life, or yet a set of moral precepts, or a secret code for mystical union with the divine. At its core Christianity is the record of what God has once and for all done in the person and work of his Son, Jesus Christ. Among these mighty acts of God, we must include the calling of the apostle Paul, for it too belongs among the foundational events of salvation history.

What this means and why it was such a hot issue in Galatia we will seek to uncover in our study of the verses that follow. Suffice it to say here that nowhere in this long historical section does Paul tell us how he felt about the events that happened to him. We can certainly speculate about this matter, imagining, for example, that he must have been greatly surprised at the appearance of the risen Christ near Damascus, or greatly angered by the false brothers who were trying to subvert the principle of Christian freedom, or deeply hurt and betrayed by Peter, who in a tense situation compromised what Paul knew were his real convictions. But the point of the narrative is not to focus on Paul's personal experience or subjective feelings, however interesting such a disclosure would be to us. Rather it is to set forth the objectively given revelation of God in and through Paul, the expressed purpose of which was to serve the furtherance of the gospel (Gal 1:16).

Galatians 1–2, then, establishes a historical context for the expressly theological content of Gal 3–4, which issues in turn in the ethical outcome of Gal 5–6. From the beginning, however, the theological issue is paramount, as we have seen already in the introductory verses. In the historical narrative also Paul was concerned not merely to recount the story of his life but to relate how "the truth of the gospel" (2:14) had manifested itself in his life story.

Paul was not quoting in these verses from his personal spiritual diary; unlike Augustine, he was not given to reminiscence and left behind no "Confessions of St. Paul." Rather he surveyed his life and selectively recounted certain incidents in order to make a theological point. The theological thrust of his presentation is seen in the fact that the historical narrative flows almost imperceptibly into his theological exposition. Thus it is unclear whether

2:15-21 constitutes the conclusion of his declaration to Peter (as the NIV has it with quotation marks around the entire passage) or the commencement of his special address to the Galatians on the theme of justification.

In any event, the entire historical narrative is evidently intended as a prolegomenon to the central thesis that "a man is not justified by observing the law, but by faith in Jesus Christ" (2:16). The polemical tone we have encountered in the early verses of chap. 1 continues to dominate Paul's rehearsal of his life and ministry here. Clearly he was responding to a certain representation of his career that his opponents had disseminated among the Galatian churches. If, as seems likely, these agitators had close ties to Jerusalem Christianity, they may well have represented themselves as the true ambassadors of the mother church there while depicting Paul as a renegade evangelist, one whose authority was wholly derived and subordinate to the Jerusalem apostles. Paul, they perhaps claimed, had totally distorted the message of these great church leaders while they, on the other hand, offered a pure replication of it.

Thus Paul was concerned to clarify his relationship to the church at Jerusalem, and especially to Peter and James. Each of these leaders is mentioned three times in the first two chapters. First, just a few years after his conversion Paul paid a "get acquainted" visit to Peter and James in Jerusalem (1:18-19). Then, well over a decade later, he encountered them again at Jerusalem in a strategic conference related to his missionary work among the Gentiles. And, finally, he confronted Peter at Antioch in a crisis over table fellowship prompted by certain individuals affiliated with James. We will have to examine more closely what these verses tell us about Paul's relationship to the church at Jerusalem and its leaders. It is clear, however, that Paul wanted to assert his apostolic independence over against Peter, James, and all other human intermediaries.

(1) Called from Above (1:11-12)

[11]I want you to know, brothers, that the gospel I preached is not something that man made up. [12]I did not receive it from any man, nor was I taught it; rather, I received it by revelation from Jesus Christ.

NOT HUMANLY DEVISED (1:11-12a). **1:11-12a** These verses introduce the theme already alluded to in the introduction and more fully developed in the following narrative, namely, that the gospel Paul preached to the Galatians was not devised by any human contrivance but came directly from God himself. In order to impress the truth of this thesis upon his readers, Paul introduced it with a solemn disclosure formula, "I want you to know."

This expression, along with its negative counterpart, "I do not wish you to be ignorant," occurs numerous times in Paul's writings (cf. Rom 1:13; 1 Cor 12:3; 15:1; 2 Cor 1:8; Eph 1:9; 1 Thess 4:13). This was Paul's way of saying, "I want to make this perfectly clear."

Despite his reputation for making overweening pronouncements, Paul could on occasion speak with great tentativeness and hesitation. For example, concerning the status of virgins in the church at Corinth, Paul frankly confessed, "I have no command from the Lord" (1 Cor 7:25). Again, concerning his own translation into the third heaven, he was uncertain about whether or not this experience was corporeal (2 Cor 12:2). But here in Galatians, Paul was not dealing with a matter of secondary importance. He was defending the very heart of the Christian faith against a sinister and subversive attack upon it.

On this issue—the nature of the gospel—there is not room for equivocation or doubt. Nothing less than the reality of the salvation secured by Jesus Christ is at stake in this unyielding assertion. Significantly, Paul addressed the Galatians as his "brothers," the same word he had used earlier (1:2) to designate the companions who joined him in addressing the churches of Galatia. This word recurs several times in Paul's direct address to his readers throughout the book (e.g., 2:15; 4:12,28; 5:11,13; 6:1,18). This word establishes an indispensable link between the apostle and the people to whom he wrote. Both were subjects of divine grace and therefore members of the same family. Despite, indeed because of, the ominous crisis that now engulfed the churches of Galatia, Paul reached out to them with all the urgency of a loyal family member seeking to rescue his loved ones from imminent ruin.

When Paul said that his gospel was not "according to man" (*kata anthropon*), he was saying something more than the NIV translation indicates, "not something that man made up." J. Bligh comes close to the correct sense of this expression in his paraphrase of the verse: "My gospel (and my preaching of the gospel) do not belong to the purely human level of existence: the gospel message did not come to me through human channels—it was not mediated to me through any man; and my preaching of the gospel has not been guided by human motives and ambitions."[44]

The *kata* in v. 11 harks back to and encompasses the twin negatives in v. 1—Paul's apostleship and his gospel was neither from (*apo*) nor by (*dia*) any human source. Paul elaborated this denial by adding two additional negative qualifications concerning the nonhuman character of his gospel: he neither received it through tradition nor was taught it through the ordinary means of

---

[44] Bligh, *Galatians*, 124.

instruction. These two additional denials both point to the same reality and are nearly identical in meaning. "'I did not receive it from any man' refers to the initial reception of the gospel, while 'nor did anyone teach it to me' refers to his growing understanding of its contents."[45]

Paul clearly was contrasting the way he received the gospel from the normal pattern of catechetical instruction commonly practiced in rabbinic Judaism. In that system the citation of venerable sources and the piling up of numerous "footnotes" were integral to the learning process: Rabbi so-and-so says this, but Rabbi so-and-so says that, and so forth. Paul here claimed an unmediated divine authority for the gospel he proclaimed, an assertion that would be utterly preposterous were it not true. Just as Jesus confronted the scribal traditions of his day with his univocal "but-I-say-unto-you" pronouncements, so Paul confounded his opponents by stressing the unilateral and vertical character of the revelation he received from the risen Lord Jesus Christ.

But was Paul really as independent as he claimed in this text? J. T. Sanders, among others, claims to have found "an absolute contradiction" in what Paul claimed in Gal 1:11-12 and his statement in 1 Cor 15:3, where he said that he passed on to the Corinthians the gospel that he too had received.[46] Both verses employ the same Greek word for "receive" (*paralambanein*), a technical term for the transmission of religious tradition. In the early church the Gnostic exegetes had a field day with Paul's claim in Gal 1:12 that his gospel was independent of the teaching and tradition of the other apostles. Earlier, they said, Paul had indeed preached "what I also received" (1 Cor 15:3) in common with the other apostles; but in Galatians he disclosed that the true gospel (i.e., the Gnostic one) had been secretly revealed to him alone. For this reason the Gnostics frequently cited Paul as the progenitor of their own interpretation of the Christian faith while rejecting the other apostles and writings of the New Testament as defective and tainted with Judaism.[47]

However, what Paul was arguing in Galatians was not that his gospel was different from that of the other apostles but rather that he had received it independently of them. Indeed, as we will see, he went to great lengths to demonstrate the basic consistency of his message and theirs. Even when he confronted Peter in Antioch (2:11-14), it was not because Peter was preach-

---

[45] D. C. Arichea and E. A. Nida, *A Translator's Handbook on Paul's Letter to the Galatians* (London: UBS, 1976), 17.

[46] J. T. Sanders, "Paul's 'Autobiographical' Statements in Galatians 1–2," *JBL* 85 (1966): 335-43.

[47] Pagels, *Gnostic Paul,* 102.

ing a different gospel from Paul but rather that he had acted inconsistently with the one gospel they both accepted and proclaimed. What, then, was the basic meaning of Paul's claim to absolute independence of all prior teaching and tradition?

It is certain that Paul knew a great deal about the Christian faith even before his conversion. It is inconceivable that he would have invested so much energy in trying to stamp out a movement he knew nothing about. No doubt the very Christians he persecuted witnessed to him of their faith in Jesus as the Messiah, God's anointed one who had been cruelly crucified but then raised from the dead by the power of the Father. Only the appearance of Christ on the road to Damascus convinced Paul that their testimony was true. He received the gospel through this firsthand encounter with the risen Christ and not from anyone else. It does not follow, however, that Paul remained ignorant or aloof from the teaching tradition of the early church. Through his contacts with Ananias and other believers in Damascus, not to mention his later visit to Peter and James in Jerusalem, Paul would have had ample opportunity to absorb the early Christian tradition as it was crystallizing in confessional statements (1 Cor 15:1-3), liturgical formulas (1 Cor 11:23-26), and hymns of praise to Christ (Phil 2:5-11). Paul's point in Galatians is not that he was opposed to or ignorant of this developing Christian tradition, but simply that he was not dependent upon it for his knowledge of Christ. The Jesus traditions which he later learned, incorporated into his letters, and passed on to his churches only served to confirm what he already knew by direct revelation to be true.[48]

BUT DIVINELY GIVEN (1:12b). **1:12b** Paul now proceeded to fill in the positive side of the contrast he was making by declaring that his gospel was made known to him "by revelation from Jesus Christ." The word for "revelation" (*apokalypsis*) literally means "unveiling, a laying bare, the removal of that which conceals or obscures, a disclosure." It is used only once in the Greek Old Testament (1 Sam 20:30) but occurs frequently in the

---

[48] Cf. F. F. Bruce's statement: "He [sc. Paul] must have distinguished in his own mind the sense in which the gospel came to him by direct revelation from that in which it came to him by tradition. . . . His explanation might be that the essence of the gospel, 'Jesus is the risen Lord,' was communicated to him from heaven on the Damascus Road: it was no human testimony that moved him to accept it. . . . But the historical details of the teaching of Jesus, the events of Holy Week, the resurrection appearances and so forth were related to him by those who had firsthand experience of them" (quoted in R. Y. K. Fung, "Revelation and Tradition: The Origins of Paul's Gospel," *EvQ* 57 [1985]: 39). In addition to Fung's excellent study, see also G. E. Ladd, "Revelation and Tradition in Paul," in *Apostolic History and the Gospel*, ed. W. W. Gasque and R. P. Martin (Exeter: Paternoster, 1970), 223-30, and P. H. Menoud, "Revelation and Tradition: The Influence of Paul's Conversion on His Theology," *Int* 7 (1953): 131-41.

New Testament, where it carries at least three nuances: (1) the coming or manifestation of a person, especially the coming of Christ (1 Cor 1:7; 2 Thess 1:7); (2) the disclosure of the true character of a person or truth (Luke 2:32; Rom 2:5); (3) the content of that which is unveiled or manifested (1 Cor 14:6; Eph 1:17).

Which of these three meanings is meant in Gal 1:12 depends on whether we read the phrase "from Jesus Christ" as an objective or subjective genitive. If it is subjective, then it means the revelation Jesus Christ himself disclosed, the revelation by Christ; if objective, then it means the revelation whose content is Jesus Christ, that is, the disclosure about Christ. Neither reading does grammatical or theological violence to the text, and some have taken it as both subjective and objective, the ambiguity perhaps being intended by Paul himself.[49] Clearly both are true. On the Damascus Road, Jesus Christ himself appeared to Paul as the revealing one; what he disclosed was the true nature of the gospel, the content of the message Paul was commissioned to preach.

Two other texts in the New Testament help to illumine this passage. The first is Jesus' comment about Peter's surprising confession at Caesarea Philippi, "You are the Christ, the Son of the Living God," to which Jesus replied, "This was not revealed to you by men, but by my Father in Heaven" (Matt 16:16-17). Obviously Peter was well acquainted with Jesus before receiving this great insight. He knew well the bare facts of his earthly ministry. He had heard Jesus teach and had seen him do great miracles. None of this sufficed, however, to bring him to a true awareness of who Jesus really was until the veil was lifted in the moment of divine disclosure. From this we learn that only God can truly reveal himself. We may preach, teach, and share the good news of Christ with others; but only God can soften a hardened heart and bring the light of divine truth to a darkened mind.

The second passage is Paul's own description of how "the mystery of Christ," unknown in earlier generations, was "now being revealed (*apekalyphthē*) to his holy apostles and prophets by the Spirit" (Eph 3:5, RSV). Though Paul considered himself the very least of all the saints, he could not deny that this great mystery had been unveiled to him by Jesus Christ. Thus what had been hidden in ages past was now being displayed, publicly and universally, for all peoples to hear and receive.

Before leaving this verse, we must ask about the exact content of the mys-

---

[49] See, for example, the comment of W. Grundmann: "The expression describes Jesus Christ as the One who has revealed Himself and made him His apostle, this revelation being an act of God's grace. Jesus Christ is the One through whom God acts" ("Χριστός," *TDNT* 9.551). Also see discussion in Burton, *Galatians,* 433-35.

tery of Christ supernaturally revealed to Paul in such a way that he could claim and proclaim it as "my gospel." We will have to return to this theme as Paul develops his argument throughout Galatians, but let us note here five essential elements of the gospel made known to Paul. (1) God has raised from the dead Jesus, the crucified Messiah, vindicating his claim to be one with the Father. (2) Jesus has been exalted to the right hand of the Father but is still vitally connected to his people on earth. The shattering insight Paul saw on the Damascus Road was this: in persecuting the Christians, he was in reality torturing Christ himself. Paul's doctrine of the church as the body of Christ undoubtedly grew out of this profound insight. (3) The risen Christ will come again in power and glory to fulfill all the messianic prophecies of the old covenant, bringing history to a climactic closure in a display of divine judgment and wrath. (4) In the meantime, God has opened the door of salvation for Gentiles as well as Jews. Paul himself had been commissioned to herald this good news to all persons, but especially to the Gentiles. (5) The basis for acceptance with God, for Jews and Gentiles alike, is justification by faith apart from the works of the law. The futility of legal righteousness is seen in a true appreciation of Christ's atoning death on the cross. The revelation of Jesus as Messiah requires a radical reorientation in how the law is seen and applied in this "dispensation of the fullness of times."

Was this gospel unique to Paul? No, for it was simply the full elaboration of the one and only gospel Jesus himself proclaimed. Paul was no neoapostle who preached "another Jesus" or a "different gospel" (2 Cor 11:4). Much of the content of Paul's message was already implied in the *kerygma* of the primitive church, which is why he could endorse and transmit it with such confidence and enthusiasm. Even the insight about the inclusion of the Gentiles was not originally Pauline, for God had also revealed this to Peter in his mission to Cornelius (Acts 10:9-48). Yet the full implications of Paul's message, especially the doctrine of justification by faith and its practical outworking in the missionary context of the early church, remained for Paul and him alone to pioneer. Undoubtedly this is why in the providence of God Paul's life and writings figured so prominently in the formation of the New Testament canon.

(2) Paul's Life before Christ (1:13-14)

[13]For you have heard of my previous way of life in Judaism, how intensely I persecuted the church of God and tried to destroy it. [14]I was advancing in Judaism beyond many Jews of my own age and was extremely zealous for the traditions of my fathers.

HIS PERSECUTION OF THE CHURCH (1:13). **1:13** Having set forth his thesis of the nonhuman origin of the gospel in the two preceding verses, Paul began a demonstration of its truth in terms of five historical proofs derived from his own life and ministry: (1) Nothing in Paul's religious background could account for his acceptance of the gospel (1:13-17). (2) Paul was not commissioned by the Jerusalem church (1:18-20). (3) Those Paul formerly persecuted glorified God because of the change wrought in him (1:21-24). (4) Paul's apostolic work was recognized by church leaders at Jerusalem (2:1-10). (5) Paul defended the gospel against Peter's vacillation at Antioch (2:11-14). Following this extensive historical excursus, Paul summarized the central theme of his letter (2:15-21) and then reminded the Galatians of how God had worked among them at his first preaching of the gospel in their midst (3:1-5). Thus the entire historical section of the letter moves from Paul the persecutor to Paul the preacher; it is the record of "the way of the gospel from Damascus to Galatia."[50]

Paul's main point in vv. 13-14 was to show that there was nothing in his religious background and preconversion life that could have in any way prepared him for a positive response to the gospel. Quite the contrary. His early career and lifestyle were shaped by a confident attachment to the strictest traditions of Judaism, which in turn had led him to take up arms against the believers in Jesus. Paul assumed that the Galatians already knew something about his past life as a persecutor; he was reminding them of something they already had heard about. Doubtless they had heard this from Paul's own lips, for, unlike many public figures, he was never one to conceal the shameful deeds that marred his past life.[51]

Paul spoke frequently and graphically of his campaign of persecution against the Christians. He told of how he had pursued them, like a bloodhound, from city to city, arresting both men and women, throwing them into prison, voting for their execution, and further harassing them even to the point of death (Acts 22:4; 26:9). Paul gave this witness not to brag on the misdeeds of his pre-Christian life, as some converts are wont to magnify their sinful past more than their rescue from it, but in order to hold high the sovereign initiative of God in reversing the murderous track of his career.

---

[50] D. Lührmann, *Galatians* (Minneapolis: Fortress, 1992), 20-27.

[51] Cf. the comment of the Puritan divine William Perkins: "Paul here makes an open and ingenuous confession of wicked life past. And hence I gather that this apostle, and consequently the rest, wrote the Scriptures of the New Testament by the instinct of God's Spirit, and not by human policy, which (no doubt) would have moved them to have covered and concealed their own faults, and not to have blazed their own shame to the world. And therefore the books of Scripture are not books of policy (as atheists suppose) to keep men in awe, but they are the very Word of God" (*Galatians,* 35).

Paul always spoke of this part of his life with great sorrow and shame, considering himself the "least of the apostles" (1 Cor 15:9) because he had "persecuted the church of God" (Gal 1:13).

Paul's use of the word "church" in the singular stands in marked contrast to his earlier address to the "churches in Galatia" (1:2). Clearly he had in mind the church universal, the body of Christ, the company of all the redeemed scattered throughout the world. However, the emphasis here is on the qualifying genitive: the church *of God*. What Paul came to realize through his encounter with the risen Christ was that the despised Christians he had been pursuing with such ardor were none other than the special people of the Holy One of Israel, "the community of God." This expression was used in the Old Testament to describe the children of Israel who stood in a special covenantal relationship to God. Paul's persecution of the Christians was designed to safeguard the purity of that very community. Now he suddenly saw that the crux of his life's work had been directed against the very "company of God" he had intended to protect: God's called-out ones. The intensity of his persecuting zeal is revealed in the next phrase, "and tried to destroy it." The word used here (*eporthoun*) means "to make havoc of." As Chrysostom put it, it signifies "an attempt to extinguish, to pull down, to destroy, to annihilate the church."[52] This word, which was used of the sacking of cities, recurs again in v. 23 as well as in Luke's parallel account of Paul's devastation of the Jerusalem Christians (Acts 8:3).[53]

HIS ZEAL FOR RELIGION (1:14). **1:14** Why did Paul seek to exterminate the Christians? This verse takes us back to Paul's pre-Christian days when, as the protégé of the famous Jewish theologian Gamaliel, Paul was no doubt regarded as the rising star of Pharisaic Judaism. This entire passage is replete with superlative words that speak of compulsive obsession and ambition: he intensely persecuted the church and tried to eradicate it; he was advancing in Judaism beyond his contemporaries by being extremely zealous. This kind of language leads us to ask: what had the Christians done to elicit this sort of fanatical response? It is important to remember that, as A. D. Nock noted, "When Paul first learned of the body which was the germ cell of later Christianity, there was no title 'Christian': that came into being at Antioch, and perhaps as a nickname."[54] What Paul did encounter was a sect within Judaism that, because of their devotion to Messiah Jesus, was redefining the boundaries of the community of Israel in ways that were profoundly disturbing to such a strict Pharisaic leader as Paul.

---

[52] NPNF 13.10.

[53] Bruce, *Galatians,* 91.

[54] A. D. Nock, *St. Paul* (New York: Harper, 1938), 35.

Two aspects of the early Christian message must have been especially galling to Paul. Not merely the claim that Jesus was the Messiah, but the triple assertion that this Messiah had been publicly condemned and crucified, then raised from the dead, and now exalted to heaven with the status of deity, which demanded the kind of worship only properly given to God—all of this amounted to the perpetuation of the same "blasphemy" that had led to Jesus' death in the first place (John 10:33). What Paul later called the "stumbling block" of the cross was offensive in the highest degree: to be crucified was to come under the curse of God, an unthinkable condition for God's anointed one from the perspective of strict Pharisaic Judaism.[55]

Paul's devotion to "the tradition of my fathers" also would have prompted him to regard as dangerous the Christian message that Christ had displaced the law as the means for right standing before God. As T. L. Donaldson has put it: "Christian preaching declared that to be part of the community destined for salvation, everyone, even those whom the Torah would declare to be 'righteous,' needed to believe in Jesus (e.g., Acts 3:17-26); therefore the Torah was not sufficient. . . . Even though the early church may not have been aware of the radical implications of its message, Paul recognized that the *kerygma* assigned this central role to Christ rather than to the Torah, and so took steps to defend Judaism from this danger."[56] The inadequacy of the law and the temple cultus as a way of salvation is evident already in Stephen's address to the Sanhedrin (Acts 7) and may well have prompted Paul to play such a major role in his execution.[57]

It is significant that Paul used the word "zealous" to describe his persecuting activity against the church. The word "zeal" is prominent in the Macca-

---

[55] Fung, *Galatians*, 58-62. This idea is further elaborated by M. Hengel, *The Atonement: The Origins of the Doctrine in the New Testament* (Philadelphia: Fortress, 1981), 40. For a different interpretation of this motif, see C. M. Tuckett, "Deuteronomy 21, 33 and Paul's Conversion," in *L'apôtre Paul: Personnalité, style et conception du ministère*, ed. A. Vanhoye (Leuven: Leuven University Press, 1986), 345-50.

[56] T. L. Donaldson, "Zealot and Convert: The Origin of Paul's Christ-Torah Antithesis," *CBQ* 51 (1989): 678-79.

[57] We cannot accept the view of F. Watson that Paul's negative assessment of the law as the focal point in the process of salvation developed out of the exigencies of his missionary labors, namely, his realization that Gentiles could be more easily converted if they were not required to observe circumcision and other requirements of the law. It was precisely against this kind of charge that Paul defended himself in Gal 1:10 when he denied being a manpleaser. Paul's theological discussion about the law was not an attempt to justify a pragmatic decision made on nontheological grounds but rather the working out of a radical reorientation already implied in the earliest proclamation of the Christian church. See F. Watson, *Paul, Judaism and the Gentiles* (Cambridge: Cambridge University Press, 1986). For a similar developmental view of Paul and the law, see H. Räisänen, "Paul's Conversion and the Development of His View of the Law," *NTS* 33 (1987): 404-19.

bean literature, where it refers to those Jewish leaders who were willing to resort to the use of force in order to defend their homeland, its temple, and law against foreign intruders. The sanctions of holy violence and even death for those who flagrantly violated the covenantal community are rooted in such Old Testament prototypes as Phinehas (Num 25), Joshua (Josh 7), and Elijah (1 Kgs 18:19).[58] No doubt Paul saw himself as standing in the tradition of these zealous leaders in his campaign of violence against the Christians who to his mind were contravening the purpose of God by subverting his holy law.

The point to be made in this discussion is that Paul's persecuting activity, carried out with great energy and dispatch, arose out of sincere religious convictions and high moral expectations. Paul was no second-rate thug or mafioso bent on vandalism and violence for its own sake. There is no evidence that he carried out his work with a guilty conscience burdened by self-doubt or hindered by second thoughts. He was a happy and successful Jew who could put on his résumé, as he later reconstructed it for the Philippians, his persecution of the church alongside his other virtues and achievements—his circumcision, his rootage in the tribe of Benjamin, his membership in the Pharisaic party, his blameless devotion to the law. All of these, including the persecutions, he counted as "profit" before he met Christ (Phil 3:4-6).[59] Thus all the greater his shame and remorse when he realized that in seeking to please God he had actually been striving against God; in aiming for the best he had sunk to the worst. Those things he had called "profit" he now realized were "loss," refuse, trash, *skubala,* human excrement fit only to be hurled onto the dung heap of his life.

(3) Conversion and Calling (1:15-17)

15But when God, who set me apart from birth and called me by his grace,

---

[58] In the New Testament too the judgment of God can fall suddenly and fatally on those who persecute God's people (cf. the death of Herod Agrippa I, Acts 12:20-23) or even believers who flaunt the holy things of God (cf. Ananias and Sapphira, who lied to the Holy Spirit, Acts 5:1-11, or the Corinthian church members who defiled the Lord's Supper, 1 Cor 11:30). In the NT church, however, such judgments are the result of God's direct intervention, not the prerogative of the Christian community. Christians are commanded to love their enemies, pray for their persecutors, and commit all vindication into the hands of God (Rom 12:14-21). For the biblical basis and historical development of this approach, see J. Piper, "Love Your Enemies," in *Jesus' Love Command in the Synoptic Gospels in the Early Christian Paranesis* (Cambridge: Cambridge University Press, 1979); G. R. Edwards, *Jesus and the Politics of Violence* (New York: Harper & Row, 1972); T. George, "Between Pacifism and Coercion, The English Baptist Doctrine of Religious Toleration," *MQR* 58 (1984): 30-49.

[59] Cf. K. Stendahl, *Paul among Jews and Gentiles, and Other Essays* (Philadelphia: Fortress, 1976), 12-13.

was pleased **¹⁶to reveal his Son in me so that I might preach him among the Gentiles, I did not consult any man, ¹⁷nor did I go up to Jerusalem to see those who were apostles before I was, but I went immediately into Arabia and later returned to Damascus.**

Paul's first proof for the nonhuman origin of his gospel, then, was a quick review of his pre-Christian past. His life before Christ was given over to utter hostility and opposition to the very gospel he now proclaimed. Only a radical transformation brought about by a supernatural intervention could account for this change in him. He now moved to the second proof in his autobiographical narration: the divine disclosure that turned him into an apostle.

THE INITIATIVE OF GOD (1:15-17). **1:15** Verses 15-17 constitute one long and rather difficult sentence in Greek. Paul's purpose was to amplify what he had said already in v. 1, namely, that his apostolic work was neither "from men nor by man, but by Jesus Christ." Thus he did not rehearse the specific details of his conversion experience but rather cited it as proof that his apostolic calling was due solely to the initiative of God and therefore did not depend on human validation.

Paul described the sovereign initiative of God in terms of three distinct acts, all of which are governed by the verb in the clause translated "he was pleased" (*eudokēsen*). God's good pleasure was manifested in that Paul was set apart, called, and received the revelation of Christ.

1. *Paul was set apart.* Paul used the word "set apart" also in Rom 1:1, where he described himself as being "set apart for the gospel of God." Literally the word means "to determine beforehand," "to fix a boundary, a frontier, to cordon off for a special purpose." The rendering of the KJV, "God, who separated me from my mother's womb," conveys the idea of a physical procedure related to the birth process. But Paul had in mind something far antecedent to the occasion of his birth, namely, God's eternal predestination and good pleasure by which "he chose us in Christ before the creation of the world" (Eph 1:4). Thus we may paraphrase the expression in this way, "God, who set me apart, devoted me to a special purpose from before my birth, and before I had any impulses or principles of my own."[60]

J. Munck, among others, has shown how this expression, and indeed the entire description of Paul's calling, echoes the Old Testament texts that describe the setting apart of the prophet Jeremiah and the suffering servant of Isaiah (Jer 1:4; Isa 49:1-6).[61] Evidently Paul felt that those texts from the history of Israel expressed his own sense of being chosen and pressed into

---

[60] K. S. Wuest, *Wuest's Word Studies from the Greek New Testament* (Grand Rapids: Eerdmans, 1966), 1:49.

[61] Munck, *Paul and the Salvation of Mankind,* 24-35.

service by God's overcoming grace. As John Calvin put it, "This separation was God's purpose, by which Paul was appointed to the apostolic office before he was aware of his own existence."[62]

The doctrine of election, which Paul touched on in this verse, has been much abused and misunderstood throughout the history of the Christian church. Some have denied its biblical basis altogether, preferring to believe that one's standing before God is determined by religious activity, good works, or some other form of moral striving. The Judaizers of Galatia were not far from this heresy, advocating their gospel of Christ plus law. Others, though, have used the doctrine of election as a pretext for a do-nothing approach to missions and evangelism. If God has chosen some to salvation before the foundation of the world, they reason, then why preach the gospel, go to church, send missionaries, or do anything?

No one was more committed to the doctrines of grace than Charles Haddon Spurgeon; but when he encountered such distorted teaching in his own day, he lamented the fact that it had "chilled many churches to their very soul," leading them "to omit the free invitations of the gospel, and to deny that it is the duty of sinners to believe in Jesus."[63] Such hyper-Calvinistic construals of the doctrines of election and predestination ignore the fact, everywhere attested in Scripture, that the God who calls to salvation by his sovereign grace also ordains the means, including the preaching of the gospel to all peoples everywhere, which will lead his chosen ones to repentance and faith. Seen in the wider context of biblical revelation, the doctrine of election is no cause for either presumption or laziness. It is neither a steeple from which to view the human landscape nor a pillow to sleep on. It is rather a stronghold in times of temptation and trials and a confession of praise to God's grace and to his glory.[64]

2. *Paul was called.* Not only was Paul chosen from eternity and set apart from his mother's womb, but he also was called by God at a specific point in his life. In Rom 1:1 his calling is mentioned before his predestination, following the sequence of the usual experiential appropriation of God's grace. But here in Galatians, where Paul was stressing the priority of the divine initiative, the calling is placed after the setting apart, indicating that Paul's

---

[62] Calvin, CNTC 11.20.

[63] Quoted in R. Brown, *The English Baptists of the Eighteenth Century* (London: The Baptist Historical Society, 1986), 23. See also the excellent discussion of Spurgeon's evangelical Calvinism in L. Drummond, *Spurgeon: Prince of Preachers* (Grand Rapids: Kregel, 1992), 636-50.

[64] See H. H. Rowley, *The Biblical Doctrine of Election* (London: Lutterworth, 1950); and T. J. Nettles, *By His Grace and For His Glory: A Historical, Theological, and Practical Study of the Doctrines of Grace in Baptist Life* (Grand Rapids: Baker, 1986).

coming to Christ was the consequence of God's electing grace. As an early Baptist confession of faith expressed it, "Election is God's gracious choice of certain individuals unto eternal life in consequence of which they are called, justified, sanctified and glorified."[65] "Calling," then, refers to that whole complex of events, including repentance and faith, by which a lost sinner is converted to Christ. In this sense Paul could refer to all the Christians in Rome as those who had been "called to be saints," just as Peter could admonish believers to "be all the more eager to make your calling and election sure" (Rom 1:7; 2 Pet 1:10).

A wonderful analogy to this calling in the life of a believer is Jesus' raising of Lazarus from the dead. There, faced with the incontrovertible reality of death (a corpse that stank!), Jesus said, "Lazarus, come forth!" and the dead man came to life. Just so, we who are "dead in trespasses and sins" have been "made alive" through the call of Christ. As if anyone could possibly miss his point, Paul emphasized again that this call is by grace. However, "irresistible grace" is a poor term to describe God's effectual calling unto salvation. It obscures the fact that God's choice of us in eternity past must become our choice of him in space and time. God's grace is often resisted stoutly (cf. Paul's "kicking against the goads"); the point of the gospel is that God's grace overcomes our sinful resistance, bringing us to a point of surrender where we can confess, in the words of W. T. Sleeper, "Out of my bondage, sorrow, and night, Jesus, I come, Jesus, I come."

3. *God revealed his Son through Paul.* What is referred to by the revelation of God's Son in Paul? Many commentators believe that Paul was here again referring to his encounter with the risen Christ on the road to Damascus. Thus "to reveal his Son in me" is just another way of describing the call Paul received at this decisive juncture of his life.

This discussion is closely related to another controverted point of interpretation. Does the expression "in me" (*en emoi*) refer to a "subjective revelation in and for the apostle or to an objective manifestation of Christ in and through him to others"?[66] Some have opted for the subjective, mystical reading of this phrase because they have dismissed out of hand the possibility that Jesus Christ could actually have appeared in person to Paul at a particular place in time. Yet this is precisely what Paul himself insisted upon again and again. "Have I not seen Jesus our Lord?" he asked (1 Cor 9:1). He evi-

---

[65] These words are from the *Abstract of Principles,* the confessional standard of The Southern Baptist Theological Seminary, Louisville, Kentucky. On this doctrinal point they echo almost verbatim the Second London Confession of 1689. See W. L. Lumpkin, *Baptist Confessions of Faith* (Valley Forge: Judson, 1959).

[66] Burton, *Galatians,* 50.

dently distinguished this encounter with Christ from a private spiritual experience or even the "visions and revelations from the Lord" he later admitted to receiving (2 Cor 12:1). Jesus appeared to Paul. He spoke to him in his native Aramaic tongue. The apostle saw him with his eyes (the meaning of *heōraka* in 1 Cor 9:1) and was afflicted with blindness as a result of this encounter. Moreover, Jesus intercepted Paul at a certain time, about midday, at a particular place, on the highway to Damascus.

To interpret Paul's encounter with Christ as something less than an actual historical event that took place in space and time as the scriptural text indicates is to opt for a docetic version of Christianity, which is far removed from the particularist, incarnational religion of the New Testament. On balance it seems better to interpret *en emoi* as "through me," linking the revelation of Christ in Paul to the divine purpose and mission God had planned for him, to preach the gospel among the Gentiles, rather than backward to his conversion and call, which has already been alluded to. By no means does this diminish the importance of the subjective appropriation of Christ for Paul or for any other minister of the gospel. While we have no reason to expect the precise duplication of Paul's experience, a one-time resurrection appearance of Jesus (1 Cor 15:8), in another, very important sense everyone who stands to proclaim the good news of Christ must do so only because God has revealed his Son to them. No one has made this point better than the Puritan divine William Perkins:

> Ministers of the gospel must learn Christ as Paul learned him. They may not content themselves with that learning which they find in schools; but they must proceed further to a real learning of Christ. They that must convert others, it is meet that they should be effectually converted. John must eat the book, and then prophesy; and they who would be fit ministers of the gospel, must first themselves eat the book of God. And this book is indeed eaten, when they are not only in their minds enlightened, but in their hearts are mortified, and brought in subjection to the word of Christ, unless Christ be thus learned spiritually and really, divines shall speak of the Word of God as men speak of riddles, and as priests in former times said their matins, when they hardly knew what they said.[67]

In sum, we can say that God revealed Christ in Paul in order to reveal him through Paul. What was the content of this revelation? Of course, it was Jesus Christ himself and the gospel he entrusted to Paul. J. A. Fitzmyer has listed six characteristic aspects of the gospel Paul proclaimed: apocalyptic, dynamic, kerygmatic, normative, promissory, and universal.[68] All six of

---

[67] Perkins, *Galatians,* 46.

[68] J. A. Fitzmyer, *To Advance the Gospel* (New York: Crossroad, 1981), 149-61.

these characteristically Pauline emphases are evident throughout Galatians.

First, the gospel is an *apocalyptic* revelation, the unveiling of good news previously unknown in the same way it has now been manifested. The whole argument of Galatians is in essence an unpacking of the confessional statement with which Paul opened the book: Christ "gave himself for our sins to rescue us from the present evil age" (1:4). The revelation "through" Paul is an integral part of the rescue mission of Christ himself.

Second, the gospel is a *dynamic* force in human history, not merely a doctrinal formula to be memorized or a code of ethics to be obeyed. The gospel has a life of its own, so to speak: it relativizes the old structures of human existence, liberates believers from the principalities and powers that tyrannize them, and creates a new community of love and forgiveness.

Third, the gospel is not merely a personal testimony but a *kerygmatic* message that conveys the good news of God's salvific work in Christ. Several confessional texts are imbedded in Galatians reflecting the liturgical practice and worship patterns of the early church (cf. Gal 1:3-5; 3:26-29; 4:4; 6:18).

Fourth, the gospel had a *normative* role in Paul's thinking as can be seen from the dreadful adjuration he hurled against those who would pervert it (1:7-9). The gospel is not information to be politely presented as one option among many. The gospel is to be listened to, welcomed, obeyed, followed, and lived out. For this reason it can brook no rivals and will not tolerate adulteration, contamination, or dilution.

Fifth, the gospel of Christ revealed through Paul, while truly a new unveiling, was not invented out of thin air. The *promissory* nature of the gospel is a major theme in Galatians as Paul showed in his discussion of the Abraham narrative and the Hagar and Sarah allegory.

Sixth, the gospel Paul proclaimed was *universal* in scope, not restricted to any one class, nationality, race, gender, or social grouping. "You are all sons of God through faith in Christ Jesus" (3:26). The heart of the controversy in Galatia was related to this very characteristic. Paul stubbornly refused to accept that any one culture had a monopoly on the gospel or that any particular ritual, such as circumcision, could be made a prerequisite to its reception. The salvation Jesus has brought is intended for Jew and Gentile alike.

PAUL'S UNIQUE COMMISSION (1:16). **1:16** The phrase "that I might preach him among the Gentiles" is a purpose clause in Greek revealing the goal or end for which Paul was set apart, called, and made the instrument of the revelation of God's Son: in order to proclaim him among the Gentiles. The scope and specificity of Paul's apostolic mission is not coincidental. He was not merely called to be an apostle but called to be an apostle *to the Gentiles*. Paul sometimes referred to himself as "the apostle to the Gentiles"

(Rom 11:13; 1 Tim 2:7). This commission was an integral part of the disclosure given to Paul by the risen Christ both on the road to Damascus and later in Paul's temple vision in Jerusalem (Acts 9:15; 22:17-21). It was precisely Paul's law-free mission to the Gentiles that brought him into conflict with the Judaizing teachers in Galatia. As we will see in Gal 2, a major breakthrough for Paul's ministry occurred when the leaders of the Jerusalem church recognized his God-given "task of preaching the gospel to the Gentiles" (Gal 2:7). This view of Paul's unique role was not shared by other groups within the Jewish Christian movement. Conflict inevitably arose when Paul's message of salvation by grace for all peoples everywhere came up against more restrictive notions of salvation through Christ plus adherence to Jewish rites and rituals.

The fact that Paul was called to pioneer evangelism among the Gentiles should not obscure his great zeal and desire for his fellow Jews to know Christ as well. On one occasion he went so far as to echo the plea of Moses, wishing himself cursed and "cut off from Christ for the sake of my brothers, those of my own race, the people of Israel" (Rom 9:3). His missionary strategy reflected the burden of his heart: wherever he could, he always preached the gospel "to the Jew first."

Perhaps earlier than anyone else in the history of Christian thought, Paul realized that the church was a "third race" consisting of completed Jews and converted Gentiles (1 Cor 10:32). What Paul recognized that others did not was that God, in the mystery of his electing grace, had chosen to use the occasion of the Jewish rejection of the Messiah to open the door for the inclusion of Gentiles as full participants in the people of God. Paul argued this case in Rom 9:11, where he concluded by referring to the temporary hardening that had fallen upon Israel "until the full number of the Gentiles has come in" (Rom 11:25). Thus Paul's worldwide mission to the Gentiles, and particularly his desire to preach the gospel where it had not yet been heard, was related to his earnest expectation of the return of Christ, which would occur only when the chosen number of Gentiles and the chosen number of Jews had alike embraced the true Messiah. As J. Munck put it, Paul's personal call coincided with "an objective eschatological necessity, namely, God's plan that the gospel is to be preached to the Gentiles before the end of the age."[69]

PAUL'S SPECIAL PREPARATION (1:17).   **1:17** A difficult interpretive problem is posed by the adverb "immediately" (*euthōs*) in this passage. In the Greek text this word stands at the beginning of the two negative statements Paul made about his postconversion activity and thus could be trans-

---

[69] Munck, *Paul and the Salvation of Mankind,* 41.

lated "immediately, without seeking human advisors, or even going to Jerusalem to see those who were apostles before me." This is an awkward construction in both Greek and English, and most modern translations have connected "immediately" with Paul's visit to Arabia. Thus, as the NEB has it, "I went at once to Arabia."[70]

If this view is pressed very far, it seems to conflict with the narrative of Paul's activities given in Acts 9:19-22. There the same word, *euthōs,* is used to describe what Paul did immediately following his baptism. "Saul spent several days with the disciples in Damascus. At once he began to preach in the synagogues that Jesus is the Son of God" (Acts 9:20). How could Paul have "at once" both preached in Damascus and gone off to Arabia?

This difficulty disappears altogether if we follow the literal sequence of the Greek text and interpret "immediately" as qualifying Paul's negative statements concerning his postconversion whereabouts. Clearly the point he was making was not that he went immediately to Arabia without doing anything at all in Damascus but rather that immediately after his conversion, he did not go to Jerusalem or consult with the apostles there. He was countering the charge of his Galatian opponents that whatever gospel he possessed, he received secondhand from those who were apostles before him. Paul wanted to show that not only was he called and commissioned by Christ himself apart from any human mediation but also that he was engaged in the ministry of preaching prior to his first meeting with the Jerusalem authorities.[71]

Some modern critics have cast aspersion on the historical accuracy of Luke's account because he nowhere mentioned Paul's journey to Arabia. However, it is important to recognize that both Luke and Paul wrote their distinctive accounts with a clearly defined purpose in mind. Neither Acts nor Galatians was intended to be a day-by-day journal of Paul's activities; each is a selective account of what Paul said and did, designed to show, in the case of Acts, his strategic role in the worldwide mission of the church and, in the case of Galatians, the divine derivation and independence of his apostolic mission. It is possible to affirm the total truthfulness and accuracy of the

---

[70] This interpretation is also favored by GNB, NRSV, JB. The NKJV and NAS follow a more literal rendering. For an excellent discussion of this issue, see *Machen's Notes on Galatians,* 68-74.

[71] Machen contends that even if the word "immediately" is taken to qualify Paul's visit to Arabia as well as his denial of consort with others, this need not imply a contradiction with the narrative in Acts. "The real point of the sentence is to deny that there was a journey to Jerusalem during those early days; it is not to establish the exact moment of the journey to Arabia. . . . When Paul uses the word 'immediately' in connection with the journey to Arabia, he is thinking not in terms of days or of hours but of journeys. His journey at that time was not to Jerusalem but to Arabia" (ibid., 70).

Bible in everything it describes without assuming that it purports to be totally exhaustive in every detail.

Why did Paul go to Arabia? In the history of interpretation two possible answers have been given to this question. Some have claimed that he withdrew to Arabia for an extended time of prayer, meditation, and reflection on the tremendous experience he had just gone through. The word "Arabia" occurs again in Gal 4:25 as the location of Mount Sinai. On the basis of this allusion, some have speculated that Paul withdrew far away into the Arabian Peninsula to Mount Sinai itself, where the law originally had been revealed to Moses. However, in the days of Paul the word "Arabia" referred to the Nabatean Kingdom, a vast expanse of territory stretching southward from Damascus toward the Arabian Peninsula. At the time of Paul's conversion this kingdom was governed by Aretas IV (9 B.C. to A.D. 40), a monarch connected by marriage to the Herodian dynasty. Paul did not say where within this territory he went or how long he stayed. A visit to Mount Sinai, while not impossible, may be considered unlikely given its far distance from Damascus, Paul's home base during his earliest days as a Christian.

A second reason has been advanced for Paul's visit to Arabia: he went there to continue the preaching ministry he had already begun in Damascus. Recent excavations have shown that the kingdom of Nabatea (*Provincia Arabia*) encompassed a thriving civilization centered around the cities of Petra and Bostra. No doubt Paul would have had ample opportunity to preach the gospel among many Gentiles in these places. We have no record of Christian communities in this territory which sprang from Paul's activity there, but there is a shred of evidence in one of Paul's own letters that his word did not go unnoticed by the governing authorities. In 2 Cor 11:32-33 Paul referred to the fact of his being lowered in a basket from the city wall of Damascus following a plot against him engineered by King Aretas (cf. Acts 9:23-25). Of course, it is impossible to date this event precisely, but it seems likely that it occurred after Paul's return from Arabia to Damascus and before his first journey to Jerusalem.

Which of the two theories should we choose? Did Paul go to Arabia on a preaching mission or for a spiritual retreat? There is no reason why we should be forced to choose between the two alternatives. We know that Paul's preaching activity began immediately after his baptism in Damascus, although he was still a new Christian at that time. However, as J. Bligh has put it, "If the illumination he had received on the road to Damascus was enough to equip him to preach in the synagogues of Damascus, it was also enough to enable him to preach to the Arabs."[72] We can safely assume that

---

[72] Bligh, *Galatians,* 135.

Paul would be just as anxious to herald the good news of Jesus Christ to whomever he met on his journey to Arabia. However, the plausibility of this scenario should not obscure the fact that even so brilliant and well-trained a thinker as Paul would also require a period of intensive preparation for the life work to which he had been called.

As we have seen, Paul did not preach another gospel but the one and only gospel of Jesus Christ, the Redeemer and Lord of the church. It is true, however, that Paul saw with greater clarity than anyone before him the full implications of this message. How was the good news of salvation through Christ related to the divinely given Torah? Have God's promises to Israel been annulled or abridged by the coming of the Messiah? What role does circumcision have in the new community (*ekklesia*) God was now calling forth? As one who had persecuted the first Christians in Jerusalem, Paul doubtless knew a great deal about the structure and leadership of the church there. How should he relate to them now? The resolution of these and other questions would require extensive time alone with God, a time for prayer and searching the Scriptures, a coming apart to be prepared for being sent back forth.

Although Paul had a unique apostolic ministry that cannot be duplicated today, we have much to learn from the rhythm of solitude and activism that we see in his life. Undoubtedly, one of the major reasons for ministerial "burnout" in the church today is a preoccupation with the demands and tasks of pastoral work to the exclusion of quality time alone with God. Pastors who are too busy to give serious and prayerful preparation to their sermons will have no power or depth in their preaching. If the study is a lounge, the pulpit will be an impertinence. But true preparation means far more than sermon planning. It is to seek the face of the Lord and to search out his divine will in every dimension of one's life. As a young ministerial student Jonathan Edwards drew up a set of resolutions by which he pledged to abide throughout his life. One of his resolutions can be applied with equal urgency to every minister of the gospel: "To study the Scripture so steadily, constantly and frequently, as that I may find, and plainly perceive myself to grow in the knowledge of the same."[73] Through such study and meditation Paul too came to know Christ more fully—in the power of his resurrection and the fellowship of his sufferings—and thus to be prepared more completely for the awesome task for which he had been set apart, called, and commissioned.

---

[73] "Resolutions of Jonathan Edwards," *Christian History Magazine*, vol. 4 (1985): 2.

(4) The First Visit to Jerusalem (1:18-24)

[18]Then after three years, I went up to Jerusalem to get acquainted with Peter and stayed with him fifteen days. [19]I saw none of the other apostles—only James, the Lord's brother. [20]I assure you before God that what I am writing you is no lie. [21]Later I went to Syria and Cilicia. [22]I was personally unknown to the churches of Judea that are in Christ. [23]They only heard the report: "The man who formerly persecuted us is now preaching the faith he once tried to destroy." [24]And they praised God because of me.

Paul's opponents in Galatia had sought to undermine his authority and his message by claiming that he dealt in a secondhand gospel, one originally derived from the apostles at Jerusalem but then changed and compromised by Paul without their knowledge or approval. Up to this point in chap. 1 Paul has responded to this charge by issuing his primary line of defense: he received his gospel by direct revelation from God, not through any human mediation, and furthermore, he had been set apart and called by God to carry this message to the Gentiles even prior to his birth.

Now, beginning in v. 18, Paul developed a second line of defense, a tightly woven alibi designed to show that his contacts with the Jerusalem church were such that he could not possibly have had the kind of subordinate leadership to its leaders that his opponents alleged. The whole argument in this passage hinges on the threefold use of the adverb *epeita,* "then" (1:18-21; 2:1). In the previous sentence Paul informed us of his immediate whereabouts following his conversion, an itinerary that involved preaching in Damascus and a sojourn in Arabia, but not a trip to Jerusalem. Now, extending that clarification, he wanted to specify precisely when he did go to Jerusalem and what the nature of his visit there was. Each of the three "then" clauses forms a crucial link in his alibi against the false charges of his Galatian adversaries.

1:18 "After three years" doubtless refers back to the date of Paul's conversion rather than to the time of his return to Damascus from Arabia. A commonly accepted practice among Jewish writers in Paul's day was to use an inclusive reckoning of time. In other words, "after three years" might well mean "in the third year," counting each segment in the measure of time as a full unit. The same rule would apply to the expression "fourteen years later," which Paul used in 2:1. This is an important point in trying to fit the events Paul rehearsed in Galatians into a comprehensive chronological account of his life.[74] In the present context, however, Paul was not concerned with

---

[74] See the excellent discussions by F. F. Bruce, "Further Thoughts on Paul's Biography: Galatians 1:11–2:14," in *Jesus und Paulus* (Tübingen: Mohr-Siebeck, 1975), 21-29; and C. J. Hemer, "Acts and Galatians Reconsidered," *Themelios* 2 (1976-77): 81-88. For a different reconstruction of Pauline chronology, see J. Knox, *Chapters in a Life of Paul* (New York: Abingdon, 1950), 47-73.

chronological precision but rather with refuting the false charges leveled against him. To do this it was only necessary for him to show that his first trip to Jerusalem occurred after a considerable lapse of time from his conversion and early preaching activity.

Paul said that he went up to Jerusalem "to get acquainted with Peter." The verb *historēsai*, "to get personally acquainted with," "to visit," is rare in biblical Greek, occurring only here and in the Apocryphal Book of 1 Esdras (1:31). While this word can mean "to inquire of," it more often means "to visit with the purpose of coming to know someone," as it evidently does here.[75]

For fifteen days Paul was a house guest of Peter in Jerusalem. How we would like to have been a fly on the wall during their dinner conversations! Paul did not need to be taught the gospel from Peter (1:12); he had already received this message along with his commission from the risen Christ himself. Still, he must have been vitally interested in Peter's account of the earthly life of Jesus, his miracles and teachings, his death and resurrection. According to church tradition, Peter was the primary source for the material that was later incorporated into the Gospel of Mark.

Paul certainly would have been fascinated to learn as much as possible about Peter's call, his confession of Christ at Caesarea Philippi, his threefold denial, and his subsequent restoration by Christ. As Jerome put it quite humorously, Paul did not go to Jerusalem "to look at Peter's eyes, cheeks, and face, to see if he was fat or thin, whether his nose was hooked or straight, whether he had a fringe of hair across his brow or was bald."[76] Paul did not seek authorization of his message or validation of his ministry from Peter. He did seek a close fellowship in the things of the Lord as well as a strategic partnership in their common apostolic mission.[77]

1:19 Paul claimed that he saw none of the other apostles except James, the brother of Jesus. The expression is ambiguous in Greek, so we cannot be

---

[75] Cf. Cole, *Galatians*, 55; G. D. Kilpatrick, "Galatians 1:18 ISTORESAI KEPHAN," in *New Testament Essays*, ed. A. J. B. Higgins (Manchester: University of Manchester Press, 1959), 144-49.

[76] PL 26-354 A. Quoted in Bligh, *Galatians*, 139.

[77] Some traditionalist Roman Catholic interpreters have seen Paul's visit to Peter as an example of his submission to the supreme Roman Pontiff. Thomas Aquinas, who was not an advocate of papal infallibility, did offer a fanciful exegesus of the "fifteen days" in this passage. "Eight is the number of the New Testament, in which the eighth day of those who will rise is awaited; but seven is the number of the Old Testament, because it celebrates the seventh day. And so he stayed with Peter fifteen days, conversing with him on the mysteries of the Old and New Testament" (*Galatians*, 28).

sure whether Paul meant to include James among the other apostles. Did he mean: "The only other apostle I saw was James," or "I saw no other apostle, although I did see James"? Probably he meant something like this: "During my sojourn with Peter, I saw none of the other apostles, unless you count James, the Lord's brother."

Who was James? Three figures in the New Testament bear the name of James. First, there is James, the brother of John and the son of Zebedee. He was the James who was put to death by the sword at the command of Herod Agrippa I (Acts 12:1-4). James, the son of Alphaeus, was also one of Jesus' Twelve Apostles (Mark 3:18). He is also known as James the Less based on a description of him in Mark 15:40. We know nothing of his later life. Calvin believed that this was the James referred to in Gal 1:19.[78] The third James, the one most likely referred to in this text, is listed among the brothers of Jesus in Mark 6:33. He is one of the most important and fascinating characters in the history of the early church although there is much about him that we do not know. However, the following facts are firmly established: (1) James was not a follower of Jesus during his earthly life. With the exception of his mother, apparently none of Jesus' earthly relatives accepted his claim to be the Messiah prior to the resurrection (John 7:5). (2) Jesus made a special resurrection appearance to James, and thus he is listed among the witnesses to the resurrection in 1 Cor 15:7. (3) James became a member of the church at Jerusalem and was among the one hundred twenty who witnessed the outpouring of the Holy Spirit on the Day of Pentecost (Acts 1:14; 2:1). (4) James quickly rose to a position of leadership within the Jerusalem church, in some sense taking the place of Peter after the latter's departure from the city (Acts 12:16-17). (5) James was known as "the Just" obviously because of his personal piety and strict observance of Jewish customs. (6) In all likelihood James wrote the general epistle that bears his name. Some have argued that this is the earliest writing of the New Testament, antedating the controversy over Paul's law-free gospel. (7) In A.D. 62 James was put to

---

[78] John Calvin, CNTC 11.22. Calvin argued that in this passage Paul consistently used the word "apostle" to refer to the highest order in the church and therefore would not have applied it to a person who was not one of the Twelve. However, as we have seen, the title apostle is not used exclusively for the Twelve but is sometimes applied to others who were sent forth for specific missionary tasks (cf. Rom 16:7; Phil 2:25; 2 Cor 8:23). To accept Calvin's reading of "apostle" in the strictest sense requires a loose interpretation of the word "brother." James, the son of Alphaeus, was not the brother of Jesus except in the general sense that all true believers share this privileged status.

death through the conniving of the Sadducees who administrated the temple.[79] This is the first of three references to James in Galatians. We will encounter him again in chap. 2, first as one of the "pillars" Paul conferred with and then as the point of reference for "certain men" who instigated controversy in the church at Antioch (2:9,12).

SO HELP ME GOD! (1:20). **1:20** Paul here affirmed in the strongest manner possible the veracity of what he had just told the Galatians concerning his dealings with the church at Jerusalem. The paraphrase of the Amplified Bible conveys the solemnity of Paul's remark: "Now—[note carefully] what I am telling you [for] it is the truth; I write it as if I were standing before the bar of God; I do not lie."

We can only surmise that Paul's adversaries had made much of the idea that he preached a derived gospel, that he was a renegade disciple of Peter and the other apostles. The timing and character of his first visit to Jerusalem were both critical in Paul's refutation of this charge. While the oath may have covered, as Burton believed, the entire narrative section beginning with v. 13, its placement immediately after Paul's account of his first visit to Jerusalem indicates that this was a particularly sore point in his exchange with the anti-Pauline party.

This verse can be compared with numerous other instances in Paul's writings where he used an oath formula to reinforce the truth of what he had said. In so doing he called God and sometimes also the holy angels as witnesses to the accuracy of his claim (Rom 1:9; 9:1; 2 Cor 1:23; Phil 1:8; 1 Tim 5:21; 2 Tim 2:14; 4:1). In an insightful study of this verse, J. P. Sampley has argued that Paul may have been using here the kind of voluntary oath (*iusiurandum voluntarium*) that was common in the Roman legal system of his day. By this device a party could settle a dispute out of court even prior to the beginning of the trial. Although we know from 1 Cor 6:1-8 that Paul did not believe Christians should take one another to court, he did not hesitate to draw an analogy to an actual legal proceeding by saying, in effect, that he was prepared to present his case with absolute confidence to the "jury" of Galatian believers who had heretofore only heard the other side of the story.[80]

A MISSION TO SYRIA AND CILICIA (1:21). **1:21** Here Paul introduced the second of the "then" clauses to show the independence of his ministry and missionary activity. In Paul's terse account of his first visit to Jerusalem, he presented only one reason for his journey to that city: to get personally

---

[79] See D. H. Little, "The Death of James the Brother of Jesus" (Ph.D. diss., Rice University, 1971). Cf. also the excursus on James in Betz, *Galatians*, 78-79.

[80] J. P. Sampley, "'Before God, I Do Not Lie' (Gal 1:20): Paul's Self-Defense in the Light of Roman Legal Praxis," *NTS* 23 (1976-77): 477-82.

acquainted with Peter. However, we know from Acts 9:26-30 that those fifteen days were filled with other activities as well. Indeed, it seems likely that Paul may well have intended to stay in Jerusalem for more than two weeks. We know that he "tried to join the disciples" there, but they rejected him, being as yet unconvinced of the sincerity of his Christian profession (Acts 9:26). Barnabas, we are told, befriended him and introduced him to the apostles, that is, to Peter and James. Paul preached freely throughout the city, as he had done in Damascus before, speaking boldly in the name of the Lord. His debates with the Hellenistic Jews led to their efforts to put him to death.

It is at this point that we should place the vision Paul had while praying in the temple. While in a trance he saw Christ, who told him to leave Jerusalem immediately since his testimony would not be received there. Paul was reluctant to obey, believing that he should remain and bear witness to those he had formerly persecuted. But the Lord replied, "Go; I will send you far away to the Gentiles" (Acts 22:17-21). When the Jerusalem Christians discovered the plot against Paul's life, they accompanied him to the port city of Caesarea and sent him off to Tarsus. Thus, in a sense, the excursion to Syria and Cilicia was really Paul's "first missionary journey," unless we use that designation for his earlier work in Arabia. From 25 B.C. to A.D. 72, Syria and Cilicia were united as a single Roman province with a common governor who was based in Syrian Antioch. Tarsus, Paul's home city, was the capital of Cilicia, which covered the southeastern region of Asia Minor.

What was the result of Paul's ministry in these places? We cannot say for sure, but it is clear from later references in Acts that Paul's witness bore fruit in the conversion of new believers and the planting of several churches. The Jerusalem Council addressed its letter "to the Gentile believers in Antioch, Syria and Cilicia." We also read of a later journey of Paul and Silas, who "went through Syria and Cilicia, strengthening the churches" (Acts 15:23-41).

Apart from these brief references we have no clue about where Paul went or what he did during these years. Perhaps it was during this time that he experienced some of the hardships he later chronicled for the Corinthians: his scourgings in the Jewish synagogues, his beatings, shipwrecks, imprisonments, and other sufferings (2 Cor 11:23-29). These years, no less than his earlier journey to Arabia and his preaching efforts in Damascus and Jerusalem, were part of a divine preparation for his later, more extensive missionary labors. God sometimes calls his servants to labor in obscure places and under difficult circumstances in order to make them ready for some particular task or assignment unknown to them at the time. It may well be that Paul would not have had the wisdom to write Romans, or the equanimity to deal with the fractious Corinthians, or the courage to withstand the false teachers of Galatia, or the endurance to face arrest in Jerusalem and martyrdom in

Rome had it not been for the ten years or so he spent laboring in little-known places with results difficult to quantify.[81]

Paul next emerged into the light of New Testament history when the peripatetic Barnabas, who had first introduced him to the church leaders in Jerusalem, was sent by the Christians at Antioch to fetch him from Tarsus (Acts 11:25-26). For a year he and Barnabas labored together in the church at Antioch. This was an important transition in Paul's apostolic ministry. Apparently a crisis in the church at Antioch gave rise to the important conference in Jerusalem Paul would describe in 2:1-10. Also at Antioch, Paul confronted Peter in a painful episode (2:11-14). And, of course, it was from Antioch that Paul and Barnabas set sail for Cyprus and from there to Asia Minor, where they first preached the good news of Jesus Christ to the people of Galatia.

REACTION TO PAUL IN JUDEA (1:22-24). In these closing verses of chap. 1 the perspective shifts away from Paul's missionary activities in faraway Syria and Cilicia back to the local environment around Jerusalem. This reminds us again of why it was necessary for Paul to tell the Galatians that he went to Syria and Cilicia. As Luther observed, "Obviously he is proving that he did not have the apostles as teachers anywhere but was himself a teacher everywhere."[82] If his preaching ministry carried him far away from Jerusalem for such an extended time, he could hardly have been working under the authority or tutelage of the apostles who were still based in Judea at that time. However, it was nonetheless important for Paul to register the reaction of the Jerusalem churches to his early ministry. He did this by referring to three facts: his lack of personal acquaintance with the Judean churches, the impression of his work that was conveyed to them, and their jubilant reaction at the report of the persecutor-turned-proclaimer.

1:22 The expression "the churches of Judea" recalls a similar expression in 1 Thess 2:14, "God's churches in Judea." The Roman province of Judea covered a geographical area roughly equivalent to the present state of Israel, including Galilee, Samaria, and Judea proper, that is, the territory surrounding the city of Jerusalem.[83] Paul referred to "churches" in the plural, reflecting his normal practice of speaking of "the 'church' (singular) in a city but the 'churches' (plural) in a province or more extensive area."[84] Doubt-

---

[81] On Paul's labors in Syria and Cilicia, see W. R. Ramsay, *A Historical Commentary on Saint Paul's Commentary to the Galatians* (Grand Rapids: Baker, 1965), 275-80.

[82] *LW* 27.197.

[83] In Acts 9:31 Luke used Judea in the strict sense of a subdivision within Palestine, "then the church throughout Judea, Galilee and Samaria enjoyed a time of peace" C. M. Stern, "The Providence of Judaea," *Compendium Rerum Judaicarum ad Novum Testamentum* (Assen: Gorcum, 1974), 1:308-16.

[84] Bruce, *Galatians,* 103.

less these were among the earliest Christian communities established in fulfillment of Jesus' command for the early believers to be his witnesses "in
Jerusalem and in all Judea" (Acts 1:8).

Some scholars have claimed that this passage flatly contradicts Luke's
account of Paul's first postconversion visit to Jerusalem, where he preached
publicly and evidently was known to a number of the believers there.[85] Others have gone to the opposite extreme, claiming that Paul must have traveled
to Jerusalem incognito and spent his two weeks there "somewhere in a back
room of Peter's house."[86] The evidence, however, demands neither that we
do violence to the historical integrity of Acts nor draw such a drastic conclusion concerning Paul's movements. Evidently Paul appeared publicly in
Jerusalem and was known to many believers there. He said that he saw none
of the apostles except Peter and James (perhaps because the others were out
of the city at the time), not that he saw no other believers except these two.
However, the province of Judea was much larger than the city of Jerusalem;
it is thus perfectly reasonable to suppose that many of the country churches
in this area, while having heard of Paul, could hardly have picked him out of
a lineup.

1:23 This verse refers to Paul's growing reputation as a preacher of the
gospel. The churches of Judea "kept on hearing" (the literal meaning of
akouontes) reports of his evangelistic activities. Doubtless some who had
been initially skeptical became convinced that Paul's conversion was for real
and his ministry indeed of God.

In our own day the dramatic turnaround in the life of such a person as
Charles Colson can only be explained by a divine intervention from above.
While many were at first wary of Colson's "born-again" experience, no
objective observer, not even his detractors, can gainsay the sincerity of his
commitment to Christ after so many years of consistent Christian living and
his positive witness for the gospel in word and deed. So it was with Paul.
What Paul, the former persecutor, now proclaimed was "the faith," not
merely his faith, not yet the church's faith, but "the" faith. Paul would use
this expression again in an absolute sense in Gal 3:23,25 to describe the
objective content of the Christian message. This is "the faith" for which Jude
urges believers to contend, the faith "that was once for all entrusted to the
saints" (Jude 3). If the Pauline expression "faith in Jesus Christ," which
occurs later in Gal 3:22, is really an objective genitive as some have claimed,

---

[85] "Paul's statement contradicts Acts 9:26-30, where it is assumed that Paul preached in
Jerusalem and moved freely in and out of the city" (Betz, *Galatians,* 80). For a sensible
response to this charge, see Machen, *Origin of Paul's Religion,* 49-54.

[86] *Machen's Notes on Galatians,* 82.

then Paul's effort to destroy the faith was in effect a campaign to destroy Christ himself.[87] This was the shattering insight that led to the disillusion of Paul's former life and his newfound zeal as an evangelist and advocate for the faith he once tried to destroy.

1:24 This verse carries us back to the worship of the early Judean Christians as they praised God for his stupendous work in the life of Paul. The chorus of praise here at the end of chap. 1 echoes the earlier doxology at the conclusion to the introduction (1:5). The first doxology is a hymn of praise for what God has done through the atoning death and triumphant resurrection of Jesus Christ. The second doxology celebrates that same victory as seen in the calling and apostolic ministry of Paul. The common thread running through both anthems of praise is the triumph of God. Against the machinations of Satan, who dominates this present evil age, against the insinuations and plots of the false teachers who would pervert the true gospel, against heresy and schism, against persecution and hardship, against all of this—our God reigns! God's kingdom, God's eternal will, God's purpose in grace, God's plan of salvation, God's building up of the church, God's transforming work in the life of every sinner, even so notorious a one as Paul the persecutor, for all of this we too, along with worshiping Christians of every age and place, can lift up our hearts in praise, adoration, and triumphant hope.

Before leaving this chapter, we should note one final reason for Paul's interest in the reaction of the Judean Christians to his apostolic work. Paul's argument had gone like this: "I received my gospel directly from Jesus Christ, not from any human sources. I only visited Jerusalem sometime after my conversion, and then only for a short time to get acquainted with Peter. Far from being a clone of the apostles, or a protégé of the churches they established in Judea, I was hardly even known to most Christians there. But when they did hear of what God was doing through me, they praised and glorified him on that account. I was no embarrassment to the church in Jerusalem nor to the brothers and sisters in Judea. Rather, through the grace of God, I was the cause of their rejoicing."

Why was it necessary for Paul to make such a point? The crisis Paul was facing in Galatia likely had its roots in a certain type of Jewish Christianity that claimed allegiance to the primitive Christian community in Jerusalem, its leaders, and its ethos. Paul wanted to show that from the beginning it was not so. The Jerusalem church leaders welcomed him as a colleague and blessed his ministry. The churches of Judea, including some Paul himself

---

[87] R. B. Hays, *The Faith of Jesus Christ: An Investigation of the Narrative Substructure of Galatians 3:1–4:11,* SBLDS 56 (Chico, Cal.: Scholars Press, 1983).

had formerly persecuted, rejoiced in the great reversal they heard about in Paul's life. While Paul wanted to assert as strongly as possible his independence from the Jerusalem church, he also wanted to claim a vital partnership with them in the service of a shared gospel and a common Lord.

4. The Apostolic Message—Confirmation and Challenge (2:1-21)

Chapter 2 continues the train of thought Paul had begun to develop concerning the independence of his apostolate and the integrity of the law-free gospel he received from Jesus Christ. The chapter divides naturally into two major sections. In the first (2:1-10) Paul recounts an important meeting he had with the leaders of the Jerusalem church. The issue of circumcision, which now dominates the appeal being made to his Galatian converts by the false teachers, surfaced at this earlier meeting with reference to Titus, a Gentile believer whom Paul refused to have circumcised despite pressure from certain "false brothers."

Despite the note of conflict that runs through this passage, the major motif is Paul's solidarity with the Jerusalem leaders and their common front in the work of the gospel. Although they "added nothing to [his] message," Paul said, "they recognized the grace given to" him. The second section of the chapter (2:11-21) centers on another meeting between Peter and Paul, this time at Antioch, where again the issue of legalism threatened to disrupt the unity of the church. Paul confronted Peter because the latter had yielded to pressures from a group of Judaizing intruders by withdrawing from table fellowship with uncircumcised Gentile believers. The incident at Antioch provided an occasion for Paul to state clearly the principle of justification by faith. Thus the closing verses of chap. 2 are transitional, leading into the major theological center of the book in chaps. 3 and 4.

(1) The Second Visit to Jerusalem (2:1-10)

[1]Fourteen years later I went up again to Jerusalem, this time with Barnabas. I took Titus along also. [2]I went in response to a revelation and set before them the gospel that I preach among the Gentiles. But I did this privately to those who seemed to be leaders, for fear that I was running or had run my race in vain. [3]Yet not even Titus, who was with me, was compelled to be circumcised, even though he was a Greek. [4][This matter arose] because some false brothers had infiltrated our ranks to spy on the freedom we have in Christ Jesus and to make us slaves. [5] We did not give in to them for a moment, so that the truth of the gospel might remain with you.

[6]As for those who seemed to be important—whatever they were makes no difference to me; God does not judge by external appearance—those men

added nothing to my message. ⁷On the contrary, they saw that I had been entrusted with the task of preaching the gospel to the Gentiles, just as Peter had been to the Jews. ⁸For God, who was at work in the ministry of Peter as an apostle to the Jews, was also at work in my ministry as an apostle to the Gentiles. ⁹James, Peter and John, those reputed to be pillars, gave me and Barnabas the right hand of fellowship when they recognized the grace given to me. They agreed that we should go to the Gentiles, and they to the Jews. ¹⁰All they asked was that we should continue to remember the poor, the very thing I was eager to do.

THE OCCASION OF THE VISIT (2:1-2). **2:1-2** In these opening verses the stage is set for the drama that is about to unfold. Let us notice the event itself, the parties involved, and the motive behind Paul's action.

The Event. The first word in the Greek text of chap. 2 is *epeita,* translated as "later" (NIV), "next" (NEB), or "after" (RSV). In fact, this is the third in a series of "then" clauses Paul stitched together to form an airtight argument for his apostolic independence from the Jerusalem church (cf. 1:18,21). In chap. 1 Paul reminded the Galatians that his first visit to Jerusalem occurred sometime after his conversion and that it lasted for only a brief time, fifteen days. Only then did he get acquainted with Peter. Then, following this visit, his ministry carried him far from the environs of Jerusalem so that the churches in that area only knew of his activities by hearsay. Then it was fourteen years before he visited Jerusalem again, that is, for a second time after his conversion.

Given the tightly woven structure of Paul's argument, we must insist that the meeting he described in chap. 2 occurred during the course of his second postconversion visit to Jerusalem. Paul was not running back and forth to Jerusalem so frequently that he could have confused the sequence of his visits, especially when such a momentous issue for his own apostolic work was at stake. Moveover, he already had taken an oath before the bar of God to verify the unerring accuracy of his narration (Gal 1:20). Still, however, different matters of interpretation remain concerning the conference in Jerusalem and where it should be placed in Paul's life. C. K. Barrett has referred to this issue as "the most celebrated and complicated historical problem in the whole epistle—perhaps in the whole of the New Testament."[88] We cannot here refer to all of the dimensions of this problem; let us briefly mention two issues that bear on our reconstruction of this event.

[88] C. K. Barrett, *Freedom and Obligation* (Philadelphia: Westminster, 1985), 10.

First, what did Paul mean by the expression "fourteen years later"? In considering the similar expression "after three years" (1:18), we noted that in the New Testament era an inclusive method of reckoning periods of time was often used. By this method any portion of a given year could be counted as a whole year. Thus 1995 would be "three years" after 1993, even though conceivably by this method no more than thirteen months might have elapsed between the two dates. This means that in Gal 1:18 the "three years" could have been slightly more than one, and the "fourteen years" of Gal 2:1 possibly could have covered only twelve.

Another chronological issue concerns the benchmark from which Paul was gauging the time of his second visit to Jerusalem. Fourteen years after what? His first visit to Jerusalem (1:18) or, as seems more likely, his conversion encounter with Christ? If we assume the latter, and factor in the inclusive reckoning of years, we can place the date for Paul's second visit to Jerusalem around A.D. 44–46, with the *terminus a quo* of his conversion occurring in A.D. 32 or 33. This would mean that the events of Gal 2:1-10 parallel the "famine visit" Paul and Barnabas made to Jerusalem as recorded in Acts 11:25-30.

This view has been convincingly argued by F. F. Bruce although it remains a minority opinion among commentators on the epistle.[89] The prevailing view equates Gal 2:1-10 with Acts 15:1-21, the famous council at Jerusalem that produced an agreement endorsed by Paul and the Jerusalem leaders alike concerning the admission of Gentile converts into the Christian community. On the surface this is a plausible hypothesis since there are marked similarities between the two passages. Both involve Paul and Barnabas on the one side and Peter and James on the other. Both meetings deal with the issue of circumcision and reflect a similar outcome, one essentially favorable to Paul.

Upon closer examination, however, the differences between Acts 15 and Gal 2 are more striking than the similarities. In Acts 15 Paul and Barnabas are sent as part of an official delegation from the church at Antioch to resolve a dispute introduced into their congregation by intruders from Judea. In Gal

---

[89] See Bruce, *Galatians,* 43-56, and "Further Thoughts on Paul's Biography," 21-29. More recently Longenecker (*Galatians,* lxxiii) has reviewed all of the relevant evidence and arrived at a similar conclusion, holding that Paul's conversion occurred two or three years after the crucifixion of Jesus (A.D. 30) and that the three and fourteen years of Gal 1:18 and 2:1 are concurrent, not consecutive. This leads him to date Galatians on the eve of the Jerusalem Council referred to in Acts 15, which probably occurred around A.D. 49. "The thesis of an early date for the writing of Galatians is supported by . . . historical, exegetical, and critical evidence. . . . And though the time spans of Gal 1:18 and 2:1 may not at first glance easily fit into such an understanding, they do not, given certain possible assumptions, discredit that thesis."

2, however, Paul himself, prompted by a divine revelation, takes the initiative for the meeting. The council of Acts 15 was clearly a public meeting involving lengthy discussions and presentations addressed to the whole assembly by Peter, Paul, Barnabas, and James. By contrast, the conference of Gal 2 was carried on in private conversation among the principal leaders.

Most telling of all, however, is the fact that nowhere in Galatians does Paul refer to the outcome of the Jerusalem Council or to the apostolic decree which, according to Acts, he and Barnabas later distributed among the churches of Syria, Cilicia, and also Galatia (Acts 16:4). As Bruce has observed, "After the publication of the apostolic decree of Acts 15:20-29, it would have been difficult for Judaizing preachers invoking the authority of the leaders of the Jerusalem church to impose circumcision on Gentile Christians."[90] It is inconceivable that Paul would have refrained from any mention of this concordat with the Jerusalem church, especially when he had gone to such pains to delineate his relationship with that Christian community and when the mere disclosure of such an agreement would have silenced those who were seeking to undermine his ministry in Galatia. On balance it is thus better to see the situation in Galatia as part of the Judaizing agitation that led up to the Jerusalem Council. That Paul nowhere alluded to this meeting or its outcome is best explained by the fact that it had not yet occurred. In fairness, however, other scholars, including some who hold to a high view of biblical authority, have interpreted Gal 2 and Acts 15 as parallel accounts of the same event.[91]

---

[90] Bruce, *Galatians*, 52.

[91] In addition to chronological difficulties, other problems have been posed concerning the correlation of Gal 2 and the famine visit of Acts 11. The equation of the two presupposes two separate conferences over the same issue with a similar outcome. Moreover, Luke makes no mention in Acts 11 of Paul's meeting with the apostles at Jerusalem. He frames that entire visit with reference to the deliverance of the love gift from Antioch, with no hint of a wider controversial agenda. Against the first objective, it may be said that the admission of Gentiles into a Jewish-dominated Christian community was a serious and recurring problem in the early church. The imposition of circumcision as a requirement for salvation was a disruptive factor not only in Antioch and Galatia but also in other Pauline communities as we gather from various references in his other writings (cf. Eph 2:11-13; 1 Cor 7:17-24; Titus 1:10-11; Col 2:11,13-14). It is not surprising that Paul would have taken the occasion of the famine visit to have a private conversation with the Jerusalem church leaders over this vexing problem. C. H. Talbert has explained the presumed discrepancies between Gal 2 and the famine visit account in Acts 11 by referring to Luke's distinctive literary and theological perspective: "The form of the visit in Acts is determined by the aims and tendencies of the author." Talbert himself equates Gal 2 and Acts 11, although he dates Galatians after the Jerusalem Council of Acts 15. He locates the *Sitz im Leben* of the epistle in the missionary situation of Acts 16:1-5 with Paul's circumcision of Timothy and his promulgation of the apostolic decree leading to charges of inconsistency and compromise from his syncretistic opponents ("Again: Paul's Visits to Jerusalem," *NovT* 9 [1967]: 26-40).

The Parties. In the narrative that follows there are three groups of principal actors, each of which plays a distinctive role in the decision of the conference and its aftermath. First, there is the Pauline party, consisting of Barnabas, Titus, and the apostle himself.

Second, there are the "false brothers" who agitated for Titus to be circumcised and later imported their Judaistic tendencies to Antioch itself. This group represented an extreme wing of the Jewish Christian movement. They had strong attachments to the church at Jerusalem, particularly to James. They were obviously zealous, law-observant propagandists who perceived Paul's law-free gospel as a serious threat to the Christian faith as they understood it. We get a glimpse of their theology from Acts 15, where we are told that "some men came down from Judea to Antioch and were teaching the brothers: Unless you are circumcised, according to the custom taught by Moses, you cannot be saved" (15:1-2). It is possible that some of these same people were among those who created the stir at Antioch that led to the breach between Paul and Peter. Like Paul they had come to Christianity out of a strict Pharisaic background. Now some of these same Jewish Christian missionaries or their close fellow travelers also had penetrated the churches of Galatia, "spying on" the Christian freedom of the new believers there just as they had done before at Antioch and elsewhere.

The third party that plays a prominent role in the narrative are the leaders of the Jerusalem church, namely, James, Peter, and John, whose prominence had given them the name "pillars." Paul's main negotiations were with these church leaders, not with his Judaizing detractors, although the close relationship between the "pillars" and some of their more zealous disciples must have created a situation of great tension for everyone involved.

The Motive. Paul made three important points concerning the motivation for his second visit to Jerusalem. First, he insists that he was prompted to call for this meeting "in response to a revelation" (v. 2). This is the same word Paul used in 1:12 to describe his epiphany of the risen Christ on the road to Damascus. Although that experience was a unique, unrepeatable event, we know that Christ appeared and spoke to Paul on other occasions as well (Acts 22:17-21; 2 Cor 12:1-10). There is no reason to doubt that Paul is here referring to a similar disclosure related to the special circumstances of his mission to the Gentiles. The Amplified Bible captures the meaning of Paul's sentiment: "I went because it was specially and divinely revealed to me that I should go." Some interpreters have seen in the word "revelation" an oblique reference to the prophecy of Agabus in Acts 11:28 concerning a forthcoming famine, a prediction that prompted the Antiochene Christians to respond with a gift of charity to their Judean brothers and sisters. However, the context in Gal 2 calls for a more specific word from the Lord, one related to the growing rift and controversy concerning Paul's message and its reception throughout the church at large.

Paul's second motivation in convening the conference is succinctly expressed: "I went . . . to set before them the gospel that I preach among the Gentiles." The verb *anethemēn,* "set before them," means literally "to declare, communicate, advocate, propound." Perhaps there were those already who were maligning Paul and his message. Their line might have gone something like this: "After his conversion we had such high hopes for Paul. After all, no one else in this generation was better trained in God's Torah than he. But now he has departed from the faith of Jesus and the apostles. He is carrying out a negative campaign against the law, totally divorcing the Messiah from the nation Israel. He is a dangerous radical who must be stopped before he completely overturns the Jewish character of our faith by bringing into the church those Gentiles who shun so basic a requirement of the law as circumcision."

Against this kind of misrepresentation, Paul found it necessary to "set forth" the true gospel he was proclaiming among the Gentiles. As we will see, Paul's gospel was the same gospel that the Jerusalem apostles also believed and preached. The implications of this message in a new missionary situation, however, were not grasped clearly by everyone at once. What we have in Gal 2 is a snapshot of the early church grappling with the problems of law and gospel, faith and freedom, historical particularity and evangelical inclusivism. The issue was not finally resolved by this conference, nor indeed by the later Jerusalem Council. Yet Paul's stubborn resistance on both of these occasions to those who would water down the gospel of grace was an indispensable factor in the triumph of the orthodox Christian doctrine of salvation.

The third motivation for the conference relates to an issue that flows just beneath the surface of the text. Paul made it abundantly clear that the conference was called at his initiative, not that of the Jerusalem leaders. He was not being summoned to headquarters to give an account for his activity. Rather, he himself sought the meeting in order to resolve a crisis that could have led to a major division within the body of Christ. Doubtless this was why Paul asked for a private meeting, not a public hearing, over these matters.

We have much to learn from how Paul handled himself in this controversy. Later he would write to the Romans, "Let us therefore make every effort to do what leads to peace and to mutual edification" (14:19). It is always wrong to provoke controversy in a belligerent, un-Christlike manner. Paul sought to avoid such a situation by sharing confidentially with trusted leaders of the church. There are occasions, however, when in order to be faithful to the gospel it is necessary to speak out publicly and even bluntly on matters that cannot be compromised. This Paul would do in his open rebuke of Peter at Antioch.

The Jerusalem Council in Acts 15 also was a public event, one fraught with great tension and controversy. Yet in the providence of God that public airing and resolution of the question of Christian liberty was a necessary antidote against the destructive teachings of those who would have reduced the Christian faith to a small sect within Judaism. How do we know when to seek private counsel and when to take a public stand? When is it right to swallow our scruples and yield to a fellow Christian on a matter of secondary importance? Conversely, when is it wrong to sit still and keep the peace when our speaking out could make a difference about whether our church or our denomination will remain faithful to the gospel? There is a time to speak and a time to keep silent. Every Christian must seek the wisdom of the Holy Spirit to know which is appropriate at a given time.

The phrase "for fear that I was running or had run my race in vain" is perplexing and has called forth various interpretations. Some have suggested that Paul went to Jerusalem seeking the approval of the leaders there without which his ministry would not have been valid. This hypothesis, however, seems to contradict the entire drift of Paul's argument in Gal 1–2. Others have given these words a more existentialist twist as though Paul were expressing here a kind of hesitation or self-doubt about his apostolic vocation. This theory also founders on what we everywhere else know about Paul as a person of robust conscience, one given to self-examination but not to psychological introspection. After all, this same apostle could write to the Corinthians, "I therefore so run, not as at an uncertainty" (1 Cor 9:26, KJV). It seems better to interpret Paul's words as an expression of concern for the new believers he had led to Christ and the young churches he had founded. What would a major division in the church mean for these Christians? Beyond that, what would it mean for the furtherance of Paul's missionary work? Doubtless he himself would not be deterred from the path he had been traveling for more than a dozen years. Yet the world mission to which he had been divinely called could well be sidetracked, if not finally thwarted, by his failure to reach a base agreement on a shared gospel with the mother-church in Jerusalem.[92] For these reasons Paul sought the unity of the church and close partnership with the Jerusalem leaders.

---

[92] See the comment of Bruce on this text: "His commission was not derived from Jerusalem, but it could not be executed effectively except in fellowship with Jerusalem. A cleavage between his Gentile mission and the mother-church would be disastrous: Christ would be divided, and all the energy which Paul had devoted, and hoped to devote, to the evangelizing of the Gentile world would be frustrated" (*Galatians,* 111). See also H. Schlier, *Der Brief an der Galater* (Göttingen: Vandenhoeck & Ruprecht, 1949), 67-70.

TITUS AND THE FALSE BROTHERS (2:3-5).   Verses 3-5 constitute a
digression in Paul's narration of his second visit to Jerusalem. This reflects
what was likely an actual interruption in his private conference with the
Jerusalem church leaders. The entire passage is fraught with syntactical difficulties and textual uncertainties, leading J. B. Lightfoot to call it "this shipwreck of grammar."[93] For example, in the Greek text v. 4 lacks both a proper
subject and verb, "this matter arose," being supplied by the NIV translators
in order to make sense of Paul's broken syntax. Paul obviously wrote these
verses under great emotional stress, thinking both of the incident at Jerusalem and also of the contemporary situation in Galatia. The intensity and
unevenness of his language here has given rise to diverse interpretations of
the Titus episode. As best we can, let us reconstruct the incident as Paul
related it, keeping in mind that this entire historical narrative was intended
to illuminate a serious theological crisis that had arisen among the churches
of Galatia.

The Case of Titus.   **2:3**   We already have been introduced to Titus in v.
1, where he appeared along with Barnabas as one of Paul's companions on
the trip to Jerusalem. Paul, a former Pharisaic Jew and now Apostle to the
Gentiles, took with him a Jewish Christian, Barnabas, and a Gentile convert,
Titus. Later, in his Letter to Titus, Paul addresses him as "my true son in our
common faith" (Titus 1:4). Titus was probably won to Christ through the
witness of Paul himself and thus became one of his most trusted coworkers
(2 Cor 8:23).[94] Titus is nowhere mentioned in Acts but he appears frequently
in Paul's letters serving as the apostle's confidential agent especially in the
gathering and administration of the love offering the Gentile churches were
collecting for the poor saints in Jerusalem (2 Cor 8:20; 12:17). It has been
well said that Titus "possessed considerable people skills . . . and was a man
of unquestioned integrity, especially with regard to financial resources."[95]

Why did Paul take Titus with him to Jerusalem? If, as we have argued, this
visit was made for the purpose of delivering famine relief to the Christians
of Judea, then it would be perfectly natural for a Gentile member of the
church at Antioch to be sent along as an expression of solidarity between the
predominantly Gentile church in Syria and the largely Jewish mother congregation at Jerusalem. However, there is also the possibility that Paul may
deliberately have included Titus in the delegation to have a living example

[93] Lightfoot, *Galatians,* 104.

[94] E. E. Ellis, "Paul and His Co-workers," *NTS* 17 (1971): 437-52. See also C. K. Barrett,
"Titus," *Essays on Paul* (Philadelphia: Westminster, 1982), 118-31, and B. Reicke, "Chronolo-
gie der Pastoral briefe," *TLZ* 101 (1976): 82-94.

[95] T. D. Lea and H. P. Griffin, Jr., *1, 2 Timothy, Titus,* NAC (Nashville: Broadman, 1992),
273.

of a Gentile convert on hand when he "set forth" his gospel to the church leaders there. He surely knew that Titus was uncircumcised, and he may well have anticipated the controversy over this issue.

On this reading, then, Paul took Titus with him as a test case for the principle of Christian freedom. In some sense this was a deliberate act of provocation although, as John Stott has said, "It was not in order to stir up strife that he brought Titus with him to Jerusalem, but in order to establish the truth of the gospel. This truth is that Jews and Gentiles are accepted by God on the same terms, namely, through faith in Jesus Christ, and must therefore be accepted by the church without any discrimination between them."[96]

Here for the first time in Galatians we encounter the issue of circumcision. It will be mentioned again later in this same chapter and also in the closing section of the book (2:7-9,12; 5:1-11; 6:12-15). Controversy over circumcision was not limited to the Galatian context. It dogged Paul wherever he went as can be seen from his discussions of it in Romans (2:25-29; 3:1,20; 4:9-12; 15:8), Philippians (3:3-5), 1 Corinthians (7:18-20), and Colossians (2:9-15; 3:10-11). In Gal 2:12 Paul identified the troublemakers in Antioch as "those who belonged to the circumcision group." The same expression recurs in his Letter to Titus (1:10), where the apostle warned his younger colleague against "many rebellious people" who oppose sound doctrine, "mere talkers and deceivers, especially those of the circumcision group." In order for us to understand more clearly what was at stake in the episode over Titus at Jerusalem, and indeed in the Galatian crisis generally, we must review briefly the role of circumcision both within Judaism and early Christianity.

Circumcision is the act of removing the foreskin of the male genital, a rite practiced among various peoples of the ancient world as a sign of initiation at puberty or marriage.[97] Among the Jewish people, however, circumcision originated in the special covenant God made with Abraham (Gen 17:1-27)

---

[96] J. Stott, *Only One Way: The Message of Galatians* (Downers Grove: InterVarsity, 1968), 42. Cf. also Barrett's comment: "Paul could see that trouble was blowing up (the next few verses will show how near it was), and went to lay his cards on the table. . . . Perhaps what he wanted was a showdown, and he took Titus with him as a deliberate provocation. Jerusalem was evidently a divided church, for we leave the authorities and come first to the false brothers (2:4), that is, people who looked like Christians, and claimed to be Christians, but (in Paul's view) were not Christians. It was these men who required that Titus, the Greek, should be circumcised, evidently taking the line that this was the only way into the Christian body, the people of God. Paul would not have it" (*Freedom and Obligation,* 11)

[97] The following summary is based on the article by R. Meyer, "Περιτέμνω," *TDNT* 6.72-84. Also see J. B. Polhill, "Circumcision," *MDB*. Also worthy of note are N. J. McEleney, "Conversion, Circumcision and Law," *NTS* 20 (1974): 319-41, and J. M. Sasson, "Circumcision in the Ancient Near East," *JBL* 85 (1966): 473-76.

whereby every male child, whether freeborn Israelite or household slave, would be circumcised on the eighth day after birth as a sign of participation in the chosen people of God. In the tradition of the great prophets of Israel circumcision is extended metaphorically to refer to the act of repentance and total consecration demanded by the Lord. Thus Jeremiah could deliver this word from the Lord for the people of his day, "Circumcise yourselves, and take away the foreskins of your heart" (Jer 4:4, KJV). Obviously the children of Israel were guilty of overreliance on the external rite of circumcision and the sacrificial system of the temple to the neglect of what Jesus would call "the more important matters of the law—justice, mercy, and faithfulness" (Matt 23:23). There may well be, as some scholars have claimed, a line of continuity between Jeremiah's spiritualizing of circumcision in terms of a genuine response of the heart and Paul's use of the term as a metaphor for the Christian life.[98]

In the Hellenistic Roman period, circumcision became more and more prominent as a distinguishing mark of Jewish identity as the people of Israel found themselves in a political environment that grew increasingly hostile. According to the Maccabean literature, the reign of terror unleashed by Antiochus IV (175–163 B.C.), included a prohibition of circumcision and a policy by which babies who had been circumcised were put to death along with the mothers who had submitted them to this sign of the covenant. In reaction to this brutal assault on Jewish identity, circumcision was raised to an even higher status as a sign of the election and purity of the nation Israel. Thus, "as a basic Jewish law, circumcision was in the Hellenistic Roman period one of the presuppositions without which intimate dealings with the Jews were not conceivable."[99]

Within the crosscurrents of political messianism and apocalyptic speculation, the idea grew that the Messiah would only come when the Holy Land had been purified of all uncircumcised Gentiles. Prior to the conquest of Pompey and the beginning of Roman rule, the Hasmonean king, John Hyr-

---

[98] See, e.g., Paul's comment in Phil 3:3: "For it is we who are the circumcision, we who worship by the Spirit of God, who glory in Christ Jesus, and who put no confidence in the flesh." Similarly, Paul can say to the Colossians that in Christ we have received a circumcision made without hands. This has happened through a putting off of the old life in the circumcision of Christ, evidently a reference to the experience of forgiveness secured by the cross and the inner transformation of the believer wrought thereby (Col 2:12-13). For Paul, regeneration, not baptism, is the New Testament antitype for which literal circumcision in the OT was the type. On how this issue has fared in recent baptismal controversies, see T. George, "The Reformed Doctrine of Believers' Baptism," *Int* 47 (1993): 242-54.

[99] Meyer, "Περιτέμνω," 78. See also the treatment of circumcision by J. J. Gunther, *Saint Paul's Opponents and Their Background* (Leiden: Brill, 1973), 82-89.

canus I, had mandated the mass circumcision of the Idumeans whom he had subjugated by force. Thus, during the period of the New Testament, circumcision was regarded by devout Jews as an indispensable precondition and seal of participation in God's covenant community. The strictest Jews insisted that even proselytes be circumcised as a rite of initiation into the special people of God. When Paul listed among his preconversion bragging points the fact that he had been "circumcised on the eighth day" (Phil 3:5), he was giving witness to the powerful emotional and ideological force this ancient rite conveyed to Jewish people everywhere.[100]

With this background in mind we can understand more clearly some of the fears and suspicions the Pauline mission provoked among what might be called the ultra-right wing of Jewish Christianity. For them Paul represented a serious threat to the character of the Christian faith, which they interpreted in terms of continuity with the Old Testament law, worship in the temple, and faithful observance of such sacred Jewish rites as circumcision. We get a glimpse of the harsh feelings these Jewish believers had for Paul from an incident that occurred during one of the apostle's later visits to Jerusalem. While Paul was received warmly by many of the Christians there, including James, they were quick to warn him of the negative press he had received among many others. "You see, brother, how many thousands of Jews have believed, and all of them are zealous for the law. They have been informed that you teach all the Jews who live among the Gentiles to turn away from Moses, telling them not to circumcise their children or live according to our customs. What shall we do?" (Acts 21:20-22). In order to show his solidarity with these scrupulous Jewish believers, Paul willingly submitted himself to the purification ritual of the temple and also paid the stipulated fee for four of the strict brothers who had taken a Nazirite vow. In this way Paul reassured the believers in Jerusalem of his personal compatibility with Jewish traditions so long as no compromise of the gospel was involved.

In fact, the rumor that Paul had instructed Jewish Christians of the diaspora to forego the circumcision of their children was patently false. As he wrote to the Corinthians: "This is the rule I lay down in all the churches. Was a man already circumcised when he was called? He should not become uncircumcised. Was a man uncircumcised when he was called? He should

---

[100] In the rabbinic Judaism of the post-NT era, this high view of circumcision was maintained. If the circumcision day fell on a Sabbath, "the duty of circumcision took precedence of the law of the Sabbath." The circumcision ceremony was a high moment of family ritual including a series of benedictions and concluding with a feast. A major contributing factor to the Bar Kochba revolt of A.D. 135 was an imperial ban on circumcision promulgated by the emperor Hadrian. This ban was lifted by his successor Antoninus Pius (Meyer, "Περιτέμνω," 79-81).

not be circumcised. Circumcision is nothing and uncircumcision is nothing. Keeping God's commands is what counts" (1 Cor 7:17-19). He explained the same principle somewhat differently in Gal 6:15: "Neither circumcision nor uncircumcision means anything; what counts is a new creation."

The phrase about "becoming uncircumcised" in the Corinthian text refers to a practice called *epispasmos,* a surgical procedure designed to conceal cosmetically the physical effects of circumcision. This procedure was sought by certain Jewish men in order to avoid embarrassment when they visited the public baths or participated in athletic games (cf. 1 Macc 1:15).[101] Paul had no sympathy for this kind of radical Hellenizing of Jewish culture and spoke against it. He honored circumcision as a sign of Jewish identity and encouraged Jewish Christians to continue to circumcise their male offspring.

Then why all the fuss over Titus? If circumcision is after all a matter of indifference, then why not submit Titus, a Gentile believer, to this harmless ritual in order to keep peace with the more scrupulous element of the Jerusalem church? The answer relates to the claims for circumcision advanced by the Judaizing party, "Unless you are circumcised . . . you cannot be saved" (Acts 15:1). To accept this verdict is to renounce the truth of the gospel, that salvation is by divine grace manifested in Jesus' completed work on the cross, the benefit of which is received through personal faith in the Redeemer, and that alone. In this case, for a Gentile believer to submit to circumcision is to "make Christ of no value to you" (Gal 5:2). Those to whom Christ is of no value are still under the curse of the law, without God and without hope in this world and the next.

Thus the dispute over Titus set the parameters for the crisis in Galatia. It brought into focus an issue that could not be avoided, a matter that would again come to the fore at the Jerusalem Council (Acts 15), the outcome of which was crucial both for the integrity of the gospel and the unity of the church. As G. Ebeling has aptly put it: "The treatment of circumcision had become a test of the Christian faith. In historical terms, it must be decided whether Christianity is something other than a new Jewish sect. In theological terms, the decision is whether one's relationship with Christ is dependent on being under the law, or the relationship to the law is dependent on being in Christ."[102]

Sneaks and Spooks (2:4). **2:4** In this verse the spotlight falls on the *pseudadelphoi,* the "false brothers," who had insisted on the circumcision of Titus. Paul reserved some of his most colorful and combative language to

---

[101] See J. Goldstein, *I Maccabees,* AB (Garden City: Doubleday), 199-200.

[102] Ebeling, *Truth of the Gospel,* 97.

describe these people. Before looking at that description, however, we must address two historical problems, both of which are made more difficult by the broken syntax and textual difficulty of this passage.

The first question concerns when the incident with Titus took place. It could refer to an event that happened either before or after this trip to Jerusalem, say, in the church at Antioch or some other Gentile mission setting. We know from the incident over table fellowship at Antioch and also from the disturbance that prompted the Jerusalem Council of Acts 15 that members of "the circumcision party" were pursuing a policy of disruption on several fronts. That their ploys had penetrated as far as Galatia was the occasion of this letter. Clearly the demand for Titus to be circumcised was not unique: this was one instance of a widespread Judaizing effort based in Jerusalem but obviously carried to strategic mission stations throughout the Eastern Mediterranean. Thus many commentators believe that Paul was here thinking of an event that happened elsewhere, most likely at Antioch, rather than during his meeting with the Jerusalem church leaders. Paul's reason for interjecting the matter into his narration of the Jerusalem meeting, however, is that it likely occurred on that very occasion.

There is the further question of whether Titus indeed was circumcised, at his own or Paul's initiative, as a gesture of conciliation made perhaps at the behest of the "pillars." Some of the early church fathers reflect an interpretation of v. 5 based on the omission of the negative *oude,* "not." However, as B. Metzger has noted, the resultant reading "because of the false brethren . . . I yielded for a brief time" seems to contradict both the drift of Paul's argument in this passage as well as his general temperament in dealing with a matter over which he is willing to hurl anathemas.[103] It has been suggested that this textual variant occurred through the mistake of some unknown copyist who wanted to harmonize the Titus incident with Acts 16:3, where we are told that Paul did agree to have Timothy circumcised "because of the Jews who lived in that area."

Why would Paul be so adamant in refusing to have Titus circumcised when he was later so concessive in submitting Timothy to the same rite? The answer, of course, is that Timothy was not Titus. We know that Timothy had a Jewish mother, which, then as now, was a recognized criterion of Jewish

---

[103] Metzger, *Textual Commentary,* 591. Bruce (*Galatians,* 113) observed that the omission of the negative in the first half of the sentence makes complete nonsense of the latter part. "It is difficult to see a logical connection between this reading of the situation and the following statement of purpose 'in order that the truth of the gospel might remain [unimpaired] with you.' How the circumcision of a Gentile Christian could have been supposed by anyone, especially by Paul, to help to maintain the gospel of free grace for Gentile Christians in general, passes understanding."

identity. Moreover, the two situations were quite different. Titus, a Gentile, was being pressured to be circumcised in order to receive salvation and full membership in the church. Timothy, however, could submit to the ancestral traditions of his mother's family without compromising the cardinal doctrine of salvation by grace. He did so with Paul's full blessing in order to enhance their missionary witness among the Jews.[104]

To summarize: during Paul's visit to Jerusalem, perhaps even during the course of his private meeting with the church leaders, certain "false brothers" made a big deal over the fact that he had brought with him an uncircumcised Gentile Christian, Titus, whom they insisted should undergo this sacred Jewish rite. Paul resisted, and their scheme came to naught: Titus was not compelled to be circumcised.

We are now ready to look more closely at Paul's description of his adversaries in Jerusalem. Paul used three unusual words to characterize the activities of the false brothers. They are all words derived from the world of political and military espionage but applied to the conflict raging in the early church. We can paraphrase Paul's assessment of the situation thus: "Now all this came about because certain false brothers, having been secretly smuggled into our ranks, disrupted our fellowship in order to spy on us and thereby subvert our freedom in Christ." The word *pareisaktos,* which the KJV translates "brought in unawares," occurs nowhere else in the New Testament. The closest New Testament parallel is 2 Pet 2:1, where a closely related word is used to describe a similar situation: "But there were also false prophets among the people, just as there will be false teachers among you. They will secretly introduce destructive heresies, even denying the sovereign Lord who bought them." The idea is that of a conspiracy of error, a secret plot concocted by enemies of the faith, informants, and double agents deliberately planted to ferret out confidential information.

The verb Paul used is a kindred word, *pareiserchomai,* "to slip in," "infil-

---

[104] On the circumcision of Timothy see the perceptive comments of J. B. Polhill (*Acts,* NAC [Nashville: Broadman, 1992], 341-43: "Many scholars have argued that Paul would never have asked Timothy to be circumcised, since he objected so strenuously to that rite in Galatians. That, however, is to overlook the fact that Galatians was written to Gentiles and Timothy was considered a Jew. There was no question of circumcising Gentiles. . . . The converse was also true: Jews would not be required to abandon their Jewishness in order to become Christians. There is absolutely no evidence that Paul ever asked Jews to abandon circumcision as their mark of membership in God's covenant people. . . . To have had a member of his entourage be of Jewish lineage and yet uncircumcised would have hampered his effectiveness among the Jews. It was at the very least a matter of missionary strategy to circumcise Timothy (1 Cor 9:20). It may have been much more. Paul never abandoned his own Jewish heritage. He may well have wanted Timothy to be true to *his* (cf. Rom 3:1f.)." See also W. O. Walker "The Timothy-Titus Problem Reconsidered," *ExpTim* 92 (1981): 231-35.

trate." It deepens the idea of a conspiratorial activity carried out for sinister purposes. True, this word can mean simply "to come in between or intercept." Paul himself used it this way in Rom 5:20 to describe the unique purpose of the "intrusion" of the law into salvation history, "The law was added so that the trespass might increase." The Galatian context, however, points unmistakably to the unworthy motives of these infiltrators. This is spelled out in the third word Paul used to describe what they did: *kataskopeō*, "to spy on, to destroy in a sneaky manner." The word *kataskopē* is closely related to another Greek word, *episkopē*, "oversight," a word Paul used in a positive sense to describe pastoral authority in the governance of a New Testament congregation. Perhaps Paul was here making a deliberate contrast between the proper oversight of a godly pastor and the arrogant usurpation of ecclesiastical power the false brothers had assumed for themselves.

Drawing together the hints we have gained from studying this verse, we can summarize what we have learned about the false brothers in the following five propositions.

1. *The false brothers were not what they seemed to be.* Paul had not hesitated to address his Galatian readers as "brothers" (1:11), even though they had broken his heart by flirting with false doctrine and departing from the Spirit-filled life they had once known. All the more striking, then, is the designation "false brothers." There is no doubt that these people were members in good standing of the Jerusalem church. They were overly scrupulous and hyperzealous for the law and the Jewish traditions of food laws, feast days, and the like. In reality they were counterfeit believers, "sneaky, phony-Christians" (Cotton Patch) for whom the freedom and truth of the gospel meant nothing.[105] It is a sad but undeniable fact that in the visible church of Jesus Christ there are false brothers as well as true ones, sham Christians alongside genuine believers. The preaching of sound doctrine and the administration of remedial discipline are intended to safeguard the church against those who would subvert its fellowship either through theological compromise or ethical misconduct. This side of heaven, however, these remedies are not foolproof; thus the church ever faces anew the same danger Paul confronted long ago.

2. *The false brothers were secretive in their work of disruption.* The Geneva Bible rendered the first part of v. 4, "For all the false brethren that crept in." They crept into the church much as a poisonous snake would creep into a lovely garden. Their heresy was clandestine, underhanded, furtive. It

---

[105] Paul used the same term, "false brothers," in 2 Cor 11:26, where they appear as one of the items in his catalog of sufferings. In the same chapter (11:13) he spoke of "false apostles, deceitful workmen, masquerading as apostles of Christ."

has been suggested that their "spying" on the delegation from Antioch led them to discover the fact that Titus was uncircumcised. While this may be true, Paul's language describes not so much a group of prurient Peeping Toms as a whole pattern of trickery and deception. Behind the plotting of the false brothers, of course, was the work of the archdeceiver himself, the thief who comes to "steal, kill, and destroy" by enticing men and women to "climb in by some other way" than that provided by God in Jesus Christ (John 10:1-10).

3. *The false brothers carried out their destructive mission step-by-step.* Paul's depiction of the false brothers suggests that their fraudulent work was deliberately planned and carried out by degrees. First, they infiltrated the church, pretending to be true believers concerned with the furtherance of the gospel.[106] Their second step was to insinuate themselves further into the fellowship in order to "spy out" the gospel liberty of Gentile believers. As D. Guthrie put it, "They were acting like intelligence-agents building up a case against slackness over Jewish ritual requirements."[107] Having succeeded in their sneaky maneuvers, they then imposed their legalistic bondage on the church.

Satan still continues to worm his way into churches and institutions founded for godly purposes in order to subvert them from within step-by-step. A new chapel was recently dedicated at a theological school, an institution founded by a major evangelical denomination for the purpose of training ministers of the gospel. Since it was decided that it would be too chauvinistic to adorn this worship space with Christian symbols, a nearby closet was partitioned and assigned to hold the liturgical accoutrements of various world religions which would make use of that common space, the spectrum stretching from Buddhism to the New Age, with Christianity dutifully apportioned its spot as merely one acceptable tradition among many. At no particular time in the long history of that institution was the original commitment to historic Christian orthodoxy officially repudiated or abandoned. Only incrementally did that institution and many others lose touch with the roots that gave birth to and nurtured a lively faith for many generations. But step-by-step the Lord of hosts was replaced by a user-friendly, equal-opportunity God.

4. *The false brothers demonstrated the connection between false teach-*

---

[106] As W. Perkins perceptively noted: "Here then the foundation they lay of all their naughty dealing is their dissembling, which Paul here notes and condemns. On the contrary, our duty is to be indeed that which we profess ourselves to be: and to profess no more outwardly than we are inwardly: and to approve our hearts to God, for that which we profess before men" (*A Commentary on Galatians,* ed. G. T. Sheppard [New York: Pilgrim, 1989], 74).

[107] D. Guthrie, *Galatians*, NCB (Grand Rapids: Eerdmans, 1973), 80.

ing and unworthy behavior. Paul called his adversaries "false" primarily because the content of their teaching was antithetical to the truth of the gospel. However, by using the language of infiltration and deception to describe their activity in the Titus affair, Paul extended his indictment also to cover their motivations and methodology. Theology and ethics can never be divorced in an ultimate sense. It is true that one can champion orthodox theology out of selfish ambition and with loveless anger, forgetting the warning of T. S. Eliot in his play *Murder in the Cathedral*, "The last temptation is the greatest treason: to do the right deed for the wrong reason."[108] Conversely, one can also propagate false doctrine out of sincere conviction. Notable heretics have sometimes been known for their kind disposition and saintly demeanor. Such persons are all the more blinded by the god of this age to the corrupting impact of their false teaching. Despite these exceptions, there is an intrinsic linkage between unbelieving theology and unethical behavior. Sooner or later and in one way or another, doctrine that derives from some source other than Holy Scripture or a view of salvation that magnifies human effort at the expense of God's grace will manifest itself in unfaithful living and disreputable methods.

5. *The heretical trajectory of false teaching.* We cannot say for sure who the false brothers were who tried to compel Titus to be circumcised. There is good reason to identify them with the Judaistic intruders at Antioch mentioned in Acts 15 as well as the troublemakers Paul was opposing in Galatia. Some have argued for a direct line of continuity between the legalistic opponents Paul confronted in his day and the later Ebionites, a group of Jewish Christian heretics in the next century who denied the pre- existence of Christ and his virgin birth.[109] Eusebius said that the Ebionites "insisted on the complete observation of the law, and did not think that they would be saved by faith in Christ alone."[110] Not surprisingly, they disparaged Paul's writings and rejected him as an apostate from the law. The Ebionite movement represents a later stage of the Jewish Christian heresy Paul confronted in his day. However, there is clearly a line of progression from the former to the latter. Having abandoned a high doctrine of salvation by grace, a low Christology inevitably followed. A low view of sin invariably implied an attenuated doctrine of atonement. Once the work of Christ has been diminished, there is lit-

---

[108] T. S. Eliot, *The Complete Poems and Plays, 1909-1950* (New York: Harcourt, Brace and World, Inc., 1971), 196.

[109] J. D. G. Dunn, *Unity and Diversity in the New Testament* (Philadelphia: Westminster, 1977), 263: "The opponents of Paul whom we meet in Gal 2, 2 Cor 10–13, and Acts 21 are in the end of the day not easy to differentiate from the later Ebionites."

[110] Eusebius, *The Ecclesiastical History* (Cambridge: Harvard University Press, 1926), 261-63.

tle reason to insist on the full deity of his person.

Freedom and Truth (2:5).   **2:5**   The parenthetical paragraph on Titus and the false brothers concludes with the introduction of two concepts that will dominate the remainder of Galatians: freedom and truth. The under-handed efforts of the false brothers were aimed at subverting "the freedom we have in Christ Jesus," a phrase that sums up the central theme of the entire letter. To submit to their demands would have been to abrogate the *No Longer* of Christ's finished work on the cross and the present reality of the Holy Spirit, who had been poured out in the lives of the Galatian believers. Paul used the example of Titus to encourage the Galatians to resist the same kind of bondage that was being urged upon them by equally subversive inter-lopers who had intruded into their midst. Later in the letter he would reiterate this theme: "Stand firm, then, and do not let yourselves be burdened again by a yoke of slavery" (5:1).

We will return to the theme of freedom, for it is much misunderstood in our own day; Galatians, "the Magna Carta of Christian liberty," has much to teach us about it. Suffice it to say here that the freedom Paul celebrated was not the kind of privatized individualism that equates liberty with doctrinal license or moral laxity. The freedom for which Christ has set us free is a lib-erty grounded in "the truth of the gospel."

The phrase "the truth of the gospel" occurs both here in v. 5 and again in 2:14 and thus connects the two major sections of the chapter: the same issue was at stake in both the Jerusalem meeting and the Antioch incident. For Paul to have yielded to the illicit demands of those who tried to force circum-cision on Titus would have involved a betrayal of the very essence of the good news he had been commissioned to proclaim. Nothing less than this same truth also was at stake in the dissimulation of those who "were not act-ing in line with the truth of the gospel" after the Judaizers made their show at Antioch. As Lightfoot observed, the truth of the gospel means "the gospel in its integrity . . . the doctrine of grace."[111] Later in this chapter (2:15-21) Paul would spell out the implications of this cardinal tenet in terms of justi-fication by faith.

Verse 5 summarizes the Titus incident in terms of its immediate result and its long-range implications: Paul's stubborn resistance ("we did not give in to them for a moment") and the result this implied for the Galatians ("so that the truth of the gospel might remain with you"). Here again Paul's pastoral concern and love for his wayward children (cf. 4:19) was foremost in his mind. No doubt the whole episode with the false brothers was a painful one for him. At this pivotal stage in his missionary career, Paul would doubtless

---

[111] Lightfoot, *Galatians,* 107.

have won many influential friends and perhaps advanced his own personal standing with many in the Jerusalem church by pursuing a more temporizing approach. Moreover, it would have been easy to rationalize such a policy given Paul's own belief that circumcision itself was a thing indifferent. Yet Paul wisely saw through the subtle tricks and devices of the false brothers and stood firm against their ploy, not out of personal pique or concern for his own status but rather because of his desire to preserve the truth of the gospel "for you," that is, for the sake of all those who had been and would be liberated from the servitude of self-justification through the transforming power of God's grace. Later Paul would speak of the agonizing "pressure of my concern for all the churches. Who is weak, and I do not feel weak? Who is led into sin, and I do not inwardly burn?" (2 Cor 11:28-29).

Here we get an insight into Paul's understanding of the unity of the church, the body of Christ concretized in many local congregations but connected and interrelated to one another through the bond of the Holy Spirit. Thus what happened in Jerusalem was not an isolated incident; it directly affected the course of the gospel and the vitality of the church in Galatia and elsewhere. The same is true today. Wherever the church languishes, or the gospel is compromised, or scandal blemishes the witness of God's people, all Christians everywhere should feel, as Paul did, the empathy of a common burden and pain.

We are reminded in these verses of another important truth: the price of theological integrity and spiritual vitality, like that of liberty, is eternal vigilance. The gates of hell will never prevail against Christ's church, nor will the truth of the gospel ever be so obscured that God is left without a witness on the earth. However, throughout the history of the church there are discernible periods of apostasy and decline and examples of many visible congregations whose candlestick has been removed by the living Lord because of their infidelity to him.

At the time of the Reformation the doctrine of justification was again at stake in the confessional struggles of that age. Like Paul, Luther and the other Reformers refused to "budge the least little bit"[112] on such an essential point of the Christian faith. Against those who urged concessions in the interest of an outward peace, Luther explained the reasons for what we might call his sanctified stubbornness: "For the issue before us is grave and vital; it involves the death of the Son of God, who, by the will and command of the Father, became flesh, was crucified, and died for the sins of the world. If faith yields on this point, the death of the Son of God will be in vain. Then it is only a fable that Christ is the Savior of the world. Then God is a liar, for

---

[112] *LW* 26.90-91.

he has not lived up to his promises. Therefore our stubbornness on this issue is pious and holy; for by it we are striving to preserve the freedom we have in Christ Jesus and to keep the truth of the gospel. If we lose this, we lose God, Christ, all the promises, faith, righteousness, and eternal life."[113]

Looking back from the perspective of two thousand years of church history, it is hard for us to see what was so decisively at stake in the whole debate over circumcision. It appears more like a tempest in the teapot of late antiquity, an obscure issue no longer relevant to our present concerns. For one thing, Paul's position seems clearly to have won the day, not only with reference to the noncircumcision of Titus but also in the church at large. By the early second century, the Epistle of Barnabas could say that "the circumcision in which they [i.e., the Jews] trusted has been abolished."[114] With the spiritualization of circumcision and the growing Gentile majority in the church, the intensity of the circumcision debate in Paul's day became more and more remote.

Today it would seem ridiculous for anyone to insist that all non-Jewish males be circumcised before they could become Christians or unite with the church. However, this historical development should not blind us to the fact that while the terms of the debate have changed, Paul's struggle for Christian liberty and the truth of the gospel is far from being a dead issue. As Luther's comments show, human beings are forever trying to add something to God's completed work of salvation. It may be Jesus Christ and the mass, or Jesus Christ and water baptism, or Jesus Christ and good works, or Jesus Christ and a charismatic experience. Paul's argument is that nothing, absolutely nothing, can be mingled with Christ as a ground of our acceptance with God. Our hope is built on nothing less—and nothing more—than Jesus' blood and righteousness.

PAUL AND THE PILLARS (2:6-9). Having interrupted his narration of the Jerusalem meeting to describe the intrusion of the false brothers and the Titus test case, Paul now resumed the flow of his account he left off at the end of v. 2. In the Greek text vv. 6-10 constitute one long, convoluted sentence with several major ideas condensed into a difficult sequence of thought. True, these verses are not plagued with the kind of textual problems and syntactical breaks we encountered in the preceding verses.[115] However,

---

[113] Ibid.

[114] *Epistle of Barnabas* 9.4., *The Apostolic Fathers,* trans. K. Lake (Cambridge: Harvard University Press, 1912), 370-71.

[115] The only significant textual variant in this passage occurs at 2:9, where several witnesses in the Western tradition replaced the Aramaic name Κηφας with the more common Greek form Πετρος. Similar textual variance on the name of Peter is found in 2:11,14. See Metzger, *Textual Commentary,* 592-93.

some scholars have suggested that Paul may have been quoting from an official report or protocol of the conference with the Jerusalem church leaders since the vocabulary he used to describe this accord seems rather stylized and out of keeping with his normal usage.[116] Whether or not this is true, it is clear that Paul crafted this sentence with great care to provide both an accurate and memorable report of the agreement he reached at Jerusalem and a refutation of the slanderous charges made against him by his Galatian opponents. The words of H. D. Betz on this point are worth noting: "The enormous care which the author has apparently devoted to this section can only be explained if the event on which he reports constitutes the center of his 'statement of facts.' If this is the case, then there must be a relationship between the events at Jerusalem and the present crisis in Galatia. Then the present agitators and their theological position must in some way be related to the authorities in Jerusalem. This relationship probably existed not only in Paul's mind, but in the mind of the agitators and the Galatians as well."[117]

Negative Considerations (2:6). **2:6** Paul drew a sharp distinction between the false brothers he had just characterized in such a derogatory way (the sneaks and spies of vv. 3-5) and the church leaders with whom he had come to Jerusalem to confer. The former clearly were pseudo-Christians and minions of Satan; the latter, on the other hand, were respected leaders and dialogue partners with Paul in this strategic missionary summit.

On four occasions within the scope of seven verses Paul used a form of the verb *dokein,* "to seem," "to appear," to describe his interlocutors at the Jerusalem meeting. In v. 2 he referred to them simply as those who seemed or appeared, the word "leaders" being supplied by the NIV translators. Here in v. 6 these same persons are identified as "those who seemed to be important," or, more literally, those who seem to be something. At the end of the verse the earlier designation of 2:2 is repeated and simply rendered by the NIV as "those men."

In v. 9 we learn for the first time the identity of these persons. They were James, Peter, and John, who are further described as "those who seem to be pillars." Some scholars have argued that Paul's repeated use of this expression indicates a disparagement or slighting of the authority of these church leaders. On this view, Paul would have been saying that they were reputed to be pillars, they appeared to be something, they seemed to be real leaders, but in reality their appearances were deceiving; the reality did not match the

---

[116] Cf. E. Dinkler, "Der Brief an die Galater," *Verkündigung und Forschung* (1953-55), 182. For a discussion of this hypothesis, see Betz, *Galatians,* 96-98, and Longenecker, *Galatians,* 55-56.

[117] H. D. Betz, *Galatians,* Her (Philadelphia: Fortress, 1979), 92.

reputation.[118] However, the expression "those who seemed" need not carry such a derogatory connotation. It may simply mean, as the Jerusalem Bible renders it, "these people who are acknowledged leaders." In other words, Paul may simply have been using a common term of respect to refer to those leaders who were indeed men of high reputation and considered to be authorities among the believers in Jerusalem. Had Paul meant this term in a decidedly negative way, he would have undercut his own argument, namely, that he and the Jerusalem "pillars" were, after all, on the same team.

The basic drift of the passage points not to opposition or confrontation between Paul and these leader but rather to their fundamental unity and reciprocity in the shared task of fulfilling the Great Commission. At the same time, it must be admitted that this way of describing the Jerusalem authorities does convey a note of reticence and hesitation. In all likelihood this reflects the polemical context of the Galatian letter. Paul was fighting for his life, so to speak, against those emissaries from Jerusalem who had exalted the status and authority of the church leaders there at his own expense. Paul himself held these leaders, including certainly the three pillars of 2:9, in highest regard. He recognized the legitimacy and authority of those "who were apostles before I was" (1:17). Yet he stubbornly refused to subject the independence of his own apostolic calling to the exaggerated and illicit veneration of the Jerusalem leaders which his opponents were promoting. This idea was foremost in Paul's mind as he made three additional points about his relationship to the leaders in question.

1. *"Whatever they were makes no difference."* The key grammatical point here is the past tense of the verb: "whatever they were at one time." Ambrose thought he could discern a note of sarcasm in this expression, as though Paul had said, "May not I just as well object that they were poor illiterate men who knew nothing but how to fish, whereas I was well taught from my boyhood under my master Gamaliel. But I pass over all that because I know that there is no respect of persons with God."[119] Paul's opponents had accused him of being a johnny-come-lately to the Christian faith. The other leaders had known Jesus from the early days of his public ministry on earth.

---

[118] See, e.g., the comment of C. K. Barrett: "The fourfold use of *Dokein* is striking and can hardly be fortuitous. . . . Paul is not impressed by the reputation enjoyed by the Jerusalem authorities since God is able to see through human appearances to the secret of the heart. Reputations may be false; what matters is not what a man appears to be or is reputed to be (*dokei einai*), but what he really is. . . . We conclude therefore that the possibility is at least hinted that those who *dokousi stuloi einai* may in fact, in Paul's view, be no such thing" ("Paul and the 'Pillar' Apostles," *Studia Paulina*, Festschrift for Johannis De Zwaan [Haarlem: De Erven F. Bohn, 1953], 2-4).
[119] See CNTC 11.29.

Paul could not claim the kind of privileged status they enjoyed because he had no such comparable knowledge of Jesus' earthly life and work.

Paul did not dispute the facts in this charge, but he did vigorously deny the inference his opponents drew from them. Paul's opponents, like some modern biblical critics, preferred the "Jesus of history" to the "Christ of faith."[120] Paul refused to divorce the two. The risen Christ who appeared to him was none other than the same Jesus who walked the dusty roads of Galilee and died on a Roman cross outside the gates of Jerusalem. While Paul doubtless knew and cherished some of the early Christian traditions about Jesus' earthly life, his teachings, and his miracles, he refused to relegate Jesus to the realm of the past. For Paul there could no merely "historical" interest in Jesus. For Paul, Jesus could never be an absent savior whose words and deeds, like those of Socrates, could be scrutinized and analyzed with dispassionate interest. No! Jesus Christ is Victor, the ever-living King of the church and Lord of the future.

2. *God is not impressed with external credentials.* Paul here used an idiom that can be literally translated, "God does not accept the face of a man." To accept the face of someone is to evaluate that person on the basis of some outward appearance or external circumstance. It has been suggested that Paul was here drawing on the Stoic ideal of indifference (*adiaphora*) in order to relativize the authority of the seemingly great ones in Jerusalem.[121] However, the Old Testament itself is replete with the principle of divine impartiality: God looks not on the outward appearance but on the heart; God does not honor outward symbols of status and privilege but rather true obedience and devotion; God expects justice to be meted out evenly to the poor and great alike (cf. Ps 51:16-17; Amos 3:13-15; Lev 19:15).

In chap. 1 we saw how Paul described his apostolic calling in language that recalled the divine commissioning of the prophet Jeremiah. In the Greek version of the Old Testament, Jeremiah's call was accompanied with the words, "Do not be afraid of their faces" (Jer 1:8). A similar image was used in the calling of Ezekiel who was told that his face would be made strong and hard against the faces of his adversaries (Ezek 3:8). Perhaps Paul had these Old Testament precedents in mind in his rejection of the exaggerated veneration of the Jerusalem authorities by his Galatian opponents.

Behind Paul's language about "external appearance," we can hear the

---

[120] See the classic statement of this issue by M. Kähler, *The So-called Historical Jesus and the Historic Biblical Christ* (Philadelphia: Fortress, 1964).

[121] Cf. Betz, *Galatians*, 94-95. See also D. M. Hay, "Paul's Indifference to Authority," *JBL* 88 (1969): 36-44. On the word "face" in this context, see E. Lohse, "Πρόσωπον," *TDNT* 6.779-82.

echo of another kind of attack his opponents may well have launched against the Apostle to the Gentiles. According to church tradition, Paul was not much to look at physically: baldheaded, bowlegged, short of stature, and beset with bodily ailments (cf. the "thorn in the flesh"). We know that Paul's opponents on Corinth criticized his speaking ability and platform appearance—"unimpressive" was the word they used (2 Cor 10:10). The Galatian adversaries likely had picked up on the same theme and were using it to make insidious comparisons between Paul and the presumably good-looking, smooth-talking "pillars" of Jerusalem. Paul too respected these men; they were his companions, not his competitors, in the work of the Lord. But he could not countenance the kind of distorted devotion his opponents had lavished on these human leaders, for it bordered on idolatry and obscured the truth of the gospel to which both they and Paul were committed.[122]

3. *No Addition to Paul's Gospel.*   Those who seemed to be something, Paul said, added nothing. In the Greek the emphatic pronoun *emoi,* "to me," stands at the beginning of the sentence to stress again the theme Paul had been developing throughout the first two chapters of the epistle: the supernatural origin of his gospel and the independence of his apostolic calling. It has often been argued that Paul's defiant denial of any extra-Pauline additive to his message stands in flat contradiction to the account of the Jerusalem conference in Acts 15. The apostolic decree promulgated on that occasion appears in fact to add four specific items from which Gentile Christians were to abstain: food polluted by idols, sexual immorality, the meat of strangled animals, and blood (Acts 15:19-20). What is the meaning of these strictures, and how can they be squared with Paul's decisive statement here about "nothing added"? In Galatians, Paul said clearly, "Trust in Christ and you will be saved apart from keeping the works of the law." Did the Jerusalem church say in effect, "Trust in Christ and, while you may not have to be circumcised, there are certain ritual requirements it will be necessary for you to observe"?

One way around the apparent difficulty of reconciling Gal 2 and Acts 15 is to recognize that they are reports of two different meetings in Jerusalem rather than dual accounts of the same meeting. If, as we have suggested, Gal 2 refers to a private meeting Paul had with the Jerusalem authorities when he and Barnabas delivered a love gift from the Antiochene Christians (Acts

---

[122] Luther characterized these various offices and social positions as the *larvae* or "masks" of God. "God wants us to respect and acknowledge them as his creatures, which are a necessity for this life. But he does not want us to attribute divinity to them, that is, to fear and respect them in such a way that we trust them and forget him. . . . Therefore, let us make use of wine, clothing, possessions, gold, etc.; but let us not trust or glory in them. For we are to glory and trust in God alone; he alone is to be loved, feared, and honored" (*LW* 26.95-96).

11:27-39), then in all likelihood the Jerusalem Council mentioned in Acts 15 occurred after Paul had written Galatians. It represents a further development and a kind of definitive solution to the vexing problem of Gentile inclusion in the church which the earlier meeting had addressed in a more general way. If this is true, we can assume that the legalistic agitators did not accept the concordat arrived at between Paul and the "pillars" but continued to push even more aggressively for their own brand of Christianity, extending their influence to the far reaches of the Pauline mission field in Asia Minor. Because the private agreement of Gal 2 was not honored, and perhaps not widely known, it became necessary to clarify the whole matter in a public assembly with all the relevant parties present.

While this interpretation provides a plausible resolution of the historical relationship between the two accounts, does it really address the deeper theological question of something being "added" to Paul's law-free gospel? Are we to suppose that Paul, after preaching such an uncompromising doctrine of justification by faith apart from works of the law in Galatians, would turn around and willy-nilly endorse a more legalistic understanding of salvation that stood somewhere between his own grace-controlled theology and the extremist views of his Judaizing opponents? The incredibility of such a supposition has prompted many modern scholars to question the accuracy of Acts, to see it as a kind of historical fiction intended to paper over the disruptive differences between Paul and his opponents.[123]

Clearly Paul would never have agreed to anything being added to the gospel of grace as a requirement for salvation, even if it were only the ritual

---

[123] This perspective can fairly be called the dominant critical view in NT studies today. See the article by P. Vielhauer, "On the 'Paulinism' of Acts," *Studies in Luke-Acts,* ed. L. Keck and J. L. Martyn (Nashville: Abingdon, 1966), 33-50. G. Bornkamm reflects the general skepticism of the historical value of Luke's account of the Jerusalem Council: "As a source the account in Acts has no independent value. [It] proves to be a product of Luke's own, composed at a time when past conflicts had long been settled and now seem no more than insignificant attempts from without to disturb what was in principle unassailable, the primitive church's unity. Luke could not, of course, avoid regarding the meeting as an impressive manifestation of the one united church led by Jerusalem, and in consequence he drew up his account on the basis of his own later idealized view of the church and its history" (*Paul* [New York: Harper & Row, 1971], 32). On the specific issue of nothing "being added," G. Ebeling has noted: "The two accounts, which are mutually contradictory on this point, cannot be harmonized. Acts 15 shows that many thought that at some time the Gentile Christians had been placed under an obligation to observe a bare minimum of the regulations governing purity. . . . According to Paul, this is out of the question. In his own conduct he could, in fact, generally follow such requirements, but he could never have agreed to add this requirement of a minimal assimilation to the Jewish way of life as a universal condition to the gospel to be proclaimed among the Gentiles" (*Truth of the Gospel* [Philadelphia: Fortress, 1984], 102-3).

requirements of the Jewish tradition and not circumcision itself. As we have seen, Paul had no objection even to circumcision per se; it was a matter of indifference that might or might not be practiced in light of the exigencies of the Christian mission and one's circumstances in that effort. What he refused to submit to even for a moment was the notion that circumcision should be added on or appended to the perfectly complete atoning work of Christ on the cross as a condition for a right standing with God. That he did not interpret the apostolic decree of Acts 15 as implying this kind of salvific supererogation is clear not only from the fact that he personally delivered the decree to the churches he had founded but also that he continued to preach consistently a message of salvation by grace through faith alone. When the jailor in Philippi asked, "What must I do to be saved?" Paul did not reply, "Believe in the Lord Jesus and also abstain from eating nonkosher foods and you will be saved." His message was simply, "Believe in the Lord Jesus, and you will be saved" (Acts 16:4-5,30-31).

The Jerusalem Council has been described as "the most important event in the history of the primitive church."[124] From its placement at the center of Luke's narrative in Acts and from its influence on subsequent developments in the apostolic age, this assessment does not appear exaggerated. However, the four prohibitions for Gentile Christians agreed to at the Council were not intended as additives to the gospel of grace. The reason for asking Gentile believers to abide by the minimal purity regulations of the Jewish tradition was spelled out by James at the Council itself: "For Moses has been preached in every city from the earliest times and is read in the synagogues on every Sabbath" (Acts 15:21).

James knew there were many Jews in the cities where this decree was to be sent. From hearing the law of Moses read week by week in their synagogues, they had come "to abhor especially certain things in Gentile life; and in order to win them the Gentile disciples of Jesus ought to refrain from those things."[125] Thus, whether or not one equates Gal 2 with Acts 15, it is clear that Paul and the Jerusalem church leaders were not divided on the essence of the gospel. Paul had clearly set the gospel he preached to the Gentiles before them, and they had embraced it with no reservations. The specific prohibitions of the decree were a matter of missionary strategy, not theological doctrine. They were in fact an example of the "accommodation" principle Paul adopted as his own *modus operandi*—"to the Jews I became

---

[124] Bornkamm, *Paul*, 31.

[125] J. G. Machen, *Machen's Notes on Galatians* (New Jersey: Presbyterian & Reformed, 1977), 124.

like a Jew, to win the Jews" (1 Cor 9:20).[126]

POSITIVE AFFIRMATIONS (2:7-9). Having stated the negative considerations related to what did not happen at his meeting with the Jerusalem leaders, Paul turned abruptly ("on the contrary") to a description of the positive outcome of the summit. The climax of the meeting was the mutual recognition symbolized by the right hand of fellowship and the agreed-upon division of labor in the worldwide missionary enterprise. In describing how this decision came about, Paul focused on the one gospel shared by all the participants, the two apostles representing the two spheres of missionary outreach, and finally the three pillars whose affirmation of Paul and Barnabas were crucial to the positive outcome of the conference.

One Gospel. **2:7** Paul referred here to the positive reception given to his ministry by the Jerusalem leaders who "saw" and "recognized" (2:9) the unique role he had been called to play in expansion of the gospel message. The pluperfect tense of the verb "had been entrusted" (*pepisteumai*) is crucial for Paul's argument here. Paul was not entrusted with this assignment by the twelve apostles or by the Jerusalem church. What they recognized and affirmed was something that had already occurred in Paul's life, namely, the divine commissioning he had received from Christ himself.

In describing the content of this recognition, Paul used an expression found nowhere else in his writings. He had been entrusted with the "gospel of the uncircumcision" just as Peter had been assigned the "gospel of the circumcision." But how can this claim be squared with Paul's earlier insistence that there really is no "other" gospel except the distorted, counterfeit gospel of the false apostles that in reality is a "bad-news gospel" (*dysangelion*) because it can only lead to eternal condemnation in hell (1:8-9). What could Paul have meant when he spoke here of one gospel for the Gentiles and another gospel for the Jews? The misunderstanding of this expression has been the source of numerous errors in the history of biblical interpretation. Let us look briefly at three of these major misunderstandings.

1. *The Gnostic interpretation.* Many of the early Gnostic teachers

---

[126] See J. Polhill's helpful discussion of this issue. Polhill summarizes the four prohibitions in this way: "The decrees were a sort of minimal requirement placed on Gentile Christians in deference to the scruples of their Jewish brothers and sisters in Christ. . . James's remark could also be taken in another sense, which would fit the context well: there are Jews in every city who cherish the Torah. Gentile Christians should be sensitive to their scruples and not give them offence in these ritual matters, for they too may be reached with the gospel" (*Acts,* NAC [Nashville: Broadman, 1992], 328-38). Polhill interprets the well-known variation in the Western text where the prohibitions are reduced to the three mortal sins of idolatry, immorality, and murder, as a reflection of a later development in the life of the church when the issues of ritual purity raised by Jewish Christianity were no longer matters of vital concern.

latched on to Paul as their favorite apostle. In their view he had been entrusted with the "pneumatic" gospel of uncircumcision, while Peter was laden with the "psychic" gospel of the Jews. The radical dualism of Gnostic soteriology thus split the gospel into two irreconcilable parts, the true gospel being the secret *gnosis* conveyed by the secret writings and esoteric doctrines of the Gnostic teachers, the other gospel being the doctrine of Christ proclaimed by the orthodox Christian community and summarized in the Apostles' Creed.

2. *The Hegelian interpretation.* In the nineteenth century F. C. Baur and his disciples interpreted the history of the early church in terms of the Hegelian dialectic. According to this view, Peter and the church at Jerusalem represented the traditionalist pole in early Christianity (thesis), while Paul and his circle stood at the opposite progressivist pole (antithesis), with the emergence of an orthodox Christian consensus in the second century seen as a kind of convergence between the two (synthesis). Galatians 2:7 is a key text for imposing this kind of bifurcated grid onto New Testament history.

3. *The Ultradispensationalist interpretation.* Dispensationalism, in its extreme forms, is a way of dividing the history of salvation into various epochs, each with its own distinct requirement of salvation. According to one dispensationalist line of argument, the gospel of circumcision that Peter preached on the Day of Pentecost was in fact a message of grace plus works (e.g., "Repent and be baptized . . . for the forgiveness of your sins," Acts 2:38). However, with the calling of Paul, this message was superseded by the gospel of *sola gratia*. On this reading, Gal 2:7 reflects a transitional period between the dispensation of law under the old covenant and the new dispensation of sheer grace that was inaugurated primarily through the preaching of Paul.

Each of these erroneous interpretations stems from the basic mistake of failing to realize that Paul's expression denotes "a distinction in the sphere in which the gospel was to be preached, not a difference in the type of gospel."[127] The gospel Paul preached was identical with that proclaimed by the primitive church at Jerusalem. Just as the leaders of that community recognized him and his unique role in the spread of the gospel, so too he elsewhere associated himself with them as a witness to the resurrection and gave thanks to God for how he had worked mightily through all of his apostolic colleagues: "Whether, then, it was I or they, this is what we preached, and this is what you believed" (1 Cor 15:11).

---

[127] Lightfoot, *Galatians,* 109. Cf. Tertullian (*De praescriptione haereticorum,* 23): "Inter se distributionem officii ordinaverunt, non separationem evangelii, nec ut aliud alter sed ut aliis alter praedicarent."

Two apostles.　**2:8**　This verse provides evidence for the fact that early on Peter and Paul were commonly recognized as the two leading figures in the primitive church. In the Roman Catholic calendar of saints the two apostles share a common feast day, June 29, reflecting an ancient tradition that they were executed on the same day during the Neronian persecution at Rome (A.D. 64). If this tradition be true, then the lives of these two great missionary-apostles converged in the common witness of martyrdom although they had been led by divine providence to labor in different places and among diverse constituencies.[128]

After playing such a dominant role in the early chapters of Acts, Peter disappears from the stage after the Jerusalem Council in chap. 15 as the spotlight falls on Paul and his missionary journeys leading finally to Rome. We do know, of course, that Peter and Paul were together on another occasion at Antioch (2:11-14). We also know that Peter later referred to the writings of Paul, describing some of them as "hard to understand" (2 Pet 3:15-16). It seems likely that the two men crossed paths in other venues as well, including Corinth, where Paul acknowledged the existence of a fractious "Cephas party" (1 Cor 1:12; 9:4).

The decision to divide the missionary task of the church into two major thrusts, one led by Peter to the Jews and the other by Paul to the Gentiles, was a matter of practical necessity and wise stewardship. It would be a mistake to press the distinction too far, as though Peter and the apostles with him would be allowed to witness to Jews only, while Paul and Barnabas could speak to Gentiles only. "It was not that the apostles said, 'All right Paul, you preach the noncircumcision gospel to the Gentiles, but stay away from the Jews, that's our territory.' The language rather suggests that they said: 'Right, Paul, you go to the Gentiles with the noncircumcision gospel, and we will go to the Jews with the circumcision gospel.'"[129] We know in fact that the gospel had first broken through to the Gentiles through the witness of Peter in his preaching to the household of Cornelius. Likewise, Paul continued to preach to the Jews, finding in their synagogues many God-fearers and proselytes who responded to his message and who frequently became the beachhead of a new Christian community in their city. Thus the missionary strategy worked out at this conference should not be taken as a "religio-political restriction on either side."[130] It was a decision taken in the interest of the maximal fulfillment of the Great Commission that Jesus had given to the entire church.

---

[128] See O. Cullmann, *Peter: Disciple, Apostle, Martyr* (Philadelphia: Westminster, 1953).
[129] G. Howard, *Paul: Crisis in Galatia* (Cambridge: Cambridge University Press, 1979), 40.
[130] Ibid.

While the strategic division of labor between the two apostles was the practical outcome of the conference, its theological basis was rooted in a more fundamental recognition: the same God who was at work in the ministry of Peter was also at work in the ministry of Paul. The two apostles proclaimed the same gospel because they worshiped the same God. While every Christian has an important role to play in missions and evangelism, we must never forget that Jesus himself is the great Missionary, the Son who has been sent from the Father; and the Holy Spirit is the true Evangelist, the divine One who convicts and converts.

Three Pillars. **2:9** James, Peter, and John are here singled out and referred to as "those reputed to be pillars." Obviously they were the ones with whom Paul met privately to set forth his gospel (2:2) and with whom the missionary concordat was negotiated. This is the second mention of James in Galatians, he being earlier identified as "the Lord's brother" (1:19). John was the son of Zebedee, the apostle identified by tradition as the "beloved disciple" of the Fourth Gospel.

Various theories have been given about why they are here called "pillars." It is possible, of course, that Paul was merely using a common metaphorical expression to refer to individuals of strength and stability who are regarded as indispensable to the life of a certain community or institution. Even today we commonly speak of certain individuals as "pillars of the church." However, two important studies of this verse have been published that point to a more nuanced and more ambiguous meaning of the term "pillars."

In "Paul and the 'Pillar' Apostles,"[131] C. K. Barrett argued that the Christians in Jerusalem spoke of their leading apostles as "pillars" because of the role they believed they would occupy in the coming messianic age. In Act 15:16 James quoted a prophetic promise about God's plans to rebuild the tent of David, which had fallen down. The word translated "pillar" (*stulos*) can also mean "tent-pole." Elsewhere in the New Testament the apostles are spoken of as foundational in the building of the church and also as occupying a special role as judges when the Son of Man returns to earth to reign in glory and power (Eph 2:20-22; Matt 19:28). In Barrett's view this originally eschatological concept derived from Jewish apocalyptic thought had become domesticated and recast in a more this-worldly, institutional form. The three pillars of Gal 2:9 are singled out because of the dominant role they came to play as organizers and administrators in the early Jerusalem church. On the other hand, Paul's own apostolic self-understanding, as one "born out of due time" (1 Cor 15:8, KJV), is more in keeping with the primitive escha-

---

[131] C. K. Barrett,"Paul and the 'Pillar' Apostles," *Studia Paulina,* Festschrift for Johannis De Zwaan (Haarlem: De Erven F. Bohn, 1953), 2-4.

tological ideal of the apostle as a unique link between the end of the old world and the beginning of the new. "This is a lofty position," Barrett observes, "which is lowered rather than exalted, distorted rather than adorned, when the apostle's office is turned into one of ecclesiastical preeminence and administrative authority."[132]

Building on Barrett's argument and extending it further, R. D. Aus has argued that the three pillar apostles in this verse were deliberately selected by the Jerusalem church as an analog to the three patriarchs of the Old Testament, Abraham, Isaac, and Jacob. Just as God had established his original covenant with Israel through these great historic figures, so he had renewed that covenant through these three outstanding church leaders. According to Aus, Paul could never accept this view of his colleagues since it implied that they possessed at least a quasisoteriological function, a role utterly invalidated by the fact that right standing with God came through faith in Jesus Christ as sole and sufficient savior.[133] Perhaps some of Paul's opponents were guilty of the kind of exaggerated veneration of the pillar apostles and used it in their efforts to minimize the ministry of Paul. It is significant, however, that Paul did not challenge the fact that James, Peter, and John really were pillars of the church. Rather, his strategy was to accept this word as a term of respect but then to develop a compelling theological argument for justification by faith alone.[134]

The pillars of the Jerusalem church extended the right hand of fellowship to Paul and Barnabas. This was more than the sealing of a "gentleman's agreement" between two competing parties. The fellowship they shared, symbolized by the clasping of hands, was nothing less than the common life of the Holy Spirit. Significantly, the same word for fellowship (*koinonia*) recurs in the apostolic benediction at the end of 2 Cor (13:14): "May the grace of the Lord Jesus Christ, and the love of God, and the fellowship of the Holy Spirit be with you all." This accord happened because the Jerusalem authorities "recognized the grace given" to Paul. Scholars are divided as to whether this expression refers to the Christian attitude Paul displayed on this

---

[132] Ibid.

[133] R. D. Aus, "Three Pillars and Three Patriarchs: A Proposal Concerning Gal 2:9," *ZNW* 70 (1979): 252-61. Concerning the salvific merit of the patriarchs, Aus points out that in the rabbinic sources Abraham is portrayed as sitting at the entrance to Gehenna to prevent any circumcised Israelite from descending to that place of judgment. See also U.Wilckens, "Στῦλος," *TDNT* 7.732-36.

[134] Aus points out that "it is one of the ironies of early Christian history that the Apostle to the Gentiles, who now rejected all merit except that acquired through the atoning death of Christ on the cross, only a few decades after his death was labeled one of the 'greatest and most righteous pillars' (of the church)" ("Three Pillars," 261). The reference is to 1 Clem 5:2.

occasion or his statement of the gospel which he set before them at the beginning of the conference, or the evidence of his labors in the display of miraculous signs and the winning of new believers. Perhaps an element of all of
these was involved. But we should not forget that the outcome of the agreement involved a recognition of the doctrine of grace Paul preached as well
as a recognition of that grace in his own life and ministry.

CONCERN FOR THE POOR (2:10).   **2:10**   Verse 10 is added as a kind of
postscript to the agreement Paul and Barnabas had concluded in v. 9 with the
pillar apostles. "They agreed that we should go to the Gentiles, and they to
the Jews" only (*monon*), that is to say, but with this additional distinction,
that we, that is, Paul and Barnabas, should remember the poor. Clearly Paul
was not saying that this request was understood as something "added" either
as a *sine qua non* for the mutual recognition he had sought and won or as a
condition for the missionary collaboration just agreed upon. Such interpretations are ruled out by Paul's explicit denial in v. 6. Nor should we think of
the solicitation of this help as an obligation imposed by the mother church at
Jerusalem on the Gentile congregations. The Jerusalem leaders shared a
need; they did not issue a demand. Jewish synagogues of the diaspora regularly sent a temple tax to Jerusalem. However, the money sent by Gentile
churches to the Christians in Jerusalem was in the form of a love gift, not an
expected fee paid to ecclesiastical headquarters.[135]

Paul and Barnabas were asked to remember "the poor," a shorthand
expression for "the poor among the saints in Jerusalem" (Rom 15:26). From
its earliest days the Jerusalem church faced a condition of grinding poverty,
as can be seen from the dispute over widows receiving sufficient food and
the practice of sharing all things in common to care for the needy (Acts 4:32-
35; 6:1-4). A land of soil deprivation and poor irrigation, Judea was also hard
hit in this period of history by famine, war, and overpopulation. To all this
must be added the ravishing of the church in the persecutions directed by
Paul and other leaders of the Jewish religious community. So chronic was the
economic deprivation of the Judean Christians that they became known collectively as "the Poor."[136]

---

[135] For a different understanding see K. F. Nickle, *The Collection: A Study in Pauline Strategy* (Naperville: Allenson, 1966). On the importance of the collection in determining Pauline
chronology, see D. Georgi, *Die Geschichte der Kollekte des Paulus für Jerusalem* (Hamburg-
Bergstedt: Reich, 1965).

[136] See F. Hauck and E. Bammel, "Πτοχός," *TDNT* 6.885-915, and L. Keck, "The Poor
among the Saints in the New Testament," *ZNW* 56 (1965): 100-29. Πτοχός is also the word
Jesus used in the first beatitude, "Blessed are the poor in spirit, for theirs is the kingdom of
heaven" (Matt 5:3). In this sense the word "poor" connoted not only physical and economic
need but also spiritual dependence, humility, and piety. See the discussion in Bligh,
Galatians, 170-71, and in R. Longenecker, *Galatians*, WBC (Dallas: Word, 1990), 59-60. On
the problem of famine in the ancient Near East see B. P. Winter, "Secular and Christian
Responses to Corinthian Famines," *TynBul* 40 (1989): 86-106.

Paul indicated that the request to remember the poor was not received as an onerous burden but rather as an activity he had already begun and was eager to carry forward. We know from his later writings that Paul devoted much time and energy to the collection of a special offering for the Jerusalem Christians (Rom 15:25-33; 1 Cor 16:1-4; 2 Cor 8:9). The churches of Galatia were among the Pauline congregations who contributed to this relief effort. For Paul this effort was an important witness for Christian unity, a tangible way for Gentile Christians to express materially their appreciation for the great blessing in which they had shared spiritually with their brothers and sisters in Jerusalem. Paul himself carried this love gift to Jerusalem on his last visit to that city, during the course of which he was arrested and began the long journey to Rome that ended with his execution.[137]

SUMMARY. Despite their unevenness and grammatical awkwardness, the first ten verses of Gal 2 form a distinct literary unit within the historical argument Paul was unfolding in defense of his apostolicity. He told of a private meeting he held on his second postconversion visit to Jerusalem with the church leaders there. The purpose of the meeting was to set before these "pillars" the gospel he had been proclaiming for some years among the Gentiles. Upon hearing his testimony they fully endorsed his message and him. From Paul's perspective this meeting was a smashing success. Not only were the false brothers unsuccessful in their efforts to compel Titus to be circumcised, a move fiercely resisted by Paul, but, equally important, he and the Jerusalem authorities arrived at a common missionary strategy to enhance the task of world evangelization. Paul eagerly agreed with the request that this practical division of labor might not result in a loss of love between Jewish and Gentile Christians. Their unity in the faith and mutual care would be demonstrated by a love offering collected on behalf of the poor saints in Jerusalem.

The two key themes in this passage are the truth of the gospel and the unity of the church. In a moment of crisis Paul found it necessary to stand adamantly, stubbornly, uncompromisingly against the heretical doctrine and illicit demands of the false brothers. It would have been easy for Paul to say: "Oh, come now; circumcision is no big deal. Let's compromise on this

---

[137] J. Munck, among others, has interpreted the Pauline collection in terms of the apostle's eschatological hope for the conversion of Israel. It has been suggested that Paul may have hoped that his deliverance of a large collection from the Gentile churches would lead to the mass conversion of many Jews in Jerusalem thus preparing the way for the dawn of the messianic age. See J. Munck, *Paul and the Salvation of Mankind* (Richmond: John Knox, 1959), 282-308.

issue in order to save face and win friends here in Jerusalem." By such an approach he might well have spared himself a confrontation, but he would thereby have forfeited the cause of Christian freedom. At the same time, Paul greatly valued the unity of the church and sought to strengthen it in every way possible. We have much to learn from this episode in the life of the early church as we seek to be faithful stewards of the missionary challenge confronting us today.

First, we can develop a pattern of cooperation around the truth of the gospel. This is not an ecumenism of convenience; Paul could not work together with the false brothers, even though they claimed to be fellow Christians, because their theological position was antithetical to the gospel message itself. However, Paul was eager to work closely together with other Christian leaders who shared with him a common commitment to the good news of salvation through Jesus Christ.

Second, the apostles found it necessary to distribute the work of evangelization by a practical division of labor. Today 1.3 billion persons in the world have never heard the name of Jesus for the first time. Evangelical, Bible-believing Christians cannot afford to fight turf wars over comity agreements and missionary zones. No one person, ministry, missions agency, or denomination can cover all the necessary bases. We must be ready to stand together and work collaboratively with Great Commission Christians everywhere in the unfilled task of world evangelization.

Finally, the word about caring for the poor points to the dual necessity of both a propositional and an incarnational dimension to the life and mission of the church. Paul steadfastly refused to divorce conversion from discipleship. His mission included both a social and an evangelistic responsibility. If he gave priority to the latter over the former, it was because he sensed so keenly the eternal destiny of every person he met and shuddered to think of the dire consequences of spurning Christ's invitation to eternal life. Still, he knew, as we must, that the gospel he preached was addressed to living persons, soul and body, in all of their broken humanity and need for wholeness.

(2) The Incident at Antioch (2:11-21)

[11]When Peter came to Antioch, I opposed him to his face, because he was clearly in the wrong. [12]Before certain men came from James, he used to eat with the Gentiles. But when they arrived, he began to draw back and separate himself from the Gentiles because he was afraid of those who belonged to the circumcision group. [13]The other Jews joined him in his hypocrisy, so that by their hypocrisy even Barnabas was led astray.

[14]When I saw that they were not acting in line with the truth of the gospel, I said to Peter in front of them all, "You are a Jew, yet you live like a Gentile and

not like a Jew. How is it, then, that you force Gentiles to follow Jewish customs?

This passage concludes the historical narrative Paul began at 1:13. The whole section, with its twists and turns, its conflicts and controversies, serves as a kind of verification for the thesis Paul was expounding in these first two chapters: "The gospel I preached is not something that man made up" (1:11). In particular, it was important for him to clarify that his gospel was not derived from the Jerusalem church or from those who were apostles before him.

Thus after describing his conversion and calling (1:13-17), Paul referred to four episodes, the first three introduced by the adverb *epeita*, "then," "at that time," which together provide a kind of chronological alibi of whereabouts at critical junctures in his ministry and also trace his developing relationship with the Jerusalem church. His argument can be summarized this way: After God called me to be an apostle, I did not even go to Jerusalem for several years. When I finally did get there, it was only for a brief get-acquainted visit with Peter, although I also bumped into James, who was present as well. After this my preaching ministry took me far to the north, to Syria and Cilicia. During this time the Christians in Judea only received hearsay reports about my work although they praised the Lord for what he was doing through me. It was well over a dozen years later when I went to Jerusalem again, this time to talk with the leaders there about how we could collaborate most effectively in the work of world evangelization. James, Peter, and John stood shoulder to shoulder with me against some false brothers who intruded into our meeting and tried to force my young friend Titus, a Gentile convert, to be circumcised. Of course, I didn't budge an inch on this crucial issue, and when the dust had cleared, the pillar apostles and I sealed our agreement with a cordial embrace. Given this outcome, you can imagine how disappointed I was when Peter came to Antioch and engaged in a kind of behavior that I knew belied his own convictions. Not even Peter, great as he is, could resist the pressure to back away from his earlier commitment to Christian liberty. So I had to oppose him publicly because in this case, no less than during my second visit to Jerusalem, the truth of the gospel was at stake.

Unlike the first three episodes in this sequence, the Antioch incident is not introduced by the word *epeita* but rather by a more indeterminate adverbial expression, *hote,* "when." For this reason some scholars have suggested that the Antioch incident should be placed chronologically prior to the events narrated in 2:1-10.[138] While we cannot be dogmatic about the chronological

---

[138] See the discussion in Bruce, *Galatians,* 128-29; Betz, *Galatians,* 105; Longenecker, *Galatians,* 71. B. Reicke relates the Antioch incident to pressures arising within the Jewish Christian movement in Palestine as a result of the intensely nationalistic movement led by the Zealots. He thus equates Gal 2:11-14 with Acts 18:22-23 assuming, of course, a later dating for

placement of the Antioch incident, it seems clear that Paul intended us to understand it as a sequel to the events just described in 2:1-10. Assuming, as we have in this commentary, that those events parallel the famine visit of Acts 11, we can reconstruct the following sequence of events:

1. Antioch was first evangelized by some of those Christians scattered abroad as a result of the persecution occasioned by Stephen's death. Almost from the beginning the church at Antioch seems to have been a mixed congregation of completed Jews and converted Gentiles (Acts 11:19-21).

2. Barnabas and, through his agency, Paul became active in the leadership of the Antiochene church. The Lord blessed the church numerically and materially so that they were able to send a love gift to their fellow Christians in Judea during a time of famine. Paul and Barnabas delivered this gift in person and during this visit concluded an agreement with the pillar apostles concerning the evangelization of Jews and Gentiles (Acts 11:22-30; Gal 2:1-10).

3. Soon after their return from Jerusalem, Paul and Barnabas were set aside and sent forth from the church at Antioch on their "first missionary journey." On this trip they visited Cyprus and southern Asia Minor and founded the churches of Galatia (Acts 12:25–14:25).

4. Upon returning to Antioch, Paul and Barnabas reported to the church "all that God had done through them and how he had opened the door of faith to the Gentiles." They stayed in the city and continued to minister to the believers there for "a long time." During this sojourn the issue of table fellowship threatened to divide the church at Antioch, resulting in a public conflict between Peter and Paul (Acts 14:26-28; Gal 2:11-14).

5. The controversy at Antioch continued to fester and became exacerbated when other men from the church in Judea arrived and began insisting that there could be no salvation for Gentiles apart from circumcision. This matter, together with the lingering issue of table fellowship, prompted the church at Antioch to send Paul and Barnabas to Jerusalem to confer with the apostles and elders there concerning the whole complex of concerns. The result was the Jerusalem Council and the apostolic decree recorded by Luke in Acts 15.

Galatians. See his "Der Geschichtliche Hintergrund des Apostelkonzils und der Antiochia-Episode, Gal 2:1-14," *Studia Paulina, Festschrift for Johannis De Zwaan* (Haarlem: De Erven F. Bohn, 1953), 172-87. More recently D. R. Catchpole ("Paul, James and the Apostolic Decree," *NTS* 23 [1977]: 428-44) has argued that the issues that prompted the confrontation between Peter and Paul at Antioch correspond so exactly to the demands promulgated by the Jerusalem Council in Acts 15 that the emissaries from James were simply delivering the apostolic decree itself to Antioch. This hypothesis can only be held if one discounts the historical value of Acts, where Peter, Paul, and James were in agreement on the substance of the apostolic decree that in turn was delivered to the Gentile churches, not by a delegation from James but rather by Paul himself. For a summary and critique of the chronological issues see J. Dupont, "Pierre et Paul à Antioche et à Jérusalem," *Recherches de science religieuse* 45 (1957): 42-60, 225-39.

Thus the incident at Antioch was an important link between Paul's earlier agreement with the Jerusalem leaders on missionary strategy and the later settlement of the Jerusalem Council regarding the inclusion of Gentiles into the Christian fellowship. Paul included it here as the concluding linchpin in his historical narrative because doubtless the Galatians had been given another, distorted version of the same episode. In order to set the record straight, Paul gave here his side of the story and that for three reasons: first, to underscore again the independence of his apostolic calling; then, to highlight the truth of the gospel that even so great an apostle as Peter was pressured to compromise; and, finally, to warn the Galatians against succumbing to the same kind of legalistic appeal being pitched to them by Paul's detractors in Galatia.

THE PROBLEM: TABLE FELLOWSHIP (2:11-13). **2:11-13** Today the small, unimpressive town of Antakiya occupies the site of ancient Antioch, which in Paul's day was renowned for its architectural splendor and strategic political importance.[139] During the New Testament period Antioch was the third largest city in the Roman Empire and boasted a population of more than half a million. Its political importance derived from the fact that it served as the capital city of the Roman province of Syria. A series of Roman emperors beginning with Julius Caesar lavished attention and resources upon this "Rome of the East," furnishing it with theaters, aqueducts, public baths, a great basilica, and a famous colonnaded main street adorned with a marble pavement and vaulted stone roofs.[140]

The Jewish community formed a significant segment of the city's population, numbering some sixty-five thousand during the New Testament era. The Jews at Antioch were generally tolerated by the Roman overlords but were occasionally harassed and persecuted there as in other large cities throughout the empire. Less than ten years before the clash between Peter and Paul, the emperor Caligula (A.D. 37–41) had instigated a virulent attack against the Jews of Antioch. During this crisis many Jews were killed and

[139] See the helpful excursus "Antioch on the Orontes" in Longenecker, *Galatians,* 65-71. Antioch remained a major center of Christian life and theological ferment during the patristic period. In the sixth century it was beset by a major fire and two devastating earthquakes. In the next century it fell, along with Jerusalem and Alexandria, to the invading forces of Islam. On the crucial role of Antioch in the development of Christian theology, see D. S. Wallace-Hadrill, *Christian Antioch: A Study of Early Christian in the East* (Cambridge: Cambridge University Press, 1982). On the nature of early Christianity in Antioch, see the excellent study by R. Brown and J. Meier, *Antioch and Rome* (New York: Paulist, 1983).

[140] Longenecker describes the promenade that distinguished the main street of Antioch: "Some of the porticoes led to the entrances of public buildings; some to homes of the wealthy. Others protected shoppers and a variety of merchants whose booths were set up between the columns. There was, in fact, no other city in the world where one could walk for two miles in such splendor under porticoes" (*Galatians,* 67).

their synagogues burned. The same kind of harassment was being carried out in Palestine as well and may account for the overly zealous attitude of many Jewish Christians there concerning issues of circumcision, food laws, and adherence to worship in the temple.

Not surprisingly, Antioch became the home base for the first major expansion of Christianity outside of Palestine. Acts tells us that the fires of persecution ignited against the first believers in Jerusalem had the effect of multiplying rather than squelching their witness. "They that were scattered abroad went everywhere preaching the word" (Acts 8:4, KJV). Some of these "missionaries by necessity" came to Antioch, where they witnessed first to the Jews but then also to the Gentiles of that city, winning many of both groups to faith in Christ. When the church in Jerusalem got wind of the spiritual awakening in Antioch, they sent Barnabas, "a good man, full of the Holy Spirit and faith" (Acts 11:24), to assist the new believers there. Barnabas in turn traveled to Tarsus where he recruited Paul, whom he had earlier introduced to the Jerusalem church leaders, to join him in the work of the ministry at Antioch. Thus Barnabas was a kind of personal go-between reaching out to Paul and the Gentile believers on the one hand and to Peter, James, and the Jerusalem church on the other. This fact may explain, although not justify, his disappointing defection from Paul during the height of the Antioch incident.

Before analyzing the events that provoked the incident between Peter and Paul, it will be helpful to identify several features of early Antiochene Christianity during this time. The first point to be made is that we are dealing with an event that occurred early in the history of the church. True, the gospel had already broken through to the Gentiles, and Peter himself had played a crucial role in this development (cf. Acts 10). However, the full implications of how Jewish Christianity and Gentile Christianity could together form a spiritual symbiosis was yet to be realized. Not even Paul's agreement with the pillar apostles over respective missionary strategies for reaching Jews and Gentiles contemplated all of the difficult and dynamic possibilities of Jewish and Gentile believers living and worshiping together in a mixed congregation. The incident at Antioch was thus a necessary if painful stage in the development of a mature New Testament ecclesiology.

Furthermore, the church at Antioch existed in a missionary situation that called for a different contextual response from the one dictated by the Judean environment. Jerusalem was the epicenter for a kind of Jewish Christianity that was decisively shaped by the presence of the temple, strong Pharisaic and Zealot influences, and a Torah-centered interpretation of Christianity. Antioch, on the other hand, was far to the north of Jerusalem; it stood at the geographical and political crossroads of East and West, a veritable melting pot of diverse civilizations and cultures. Looking back from the distance of two millennia, we can see now that the controversy at Antioch was more than a clash between two apostles; it was a collision between two ways of being Christian. Thus it raises for us the ever-pressing question of the tension between Christ and culture.

Finally, it is not coincidental that believers in Jesus were first called Christians at Antioch. The designation of Palestinian believers as followers of "the Way" evidently was not transferred to the residents of Antioch who came to believe in Jesus as Messiah. Obviously a new reality had come into being with this new called-out company of Jews and Gentiles whose identity and self-definition centered neither in their Jewishness nor their Gentile character but rather in their common devotion to the one in whose name they shared a common meal. Thus they were called *Christianoi,* "the folks of Christ," originally perhaps a term of derogation that soon came to be owned with pride by believers everywhere because it was so evidently appropriate.

Without idealizing the early Antiochene church—the fact that its fellowship could be so easily disrupted is a sure sign that it was far from perfect—we can say that part of what was at stake in the quarrel over table fellowship was nothing less than the unity and indivisibility of the body of Christ. What does it mean when the people of God, redeemed by the blood of Christ and sealed by the Holy Spirit, cannot share together a common loaf at a single table? In looking at what led to the conflict, let us consider the issue of table fellowship, Peter's open-table practice, and his capitulation to pressure.

The Issue of Table Fellowship. In the fast-food culture of modern Western civilization, it is difficult to appreciate the religious significance ancient peoples associated with the simple act of eating. This was especially characteristic of Judaism, as Jeremias observed: "In Judaism table-fellowship means fellowship before God, for the eating of a piece of broken bread by everyone who shares in the meal brings out the fact that they all have a share in the blessing which the master of the house has spoken over the unbroken bread."[141]

Traditional Jewish strictures against the eating of unclean food covered a variety of culinary practices, such as the consumption of pork, eating food offered to idols, and partaking of meat from which the blood had not been properly drained in accordance with the law of Moses (cf. Lev 3:17; 7:26-27; 17:10-14), as well as partaking of food not properly tithed or eating a meal without observing the ritual cleansing of the hands. Devout Jews of this period would have remembered the story of Daniel and his friends, who

---

[141] J. Jeremias, *New Testament Theology: The Proclamation of Jesus* (London: SCM, 1971), 115, quoted in J. D. G. Dunn, "The Incident at Antioch (Gal 2:11-18)," *JSNT* 18 (1983):

refrained from partaking of the royal table of a Gentile king because of their religious scruples, as well as the story of the Maccabean revolt when many pious Israelites resisted foreign (i.e., Gentile) efforts to Hellenize their homeland. These determined patriots refused to eat any unclean food. "They welcomed death rather than defile themselves and profane the holy covenant, and so they died" (Dan 1:3-16; 1 Macc 1:62-63).

These traditions were pressed into even stricter requirements by the Pharisaic teachers who forbade any observant Jew from having table fellowship with anyone outside of the covenant of Israel. While some forms of social intercourse were permitted between observant Jews and Gentiles who were either proselytes or God-fearers, the importance of observing strict limits on table fellowship with those who observed the law in the way native-born Jews did was increasingly stressed in the period leading up to the Jewish revolt of A.D. 66–70.

It must be remembered that many of the Palestinian Jews who entered the Christian community there came like Paul from a strict Pharisaic background. However, unlike the apostle their conversion was neither so dramatic nor so thorough as to lead them to question the normative status of the law in their daily lives. Without questioning the sincerity of their convictions in every case, though Paul's description of the "false brothers" suggests that he saw them as sham Christians and not true believers, we can generally say that these people were Jews first and Christians second. If Gentiles were to be accepted into the Christian fellowship at all, it could only be on the basis of their strict adherence to the Mosaic law. For the strictest Jewish Christians this meant that all Gentile Christian males must be circumcised else they would lack the divinely ordained seal of the covenant; apparently for an even larger number of Jewish Christians, it meant that there could be no table fellowship with Gentile believers who disregarded the scrupulous observance of the dietary laws.

Peter's Open-Table Practice.   When Peter came to Antioch, he found Jewish and Gentile believers eating together at the same table, and he freely joined them in this practice. We do not know the precise nature of these meals, but they very likely included the *agapē,* or Christian love, feast, of which the celebration of the Lord's Supper was an integral part (cf. 1 Cor

---

12. I am indebted to Dunn for his thorough elucidation of the Antioch episode even if I cannot follow his conclusions at every point. For two important rejoinders to Dunn's analysis, see D. Cohn-Sherbok, "Some Reflections on James Dunn's 'The Incident at Antioch (Gal 2:11-18),'" *JSNT* 18 (1983): 68-74, and J. L. Houlden, "A Response to James D. Dunn," *JSNT* 18 (1983): 58-67. More recently E. P. Sanders has entered the debate. See his "Jewish Association with Gentiles and Gal. 2:11-14," in *The Conversation Continues: Studies in Paul and John in Honor of J. Louis Martyn*, ed. R. T. Fortna and B. Gaventa (Nashville: Abingdon, 1990).

11:20-21).[142] What is often not discussed in relation to this incident is the extent to which the Christians of Antioch were replicating the pattern of table fellowship practiced by Jesus himself.

God's revelatory presence in Jesus was manifested in numerous ways during his earthly ministry. Chief among these, however, was Jesus' celebration of the eschatological meal with tax collectors and sinners, a scandalous act that drew a critical response from the Pharisees and teachers of the law: "This man welcomes sinners and eats with them!" (Luke 15:2).[143] By freely associating with notorious sinners and Gentile "dogs" in the fellowship of a shared meal, Jesus was in effect announcing the arrival of the kingdom of God in his own person. By this radical act he also was saying that the basis of one's true standing before God could no longer be measured in terms of obedience to the law. Of far greater eternal significance was one's relationship with Jesus, the only person who perfectly fulfilled the law.[144]

Clearly Jesus' disciples did not immediately grasp the full implications of his practice of open table fellowship, nor did they easily imitate him in this regard. When in a vision Peter was told he could eat all kinds of animals, his reply reflected the typical practice of Jewish Christians at that time: "Surely not, Lord! I have never eaten anything impure or unclean" (Acts 10:14). This revelation was a critical breakthrough for Peter and for the early church. It meant that the door of salvation had been opened to the Gentiles and that a new basis of Christian fellowship had been established: not the observance of Jewish rituals but the outpouring of the Holy Spirit which, as Peter witnessed at the household of Cornelius, was given indiscriminately upon Jews and Gentiles alike. As Peter put it: "Can anyone keep these people from being baptized? They have received the Holy Spirit just as we have" (Acts 10:47).

---

[142] Dunn ("Incident at Antioch," 31-33) has suggested that the Gentile believers at Antioch were already observing the basic food laws prescribed by the Torah, such as abstention from pork and the koshered preparation of other meats. They would have done so out of consideration for the scruples of their Jewish brothers and sisters. In this case, what the "men from James" demanded was an even stricter observance of the Pharisaic traditions of ritual purity and the dietary laws. However, assuming, as we do in this commentary, that the apostolic decree of Act 15 was in some measure an answering solution to the incident at Antioch, it appears that there was no consensus among Gentile Christians concerning food regulations prior to this occasion. In any event, Jewish believers at Antioch were openly sharing meals with uncircumcised Gentiles, which itself violated the strictest Pharisaic interpretations.

[143] The Pharisaic critique of Jesus' table fellowship is a persistent theme in the Synoptic tradition (e.g., Mark 2:16; Matt 11:19/Luke 7:34), as is their condemnation of his practice of eating with unwashed hands (Mark 7:2-5; Luke 11:38).

[144] W. Pannenberg refers to Jesus' celebration of the eschatological meal as one aspect of "the proleptic element of Jesus' claim to authority" (*Jesus—God and Man* [Philadelphia: Westminster, 1974], 53-66).

What happened with Cornelius at Caesarea sent shock waves through the church at Jerusalem. Peter was confronted and given a stern reprimand: "You went into the house of uncircumcised men and ate with them" (Acts 11:3). Peter explained what had happened and concluded, "So if God gave them the same gift as he gave us, who believed in the Lord Jesus Christ, who was I to think that I could oppose God?" (Acts 11:17). Apparently the compelling logic of Peter's reply stilled the objections of his critics, but, as we know, this was only a temporary calm before the next storm.

After the Cornelius incident apparently nearly everyone agreed that Gentiles could indeed be saved. But on what basis salvation was to be extended to them and under what conditions table fellowship was to be shared with them, remained matters of deep division and controversy. However, the crucial point for understanding Peter's action at Antioch is the fact that he himself had pioneered the sharing of the gospel with the Gentiles and had already worked through to a position of Christian liberty concerning unbroken table-fellowship within the body of Christ.

Peter's Capitulation to Pressure.   Three interrelated events precipitated the confrontation between Peter and Paul: the arrival of the Jerusalem delegation, Peter's withdrawal from common table fellowship, and the wholesale defection of Barnabas and other Jewish Christians. Who were the "men from James" whose coming to Antioch put Peter under such pressure? We should not automatically equate these persons with the false brothers who earlier had clamored for Titus to be circumcised (2:3-4). A sinister reading would see these men as agents-provocateurs, a delegation from headquarters deliberately dispatched to Antioch to "spy out" Peter's libertarian tendencies just as earlier the false brothers had tried to undermine the gospel freedom of Titus.

This interpretation goes beyond the clear reading of the text. Nor should we assume that James had engineered their action as a ploy to win Peter back to a more hard-line position on Gentile fellowship.[145] Obviously these visitors felt some attachment to James, respected his leadership of the church in Jerusalem, and perhaps even carried letters of recommendation from him (cf. 2 Cor 3:1-3). Later at the Jerusalem Council, James, writing to the believers in Antioch, referred to certain persons who "went out from us without our authorization and disturbed you, troubling your minds by what they said" (Acts 15:24). It is likely then that the "men from James" were zealous

---

[145] Some manuscripts read τινα . . . ἦλθεν, "a certain one came," as opposed to the plural τινας . . . ἦλθον, reinforcing the idea that James may have delegated a single troubleshooter to deal with the problem at Antioch. Although the plural form is the preferred reading, neither variant lends credence to a personal involvement of James in the matter. See Metzger, *Textual Commentary,* 592-93.

members of the ultra-right wing party within the Palestinian movement.

The "men from James" were shocked when they saw how freely Peter was sharing table fellowship with uncircumcised believers in evident disregard for the usual practice of Jewish Christians at home. We do not know what, if anything, they said to him about this matter; perhaps their very presence was sufficiently intimidating to lead Peter to withdraw from eating with the Gentile believers. In the Greek text the verbs "began to draw back" and "separate himself" are in the imperfect tense, indicating that Peter's action may have happened gradually as, little by little, he reacted to the increasing pressures of the Jerusalem visitors until finally "he drew back and began to hold aloof" (NEB). As if Peter's pressured withdrawal from table fellowship with Gentile believers was not enough, all of the other Jewish Christians at Antioch were swept along with him in this shameful playacting.

At this point Paul inserted what is perhaps the most poignant line in the entire epistle, "By their hypocrisy even Barnabas was led astray." *Even Barnabas!* Paul's sorrow and embarrassment over the defection of his close friend and colleague was still a painful memory as he related it to the Galatians. Barnabas had introduced Paul to the Jerusalem believers when others in that city thought he was still a persecutor in disguise. It was Barnabas who had sought out Paul in Tarsus and persuaded him to become a part of the ministry team at Antioch. Barnabas too had stood with Paul in Jerusalem when he defended the liberty of the gospel against the false brothers. And, of course, Barnabas had accompanied Paul on the first missionary journey when many Gentile believers were won to Christ and the churches of Galatia themselves were established. For "even Barnabas" to be carried away was a severe blow![146]

Some commentators have related Barnabas's defection at Antioch to their "sharp disagreement" over John Mark at the beginning of the second missionary journey (cf. Acts 15:36-41). While there may well have been some lingering friction between the two men following the Antioch incident, there is no reason to confuse the two events. We have good evidence that the rupture was not permanent: Barnabas again stood with Paul at the Jerusalem Council, and Paul later associated himself with Barnabas in a positive manner (Acts 15; 1 Cor 9:5-6). Still, the fact that "even Barnabas" could be pres-

---

[146] R. Bauckham has argued that the minor role Barnabas occupies in Galatians reflects Paul's severe disappointment over his behavior in the crisis in Antioch. The fact that Paul did not explicitly appeal to Barnabas in his defense of Gentile freedom from the law is said to imply a continuing rift between the two cofounders of the Galatian congregations ("Barnabas and Galatians," *JSNT* 2 [1979]: 61-70). See also G. M. Burge, "Barnabas," *DPL,* 66-67, and F. F. Bruce, *Men and Movements in the Primitive Church: Studies in Early Non-Pauline Christianity* (Exeter: Paternoster, 1979), 49-85.

sured to yield over the issue of table fellowship indicates both the strong influence exerted by the legalistic Jewish Christians and the loneliness of Paul's resistance to their demands.

THE PROTEST: TWO APOSTLES COLLIDE (2:14). **2:14** Verse 14 is an extended explanation of what Paul had already stated as the climax of the Antioch incident: he opposed Peter to his face because Peter was clearly in the wrong. Various motivations have been suggested for Peter's withdrawal from table fellowship with the Gentile Christians at Antioch. Paul said that Peter was "afraid of those who belonged to the circumcision group." But what was the nature of this fear? Was Peter reacting to the fact that Jewish Christians in Judea were scandalized by his open fellowship with Gentile believers elsewhere so that his position as a leading "pillar" of the Christian community back home was in jeopardy? Was he afraid if he would not be able to fulfill his assigned role as "apostle to the Jews" that he sat so loose by the obligations to Torah obedience required by devout Jews? Did the "men from James" bring news of an insurgent Jewish nationalism, a Zealot-led movement that placed great pressure on Jewish Christians to follow strictly the defining traits of Judaism? If so, then word of Peter's public consorting with Gentiles could have triggered an act of reprisal either against him personally or against the Jewish Christian communities of Palestine.

Peter may have used these and other excuses to justify what might well seem to an outside observer to be a reasonable course of action. However, we do well to listen to Calvin's analysis at this point: "It is foolish to defend what the Holy Spirit has condemned by the mouth of Paul. This was no human business matter but involved the purity of the gospel."[147]

Paul used two very strong words in his public condemnation of Peter and the other Jewish Christians at Antioch who had separated from their Gentile brothers and sisters: playacting and crooked walking. The word in v. 13 translated "hypocrisy" (*hypokrisis*) comes from the world of the theater, where it refers to the act of wearing a mask or playing a part in a drama. By negative transference it came to mean pretense, insincerity, acting in a fashion that belies one's true convictions.[148] Here is the brunt of Paul's charge against Peter: He should have known better! Peter was not guilty of an honest mistake, nor was there any evidence that he had changed his mind about the extension of salvation to the Gentiles, a truth revealed to him by a special revelation. Peter had donned a mask of pretense; he was shamefully acting a part contrary to his own true convictions. What Paul rebuked was the inconsistency of his conduct.

---

[147] See Calvin, CNTC 11.36.
[148] See the article by U. Wilckens, "ὑποκριτής" *TDNT* 8.565.

O. Cullmann has observed that Peter's conduct in this situation was a throwback to his earlier pattern of vacillation and denial that marked his character during the earthly ministry of Jesus.[149] On three separate occasions Peter fell into serious trouble when his devotion to Christ was distracted by other factors. First, when he took his eyes off Jesus and began to look at the circumstances of the storm, he started to sink into the lake; then, when he took his eyes off Jesus and started to focus on himself, in a moment of pressure he denied that he had ever known the Lord; and, finally, when he took his eyes off Jesus and began to look at other people, notably John, Christ had to recall him to the first imperative of discipleship, "Follow me!" (Matt 14:22-36; Luke 22:54-62; John 21:19-23). Here again at Antioch the rock man had become a wave. Again, he took his eyes off Jesus and became obsessed with external circumstances, his own personal position, and other people ("the men from James"). All of this led to the disastrous result of Peter's "not acting in line with the truth of the gospel."

The word translated "acting in line with," *orthopodein,* literally means "to walk with straight feet," thus to "walk a straight course." Transliterating this word into a modern medical term, we could render Paul's statement thus: "But when I saw that they were not walking orthopedically, that is, in a straightforward, unwavering, and sincere way."[150] Elsewhere in his letters Paul had much to say about the importance of the Christian's "walk" (Eph 4:1,17; Col 1:10; 2:6; Rom 13:13). Later in Galatians he also would admonish his readers to "keep in step with the Spirit" (Gal 5:25). Like Peter before Antioch, they too were "running a good race" until someone "cut in" on them and threw them into confusion (Gal 5:7-10).

The expression "when I saw" gives the impression that Paul was caught off guard by the defection of Peter, Barnabas, and the other Jewish Christians at Antioch. This may indicate that he was out of the city on a preaching mission when the men from James first arrived so that he was not present to argue the other side of the case when their intimidation began. Had he left a congregation where Jews and Gentiles were fully integrated in common worship and shared fellowship only to return to a church where the old pattern of segregation had been reintroduced?[151]

---

[149] O. Cullmann, *Peter: Disciple, Apostle, Martyr,* 50-53. Cf. also G. S. Bishop, *Grace and Galatians* (Swengel, Pa.: Reiner Publications, 1968), 30-33.

[150] *Wuest's Word Studies,* 1:74; G. D. Kilpatrick, "Gal 2:14 *orthopodousin*," *Neutestamentliche Studien für Rudolf Bultmann* (Berlin: Tüpelmann, 1957), 269-74. This word is found nowhere else in the NT, although a similar expression occurs in 2 Tim 2:15: ὀρθοτομοῦντα τὸν λόγον τῆς ἀληθείας, "Be straightforward in your proclamation of the truth" (NEB).

[151] Clarence Jordan's paraphrase of this passage, written during the struggle for civil rights, makes an explicit analogy to the contemporary issue: "But in spite of all of this, when Rock

2:14

In any event, Paul exploded with righteous indignation, calling Peter to account in front of the whole assembly. It seems likely that Paul had first remonstrated with Peter privately in accordance with Jesus' instruction on church discipline in Matt 18:15-20. If so, we may assume that this personal appeal was to no avail. Paul had to confront Peter publicly because the issue at stake was not merely a personality clash between the two apostles but rather the truth of the gospel and the unity of the church. What Peter lacked, Paul possessed in full measure: the courage of his convictions. Earlier, in Jerusalem, Paul had sought a private conference with the pillar apostles to prevent the least appearance of disharmony among the leaders of the church. Here, however, he did not shrink from a public confrontation with the most prominent pillar of them all because to have done so would have involved the compromise of his own conscience and the approval by connivance of a deep and permanent rift within the body of Christ. No one should appeal to Paul's example here as a pretext for disrupting the peace of any congregation or denomination over trivial theological issues or personality quirks. But neither should anyone take comfort in Peter's dissembling action when we are really confronted with a situation that calls for a clear, uncompromising stand for the faith once delivered.

But was the gospel really at stake in this situation? Could not Peter have appealed to Paul's own principle of accommodation (1 Cor 9:19-23), according to which Christians willingly forego the exercise of their liberty out of respect for the scruples of their "weaker" brothers and sisters? On the specific issue of eating food that had been sacrificed to idols, Paul declared that while he himself had a clear conscience about partaking of this kind of cuisine, he would refrain from doing so if his eating became a stumbling block to other believers whose consciences were less well informed (1 Cor 8). Is there a contradiction between Paul's bold stand in Gal 2 and his concessive appeal in 1 Cor 8?

To answer this question, we must keep in mind that the issue at Antioch was not so much *what* one ate as *with whom* one ate. Just as circumcision was neither good nor evil in itself, the eating of nonkosher foods carries neither an intrinsically positive nor an intrinsically negative value for the believer. However, when either issue is presented in such a way that it undercuts the very basis of the Christian life, that is, the doctrine of salvation by grace

---

came to Albany, I had to rebuke him to his face, because he was clearly in error. For, before the committee appointed by Jim arrived, he was eating with Negroes. But when they came, he shrank back and segregated himself because he was afraid of the whites. He even got the rest of the white liberals to play the hypocrite with him, so that even Barney was carried away by their hypocrisy" (Cotton Patch, 96).

alone, then it can no longer be treated as a thing indifferent. The principle of accommodation cannot be stretched to include solidarity with a practice or belief that stands in contradiction to the gospel itself.

When Paul spoke of becoming as a weak one to the weak ones in order that he might win some, it is imperative to understand what he meant by such a winning. As Ebeling has put it so well: "To win them for the gospel means to bring the gospel to them, to deliver them, to see that they are changed from what they were to what they are. To strengthen the Jews in their devotion to the law through accommodation, to strengthen the Gentiles only in their libertinism (cf. Rom 1:18ff.) or their soaring speculations, to strengthen the weak, only in a weakness that they wrongly consider strength—that would win nothing."[152] Thus what was implicit in Peter's withdrawal from table fellowship with Gentile believers was not simply a laudable honoring of the scruples of the "weaker" Jewish Christians but rather the imposition of an alien theology of salvation, one that reintroduced the very bondage from which Christ had died to make us free.

Though the circumstances were different, what was at stake in Antioch was the same principle for which Paul had contended against the false brothers in Jerusalem: God redeems Jews and Gentiles alike on precisely the same terms, namely, personal faith in Jesus Christ and him alone. That Peter's vacillating and expedient behavior was a denial of this basic gospel truth is evident from two key words Paul used in this passage. By his withdrawal from table fellowship, Paul averred, Peter would "force Gentiles to follow Jewish customs." The word "force" or "compel" (*anangkazō*) is precisely the same term Paul used earlier in this chapter (2:3) to describe the demands of the false brothers for Titus's circumcision.[153]

The second word that indicates that the matter in Antioch was more than a simple controversy about social graces is the verb *Ioudaizein*, "to become a Jew," "to turn Jew," the full force of which becomes evident in the following verse when he contrasted those who are Jews by birth from Gentile sinners (2:15). The NIV renders the term "Gentile sinners" in quotations, indicating that it was likely a technical term in the Antiochene debate over

---

[152] Ebeling, *Truth of the Gospel,* 114-15.

[153] Betz points out that this word was prominent in the Maccabean period as a description of compulsory hellenization imposed upon the Jewish people (cf. 1 Macc 2:25; 2 Macc 6:1, 7, 18; 4 Macc 5:2, 27; *Galatians,* 112). If indeed Peter had succumbed to pressures originated in the context of zealous Jewish nationalism in Palestine, then there is great irony in Paul's use of this particular term. By forcing the Gentile believers to "Judaize," Peter is guilty of a kind of reverse discrimination: what the enemies of Israel did and were still doing to the Jewish people, Peter was in effect doing to his Gentile brothers and sisters in Christ. Ἰουδαΐζειν is a hapax legomenon in the NT.

table fellowship. What was so insidious in the separatism of Peter and his associates was the fact that they were acting as if their Gentile Christian brothers and sisters were still sinners while they, because of their ritual purity and obedience of the law, stood in a different, more favorable relationship to God. Yet Jews and Gentiles alike had been redeemed by the same Christ, regenerated by the same Holy Spirit, and made partakers of the same fellowship. Who then could dare say they should not come to the same table to partake of the same Lord's Supper just as already they had been baptized into the name of the same one triune God? Who shall separate us from the love of Christ, or from one another? It is God who justifies . . . it is Christ Jesus who died (Rom 8:33-34).[154]

What was the upshot of the Antioch incident? It is significant that Paul did not say how the drama was resolved but passed, almost imperceptibly, from his rebuke of Peter into his theological address to the Galatians. Because of this silence, many scholars, beginning with F. C. Baur and the Tübingen critics of the nineteenth century, have assumed that the Antioch incident marked a permanent fissure between the two great apostles leading to an equally polarized church divided into Petrine and Pauline branches. However, from Peter's stance at the Jerusalem Council of Acts 15 and, even more, from the content of the two letters he contributed to the New Testament canon, we have reason to believe that there was no permanent rupture with Pauline Christianity. Peter had fallen before and repented before, and we may assume that a similar pattern of remorse and renewal followed Paul's stern rebuke.

Yet the question persists: If Paul "won" at Antioch, why did he not mention it in Galatians? It could be, of course, that his "victory," if that it was, was not yet apparent or complete when he wrote Galatians, assuming that the letter should be dated on the eve of the Jerusalem Council. Or he may simply

---

[154] See Dunn, who comments perceptively on this passage: "If Gentiles are 'in Christ' (v. 17) and yet still 'sinners,' then we who are with them 'in Christ' are thereby found to be sinners too, and Christ has become an 'agent of sin' (*hamartias diakonos*). But that cannot be right (v. 17). I cannot live my life 'in Christ' and at the same time give the law the significance it had when I was a Pharisee, for the law neither gives nor expresses life in Christ but simply shows me up as a transgressor" ("Incident at Antioch," 36). Dunn further suggests that the Antioch episode was a breakthrough for Paul because through it he came to see for the first time the implications of justification by faith not simply as the basis of conversion but as a regulative principle for the whole of the believer's life. While it is surely likely that his painful conflict with Peter reinforced this doctrinal principle as a nonnegotiable fundamental of the apostle's life and ministry, the whole issue arose in the first place because justification by faith was already the theological lodestar in Paul's body of divinity. On this controverted issue in Pauline theology, see Dunn's, "The New Perspective on Paul," *BJRL* 65 (1983): 95-122, and the magisterial study by P. Stuhlmacher, *Gerechtigkeit Gottes bei Paulus* (Göttingen: Vandenhoeck & Ruprecht, 1966).

have refrained from gloating in victory out of deference for Peter, preferring to "restore him gently" (6:1) rather than exacerbate the tensions being exploited by his Galatian opponents. G. Howard has given this apt summary of the outcome: "The surprising thing is not that [Peter] wavered in his understanding of the Christian faith on this occasion but that such waverings were apparently confined to this general time-period and in fact amounted to so little. You hear of no other such crisis in the church, and from all appearances Paul's one public rebuke of Peter was enough eventually to bring him around."[155]

Beyond all of these considerations, we must remember that the Antioch incident was never merely a personality clash or power play between these two great leaders. From first to last the issue was theological, and Paul treated it as such. That Paul's historical narrative flows so smoothly into his theological exposition indicates that the two, history and theology, were inextricably bound together in Paul's defense of the gospel. In summary, what lessons can we learn for today from this vivid account of Paul's confrontation with Peter at Antioch? Let us look at three practical truths we can apply from this passage to the life of the church today.

1. *Great leaders can fall.* There was every reason for Peter to resist the pressure to compromise his convictions in the face of pressure. He had been in the intimate circle of Jesus' closest disciples. He was a primary witness to the resurrection. He had witnessed the outpouring of the Holy Spirit on the Day of Pentecost. He had even been used by God as the instrument of evangelistic breakthrough to the Gentiles. Yet in a moment of crisis he failed and by the force of his example led many others astray as well. Paul's warning to the Galatians is clear: what happened to Peter can happen to you! He "that thinketh he standeth, take heed lest he fall" (1 Cor 10:12, KJV). In recent years the church of Jesus Christ has witnessed the downfall of many greatly gifted and highly visible leaders. Their lapse is not only a matter of personal tragedy but also a blight on the body of Christ. May God help us to test every message we hear by the touchstone of his Word and save us from exalting any human leader above measure.

2. *God's grace means no second-class Christians.* The withdrawal of Jewish believers from table companionship with their Gentile brothers and sisters precipitated a serious breach within the Antiochene church. Throughout the history of the church, and especially in missionary settings, the sharing of a simple meal has often symbolized the unity and fellowship implied in the message of salvation through Christ. When William Carey and his associates carried the gospel message to India, they confronted a situation

---

[155] Howard, *Paul: Crisis in Galatia,* 43.

very similar to that reflected in this passage. From the beginning Carey felt that the holding of caste was incompatible with faith in Christ. He thus refused to baptize anyone who continued to maintain caste distinctions that included the refusal to share together in a common meal. Yet for a Hindu to eat with a European in that culture meant the foreswearing of his caste. When Carey's first Hindu convert, a man named Krishna Pal, became a Christian and decided to break caste by taking dinner with the missionaries, William Ward, one of Carey's fellow workers, exclaimed in words that breathe the spirit of the New Testament: "Thus the door of faith is open to the Gentiles. Who shall shut it? The chain of caste is broken; who shall mend it?"[156] Racism of any brand in any culture is incompatible with the truth of the gospel. Later in Galatians (3:26-29) Paul would spell out the implications of Christian unity in terms of the promise of grace fulfilled in Jesus Christ. Any religious system or theology that denies this truth stands in opposition to the "new creation" God is bringing into being, the body of Christ based not on caste, color, or social condition but on grace alone.

3. *Standing for the gospel can be a lonely business.* When the crisis became more intense, Barnabas sided with Peter in the confrontation with Paul. The Apostle to the Gentiles stood alone on behalf of the gospel. In the fourth century Athanasius stood *contra mundum,* "against the world," when the deity of Christ was at stake in the Arian struggle. In the sixteenth century Luther stood alone at the Diet of Worms because, as he said, his conscience was captive to the Word of God. In victorian England Charles Haddon Spurgeon stood alone during the Downgrade Controversy to protest "the boiling mud-showers of modern heresy" that were beginning to descend on Baptist life in his day.[157] Thank God for these brave warriors of the faith who did not flinch in the hour of temptation, who refused to flirt with the false gods of their age and thus have passed on to us a goodly heritage of courage and faith.

EXCURSUS 2: LUTHER AND CALVIN ON PETER AND PAUL. Galatians, like Romans, is a book that has created shock waves throughout the history of the church. As is well known, Martin Luther had a love affair with Galatians, referring to it as "my own epistle to which I have plighted my troth; my Katie von Bora," Katie being his beloved wife.[158] Near the end of his life Luther commented on plans to publish a complete edition of his writings in Latin: "If they took my advice, they would print only the books containing doc-

---

[156] Quoted in T. George, *Faithful Witness: The Life and Mission of William Carey* (London: InterVarsity, 1991), 130-31.
[157] C. H. Spurgeon, *Autobiography* (London: Passmore and Alabaster, 1900), 4:261-62.
[158] WA 40/1, 2. See the discussion in Longenecker, *Galatians,* lii-lvii.

trine, like Galatians."[159] Luther, in fact, lectured repeatedly on Galatians and published two major commentaries on the epistle: one in 1519, just on the eve of his break with Rome, and the other in 1535 (revised in 1538), a work that reflects years of struggle and hard-won victories for the doctrine of justification by faith. Concerning this important book, H. D. Betz has written: "Luther's commentary is more than a scholarly commentary upon Galatians. It is a recreation of Galatians in the sixteenth century. Luther speaks as Paul would have spoken had he lived at the time when Luther gave his lectures."[160] Luther's younger contemporary, John Calvin, was, if anything, a more penetrating biblical scholar than even the great German Reformer. He himself was not unaware of his great abilities as can be seen from this comment from the dedicatory epistle to his commentary on Galatians, published at Geneva in 1548: "Of my commentaries I shall only say that perhaps they contain more than it would be modest in me to acknowledge."[161] Both Luther and Calvin dealt at length with the Antioch episode, applying the lessons learned therefrom to their own pastoral and confessional contexts in the sixteenth century.

In the Galatians commentaries of Luther and Calvin we can hear the echo of a major patristic dispute over Paul's treatment of Peter at Antioch. Jerome, following Origen, proposed the theory that Peter merely pretended to compromise his convictions in order to give Paul the opportunity to correct him in a feigned, well-staged pretense of his own. This interpretation, which was followed by Erasmus in the sixteenth century, derived from a dubious reading of the Greek words *kata prosopon,* "I opposed him to his face." Jerome read this to mean "I opposed him to outward appearances," that is, I made a show of opposing him, presumably in order to turn the situation into an occasion for clearly articulating the doctrine of justification. Augustine disagreed strongly with Jerome's interpretation of this incident, noting that Paul had put himself under an oath (1:20) to assure the accuracy of his historical narration. In the period of the Reformation, Erasmus and other Roman Catholic commentators followed Jerome on this point while Luther and Calvin echoed Augustine.

Behind the flimsy exegesis of Jerome was the dreaded shock of believing that this passage could mean what it says, namely, that so weighty an apostle as Peter could be upbraided so brazenly—even by another apostle! In Luther's day Peter was even more highly regarded, not only as a pillar apostle but also as the first pope, the visible head of Christ's church on earth. But Luther insisted that even an apostle could err. In the same year in which his first com-

---

[159] Ibid., lii.
[160] Betz, *Galatians,* xv.
[161] See Calvin, CNTC 11.1.

mentary on Galatians appeared (1519), Luther debated publicly with John Eck at Leipzig over the issues of church tradition and religious authority. In the course of that debate he declared, for the first time so boldly, that popes could be wrong and had been wrong, that church councils could err and had erred, that only Holy Scripture alone (*sola scriptura*) could be appealed to as the normative authority in matters of faith and practice. Thus Paul was correct to have challenged Peter so openly since far more than personal pride or ecclesiastical position was at stake: "This is the issue at stake here: Either Peter must be severely rebuked, or Christ must be removed entirely. Rather let Peter perish and go to hell, if need be, than that Christ be lost."[162]

Luther drew two corollaries from this episode that have important implications within his larger theological perspective: the fragility of faith and the priority of revelation over reason. The fact that so great a leader as Peter could fall is evidence that the church itself is at once both righteous and sinful. As Luther put it, we must pray the Lord's Prayer every day, "Forgive us our sins." Luther called justification by faith "the most important doctrine of Christianity," but he realized how constantly it is being threatened and undermined from every side. "I am making such a point of all this to keep anyone from supposing that the doctrine of faith is an easy matter. It is indeed easy to talk about, but it is hard to grasp; and it is easily obscured and lost. Therefore let us with all diligence and humility devote ourselves to the study of Sacred Scripture and to serious prayer, lest we lose the truth of the gospel."[163] Luther realized also that the stand Peter took at Antioch could well be justified on the basis of human reasoning, although it stood in flat contradiction to the doctrine of grace mediated by special revelation. The polarity between law and gospel, which dominates Luther's discussion here, comes into play as he speaks of the gospel leading us into "the darkness of faith." Luther seized on Paul's abrupt "No!" to Peter at Antioch to reinforce his construals of the either/or of law versus gospel and reason versus faith. As he put it in one of his most memorable one-liners: "As soon as reason and the law are joined, faith immediately loses its virginity."[164]

Turning to Calvin's treatment of the Antioch episode, we find him characteristically giving close attention to the implications of church order and discipline in this passage. Whereas Luther accepted the traditional identification of Gal 2:1-10 with the Jerusalem Council of Acts 15, Calvin opted for the famine visit of Acts 11 as the occasion for Paul's meeting with the pillar apostles. Noting the prominence of James in the listing of the pillars, he

---

[162] *LW* 26.119. On the importance of the Leipzig debate for Luther's theological development, see S. H. Hendrix, *Luther and the Papacy* (Philadelphia: Fortress, 1981), 71-94.
[163] *LW* 26.114.
[164] Ibid., 113.

commented, "And as a people must not lack a pastor, so the assembly of pastors requires a controller *(moderator)*."[165]

Here, as elsewhere, Calvin too eagerly read a proto-presbyterian polity back into the New Testament. However, Calvin, no less than Luther, found in Peter's inconsistency a repudiation of papal authoritarianism. Since Peter was called the apostle of the circumcision, the pope, to rightly claim the possession of his primacy, should "assemble churches from the Jews." Paul's public chastisement of Peter was not simply a personal rebuke, Calvin averred, but rather a matter of church discipline. "The aim is that their sin may not, by remaining unpunished, do harm by its example. As elsewhere (1 Tim 5:20) Paul expressly says that this should be observed in regard to elders, because the office they hold makes their bad example more harmful. It is especially useful that the good cause which concerned them all should be frankly defended in the presence of the people, so that Paul might make it quite clear that he did not shrink from the light."[166]

The burden of Calvin's comments focused on the primary issue at stake: the righteousness of God received through grace alone. Although elsewhere Calvin could speak (as Paul did) of the law in a positive sense as the guiding principle of Christian behavior, he recognized that in this context the "works of the law" included not only its ceremonial aspect but the law in its entirety. "Paul was worried not so much about ceremonies being observed as that the confidence and glory of salvation should be transferred to works." For this reason Calvin rejected the "semi-righteousness" medieval Catholic theologians taught that human beings could merit as a first step toward justification. He defended Luther's use of *sola,* by grace alone, by faith alone, by Christ alone. Thus on the core issue of how one obtains a right standing before God, Calvin stood together with Luther in his advocacy of a theology of either/or: "Consequently we have to ascribe either nothing or everything to faith or to works."[167]

[15]"We who are Jews by birth and not 'Gentile sinners' [16]know that a man is not justified by observing the law, but by faith in Jesus Christ. So we, too, have put our faith in Christ Jesus that we may be justified by faith in Christ and not by observing the law, because by observing the law no one will be justified. [17]"If, while we seek to be justified in Christ, it becomes evident that we ourselves are sinners, does that mean that Christ promotes sin? Absolutely not! [18]If I rebuild what I destroyed, I prove that I am a lawbreaker. [19]For through the

---

[165] Calvin, CNTC 11.33.

[166] Ibid., 36.

[167] Ibid., 40. On medieval construals of the doctrine of justification, see H. A. Oberman, *The Harvest of Medieval Theology* (Cambridge: Harvard University Press, 1962).

law I died to the law so that I might live for God. [20]I have been crucified with Christ and I no longer live, but Christ lives in me. The life I live in the body, I live by faith in the Son of God, who loved me and gave himself for me. [21]I do not set aside the grace of God, for if righteousness could be gained through the law, Christ died for nothing!"

THE PRINCIPLE: JUSTIFICATION BY FAITH (2:15-21).   In this concluding section of chap. 2 Paul brings to a conclusion the historical argument he has been pursuing and launches into the theological exposition that will preoccupy him in the next two chapters. It is difficult, if not impossible, to say where the history stops and the theology begins, for the two are inextricably interwoven in Paul's own mind. The NIV includes the entire section (vv. 15-21) in quotations, indicating that we have here a summary, if not a transcript, of Paul's address to Peter at Antioch. While this may be true, we should bear in mind that Paul's reason for rehearsing the Antioch episode in the first place was to show its relevance to the situation in Galatia. Thus what begins as an address to Peter in 2:15, "We who are Jews by birth," ends with an appeal to Paul's readers in 3:1, "You foolish Galatians!"

In these seven verses Paul used some of the most compressed language found anywhere in his epistles to set forth the central thesis he wanted to impress upon the Galatians: acceptance with God is effected through a simple act of trust in Jesus Christ and not through anything else. One would think that such a compelling idea so clearly put would cause little problem for interpreters of this passage. However, nearly every word in these few verses is a land mine on the battlefield of biblical scholarship.

What did Paul mean by the terms *justification, works of the law,* and *faith?* In what sense could Paul have "died to the law" or been "crucified with Christ"? What is the relationship between acceptance with God and the life of faith that follows from it? These are the questions Paul will be unpacking in detail in the four concluding chapters of Galatians. He introduces them here in chap. 2 to show that what is at stake for the Galatians is nothing less than the truth of the gospel. Paul's defense of his apostolic authority has led him to this definitive declaration of doctrine. The central theme is justification by faith, the very principle posed by the problem of table fellowship at Antioch and brought to the fore in Paul's protest against Peter.[168]

---

[168] In terms of structure recent commentators such at Betz and Longenecker have interpreted this passage as the *propositio* of Galatians, that transitional section of an apologetic letter that "sums up the *narratio*'s material content" and "sets up the arguments to be discussed later in the *probatio*" (Betz, *Galatians,* 114). A slight variation on this theme is set forth by G. A. Kennedy, who interprets Galatians not as an apologetic letter of self-defense but rather as an example of deliberative rhetoric. In other words, Paul intended by his arguments to persuade

We should remember that the problem in Galatia was not the overt repudiation of the Christian faith by apostates who formerly professed it but rather the dilution and corruption of the gospel by those who wanted to add to the doctrine of grace a dangerous admixture of "something more." In order to counter this tendency, Paul developed a series of daring contrasts throughout this passage.[169] Thus "Jews by birth" are contrasted to "Gentile sinners"; justification "by observing the law" is contrasted to justification "by faith in Jesus Christ." The rebuilding of the old structures of salvation by works is contrasted to their destruction by the gospel. And, finally, Paul's "dying to the law" is contrasted to his "living for God." All of this was intended to impress upon the Galatians the radical choice that confronted them. This is the reason Paul immediately, without so much as a break in his narrative, extrapolated the doctrine of justification from the incident at Antioch.

What was under dispute at Antioch was now the burning question in Galatia: not the personal clash between two leading apostles or even the rift between two sections of the church (the "men from James" versus the Pauline party) but rather the one and only basis of salvation for all peoples everywhere. Paul drew his argument to a crushing conclusion in 2:21. If the doctrine advanced by the Galatian agitators, and encouraged at least implicitly by the inconsistent behavior of Peter and Barnabas, were true, then Jesus Christ had no business dying on the cross! In order to see how Paul arrived at this startling conclusion, let us look more closely at his declaration (vv. 15-16) and defense (vv. 17-20) of the doctrine of justification by faith.

The Doctrine Declared. **2:15-16**   Paul began his definition of justification by identifying himself with his fellow Jewish Christians, including no doubt Peter, with whom he was locked in conflict at Antioch. He acknowledged the fact that those who were Jews by heritage and birth had a great advantage over those who were mere "Gentile sinners." From the Jewish perspective, Gentiles were sinners simply by virtue of the fact that they were Gentiles. Later in Ephesians Paul described the desperate condition of those who were "Gentiles by birth": they stood under the judgment of God because they had been excluded from citizenship in Israel; they were "foreigners to the covenants of the promise, without hope and without God in the world" (Eph 2:11-12).

---

the Galatians to resist the encroachments of his opponents. In this sense 2:15-21 introduces for the first time the question Paul had heretofore avoided mentioning in the letter, namely, the purpose and status of the law. See G. A. Kennedy, *New Testament Interpretation through Rhetorical Criticism* (Chapel Hill: University of North Carolina Press, 1984), 144-52.

[169] D. B. Bronson, "Paul, Galatians and Jerusalem," *JAAR* 35 (1967): 119-28.

On the other hand, those who were Jews by nature (as the Greek literally reads here[170]) were on an altogether different plane. They were, we might say, soteriologically privileged in that they had received the law of God, the Old Testament Scriptures, as well as circumcision, the sign of the covenant. We must not ignore the significance of this distinction by mentioning too quickly Paul's conclusions. Paul certainly was not saying that Jews were perfect or free from sin. He knew very well that both the Old Testament and rabbinic tradition had much to say about repentance, forgiveness, and atonement. Indeed, the entire cultic system and sacrificial practices of temple worship, which were still in effect when Paul wrote to the Galatians, presupposed the need to seek God's mercy and righteousness in accordance with the prescripts of the divine law. Nowhere else in all of the ancient world was there such a pervasive seeking after God than in the Jewish religion. Nor should we reduce such religious strivings to the kind of sanctimonious piety that produced pretentious hypocrites who were more obsessed with the minutia of the law than with its true content. Doubtless there were such people, especially among the religious leaders of Jesus' day, and the Synoptic Gospels portray them with full accuracy. However, we cannot adduce Paul himself as a primary witness for this kind of perverted religion. When he cataloged the benefits he enjoyed as a "Jew by birth" in his life before Christ, he spoke only in positive terms. He was sincere, zealous, observant, subjecting himself to the law of God and its demands in every respect. Moreover, the other benefits he listed, such as his circumcision and membership in the tribe of Benjamin, were certainly not the result of any kind of legalistic exertions. Rather, they were evidences of Paul's placement within the covenanted community of Israel, a special status enjoyed by all Jews quite apart from their own moral endeavors.[171]

Given all these wonderful benefits of "life under the law," why should Jewish Christians have moved beyond the law to faith in Jesus Christ? Obviously they should have because there was a fundamental disjunction between the best that could be obtained by observing the law and the gift of salvation freely offered through Jesus Christ. This is the point Paul was making in Gal 2:15-16. We can paraphrase his argument thus: "Forget the Gentile sinners. We know they are outside the covenant and hopeless before

---

[170] H. Koester, "φύσις," *TDNT* 9.272.

[171] The pattern of religion that prevailed among Paul's Jewish contemporaries has been dubbed "covenantal nomism" by E. P. Sanders in his monumental *Paul and Palestinian Judaism.* The great achievement of Sanders' work has been to recast the Judaism of NT times in a more positive light. His interpretation of Paul, however, is more problematic. Among the more telling critiques of Sanders' position are the studies of F. Thielman, *From Plight to Solution* (Leiden: Brill, 1989), and T. Schreiner, *The Law and Its Fulfillment* (Grand Rapids: Baker, 1993).

God. But even we Jews who could claim all the privileges of the chosen people, even we had to realize that no one could be justified by observing the law. We too, no less than the Gentiles, have been accepted by God through faith in Jesus Christ."

What Paul came to realize in coming to faith in Christ was not so much God's judgment against his wickedness, for that was a standard assumption of rabbinic Judaism, but rather God's indictment of Paul's goodness. For this reason he considered as garbage that which he formerly counted as the most precious cargo of life. That which was dearest and most precious to him, he came to realize, could not produce a right standing before God. In light of God's justifying grace, all that had been "gain" was now "loss." As Karl Barth summarized Paul's autobiographical confession in Phil 3:7: "The heights on which I stood are abysmal. The assurance in which I lived is lostness; the light I had darkness. It is not that nil takes the place of the plus, but the plus itself changes to a minus."[172]

Paul clinched his argument at the end of 2:16 by quoting a verse from Ps 143:2 (Ps 142:2 in the LXX): "Do not bring your servant into judgment," the psalmist had prayed, "for no one living will be justified before you." In Paul's rendering of this verse, however, he changed the quotation to read "no flesh will be justified." This significant change is lost in the NIV translation, which seems totally to ignore what the Greek text says and translates the Septuagint instead of Paul.[173]

What did Paul mean by the expression "no *flesh* shall be justified" (italics added)? In Gal 5:17-21 Paul contrasted the works of the flesh (which the NIV again weakly translates "acts of the sinful nature") to the fruit of the Spirit. For Paul, flesh was that realm of human existence that was most vulnerable to the ravages of sin. Flesh was not evil in itself since it was created by a good God, but in its fallen state it was subject to the debilitating forces of desire, decay, and death. Thus in Gal 2:16 "Paul takes pain to change the wording of the Septuagint in order to say that humanity, because of its weakness and susceptibility to sin, cannot keep the law."[174] In Rom 8:3 Paul would spell out more fully what he announced here in Gal 2:16, "For what the law could not do, weak as it was through the flesh, God did: sending his own Son in the likeness of sinful flesh and as an offering for sin, he condemned sin in the flesh" (NASB). Paul's point was that no one could find salvation by keeping the

---

[172] K. Barth, *The Epistle to the Philippians* (Richmond: John Knox, 1962), 97.

[173] The LXX reads ὅτι οὐ δικαιωθήσεται ἐνώπιόν σου πᾶς ζῶν, but Paul rendered it ὅτι ἐξ ἔργων νόμου οὐ δικαιωθήσεται πᾶσα σάρξ.

[174] Thielman, *From Plight to Solution,* 63.

law simply because no one can keep the law.

F. Thielman has shown how the wider context of the psalm Paul quoted supports this thesis. Psalm 143 is a petition to God for deliverance from the enemy. The rescue envisioned there depends entirely on God's faithfulness and righteousness. "For your name's sake, O Lord, preserve my life; in your righteousness, bring me out of trouble" (Ps 143:11). Thus rather than merely snatching a proof text to support his predetermined conclusion, Paul had in mind the motif of unilateral rescue and divine deliverance that pervades the entire Psalm.[175]

Because of the programmatic character of 2:16, we must look more closely at three of the expressions Paul used in this verse, each of which is crucial for understanding the flow of his argument in the rest of the letter. The three terms are *justified/justification, the works of the law,* and *faith in Christ.* Each is used here for the first time in Galatians.[176] While their full meaning will become clearer in the course of Paul's argument, it will be helpful to subject each of them to a brief preliminary sounding at this point.

Justification. In its most basic meaning, justification is the declaration that somebody is in the right.[177] A. E. McGrath observes that in Pauline vocabulary the verb *dikaioō* "denotes God's powerful, cosmic and universal action in effecting a change in the situation between sinful humanity and God, by which God is able to acquit and vindicate believers, setting them in a right and faithful relation to himself."[178] In Pauline usage the term has both forensic (from Latin *forum,* "law court") and eschatological connotations. Justification should not be confused with forgiveness, which is the fruit of justification, nor with atonement, which is the basis of justification. Rather it is the favorable

---

[175] Ibid., 64-65. On Paul's use of Scripture in another context see J. D. G. Dunn, "'Righteousness from the Law' and 'Righteousness from Faith': Paul's Interpretation of Scripture in Romans 10:1-10," in *Tradition and Interpretation in the New Testament: Essays in Honor of E. E. Ellis,* ed. G. F. Hawthorne (Grand Rapids: Eerdmans, 1987), 216-28. Paul repeated his quotation of Ps 143:2 in Rom 3:20. On the meaning of "flesh" in Paul, see K. G. Kuhn, "New Light on Temptation, Sin and Flesh in the New Testament," in *The Scrolls and the New Testament,* ed. K. Stendahl (New York: Harper, 1957), 94-113; E. Schweizer, R. Meyer, F. Baumgärtel, "σάρξ," *TDNT* 7.98-151; R. J. Erickson, "Flesh," *DPL,* 303-6. Erickson claims that "the employment of *sarx,* then, to indicate fallen humanity and the evil worldly system of values is a decidedly Pauline phenomenon, with its roots in Jewish apocalyptic. It is imitated perhaps, but not wholeheartedly adopted by any of the other early Christian writers."

[176] The word "faith" does occur earlier in 1:23. There, however, it refers to the objective content of the Christian *kerygma,* "the faith," rather than the faith by which one personally appropriates the saving work of Christ.

[177] I have borrowed this definition from the fine essay by N. T. Wright, "Justification: The Biblical Basis and Its Relevance for Contemporary Evangelicalism," in *The Great Acquittal: Justification by Faith and Current Christian Thought* (London: Collins, 1980).

[178] *DPL,* 518.

verdict of God, the righteous Judge, that one who formerly stood condemned has now been granted a new status at the bar of divine justice.

The classical Protestant understanding of justification is set forth with great clarity in Question 60 of the *Heidelberg Catechism:* "How are you righteous before God?" The following answer is given:

> Only by true faith in Jesus Christ. In spite of the fact that my conscience accuses me that I have grievously sinned against all the commandments of God, and have not kept any one of them, and that I am still ever prone to all that is evil, nevertheless, God, without any merit of my own, out of pure grace, grants me the benefits of the perfect expiation of Christ, imputing to me his righteousness and holiness as if I had never committed a single sin or had ever been sinful, having fulfilled myself all the obedience which Christ has carried out for me, if only I accept such favor with a trusting heart.[179]

According to this definition, justification is by imputation, that is, the righteousness of Christ is counted or reckoned to the sinners so that their standing before God is "as if" they possessed the kind of standing before the Father that would allow him to say of them, as he did of Christ, "This is my beloved Son in whom I am well pleased."

The radical character of this doctrine was as shocking to Paul's opponents as it was to Luther's and as it still is to many people today. It goes squarely against the gospel of self-esteem and undercuts all programs of autosalvation. Beginning with Albrecht Ritschl in the nineteenth century, many Protestant theologians have joined their Roman Catholic counterparts in protesting the forensic understanding of justification, preferring to emphasize the infusion of God's grace rather than the imputation of what Luther called an "alien righteousness."[180] However, as G. C. Berkouwer has pointed out, it is well to remember that "many objections to declarative justification are part and parcel with a rejection of the substitutionary suffering and death of Jesus Christ. Terms common to jurisprudence have been used in connection with Christ's death: satisfaction, sufficiency, payment, purchase, ransom, and punishment. And these terms have made men angry."[181]

---

[179] *The Book of Confessions* (New York: The General Assembly of the PCUSA, 1983), Lord's Day 23.

[180] See D. L. Mueller, *An Introduction to the Theology of Albrecht Ritschl* (Philadelphia: Westminster, 1969). Ritschl's magisterial study of this theme appeared in English as *A Critical History of the Christian Doctrine of Justification and Reconciliation,* trans. J. S. Black (Edinburgh: Edmonston & Douglas, 1872).

[181] Berkouwer, *Faith and Justification,* 89-90. Much discussion has been given to whether in Paul's vocabulary the verb "to justify" means "to make righteous" or "to declare righteous." However, Paul's use of the term in Rom 3:4, where he quoted Ps 51:4, reinforced the forensic or declarative character of justification, "So that you may be proved right ['justified,' KJV]

It is equally important to grasp the eschatological character of justification in Paul's thought. Deeply embedded in Jewish apocalyptic thinking was the idea of a future judgment at which God would finally vindicate his people, right all the wrongs of human history, and render his final and eternal verdict on the fate of all peoples, that is, the sorting out of the sheep and goats (cf. Matt 25:31-46). While Paul fully accepted the futurity of the final judgment, along with the alternative destinations of heaven and hell, he believes that the ground of God's final judgment has moved from the end of history to its center, that is, from the parousia to the cross and resurrection. Not only is the event of Jesus Christ the "climax of the covenant," to use Wright's suggestive term, it is also the "climax of the cosmos." On the cross the debt of sin has been fully paid, Satan has been unmasked, and hell has been put on notice that time is running out. In the meantime, between the *No Longer* and the *Not Yet,* God's righteous verdict of justification has been pronounced upon all those who place their trust in the crucified and coming Messiah. This does not mean that Christians will be exempted from accountability, for "we must all appear before the judgment seat of Christ" (1 Cor 3:12-15). However, it does mean that the basis of our standing before God has shifted from the future (last judgment) and the present (our moral strivings) to the past (the finished work of Christ on the cross). This was, of course, the very point that so irritated the Judaizers who wanted to make obedience to the law the prerequisite of a right standing with God.

The works of the law. Galatians 2:16 is a stylistically convoluted verse because Paul repeated himself. Within the space of one sentence he said the same thing in three slightly different ways: We (Jewish Christians) know that a person is not justified by observing the law . . . for this reason even we have trusted in Christ in order that we could be justified by faith rather than by the works of the law . . . since (as the psalmist said) no human being can be justified by the works of the law. What did Paul mean by "the works of the law"?

The word "law" (*nomos*) is found 119 times in Paul's letters, where it means variously the Old Testament Scriptures, the will of God, or a general principle or authority (cf. Rom 7:21). However, the law in Paul usually refers to "the sum of specific divine requirements given to Israel through

---

when you speak and prevail when you judge." Clearly God cannot be "made righteous," but he can be declared or recognized as righteous because all of his actions are fully consistent with his holy character. On the intertwining of forensic and eschatological motifs in this passage, see E. Käsemann, *Commentary on Romans* (Grand Rapids: Eerdmans, 1980), 80-82. See also the more recent studies by M. Seifrid, *Justification by Faith: The Origin and Development of a Central Pauline Theme* (Leiden: Brill, 1992).

Moses."[182] Paul claimed that the law is holy and righteous containing, as it does, the precepts of a holy and righteous God (Rom 7:12-14). However, the entire burden of Paul's argument in Galatians was to show that the nature of the law is such that it cannot produce a right standing before God. As Paul showed in Gal 3, the law was given by God in order to play a special role in the divine economy of salvation, namely, to lead us to Christ, who is the "end [*telos*] of the law" (Rom 10:4). We must postpone until later a discussion of what continuing role, if any, the law has in the life of the believer. Concerning the text before us, three major interpretations have been put forth about what Paul meant here by "the works of the law."

First, it has been argued that Paul was referring here not to the requirements of the law as such but rather to a distorted obsession with the law, that is, to legalism.[183] H. Räisänen has introduced a helpful distinction between "hard" legalism and "soft" legalism. The former refers to use of the law in a self-centered, boastful manner seeking to earn a righteous standing before God in this way. "Soft" legalism, on the other hand, is the kind of sincere piety that seeks to fulfill God's commandments out of love and obedience without trying thereby to manipulate God or merit salvation.[184] But Paul's strictures against "the works of the law" cannot be understood as merely a condemnation of legalism, whether of the hard or soft variety. Paul did not contrast faith to legalism but rather faith to works. His point was that no human deeds, however well motivated and sincerely performed, can ever achieve the kind of standing before God that results in the verdict of justification.

Equally inadequate is the view of Dunn that by "works of the law" Paul intended his readers "to think of particular observances of the law like circumcision and the food laws," rituals that were "widely regarded as characteristically and distinctively Jewish."[185] According to this view, Paul was not concerned with the problem of faith versus works as alternative avenues of salvation; rather he was protesting Jewish exclusivism by denouncing the way such "identity markers" as circumcision and the food laws had produced a "too narrow understanding of God's covenant promise and of the law in nationalistic and racial terms."[186] It is true that Paul stood against the exclu-

---

[182] S. Westerholm, *Israel's Law and the Church's Faith: Paul and His Recent Interpreters* (Grand Rapids: Eerdmans, 1988), 108.

[183] See, esp., C. E. B. Cranfield, "St. Paul and the Law," *SJT* 17 (1964): 43-68. D. P. Fuller advocates a similar view in his "Paul and 'The Works of the Law,'" *WTJ* 38 (1975-1976): 28-42.

[184] H. Räisänen, "Legalism and Salvation by the Law," in *Die Paulinische Literatur und Theologie,* ed. S. Pedersen (Aarhus: Aros, 1980), 63-83. See also the discussion in Westerholm, *Israel's Law,* 132-34.

[185] J. D. G. Dunn, "The New Perspective on Paul," *BJRL* 65 (1983): 107.

[186] Ibid., 121. H. Räisänen has observed that "the problem of the 'identity marker' may

sivism of Jewish Christians at Antioch whose loyalty to a particularist culture led to segregation from their Christian brothers. It is also true that circumcision, and to a lesser extent Sabbath keeping and food laws, were prominent features of the crisis in Galatia. By Paul's own witness, however, "works of the law" cannot be restricted to these three issues. As he would later tell the Galatians, circumcision implies an obligation to obey the whole law, and, moreover, the curse of the law will fall with equal weight on everyone who does not persevere in all of the commandments of the law (5:3; 3:10).

The "works of the law," then, refer to the commandments given by God in the Mosaic legislation in both its ceremonial and moral aspects, precepts commanded by God and thus holy and good in themselves. Because of the fallenness of human beings, however, "no flesh" could ever be justified by observing the law. Moreover, God himself knew and intended for it to be thus from the beginning. But why would God give a law no one could keep or issue commands no one could obey? Paul would struggle with this question in Gal 3 and 4 as he described the divine purpose for the law in the history of salvation.

Faith in Christ. This expression is a good example of the relationship between grammar and theology in the proper exegesis of a New Testament text. Paul said that we are not justified by works of the law but rather *dia pisteōs Iēsou Christou,* which the NIV translates "by faith in Jesus Christ." This translation assumes the traditional view that *Iēsou Christou* is an objective genitive, so that the faith in question is that of those who believe in Jesus Christ. More recently, however, other scholars have argued that this expression should be read as a subjective genitive, referring to the faith or faithfulness of Jesus Christ.[187] While the faithfulness of Jesus Christ is a prominent theme in Paul's theology (cf. the kenotic hymn of Phil 2:5-11), what is being contrasted in Galatians is not divine fidelity versus human fickleness but rather God's free initiative in grace versus human efforts toward self-salvation. Thus when Paul spoke of faith as essential for justification, he was thinking of the necessary human response to what God has objectively

---

well once have been the starting point for Paul's theologizing about the law, but finally he arrived at very negative statements on the law as such and as a whole." See his "Galatians 2:16 and Paul's Break with Judaism," *NTS* 31 (1985): 548.

[187] The extensive literature on this hotly debated topic is summarized in Longenecker, *Galatians,* 87-88, who himself opts for the subjective alternative. Among other advocates of this view are E. Fuchs, "Jesu und der Glaube," *ZTK* 55 (1958): 170-85; G. E. Howard, "On the 'Faith of Christ,'" *HTR* (1967): 459-65; and especially R. B. Hays, *The Faith of Jesus Christ: An Investigation of the Narrative Substructure of Galatians 3:1–4:11* (Chico, Cal.: Scholars Press, 1983), 139-224. The traditional view has been restated by E. deW. Burton (*A Critical*

accomplished in the cross of Christ. At the same time, it is crucial to recognize the instrumental character of such faith. Paul always says that we are justified "by" faith (*dia* plus the genitive), not "on account of" faith (*dia* plus the accusative).[188] Evangelical Christians must ever guard against the temptation to turn faith itself into one of the "works of the law." Saving faith is a radical gift from God, never a mere human possibility (Eph 2:8-9). Faith is not an achievement that earns salvation anymore than circumcision is. Rather faith is the evidence of saving grace manifested in the renewal of the heart by the Holy Spirit.

Objections Answered (2:17-18).   **2:17-18**   In vv. 15 and 16 Paul set forth the doctrine of justification by faith as a matter of common agreement between him and other Christian believers. He said in effect, "Despite the great advantages we Jewish Christians have enjoyed as heirs of the commonwealth of Israel, and the great blessings we have received from hearing and knowing the law of God from our youth up, we too, no less than the Gentiles, have been placed in a right standing with God only through faith in Jesus Christ." Put otherwise, if a Torah could have produced righteousness before God, why should anyone have turned from Judaism to Jesus in the first place? Having assumed this basic agreement as the foundation for his declaration of justification by faith, Paul now turned to meet specific objections that had been hurled against this teaching.

Verses 17-18 take us back to the troubles in the fractured church at Antioch. We may well have here in Paul's coded language an actual piece of the debate that raged in Antioch. Thus v. 17 might contain an echo of the kind of argument Peter had cast in his teeth by the "men from James" or other law-observant spectators: "Peter, don't you realize that your open table fellowship with Gentiles is a repudiation of the law of God? You are actually engaging in sin, my brother! And, furthermore, when you try to justify this kind of behavior by appealing to our common faith in Christ, you are really making our Lord an agent of sin!" Paul responded to this line of thinking with one of the strongest negations in his vocabulary: *God forbid!* Christ has not led us into sin, but his cross has revealed to us the depth of our own depravity. In a very real sense, then, there is no difference, soteriologically speaking, between Jews and Gentiles. Both indeed are sinners and helpless to effect their own redemption. It was for this reason that we too have believed in Jesus Christ.

---

and Exegetical Commentary on the Epistle to the Galatians, ICC [Edinburgh: T & T Clark, 1921], 121); Betz (*Galatians,* 118). See also comments by Westerholm, *Israel's Law,* 111-12.

[188] See the discussion of faith in R. Bultmann, *Theology of the New Testament* (New York: Scribners, 1951), 314-30.

However, the fact that we Jewish Christians now share table fellowship with Gentile believers does not make us sinners. Rather it is an expression of the Christian freedom that is ours through the righteousness of faith.

In v. 17 Paul had in mind the earlier phase of the Antioch situation when Jewish and Gentile Christians enjoyed a shared fellowship around a common table. Now v. 18 recalls the later development that shattered that unity and brought the two great apostles into open conflict. By seeking to reinstate the requirements of the law as a test of fellowship within the Christian community at Antioch, Peter, Barnabas, and the other Jewish Christians who withdrew from table fellowship with their Gentile brothers and sisters had dishonored Christ and had actually transgressed his command.

Paul doubtless knew about the revelation of Christ to Peter at Joppa and the Lord's prohibition against calling unclean that which he had cleansed. Peter had earlier been obedient to this vision but under pressure had vacillated and then transgressed the Lord's command. However, the fact that Paul spoke in the first person here rather than the accusatory "you" may indicate the pressure he himself felt to compromise on this controverted matter. Speaking in paradoxical language, Paul said that to go back on this fundamental commitment would be, in effect, to build back the old structures of repression and slavery, structures that have been once and for all shattered by Christ's death on the cross and the pouring out of his Spirit upon his people. To yield on this point would be like trying to put the plan of salvation into reverse! The very thought was no less blasphemous than imagining Christ as the agent of sin. May it never be! God forbid!

2:19-20 In these verses Paul took up another major objection to his doctrine of justification by faith. By denigrating the law as the proper channel for a right standing before God, had not Paul undermined the very basis for living a righteous life? Did not Moses command the children of Israel to walk in God's ways and "to keep his commands, decrees and laws" in order to live (Deut 30:16)? Had Paul so emphasized the forensic aspect of justification that he had no place left for the practical outworking of faith in the life of the believer? Similar objections to Pauline theology have resounded throughout the history of the church. In the sixteenth century Duke George at Saxony summed up this protest well in his pithy comment on Luther's doctrine of justification: "It's a great doctrine to die by, but a lousy one to live with!"

Following the analysis of Betz, let us look at the four theses Paul set forth in these verses to refute this objection to his doctrine.[189]

---

[189] Betz, *Galatians*, 121-27.

1. "Through the law I died to the law so that I might live for God." Paul used here the emphatic pronoun for "I" (*ego*) in order to distinguish this confessional statement from his more generalized use of the first person singular in the preceding verse. Thus these verses reach back to Paul's earlier discussion of his conversion and calling when, as he put it, God was "pleased to reveal his Son in me" (1:15-16). However, without attenuating the personal and autobiographical element here, we should realize that Paul was speaking of his experience in a paradigmatic way. He was not here talking about his unique apostolic calling or the special revelations he had received from the Lord; rather, he was describing what might be called the normal Christian life. What was true for Paul is true for all believers who have been justified by faith in Jesus Christ.

What did Paul mean when he said, "I died to the law"? We must avoid two errors in interpreting these words.[190] In the first place we must avoid reducing the law in this context to its ceremonial aspect. True, the burning issues in Galatia were circumcision, feast days, and food laws, all of which were external rites or ceremonies called for by the law of Moses. However, the issue at stake was not these ceremonies as such, for to Paul they were "things indifferent"; his concern was rather the theological baggage the false teachers were placing on such rites. As J. G. Machen put it, "Paul is contending in this great epistle not for a 'spiritual' view of the law as over against externalism or ceremonialism; he is contending for the grace of God as over against human merit in any form."[191]

When Paul said he died to the law, he was referring to nothing less than the God-given commandments and decrees contained in Old Testament Scriptures. However, he was not saying here that the law of God had lost all meaning or relevance for the Christian believer. This is the error of antinomianism, which Paul was at pains to refute both here in Galatians as well as in Romans. Later in Galatians, Paul would exhort his readers to carry one another's burdens and thus "fulfill the law of Christ" (6:2). There is an ethical imperative in the Christian life that flows from a proper understanding of justification. Paul would return to this theme in the last two chapters of the epistle.

Elsewhere Paul used the expression "to die to" not only with reference to

---

[190] Machen, *Machen's Notes on Galatians,* 156-57.

[191] Ibid., 156. Cf. the similar comment by Calvin: "Paul was worried not so much about ceremonies being observed as that the confidence and glory of salvation should be transferred to works. . . . Paul therefore is not wandering from the point when he brings a disputation on the law as a whole, whereas the false apostles were arguing only about ceremonies. Their object in pressing ceremonies was that men might seek a salvation in the observance of the law, which they made out to be a meritorious service. Therefore Paul opposes to them the grace of Christ alone, and not the moral law" (CNTC 11.39).

the law but also in relation to the self, sin, and the world.[192] In each of these cases Paul meant that his relationship to these entities—self, sin, world, law—had been so decisively altered by his union with Christ that they no longer control, dominate, or define his existence. By saying that he died to the law "through the law" Paul is anticipating his later discussion of the provisional role of the law in the history of salvation. The law itself, by revealing the inadequacy of human obedience and the depth of human sinfulness, set the stage, as it were, for the drama of redemption effected by the promised Messiah who fulfilled the law by obeying it perfectly and suffering its curse vicariously.

2. "I have been crucified with Christ." In the Greek text this expression, along with the one just before it, "so that I might live for God," are a part of v. 19, thus completing Paul's earlier thought. Thus the flow of the sentence would be: "I have died to the law in order that I might live for God having been crucified together with Christ." The new life Paul had received flowed from his identification with the passion and death of Christ. Elsewhere Paul could speak of being buried and raised with Christ, an identification portrayed liturgically in the ordinance of baptism (Rom 6:1-6). Indeed, Betz has suggested that Paul's more developed baptismal theology in Romans may have evolved from this more succinct statement in Galatians.[193]

But what does it mean to be "crucified with Christ"? In one sense this is presumptuous language because the mystery of atonement requires that the death of Christ be unique, unrepeatable, and isolated. The two thieves who were literally crucified with Christ did not bear the sins of the world in their agonizing deaths. On the cross Christ suffered alone forsaken by his friends, his followers, and finally even his Father, dying, as J. Moltmann puts it, "a God-forsaken death for God-forsaken people."[194] With reference to his substitutionary suffering and vicarious death, only Jesus, and he alone, can be the Substitute and Vicar. And yet—this was Paul's point—the very benefits of Christ's atoning death, including first of all justification, are without effect unless we are identified with Christ in his death and resurrection. As Calvin put it, "As long as Christ remains outside of us, and we are separated from him, all that he has suffered and done for the salvation of the human race remains useless and of no value for us."[195] Thus to be crucified with Christ

---

[192] See C. F. D. Moule, "Death 'To Sin,' 'To Law,' and 'To the World': A Note on Certain Datives," *Mélanges Bibliques en hommage au R. P. Béda Rigaux* (Gembloux: Duculot, 1970), 367-75.

[193] Betz, *Galatians*, 123: "Gal 2:19 may contain the theological principle by which Paul interprets the ritual of baptism in Romans 6."

[194] J. Moltmann, *The Crucified God* (New York: Harper & Row, 1974), 145.

[195] *Institutes* 3.1.1.

is, as Paul said elsewhere, to know him in the "fellowship of his sufferings" (Phil 3:10). To be crucified with Christ is the same as being dead to the law. This means that we are freed from all the curse and guilt of the law and, by this very deliverance, are set free truly to "live for God." As Calvin said again, "Engrafted into the death of Christ, we derive a secret energy from it, as the shoot does from the root."[196] It is this experience of divine grace that makes the doctrine of justification a living reality rather than a legal fiction.

3. "I no longer live, but Christ lives in me." Paul set forth in this expression his doctrine of the indwelling Christ. Probably no verse in the Letter of Galatians is quoted more frequently by evangelical Christians than this one. Much harm has been done to the body of Christ by well-meaning persons who have perpetuated erroneous interpretations of these words. Properly understood, Paul's words give sanction neither to perfectionism nor to mysticism. Paul was not saying that once a person becomes a Christian the human personality is zapped out of existence, being replaced somehow by the divine *logos*. The indwelling of Christ does not mean that we are delivered from the realm of suffering, sin, and death. Paul made this abundantly clear in his very next phrase, "the life I now live in the flesh" (NRSV). So long as we live in the flesh, we will continue to struggle with sin and to "groan" along with the fallen creation around us (Rom 8:18-26). Perfectionism this side of heaven is an illusion.

Nor did Paul advocate here the kind of Christ-mysticism that various spiritualist leaders have advanced throughout the history of the church. We are crucified with Christ, that is, identified with his suffering and death, which occurred once for all outside the gates of Jerusalem some two thousand years ago. Christ is not crucified in us. Similarly, we must be born again: Christ has no need to be born anew, in the "core of the soul."[197] The doctrine of justification by faith stands opposed to every idea of mystical union with the divine that obscures the historicity of the incarnation, the transcendence of God, or the necessity of repentance and humility before an awesome God whose "ways are not our ways and whose thoughts are not our thoughts."[198]

---

[196] Calvin, CNTC 11.42.

[197] "How does God beget his Son in the soul? God begets his Son through the true unity of the divine nature. See! This is the way: He begets his Son in the core of the soul and is made one with it. . . . [for this to happen] you must get into the essence, the core of the soul, so that God's undifferentiated essence may reach you there, without the interposition of any idea" (*Meister Eckhart*, trans. R. B. Blakney [New York: Harper and Row, 1941], 98).

[198] I realize, of course, that mysticism is a fluid term in the history of Christian thought and can be used to describe patterns of piety that do not violate the great principles of Christian orthodoxy. However, many of the spiritualist and mystical movements so popular today draw heavily from the spiritual traditions of the East or from the heretical strain of mystical theology epitomized in the West by Meister Eckhart.

Having discounted these false interpretations, we must give full weight to the meaning of Paul's words. Being crucified with Christ implies a radical transformation within the believer. The "I" who has died to the law no longer lives; Christ, in the person of the Holy Spirit, dwells within, sanctifying our bodies as temples of the Holy Spirit and enabling us to approach the throne of God in prayer. Paul gave a fuller explanation for what it means for Christ to live in us: "Because you are sons, God sent the Spirit of his Son into our hearts, the Spirit who calls out 'Abba, Father'" (Gal 4:6).

4. "The life I now live in the body I live by faith in the Son of God, who loved me, and gave himself for me." In this fourth thesis Paul described the modality of the Christian life and again reiterated its objective source in the living Son of God and the love that sent him to the cross. While the Christian life takes place "in the flesh" (*en sarki*), it is nonetheless lived "by faith" (*en pistei*). Not only are we justified by faith, but we also live by faith. This means that saving faith cannot be reduced to a one-time decision or event in the past; it is a living, dynamic reality permeating every aspect of the believer's life. As Calvin put it nicely, "It is faith alone that justifies, but the faith that justifies is not alone."[199] The object of this faith is Jesus Christ, the Son of God, "who loved me and gave himself for me." This is a rich expression that contains in summary form the whole doctrine of atonement. No impersonal force or cosmic law or external necessity compelled Christ to die. It was the love of God, unmerited, immeasurable, infinite, that sent Jesus to the cross. Not for his own sake but "for me" he endured the rigors of Calvary.

The Terrible Alternative. **2:21** As we have seen, grace is the operative word in Galatians, and here in the concluding verse of chap. 2 Paul defended himself against the charge that by displacing the law as a means of salvation he himself had thwarted God's grace. The exact opposite was true, Paul said. If it were possible to obtain a right standing by God through the works of the law, then Christ had no business dying! Here everything is at stake. Was Christ a false messiah, a common criminal, a nonentity whose death was merely a trivial footnote in the history of late antiquity? Any true Christian must tremble in horror at such a prospect. Yet Paul said that if we persist in building again the wall that Christ has torn down, if we try to climb up to heaven "by some other way," if we add works of the law to the sacrifice of the cross, then indeed we make a mockery of Jesus' death just as the soldiers who spat upon him, the thieves who hurled insults at him, and the rabble who shouted, "Come down from the cross!"

---

[199] *"Fides ergo sola est quae justificat; fides tamen quae justificat, non est sola"* (*CO* 8:488).

SUMMARY. We have now come to the end of the first major section of Paul's Letter to the Galatians, having followed the path of the gospel from Damascus to Galatia via Jerusalem and Antioch. Throughout this long autobiographical narrative, Paul defended his apostolic authority and independence over against those who had characterized his message as a distorted version of the true Christian gospel proclaimed by the Jerusalem apostles. Paul declared that his gospel was received directly from Jesus Christ, who called and commissioned him to be the apostle to the Gentiles. This message brooks no competition but demands obedience and unalloyed allegiance from all who have heard and embraced it. Despite the unique provenance of his own calling, Paul had been careful to stress the basic agreement he and the other apostles shared concerning the essence of the gospel. Even at Antioch, where Paul came into open conflict with Peter, the issue was not Peter's defection from the faith but rather his inconsistency or, as Paul called it, hypocrisy. Thus when Paul stated in the clearest possible terms the doctrine of justification by faith, applying it equally to Jews and Gentiles, he couched it in the form of a theological consensus that he shared with Peter.

At the same time there is a dark shadow that falls across these first two chapters, an insidious opposition to the gospel that forms the backdrop of Paul's passionate appeal to the Galatians. "Some people" had evidently thrown Paul's recent converts into confusion by imposing addenda to the message of grace he had proclaimed to them. Who these people were we do not know, but we can fairly assume that they had some kinship with the "false brothers" who sought to impose circumcision on Titus at Jerusalem and the "circumcision group" that intimidated Peter at Antioch. In the face of their demands Paul would not budge an inch. Because the truth of the gospel was at stake, no concession or compromise could be considered.

Galatians 2:15-21 summarizes the themes developed thus far and introduces the theological exposition of justification by faith that Paul would pursue in Gal 3–4. Thus 2:16, the key verse in this section, contains both an appeal to Christian experience ("We, too, have put our faith in Christ Jesus") and an argument from Scripture, the quotation from Psalm 143:2 about no flesh being justified by observing the law. Paul also anticipated objections to his doctrine of justification and emphasized the life of faith to which he would return in greater detail in Gal 5–6. We are now ready to look at the centerpiece of Paul's doctrine of justification which he unfolds in the next two chapters.

—— **II. THEOLOGY: JUSTIFICATION BY FAITH (3:1–4:31)** ——

Having established the historical authenticity and integrity of his apostolic calling and mission, Paul had already made the transition to theology proper that began with his response to Peter (2:16) but led into his direct address to the Galatians (3:1). As we have seen, these verses contain in some of the most compressed language found anywhere in Paul's writings what the eighteenth-century Pietist commentator J. Bengel once described as "the sum and marrow of Christianity."[1] In these verses Paul stated what he now had to prove: that the only way for anyone, Jew or Gentile, to be declared righteous before God is through personal faith in Jesus Christ. In order to accomplish this task, Paul would set forth a series of arguments or proofs drawn primarily from Scripture and intended to show that the message of salvation he had proclaimed to the Galatians was no novel doctrine but one based firmly on the holy oracles and divine promises of God himself.

But why was it necessary for Paul to take this approach in his appeal to the Galatians? One scholar has commented that Paul could well have closed his epistle at the end of chap. 2, having refuted the false charges brought against him and produced such a masterful statement of the doctrine of justification.[2] Others have noted the unevenness and complexity of Paul's argumentation in this *probatio* section of the letter. One scholar characterized it as "a maze of laboured exegesis, puzzling illustration, and cryptic theological shorthand."[3]

We should be wary, however, lest such a verdict lead us to an attitude of despair in studying the text before us. We will be helped immensely if we remember three basic principles. First, Paul along with all other New Testament writers regarded the Old Testament Scriptures as the divinely inspired,

---

[1] Bengel, quoted in J. G. Machen, *Machen's Notes on Galatians* (Nutley, N.J.: Presbyterian & Reformed, 1977), 164.

[2] R. A. Cole, *The Epistle of Paul to the Galatians,* TNTC (Grand Rapids: Eerdmans, 1965), 84.

[3] T. L. Donaldson, "The 'Curse of the Law' and the Inclusion of the Gentiles: Galatians 3:13-14," *NTS* 32 (1986): 94. H. D. Betz has identified Gal 3:1–4:31 as the *probatio* of Galatians, containing as it does the proofs or arguments introduced by the *propositio* of 2:15-21 (*Galatians,* Her [Philadelphia: Fortress, 79], 128-30). He admits, however, that "an analysis of these chapters in terms of rhetoric is extremely difficult." Part of the difficulty stems from the digressions, interruptions, and diverse forms of argumentation Paul used. Longenecker adopts Betz's analysis of Galatians as an apologetic letter but limits the central arguments of the *probatio* to 3:1–4:11. He also points out that in this section Paul "seems much more heavily influenced by Jewish forms of argumentation and Jewish exegetical practices," thus accounting for his divergence from the more classical rhetorical conventions employed in Gal 1 and 2. See R. Longenecker, *Galatians,* WBC (Dallas: Word, 1990), 97.

error-free Word of God. Moreover, they saw this Word not as a static document from the past but rather as a living, dynamic reality in the present (cf. Heb 4:12). Thus when Paul quoted Old Testament texts and examples, drawing on the best traditions of rabbinic exegesis in which he was trained, he fully expected that such proclamation, whether verbal or written, would have a spiritually transforming effect on his hearers and readers. In Gal 3 and 4 Paul did not merely provide footnotes to a theological discourse; he declared "thus saith the Lord" with power, conviction, and expectancy. Second, we must remember that Paul was not doing theology in abstraction but was writing to a particular context and setting of which we have only partial awareness. No doubt, Paul developed some of his arguments in direct response to the message of the Galatian agitators. We are overhearing, as it were, one-half of a conversation, and that largely directed against the position of a third party. Various phrases and turns of argument which may be ambiguous to us were doubtless perfectly clear to the Galatians. They, after all, had heard Paul preach, perhaps on these same themes, and could easily compare his response to the message of his opponents. Third, it is important for us to remember that the Holy Spirit has inspired every single word of Scripture, including the more obscure and difficult passages, for our benefit. For this reason we must study the Scriptures with both diligence and reverence ever seeking to handle correctly the Word of truth (2 Tim 2:15).

1. The Argument from Conversion (3:1-5)

(1) A Bewitched Congregation (3:1)

¹You foolish Galatians! Who has bewitched you? Before your very eyes Jesus Christ was clearly portrayed as crucified.

3:1 At two points in the theological section of the letter Paul stepped back from his tight-knit argument and appealed directly to the Galatians. In both passages (3:1-5; 4:12-20) Paul sounded exasperated and perplexed: "You foolish Galatians!"; "What has happened? . . . Have I now become your enemy? . . . I am perplexed about you." On two other occasions in his writings Paul used the vocative case to appeal directly to his readers (2 Cor 6:11; Phil 4:15), but only here in Galatians did he add the prefixed "Oh" (Gk., Ō; cf. Moffatt; Williams), an emotive particle that reinforces the apostle's mood of indignation and concern.

Paul not only addressed his readers by name; he also characterized them in a very unflattering way as foolish, stupid, senseless, silly. Or, as J. B. Phillips puts it, "Oh you dear idiots of Galatia . . . surely you cannot be so idiotic?" The bluntness of Paul's language should not blind us to the fact that he had earlier referred to the Galatians as "brothers" (1:11) and that he would later call them his children (4:19). Paul's language here does not contradict his principle of restoring with gentleness those believers who have lapsed into error and sin (6:1). Paul loved the Galatians and wanted them to be restored to spiritual and theological soundness. To accomplish this, however, something more stern than mushy sentimentality was required. Paul's harsh rebuke is an example of tough love. He confronted the Galatians with their folly so that by this means he might win them back to the truth they were in danger of forsaking.

In calling the Galatians foolish or stupid, Paul was not casting aspersions on their intelligence. No one can read the Letter to the Galatians without realizing that Paul presupposed a high level of intellectual ability on the part of his readers.[4] The Galatians were not lacking in IQ but in spiritual discernment. They were like the disciples on the road to Emmaus whom the risen Christ characterized as "foolish . . . and . . . slow of heart to believe all that the prophets have spoken" (Luke 24:25).

As these opening verses of chap. 3 indicate, the Galatians were obviously enthralled by the supernatural manifestations of the Holy Spirit in their midst. At the same time, their grasp on the fundamental truths of the gospel was woefully inadequate. One of the most dangerous dichotomies in the Christian life is for the spiritual to be divorced from the doctrinal, experience from theology. In the most explicitly charismatic passage in the New Testament, Paul insisted that we should sing and pray not only in the spirit but also with our minds (1 Cor 14:15-19). Paul did not say that the Galatians had had less than a fully genuine experience of the Holy Spirit. Indeed, he argued from precisely the opposite premise: since they had certainly received the Holy Spirit and witnessed his mighty works, why were they now retrogressing back from the Spirit to the flesh, that is, from faith back to works and from grace back to law? The answer is implied in Paul's critical word of address: somehow the balance between sound doctrine and Spirit-filled living had gotten out of kilter among the churches of Galatia. Not being firmly grounded in the faith, they

---

[4] J. B. Lightfoot cited this text as evidence that Paul had addressed his letter to descendants of the ancient Celts, a tribe known for their fickle character and dull intelligence: "Ye senseless Gauls, who did bewitch you?" (*Saint Paul's Epistle to the Galatians* [1890; reprint, London: Macmillan, 1986], 15). Martin Luther interpreted "Galatians" in a similar way, transferring these stereotypical qualities to the Germans rather than the Gauls. Just as the Cretans were known as liars (Titus 1:12), the peculiar national vice of the Galatians was stupidity (*LW* 26.188). W. M. Ramsay has argued convincingly that Paul used the word "Galatians" in this verse as a collective noun referring to the residents of the Roman province of Galatia rather than as a term of ethnicity (*A Historical Commentary on St. Paul's Epistle to the Galatians* [London: Hodder & Stoughton, 1900], 308-13).

had been led astray by undisciplined thinking and careless theology to the
point where they were now on the verge of embracing dangerous doctrines.
But how had this happened? Paul was not content to explain the situation
solely in human terms. "Who has bewitched you?" he asked, implying that
the Galatians had become the objects of a sinister, supernatural ploy. The
word for "bewitched" is a hapax legomenon, a word found nowhere else in
the New Testament.[5] Literally the word means "to give someone the evil
eye, to cast a spell over, to fascinate in the original sense of holding someone spellbound by an irresistible power."[6]

Someone had misled the Galatians, leaving them deficient in understanding and judgment and vulnerable to the evil forces at work in their midst. On
one level the answer to Paul's rhetorical question was very simple. The false
teachers, those heretical interlopers, had sown confusion and doubt among
the believers of Galatia, leading them to their present state of spiritual disar-
ray. However, the "who" in Paul's question is singular, suggesting that behind
the work of the Galatian agitators was the devil himself, the father of lies who
walks about as a roaring lion seeking someone to seize upon and devour (1
Pet 5:8). Later Paul would warn the Corinthians of this very danger: "Just as
Eve was deceived by the serpent's cunning, your minds may somehow be led
astray from your sincere and pure devotion to Christ" (2 Cor 11:3). This verse
is a solemn warning to every congregation that gathers for worship and every
preacher who stands behind a sacred desk to proclaim God's Word. However
large or small the congregation, however powerful or ineffective the preacher,
a contest of eternal moment is being waged, with the souls of men and
women in the balance. With so much at stake, the content of our preaching
must be nothing less than Jesus Christ and him crucified (1 Cor 2:2).[7]

---

[5] G. Delling, "Βασκαίνω" *TDNT* 1.594–95. This word has the connotation of harming someone by means of a hostile look, of giving someone an evil eye, thus casting a magic spell or
unleashing demonic forces. Concerning its use in Gal 3:1, Delling writes: "This is not merely an
exaggerated metaphor, for behind magic stands the power of falsehood and this has been exercised
by the τίς (or the group behind the τίς) to do real harm to the νοῦς of the Galatians (ἀνόητοι).
This is certainly not to be understood in a naively realistic way as mechanical magic. The dangerous feature is that the Galatians have willingly yielded to these magicians and their influence without realizing to what powers of falsehood they were surrendering. The characteristic point of the
βασκανία is that it exerts its influence without extraordinary means."

[6] Cf. the Vg rendering: *"O insensati Galatae, qui vos fascinavit?"* and the French: *"O Galates
insensés! Qui vous a ensorcelés?"*

[7] At this point in the text the KJV inserts a phrase found in some of the later Greek manuscripts,
"that ye should not obey the truth." Most scholars believe this to be an addition to the original text
evidently influenced by the same phrase in Gal 5:7. There Paul asked the Galatians, "Who cut in
on you and kept you from obeying the truth?" While the textual evidence suggests that the phrase
does not belong in 3:1, its meaning is certainly congruent with the context there. The Galatians'
lack of ability to distinguish truth from error was the result of their willful blindness. They had
become "fascinated" by the false teachers because they did not obey the truth as it was originally
proclaimed to them by Paul and Barnabas. See B. Metzger, *A Textual Commentary on the Greek
New Testament* (New York: UBS, 1971), 593.

Had Paul continued his autobiographical narrative into chap. 3, at this point he would have been ready to describe his bringing of the gospel to the Galatians. We may be surprised that Paul did not in fact continue the sequence of events he had begun: his conversion, calling, early ministry, the missionary summit at Jerusalem, the incident at Antioch, the first missionary journey that brought him and Barnabas to the cities of South Galatia. As we have seen before, however, Paul had no interest in writing "A History of my Life and Labors." In Galatians he wanted to provide the churches he founded with the theological weapons they needed to withstand the seductive influences that would shipwreck their souls. However, before launching into his theological exposition proper, Paul gave a brief backwards glance to his evangelization of the Galatians. Doubtless referring to the message he and Barnabas had proclaimed when they first brought the gospel to the Galatians, he reminded them of how, right before their very eyes, Jesus Christ was graphically set forth as crucified.

Everything else Paul said in Galatians 3 and 4 was predicated on the message he first preached to the Galatians, which he summarized in this familiar formula. Each of the three elements in this sermon summary are worthy of close attention. First, Paul preached Jesus Christ. It has been well said that "the universe of Paul's thought revolved around the Son of God, Jesus Christ."[8] Before his encounter with the risen Christ on the road to Damascus, Paul had regarded Jesus as a failed messiah, a foolish rabbi who deceived himself and others. All of this was changed when "God was pleased to reveal his Son in me" (1:16). The prominent Christological titles Paul attributed to Jesus—Christ, Lord, Son of God, Savior—reflect his belief that Jesus was fully divine and thus a proper object of worship and prayer. In Rom 9:5 Paul could speak of "Christ, who is God over all, forever praised!"[9] Paul's doctrine of justification makes no sense apart from the high Christological assumptions on which it is based.

Second, Paul said that Jesus Christ "was clearly portrayed before your eyes." The word "portrayed" (*prographō*) can mean either "write before-

---

[8] B. Witherington, III, "Christology," *DPL*, 103.

[9] Paul usually prefers functional to ontological language in referring to Christ, but the former is directly dependent on the latter. On the controverted interpretation of the Romans text, see B. M. Metzger, "Punctuation of Rom 9:5," in *Christ and the Spirit in the New Testament*, ed. B. Lindars and S. S. Smalley (Cambridge: Cambridge University Press, 1973), 95–112.

hand" (in a temporal sense) or "portray publicly" (the prefix *pro* as locative, not temporal). The former sense in terms of predictive prophecy is consonant with Paul's use of the Old Testament especially in the present context (cf. 3:8, where we read, "The Scripture foresaw [*proidousa*] that God would justify the Gentiles by faith, and announced the gospel in advance [*proeuēngelisato*] to Abraham"). When we read Luke's account of Paul's preaching among the Galatians in Acts 13–14, we find him quoting freely from the Prophets and the Psalms, declaring to the people, "We tell you the good news: what God promised our fathers, he has fulfilled for us" (Acts 13:32). However, in 3:1 the word *prographō* more likely carries the locative meaning "to display publicly as on a placard." Paul likely was referring to the vivid, unforgettable way in which he first presented the story of Jesus' suffering and death to the Galatians. In effect, he was saying to them, "How can you have been so deceived by these heretics when in your mind's eye Jesus was, as it were, impaled on the cross of Calvary right before you? Yes, you have actually seen Christ crucified plastered on a billboard; how could you ever lose sight of that?" Of course, it is not merely the gruesome facts about Jesus' death but rather the supreme truth that "God was in Christ, reconciling the world unto himself" (2 Cor 5:19, KJV) that gives power to such portrayals of the crucifixion.

Finally, Paul put special stress on the finality of the cross. He proclaimed Jesus Christ as *estaurōmenos,* literally, as having been crucified. This perfect participle relates to Jesus' cry from the cross, "It is finished!" The work of redemption was completely accomplished through that perfect atoning sacrifice.

> Complete atonement Christ has made,
> And to the utmost farthing paid
>   whate'er his people owed;
> How then can wrath on me take place,
> If sheltered in his righteousness,
>   and sprinkled with his blood?[10]

(2) Why the Spirit? (3:2-5)

²I would like to learn just one thing from you: Did you receive the Spirit by observing the law, or by believing what you heard? ³Are you so foolish? After beginning with the Spirit, are you now trying to attain your goal by human effort? ⁴Have you suffered so much for nothing—if it really was for nothing? ⁵Does God give you his Spirit and work miracles among you because you

---

[10] Quoted, G. S. Bishop, *Grace in Galatians* (Swengel, Pa.: Reiner, 1968), 25.

observe the law, or because you believe what you heard?

In these verses the term "Spirit" is introduced for the first time in Galatians. It appears again at critical junctures throughout the book (3:14; 4:6,29; 5:5; 6:8) and is central to Paul's description of the life of freedom and love to which every believer is called (5:16-26). When Paul spoke of the Spirit, he was talking about the Holy Spirit of God to whom he attributed the personal characteristics of deity. The Holy Spirit leads believers and may be grieved by their sin; he reveals the mystery of the gospel and intercedes for the saints in prayer; he baptizes, indwells, seals, fills, and empowers Christians to live a life pleasing to God. Above all, the Holy Spirit enables the church to confess Jesus as Lord (1 Cor 12:3). Without his vivifying presence these words are but an empty slogan. Thus here, and also later in Galatians, the Holy Spirit is introduced in the context of the doctrine of the Trinity. Paul had just spoken of his proclamation of the cross of Christ; in 3:5 he would refer to the Father who gave his Spirit to the Galatians. While Paul had in mind the observable manifestation of miracles at this point, he would later refer to the more fundamental gift of divine sonship the Holy Spirit bestows on all who trust in Christ. "Because you are sons, God sent the Spirit of his Son into our hearts" (4:6).[11]

In 3:1-5 Paul asked the Galatians a series of six rapid-fire questions, all of which he expected them to answer on the basis of their Christian experience. He had just spoken of the placarding of Christ "before their eyes." In a moment he would remind them of their "hearing of faith." Paul was reminding the Galatians of something they could not deny: the reality of the new life they had received in Jesus Christ. Still, we might think that Paul had entered a slippery slope by appealing so blatantly to the experience of the Galatians. Was not this the very thing that had gotten them into trouble? Weren't they so entranced by their spiritual experiences that they had lost their theological footing? In any event, an appeal to mere experience was invariably a dangerous method of deciding a theological issue.

To this line of reasoning two responses can be made. First, Paul always promoted the coherence of sound doctrine and holy living. While it is true that experience minus theology will surely lead to a distorted spirituality, it is also true that theology minus experience can only issue in a dead orthodoxy. Paul anticipated what he would say about the life of the Spirit in Gal 5–6 by referring to the outpouring of the Spirit in the Galatians' early Christian experience.

---

[11] T. Paige, "Holy Spirit," *DPL,* 404-13. See also J. D. G. Dunn, *Jesus and the Spirit* (Philadelphia: Westminster, 1975), and E. Schweizer, "πνεῦμα, πνευματικός," *TDNT* 6.396-451. On the function of the Holy Spirit in Paul's argument in Gal 3, see the important article by S. K. Williams, "Justification and the Spirit in Galatians," *JSNT* 29 (1987): 91-100.

GALATIANS 3:2

Granting this important principle, however, a closer examination of this passage reveals that Paul was not so much arguing from experience as he was asking the Galatians to examine the basis of their Christian experience. Thus his six questions can be reduced to one (which he twice repeated): "I would like to learn just one thing from you: Did you receive the Spirit by observing the law, or by believing what you heard?" If only this one question could be resolved, Paul thought, the whole trouble with the Judaizers would soon be over. However, to answer this question the Galatians had to reflect theologically on the experience of the Spirit in their midst. This Paul led them to do by posing three contrasts for them to consider.

BY WORKS OF THE LAW OR HEARING OF FAITH? (3:2). **3:2** Paul posed here the one question (which he repeated in a slightly expanded form in v. 5) that could decisively settle the whole dispute: "Did you receive the Spirit by observing the law, or by believing what you heard?" This question brings into sharp antithesis two prepositional phrases, each of which represents an alternative way for the Galatians to interpret their initial reception of the Holy Spirit. Did this happen by the works of the law (*ex ergōn nomou*) or by the hearing of faith (*ex akoēs pisteōs*)? The implied answer to this question was undisputed for one reason: the Galatians had been saved and blessed with the Spirit as a result of Paul's preaching of "Christ crucified" long before the Judaizing disturbers of their faith had appeared in their midst.

Two key words in Paul's question underscore the theology of grace that characterized his doctrine of the Spirit. The first is the simple verb "received" (*elabete*). This word occurs again in 3:14, where Paul referred to receiving by faith the promise of the Spirit. "To receive" in these texts does not refer to a self-prompted taking but rather to a grateful reception of that which is offered. The same verb occurs in 1 Cor 4:7, where Paul posed this penetrating question to the Corinthians: "What do you have that you did not receive? And if you did receive it, why do you boast as though you did not?" This verse had a powerful effect on Augustine in opening up for him the mystery of God's grace; later it was a crucial weapon in his struggle against the Pelagians.[12] Thus the Galatians received the Holy Spirit as an unfettered gift from the sovereign God quite apart from any contribution of good works or human merit on their part.

And how did this marvelous outpouring of the divine Spirit come about? It happened, Paul said, through the hearing of faith. Much has been written on this expression, which could mean variously "the faculty or organ of

---

[12] See Augustine's treatise "On the Spirit and the Letter," chaps. 57–61 in NPNF 5.108-11. Cf. the essay by J. M. Rist, "Augustine on Freewill and Predestination," in *Augustine: A Collection of Critical Essays,* ed. R. A. Markus (New York: Doubleday, 1972), 218-52.

hearing," or "the act of hearing," or "the content of what is heard."[13] However, while the content of what is heard is crucial, Paul was rather thinking here of the process by which one comes within the orbit of God's saving grace. As Paul said elsewhere, faith comes by hearing and hearing by the Word of God (Rom 10:17). The term "hearing" refers to the passive posture of the recipient. Thus Luther could write that the only organs of a Christian man are his ears. The focus is not merely on the physical faculty of hearing but on the awakening of faith that comes through the preaching of the gospel. Thus the contrast Paul was drawing was between doing works and believing in Christ. However, these are not merely two kinds of human activities but rather alternative ways of approaching God.[14]

FROM START TO FINISH (3:3). **3:3** Since the answer to the previous question was so patently obvious, Paul returned to his opening theme of the folly of the Galatians and bluntly asked again: "Are you so foolish?" "Since then you have received the Spirit as a gift and not as a reward, being saved through your ears, as it were, and not by your hands, have you now gone completely crazy?" Paul now posed a question that went to the heart of their motivation for abandoning the gospel of free grace he had preached to them: "Having begun in the Spirit, are ye now made perfect by the flesh?" (KJV).

There is a twofold contrast in this question: beginning/completing and spirit/flesh. Paul told the Philippians that "he who began a good work in you will carry it on to completion" (Phil 1:6). The Galatians, however, having begun so well with their life in the Spirit, were being tempted to turn back to those weak and miserable principles which dominated their existence before they became Christians in the first place. By turning to a different gospel, they have not advanced forward in the life of the Spirit but, on the contrary, lapsed into the realm of the flesh. While the word "flesh" in this context may refer, as many commentators believe, to the issue of circumcision, it also has the wider meaning of "an independent reliance on one's own accomplishments over against a spirit of dependance upon and submission to his rule."[15]

The contest between Paul and his opponents reverberates in the background of this verse. There is no evidence that these law-observant teachers

---

[13] Longenecker, *Galatians,* 103. See also S. K. Williams, "The Hearing of Faith: AKOH ΠΙΣΤΕΩΣ," *NTS* 35 (1989): 82-93.

[14] F. Matera, *Galatians,* Sacra Pagina (Collegeville: Liturgical, 1993), 116. Cf. Betz's comment on this passage: "The phrase *ex akoēs pisteōs* may be constructed in antithesis to *ex ergōn nomou*; while the Torah requires man to do 'works of [the] law,' the Christian message 'gives' Spirit and faith to man (cf. 3:21-22; Rom 10:8-18)" (*Galatians,* 133).

[15] R. J. Erickson, "Flesh," *DPL,* 306. See also R. Jewett, *Paul's Anthropological Terms: A Study of Their Use in Conflict Settings* (Leiden: Brill, 1971).

denied either the fundamental fact of "Christ crucified" or the manifestation of the Spirit among the Galatians. Their claim was rather that the entry-level gospel proclaimed by Paul was insufficient for the higher spiritual realities offered only through the works of the law. They would have abhorred Paul's antithesis between the gift of the Spirit and the works of the law. For them the granting of the Spirit was merely a preliminary initiation into the Christian faith, one that remained vacuous and incomplete until it was perfected by receiving the sign of physical incorporation into the people of Israel. As we have seen, it was the soteriological value attached to circumcision, and not the rite itself, that prompted Paul's negative reaction to the reforming mission of his opponents. The "higher life" they were promoting was in reality a step backwards into the negative sphere of human self-justification and rebellion against the grace of God.

ALL FOR NAUGHT? (3:4-5). **3:4** The word *paschō* in this verse can mean either simply "to experience" or more specifically "to suffer." Biblical scholars are divided about which sense was intended here. If the former, then Paul was asking, "Have you experienced such great things [the gift of the Spirit, the ensuing mighty works] to no purpose?"[16] However, the NIV probably is correct in opting for the other meaning, "Have you suffered so much for nothing?" assuming that Paul's Galatian converts had been called upon to endure periodic persecutions at the hands of non-Christian Jews or the Roman authorities in Galatia.

While there is no positive evidence that the Galatian Christians actually suffered such external persecutions, it is not unreasonable to suppose that they would have been subjected to the same kind of harassment and violent assaults that Paul and Barnabas experienced when they first brought the gospel into that region (cf. Acts 13:14). By accepting circumcision, however, they might well have reduced the brunt of such persecution since they would then have appeared more as normal proselytes in submission to the Jewish rituals of the synagogue. According to Paul, avoidance of persecution was a major motive of the false teachers themselves (6:12). Thus Paul would have been saying something like this: "Having received with me the brand marks of Christ in your bodies, being persecuted for the cause of Christ, are you now going to accept a practice that could have spared you all these persecutions in the first place? Has all this been for naught?"

Paul added a brief conditional clause—"if it really was for nothing?"— which indicates that the situation in Galatia was not yet hopeless. Although the situation was desperately bad, it was not beyond the reach of divine res-

---

[16] F. F. Bruce, *The Epistle to the Galatians,* NIGTC (Grand Rapids: Eerdmans, 1982), 150. See also W. Michaelis, "Πάσχου," *TDNT* 5.905.

cue. Throughout the history of the church, periods of doctrinal decline and spiritual apathy have often preceded reformation and revival. There is hope from anywhere the Christian stands because God is sovereign. His purpose cannot be thwarted nor his Word returned void. Three times in Galatians Paul has raised the specter of the absurd consequences of justification by works. In 2:2 Paul raised the possibility that his missionary labors may have been in vain. In 2:21 he raised the stakes and suggested that if righteousness could be gained through the law, then even Christ would have died in vain. Now here in 3:4 he queried the Galatians about whether the Spirit had not been given to them in vain. In effect, he was saying to them: "See where this kind of theology will lead you! If salvation is not the work of God from first to last, then the preaching of the gospel is vanity, the cross of Christ was a farce, and the gift of the Holy Spirit means nothing!" By presenting these terrible alternatives to the Galatians in such a startling way, Paul sought to jar them from their folly and break the spell that had left them bewitched.

3:5 Paul brought his argument from experience to a conclusion by asking again the question he had posed in v. 2. Here in summary he said to them: "Remember how you came to Christ in the first place. Barnabas and I came to Galatia preaching the gospel of Jesus Christ and him crucified. You heard our words, believed the message, and God poured out his Holy Spirit among you. The evidence of his presence and power was unmistakable. Moreover, none of this was conditioned on your acceptance of circumcision or your obedience to the law. You have begun in the Spirit, now don't turn back to the flesh! Even the scars of persecution you bear are trophies of God's grace. Don't blow it all by following these false teachers who, like evil magicians, are trying to seduce you from the way of Christ to a counterfeit gospel."[17]

---

[17] Paul's reference to the fact that God "works miracles" among the Galatians has been interpreted variously by commentators on this passage. Some see this as a reference to the exorcism of evil spirits, others to ecstatic phenomena or divine healings and the like. Whatever they were, Paul was not speaking merely of the miracles he performed in Galatia, some of which are recorded in Acts, but of the continuing miraculous manifestations of the Spirit among the believers of Galatia. Such miraculous signs often accompany the initial evangelization of a particular region. There is no more reason to assume that such miracles were limited to the days of the apostles than there is to teach that the Great Commission has expired with them. At the same time, it is important to note that while Paul, here and elsewhere, accepted the validity of miraculous manifestations of the Spirit, he did not separate this dimension of the Spirit's ministry from the sanctifying work of inner transformation. As E. deW. Burton put it, "Yet it must also be borne in mind that in the view of the apostle it was one spirit that produced alike the outward charismata and the inward moral fruit of the Spirit (5:22-23)" (*A Critical and Exegetical Commentary on the Epistle to the Galatians,* ICC [Edinburgh: T & T Clark, 1921], 151). See also W. Grundmann, "δύναμαι," *TDNT* 2.304-17, and D. J. Lull, *The Spirit in Galatia: Paul's Interpretation of Pneuma as Divine Power* (Chico, Cal.: Scholars Press, 1980).

2. The Case of Abraham (3:6-9)

We now come to an important transition in Paul's argument in Galatians. Paul reviewed his special calling and unique apostolic ministry from his encounter with the risen Christ near Damascus through his confrontation with Peter at Antioch. Here he concluded the opening historical section of his letter by stating clearly that justification was not secured by human works of any kind but only through faith in Jesus Christ (2:16). This was the central thesis Paul was defending against certain Jewish-Christian missionaries who had come into Galatia insisting that Paul's converts there submit to circumcision and other observances of the Jewish law in order to achieve a right standing before God. Paul saw in this false teaching the sinister scheme of the Evil One and appealed to the Galatians to remember how the presence of the Holy Spirit was manifested among them as an act of God's sheer mercy quite apart from any works they had done (3:1-5).

While this argument from experience was necessary, and certainly valid, it was not sufficient to reanchor the Galatians in the truth of the gospel. Why not? Because in New Testament times, just as in ours, the genuine work of the Holy Spirit is often confused with spiritual experiences of dubious origin. That this was true in Galatia is evident from the fact that Paul considered the Galatians to have been robbed of their senses by some uncanny force of darkness: "Who has bewitched you?" (3:1). Thus to his preliminary appeal to experience Paul added a lengthy and substantial argument from Scripture. While the two arguments complement each other, they were not of equal weight in Paul's mind. From this point on to the end of chap. 4 the doctrine of justification will be presented in the context of a battle for the Bible. For Paul the verdict of Holy Writ is the court of final appeal in all matters related to God and the revelation of his will to human beings.

In the main section of Galatians, Paul used three major arguments from Scripture to demonstrate the doctrine of justification by faith. The first argument, which begins in v. 6 and ends with the twofold conclusion of v. 14, focuses on Abraham's faith and the blessing that comes through it over against the curse of the law that Christ has borne through his death on the cross. The second argument, 3:15-25, picks up on the theme of the law and discusses its foreordained purpose within the economy of redemptive history. The third major argument from Scripture (4:21-31) brings to a conclusion Paul's theological exposition by means of an allegory on two mothers, Hagar and Sarah, and their two sons, Ishmael and Isaac, who are taken as prototypes of those who appeal to the patrimony of Abraham today.

The three arguments Paul developed employ various exegetical devices and marshall diverse texts of Scripture ranging from Genesis to Habakkuk.

However, they all share one theme in common: an appeal to the patriarch Abraham. Indeed, Paul's intricate argumentation in Gal 3 and 4 can be reduced to one simple proposition: those who believe in Jesus Christ share fully in the blessings God promised to Abraham. Each of these three sections poses a distinct but interrelated question: How was Abraham made right with God? (3:6-14). What is the true purpose of the law? (3:15-25). Who are the real heirs of the promise? (4:21-31).

Galatians 3:26–4:20 stands as a parenthesis in the elaboration of Paul's scriptural proofs. The parenthesis is further divided into subsections: 3:26–4:7, where Paul drew on early baptismal and confessional formulas to emphasize the unity of the church, and 4:8-20, in which the apostle again expressed in terms of personal intimacy his enduring concern for the Galatians. Throughout Gal 3 and 4 Paul greatly expanded the vocabulary of salvation he had already introduced in the letter. Not only gospel, faith, and justification but also the Spirit, redemption, promise, covenant, inheritance, sonship, and freedom would dominate his discussion of God's gracious initiative to rescue lost individuals from the prison of sin to the praise of his glory.[18]

(1) A Text from Genesis (3:6)

6Consider Abraham: "He believed God, and it was credited to him as righteousness."

3:6   The patriarch Abraham, who is mentioned nineteen times in Paul's letters, is the pivotal figure in all of Paul's arguments from Scripture in Galatians. But why Abraham? It has been suggested that Paul was exercising theological one-upmanship in his appeal to the father of the Jewish people. In other words, if his opponents claimed the authority of Moses, the giver of the law, he would do them one better by going even further back to Abraham.[19] It is much more likely, however, that Paul developed his unique

---

[18] J. Bligh has argued that Gal 3–4 (minus the personal parenthesis of 4:11-20) is a continuation of Paul's Antioch discourse that began at 2:15 (*Galatians: A Discussion of St. Paul's Epistle* [London: St. Paul, 1969], 235-36). He claims that the OT quotations and the Midrashic interpretations of them which Paul's exegesis reflects would have been more intelligible to Jewish Christians at Antioch than to Gentile converts in Galatia. Bligh's argument allows him to interpret Paul's first person pronouns "we" and "us" in 3:13,24 and 4:4 to mean "we Jews" and "us Jews" rather than in a more inclusive sense. However, as we shall see, the mutual implication of God's redemptive work for Jews and Gentiles in these two chapters is more complex than this simple analysis will bear. Paul was not arguing for two separate ways of salvation, one for Jews and another for Gentiles, but rather for a new reality effected by faith in Jesus Christ that has completely relativized the old distinctions of race, class, and gender (3:28). Nonetheless, Bligh correctly points to the centrality of the Antioch episode in setting forth the issues that concerned Paul in the central section of the Galatian epistle.

[19] This, for example, is the suggestion of J. Stott (*Only One Way: The Message of Galatians*

understanding of Abraham's role in the history of salvation over against the appeal to Abraham in the theology of his opponents. Thus Paul's main purpose was not so much to oppose Abraham to Moses as it was to set the Abraham of "faith alone" over against the Abraham of rabbinic exegesis who was blessed by God because of his meritorious deeds.[20]

In the postexilic period the Pentateuchal patriarchs became the focus of extensive study and speculation. In a time of national conflict and identity crisis, the Jewish people sought an answer to the question, What does it mean to be in covenant with the "God of Abraham, Isaac, and Jacob"? Abraham, of course, was not only the father of the Jewish nation, but he also was the original source of blessing for the Jewish people. In the Jewish literature of this period Abraham is invariably depicted as the "hero of faith" whose fidelity and obedience merited the favor of God and brought divine blessing on him and his posterity. Abraham is extolled as the "friend of God," a man of hospitality, virtue, and conviction.

Two incidents in Abraham's life were singled out as illustrations of his faithful obedience and worthiness before God. The first event is referred to in a lyrical passage from the apocryphal book called Sirach (Ecclesiasticus), where Abraham is praised as one of the great heroes of Israel's past:

> Great Abraham was the father of many nations;
> no one has ever been found to equal him in fame.
> He kept the law of the Most High;
> he entered into covenant with him,
> setting upon his body the mark of the covenant;
> and, when he was tested, he proved faithful.
> Therefore, the Lord swore an oath to him,
> that nations should find blessing through his descendants,
> that his family should be countless as the dust of the earth
> and be raised as high as the stars,
> and that their possession should reach from sea to sea,
> from the Great River to the ends of the earth. (Sir 44:19-21, NEB)

The "mark of the covenant" that was set upon Abraham's body is an

---

[Downers Grove: InterVarsity, 1968], 72). Paul does not mention Moses by name in Galatians, although he is referred to by inference in 3:19-20. For other Pauline references to Moses see especially Rom 5:13-14 and 2 Cor 3:6-18. On the place of Moses in Paul's covenant theology, see P. Démann, "Moïse et la loi dans la pensée de saint Paul," in *Moïse, l'homme de l'alliance*, ed. H. Cazelles (Paris: Desclé, 1955), 189-242.

[20] On this theme see the excursus and literature cited in Betz, *Galatians*, 139-40, and Longenecker, *Galatians*, 110-12. On Paul's use of Abraham as a key figure in the development of his theology see G. W. Hansen, *Abraham in Galatians: Epistolary and Rhetorical Contexts* (Sheffield: JSOT 1989) and the excellent summary article by N. L. Calvert on "Abraham" in *DPL*, 1-9.

explicit reference to Abraham's acceptance of circumcision as recorded in Gen 17:4-14. This was doubtless a critical text for Paul's opponents, for it suggested that circumcision was an indispensable sign of the covenant. If Gentile converts wanted to receive the full blessing of the people of God, they had to submit themselves to the God-ordained sign of his covenant as Father Abraham had done long ago. The text from Sirach also declares that Abraham had "kept the law of the Most High." Of course, Abraham lived before the actual giving of the Mosaic law, but it was believed that he had fulfilled it proleptically through his exemplary obedience and faithfulness before the Lord.[21]

Abraham's anticipatory obedience of the law was further illustrated by the ten trials or tests that proved Abraham's trustworthiness, the ten trials corresponding to the Ten Commandments, which would be broken by the children of Israel.[22] In rabbinic writings the last of the ten trials was always the "*Aqēdâ* Isaac," the "binding" and sacrifice of Abraham's beloved son as recorded in Gen 22:1-19. These two things, Abraham's obedience to the law and his sacrifice of Isaac, were brought together in the story of Mattathias, the father of Judas Maccabeus, who organized an army of liberation to wage guerilla war against the Gentile invaders of Israel. First Maccabees 2 describes how these "freedom fighters" swept through the land, pulling down pagan altars and forcibly circumcising all the uncircumcised boys found within the frontiers of Israel. Thus they "saved the law from the Gentiles and their kings and broke the power of the tyrant." On his deathbed Mattathias gathered his sons about him, exhorting them to be zealous for the law and give their lives for the covenant of their fathers. He reviewed the catalog of Israel's heroes whom God blessed because of their obedience to the law: Joshua kept the law and became a judge in Israel; Elijah was zealous for the law and was taken up to heaven; Daniel was an observant Jew in a pagan culture and was rescued from the lions' jaws. At the head of the list, of course, stands Abraham: "Did not Abraham prove steadfast under trial, and so gain credit as a righteous man?" (1 Macc 2:45-64). Here again is the standard portrayal of Abraham—the valiant warrior of faith who received

---

[21] Cf. Jubilees 23:10: "For Abraham was perfect in all his deeds with the Lord, and well-pleasing in righteousness all the days of his life."

[22] The following dialogue between Moses and God is reported by Rabbi Abin as an example of the merit of Abraham's faithfulness: "But Moses pleaded: 'Lord of the Universe! Why art thou angry with Israel?' 'Because they have broken the Decalogue,' He replied. 'Well, they possess a source from which they can make repayment,' he urged. 'What is the source?' He asked. Moses replied: 'Remember that Thou didst prove Abraham with ten trials, and so let those ten [trials of Abraham] serve as compensation for these ten [broken commandments]'" (*Exod Rab* 44.4).

the reward of righteousness because of his obedience and steadfastness under testing, even to the limits of sacrificing his own son.

No doubt Paul was well aware of this traditional portrait of Abraham. Very likely it had been cast in his teeth by his Judaizing opponents. Paul did not ignore their appeal to Abraham, but he shifted the point of departure to an earlier event in Abraham's life. Nowhere did Paul refer explicitly to Abraham's sacrifice of Isaac, nor in Galatians did he cite the covenant of circumcision mentioned in Gen 17.[23] For Paul the critical verse was Gen 15:6: "He believed God, and it was credited to him as righteousness." This quotation is introduced by the correlative conjunction *kathōs,* "just as," which connects the faith of Abraham to the experience of the Galatians that Paul had just reviewed. He was saying, in effect, that just as the Galatians had trusted God's Word, which they heard through Paul's preaching, so also Abraham believed what God said and was counted righteous, just like the Galatians, through the "hearing of faith," not by the doing of deeds.

How did Paul understand Abraham's faith? In Rom 4:3 he again quoted this same text from Genesis and described more fully how faith became the instrument of Abraham's justification. Thus the best commentary on Gal 3 is Rom 4. Looking at both passages in the total context of Paul's theology, we can learn three important principles about faith from the example of Abraham.[24]

---

[23] In a suggestive article, however, M. Wilcox has pointed to several possible allusions of the sacrifice of Isaac in Paul's writings including the word for "cross" or "tree" (ζύλον) in Gal 3:13 ("'Upon the Tree'—Deut 21:22-23 in the New Testament," *JBL* 96 [1977]: 85-99). This word can also mean "wood," which was used in Midrashic interpretations to refer to the wood of the burnt offering that Abraham loaded onto Isaac for their excursion to Mount Moriah. Tertullian spells out the significance of this act for Christian typology: "Isaac, when led by his father as a victim, and himself bearing his own 'wood' (*lignum*) was even at that period pointing to Christ's death; conceded, as he was, as a victim by the Father; carrying, as he did, the 'wood' of his passion" (*Adversus Iudaeos* 10.6). Wilcox also finds a Pauline reference to Isaac in Rom 8:32, where God is described as the one "who did not spare his own son, but handed him over for the sake of us all."

[24] In interpreting Gal 3 by means of Rom 4, I presuppose the essential coherence of Paul's thought while allowing for the occasional and contextual character of both Galatians and Romans. Important differences exist in the way Paul treated the Abraham story in these two epistles, but his interpretations are complementary rather than contradictory. J. C. Beker has argued that Paul's polemical attack against the law in Galatians reflects the contingency and particularity of his defense of the gospel against the Judaizers (*Paul the Apostle: The Triumph of God in Life and Thought* [Philadelphia: Fortress, 1980], 99). Romans, on the other hand, is more irenic and positive in its treatment of circumcision and the law because it was written as a dialogue with converted Jews rather than as an *apologia* for Gentile Christians. While Beker's analysis is helpful in accounting for the different tone and nuances of the two letters, he goes too far in claiming that "Romans 4 allows for the continuity of salvation-history, whereas Galatians 3 focuses on its discontinuity." In neither Romans nor Galatians did Paul ever lose

1. *Faith excludes boasting.* The theme of boasting is a major motif in Paul's writings, not only in Galatians and Romans but also in the Corinthian correspondence and Philippians as well.[25] To boast is to glory, to take credit for, to claim the right of self-determination, to brag about one's autonomy and self-sufficiency. While few people are so brazen as to claim outright, "I am the master of my fate; I am the captain of my ship" (Thomas Henley), this thought lies just beneath the surface in every unregenerate heart. But the faith by which Abraham was justified stands in absolute contradiction to every kind of self-glorification. Just prior to quoting Gen 15:6 in Rom 4, Paul made this very point. If indeed Abraham had been justified by works, he would have had reason to boast. Yet this is precisely what Abraham could not do because God called him, as Paul would show later in Gal 3, four hundred thirty years before the law was given, even twenty-nine years, according to the reckoning of the rabbis, before the sacrifice of Isaac. Thus, contrary to the traditional interpretation, Paul did not present Abraham as a paragon of virtue or a model of religious activism. Rather, it happened this way: God spoke, Abraham heard and believed, and on the basis of mere faith (*sola fide*) he received God's justifying verdict.

2. *Faith transcends reason.* In his exegesis of this verse, Martin Luther introduced a second antithesis: not only faith versus works but also faith versus reason. "To attribute glory to God is to believe in him, to regard him as truthful, wise, righteous, merciful, and almighty, in short, to acknowledge him as the Author and Donor of every good. Reason does not do this, but faith does. . . . Faith slaughters reason and kills the beast that the whole world and all the creatures cannot kill."[26]

---

sight of the Jews' and Gentiles' special place in God's salvific economy. H. Hübner proposed a developmental scheme of Paul's thought that bifurcates Galatians and Romans in an even more extreme manner (*Law in Paul's Thought* [Edinburgh: T & T Clark, 1984], 51–57). He sees great inconsistency in Paul's treatment of the law in these two letters and attributes this disjunction to the apostle's fundamental rethinking of the relationship of Gentile Christianity to its Jewish counterpart. Galatians was written rather late in Paul's apostolic career even if, as we have argued, it may have been the first of his extant letters. By the time he wrote Galatians, he had behind him many years of missionary preaching, the synod on the Gentile mission at Jerusalem, and the confrontation with Peter at Antioch. It is inconceivable that he would not yet have given thought to the "inconsistencies" in his attack on the law on the one hand and his appeal for the unity of Jewish and Gentile Christianity on the other. Galatians reflects a mature, if passionate, theology that is anything but half-baked.

[25]See R. Bultmann, *Theology of the New Testament* (New York: Scribners, 1955); E. Käsemann, *Romans* (Grand Rapids: Eerdmans, 1980), 64. Cf. Gal 6:13–14; Rom 2:23; 3:21–31; 4:1–6; 1 Cor 1:29–31; 2 Cor 10:7–18; 11:16–30; Phil 3:3–9.

[26]*LW* 26.227–28. On the various ways Luther used the word "reason" (*ratio, Vernunft*), see the excellent study of B. A. Gerrish, *Grace and Reason* (Chicago: University of Chicago Press, 1979). See also H. Oberman, ed., *Luther: Sol, Ratio, Erudio, Aristoteles* (Bonn: Bovier, 1971).

Such language can easily be misunderstood if we take it as a blanket condemnation of logical thinking or rational discourse. Clearly both Paul and Luther made good use of their God-given ability to think clearly and argue cogently by means of human reasoning. But Luther was right to oppose faith to reason where the latter is understood as an autonomous principle of doing theology apart from the special revelation of God in his Word.

Abraham's faith was not based on his independent inquiry into the structure of reality nor his construal of various arguments for or against the existence of God. Abraham's listening to God and finding God in the right was thus "contrary to all self-assessment and the verdict of human probability."[27] In Rom 4 Paul gave the example of Abraham's trust that God would fulfill his promise to give him descendants as numerous as the stars in the heavens or the sands along the seashore even when he and Sarah were well past the normal age of childbearing. When reason would have counseled doubt and despair, Abraham "was fully persuaded that God had power to do what he had promised" (Rom 4:21). The sacrifice of Isaac must be interpreted along these same lines. Abraham was willing to slay his son of promise at God's command, believing that, if necessary, God could raise him back to life in order to fulfill his word. This is the kind of faith Jesus spoke of when he announced that, contrary to every canon of reason, God was able to raise up sons to Abraham by the power of his word from inanimate objects such as lifeless stones. Thus Luther invites us to enter with Abraham into "the darkness of faith," saying to reason, "You keep quiet. Do not judge; but listen to the Word of God, and believe it."[28]

3. *Faith issues in obedience.* By emphasizing so strongly the unilateral action of God in justifying sinners by faith alone apart from works, did not Paul undercut the basis of Christian morality and leave himself open to the charge of antinomianism? Clearly he faced just such an objection in his own day as he himself indicated: "Shall we go on sinning so that grace may increase? By no means!" (Rom 6:1–2). In Gal 5 and 6 he would spell out the dimensions of the Spirit-led life and encourage his readers to "test their own actions, serve one another in love, and fulfill the law of Christ" (6:4; 5:13).

---

[27] G. Ebeling, *The Truth of the Gospel: An Exposition of Galatians* (Philadelphia: Fortress, 1984), 176.

[28] *LW* 26.228. In his excoriation of unbridled reason, Luther sometimes praises faith in a way that seems inappropriate as when he calls it "the creator of the deity, not in the substance of God but in us." Early in his reforming career Luther had broken with the mystical doctrine that within every human soul there remained a spark of divinity. His language about "faith creating deity" represents an awkward attempt to read an evangelical meaning into a pre-Reformation conceptual framework. See T. George, *Theology of the Reformers* (Nashville: Broadman, 1988), 62–73.

It is in this context that we must place the presumed contradiction between Paul's doctrine of justification by faith and James's statements about justification by works (Jas 2:14-26). As is well known, Luther criticized James as "a right strawy epistle" that was hardly worthy to be included in the canon since it contradicted Paul in ascribing justification to works.[29] Calvin, on the other hand, held that James was not opposing works to true faith but rather to a false conception of faith. Calvin contended that James's intention was not to show the source or manner of one's attainment of righteousness but simply to stress a single point, that true faith is confirmed by good works.

> When the Sophists set James against Paul, they were deceived by the double meaning of the term 'justification.' When Paul says that we are justified by faith, he means precisely that we have won a verdict of righteousness in the sight of God. James has quite another intention, but the man who professes himself to be faithful should demonstrate the truth of his fidelity by works. James did not mean to teach us where the confidence of our salvation should rest—which is the very point on which Paul does insist. So let us avoid the false reasoning which has trapped the Sophists, by taking word of the double meaning: to Paul, the word denotes our free imputation of righteousness before the judgment seat of God, to James, the demonstration of righteousness from its effects, in the sight of men.[30]

If Luther understood better than anyone since Paul himself the radical character of justification by faith alone, Calvin had a better grasp of how this vital doctrine related to the overall structure of Pauline thought and New Testament theology. We are justified by faith alone, but the faith that justifies is not alone. E. Käsemann has captured well the meaning of this dictum for

---

[29] *LW* 35.362. For Zwingli, Calvin and the Anabaptists on James, see T. George, "'A Right Strawy Epistle': Reformation Perspectives on James," *RevExp* 83 (1986): 369-82.

[30] CNTC 3.285. Echoes of Luther and Calvin can be heard in recent scholarly discussion of the James-Paul issue. After surveying this literature P. H. Davids has concluded that there is "no real conflict between James and Paul on the issue of works. . . . The two authors used their terms in different ways because they addressed different issues." Concerning the use both James and Paul made of Gen 15:6, he notes how the example of Abraham functioned differently for the two biblical writers. For Paul the critical issue was the fact that Abraham was declared righteous before the rite of circumcision was instituted; for James the critical issue was to show that the faith of Abraham was not mere orthodoxy but rather a trust leading to actual righteous deeds. "In other words, the two men come at the Abraham narrative from different directions, using definitions of faith with different emphases, and as a result argue for complementary rather than contradictory conclusions." See P. H. Davids, "James and Paul," *DPL*, 457-61.

Paul's overall understanding of faith: "Faith is constituted by the fact that with the preaching of the gospel the Lord who is the basis of the gospel comes upon the scene and seizes dominion over us. . . . Faith is living out of the word which bears witness to his lordship, nothing more and nothing less."[31]

(2) True Children of Abraham (3:7-9)

⁷Understand, then, that those who believe are children of Abraham. ⁸The Scripture foresaw that God would justify the Gentiles by faith, and announced the gospel in advance to Abraham: "All nations will be blessed through you." ⁹So those who have faith are blessed along with Abraham, the man of faith.

3:7 In this verse Paul extended his argument from Abraham to his posterity and raised for the first time the question that would dominate the remainder of Gal 3 and 4: Who are the true children of Abraham? This train of thought will find a conclusion in the allegory of the two mothers, Sarah and Hagar, and their two sons, Isaac and Ishmael (4:21-31).

Appealing to the traditional Jewish exegetical tradition about Abraham, Paul's opponents had evidently been saying to the Gentile believers of Galatia: "So you want to become Christians? Great! We will show you how to become true sons of Abraham. You must receive the seal of circumcision, the indispensable sign of God's covenant with his people, and, like Father Abraham, keep the commands of the holy law." Against this "orthodox" theology of Abraham, Paul offered a counterinterpretation. "All right," he said; "you think being a son of Abraham is such a big deal? Well, let's go back to Abraham himself. How was he declared righteous before God in the first place? Was it because he forsook his fatherland, his family, and all his friends back in Ur of the Chaldees? Was it because he accepted circumcision and observed the law? Was it because he was ready, at the command of God, to sacrifice his son Isaac? No! Abraham was justified not on account of his outstanding virtues and holy works, but solely because he believed God. And his faith was reckoned as righteousness long before he knew anything about circumcision or had taken the first step in his long journey toward the promised land. Although he became the father of the Jews, he was justified when he was still a Gentile!—just like you Galatians, who were justified and received the Holy Spirit through the hearing of faith, not through works of the law."

Paul's rebuttal was a stinging rebuke to the theology of the Judaizers. Descent by blood or physical procreation does not create sons of Abraham

---

[31] Käsemann, *Romans,* 108.

in the sight of God any more than the alteration of one's private parts does. The true children of Abraham are those who believe, literally, those who ground their relationship with God and thus their very existence itself on the basis of faith. Paul's argument resonates with the discussion Jesus held with the Jewish leaders of his day concerning their status as children of Abraham. If Abraham were your real father, Jesus said, you would act more like him, you would embody his characteristics—rather than those of the devil to whom you really belong (John 8:31-47). Paul already had hinted at the presence of the Evil One in Galatia (cf. the "bewitcher" of 3:1). Now he suggested that those who seek to be right with God through physical lineage or human effort will at the end of the day be found outside the people of God altogether, locked up forever in "this present evil age" of darkness and sin (1:4).[32]

3:8 Here in a remarkable figure of speech Paul attributed divine foresight to the written Word of God: "The Scripture foresaw that God would justify the Gentiles by faith and announced the gospel in advance to Abraham." Whether the word Paul used for Scripture, *graphē*, refers to the specific verse he quoted (actually a conflation of Gen 12:3 and 18:18) or, as seems more likely, to Scripture as a whole, it is clear, as Bruce rightly observes, that Paul used "Scripture" here "more or less as an extension of the divine personality."[33]

The doctrine of biblical inspiration that Paul elaborated in 2 Tim 3:15-17 is clearly implied in this text by his absolute identification of "Scripture" with the speaking God. Otherwise Paul's language makes no sense at all. How can an inanimate object, a written text, "foresee" anything? Clearly it was God himself who spoke to Abraham the words attributed here to Scrip-

---

[32] R. A. Cole has suggested that υἱοὶ Ἀβραάμ should perhaps be translated not so much children or sons of Abraham as "real Abrahams" (*The Epistle of Paul to the Galatians,* TNTC [Grand Rapids: Eerdmans, 1965], 93). This would follow the normal Semitic pattern by which, for instance, Jews were referred to as "sons of David" or wicked persons called the "sons of Belial." On the significance of the John 8 passage in Paul, see F. Leenhardt, "Abraham et la conversion de Saul de Tarse, suivi d'une note sur Abraham dans Jean 8," *Revue d'histoire et de philosophie religieuse* 53 (1973): 331-51.

[33] Bruce, *Galatians,* 156. The term γραφή is used variously in the NT to refer to Holy Scripture in its totality and unity as well as to designate individual passages of Scripture. Galatians 3:8 seems to parallel Rom 9:17 and 10:11, where clearly Paul identified the Scripture with God's own speaking. See G. Schrenk, "γραφή," *TDNT* 1.749-61. On the doctrine of Scripture in Pauline theology, see the classic study by E. E. Ellis, *Paul's Use of the Old Testament* (Edinburgh: Oliver & Boyd, 1957), and, more recently, W. C. Kaiser, Jr., *The Uses of the Old Testament and the New* (Chicago: Moody, 1985), and C. D. Stanley, *Paul and the Language of Scripture: Citation Technique in the Pauline Epistles and Contemporary Literature* (Cambridge: Cambridge University Press, 1992).

ture. Indeed, when those words were first spoken, there was as yet no written revelation in existence. Obviously, then, what Paul meant was "God, as recorded in Scripture, said." Paul's language does not require us to posit a Koran-like Bible that exists independently of God himself. However, we are left with the irresistible impression that for Paul the words recorded in Holy Scripture are nothing less than the living voice of God. It is God who speaks in Scripture and for this reason it has an unassailable validity and normative significance for the people of God.[34]

What was it that the Scriptures "foresaw" and "preached beforehand" to Abraham? Simply this: the good news of salvation was to be extended to all peoples, including the Gentiles, who would be declared righteous by God, just like Abraham, on the basis of faith.[35] Thus Paul interpreted the Genesis quotation "All nations will be blessed through you" in a far richer sense than traditional Jewish exegesis allowed. Through the Jewish people the world had received many wonderful benefits, above all the sacred Scriptures and the religion of monotheism. However, Paul went much further when "he simply identifies the blessing with God's 'grace' and his 'justification by faith.'"[36] Abraham was special because centuries before Jesus was born he received in this word from God the promise of the Messiah and believed. Paul's exegesis at this point is really a commentary on the declaration of Jesus: "Abraham was overjoyed to see my day; he saw it and was glad" (John 8:56, NEB). In Paul's mind, of course, the "day" of Christ had inaugurated a new epoch in the history of salvation which, as he had shown already in Gal 1, included his own calling and special mission to the Gentiles. He was now ready to apply the lesson of Abraham to the Gentile Christians of Galatia.

3:9 This verse presents the conclusion ("so," Gk., *hōste*) to the Abraham-argument Paul introduced in v. 6. Clearly he was not through with Abraham, as the unfolding of his argument in Gal 3 and 4 will show. However, in these few short verses he had already made two critical points that

---

[34] B. B. Warfield's statement is still relevant to this theme: "It would be difficult to invent methods of showing profound reverence for the text of Scripture as the very Word of God, which will not be found to be characteristic of the writers of the New Testament in dealing with the Old. . . . God and the Scriptures are brought into such conjunction as to show that in point of directness of authority no distinction was made between them" (*The Inspiration and Authority of the Bible* [Philadelphia: Presbyterian Reformed, 1948], 299).
[35] Betz notes that προευηγγελίσατο is a hapax legomenon in the NT, although it does occur in Philo (*Galatians*, 143). Cf. J. Locke's paraphrase of this text: "For it being in the purpose of God to justify the Gentiles by faith, he gave Abraham a foreknowledge of the gospel" (J. Locke, *Paraphrase of Paul* [Oxford: Clarendon, 1987]), 136-37).
[36] Betz, *Galatians,* 142.

will be elaborated in the following passages. First, he redefined the Abrahamic family in such a way as to undercut the appeal of his opponents to this biblical paradigm. The true children of Abraham are those who, like the great patriarch, have been declared righteous by faith, that is, by God himself in his grace. Put otherwise, "the authentic descendants of Abraham are soul brothers rather than merely blood brothers."[37] Second, Paul interpreted the blessing promised through Abraham to "all the nations" as a prophecy of his own law-free mission to the Gentiles. Through the unerring word of God, Abraham not only received the promise of the gospel but also anticipated its fulfillment in Jesus Christ, a fulfillment that was being realized in part among the Galatians themselves who had been justified by faith through their hearing of the gospel by the ministry of Paul.[38]

Paul's entire argument in this passage hinges on one tremendous assumption: the continuity of the covenant of grace. It is not surprising that Marcion, for all his adulation of Paul, wanted to excise all reference to Abraham as the prototype of faith.[39] By rejecting the Old Testament completely, Marcion presented Christianity as the religion of the "alien Father" of Jesus, a deity who stood in total opposition to the God of the Old Testament as well as to the world of matter that he had neither created nor was interested in redeeming.

Paul, however, would have none of this. From the creation of Adam and Eve until the second coming of Christ, God has provided one and only one way of salvation for all peoples everywhere: the atoning death of his Son on the cross applied to all of the elect through the regenerating ministry of the Holy Spirit. Thus Paul could claim that the faith of Abraham was the same as ours with this noticeable difference: he believed in the Christ who was to come, just as we trust in the One who has already come. As Calvin put it, the patriarchs of old "participated in the same inheritance and hoped for a common salvation with us by the grace of the same Mediator."[40] Paul's insistence on the continuity of salvation history had a profound impact on the future course of the Christian faith. It prevented it from becoming just

---

[37] P. R. Jones, "Exegesis of Galatians 3 and 4," *RevExp* 69 (1972): 476.

[38] This point has been well made by J. M. G. Barclay in his excellent study, *Obeying the Truth: A Study of Paul's Ethics in Galatians* (Edinburgh: T & T Clark, 1988), 87-88.

[39] See Tertullian, *Adversus Marcionem* (chap. 4): *ANF* 3.435-38. In Gnostic exegesis of this passage, Paul's reference to Abraham is taken as a figurative representation of the demiurge while the "children of Abraham" are the psychics, those unenlightened souls who can only believe since they are not yet "in the know." The early Gnostic commentator Heracleon rejected justification by faith, snidely remarking, "The demiurge believes well" (Pagels, *Gnostic Paul*, 106).

[40] John Calvin, *The Institutes of the Christian Religion*, 2.10.1.

another mystery religion from the East by binding it to God's mighty acts in the past while at the same time extending it into a worldwide missionary movement by recognizing that "the holy one of Israel" was none other than "the God of all the earth" (Isa 54:5).

3. Christ and the Curse (3:10-14)

In vv. 6-9 Paul set forth a positive argument for justification by faith. In vv. 10-14 he turned the tables and argued negatively against the possibility of justification by works.[41] The formal structure of this pericope resembles the compositional complexity of a Bach fugue and refutes the idea that Paul here pulled together a hodgepodge of disparate verses to support his makeshift argument.

On one level the passage can be analyzed in terms of four major propositions, each of which is confirmed and elucidated by a citation from the Old Testament. Thus (1) those who rely on observing the law are under a curse. Why so? The Bible says that those who do not continue to do everything written in the book of the law are cursed (Deut 27:26); (2) no one can be justified by means of the law anyway. Why not? The Scripture declares that the righteous ones live by faith (Hab 2:4); (3) law and faith are not mutually compatible ways to God. How can you be so sure? Because the law itself says that those who keep the commandments will live by them (Lev 18:5); (4) Christ redeemed us from the curse of the law. How did this happen? He became a curse for us by hanging on a tree (Deut 21:23). A closer examination of these propositions will show that (1) and (4) are closely related as problem and solution, while the two scriptural texts cited in support of (2) and (3) stand in apparent contradiction to each other. The entire passage is brought to a concluding crescendo in v. 14, which reaffirms the key element in proposition (4), Christ redeemed us, and then adds two purpose clauses—in order that the blessing of Abraham might come to the Gentiles and that by faith we might receive the promised Spirit.

Before looking at these verses in greater detail, it is important to recognize that, from another perspective, 3:10-25 constitutes a long parenthesis in the overall structure of Paul's argument concerning the true children of Abraham. As we saw earlier, Paul had been arguing from the continuity of the covenant of grace with Abraham cited as the paradigm of justification by faith. The blessing he received was not only for the Jews but for "all nations"

---

[41] So Lightfoot: "Having shown by positive proof that justification is of faith, he strengthens his position by the negative argument derived from the impossibility of maintaining its opposite, justification by law" (*Galatians,* 137).

(*ethnē*, "Gentiles"). Thus today those who believe as Abraham believed are declared righteous before God just as he was. From a strictly logical point of view, it would have made good sense for Paul to move directly from 3:9 to 3:26—"Those who have faith are blessed along with Abraham. . . . You are all sons of God through faith in Christ Jesus." Paul deliberately did not do this but rather indulged in an intricate digression on the law, a passage that, as N. T. Wright has observed, must surely rank high on any list of "the most complicated and controverted passages in Paul."[42] Why did Paul not argue, as the sequence of his thought in Gal 3:1-9 would have implied, from Abraham directly to Christ and hence to the Gentile Christians of Galatia? Why the long detour through the law and the curse?

The answer to this question must be found in the particularity of God's special revelation to his people Israel. Once the Old Testament is appropriated as Christian Scripture, there is no way for Christian theology to avoid serious engagement with the sacred history recorded in those holy texts. The church cannot be "the Israel of God" (6:16) without taking with utmost seriousness the God of Israel. Thus Paul's argument in Gal 3 follows the history of God's ancient people. It begins with Abraham, moves on to Moses (not mentioned by name in this letter but cf. 2 Cor 3:7-18), and culminates in Christ. Paul could not avoid discussing the law because the law was integral to the history of God's people. No Christian can disregard this history as pertaining only to "those Jews," for in the fullness of time God sent his Son into the very thick of this history—our history—as one born of a woman and born under law.

At this point Paul's Galatian opponents could well chime in: "Of course! That's just what we've been saying all along. The history of salvation does not run from Abraham to Christ but from Abraham through Moses to Christ. The way for the Gentiles to receive the blessing of Abraham is by way of the law. The law is not opposed to faith but rather supplements and strengthens it by making demands of it."

Paul could well have responded to the arguments of his opponents in one of two ways. He might have replied: "Yes, I agree that Moses played a pivotal role as the lawgiver in the history of God's people. But now Jesus is the New Moses! He has inaugurated a new morality, a higher set of precepts and commandments for us to obey."[43] Conversely, Paul might have argued for the complete annulment of the law, that is, that Jesus had come not only to fulfill but also to destroy the law. But Paul opted for neither of these alternatives. Instead, he took a different tact. Paul could not ignore the law because

---

[42] N. T. Wright, *The Climax of the Covenant: Christ and the Law in Pauline Theology* (Minneapolis: Fortress, 1991), 137. While I am indebted to Wright for his lively and insightful discussion of this passage, I have not been able to follow his conclusions at several controverted points.

it was crucial for his understanding of salvation and Christ—not, however, as the source of obtaining righteousness but rather as the gauge of damnation. The law tells us what we are being saved from—the curse. This takes us to the heart of Pauline soteriology. "The faith that justifies comes only through deliverance from the curse. Those who know nothing of the curse also know nothing of the blessing. Only the Christ who bears the curse can be the bearer of the blessing."[44]

(1) The Curse of the Law (3:10-12)

[10]All who rely on observing the law are under a curse, for it is written: "Cursed is everyone who does not continue to do everything written in the Book of the Law." [11]Clearly no one is justified before God by the law, because, "The righteous will live by faith." [12]The law is not based on faith; on the contrary, "The man who does these things will live by them."

3:10 As we have seen throughout Galatians, Paul frequently assembled an argument from contraries and developed his theology in terms of antitheses: crucified with Christ/alive to God, the hearing of faith/the doing of works, beginning in the Spirit/ending in the flesh, promise/fulfillment, and so on.[45] Just so, there are two decisive contrasts in vv. 9 and 10 that provide a connection for what would otherwise be a rather abrupt transition in Paul's train of thought.[46] Verse 9 is about "those who have faith," while v. 10 concerns those who observe the law; the former are said to be blessed, while the latter are cursed.

For anyone familiar with the Torah, the juxtaposition of blessing and curse would immediately evoke the *locus classicus* of Deut 27–28. In this

---

[43] Significantly, Paul nowhere used Moses as a type of Christ, although he did say that the children of Israel were "all baptized into Moses" when they passed through the sea on their way out of Egypt (1 Cor 10:2). Hebrews, of course, does compare Moses the servant to Jesus the Son, although the key reference to Moses in Hebrews is to his promulgation of the covenant by means of blood, a ritual that foreshadowed the sacrifice of Christ on the cross (Heb 3:1-6; 9:18-28). See L. L. Belleville, "Moses," *DPL,* 620-21.

[44] Ebeling, *Truth of the Gospel,* 171. Ebeling's reading of Galatians reflects Luther's interpretation. For example, Luther referred to "the chief and proper use of the law" as the revelation of "sin, blindness, misery, wickedness, ignorance, hate and contempt of God, death, hell, judgment, and the well-deserved wrath of God. . . . The law is a hammer that crushes rocks, a fire, a wind, and a great and mighty earthquake that overturns mountains." Nonetheless, "this use of the law is extremely beneficial and very necessary" (*LW* 26.309-10).

[45] So Luther: "It is the mark of an intelligent man to discern the antitheses in Scripture and to be able to interpret Scripture with their help" (ibid.).

[46] R. B. Hays has noted that "the blessing/curse opposition in that subtext [i.e., Gen 12:3] sublimely smooths the otherwise abrupt transition" (*Echoes of Scriptures in the Letters of Paul* [New Haven: Yale University Press, 1989], 109). See also Wright, *Climax of the Covenant,* 142.

passage the twelve tribes of Israel are depicted as an antiphonal choir, six standing on Mount Gerizim, six on Mount Ebal. The Levites were then to recite the litany of blessings for obedience and the catalog of curses for disobedience, at which the tribes on Mount Gerizim would ratify the blessings, and those on Mount Ebal the curses, with a hearty "Amen!" If there were any doubt that Paul had this passage in mind, he quoted the concluding curse as a confirmation of his statement that those who relied on their performance of the law for acceptance with God were under a curse: "Cursed is everyone who does not continue to do everything written in the Book of the Law."[47] As Longenecker has pointed out, Paul may well have had the words of the Deuteronomic curse painfully impressed upon his memory, not only from his rabbinical training but also from the five times he received "forty lashes minus one" at the hands of certain synagogue authorities (cf. 2 Cor 11:24). The synagogal manual outlining detailed procedures for such lashings required that the curses of Deuteronomy be read intermittently while the punishment was being meted out.[48]

Paul's argument in this verse hinges on an unstated premise that he assumes as self-evident. We can reconstruct his argument thus: the Bible says that those who do not perfectly obey the law are cursed, and in fact those who seek to be justified by works really are under such a curse because no one (except Jesus) ever has or indeed can fulfill the entire law. The idea of the unfulfillable character of the law was not unique to Paul. It was held by a number of rabbis and Jewish teachers of Paul's day, especially those of the school of Shammai, and is plainly taught in another New Testament text: "Whoever keeps the whole law and yet stumbles at just one point is guilty of breaking all of it" (Jas 2:10).

The traditional view that human beings cannot be justified by works because they are destitute of the power of keeping the law was expressed by Calvin in his Galatians commentary: "And so [Paul] concludes boldly that all are cursed because all have been commanded to keep the law perfectly, and this is because, in the present corruption of our nature, the ability is wanting. Hence we conclude that it is accidental that the law should curse,

---

[47] Bruce has suggested that the pronouncement of blessings and curses may not have been just a one-time event but rather a standard liturgy repeated periodically as part of a covenant-renewal ceremony (*Galatians,* 158). Paul was obviously quoting from a variant of the LXX, which contains two words not found in the MT: "Cursed be every one who does not abide by all the words of this law, in order to do them." However, the word "all" is found in the very next verse following the pronouncement of the twelfth curse: "If you fully obey the Lord your God and carefully follow all his commands" (Deut 28:1). Thus Paul may simply have conflated the two texts into a single quotation as he did earlier in 3:8 with Gen 12:3 and 18:18.

[48] Longenecker, *Galatians,* 117.

though at the same time perpetual and inseparable. The blessing which it offers us is excluded by our depravity, so that only the curse remains."[49]

In recent years this traditional view of Gal 3:10 has been challenged by a host of scholars who have wondered how Paul could have thought that a single infraction of the law would place one under its curse when the law itself provided the remedy of repentance on the one hand and the whole sacrificial system on the other. "No Jew who failed to keep Torah, and knew that he or she was failing to keep Torah, needed to languish for long under the awful threat of either exclusion from covenant people or, for that matter, eternal damnation. . . . How then can Paul imply that anyone who fails to keep Torah has this curse suspended forever over his or her head?"[50]

The answer to such objections has to do with both the universality and radicality of human sinfulness as seen from the perspective of the cross. As the Epistle of Hebrews explains in graphic detail, cultic sacrifices of the Old Testament were never intended to expiate the guilt of sin from any transgressor. They were instituted as a way of "announcing the gospel in advance" to the chosen people who lived before the advent of the Messiah, the true Lamb of God, who took away the sin of the world (John 1:29). The repetition of the temple sacrifices was a daily reminder of their provisionality and inherent inadequacy. For Paul, Christ was the "end" (*telos*) of the law precisely because he brought to fruition and completion what the law itself could not do (Rom 10:4). This he did by bearing the curse of the law that had justly fallen on everyone who had not fulfilled "everything written the book of the law." Thus only in the light of Jesus Christ can we understand either the true nature of humanity as God intended it to be or the radical character of human rebellion in this fallen world. It is not so much that we must paint the world as dark as possible in order to illuminate the glory of Christ; rather it is only in the light of Calvary that we grasp fully, insofar as God grants to us mortals the ability to understand such mysteries, the holiness of God, the horror of sin, and the depth of divine grace that caused all three to meet in a man on a tree.[51]

---

[49] See Calvin, CNTC 11.53.

[50] Wright, *Climax of the Covenant,* 145. Wright cites a statement by G. F. Moore that Paul's argument in Galatians was such a distortion of Jewish teaching on repentance that it would have been unintelligible to a Jewish audience. See G. F. Moore, *Judaism in the First Centuries of the Christian Era* (Cambridge: Harvard University Press, 1927-30), 3:150-51.

[51] Among others, E. P. Sanders has argued that Paul did not teach that it was impossible to keep the law perfectly (*Paul, the Law, and the Jewish People* [Philadelphia: Fortress, 1983], 17-29). He argues that Paul's polemic was not against Judaism, which did not teach that salvation could be merited by good deeds anyway, but rather against fellow Christian missionaries who were insisting that circumcision was a necessary entrance rite into the covenanted people of God. The OT citations in Gal 3:10-13 were thus intended to demonstrate that God justifies

More recently, N. T. Wright and F. Thielman have suggested a different line of interpretation for this passage, one that connects the "curse" of Galatians to the covenant theology of Israel.[52] According to this view, the curses of Deuteronomy had already been fulfilled in the history of the Jewish people. Not merely individual Jews but Israel as a whole had failed in its mission to bring light to the nations. The entire history of Israel from the exodus to the exile was a commentary on the unleashing of the curses predicted in Deuteronomy—plagues, military defeat, national disgrace, anxiety, slavery, and dispersion. One of the curses of Deuteronomy declared that God would bring a nation "from far away, from the ends of the earth, like an eagle sweeping down, a nation whose language you will not understand" (Deut 28:49) to devour the land and subjugate the people. Could any patriotic Jew of Paul's day walk through Jerusalem and see the Roman eagle ensconced near the temple precincts without thinking of that prophecy and its dire fulfillment? Thus in Gal 3:10 Paul was "reminding the Galatian 'agitators' of something which they, of all people, should know: the attempt to keep the law—to do its 'works'—in Israel's history had only led to failure and to the curse which the law pronounces on those who fail to do it."[53]

---

the Gentiles by faith, not that the law was unfulfillable. Having concluded on other grounds that salvation came only through Christ, Paul had no choice but to oppose justification by means of the law. Thus he argues "from solution to plight," stitching together various proof texts to bolster a position reached on dogmatic rather than exegetical grounds. In two important articles T. R. Schreiner has offered a conclusive refutation of Sanders: "Is Perfect Obedience to the Law Possible? A Re-examination of Galatians 3:10," *JETS* 27 (1984): 151-60; "Paul and Perfect Obedience to the Law: An Evaluation of the View of E. P. Sanders," *WTJ* 47 (1985): 245-78. The importance of Sanders' work for the "new perspective" on Paul should not be underestimated. Especially influential has been his definition of Palestinian Judaism as a religion of nonlegalistic "covenantal nomism," the idea that participation in the covenanted community was based on God's grace, not human merit, although remaining in the covenant did presuppose continuing obedience. Hardly anyone can deny that Sanders' work has been an important corrective to earlier stereotypical and monolithic perspectives on Second Temple Judaism. On the other hand, Sanders' view that Paul "abandoned Judaism simply because it was not Christianity" is less than satisfying as is his depiction of Pauline theology in general.

[52] F. Thielman, *From Plight to Solution* (Leiden: Brill, 1989), 65-72; Wright, *Climax of the Covenant,* 144-56.

[53] Thielman, *From Plight to Solution,* 69. According to Wright, the climax of the exile, and hence the beginning of restoration, had taken place when Jesus, the representative Messiah, took on himself the curse that hung over Israel through his death on the cross. "Because the Messiah represents Israel, he is able to take on himself Israel's curse and exhaust it. Jesus dies as the King of the Jews, at the hands of the Romans whose oppression of Israel is the present, and climactic form of the curse of exile itself. The crucifixion of the Messiah is, one might say, the quintessence of the curse of exile, and its climactic act" (*Climax of the Covenant,* 151).

While the national and corporate character of the curse truly belongs to the background of this text, we must not allow this fact to blind us to the deeper doctrinal truth Paul was presenting here. What happened outside the gates of Jerusalem just a few decades before Paul wrote Galatians was not merely another episode in the history of Israel. It was an event of universal human, indeed cosmic, significance. While Paul posed the problem, as he had to, in Jewish terms of blessing and curse, law and faith, it is clear from Abraham on that God's dealings with Israel had paradigmatic meaning for all peoples everywhere. As Paul argued in Rom 1–3, both Jews and Gentiles are "under the law," albeit in very different ways.[54] Thus when Paul spoke of the curse of the law he was not thinking merely of Jews, anymore than when he showed how one becomes a true child of Abraham through faith he had only Gentiles in mind. Thus the "us" of 3:13—those whom Christ has redeemed from the curse of the law—are not merely Jewish Christians but instead all the children of God, Jews and Gentiles, slaves and freed ones, males and females, who are Abraham's seed and heirs according to the promise because they belong to Christ through faith (3:26–29).[55]

3:11-12 The curse of the law, announced in v. 10, will find a remedy in the countercurse of v. 13, Christ's redeeming death on the cross. In between Paul sandwiched two verses both containing a quotation from the Old Testament, the first from the Prophets (Hab 2:4) and the second from the Law (Lev 18:5), two texts that seem on the surface to offer two alternative ways of salvation. The two quotations are linked by a common verb, "will live," but the two subjects form another of Paul's antitheses: the one who is righteous by faith versus the one who does the things of the law. How do these two verses relate to the central theme of the pericope, our redemption from

---

[54] See esp. Rom 2:14–15. Paul applied the law to unconverted Gentiles even more explicitly in Col 2:13–15. See the discussion by R. Melick, *Philippians, Colossians, Philemon,* NAC (Nashville: Broadman, 1991), 262–66. Wright, arguing that Col 2:14–15 is "not such an easy passage as to provide a basis for the exegesis of Galatians or Romans," restricts the "us" of 3:13 to Jews and the "we" of 3:14 to Jewish-Christians (*Climax of the Covenant,* 143). Later he seems to waver on the latter text, allowing that the "we" there could quite well be inclusive—"all we Christians" (p. 154).

[55] Cf. Ebeling's perceptive comment: "The Gentiles must deal with the Old Testament tradition in the specifically Jewish problems that grow out of it; the Jews must likewise draw on the example of the Gentiles to comprehend what the gospel free of the law implies. In Christ both have grown together into a single body so as to serve each other" (*Truth of the Gospel,* 174). See also R. Y. K. Fung, "The curse of the law is envisaged in Gal 3:10 as resting, not exclusively on Jews, but on Gentiles as well, so that when Christ is said to have redeemed "us" from the curse of the law "by becoming for our sake an accursed thing," the first person plural pronouns are most naturally understood as referring to both Jews and Gentiles" ("Cursed, accursed, anathema," *DPL,* 199).

the curse by Christ?

Habakkuk 2:4 is quoted three times in the New Testament, once again by Paul in Rom 1:17, a key text in Luther's "discovery" of the doctrine of justification, and in Heb 10:37, where the Old Testament prophecy is set forth as an antidote to discouragement in light of the delayed return of Christ. C. H. Dodd believed that Hab 2:4 was frequently used in primitive Christian times as a *testimonium* both to the certainty of Christ's coming and as a confirmation of salvation by faith.[56] Clearly Paul intended the latter sense in Galatians with "the righteous one" (*dikaios*) understood in a forensic sense, that is, "the one regarded by God as righteous will live by faith."[57] Significantly, both here and in Rom 1:17 Paul omitted the possessive pronoun that is found in variant forms both in the MT ("The righteous one will live through his faith") and the preferred LXX reading ("The righteous one will live through my [God's] faith/faithfulness").[58] While the inclusion of the possessive pronoun in either form would have done no damage to Paul's argument, he obviously regarded them as superfluous to his purpose here. In the overall context of Paul's argument, Hab 2:4 is a critical text because it links together three key terms already introduced in 2:20-21: righteousness-faith-life. Although the declarative aspect of justification is paramount in Gal 3, it can never be divorced from that new life in the Spirit with which Paul began his appeal to the Galatians in the opening verses of this chapter (cf. also 5:5).

No doubt there were some people in Paul's day, as there are in ours, who held that justification by faith was a good idea so long as it was not taught to

---

[56] C. H. Dodd, *According to the Scriptures* (London: Nisbet, 1952), 50-51. The Hebrew text of Hab 2:4 also occurs in the literature of Qumran (1 QpHab). The context of the Qumran text declares that God will save all doers of the law because of their faithfulness to the Teacher of Righteousness who guarantees the correct exposition and proclamation of the Torah. E. Käsemann has suggested that Paul took over this text "from the Jewish-Christian mission, which found in Hab 2:4 a prophecy of salvation by faith in the Messiah just as Qumran found salvation and commitment to the Teacher of Righteousness" (*Romans,* 31).

[57] Beginning with Theodore Beza in the sixteenth century, a number of exegetes have read ἐκ πίστεως as modifying Ὁ δίκαιος rather than the verb ζήσεται. The KJV and NIV follow the traditional interpretation while the RSV and NEB reflect the revisionist reading. Thus "he who through faith is righteous shall live" (RSV). As J. Brown observed, the traditional rendering better captures the intention of Paul both in Galatians and Romans: "The man who is the object of God's favorable regard in consequence of his faith, that man shall live, or be happy" (*An Exposition of the Epistle to the Galatians* [Marshallton, Del.: Sovereign Grace, 1970], 126). For a review of this issue in recent scholarship, see H. C. C. Cavallin, "'The Righteous Shall Live By Faith': A Decisive Argument for the Traditional Interpretation," *ST* 32 (1978): 33-43.

[58] Less preferable is this reading from the Septuagint: ὁ δε δίκαιος μου ἐκ πίστεως ζήσεται, "my righteous one will live by faith."

the exclusion of justification by works. "God helps those who help themselves" is a maxim of theology as well as economics. Paul, however, would tolerate no such theory because, as he said, "the law is not based on faith." In support of this statement, he quoted from Lev 18:5. He introduced this verse with a strong adversative, *alla*, "on the contrary," "but," in order to show that the method of justification called for by the law is wholly at variance with that established through faith. "The one who does these things, that is, the works of the law mentioned earlier in 2:16; 3:2,10, will live by them." In connection with v. 10 this statement can be understood as a hypothetical contrary-to-fact condition: if someone really were to fulfill the entire corpus of Pentateuchal law, with its 242 positive commands and 365 prohibitions (according to one rabbinic reckoning), then indeed such a person could stand before God at the bar of judgment and demand admittance to heaven on the basis of his or her performance. Yet where on earth can such a flawless person be found?

Leviticus 18:5 is in fact quoted two other times in the New Testament, and both of these references shed light on its use by Paul in Gal 3. The first instance is the prologue to the parable of the good Samaritan when Jesus encountered an expert in the law who asked him what he could do to inherit eternal life. Jesus replied, "What is written in the law?" The lawyer replied by correctly reciting the two great commandments about love of God and neighbor. Jesus replied: "You have answered correctly. Do this and you will live" (Luke 10:25-28). Immediately the man began "to justify himself," a dead giveaway that his own life record was far from spotless. Then, in response to his question, "Who is my neighbor?" Jesus told the story of the good Samaritan—not to show how much our good works and charitable deeds resemble those of the good Samaritan and so to encourage the self-justifying attitude of the lawyer, but rather to indicate how radically different his act of total self-expenditure was from the best efforts we can put forth.

If Paul had given a sermon on this parable, he would have encouraged his hearers to identify not with the good Samaritan, or even with the priest and Levite, but instead with the damaged man in the ditch. Unlike the lawyer whose question prompted the story, this man knew that he could not "justify himself" but had to receive a new standing and a new life from a source outside of himself.[59]

---

[59] On the quotation of Lev 18:5 in Luke 10:28, see Bruce, *Galatians*, 163. On the parable of the good Samaritan see the interpretation of A. C. McGill, *Suffering: A Test of Theological Method* (Philadelphia: Westminster, 1982), 99-111. W. C. Kaiser, Jr., has argued that the law was never intended as an alternative method of obtaining salvation or righteousness, not even hypothetically; see his "Leviticus 18:5 and Paul: 'Do This and You Shall Live' (Eternally?)," *JETS* 14 (1971): 19-28.

The second citation of Lev 18:5, more closely paralleling Gal 3:12, is found in the heart of Paul's great discourse on salvation and election in Rom 9–11. Having just declared that Christ is the end of the law, he set up another antithesis: "Moses describes in this way the righteousness that is by the law: 'the man who does these things will live by them'" (10:5). He then showed how the way of justification by faith has been opened up for Jew and Gentile alike since "the same lord is lord of all and richly blesses [i.e., *justifies*)] all who call on him" (10:12).

K. Barth, followed by C. E. B. Cranfield, has argued that Paul's citation of Lev 18:5 both in Romans and Galatians is a veiled reference to Christ himself. Thus rather than assuming the unfulfillability of the law, Paul was pointing by means of this text to the one person in human history who has indeed obeyed the law completely and fulfilled it perfectly, qualifying thereby to bear the curse of the law for others.[60] While the exegesis behind this interpretation seems strained, the instinct to focus on Jesus Christ as the perfect fulfiller of the law is sound. Apart from Jesus' perfect obedience of the law, what happened at Calvary would have had no more redemptive significance than the brutal crucifixion of thousands of other young Jews before, during, and after the earthly life of Christ.[61]

(2) Redemption through the Cross (3:13-14)

[13]Christ redeemed us from the curse of the law by becoming a curse for us, for it is written: "Cursed is everyone who is hung on a tree." [14]He redeemed

[60] C. E. B. Cranfield, *Romans,* ICC, 2 vols. (Edinburgh: T & T Clark, 1975, 1979), 521; "The man who accomplishes the righteousness which is of the Law, i.e., the merciful will of God expressed in the law, is the One to whom the statement basically refers as the One whom God means and wills in his law, for the sake of whom he has placed Israel under this law, who from the first has secretly been the meaning, fulfillment and authority of the law, and who has now been revealed as all this—the messiah of Israel . . . since he is the meaning, the authority, the fulfiller and the way to the fulfillment of the law, he is himself the righteousness before God, the divine justification that everyone is to receive and can receive through faith" (K. Barth, *Church Dogmatics II/2* [Edinburgh: T & T Clark, n.d.], 245).

[61] F. Thielman has shed new light on Paul's citation of the Habakkuk and Leviticus texts by placing them in the broader framework of the history and hope of Israel (*From Plight to Solution,* 65-72). Thus Habakkuk, who prophesied in a time of national disaster, encouraged his readers to trust in the faithfulness of God for deliverance and salvation. Paul wanted the Galatians to know that the eschatological deliverance promised by Habakkuk had come to pass through the death of Christ on the cross. That no one can obey the law perfectly and so receive life on this basis (Lev 18:5) is demonstrated on a national scale by Israelites who, no less than the Canaanites, had polluted the holy land and had been expelled therefrom because of their sin. Thus both of these texts point to Israel's historical plight and God's eschatological solution as the context for Paul's presentation of the work of Jesus Christ.

us in order that the blessing given to Abraham might come to the Gentiles through Christ Jesus, so that by faith we might receive the promise of the Spirit.

3:13 Verses 10–12 have painted a very grim picture of the human situation. The law requires a life of perfect obedience in order to be right with God. Yet no person can meet such a high standard. Consequently, everyone in the world has become "a prisoner of sin" (3:22), suffering the just condemnation of the curse of the law. Given this state of affairs, we are prompted to ask with the disciples, "Who then can be saved?" (Luke 18:26). If what Paul said about the gravity of sin and the certainty of judgment is true, then human beings can only despair of ever obtaining divine favor. Like the character of Sisyphus in Greek mythology, they are forever consigned to rolling a huge boulder up a mountain only to have it come crashing down upon their heads again and again. Now this is precisely the situation of all persons who are under the curse of the law, a verdict that is universal in scope including, as we have seen, Jews and Gentiles.[62]

Paul's answer to the dilemma he had just posed came in the form of a confessional statement that may well have circulated in early Jewish Christian communities as a kind of shorthand summary of the gospel itself: "Now Christ has redeemed us from the curse of the law by himself becoming a curse for us."[63] This is the first time in Galatians Paul used the word "redeemed," although the idea of rescue and deliverance through the self-sacrifice of Christ has been presupposed from the beginning (1:4; also 2:20). The word "redeemed" means literally "to buy off," "to set free by the payment of a price." The root word for redemption in Greek is *agora*, "marketplace," the site of the slave auction where everyday in ancient Rome human beings were

---

[62] In Rom 3:9–24 Paul showed in greater detail how the ill effects of the law apply equally to Jews and Gentiles. Note esp. Rom 3:19: "We know that whatever the law says, it says to those who are under the law, so that every mouth may be silenced and the whole world held accountable to God." On the idea that outside of Christ Gentiles as well as Jews are ὑπὸ νόμον, see B. L. Martin, *Christ and the Law in Paul* (Leiden: Brill, 1989), 100–104. Commentators are rather equally divided on this pivotal point with Bruce (*Galatians*, 166–67), D. Guthrie (*Galatians*, NCB [Grand Rapids: Eerdmans, 1973], 102–4), and H. Schlier (*Der Brief an der Galater*, KEK 7, 10th ed. [Göttingen: Vandenhoeck & Ruprecht, 1949], 136–37) arguing for the more inclusive meaning, while Burton (*Galatians*, 169), Betz (*Galatians*, 148), and G. S. Duncan (*The Epistle of Paul to the Galatians*, MNTC [London: Hodder & Stoughton, 1934], 99–102) restrict both the curse and the redemption procured by Christ in v. 13 to the Jewish people.

[63] On the idea that this statement may have originated as a pre-Pauline, Jewish Christian confession, see Longenecker, *Galatians*, 121–22. The *Apocryphon of James* preserves, independently of Paul, a similar statement that is placed in the mouth of Christ: "I have given myself up for you under the curse, in order that you might be saved" (cf. Betz, *Galatians*, 150, n. 120).

put up for sale to the highest bidder.[64] The word "redemption" declares that we have been bought with a price. "We are not saved by the Lord Jesus Christ by some method that cost him nothing."[65] The "ransom" for our sins was nothing less than the very life blood of the Son of God himself.

But in what sense could Christ have become a curse for us? Although Jesus was born "under the law" (4:4), he did not merit the curse of the law for any wrongdoing he had committed because he was as "a lamb without blemish or defect" (1 Pet 1:19). Yet both the fact and the manner of his death brought him inexorably under the curse of the law. To prove this point from Scripture, Paul again reached back to Deut 21:23 and quoted the text: "Cursed is everyone who is hung on a tree." Admittedly, the original reference was not to crucifixion, a Roman style of execution abhorrent to the Jewish people. The Talmud recognizes four modes of capital punishment that were sanctioned by the Jewish people: stoning, burning, beheading, and strangling the criminal as he stood on the ground. After the execution had been carried out, the corpse of the criminal would then be hoisted onto a piece of timber, a stake or "tree," as an indication that this person had been justly condemned as a transgressor of the divine law.[66] It was important that the criminal's corpse not be exposed beyond sundown because this would dishonor God and defile the land. Thus, according to John's Gospel, the bodies of Jesus and the two thieves crucified with him were removed from their crosses before nightfall so as not to desecrate the Passover Sabbath (John 19:31). Thus by being impaled on a cross, becoming a gory spectacle for all to see, Jesus exposed himself to the curse of the law.

Paul's citation of the text from Deuteronomy shows that there was nothing accidental or coincidental about the death of Christ. The reference to Jesus' death as a "hanging on a tree" occurs frequently in early Christian presentations of the *kerygma* (cf. Acts 5:30; 10:39; 13:29; 1 Pet 2:24) as a witness to the fact that Christ's death on the cross was a fulfillment of Old Testament Scripture. While it is true that being hung on a tree was not the

---

[64] B. B. Warfield's classic study, "The New Testament Terminology of 'Redemption,'" is still unsurpassed in perception and depth. See his *Biblical Doctrines* (New York: Oxford University Press, 1929), 327-72. See also L. Morris, "Redemption," *DPL*, 784-86.

[65] Machen, *Machen's Notes on Galatians,* 180.

[66] See J. A. Fitzmyer, "Crucifixion and Ancient Palestine, Qumran Literature, and the NT," *CBQ* 40 (1978): 493-513. The Temple Scroll found at Qumran refers to "hanging a man on a tree, that he may die," indicating that death by crucifixion was apparently accepted by some Jews in the postexilic period. F. F. Bruce has pointed to Joshua's treatment of the body of the king of Ai (Josh 8:29) as an example of how the ancient Israelites applied the text of Deut 21:23 ("The Curse of the Law," in *Paul and Paulinism: Essays in Honor of C. K. Barrett* [London: SPCK, 1982], 27-36).

curse itself but rather the public proof that the one so impaled had incurred the curse, the clear inference of the New Testament is that the death of Jesus by crucifixion was not a quirk of fate but instead the deliberate design of God. Thus in Peter's sermon on the Day of Pentecost, he declared that Jesus was handed over to his executioners to be put to death by crucifixion "in accordance with God's set purpose and foreknowledge" (Acts 2:23).

To wonder whether Christ could have accomplished the work of redemption by dying in some other manner, say, being drowned on the Sea of Galilee, or hurled to his death from the precipice of Nazareth, or butchered as an infant by Herod, is like asking whether God could have become incarnate in a pumpkin—vain curiosity bordering on blasphemy.[67] Jesus moved through his public ministry dodging bullets right and left, so to speak, because his "hour had not yet come." The cross was neither an accident of history nor a divine emergency measure brought in to remedy an unforeseen situation. There was a cross in the heart of God from all eternity, for Jesus was "the Lamb of God slain from the foundation of the world."[68]

As Bruce and others have suggested, Paul may well have worked out his understanding of the relationship of the curse and the cross long before he wrote Galatians.[69] Why was the cross such a stumbling block (*skandalon*) to the Jews, including presumably Saul of Tarsus before he met Christ? Christians claimed that Jesus was the Messiah, and yet it was known to all that their Messiah had been brutally crucified by the Romans outside the gates of Jerusalem. The Messiah was the epitome of blessing, but one "hung on a tree" was by definition "accursed by God." According to a later tradition preserved in the Mishna, even an innocent person crucified by a miscarriage of justice still blasphemed the divine Name. Thus "when Paul was compelled to recognize that the crucified Jesus, risen from the dead, was Messiah and Son of God, he [was] faced with the problem how and why he nevertheless had died under the divine curse."[70]

---

[67] On the christological speculations of scholastic theology, including the possibility of God's assumption of an irrational being in a hypostatic union, see H. A. Oberman, *The Harvest of Medieval Theology* (Cambridge: Harvard University Press, 1962), 255-58.

[68] Even Bruce considers the precise form of Jesus' death "of secondary importance," as though there were "a certain accidental quality about it" ("The Curse," 32). However, this is to ignore the way in which Paul saw in the event of the cross the intersection of election, providence, and atonement. On the elaboration of this theme, see L. Morris, *The Apostolic Preaching of the Cross* (Grand Rapids: Eerdmans, 1965).

[69] Bruce, *Galatians*, 166; Longenecker, *Galatians*, 122. On the contrary, see Wright, *Climax of the Covenant*, 152.

[70] Bruce, *Galatians*, 166.

The only explanation could be that the Messiah had willingly taken upon himself the dreaded curse that rightly belonged to others. Here, *in nuce,* is the genesis of the Christian doctrine of penal substitutionary atonement. Indeed, as Stott has suggested, it may well have been reflection on the very text Paul cited in Gal 3:13 that led the early Christians to understand the death of Jesus in this way. "The apostles were quite familiar with this legislation [Deut 21:22-23], and with its implication that Jesus died under the divine curse. Yet, instead of hushing it up, they deliberately drew people's attention to it. So evidently they were not embarrassed by it. They did not think of Jesus as in any sense deserving to be accursed by God. They must, therefore, have at least begun to understand that it was our curse which he was bearing."[71] The shocking offence of a crucified Messiah may also help explain the strange slogan Paul quoted in 1 Cor 12:3, "Jesus be cursed." No one, Paul said, can utter such an anathema under the guidance of the Holy Spirit. Yet evidently this blasphemy was making the rounds in Corinth as a piece of anti-Christian polemic. As late as the time of Jerome (d. 420) the shocking image of a crucified and accursed Messiah was a major point of contention between the church and the synagogue.[72]

However, it is not only Jews of antiquity who have stumbled over Paul's theology of the cross. For example, the liberal Baptist scholar E. deW. Burton rejected the idea that the curse of the law was in any sense the real judgment of God. "To miss this fact is wholly to misunderstand Paul. But if the curse is not an expression of God's attitude towards man, neither is the deliverance from it a judicial act in the sense of release from penalty, but a release from a false conception of God's attitude."[73] According to this view, Christ's work on the cross must be seen in purely ethical, not forensic, terms. No ransom was paid, no transaction occurred, no substitution was made. What Christ did by dying on the cross was to demonstrate the divine character of self-giving love and the divine attitude of forgiveness that flows from it.

Surely there is an element of truth in this way of putting things. Jesus' death on the cross is a window into the character of God, and the example of his forgiving love is a vital force in the life of believers (cf. Eph 4:32). The problem with such a view, however, is that it trivializes the death of

---

[71] J. R. W. Stott, *The Cross of Christ* (Downers Grove: InterVarsity, 1986), 34. P. Patterson has correctly interpreted penal substitution as the primary motif of atonement theology in the NT, including Gal 3:10-13 (see "Reflections on the Atonement," *CTR* 3 [1989]: 315-20).

[72] Jerome recorded a dialogue between a certain Jewish Christian named Jason and his interlocutor Papiscus, a Jew of Alexandria. Referring to the death of Christ the latter is reported to have said "the execration of God is he that is hanged" (ANF 8.749).

[73] Burton, *Galatians,* 168.

Christ by reducing it to the significance of an advice column or a well-meant lecture on good behavior. Jesus did not need to get himself "strung up on a tree like a damned fool" (Cotton Patch, 98), to quote Clarence Jordan's jarring but accurate translation of 3:13, in order to pass on pious platitudes about how human beings should get along with one another and make the world a better place in which to live. No, "God was in Christ reconciling the world unto himself" (2 Cor 5:19, KJV).

Bringing several of these strands of thought together, we can summarize Paul's understanding of Christ's death in this passage in three affirmations.

1. *Christ was cursed.* As we have seen, Paul related the curse of the law to the specific prophecy concerning a criminal who had been "hung on a tree." However, the curse in this context assumes an almost personified form (like "Scripture" in v. 8), indicating the totality of God's righteous judgment and wrath that finally will be displayed in the blazing fire and eternal punishment of those "who do not know God" and reject "the gospel of our Lord Jesus" (2 Thess 1:7-9). Throughout the Old Testament the curse is associated with human rebellion and disobedience, from the curse on Adam and Eve in Gen 3 to the very last threatening word of the Old Testament, "Else I will come and strike the land with a curse" (Mal 4:6). As we have seen, this curse has fallen on all peoples everywhere, for "all have sinned and come short of the glory of God" (Rom 3:23). As Paul would explain shortly, the curse of the law for Jews had resulted in their bondage to the Mosaic legislation; for Gentiles the curse had resulted in their slavery to the principalities and powers who hold sway in "this present evil age." In both cases the curse of the law is damning, irrevocable, and inescapable.

2. *Christ was cursed by God.* Some scholars have made much of the fact that Paul omitted the words "by God" in his quotation of Deut 21:23.[74] However, the curse of the law that he bore was the curse of God's law. Although he was put to death by wicked men in a horrible miscarriage of justice, this happened, as we have seen, in accordance with the eternal purpose and predetermined plan of God. Thus Gal 3:13 should be interpreted in the light of 2 Cor 5:21: "God made him who had no sin to be sin for us, so that in him we might become the righteousness of God." From the perspective of salvation history, then, the curse Christ bore upon the cross was not a curse that wrongly rested upon him; it was a curse that rightly rested upon him as the

---

[74] Thus Longenecker (*Galatians,* 122): "Also he omits ὑπὸ θεοῦ ("by God") after Ἐπικατάρατος [LXX, κεκατηραμένος], either to avoid saying directly that Christ was cursed by God—though, of course, 'the curse of the law' is another way of saying 'cursed by God'—or to highlight the absolute nature of the curse itself."

sinless substitutionary sacrifice "sent" by the Father for this very purpose.[75]

3. *Christ was cursed by God for us.*   As we have seen, the dilemma of v. 10—all are under a curse—is resolved by the remedy of v. 13—Christ redeemed us from the curse. Put otherwise, the curse of Deut 27:26, quoted in v. 10, has been cancelled by the countercurse of Deut 21:23, cited in v. 13. Paul was working here with the idea of an "exchange curse" by which the sin, guilt, and hell of lost men and women are placed upon Christ while his righteousness, blessing, and merit are imputed to those in whose place he stands. Luther spoke of this atoning transaction as "a happy exchange." It was an exchange that involved a fierce struggle with the powers of darkness in which "not only my sins and yours, but the sins of the entire world, past, present, and future, attack him, try to damn him, and do in fact damn him."[76] Yet Christ emerged victorious over sin, death, and the eternal curse. This he did "for us." For this reason the doctrine of atonement can never be merely a matter of cool theologizing or dispassionate discourse. *For us* the Son of God became a curse. *For us* he shed his precious blood. *For us* he who from all eternity knew only the intimacy of the Father's bosom came "to stand in that relation with God which normally is the result of sin, estranged from God and the object of his wrath."[77] All this—*for us!* What response can we offer except that of wonder, devotion, and trust!

3:14   Here Paul summarized in a concentrated conclusion the entire train of thought he had developed thus far in chap. 3. The argument he had just concluded concerning the curse and the cross is here recapitulated in two purpose clauses that point to the benefits secured by Christ's atoning death: (1) that the blessing of Abraham might be extended to the Gentiles through Christ and (2) that the promise of the Spirit might be bestowed by faith.

Here, as before, Paul had in mind all Christians, Jews and Gentiles alike, since all believers have been redeemed from the curse through the death of

---

[75] Calvin quoted from Augustine's commentary on John to show how the propitiation offered by Christ to the Father was grounded in God's prior love: "God's love is incomprehensible and unchangeable. For it was not after we were reconciled to him through the blood of his son that he began to love us. Rather, he has loved us before the world was created, that we might also be his sons along with his only-begotten son—before we became anything at all. The fact that we were reconciled through Christ's death must not be understood as if his son reconciled us to him that he might now begin to love those whom he had hated. Rather, we have already been reconciled to him who loves us, with whom we were enemies on account of sin. . . . Therefore, he loved us even when we practiced enmity toward him and committed wickedness. Thus in a marvelous and divine way he loved us even when he hated us" (*Institutes* 2.16.4). Cf. Calvin's further comment along this same line: "For, in some ineffable way, God loved us and yet was angry toward us at the same time, until he became reconciled to us in Christ" (*Institutes* 2.17.2).

[76] *LW* 26.281.

[77] C. K. Barrett, *The Second Epistle to the Corinthians* (London: Harper & Row, 1957), 180.

Christ, and all true Christians have also received the gift of the Holy Spirit (cf. Rom 8:9). God's program of salvation does not run along two tracks, one for Jewish people and the other for Gentiles. Within the body of Christ the differences between these two groups have not been obliterated—how could they be?—but they have been relativized by the events of Calvary, Easter, and Pentecost so that we are "all sons of God by faith in Christ Jesus" (3:26). Thus 3:14 anticipates 3:28, where that which unites true believers, our oneness in Christ, far outweighs those tokens of distinction that, in some respects very legitimately, still divide us.

The other notable thing about this verse is the way Paul carefully intertwined the status of justification and the reception of the Holy Spirit. In vv. 1-5 Paul appealed to his Galatian converts to recall how the Holy Spirit was poured out upon them when they first heard the preaching of the cross. In vv. 6-13 he has shown how on the basis of Christ's redemptive work God reckons as righteous those who have faith. Here he linked the two, being justified and receiving the Spirit, in the closest possible way. As S. Williams has put it: "The experience of the Spirit and the status of justification are, for the apostle, inconceivable apart from each other. Each implies the other. Those persons upon whom God bestows the Spirit are justified; the persons whom God reckons righteous have the Spirit poured out upon them."[78]

Still, these terms are not identical, nor can they be used interchangeably. Indeed, we can say that here in v. 14 Paul brought together three key soteriological concepts that will dominate the later discussion in Galatians: justification, redemption, and regeneration. Each represents a distinct dimension of the salvation effected by Christ. Through pardon and acquittal Christ has removed our condemnation (justification). He has also set us free from the power of sin and death (redemption) and bestowed upon us a new life in the Spirit (regeneration). The good news of how this has happened and what it means Paul called "gospel" and "blessing." Now for the first time he introduced a new word, "promise," which both reaches back to the gospel of grace revealed in the blessing of Abraham and looks forward to the new life of liberty and love to which those who are in Christ have been called.

4. The Law and the Promise (3:15-25)

Paul now moved to a second level of argument in his long parenthesis (3:10-25) on the validity of the law in the context of the nature of salvation as God's free and gracious favor promised to Abraham, secured by Christ,

---

[78] S. K. Williams, "Justification and the Spirit in Galatians," *JSNT* 29 (1987): 97.

and sealed in the hearts of believers by the Holy Spirit. In vv. 6-14 Paul had argued exclusively from the Scriptures, quoting from the Law five times and from the Prophets once in order to show how God's promise to Abraham that all peoples would be blessed through him has been fulfilled by Christ whose death on the cross has wrought redemption and justification by faith for Jews and Gentiles alike. Paul would now zero in on this same theme showing first how God's covenant with Abraham stands in stark contrast to the law of Moses and yet how, in the providence of God, even the law played a crucial role in the unfolding drama of redemption. There is a noticeable shift in the style of Paul's argumentation throughout this passage. With the exception of his exegetical comment on Abraham's "seed" in v. 16, he did not appeal to specific quotations from the Old Testament but argued instead from broader historical and theological considerations concerning the relationship of Abraham, Moses, and Christ. In the first pericope (vv. 15-18) Paul introduced three new terms that would dominate the remainder of his discussion in the central theological section of the letter: promise, already anticipated in v. 14, covenant, and inheritance. All of these were loaded terms in Paul's vocabulary. Together they underscore the legal and historical train of thought that led Paul toward the personal, existential application he would pursue in 3:26–4:11.

(1) The Priority of the Promise (3:15-18)

[15]**Brothers, let me take an example from everyday life. Just as no one can set aside or add to a human covenant that has been duly established, so it is in this case.** [16]**The promises were spoken to Abraham and to his seed. The Scripture does not say "and to seeds," meaning many people, but "and to your seed," meaning one person, who is Christ.** [17]**What I mean is this: The law, introduced 430 years later, does not set aside the covenant previously established by God and thus do away with the promise.** [18]**For if the inheritance depends on the law, then it no longer depends on a promise; but God in his grace gave it to Abraham through a promise.**

THE IRREVOCABILITY OF THE COVENANT (3:15-16).   **3:15**   We are struck by the fact that Paul addressed the Galatians here as "brothers," a term of endearment he had not used since 1:11, although it would occur again seven other times in the letter (4:12,28,31; 5:11,13; 6:1,18). Although the Galatians were confused, foolish, and bewitched, and although Paul felt betrayed, perplexed, and forlorn about them, still they were *adelphoi,* "brothers." This term of relationship is especially appropriate at the beginning of a passage that will seek to answer the questions: "What makes a family a family? Who are the true children of Abraham, the heirs of the promise, and thus entitled to call one another brothers and sisters?"

If indeed Paul was here responding to a specific argument set forth by his opponents, he beat them at their own game as it were. Paul's argument was really quite straightforward even if the legal context from which he spoke remains obscure to us. In Genesis, God made a promise to Abraham, a promise, as Paul had shown already, not based on Abraham's meritorious deeds, lifelong obedience, or indeed anything other than God's own gratuitous good pleasure. This promise, or covenant, as Paul called it here for the first time, was unconditional: no ifs, ands, and buts; no strings attached. Abraham simply believed that God would do what he had promised. Then comes Exodus, Mount Sinai, and Moses, who delivered a new and different covenant, one encumbered with burdensome requirements, a code of behavior that makes demands and issues threats.

However the law is to be understood, and Paul would spell this out in vv. 19-25, it cannot be interpreted as countermanding the covenant relationship established with Abraham. Why not? For two reasons: first, once a will or covenant (the Greek *diathēkē* covers both concepts, hence the intentional play on words here) has been ratified, it cannot be altered; and, second, the law, as a temporary expedient, was accidental, not essential, to the unconditional covenant granted to Abraham. Paul argued the former reason in vv. 15-16 and the latter in vv. 17-18.

Again, Paul's argument in v. 15 is that once someone's last will and testament has been duly promulgated, no one, not even the original testator, can change or revoke it. If this is true even of such human agreements, then, *a fortiori*, it applies all the more to God's covenant with Abraham. Modern scholars have been baffled by Paul's argument because it seems to presuppose a legal situation unknown to both Greek and Roman jurisprudence in the ancient world. Then, as now, it was possible for people to change or revoke their wills in view of altered circumstances or reconsidered preferences.[79]

---

[79] Commentators on Galatians have spent a great deal of time trying to sort out the legal background of Paul's covenant analogy in this text. Some have attempted to link his presumed reliance on Roman jurisprudence to the North Galatian theory of destination, whereas others have argued for the South Galatian hypothesis on the basis of his alleged acquaintance with Greek legal practice. After surveying several of these theories Longenecker concludes: "It may be that Paul felt no compulsion to speak in precise legal parlance, and that his readers would have felt the same. We today often use terms pertinent to a particular discipline with less precision than purists rightly called for, even though we might know better. . . . The point of Paul's example in its application is clear: that God established his covenant with Abraham in an irrevocable manner, so it can never be annulled or added to" (*Galatians*, 130). See also Bruce, *Galatians*, 169-71, and Betz, *Galatians*, 154-57.

E. Bammel, however, has pointed to a procedure of Jewish inheritance laws known as *mattenat bāriʾ* by which a person could make an irrevocable testament to another prior to death. It was precisely this kind of legal transaction Jesus alluded to in the parable of the prodigal son, where the father prematurely divided his property between his heirs, an act all the more momentous because it was unalterable. Assuming that Paul had some kind of legal procedure such as this in mind, another problem comes into view: When was God's covenant with Abraham ratified? Ordinarily a last will and testament is validated, or probated as we say, only after the death of the testator. But since the living God cannot die, the only kind of irrevocable will he could make was something analogous to the *mattenat bāriʾ*.[80]

It would be a serious mistake, however, to disassociate the motif of death from the covenant theology Paul was pursuing in this passage. The chapter began with his reminding the believers of Galatia that Christ had been portrayed as crucified before their very eyes. And just two verses before, he had inextricably linked Christ's death on the cross with his bearing of the law's curse. In Heb 9:15–28 the writer worked out in greater detail than Paul did in Galatians the role of Christ as the mediator of the new covenant whose death was a liberating ransom bringing salvation for all who believe in him. In Hebrews the contrast is between the Mosaic covenant, which required the shedding of blood for the forgiveness of sins, and the great High Priest, who obtained eternal redemption by shedding his own blood once for all.

Yet all of this was present, in shadow and type but nonetheless real and effective for all that, in the Abrahamic covenant as well. Beginning in Gen 12, in the context of the promised blessing, we read a phrase that occurs again and again in the Abraham narrative: "So he built an altar there to the Lord" (12:7). Abraham built an altar at Shechem, another at Bethel, another at Hebron, and still another on Mount Moriah. God's covenant with Abraham was not ratified by a bloodless word but rather by a series of altar rituals strung across the Middle East, all pointing forward to that other altar on Mount Moriah where "God, in bloody garments dressed didst purge our crimson stains."[81] That is why Paul could stress with such passion the continuity and irrevocability of God's covenant with Abraham: "If you belong to Christ, then you are Abraham's seed, and heirs according to the promise" (4:29).[82]

3:16 Having just argued from the dual meaning of *diathēkē* as both "last will" and "covenant," Paul proceeded to a piece of exegetical finesse that

---

[80] Thus Matera, *Galatians,* 130–31.

[81] See E. Bammel, "Gottes *Diathēkē* (Gal 3:15–17) und das jüdische Rechtsdenken," *NTS* 6 (1959–60): 313–19.

[82] Ibid.

may seem on the surface little more than theological hairsplitting. In v. 16 Paul said nothing about the content of the Abrahamic covenant focusing entirely on the procedural matter of its irrevocability. In v. 17 the substance of the covenant itself comes into view with the word "promises," clearly an allusion to the blessings God promised to Abraham in Gen 12 and reiterated in greater detail in Gen 17. Specifically the promises embraced the gift of the land, a multitudinous progeny, and making Abraham a channel of blessing for all the nations.

As we have seen already in v. 8, Paul had interpreted this last promise to mean that the message of the gospel, that is, justification by faith, would be preached to the Gentiles as well as to Abraham's natural descendants. However, here in v. 16 Paul's main point was that all of these promises applied not only to one man, Abraham, but also to his "seed." Now here is the hairsplitting point: the word "seed," he observed, is singular, not plural; therefore in its deepest and fullest meaning it refers to one person, not to many. And that one person, Paul contended, Abraham's true seed, is Christ himself.

Of course, Paul was aware that the word "seed" (*sperma*), in Hebrew and Greek as well as English, could be used as a collective noun as he himself employed it elsewhere (cf. Rom 4:13-18). It was not uncommon in rabbinic exegesis for a theological argument to be based on the singular or plural form of a particular word in the scriptural text. Paul may well have been responding here to the popular Jewish claim that they alone, along with a few proselytes, were the "true sons of Abraham." Paul wanted to show that the greater fulfillment of the promise is not biological but Christological.[83]

Paul's emphasis on the single seed brings together two ideas that serve as a unifying theme throughout Gal 3 and 4: solidarity in Christ and unity in the church. Elsewhere Paul contrasted Adam and Christ as two heads of humanity. Adam is viewed as the head of sinful humanity that is doomed to die, and Christ is viewed as the head of a new humanity that has the promise of eternal life (Rom 5:12-21). Here in Gal 3 the contrast is not between Adam and Christ but Abraham and Moses or, as Paul expressed it in vv. 9-10, the contrast between those who seek their identity in the world and thus before God on the basis of, out of (*ek*), works and those who relate to these matters of ultimate concern out of faith. Either way, though, such an identification

---

[83] See S. Schulz, "σπερμα," *TDNT* 7.545-47, and M. Wilcox, "The Promise of the 'Seed' in the New Testament and the Targumim," *JSNT* 5 (1979): 2-20. Some scholars have interpreted Paul's insistence on the singular meaning of "seed" as a veiled reference to Isaac and thus an implicit allusion to the Isaac-Christ typology. While this makes good theological sense within the broader context of Pauline hermeneutics (cf. Rom 8:32), Paul's second reference to σπέρμα in 3:19, "until the Seed to whom the promise referred had come," cannot be stretched to embrace Isaac who only appears in Galatians, and then not by name, in the Hagar-Sarah allegory.

involves far more than an individual decision made in isolation from all others. To be "under the curse" is to belong to a family, to be implicated in a corporate solidarity that includes the whole human race and, for that matter, the world of nature as well (cf. Rom 8:18-27). In the same way, to be "in Christ," the true Seed (singular) of Abraham, is to find a new family, to become a child and heir of the promise through the adoption of grace.

Our solidarity in Christ implies unity in the church. As N. T. Wright has shown, the oneness of the "seed" in v. 16 must be linked to the oneness of God in v. 20 and the oneness of the body of Christ in v. 28. According to this view, the original covenant with Abraham envisaged one seed, that is, a single family of faith, a unitary people of God. This is why Paul was so upset over the issue of table fellowship at Antioch. To assume that the "works of the law" have an abiding validity after Christ has come is to divide the church permanently into Jew and Gentile, not to say "Athenian and Roman, Galatian and Ephesian, African and Scythian, and so on *ad infinitum*."[84] Paul was not saying, of course, that such distinctions, and others we could think of (white and black, rich and poor, First World and Third World, and so on) have lost all their significance for those who are in Christ. Clearly they have not. What they have lost, however, is the ability to define absolutely, to circumscribe definitively. To be of the seed of Abraham means to belong to Christ, to have a share in the new humanity of the Last Adam, in whom there is no East or West, no South or North, "But one great fellowship of love Thro'-out the whole wide earth" (J. Oxenham).

THE SENIORITY OF THE COVENANT (3:17-18). **3:17** Paul here picked up and completed the train of thought he began in v. 15, applying it specifically now to the giving of the Mosaic law that occurred nearly half a millennium later than the original promise to Abraham.[85] By stressing the seniority of the Abrahamic covenant over the Mosaic law, Paul was extolling the God who keeps his promises. For the Judaizers the revelation of the law at Mount Sinai marked the real beginning of Israel's history in the sense that that event gave them a true national identity and established their unique role in the economy of salvation. The patriarchal period was seen as a mere prelude and adumbration of the definitive covenant giving at Sinai. To this line of reasoning Paul replied, in effect: "Look! You say God made a promise to Abraham

[84] Wright, *Climax of the Covenant,* 165.
[85] Paul's figure of 430 years is based on the Septuagintal reading of Exod 12:40. Acts 7:6, in keeping with the reckoning of Gen 15:13, rounds the number off at four hundred, according to Longenecker (*Galatians,* 133). Longenecker surveys various ways of reconciling this apparent discrepancy and concludes that "Paul here is probably not relying on Exod 12:40 versus Gen 15:13 but only repeating the traditionally accepted number of years for the time span between the Abrahamic covenant and the Mosaic law."

and then came along hundreds of years later and added to it burdensome requirements no one could fulfill perfectly anyway, thus radically altering the character of his relationship to his people. But this is to turn God into a dishonest broker who goes back on his word once it is given. How dare we attribute to God the kind of chicanery we do not even tolerate among sinful human beings?"

Although Paul focused here on the great time span between the two divine disclosures as a way of stressing the fidelity of God, the contrast between the Abrahamic promise and the Mosaic law is not only one of timing but also of character. In other words, for Paul the law was not merely a late addition in the history of salvation; rather it was a completely different kind of covenant than the one God had concluded with Abraham centuries before. G. E. Mendenhall has described the contrast that was at the heart of Paul's distinction between the two covenants:

> It is not often enough seen that no obligations are imposed upon Abraham. Circumcision is not originally an obligation, but a sign of the covenant, like the rainbow in Genesis 9. It serves to identify the recipient(s) of the covenant, as well as to give a concrete indication that a covenant exists. It is for the protection of the promise, perhaps, like the mark of Cain in Genesis 4. The covenant of Moses, on the other hand, is almost the exact opposite. It imposes specific obligations on the tribes or clans without binding Yahweh to specific obligations.[86]

3:18 In this verse Paul brought together by way of conclusion the three main points he had made in this short pericope: the faithfulness of God, the lateness of the law, and the gratuity of the promise. At this point Paul introduced for the first time in Galatians the term "inheritance," which along with the verb "to inherit" and the derivative noun "heir" dominate much of the discussion in the following chapters (cf. 3:29; 4:1,7; 5:21).[87] The inheritance is the blessing promised by God and ratified to him and to his "seed" by means of an unconditional covenant.

For Paul it was crucial that this original "covenant of promise" be distinguished from the law of Moses.[88] The law demands, "Do this!" The promise

---

[86] G. E. Mendenhall, "Covenant Forms in Israelite Tradition," *BA* 17 (1954): 62. See also the discussion in Bligh, *Galatians,* 274-81.

[87] On the meaning of these terms in Paul see Burton, *Galatians,* 185-86, and J. D. Hester, "Paul's Concept of Inheritance," *SJT* Occasional Papers 14; (Edinburgh: Oliver & Boyd, 1961).

[88] The term "covenant of promise" occurs in C. K. Barrett, *From First Adam to Last* (New York: Scribners, 1962), 60. M. D. Hooker has challenged the propriety of translating διαθήκη as "covenant" with respect to God's promise to Abraham ("Paul and 'Covenantal Nomism,'" in *Paul and Paulinism,* 51).

grants, "Accept this!" Here in v. 18 Paul drew the two into sharpest antithesis: If law . . . not promise; if works . . . not grace. In Luther's commentary on this text he drew the individual believer into the sequence of salvation history Paul had outlined and encouraged those who felt condemned by the accusation of the law to reply: "'Lady Law, you are not coming on time; you are coming too late. Look back 430 years; if these were rolled back, you could come. But you are coming too late and tardily; for you have been preceded for 430 years by the promise, to which I agree and in which I gently rest. Therefore you have nothing to do with me; I do not hear you. Now I am living after Abraham a believer; or rather, I am living after the revelation of Christ, who has abrogated and abolished you.' Thus let Christ always be set forth to the heart as a kind of summary of all the arguments in support of faith and against the righteousness of the flesh, the law, works, and merits."[89]

(2) The Purpose of the Law (3:19-25)

[19]What, then, was the purpose of the law? It was added because of transgressions until the Seed to whom the promise referred had come. The law was put into effect through angels by a mediator. [20]A mediator, however, does not represent just one party; but God is one.

[21]Is the law, therefore, opposed to the promises of God? Absolutely not! For if a law had been given that could impart life, then righteousness would certainly have come by the law. [22]But the Scripture declares that the whole world is a prisoner of sin, so that what was promised, being given through faith in Jesus Christ, might be given to those who believe.

[23]Before this faith came, we were held prisoners by the law, locked up until faith should be revealed. [24]So the law was put in charge to lead us to Christ that we might be justified by faith. [25]Now that faith has come, we are no longer under the supervision of the law.

These verses have been called "a new and extraordinary section in Paul's argument" (Betz) and "the *crux interpretum* for Paul's response to the problems in Galatia" (Longenecker). Structurally this passage divides neatly into three parts as the paragraphing of the NIV indicates. The first two sections are each introduced by a leading question: "What, then, was the purpose of the law?" (vv. 19-20), and "Is the law, therefore, opposed to the promises of God?" (vv. 21-22). The concluding paragraph (vv. 23-25) continues the thought of the second paragraph, summing up the function of the law in terms of a new metaphor, that of the *paidagōgos*. These verses will bring to a conclusion Paul's long parenthesis (vv. 10-25) on the nature and function of the law in the history of salvation. In the remainder of the central theolog-

---

[89] *LW* 26.302.

ical section of the book, Paul would show how the benefits of Christ's redemptive work applied to believers in the church (3:26–4:11); then, following his passionate personal appeal to the Galatians (4:12-20), he would round off the discussion by means of an exegetical excursus reminding his readers of their true identity as heirs of the covenant of promise (4:21-31). To be sure, the law does not drop out of sight in the unfolding of Paul's argument (e.g. 4:4,24-25), but it is interpreted in light of the fundamental clarification it has received in 3:19-25.

Before launching into our investigation of these verses, we need to post two warnings. First, Paul seemed to be speaking in a kind of theological shorthand that is not easy for us to unpack in detail. F. Thielman has wisely reminded us that "phrases which probably communicated paragraphs of information to the Galatians remain for us, nearly twenty centuries later, epigrammatic and obscure."[90] For this very reason, while not forgetting the contextual character of Paul's argument here, we again will find that the best commentary on Galatians is Romans, where Paul developed in a less compact way many of the ideas he first set forth in this passage. Second, we must realize that these verses do not constitute a programmatic essay "On the Law," as though Paul had here disclosed his entire thinking on this subject. In this context, for example, Paul was not dealing with the (very important) question of the role of the law in the life of the believer. Later he would tackle that issue (cf. 5:14; 6:2). But here he was dealing with another issue, namely, what is the function of the law in the history of salvation? Failure to make this distinction has led to great confusion in the history of theology from traditional Roman Catholic discussions of so-called "first" and "second" justification to contemporary evangelical debates on lordship salvation. Calvin's comment on this passage is still worth heeding: "The law has many uses, but Paul confines himself to one which serves his present purpose. . . . [But] this definition of the use of the law is not complete and those who acknowledge nothing else in the law are wrong."[91]

WHY THEN THE LAW? (3:19-20). **3:19** Paul's question, "What, then, was the purpose of the law?" or, as the KJV has it, "Wherefore then serveth the law?" arises inexorably from the logic of Paul's argument which he has pursued relentlessly since 2:16. Let us review his argument step by step. Everyone who has been declared righteous before God, Jews and Gentiles alike, has come into this relationship through faith in Jesus Christ and not by observing the law. Even you Galatians, though you may have been hoodwinked about this, have to admit that you received the Holy Spirit and wit-

[90] Thielman, *From Plight to Solution,* 73.
[91] See Calvin, CNTC 11.61.

nessed his miraculous works through the hearing of faith and not by works of the law. You want chapter and verse? Consider Gen 15:6. Abraham believed God and was justified by faith. Furthermore, the law imposes a curse on everyone who does not obey it perfectly, which is to say, everyone. Why else did Christ die except to redeem us from the curse of the law? Don't think for a minute that the law, which was given centuries later anyway, can alter God's original promise to Abraham. No, you have to make a choice. It is either law or promise, works or faith, grace or merit.

The posing of these mutually irreconcilable alternatives leads inevitably to the question of v. 19 (literally), "Why then the law?" If we are not justified by law, if our receiving the Holy Spirit had nothing to do with the law, if Christ was cursed because of the law, if our very inheritance depends on grace and promise not on works and law, then "wherefore then serveth the law?" Has Paul painted himself into a theological corner? Has Paul so totally dismissed the law that it no longer has any place within God's overall redemptive scheme?

These were not merely idle questions raised in the context of an academic debate. Later in his ministry, when Paul returned to Jerusalem to deliver the love gift from the Gentile churches, he was accosted in the temple precincts by some Jewish partisans who shouted, "This is the man who teaches all men everywhere against our people and our law" (Acts 21:28). Very likely Paul's opponents in Galatia made the same kind of accusation against him. To their mind Paul had so fused Abraham and Christ that there was no room left for Moses! Yet C. K. Barrett is right to observe that Paul was doing more than rebutting his foes on this score. As one who had devoted his early life to "the traditions of my fathers" and who as a strict Pharisee had been "faultless" in his observance of the law, Paul was dealing with questions that had arisen in his own mind.[92] That a certain trajectory of Pauline theology could indeed lead to a total disparagement of the law, and even the excision of the Old Testament as Christian Scripture, was borne out by Marcion in the second century. It is not surprising that Paul would have anticipated this kind of distortion of his teaching and that he would have sought to forestall it by the sort of argument he developed in this passage.

So Paul had an answer to the question he had posed. It is an answer flung out in four statements of terse, almost cryptic language. Why the law? It was (1) added because of transgressions (2) until the Seed had come; moreover, it was put into effect (3) through angels (4) by a mediator. While Paul would explain items 1 and 2 more fully in the following passage (vv. 21-25), let us examine briefly each of these four components.

---

[92] C. K. Barrett, *Freedom and Obligation* (Philadelphia: Westminster, 1985), 33.

1. *The Law Was Added because of Transgressions.* As the context makes clear, the law in question is the law of Moses, which was "added" 430 years after the Abrahamic covenant, added not as a codicil is appended to a will in order to alter its provisions but added in order to accomplish some other subordinate and supplementary purpose. This meaning is further clarified when we look at the parallel verse in Rom 5:20: "The law was added so that the trespass might increase." In Romans the word for "added" (*pareisēlthen*) means literally "came in by a side road."[93] The main road is the covenant of promise—inviolate, irrevocable. The law has the character of something additional, a side road intended to carry extra traffic and excess baggage and, if we may anticipate Paul's argument, designed not to lead to a separate destination but to point its travelers back to the main road.

The next phrase, "because of transgressions," can mean one of two things depending on whether the postpositive preposition *charin*, "because," "on account of," is given a causal (looking backward) or telic (looking forward) force.[94] In the former case the law would have primarily a preventive function: the law was promulgated to curb or hold in check misdeeds that were already being done, in other words, to keep a bad situation from getting even worse. But if "because" is given a telic meaning, the opposite would hold true. The law would have a provocative purpose, its function being not to prevent sins but actually to increase them, in other words, to make an already bad situation much, much worse.

The preventive and provocative functions correspond to the civil and spiritual uses of the law as developed by Luther.[95] Clearly, Luther thought, God has ordained civil laws for the purpose of restraining evildoers. Just as a rope or chain prevents a wild animal from attacking an innocent bystander, so too the law with its "thou shalt nots" and penal code prevents sinful humanity from going on a rampage and completely destroying itself. Obviously without the civil use of the law, human society could not be sustained. Thus Luther referred to the state as the "left hand of God" and to those who bear temporal rule as "God's jailers and executioners."[96] But as important as

[93] A. Oepke has compared this expression with Paul's description of the false brothers of Gal 2:4 who "infiltrated our ranks to spy on the freedom we have in Christ." In a similar way, "also the law sneaked in from behind" (*Der Brief des Paulus an die Galater* [Berlin: Evangelische Verlagsanstalt, 1973], 115). As Betz has pointed out, however, this interpretation may lean too far in the Marcionite direction (*Galatians*, 167, n. 43).

[94] See the discussion in Burton, *Galatians*, 188, and Thielman, *From Plight to Solution*, 74.

[95] *LW* 26.308–11.

[96] *LW* 45.113. See also George, *Theology of the Reformers*, 98–102, and T. A. Brady, Jr., "Luther and the State: The Reformer's Teaching in Its Social Setting," in *Luther and the Modern State in Germany* (Kirksville, Mo.: Sixteenth Century Journal, 1986), 31–44.

the civil use of the law may be for the ordering of human society, it is at best a stopgap measure completely unable to render one righteous before God. The "chief and proper use of the law," Luther said, is its provocative function, actually to increase transgressions, to make a terrible situation even more desperate, and thus to reveal to human beings their "sin, blindness, misery, wickedness, ignorance, hate and contempt of God, death, hell, judgment, and the well-deserved wrath of God."[97] But how can a holy law given by divine sanction in order to multiply human transgressions really have a redemptive function without making God the author of sin? Paul could not dodge this question and would provide an answer to it in vv. 21-25.

2. *The Law Was Added until the Seed Had Come.*   Paul here spoke of the temporal parameters and limited duration of the law. Just as it had a point of origin on Mount Sinai, so also it had a point of termination—Mount Calvary. The Seed (rightly capitalized in the NIV) is used as a metonymy for Christ, echoing Paul's earlier identification in v. 16. Thus Paul interpreted the law eschatologically in terms of its fulfillment and cancellation (cf. Col 2:14) in the messianic mission of Jesus. As W. D. Davies put it, "Paul's controversial view of the law was inextricably bound up with the significance which he ascribed to Jesus as Messiah and with the challenge this issued to all the fundamental symbols of Jewish life."[98]

What was to be the status of the Torah in the age of the Messiah? Paul may have debated this very question in his pre-Christian rabbinic training because it was a burning issue in the thought world of second-temple Judaism. Some believed that when Messiah came the old law would be modified or a new one promulgated. Still others divided the history of the world into three epochs, each lasting some two thousand years: the age of chaos, the age of law, and the messianic age. According to this view, there was to be a major break between the second and third epochs so that "if the Torah still retained its validity, it was proclaimed thereby that the Messiah had not yet arrived."[99] Whether or not Paul had once subscribed to such a view, his personal encounter with the crucified and risen Messiah necessitated a major

---

[97] *LW* 26.309.

[98] W. D. Davies, "Paul and Law: Reflections on Pitfalls in Interpretation," in *Paul and Paulinism*, 7.

[99] Bruce, *Galatians*, 176. See also W. D. Davies, *Torah and the Messianic Age* (Philadelphia: Westminster, 1952). R. Banks has shown that much of the evidence cited by Davies in support of his thesis that the messianic age would usher in a new Torah or at least a major modification of the old law reflects later rabbinic speculations. This does not mean, however, that such ideas could not have been present in Paul's time as well. See R. Banks, "The Eschatological Role of Law in Pre- and Post-Christian Jewish Thought," in *Reconciliation and Hope: New Testament Essays on Atonement and Eschatology* (Grand Rapids: Eerdmans, 1974), 173-85.

reevaluation of the law in terms of God's decisive act of salvation in the cross and resurrection of Jesus.

L. Martyn has suggested that the central question of the entire Galatian Letter is, *What time is it?*[100] It is sometimes pointed out that there are few, if any, explicit references to the second coming of Christ in Galatians (though cf. 5:5), no imminent parousia (1 Thess 4), no treatise on the resurrection (1 Cor 15), and no warning about the Antichrist (2 Thess 2). The reason for such a glaring omission is obvious: because of the peril that had befallen the Galatians, Paul had to focus on first things rather than last things in this letter.[101] All the same, Paul everywhere in Galatians presupposed the decisiveness of Jesus' death and resurrection on the one hand and the hope of his return in glory on the other. The entire letter in fact is bracketed by two powerful apocalyptic signals: the opening announcement that the Lord Jesus Christ "gave himself for our sins to rescue us from the present evil age" (1:3) and the closing declaration that "what counts is a new creation" (6:15). Here, in the very center of the book, we are reminded that the purpose of the law must be defined both Christologically and eschatologically—"until the Seed to whom the promise referred had come." Indeed, the entire section that this statement introduces (3:19–4:11) virtually brims with the language of expectation transmitting the historical tension between the *No Longer* and the *Not Yet* of Christ's first and second coming into the experiential tension in the life of every believer—"until . . . before . . . no longer . . . formerly . . . but now."[102]

3. *The Law and the Angels.* The last two elements in Paul's answer to

---

[100] J. L. Martyn, "Apocalyptic Antinomies in Paul's Letter to the Galatians," *NTS* 31 (1985): 410-24.

[101] Martyn points out that at several crucial points in Galatians Paul employed the noun ἀποκάλυψις and the verb ἀποκαλύπτω to describe the new creation and end-time reality inaugurated by the advent of Christ and the coming of the Spirit (e.g., 1:13,16; 3:23; 6:14; "Apocalyptic Antinomies"). For further elaboration of this theme, see R. E. Sturm, "An Exegetical Study of the Apostle Paul's Use of the Words *Apokalyptō/Apokalypsis*" (unpublished Ph.D diss., Union Theological Seminary, 1984).

[102] Most commentators interpret Paul's emphasis on the historical contingency and temporariness of the law as a deliberate break with the concept of the eternal and immutable character of the law, an idea found in many Jewish writers from Josephus and Philo to the books of Wisdom and Jubilees. Evidently this was a commonly held belief in Judaism. As Longenecker remarks, "It would, in fact, be difficult to find any Jew who thought otherwise" (*Galatians*, 139). With reference to Paul it is important to distinguish the law as the revealed will of God, Holy Scripture which can be used as a metonym for God himself (3:8,22), and law in terms of its adversative function in the history of salvation. It is in this latter sense that Paul viewed the law as a temporary expedient now rendered defunct by Christ's having assumed its curse on the cross. See Betz, *Galatians*, 167-70; Bruce, *Galatians*, 176, and F. Thielman, "Law," *DPL*, 529-42.

his question, "Why then the law?" show the inherent inferiority of the law in terms of the way it was given and administered. Although countless explanations have been put forth for these two cryptic statements, Paul's meaning is essentially clear: the law is not on the same par with the covenant of promise not only because it was chronologically limited but also because it was handed down by angels with a man acting as a go-between.[103]

The Hebrew text of Exod 19, which contains the scriptural account of the giving of the law, does not refer to angels, but it does describe Mount Sinai as surrounded by thunder, lightning, a thick cloud, and billows of fire (Exod 19:16-19). Later Old Testament texts, notably the Septuagintal version of Deut 33:2 and Ps 68:18, interpret these natural phenomena to mean that a large number of angels, the fiery hosts of heaven, accompanied God in his giving of the law at Sinai.[104] The participation of the angels in the giving of the law was not merely a piece of pious Jewish folklore, for it is confirmed elsewhere in the New Testament (cf. Acts 7:38,53; Heb 2:2). Paul accepted this tradition and repeated it here not, however, for the purpose of enhancing the law by associating it with the glory of angels but rather to indicate how superior promise is to law since the latter required a creaturely mediation.

Paul did not say whether the angels in question were good ones or bad ones, but later Gnostic writers identified the angels who dispensed the law as evil cosmic powers who acted on their own, not at God's behest, in devising the legal code and imposing it on the Jewish people. Marcion believed the law to be the work of the demiurge, a fallen angelic being who gave the law to the Jews as a way of holding them in bondage to his tyrannical will.[105]

---

[103] *Translators Handbook,* 75. For various theories on the angelic conveyance of the law, see J. W. MacGorman, "Problem Passages in Galatians," *SWJT* 15 (1972): 35-51; A. Vanhoye, "Un médiateur des anges en Gal 3, 19-20," *Bib* 59 (1978): 403-11; T. Callan, "Pauline Midrash: The Exegetical Background of Ga. 3:19b," *JBL* 99 (1980): 549-67.

[104] Callan has surveyed various rabbinic interpretations of the function of the angels in the giving of the law ("Pauline Midrash," 551-52). They were variously understood as assisting Israel to receive the law, honoring the law by their presence, wreaking vengeance on those who rejected the law, representing the rulers of the world as the distinct angels of various nations, etc. A text from Josephus that closely resembles Paul's language has Herod reminding his soldiers that the Jews have learned the noblest of their doctrines and the holiest of their laws δι᾽ ἀγγέλων παρὰ τοῦ θεοῦ (*Antiquities* 15.136). W. D. Davies has argued that "angels" in this text should be read as "messengers," referring to the prophets or the priests of the people. See his "Note on Josephus, *Antiquities* 15.136," *HTR* 47 (1954): 135-40. See also the article by D. G. Reid, "Angels, Archangels," *DPL,* 20-23.

[105] Marcion drew a sharp contrast between the Creator-God of the Old Testament, the "ruler of the universe," and the "alien" Father of Jesus Christ; the former was judicial, harsh, mighty in war; the latter, mild, placid, and simply good and excellent. See J. Pelikan, *Emergence,* 73-74. The early Gnostic commentator Heracleon also interpreted the "angels" of Gal 3:19 as minions of the demiurge. See Pagels, *Gnostic Paul,* 107.

A host of modern scholars, taking their cue from early Gnostic interpretations, have also viewed Paul's reference to the angelic mediation of the law in a purely negative sense.[106] In a sentence with three exclamation points, H. Hübner expresses his shock at the thought: "This has a very cynical note about it: a God who—although he is the holy one!—puts men in the (literally!) damnable and immoral situation of sinning only so that he can show his divinity through his kindness and unsurpassable grace!" Hübner then continues, "this consequence would of course no longer result if not God but the angels were the legislators."[107] However, such a view cannot be sustained either exegetically or theologically. The subject of the aorist participle translated "ordained" (*diatageis*) can only be God: God ordained the law through angels by the hand of a mediator. Put otherwise, God used angels in passing on the law to Moses. The angels, whether good or bad, are not the source of the law but only secondary agents through whom it was given. Any other reading would have to presuppose the kind of radical dualism Paul is everywhere, including the very next verse, concerned to disallow.

The Role of a Mediator. **3:20** The only other place in Paul's writings where he used the word "mediator" (*mesitēs*) is 1 Tim 2:5, where it appears as a title for Jesus. For this reason, no doubt, Luther and Calvin, following Origen and Chrysostom, interpreted the word "mediator" here as a reference to Christ as well. But this meaning does great violence to the context that portrays Christ as the Seed of the Abrahamic covenant (vv. 16,19), not as the middle man of the Mosaic one. Here the mediator could only be Moses whom Paul could elsewhere refer to quite positively as a type of Christ.[108] Here, however, Moses stands as a contrastive figure to Christ. As Paul would explain more fully in 2 Cor 3:7-18, the ministry or covenant negotiated by

---

[106] See the discussion in Westerholm, *Israel's Law,* 176-79, citing Schweitzer, Schoeps, Drane, and Hübner. Thus the law was given by demonic angelic powers who in contrast to God do not desire the salvation of human beings but only their further subjugation. In terms of theodicy, this view has the advantage of ridding God of the blame. For, as we saw earlier, the concept of a god who deliberately provokes transgressions of some ulterior motive is difficult to square with ordinary standards of human morality.

[107] H. Hübner, *Law in Paul's Thought,* 26. Hübner sees the angelic provenance of the law in Galatians as an early Pauline accretion that he later abandoned in Romans. "In Galatians Paul denigrates the Law as an angelic Law while in Romans he sets the greatest store on its being holy, just and good . . . in each of the two letters the function of the *nomos* is set forth too divergently, not to say incompatibly, to suppose anything else" (p. 79).

[108] In 1 Cor 10:2 Paul said of the children of Israel that "all were baptized into Moses," an expression he used elsewhere (e.g., Gal 3:27) to refer to the believers' incorporation into and union with Christ. At least in one respect Moses was also a type of Paul: just as Moses desired to be blotted out of Yahweh's book in order that the children of Israel might be spared, so too Paul yearned to be severed from Christ for the sake of his fellow Jews (Exod 32:30-35; Rom 9:3). See L. L. Belleville, "Moses," *DPL,* 620-21.

Moses is characterized by death, condemnation, and evanescence—it is "fading away." On the other hand, the new covenant that Christ has ushered in is marked by life, justification, and a radiance of "ever increasing glory, which comes from the Lord, who is the Spirit."

Paul did not intend to denigrate Moses as a person but rather to show again the transitory and totally inadequate character of the law as a system of salvation. The Epistle to the Hebrews picks up on one of Paul's favorite antinomies, that of servant and son, and applies them to Moses and Christ in precisely this way: "Moses was faithful as a *servant* in all God's house, . . . but Christ is faithful as a *son* over God's house" (Heb 3:5-6; italics added). Here in Galatians Paul did not develop these themes but focused instead on the unity of God, quoting from the Shema, the most basic confession of the Hebrew faith, "Hear, O Israel: the Lord our God, the Lord is one" (Deut 6:4). Paul's point was this: the promise to Abraham came directly from God, not through angels, nor by means of a merely human mediator such as Moses.

Here is another reason why the law could not annul the covenant of promise. The latter was unconditionally given and thus stands just as steadfast and sure as the unity and sovereignty of God himself. As W. Perkins summed it up in his comment on this verse, "God's unchangeableness is the foundation of our comfort."[109] For Christians the implication of this foundational truth is astounding. Through Jesus Christ we may approach the throne of grace with boldness. In the Holy Spirit we can know God with the same kind of immediacy that Abraham enjoyed. But how can this be? Because in Jesus Christ, God did not send a substitute or a surrogate, no angelic mediation, no merely human go-between. In Jesus Christ, God, the one and only God, came himself.

THE THREE FUNCTIONS OF THE LAW (3:21-25). We come now to the third question Paul posed in Gal 3. He opened the chapter by asking the Galatians, "Did you receive the Spirit by observing the law, or by believing what you heard?" (3:2). It was a question they could answer for themselves based on their experience of God's working in their midst. The second query, "What, then, was the purpose of the law?" (v. 19), could not be so self-evidently answered and thus required a fuller explanation from the apostle. The third question, "Is the law, therefore, opposed to the promises of God?" elicits an immediate and indignant response, "Absolutely not!"

The Greek expression Paul used, *mē genoito,* conveys horror and shock at the very concept under consideration.[110] Of its fifteen occurrences in the New

---

[109] W. Perkins, *Galatians* (1604; reprint, New York: Pilgrim, 1989), 193.

[110] Note the various translations given to this use of the optative to express an emphatic negative wish: "certainly not" (Phillips); "of course not" (JB); "unthinkable!" (NAB); "no, never!" (NEB); "das sei ferne!" (Luther). For once, Clarence Jordan's Cotton Patch transla-

Testament, thirteen are in Paul's writings, invariably translated "God forbid!" by the KJV: "Is God unrighteous who taketh vengeance? God forbid" (Rom 3:6). "Do we then make void the law through faith? God forbid" (Rom 3:31). "Shall we continue in sin, that grace may abound? God forbid" (Rom 6:1-2). "Is there unrighteousness with God? God forbid" (Rom 9:14). "Is therefore Christ the minister of sin? God forbid" (Gal 2:17).

In the present context the question that has drawn such a strong negative response, "Is the law, then, opposed to the promises of God?" seems to follow logically from the argument Paul has pursued relentlessly from 3:10 up to this point. Having argued strenuously for both the discontinuity and inferiority of the law compared to the covenant of promise, Paul might well have expected one of his opponents to interrupt: "Why don't you come clean, Paul, and say what you think? What you are really saying is that God's laws and God's promises are totally against each other. Everything you have said thus far is a put-down of Moses and the Torah. What else are we to think?"

More than one commentator has at least implicitly agreed with Paul's presumed interlocutor, noting that, given the drift of Paul's argument in Gal 3, we rather expect Paul to have replied to the question of v. 21 with, "Well, yes, that's right" rather than his huffy "God forbid!"[111] However, we must remember that Paul had just confessed, in the powerful words of the Shema, the oneness of God: the God of the promise is also the God of the Torah. Paul was not preparing to take back anything he had said concerning the disjunction between the two covenants, for that is fundamental to this theology of grace. However, he was now ready to give a more complete answer to the question of v. 19, "Why then the law?" It is an answer designed to show how the law, far from contradicting the promise of God, actually served its fulfillment, not by producing righteousness (which it could not do) but fulfilling other vitally important, if subordinate, ends.[112]

---

tion misses the mark for being too weak: "not necessarily." On the wider use of this term in the NT, see C. F. D. Moule, *An Idiom-Book of New Testament Greek* (Cambridge: Cambridge University Press, 1953), 23.

[111] Thus Bruce, *Galatians,* 180: "The direction of the argument thus might prepare us for an affirmative answer, rather for Paul's emphatic *mē genoito.*"

[112] For the subdivision of this next section I am indebted to the brief but superb study by E. F. Kevan, *The Law of God and Christian Experience* (London: Pickering & Inglis, 1955). My understanding of this crucial passage has also been greatly enriched by the insightful analysis of Westerholm, *Israel's Law,* 179-97, and Thielman, *From Plight to Solution,* 72-88. Both Westerholm and Thielman, while not agreeing with one another on every point, have attempted to place Paul's statements about the law within the context of his Jewish religious background as well as the larger corpus of his writings. The result is a more consistent and coherent account than one finds, for example, in the revisionist studies of Hübner, Räisäen, and Sanders.

The Law Enters That It Might Fail.   **3:21**   By no means can the law be against the promises of God or in hostile competition with them, for this simple reason: no law can be found that is able to bestow the eternal life and blessing promised by grace alone. Paul used a contrary-to-fact-conditional sentence to make his point. If law had been given that had power to bestow life, then indeed one could be justified by keeping that law. But such is clearly not the case.[113] True, the law says, "Do this and you shall live"; but, as Paul had shown already in 3:10–13, fallen human beings are utterly incapable of the "doing" contained in such a commandment and thus have fallen under the law's curse.

Paul's comment raises the serious theological question of the function of the law both in the process of salvation and in the intention of God. In Rom 7:10 Paul brought together in one verse the four elements of the paradox he was dealing with here: life, death, law, and intentionality. Speaking perhaps autobiographically but in a sense that carries a universal application, Paul said: "Once I was alive apart from law; but when the commandment came, sin sprang to life, and I died. I found that the very commandment that was intended to bring life actually brought death."[114]

The "commandment" in Rom 7:10 refers to the tenth commandment, "Thou shalt not covet," which Paul had just confessed his inability to obey. Thus the very law that from one perspective was supposed to bring life—"do this and you shall live"—in reality became the occasion of death. Just as a cancer patient who receives chemotherapy in hopes of being cured of a dread disease only to discover that the very drugs that were supposed to bring renewed health have become the agent of further debilitation and death, so Paul said that the law made my desperate plight of sin and alienation from God even worse.

But by this line of argument had not Paul fallen into the very dualism from which he had just recoiled in horror and shock? No, and for two reasons. First, he insisted that there was no defect in the law; rather, it was "holy, righteous, and good" (Rom 7:12). The problem is not the law but our sinful disobedience that the law brings to light and further exacerbates in

---

[113] See the statement of Käsemann, *Romans,* 158: "In a way that is blasphemous to Jews, Paul finds in the law no legitimate answer to the question of eternal life. It does not mark the way of salvation but belongs in both fact and effect to the side of sin and death."

[114] The autobiographical interpretation of Rom 7 has been convincingly set forth by R. H. Gundry, "The Moral Frustration of Paul before His Conversion: Sexual Lust in Romans 7:7–25," *Pauline Studies* (Grand Rapids: Eerdmans, 1980), 228–45. See also J. C. Beker, *Paul the Apostle* (Philadelphia: Fortress, 1980), 236–43. On the general exegesis of Rom 7 see C. K. Barrett, *A Commentary on the Epistle to the Romans* (New York: Harper & Row, 1957), 138–534, and J. D. G. Dunn, "Rom 7:14–25 in the Theology of Paul," *TZ* 31 (1975): 257–73.

order to show us how hopeless we are apart from the interposition of divine grace. Second, none of this has caught God off guard or taken him by surprise. From the beginning God knew and intended for the law to function in just this way. Thus E. P. Sanders sums up the thrust of Paul's argument in Gal 3:21-25 in this way: "God always intended to save by faith, apart from law. God gave the law, but he gave it in order that it would condemn all and thus prepare negatively for redemption on the basis of faith (3:22,24, the purpose clauses conveying God's intention). The law was not given to make alive (3:21)."[115]

Thus from the beginning God intended for the law to fix upon us what A. R. Vidler has called "the bondage of a salutary despair." "It rivets upon us the conviction that we cannot be justified by anything we can do. Like the Israelites in Egypt, we are commanded to make bricks without straw, to be perfectly holy when we have none of the makings of holiness—to love God with all our hearts and the neighbor as ourselves when we are without divine charity."[116] The law entered, then, that it might fail, but that failure has been turned into blessing. The "side road" of the law, which (had we remained there) could only lead us to the gallows, has by the great mercy of God directed us back toward the royal road of salvation, toward the *Via Dolorosa* and another set of gallows designed for the Prince of Glory.

The Law Condemns That It Might Save.   **3:22-23**   The adversative *alla,* "but," separates Paul's negative argument against a false conclusion in v. 21 from his positive statement of the law's function in v. 22. As R. Fung said, Paul used the image of a jail sentence to make his point here, with Scripture as the magistrate, "the whole world" as the inmates, and sin as the jailor who carries out the verdict.[117] Scripture, in this context, is neither a synonym for the law nor an allusion to some specific text, such as Ps 143:2 or Deut 27:26, both of which Paul quoted earlier in Gal 2:16 and 3:10. Here, as in v. 8, Paul personified Scripture as a metonymy for God himself.[118]

We may gather two important principles from this striking and unusual use of the word "Scripture." First, we are reminded again of Paul's theological methodology. Although he had spoken in tongues more than all the Corinthians and could "boast" of rapturous ecstasies in the third heaven, none of these experiences could displace the written Word of God as the wellspring

---

[115] E. P. Sanders, *Paul, the Law, and the Jewish People* (Philadelphia: Fortress, 1983), 68. Sanders' exegesis of Rom 7 is less satisfying given his thesis of Paul's general inconsistency throughout that epistle. See the critique of Thielman, *From Plight to Solution,* 87-116.

[116] A. R. Vidler, *Christ's Strange Work* (London: Longmans, Green, and Co., 1994), 42.

[117] Fung, *Galatians,* 164.

[118] See, for example, the parallel verse in Rom 11:32: "For God has imprisoned all in disobedience that he may be merciful to all."

of his theology. How did Paul know about the universality of human sinfulness that he here asserted? Because he had read Psalms, Isaiah, and Ecclesiastes, from each of which he quoted in Rom 3:10-18 to show that all peoples everywhere have incurred guilt by transgressing the will of a holy God.

Contrary to many modern interpreters who portray Paul as an idiosyncratic thinker given to extravagant theories and bizarre speculations, he was in fact a biblical theologian whose special vocation was to listen for and expect to find the revealed will of God in the inspired documents of the faith. Second, by bringing into view not just an isolated verse or even the five books of Moses but instead the entire corpus of sacred writings, that is, Holy Scripture, Paul showed that only from the perspective of the whole scope of scriptural revelation can the specific role of the law be assessed.

This does not mean that Paul pitted one part of Scripture against another in an invidious way. Already we have seen how Paul argued from the law against the law, just as earlier he declared, "Through the law I died to the law" (2:19). For Paul every word of Holy Writ was of permanent and unassailable validity, carrying normative significance for faith and doctrine (witness, for example, the enormous theological weight placed on the singular number of a particular noun in 3:16). Yet in the final analysis the Bible is not merely a collection of disparate documents written across several millennia in various languages of antiquity. No, it is the rule of faith, the deposit of truth, a definitive canon, a sure word of promise. From beginning to end Scripture presents one coherent theme: the sovereign unfolding of God's eternal purposes in Jesus Christ, to the praise of his glory. This is the staggering overview Paul had in mind when he wrote "the Scripture declares."

From the total perspective of Scripture, then, we can see that the purpose of the law is to "conclude" (KJV) or "consign" (RSV) the whole world under sin. Paul used the verb *sunkleiō*, "to shut up together," or "to shut up on all sides." In the LXX it is applied to cities whose gates are closed and walls guarded because they are besieged by a hostile army (Josh 6:1; Isa 45:1). In other contexts it refers to those who are bound or kept in chains (Job 8:8), to the cattle of the Egyptians who were "given over" to death by hail and lightning (Ps 78:48), and to a large catch of fish enclosed in a net (Luke 5:6).[119]

This image thus brings together both the judicial and the punitive dimensions of the law's condemning function. Not only does the law declare us guilty before God, thus placing us under its curse, but it also locks us up in prison, preventing our escape. Jewish thought had developed the idea of the

---

[119] See other examples cited by Thielman, who defines the meaning of συνκλείω as "the action of surrounding and preventing the escape of something from its present location or state of existence" (*From Plight to Solution*, 74-75).

law as a fence, a protective wall designed to cordon off the people of Israel from the corruptions of the surrounding nations. The emphasis on circumcision as a rite of initiation, the detailed regulations regarding clean and unclean foods, the prohibition against eating with "Gentile sinners," all these measures were based on the understanding of the law as a prophylactic protection for the chosen people. Paul took the metaphor of the fence, however, and radicalized it by turning it into a barbed-wire prison wall. Its purpose was not to make the unjustified sinner pure and holy, to "impart life," but rather to condemn, enclose, and punish.

Moreover, if Paul radicalized the function of the law, he also universalized its scope. The whole world, *ta panta* in Greek (a neuter plural that may signify the created realm as well as the totality of humanity), has been shut up under its dominion. Traditionally, of course, the law was understood as the special preserve of the Jews, and in fact Paul could on other occasions speak this way himself (cf. his contrasting behavior among Jews who were "under the law" and Gentiles who were "outside the law" (1 Cor 9:20-21). Yet the same sinful disobedience that characterized the Jews who were given the specific revelation of the Mosaic law has spread throughout all cultures and among all peoples everywhere.

To be sure, the precise form of bondage differs greatly. For the Jews, it is the Mosaic legislation with its burdensome requirements; for the Gentiles, it is slavery to the *stoicheia*, the pagan deities and demonic forces that hold sway in "this present evil age." In one sense the law itself, though it remains holy, righteous, and good as a divinely sanctioned mandate, has become one of these evil powers insofar as it serves as an instrument of condemnation, judgment, and death.[120]

Had Paul concluded his statement with his description of the law as an instrument of imprisonment and condemnation, then the human situation

---

[120] We need not accept every aspect of E. P. Sanders' general thesis, that Paul thought backwards from solution to plight in construing a distinctively Christian theology regarding the Judaism of his day, to appreciate his observation: "One of the most striking features of Paul's argument is that he puts everyone, whether Jew or Gentile, in the same situation. . . . Since Christ came to save all, all needed salvation. The point of the parallel between the *stoicheia* and the law is perceived when one focuses on Paul's conviction that the plight of Jew and Gentile must be the same, since Christ saves all on the same basis" (*Paul, the Law, and the Jewish People,* 68-69). See also the discussion in Westerholm, *Israel's Law,* 192-95. T. L. Donaldson has argued strenuously that the Pauline expression ὑπο νόμον cannot be applied indiscriminately to Jews and Gentiles alike ("The 'Curse of the Law'"). However, his contention that "Israel's plight is a special form of the universal plight," might be better put in reverse: the universal condition of sin was most clearly manifested in the history of Israel—not that the Jewish people were more wicked than others but because the presence of God's law brought to light the magnitude and horror of sin itself.

would indeed be bleak beyond all hope. However, just as the law enters that it might fail, so too it condemns that it might save. And how did the law perform this "strange work"? By so provoking transgressions, by so exposing human wickedness to the scrutiny of divine holiness, by so eliminating every avenue of self-justification that the sinner is drawn, conscience-stricken and impoverished, to the only place where authentic redemption and liberation can be found.

> Nothing in my hand I bring,
> Simply to thy cross I cling:
> Naked, come to thee for dress;
> Helpless, look to thee for grace;
> Foul, I to the fountain fly:
> Wash me, Savior, or I die! (A. M. Toplady)

Thus we cannot move from Abraham to Christ, from promise to fulfillment, without going through the law after all. However secondary and subordinate in God's overall economy of salvation, the law nonetheless has a necessary and irreplaceable role to play. For, as Luther said, "God wounds in order to heal; he kills in order to make alive."[121]

The parallel conclusion of vv. 23-24 expresses, first on the level of personal appropriation and then in terms of historical fulfillment, Paul's definitive answer to the question of v. 21: Is the law against the promises of God? Perish the thought! In the eternal design of God, the law entered that it might fail. It put to death so that there could be a resurrection. The law also condemned and imprisoned so that "what was promised . . . might be given to those who believe." We were locked up in prison by the law until faith should be revealed. G. G. Findlay in his commentary on Galatians explains how in Paul's mind the penultimate pain of the law was meant to yield an ultimate blessing:

> The law was all the while standing guard over its subjects, watching and checking every attempt to escape, but intending to hand them over in due time to the charge of faith. The law posts its ordinances, like so many sentinels, round the prisoner's cell. The cordon is complete. He tries again and again to break out; the iron circle will not yield. The deliverance will yet be his. The day of faith approaches. It dawned long ago in Abraham's promise. Even now its light shines into his dungeon, and he hears the word of Jesus, "Thy sins are forgiven thee; go in peace." Law, the stern jailor, has after all been a good friend, if it has reserved him for this. It prevents the sinner escaping to a futile and illusive freedom.[122]

---

[121] *LW* 26.348.

[122] G. G. Findlay, *The Expositors Bible: Galatians,* 223; quoted in Kevan, *Law of God,* 53.

The Law Disciplines That It Might Set Free. **3:24-25** Paul now shifted his image of the law from that of a surly sergeant keeping watch over prisoners to that of the *paidagōgos,* a slave charged with the rearing and discipline of children. I have chosen to transliterate this word because none of the English equivalents adequately conveys what Paul had in mind. "Disciplinarian" (NAB, NRSV) comes closer than "custodian" (RSV), "tutor" (NEB), "schoolmaster" (KJV), "teacher and guide" (TLB). What was there about a *paidagōgos* that led Paul to use it as a metaphor for the law?

In ancient Greece and Rome wealthy parents often placed their newborn babies under the care of a wet-nurse who in turn would pass them on to an older woman, a nanny who would care for their basic needs until about the age of six. At that time they came under the supervision of another household servant, the *paidagōgos,* who remained in charge of their upbringing until late adolescence.[123] The pedagogue took over where the nanny left off in terms of offering menial care and completing the process of socialization for his charge. For example, one of the functions of the pedagogue was to offer instruction in the basics of manners as this description from Plutarch reveals: "And yet what do tutors [*hoi paidagōgoi*] teach? To walk in the public streets with lowered head; to touch salt-fish but with one finger, but fresh fish, bread, and meat with two; to sit in such and such a posture; in such and such a way to wear their cloaks."[124] The pedagogues also offered round-the-clock supervision and protection to those under their care. In this regard Libanius described the pedagogues as guardians of young teenage boys who warded off unsolicited homosexual advances their charges regularly encountered in the public baths, thus becoming "like barking dogs to wolves."[125]

No doubt there were many pedagogues who were known for their kindness and held in affection by their wards, but the dominant image was that of a harsh disciplinarian who frequently resorted to physical force and corporal punishment as a way of keeping his children in line. For example, a certain pedagogue named Socicrines was described as a "fierce and mean old man" because of his physically breaking up a rowdy party. He then dragged

---

[123] There is a large literature on Paul's analogy of the παιδαγωγός. In addition to the standard commentaries, see especially L. G. Bertram, "παιδεύω" *TDNT* 5.596-625; R. N. Longenecker, "The Pedagogical Nature of the Law in Galatians 3:19–4:7," *JETS* 25 (1982): 53-61; D. J. Lull, "'The Law Was Our Pedagogue': A Study in Galatians 3:19-25," *JBL* 105 (1986): 481-98; L. L. Belleville, "'Under Law': Structural Analysis and Pauline Concept of Law in Galatians 3:21–4:11," *JSNT* 26 (1986): 53-78; N. H. Young, "PAIDAGŌGOS: The Social Setting of a Pauline Metaphor," *NovT* 29 (1987): 150-76; Westerholm, *Israel's Law,* 195-97; Thielman, *From Plight to Solution,* 77-79.

[124] Plutarch, *Mor.* 439f-440, cited in Young, "PAIDAGŌGOS," 160-61.

[125] Ibid., 159.

away his young man, Charicles, "like the lowest slave" and delivered the other troublemakers to the jailer with instructions that they should be handed over to "the public executioner."[126] The ancient Christian writer Theodoret of Cyrrhus observed that "students are scared of their pedagogues."[127] And well they might have been because pedagogues frequently accomplished their task by tweaking the ear, cuffing the hands, whipping, caning, pinching, and other unpleasant means of applied correction.

Thus the metaphor of the law as pedagogue is colored by the preceding image of the prison guard. The unfortunate translation of *paidagōgos* as "schoolmaster" (KJV) has misled many preachers and exegetes to interpret this metaphor in terms of educational advance or moral improvement. As we shall see in Gal 5–6, the law continues to have a vital role for every believer in the process of sanctification. However, that function is clearly not within the scope of Paul's meaning here. The fundamental error of Pelagius was to see the law, and for that matter Christ himself, as an external standard given to human beings as an incentive for self-improvement. Paul has already shown the utter folly of this approach to justification. No, in Gal 3 the law is a stern disciplinarian, a harsh taskmaster. Yet in its very harshness there is a note of grace, for the function of discipline, as opposed to mere torture, is always remedial. "With its whippings," Luther said, "the law draws us to Christ."[128]

This brings us to the primary purpose of the *paidagōgos* motif in Paul's analogy. The law was "a strict governess" (Phillips), a stern baby-sitter (Dunn)—*eis Christon*. The preposition *eis* can have either a purposive, "unto Christ," or a temporal, "until Christ," meaning. The NIV opts for the former in its rendering of this text: "So the law was put in charge to lead us to Christ." As we have just shown, this statement does ring true to the theological purpose of the law as Paul unfolded it in Gal 3, so long as we do not misunderstand the "leading unto Christ" as a kind of gradual moral or educational development by which one was brought into right standing with God.[129] In a proper sense the law does lead us to Christ not by weaning us

---

[126] This incident is cited by Alciphron in EP. 3.7.3-5, quoted by Lull, "'The Law Was Our Pedagogue,'" 489-90.

[127] Epistle 36; Young, "PAIDAGŌGOS," 162, n. 138. Cf. Libanius's likening of the pounding of the boat's oars on the sea to the pedagogue's lash upon a child's back (Epistle 1188, 3-4; ibid.).

[128] *LW* 26.346.

[129] Ramsay's otherwise helpful comments on this passage are marred by this interpretation: "The one man [Adam] at first needed no schoolmaster: he was able to respond at once to the requirements of God. But the nation, when it came to exist, was not able in itself to rise to the conditions which God demanded. It needed education and the constant watching of the careful guardian. The law was given to watch over the young nation as it was being trained and educated in the school of life" (*Galatians,* 385).

from our sins but rather revealing them clearly and even causing them to be multiplied and increased to the point where we stand before God utterly void of any hope of self-reclamation. Yet this convicting, condemning, killing function of the law is not an end in itself but rather, as A. Schlatter once put it, "the silent preparation for the revelation of faith."[130]

In the present context, however, *eis Christon* should be translated "until Christ" rather than "unto Christ," for Paul was again stressing the temporary nature of the law that in the unfolding of redemptive history had both a *terminus a quo*, Mount Sinai, and an equally punctiliar *terminus ad quem*, Mount Calvary. Paul was saying to the Galatians: "Look! About twenty years ago something happened in Jerusalem that has forever changed the history of the world. God's promised Messiah appeared on earth. He was born under the law and fulfilled its every jot and tittle to utter perfection. For our sake he suffered the curse of the law in his own body on the cross so that we might be justified and set free from the bondage from sin and death that the law had justly imposed upon us because of our rebellion and unbelief."

Paul described the whole complex of events surrounding the life, death, and resurrection of Jesus as "the coming of faith." He did not mean, of course, that the Old Testament saints were justified by works and we who live on this side of Good Friday and Easter are justified by faith. From 3:6 onward he strenuously argued the contrary: we are all the children of Abraham and heirs of the promise, by faith and not by works. Yet there is a critical difference. What Abraham glimpsed from a distance, we have seen up close; what he beheld in figures and types, we have received in fulfillment and reality. Before our very eyes Jesus Christ has been clearly portrayed as crucified (3:1). What God decreed in eternity past, what the patriarchs and prophets longed for in days gone by, and what the law was powerless to do—not because it was defective in any way but because it was "weakened" by human depravity (Rom 8:3)—God himself has in fact done. This has really happened not only theoretically but historically so that "now . . . we are no longer (*ouketi*) under the law" as a pedagogue. In the section that follows (3:26–4:11) Paul expanded on this theme to show how the "coming of faith" has set us free not only from the law but also for the inheritance and freedom of the children of God.

Before we leave these verses, we must touch upon two difficult herme-

---

[130] Quoted in H. Ridderbos, *Paul: An Outline of His Theology* (Grand Rapids: Eerdmans, 1975), 153. Based on Ridderbos, Schlatter, however, goes too far in claiming that "under the law we were guarded because it shut us off from God like a wall. It did not allow us access to his love." On the contrary, the law itself was a manifestation of divine love, its enslaving and condemning operation a necessary function in the economy of God's grace.

neutical issues that have plagued interpreters of this passage across the centuries. If taken in isolation from the rest of Paul's writings, Gal 3:10–25 can be, and sometimes has been, read as a manifesto of antinomianism. If the law cannot save but only condemn, if it cannot remove transgressions but actually increases them, if we are no longer under its harsh discipline, if Christ is the end (*telos*) of the law for all who believe, then does the law have any continuing normative significance for the Christian? While we will return to this question in Galatians 5 and 6, we may at this point introduce two important distinctions concerning New Testament teaching on the law.

As we have seen, the Reformers distinguished between the civil or political use of the law, according to which criminals are restrained and human society kept from complete chaos, and the theological or spiritual use of the law, according to which sinners incurred the full penalty of God's righteous judgment and became liable to his curse because of their transgressions. Clearly it is this second, theological use of the law that Paul had been developing in Galatians 3. However, Calvin and Reformed theologians especially also spoke of a third use of the law (*tertius usus legis*) by which they referred to the abiding significance of the law as a standard of moral uprightness and as a source of spiritual counsel and instruction precisely for those who have been freed from the "bondage" of the law.

However, if one accepts the validity of the third use of the law, it becomes immediately necessary to distinguish further various dimensions or layers of the law as found in the Old Testament. The most commonly accepted schema finds within the law a threefold distinction: the ceremonial law, which included the sacrificial cultus and other regulations such as circumcision that related to the ethnic particularism of the Jewish people; the civil law, which contained the code of behavior and penal sanctions given to Israel as a national entity; and the moral law, the eternal standard of God's righteous rule embodied succinctly in the Ten Commandments. When we speak of the third use of the law, that is of the continuing validity of the law as a moral guide in the life of the believer, we are speaking of the moral law of God and not the law in its civil or ceremonial aspects.[131] Both of these construals, the threefold use of the law and the threefold differentiation within the law, are

---

[131] Theonomists regularly include the civil along with the moral law of God in their design for restructuring contemporary society on the basis of the divine will. A plethora of literature on this topic continues to be hotly debated among evangelical theologians. See W. G. Strickland, ed., *The Law, the Gospel, and the Modern Christian: Five Views* (Grand Rapids: Zondervan, 1993). See also the very sensible study by W. J. Chantry, *God's Righteous Kingdom: The Law's Connection with the Gospel* (Edinburgh: Banner of Truth, 1980). On the third use of the law see the classic study by G. Ebeling, "On the Doctrine of the *Triplex Usus Legis* in the Theology of the Reformation," *Word and Faith* (Philadelphia: Fortress, 1964), 62–78.

patterns of interpretation derived from the history of exegesis. While they do reflect an accurate distillation of the overall teaching of the Scripture, they must be used with great caution when applied to a particular text.

Thus it would be a mistake to say, as exegetes from Origen onward have done, that Paul only had in mind the ceremonial law in his strongly negative assessment in Galatians 3. The law is here a unitary whole. The law in all of its aspects—civil, ceremonial, moral—was implicated in Christ's curse bearing on the cross. When he cried, "It is finished!" Christ brought to an end the epoch of the law in its entirety as prison guard and pedagogue. To those who would downplay the decisiveness of that event by taking on again the former yoke of bondage, Paul said emphatically, "No Longer!" However, to others—libertines, spiritualists, Gnostics—who assume that Christians have already been removed from the realm of temptation and struggle, Paul answered just as strongly, "Not Yet!" While the former error was clearly Paul's primary burden in Galatians, the latter was never far from the surface, and he tackled it head-on in the closing chapters of the epistle.

The second hermeneutical issue also relates to the eschatological tension present throughout Paul's discussion of the law and gospel in Galatians. On the most basic, fundamental level Paul was describing a historical process within the covenant nation of Israel. God made a promise to Abraham. He gave the law to Moses. Now he had brought both, promise and law, to their intended consummation in Jesus Christ. Elsewhere, in Rom 9–11, Paul explained how the specific promises made to the nation of Israel relate to the "engrafting" of the Gentiles into the covenant of promise. In Galatians 3–4 he was concerned to show how what happened concretely within the history of the Jewish people, and especially to one Jewish man named Jesus, had universal application for all peoples everywhere. Thus it not only was Jews who were held prisoners under sin, under the law, and under the curse but Gentiles as well. Even so, the promise has been extended through faith to all those who believe in Jesus Christ. For this reason we must read Paul closely and carefully, for he brings together in delicate balance both the corporate and individual perspectives. When Paul spoke about the duration of the time of the law, we must understand it both historically and existentially. In its function as a pedagogue the law lasted until Christ. Yet the severity of the law and its curse remain in force for all of those who are outside of Christ. What happened historically must be appropriated personally else it is of no benefit to anyone. Hence the urgency of Paul, the ambassador of Christ, in imploring men and women on behalf of his Lord, "Be reconciled to God" (2 Cor 5:20).

But to all who have looked to Christ alone for pardon and forgiveness, who by faith have heard God's gracious verdict of acquittal and have received the promised Holy Spirit, the law may no longer exercise its tyrannical rule. Luther put it best:

> Here one must say: "Stop, law! You have caused enough terror and sorrow." . . . Then let the law withdraw; for it was indeed added for the sake of disclosing and increasing transgressions, but only until the point when the Offspring would come. Once he is present, let the law stop disclosing transgressions and terrifying. Let it surrender its realm to another, that is, to the Blessed Offspring, Christ; he has gracious lips, with which he does not accuse and terrify but speaks better things than the law, namely, grace, peace, forgiveness of sins, and victory over sin and death.[132]

SUMMARY.   We have now come to the midpoint of Paul's theological exposition in Gal 3 and 4. He began this section of the epistle by pointing the Galatians back to their initial experience as Christian believers. They received the Holy Spirit through the preaching of the gospel, the hearing of faith, not by performing the works of the law. Having begun in the Spirit, they must not slide back into a dependence on the flesh. Being a Christian means belonging to the people of God, the family of faith that traces its spiritual lineage back to Abraham, who believed God and was thus justified by faith. How has this come about? Through the redeeming work of Christ on the cross. There Jesus willingly took upon himself the curse of the law on behalf of guilty sinners. Through his death the way has been opened for Jews and Gentiles alike to become children of Abraham and receive the promised Holy Spirit by faith alone. Thus God's promise to Abraham finds its true fulfillment in his Seed, Jesus Christ. The Sinaitic covenant, established centuries later through angels and a human mediator, cannot abrogate God's unconditional promise to Abraham. Yet the Mosaic law does serve a necessary and salutary purpose in the economy of salvation. It was given "on account of transgressions," that is, to reveal and condemn sin in all of its horror so that the promise of faith in Jesus Christ might be given to those who believe. The law is a harsh taskmaster: a prison warden, a public executioner, a pitiless pedagogue. But the condemnatory character of the law was a part of God's design from the beginning, and the coming of Christ has forever altered its former claim and status. To seek to go back under the tutelage of the law is to deny the efficacy of Christ's death. We who are the true children of Abraham through faith are no longer under the law or its curse. No longer slaves or truant children now, we have been set free, redeemed by the blood of Christ, and adopted as heirs of God himself.

---

[132] *LW* 26.317.

5. Sons and Servants (3:26–4:11)

The NIV correctly notes a major break in Paul's argument at this point, a new turn in his continuing scriptural demonstration of the doctrine of justification by faith. Up to this point Paul has presented the grand sweep of redemptive history from Abraham to Christ. He had used the forensic language of justification, covenant, and inheritance. Now the focus shifts from the historical to the personal, from the institutional to the individual. Paul has discussed the inheritance promised to the children of Abraham; now he zooms in on the heir who claimed his bequest. The historical and the personal merge into an indissoluble unity just as they do in the event of the gospel itself. Thus just as God sent his Son into our history to redeem us, so also has he sent the Spirit of his Son into our hearts to regenerate us (4:4-6). The following diagram illustrates the flow of Paul's argument in these two chapters:

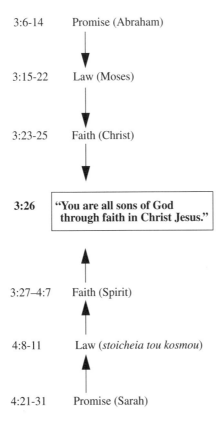

3:6-14   Promise (Abraham)

3:15-22   Law (Moses)

3:23-25   Faith (Christ)

3:26   **"You are all sons of God through faith in Christ Jesus."**

3:27–4:7   Faith (Spirit)

4:8-11   Law (*stoicheia tou kosmou*)

4:21-31   Promise (Sarah)

In 3:6-25 Paul traced the actual course of salvation history from Abraham
through Moses to Christ, that is, from promise through law to faith. "Faith"
in fact is the key word linking together the two halves of Paul's theological
exposition. In 3:25 he declared: "Now that *faith* has come, we are no longer
under the supervision of the law" (italics added). As we have seen already,
faith in this verse is a code word for the whole complex of events related to
the life, death, and resurrection of Christ. In the immediately following verse
(3:26) Paul extrapolated from this objectively accomplished redemption to
its subjective appropriation: "You are all sons of God through *faith* in Christ
Jesus" (emphasis mine). Thus Paul picked up directly where he left off, that
is, with the radical good news of how God's promise to Abraham has found
its fulfillment in Jesus Christ, whose finished work is the basis for a new relationship with God.

From 3:26 to 4:31, Paul would now argue backwards as it were from the
realization of faith through the former bondage, now portrayed as subjection
to "the basic principles of the world" in lieu of the law, toward a final restatement of the promise and its counterpart, exemplified through the allegory of
Abraham's two sons, Isaac and Ishmael.[133]

Why did Paul argue in this fashion, reversing his course and retracing his
steps back through this well-worn historical sequence to his original point of
departure? We know that the churches of Galatia were made up primarily of
Gentile converts, although there was also a mingling of Jewish believers
among them as well. Moreover, the agitators from outside who were attacking Paul's apostolic authority and his theology of grace were most likely
Jewish Christian missionaries with strong ties to Palestinian Christianity.
They preached the necessity of circumcision for salvation, arguing strenuously from the Old Testament and the history of God's covenant with Israel.
We have seen already that Paul would give no countenance to their spurious
arguments from Scripture. To the contrary, he stood his ground with them toe
to toe and text to text, proving that the doctrine of justification by faith is no
newfangled teaching or novel ideal but a fundamental truth derived from the
very fabric of Holy Scripture itself.

---

[133] I follow here the general analysis of Ebeling, *Truth,* 207-24. Bligh has offered an elaborate outline of Galatians relating this central passage to the overall chiasmic structure of the
epistle (*Galatians,* 330-415). See also the structural analysis of Betz, *Galatians,* 14-26. Betz
finds here an argument from Christian tradition (3:26–4:11) followed by an argument from
friendship (4:12-20) and a concluding allegorical argument from Scripture (4:21-31). The
analyses of Bligh and Betz are not convincing in every aspect, but they are sound correctives
to other views in showing "that Paul did not pour forth his thoughts tumultuously with no concern for orderliness of exposition, but instead arranged them with careful attention to form."
See also W. E. Hull, "A Teaching Outline of Galatians," *RevExp* 69 (1972): 429.

With this in mind we can see more clearly how Paul's argument in 3:6-25 is developed with primary focus on the Jewish Christian situation. True, the Gentiles could not stand aloof from the history of Israel; indeed, they had been drawn into it and implicated by it, for "the Scripture declares that the whole world is a prisoner of sin" (3:22). Nonetheless, the law of Moses was given to the people of Israel at a specific moment in their national history. No Jewish Christian of the first century could ignore the fact that Jesus the Messiah was a Jew and that he had come to fulfill the law, not to destroy it (Matt 5:17-20). In 3:26–4:31, however, Paul turned the spotlight on the Gentile Christian community. If Jews could only be justified by faith alone, how much more so the Gentiles (recall Paul's statement of this thesis in his earlier encounter with Peter at Antioch; cf. 2:16-21). Yet in the great mercy of God, they have been drawn into the new community where their former alienation from the commonwealth of Israel has been nullified by the divinely given unity in Christ Jesus.

(1) Baptism and the New Community (3:26-29)

²⁶**You are all sons of God through faith in Christ Jesus, ²⁷for all of you who were baptized into Christ have clothed yourselves with Christ. ²⁸There is neither Jew nor Greek, slave nor free, male nor female, for you are all one in Christ Jesus. ²⁹If you belong to Christ, then you are Abraham's seed, and heirs according to the promise.**

3:26 The Greek text connects this verse with the preceding one by the explanatory particle *gar,* "because," "for." Why is it that the law of Moses no longer serves as a prison guard or pedagogue? It is because now "you are all sons of God through faith in Christ Jesus." Some scholars believe that this expression, like the baptismal formula that follows it, may well have come from the confessional and liturgical life of the early church.[134] In structure it resembles the five "trustworthy sayings" recorded in the Pastoral Epistles (e.g., 1 Tim 1:15, "Christ Jesus came into the world to save sinners"; cf. also 1 Tim 3:1; 4:9; 2 Tim 2:11; Titus 3:8). But whether this statement was original with Paul or adapted by him from the worship services of the first Christian congregations, it reflects an affirmation of great importance for all believers.

The emphatic "all" (*pantes*) that opens the statement underscores the fact that Jews and Gentiles alike have been admitted to a new spiritual status as equal partners "in Christ Jesus." We should not read too much into Paul's noticeable transition from first person plural in v. 25 ("we") to second person

---

[134] Longenecker, *Galatians,* 151-53.

plural ("you are") in v. 26. As we have suggested, this passage does mark a shift in Paul's presentation: what he had just described in terms of the Jewish Christian perspective he would now restate from the standpoint of converted Gentiles. However, even in Gal 4, Paul would move from "we" to "you" language with no discernible difference in meaning. He could do this because the fundamental human reality is the same for Jews and Gentiles alike. The Scripture has concluded all under sin, all under the curse, all in bondage. Conversely, the redemptive work of Christ and incorporation into his body have relativized the former distinctions of race, rank, and role.

In this brief verse Paul made three astounding statements regarding the new status of "all" true believers.

1. *You are all sons of God.* The term "Son of God" has been used twice before in this letter, both times as a proper title for Jesus Christ (1:15-16; 2:20). In all Paul referred to Jesus as the "Son of God" seventeen times in his letters. Jesus is uniquely and exclusively *the* Son of God, equal with the Father from all eternity, unrivaled by any creatures in his essential deity. All the more remarkable, then, is Paul's description of the redeemed as "sons of God." He developed this theme in the verses that follow by showing how the sonship of Christians is derived from the sonship of Christ.[135]

In the present context Paul's description of the enfranchisement of elect believers as "sons of God" carries two other meanings as well. Galatians 3–4 resonates with the theme of family—the promised seed, the inheritance, adoption, heirship, motherhood. Galatians 3:26 is the fulcrum verse of both chapters. Everything Paul had said from 3:6 through 3:25 flows into this verse, just as everything that follows from 3:27 to 4:31 issues from it. This verse says plainly what Paul was arguing for throughout this central section of the letter: the true children of Abraham are really the children of God. However, in the immediate context of the pedagogue analogy, the language of sonship has still another connotation. Now that we have entered into full adult sonship, we no longer need a baby-sitter. The law of God still has a positive role to play in the life of the believer, but it may no longer condemn, imprison, or destroy. To be reshackled in that former bondage, as the Galatians were being "bewitched" to do, was to turn life in Christ into a sordid anachronism.

---

[135] In 2 Cor 6:14-18 Paul spoke of believers as "sons and daughters" of God in the context of their separation from the world as the living temple of the Holy God. On this theme see further E. Schweizer, "υιος, υιοθεσια," *TDNT* 8.334-99; M. Hengel, *The Son of God* (Philadelphia: Fortress, 1976); A. D. Nock, "'Son of God' in Pauline and Hellenistic Thought," in *Essays on Religion and the Ancient World,* ed. Z. Stewart (Oxford: Clarendon, 1972), 2, 928-39.

2. *You are all sons of God through faith.* Not by natural descent nor human contrivance but through faith alone have we entered into this new relationship with the Heavenly Father. "To those who believed in his name, he gave the right to become children of God" (John 1:12; cf. Hos 1:10).

3. *You are all sons of God through faith in Christ Jesus.* The expression "in Christ" is found 172 times in Paul's writings. Sometimes this expression is used in the instrumental sense of "by" or "through Christ," as we find in Gal 2:17 and 3:14. More often, however, it is used to describe that participation in and union with Jesus Christ that is effected for every believer by the indwelling of the Holy Spirit.

The New Testament uses a variety of metaphors to describe what Paul meant by "in Christ." John spoke of believers "abiding" in Christ as branches of a vine (John 15:1-17); Peter spoke of our new birth into a living hope that results in an inexpressible and glorious joy (1 Pet 1:3-9); Paul elsewhere spoke of the church as the body of Christ with its various members functioning as vital parts of a living organism (1 Cor 12:12-27). For Paul, to be "in Christ" meant far more than to imitate Christ, although that idea is not absent from his thought (cf. Phil 1:29). But, as Dunn has rightly noted, "The religious experience of the Christian is not merely experience like that of Jesus, it is experience which at all characteristic and distinctive points is derived from Jesus the Lord, and which only makes sense when this derivative and dependent character is recognized."[136]

3:27 This verse contains the only explicit mention of baptism in Galatians and one of the most important references to this important Christian ordinance in all of Paul's writings. It is not accidental that baptism stands at the very intersection where the historical and corporate character of salvation is brought into closest relation to the personal and confessional dimensions of new life in Christ.

---

[136] J. D. G. Dunn, *Jesus and the Spirit* (London: SCM, 1975), 342. In the ongoing efforts of Pauline scholars to locate a definitive center of the apostle's theology, the forensic language of justification sometimes is played off over against the participationist motif reflected in the "in Christ" formula. Thus E. P. Sanders regards Gal 3:24-27 as a more normative pattern of Paul's thinking in contrast to Rom 5 and other passages that reflect a more juridical statement of soteriology. See his *Paul and Palestinian Judaism,* 506, n. 68. However, while we do well to distinguish justification and participation (or incorporation) as separable categories in Paul's theology, we err gravely by turning them into polar opposites or emphasizing one to the diminution of the other. Drawing on Paul's autobiographical reflection in Phil 3, Bruce has observed: "It is because he no longer had 'a righteousness of my own, based on law, but that which is through faith in Christ,' that he could make it his settled purpose in life to advance in the knowledge of Christ 'and the power of his resurrection, and the fellowship of his sufferings'" (*Galatians,* 185). Cf. also A. Oepke's succinct summary statement, "Forensic justification leads to pneumatic fellowship with Christ" ("βαπτω, βαπτιζω" *TDNT* 1.541).

Baptism in the New Testament invariably implies a radical personal commitment involving a decisive no to one's former way of life and an equally emphatic yes to Jesus Christ. Historically, however, the doctrine of believers' baptism has also implied a gathered church, a community of intentional disciples marked off from the world by their commitment to Christ and to one another. Baptism is the liturgical enactment of the priesthood of all believers, not the priesthood of "the believer," a lonely, isolated seeker of truth, but rather of a band of faithful believers united in a common confession as a local, visible *congregatio sanctorum* ("gathering of saints"). Paul's discussion of baptism in Galatians comes at a critical juncture in his quest to redefine the people of God, the family of faith, the true children of Abraham. For him baptism was an outward sign not only of the personal response of faith but also of the new community that belongs to Christ by virtue of grace alone.

The precise relationship between faith in v. 26 and baptism in v. 27 has been vigorously debated throughout the history of the church. Does the *gar* ("for") that introduces v. 27 indicate that the status of divine sonship is contingent upon the ritual of water baptism? A. Schweitzer, among others, contended that Paul had developed his doctrine of baptism from the sacramental practices of the Hellenistic mystery religions that permeated the Roman world in his day. A new convert being initiated into the cult of a particular deity (Isis or Mithras, for example) would undergo a ritual ablution, usually through immersion, during which the person was "born again" and joined in mystical union with the god or goddess in question. The sacraments of the mystery religions worked like magic to assure the devotee of immortality.[137] Over time a similar type of sacramental realism was attributed to the Christian ordinances. This tendency is evident, for example, in Ignatius of Antioch's famous description of the Lord's Supper as "the medicine of immortality" and Augustine's consignment of all unbaptized babies dying in

---

[137] Tertullian, writing in the early third century, reported on the baptismal practices of the mystery religions still in vogue in his day: "For washing is the channel through which they are initiated into some sacred rites—of some notorious Isis or Mithras. The gods themselves likewise they honor by washings. Moreover, by carrying water around, and sprinkling it, they everywhere expiate country-seats, houses, temples, and whole cities: at all events, at the Apollinarian and Eleusian games they are baptized; and they presumed at the effect of their doing that is their regeneration and the remission of the penalties dues to their perjuries" (*De Baptismo,* 5, *ANF* 3, 671). See also T. R. Glover, *The Conflict of Religions in the Early Roman Empire* (Boston: Beacon, 1909). For Schweitzer see his *Paul and His Interpreters,* 214–30. For a recent review of NT baptism against its Greco-Roman background, see A. J. M. Wedderburn, "The Soteriology of the Mysteries in Pauline Baptismal Theology," *NovT* 29 (1987): 53–72.

infancy to the region of limbo.[138]

However important these ideas became for later sacramental theology, though, they were far removed from Paul's concern with baptism in Galatians. The whole burden of the letter has been to say that salvation is received through faith in Christ alone apart from the works of the law including specifically the requirement of circumcision. After all that Paul had said against the Judaizers and their interposition of circumcision as a prerequisite for a right standing with God, did he here set forth his own rite of initiation into God's favor? Was he saying to the Galatians: "My opponents were wrong in trying to circumcise you. What you really need is to be baptized! The requirement of baptism has replaced that of circumcision. If you want to be right with God, you must trust in Jesus Christ *and* be baptized with water"?

Yet this is precisely what Paul did *not* say to the Galatians. To believe in Jesus Christ *and* water, Jesus Christ *and* bread and wine, Jesus Christ *and* church membership, Jesus Christ *and* anything else is to profane the grace of God and render useless the death of Christ (2:21). Thus Karl Barth is correct in claiming that Gal 3:27 is looking back to the divine change, to that putting on of Christ, which in Jesus Christ himself has been effected objectively and subjectively for the recipients of the epistle by his Holy Spirit. Baptism is recalled as the concrete moment in their own life in which they for their part confirmed, recognized, and accepted their investing with Christ from above, their ontic relationship to him, not only in gratitude and hope but also in readiness and vigilance.[139]

Where the "water theology" of sacramentalism insists upon the necessity of baptism as the instrumental cause of regenerating grace, Paul pointed to the sufficiency and uniqueness of Christ's atoning death on the cross and the immediacy of the Holy Spirit as the divine carrier and agent of salvation.[140]

---

[138] Ignatius of Antioch, *Ephesians,* 20. Ignatius also described the eucharist as "the flesh and blood of our Savior, the flesh which suffered for our sins and which the Father raised from the dead" (*Smyrnaeans,* 6). For Augustine see *Enchiridion Theologicum Sancti Augustini,* ed. F. Moriones (Madrid: Biblioteca de Autores Cristianos, 1961), 565-86. For the general development of all seven sacraments see the excellent studies by J. Martos, *Doors to the Sacred* (New York: Doubleday, 1981), and A. Kavanagh, *On Liturgical Theology* (New York: Pueblo, 1984).

[139] Karl Barth, *Church Dogmatics* IV/4, 116.

[140] I agree with the substance of J. Dunn's comment that the Pauline expression "baptized into Christ" is "simply a metaphor drawn from the rite of baptism to describe . . . the entry of the believer into the spiritual relationship of the Christian with Christ, which takes place in conversion-initiation" (*Baptism and the Holy Spirit* [Naperville, Ill., 1970], 109-11). However, to refer to Christian baptism as "simply a metaphor," or, to use another popular designation, "merely a symbol," is to minimize its true meaning and real importance in the life of the church. Apart from the thief on the cross, there is no one in the NT who repented and believed in Christ without also becoming a baptized follower of him. Baptism is no more optional than discipleship is; indeed, they are integrally related to each other. See T. George, "The Reformed Doctrine of Believers' Baptism," *Int* 47 (1993): 242-54.

For Paul the baptismal rite, with its evocation of, and association with, the death, burial, and resurrection of Christ, models justification although it can never mediate it. For the New Testament believer's baptism with (or "in" or "by"; cf. 1 Cor 12:13) the Holy Spirit is antecedent to baptism with water, the latter being a confession and public witness to the former. We have no record of the baptism of the Galatians, but we may assume that many of them were baptized by Paul and Barnabas or the elders they appointed to care for the churches soon after the initial evangelization of that area (cf. Acts 14:21-23). However, in the opening verses of Gal 3, when Paul reminded the Galatians of the very beginning of their Christian experience, he did not say, "Were you baptized?" but rather, "Did you receive the Spirit?" (3:2-3). The objective basis of faith is not the ordinance of baptism but rather that to which baptism bears witness, namely, the whole Christological-soteriological "event" summarized in the phrase "God sent his Son" (4:4), together with the gift of the Holy Spirit who through the preaching of the gospel has awakened faith in the elect.[141]

With all this in mind, the question naturally arises: If one has already received the gift of the Spirit and has trusted Christ for salvation, then why be baptized with water at all? Certain Christian groups, notably Quakers and the Salvation Army, having drawn such a radical conclusion from these very premises, have dispensed with baptism altogether. However, the nonpractice of baptism can in no way be justified on the basis of the New Testament,

---

[141] H. Schlier has claimed that faith is merely the vestibule of salvation through which the believer is brought into the true event of divine transformation, i.e., baptism (*Galater,* 127-28). While not going as far as Schlier, G. R. Beasley-Murray also stresses the indissoluble alliance of faith and baptism, arguing that this connection prevented Christianity from evaporating into "an ethereal subjectivism on the one hand and from hardening into a fossilized objectivism on the other" (*Baptism in the New Testament* [Grand Rapids: Eerdmans, 1973], 151). While Beasley-Murray offers a helpful corrective to certain minimalist views of baptism, he goes too far in affirming that "baptism is the moment of faith in which the adoption is realized." As R. Fung has noted, this view leads logically to the conclusion that baptism by water is indispensable for incorporation into Christ (*The Epistle to the Galatians,* NICNT (Grand Rapids: Eerdmans, 1988) 173-74). Over against those who see the objective pole in salvation exemplified in baptism rather than in faith, Betz has aptly observed: "Faith in Christ can only be grounded in Christ himself, not in a reality outside of him. Paul does not share and would even oppose calling the ritual of baptism 'sacramentally objective' and faith in Christ 'subjective.' If one wants to employ these categories at all, Paul would call 'faith in Christ' the objective basis, because it is predicted by Scripture and because it has become a historical reality through Christ's coming (3:23,25; 4:4-5) and his self-sacrifice on the cross (1:4; 2:20; 3:13). The individual Christian existence was brought into contact with salvation by the preaching of the word and the gift of the Spirit (3:2-5; 4:6). Also these factors would be named by Paul as 'objective.' The Christian's subjectivity, in Paul's view, cannot be separated from this whole process, but is woven into it" (Betz, *Galatians,* 187-88).

which attaches great importance to this crucial event. Why be baptized? The most basic answer, of course, is that the Lord Jesus Christ ordained (hence the Baptist preference for "ordinance" as opposed to sacrament) and commanded it. Just as Jesus identified himself with our wretched sinful condition in his own baptism, thereby proclaiming in advance his death, burial, and resurrection, so too we are identified with Christ by our baptism, declaring the salvation Christ has wrought in three tenses—the drama of redemption accomplished once and for all, our own deliverance from the bondage of sin, and the consummation and final resurrection that is yet to come.

Paul described all that baptism was given to represent in one of the most striking metaphors found anywhere in the New Testament, that of "putting on" Christ. In Rom 6–8 Paul connected the concept of putting on Christ with that of "dying and rising with Christ," both of which are liturgically portrayed in the act of baptism. The language of "putting off" and "putting on" is frequently found in Paul where it often connotes the ethical transformation expected of a true believer, for example, putting off the deeds of darkness and putting on the armor of light in Rom 13:11-14. A parallel passage is Eph 6:11-14, where Christians are exhorted to put on the full armor of God in order to resist the spiritual forces of evil. However, in both Romans and Ephesians the verb for "put on" is in the imperative, whereas Gal 3:27 uses it in the indicative, "You . . . have clothed yourselves with Christ."[142] Throughout Paul's writings the imperative presupposes the indicative. We must live and walk in the Spirit, not in order to achieve a verdict of acquittal on account of our good deeds but because having trusted in Christ we have already been delivered out of darkness into his marvelous light. We have put on Christ; therefore we must put on the full armor of God.

Paul's comparison of Christian baptism to a "putting on" of Christ could have recalled several parallel practices that would have been familiar to his Gentile converts in Galatia. We have already referred to the ritual washings that were a part of the initiation ceremonies in the Hellenistic mystery religions. After being baptized in the name of the respected deity, the neophyte would then put on the distinctive garb of the god, thus identifying himself publicly with the god's persona. Thus Apuleius described his initiation into the religion of Isis: "When morning came and solemnities were finished, I came forth sanctified with twelve stoles and in a religious habit . . . in my right hand I carried a lighted torch, and a garland of flowers was upon my head, with white palm-leaves sprouting out on every side like rays."[143]

---

[142] See article on "Baptism" by G. R. Beasley-Murray in *DPL*, 60-66. See also W. Bieder, "βαπτιζω," *TDNT* 1.192-96.

[143] Apuleius, *The Golden Ass*, 11, 22-26, quoted in C. K. Barrett, *The New Testament Background: Selected Documents* (London: SCM, 1958), 99.

Equally familiar to Paul's readers would have been the custom whereby a Roman youth, nearing the end of adolescence, would remove the crimson-bordered garment of childhood and would put on the *toga virilis* to mark his entrance into full manhood. This practice would connect naturally to the image of the pedagogue Paul had just elaborated in Galatians. Just as the role of the pedagogue was completed when his charge had been invested in the garment of adulthood, so also the law no longer functions as a truant officer and agent of condemnation for those who have become the sons of God through faith in Jesus Christ. Paul further developed this theme in the following verses (4:1-7).

In the present context, however, the likening of baptism to a "putting on" of Christ most nearly approximates the ancient practice of stripping off old clothes and putting on fresh ones as a part of the baptismal rite itself. Baptism by immersion, the normal pattern in apostolic times, required of necessity a changing of garments. Moreover, from very early times many Christians practiced baptism in the nude. This practice may have been adapted from Jewish proselyte baptism which G. R. Beasley-Murray has described thus: "When women were baptized the rabbis turned their backs on them while the women entered the water to their necks, and the latter were questioned and gave answers; they had to have their hair loose, to insure that no part of their bodies was untouched by water. Cyril of Jerusalem later remarked that it was appropriate for Christians to be baptized in the nude since their Savior had been crucified in this condition."[144]

By the late second century the stripping off of one's clothes prior to baptism had been incorporated into an elaborate baptismal process that involved the following ten steps:

1. *Catechesis.*   This process included a period of intense instruction in the rudiments of the Christian faith, a time of probation sometimes lasting for several years. This practice is still maintained by many Baptist and evangelical missionaries who are reluctant to baptize converts from non-Christian religions and pagan worldviews until they have given evidence of a thorough grounding in the faith.

2. *Fasting and Prayer.*   Since baptism often was done on Easter eve, the forty days prior to this event was dedicated to rigorous spiritual exercises, especially fasting, prayer and the reading of Scripture. The liturgical season of Lent eventually developed from this period of prebaptismal preparation.

3. *Renunciation.*   When the time for baptism itself arrived, the candidate would be called upon to renounce the devil and all his pomp. Facing westward, the direction in which the sun went down, he would exclaim, "I

---

[144] G. R. Beasley-Murray, "Baptism," 62.

renounce thee, O Satan, and all thy works." Then he would spit three times in the direction of darkness, signifying a complete break with the powers of evil and their former claim on his life.

4. *Credo.*   Next, turning toward the sunrise, he would say, "And I embrace thee, O Lord Jesus Christ." At this point the one to be baptized would recite a baptismal confession of faith, sometimes presented in the form of questions and answers. "Do you believe in God the Father Almighty, maker of heaven and earth?" Answer: *"Credo,"* "I believe," and so forth. What later became known as the Apostles' Creed originally derived from this kind of baptismal inquiry.

5. *Disrobing.*   The candidate would next remove all clothing and enter naked into the baptismal waters.

6. *Immersion.*   In some churches at least the candidate would be immersed three times in the name of the Triune God. Evidently an order of godly women known as widows or deaconesses assisted the women candidates, while the men were immersed by deacons and elders assigned to this task.

7. *New Robe.*   Coming up out of the baptismal waters, the candidates would be invested in a new white robe symbolizing their "putting on" of Christ in a newness of life.

8. *Anointing.*   When all the candidates had come through the waters of baptism, each would then be anointed with oil symbolizing the presence of the Holy Spirit within them.

9. *Laying on of Hands.*   Originally this act represented a sealing and blessing given to each newly baptized Christian. It also connoted a kind of unilateral commissioning of every baptized believer to go forth from the baptismal waters as a sent-forth witness for Christ and his truth. Many early Baptists in both England and America practiced the laying on of hands for all baptized Christians as a ceremony quite distinct from ordination to the gospel ministry.

10. *The Lord's Supper.*   It was the universal practice of early Christians that only those properly baptized should partake of the Lord's Supper. Thus their "first communion" often occurred at an Easter sunrise service when the newly baptized Christians joined the other members of the congregation around the table of the Lord to celebrate the presence of the risen Christ.[145]

---

[145] The ten steps outlined here are a conflation of several baptismal traditions reflected in documents such as Tertullian's *De Baptismo,* Hippolytus's *Apostolic Tradition,* Cyril of Jerusalem's *Catechetical Lectures,* and Chrysostom's *Baptismal Homilies.* See also E. C. Whitaker, *Documents of the Baptismal Liturgy* (London: SPCK, 1960), and E. G. Hinson, *The Evangelization of the Roman Empire* (Macon: Mercer University Press, 1981), 73-95.

Certainly not all features of the patristic baptismal practice outlined here can be read back into the Pauline congregations. Yet baptism that symbolized so graphically the very "putting on" of Christ was far more than an empty ritual casually performed as a Sunday-evening afterthought. For Paul baptism was "the frontier between two worlds, between two entirely different modes of life, or, rather, between death and life."[146] During this entire period, being a Christian was very risky business. Paul himself was hounded from pillar to post, and the Galatians themselves had known their share of persecution (3:4). For Paul baptism was far more than an initiatory rite of passage; rather it involved a decisive transition from an old way of human life to a new way. It was an act of radical obedience in which a specific renunciation was made and a specific promise given. For Paul and his contemporaries, to "put on Christ" in baptism involved a willingness "not only to believe on him, but also to suffer for his sake" (Phil 1:29).

3:28 Particularly in recent years this verse has received much attention, being frequently jerked out of context and used to support all sorts of political and ideological agendas. By all accounts it is an astounding statement, and we must do nothing to dampen its radical or revolutionary implications. To grasp its true meaning, though, we must see how it fits within the flow of Paul's general argument in this passage. Thus before examining in detail the triple negation—neither Jew nor Greek, slave nor free, male nor female—let us look more closely at the statements that immediately precede and follow this startling declaration of Christian unity.

In the Greek text v. 28 follows immediately the baptismal affirmations of v. 27. Indeed, some scholars have argued that the neither-Jew/Greek, slave/free, male/female formula was itself probably derived from the baptismal liturgy of the early church. Paul used similar though not identical language in 1 Cor 12:12-13 and Col 3:11, two other texts also laden with baptismal allusions. In any event, whatever Paul wanted to say regarding the relativizing of the distinctions he listed in v. 28 is consequent to what he already had said concerning the meaning of baptism in v. 27. Paul was not making a general anthropological claim that can be extrapolated without remainder into political philosophies and social programs. Although Paul was a citizen of two worlds and consorted frequently with the high and mighty as well as the weak and lowly, he had no intention of reforming the Roman Empire. He was awaiting the Lord from heaven and regarded "this world in its present form" as "passing away" (1 Cor 7:31). This is not to say that the baptized community in which these various distinctions have ceased to play the kind of role they formerly enjoyed does not have a vital witness to bear in this

---

[146] C. Jones et al., eds., *The Study of Liturgy* (New York: Oxford University Press, 1978), 82.

"present evil age." However, Paul's primary preoccupation was the *nova creatura,* "the new creation" (6:15) that is effected by the Spirit and confessed to in baptism.

The first half of v. 28 speaks negatively of categories that have been transcended in Christ; the latter half speaks positively of a new reality that has come into being, "for you are all one in Christ Jesus." Again, baptism is the event where this divinely given unity is acknowledged, proclaimed, and celebrated. At this point we may draw on the congruence of meaning between the word *baptizō* literally "to dip" or "immerse," and a closely related word *baptō* "to dip or dye." As a part of the "putting on" metaphor, Paul may have regarded baptism as analogous to the dyeing of clothes. As J. Bligh put it, "When a person is dipped in the bath of baptism, he comes out a changed man: his former color disappears, he comes out the color of Christ. Whether the person before dipping was a Jew or a Gentile, a slave or a free man, a man or a woman, no longer matters."[147]

As we have seen already, baptism per se does not effect this transformation in some magical and mechanistic way. Rather it bears witness to a prior and deeper cleansing, a washing in the precious blood of the Lamb. Baptism is the place where what has happened individually in regeneration is validated corporately within the fellowship of the community of faith. What Paul was really saying is this: "As far as your being joined to Christ Jesus is concerned, there is no difference between how this takes place for Jews and Gentiles, for slaves and free men, for males and females; you are all just like one person in being joined closely to Christ Jesus."[148]

Herein lies the basis for true church unity as opposed to mere ecumenical togetherness. *One lord, one faith, one baptism!* This kind of unity cannot be contrived but only received as a gift from the Lord of the church, who desires for his bride to be presented unto him "without stain or wrinkle or any other blemish, but holy and blameless" (Eph 6:27). In this sense every true Christian may join in the prayer for the church found in the *Book of Common Prayer:* "Gracious Father, I humbly beseech thee for thy Holy Catholic Church; fill it with all truth, in all truth with all peace. Where it is corrupt, purge it; where it is in error, direct it; where it is superstitious, rectify it; where anything is amiss, reform it; where it is right, strengthen and confirm it; where it is in want, furnish it; where it is divided and rent asunder, make up the breaches of it; O Thou Holy One of Israel. Amen."[149]

Those who belong to the community of baptized believers, those who

---

[147] Bligh, *Galatians,* 324.

[148] Arichea and Nida, *Translators' Handbook,* 85.

[149] An adaptation of a prayer by W. Laud first published in *A Summarie of Devotion* (1677).

have been dipped and dyed in the color of Christ, have put off their former selves and now stand in a fundamentally different relationship to the world than formerly obtained. As Paul put it in 2 Cor 5:17, "The old has gone, the new has come!" And this is true not only of individual Christians but also of the church as the called-out people of God. Something radically new and different has occurred within this baptized community so that "there is neither Jew nor Greek, slave nor free, male nor female." In some sense these fundamental human distinctions have been altered or superseded by the new relationship of being "in Christ." This is beyond dispute. However, in *what* sense this is true is a matter of great dispute among interpreters of this verse.[150]

Why did Paul enumerate these precise categories of distinction? It is easy to see the relevance of the Jewish-Gentile issue to his argument in Galatians. But what of the other two? Did Paul get "so carried away with the message of faith" that he extended the formula of Christian unity to two other prominent distinctions, namely, those created by the social institution of slavery and the biological fact of gender?[151] Or did Paul include the second and third couplets merely because they were a part of a pre-Pauline Christian confession that would have been familiar to his readers although they had no relevance for his immediate argument in Galatians?[152] Both of these ideas must be rejected, for Paul was never one to waste words anymore than mince them. Let us look more closely at what these three bifurcations represent.

The three pairs of opposites Paul listed stand for the fundamental cleavages of human existence: ethnicity, economic capacity, and sexuality. Race, money, and sex are primal powers in human life. No one of them is inherently evil; rather, they are the stuff of which life itself is made. The very propagation of the human race itself is based on the distinction between male

---

[150] In addition to the standard commentaries the following specialized studies are worthy of note: P. K. Jewett, *Man as Male and Female: A Study in Sexual Relationships from a Theological Point of View* (Grand Rapids: Eerdmans, 1975); R. Jewett, "The Sexual Liberation of the Apostle Paul," *JAAR* 47 (1979): 55-87; K. R. Snodgrass, "Galatians 3:28: Conundrum or Solution?" in *Women, Authority and the Bible,* ed. A. Mickelsen (Downers Grove: InterVarsity, 1986); S. B. Clark, *Man and Woman in Christ: An Examination of the Roles of Men and Women in Light of Scripture and the Social Sciences* (Ann Arbor: Servant, 1980); B. Witherington, "Rite and Rights for Women—Galatians 3:28," *NTS* 27 (1981): 593-604; W. A. Meeks, " 'Since then you would need to go out of the world': Group Boundaries in Pauline Christianity," in *Critical History and Biblical Perspective,* T. J. Ryan, ed. (Villanova, Pa.: College Theology Society, 1979), 4-29; S. L. Johnson, "Role Distinctions in the Church: Galatians 3:28," in *Recovering Biblical Manhood and Womanhood: A Response to Evangelical Feminism,* J. Piper and W. Grudem, eds. (Wheaton: Crossway, 1991), 154-64.

[151] Arichea and Nida, *Translators Handbook,* 85.

[152] So Longenecker, *Galatians,* 157.

and female. And, while slavery is a gross perversion of God's material blessing, the ability to work hard, invest wisely, and plan carefully is essential to the well-being of any economic order. Likewise, the rich cultural and ethnic diversity of the human family has inspired some of the greatest music, some of the finest art, and some of the best literature of the ages. Yet each of these spheres of human creativity has become degraded and soiled through the perversity of sin.

Nationality and ethnicity have been corrupted by pride, material blessings by greed, and sexuality by lust. This has led to the chaotic pattern of exploitation and self-destruction that marks the human story from the Tower of Babel to the streets of Sarajevo and Soweto. Indeed, outside of Christ the primal forces represented by these three polarities are controlled and manipulated by the elemental spirits of the universe (*stoicheia tou kosmou*; Gal 4:3,9). However, all of those who have become children of God through faith in Jesus Christ have been liberated from enslavement to these evil powers. A new standard and pattern of life now distinguishes the baptized community that is still in the world but not of it. Here, as nowhere else, we are empowered by the Holy Spirit to "bear one another burdens and so fulfill the law of Christ" (Gal 6:2). The boundaries of baptism define "the existence of a place in the world where things are different: Jews and Gentiles share the same table; slaves and free citizens are treated equally as brothers and sisters; women are accorded a respect that is more substantial than a merely outward and sometimes two-edged 'equality.' "[153]

Paul's triad of Christian equality stands in marked, and probably deliberate, contrast to commonly accepted patterns of privileged status and self-assertive prejudice in the ancient world. For example, Hellenistic men regularly thanked the gods for allowing them to be born as human beings and not beasts, Greeks and not barbarians, citizens and not slaves, men and not women. By the middle of the second century A.D., Rabbi Judah ben Elai had incorporated a similar pattern of "benedictions" that in slightly revised form can still be found in the Jewish cycle of morning prayers:

Blessed art thou, O Lord our God, King of the universe, who hast not made me a foreigner.

Blessed art thou, O Lord our God, King of the universe, who hast not made me a slave.

Blessed art thou, O Lord our God, King of the universe, who hast not made me a woman.

Should Jewish women desired to address the Lord, they were encouraged to pray, "Blessed art thou, O Lord our God, King of the universe, who hast

---

[153] Ebeling, *Truth,* 215.

made me according to thy will."[154] Given the pervasive significance of such ethnic, social, and sexual barriers within both Jewish and Hellenistic culture, it is all the more remarkable to read Paul's sweeping declaration of ecclesial unity and spiritual equality that cuts across the hostile divide of such fundamental human differences.

EXCURSUS 3: WAS PAUL A FEMINIST?   In recent years Gal 3:28 has become a lonely text, a battleground for competing views of feminism, social egalitarianism, and women in ministry. Frequently the Paul of Galatians is pitted against the Paul of 1 Corinthians and the Pastorals (where the Pastorals are still regarded as Pauline or even canonical in any meaningful sense) as though Paul had given in one epistle what he took away in several others.

Was Paul a liberationist or a chauvinist? Can Gal 3:28 be treated legitimately as the *locus classicus* of feminist hermeneutics? To answer these questions in detail would require a complete volume at least, but to ignore them entirely would be irresponsible in a commentary that aims to relate the Word of God to the pressing issues of ministry and church life today. Thus in this brief excursus we may register concerns that in turn will point to further investigations and open up new vistas for approaching this controverted theme.

The rise of the modern women's movement has had a profound impact on the Christian community. The majority of the world's Christians (e.g., Orthodox, Roman Catholics, and many Protestant evangelicals, including Missouri Synod Lutherans, conservative Presbyterians, and Southern Baptists) still do not usually admit women to church leadership roles traditionally assigned to men. But this issue has become a matter of heated debate within many of the these traditions, resulting in a veritable "battle of the Bible" with text being hurled against text and history and tradition pitted against politics and ideology. A new and distinctive way of reading the Bible through the lenses of contemporary women's concerns—feminist hermeneutics—has led some to reject the authority and truthfulness of Scripture altogether. Others, reluctant to sever all ties with historic Christian institutions, have offered new interpretations of the Bible to allow for great participation of women in ministry.

The rise of contemporary feminist hermeneutics can be traced back to *The Woman's Bible,* a revisionist rendering of the Scriptures edited by Elizabeth Cady Staton and published in the 1890s.[155] The purpose of this project was

---

[154] *The Authorized Daily Prayer Book of the United Hebrew Congregations of the British Commonwealth of Nations,* tr. S. Singer (London: Eyre & Spottiswoode, 1962), 6-7. See Longenecker, *Galatians,* 157, and Bligh, *Galatians,* 322-23.

[155] E. C. Staton, ed., *The Original Feminist Attack on the Bible: The Woman's Bible,* Facsimile ed. (New York: Arno, 1974). For further discussion see J. Smylie, "The Woman's Bible and the Spiritual Crisis," *Soundings* 59 (1976): 305-28, and E. S. Fiorenza, *In Memory of Her: A Feminist Theological Construction of Christian Origins* (New York: Crossroad, 1989), 7-36.

to present the Bible as a weapon in the struggle for women's liberation. In order to accomplish this goal it was necessary to "deconstruct" the texts of Scripture that were seen as products of an ancient patriarchal culture and androcentric religion inimical to the higher aspirations of women. Thus, Elizabeth Staton boasted, *The Woman's Bible* would reveal to the modern woman that "the good Lord did not write the book; that the garden scene is a fable; that she is in no ways responsible for the laws of the Universe. . . . Take the snake, the fruit tree and the woman from the tableau, and we have no fall, no frowning Judge, no Inferno, no everlasting punishment—hence no need of a Savior. Thus the bottom falls out of the whole Christian theology."[156] One hundred years after the publication of *The Woman's Bible,* the "depatriarchializing" of Scripture has led to the Christless Christianity and postbiblical feminism that flourishes in many mainline Protestant denominations today. A typical expression of this kind of woman's spirituality is found in an essay by C. P. Christ:

> The simplest meaning of the symbol of goddess is the acknowledgment of the legitimacy of female power as a beneficent and independent power. A woman who echoes Ntosake Shange's dramatic statement, "I found God in myself and I loved her fiercely" is saying, "Female power is strong and creative." She is saying that the divine principle, the saving and sustaining power, is in herself, that she will no longer look to men or male figures as saviors.[157]

The radical feminism of goddess worship and Scripture bashing has moved well beyond the pale of anything recognizably Christian. Other feminists, however, have been reluctant to follow this trajectory to its logical conclusion. Instead, they have sought to "rescue" the Bible from its feminist critics, arguing that there is a "canon within the canon," an Archimedean point that allows one to distinguish the patriarchal, that is, sexist, form of the biblical text from it egalitarian content. According to this perspective, Gal 3:28 may be trumpeted as an egalitarian manifesto, the highest peak in the mountain range of revelation, while the less appealing subordinationist passages in Colossians, Ephesians, 1 Peter, 1 Corinthians, and the Pastorals can be treated as historically relative, situation-variable texts with no binding authority on Christian believers today. On this reading, Gal 3:28 is Scripture; the other passages are merely script. This "neo-Orthodox" model of feminist interpretation encourages the relativizing of biblical authority in other ways

---

[156] A. S. Kraditor, ed., *Up from the Pedestal: Landmark Writings in the American Women's Struggle for Equality* (Chicago: Quadrangle, 1968), 119.
[157] C. P. Christ, "Why Women Need the Goddess: Phenomenological, Psychological, and Political Reflections," in C. P. Christ and J. Plaskow, *Womanspirit Rising: A Feminist Reader in Religion* (San Francisco: Harper & Row, 1979), 277.

as well, including insistence upon gender-inclusive language for God, the legitimization of homosexual practice, and the gutting of traditional worship and prayer traditions of the church in favor of feminist-friendly formulas.[158]

In his recent study on controversies that come between Christians, R. H. Nash correctly separates his discussion of radical feminism from his analysis of the intraevangelical debate over women leaders in the church.[159] For evangelicals committed to the authority of Scripture the question of whether women should serve as pastors and/or deacons cannot be decided on "Well, isn't everyone else doing it?" but rather by "What does the Bible say about it?" Evangelicals, including advocates of biblical inerrancy, are divided on the latter question, and two groups have been formed in recent years to promote opposing positions—the Christians for Biblical Equality and the Council on Biblical Manhood and Womanhood. A welter of literature has been produced on both sides as the issue has become more and more divisive within many churches and denominations.

It is not fair for those who hold to traditional views on this subject to equate biblical egalitarians (a better term than "evangelical feminists") with goddess worshipers and advocates of homosexual ministers. At the same time, biblical egalitarians who are committed to a high view of Scripture must guard against being seduced by the subbiblical and antibiblical perspectives of contemporary feminism. Heretofore, most of the rhetoric from the egalitarian side has been directed almost exclusively against the traditionalist position on the role of women in ministry. As a cursory glance at contemporary feminist theologies will show, the issues raised by this heretical ideology go far beyond the debate over women leaders in the church. Those who are committed to the authority of Scripture should speak out strongly against feminist extremism that calls into question the normative character of biblical revelation, the historical particularity of the Christian faith, and indeed the very nature of God.[160]

---

[158] See the discussion in Fiorenza, *In Memory of Her,* 14–21. In this analysis of the feminist landscape Protestant L. Russell and Roman Catholic R. R. Ruether are both classified as "neo-Orthodox feminists."

[159] R. H. Nash, *Great Divides: Understanding the Controversies That Come between Christians* (Colorado Springs: Navpress, 1993), 39–76.

[160] On how this issue plays out in the Southern Baptist Convention, see T. George, "Conflict and Identity in the Southern Baptist Convention: The Quest for a New Consensus," in R. B. James and D. S. Dockery, eds., *Beyond the Impasse?: Scripture, Interpretation, and Theology in Baptist Life* (Nashville: Broadman, 1992), 195–214. The naiveté of biblical egalitarians concerning the dangerous doctrinal deviations of radical feminism is evident, for example, in the following two studies, both of which were written by women of faith thoroughly committed to evangelical principles: M. S. Van Leeuwen, *Gender and Grace* (Downers Grove: InterVarsity, 1990), and R. A. Tucker, *Women in the Maze: Questions and Answers on Biblical Equality* (Downers Grove: InterVarsity, 1992). More balanced is the treatment of feminist hermeneutics in the recent survey by W. W. Klein, C. L. Blomberg, and R. L. Hubbard, Jr., *Introduction to Biblical Interpretation* (Dallas: Word, 1993), 453–57.

How does Gal 3:28 fit into this discussion? The violence with which this verse has been taken out of context and misrepresented as a manifesto for contemporary social egalitarianism is seen in a new translation of the Bible that renders Paul's words thus: "There is no distinction between heterosexual and homosexual, cleric and lay, white and multicultural."[161] According to this invidious translation, what Paul elsewhere recognized and condemned as heinous and sinful he here embraced as acceptable and blessed!

Leaving aside this kind of obvious distortion, does Gal 3:28 really teach that being "in Christ" eliminates the three distinctions mentioned in this text? It is clear from the larger corpus of Paul's writings that it does not. Paul himself did not cease to be a Jew once he became a Christian. When the missionary situation called for it, he was quite willing to conform to certain Jewish rituals for the sake of a wider evangelistic witness (cf. 1 Cor 9:19–23; Acts 21:26), although he never renounced his Christian freedom in doing so. Neither did Paul anywhere argue outright for the abolition of slavery. Rather he instructed Christian masters and Christian slaves to relate to one another in a way that is informed by their mutual faith and service to Christ (cf. Col 3:22–4:1). For example, he admonished the slave Onesimus to return to his master Philemon, while the latter is charged to receive his runaway servant as a brother, in fact as he would receive Paul himself (Phlm 16). True enough, Paul's instructions to Philemon certainly carried within them the seeds of the dissolution of the very institution of slavery. Nowhere did Paul treat slavery as a divinely ordained institution, and, at least on one occasion, he declared that a slave could properly become free (1 Cor 7:21). We know of certain slaves in the second century whose freedom was purchased by the churches to which they belonged. All this notwithstanding, it remains true that Paul waged no campaign to eradicate slavery from the Roman Empire. Rather he simply gave instructions on how to carry out assigned work duties with appropriate Christian attitudes in the then-existing institution of slavery.[162]

What about the third distinction, that between males and females? It is frequently argued that just as slavery has now been abolished in light of

---

[161] Sister Fran Feder, "Future of the American Church Conference," *First Things* 40 (1994): 58.
[162] G. W. Knight III, "Husbands and Wives as Analogues of Christ and the Church," in *Recovering,* 165–78; J. Murray, *Principles of Conduct* (Grand Rapids: Eerdmans, 1957), 259–62.

a fuller understanding of Christian love and brotherhood, so also all gender-related differentiation should now be eliminated in the roles men and women play both in family and church life. It is important to note, however, that the first two couplets of Gal 3:28 are quite distinct from the last one. This is evident even from the grammatical structure of the sentence that literally reads "neither Jew nor Greek, neither slave nor free, neither male *and* female."

This slight variation in construction doubtless reflects the reading of Gen 1:27, "He made them male and female," recalling the original creative act by which God made sexuality constitutive for the human condition.[163] The difference, then, between male and female, unlike that between master and slave, and distinct as well from that of Jew and Gentile, is grounded in the ordinance of creation and is essential for the perpetuation of the human family. Moreover, this distinction was introduced by God prior to the fall, that is, prior to the entrance of sin and the curse that has since fallen upon every son and daughter of Adam and Eve, Jesus alone excepted.

There is at least one hint in the New Testament that the distinction of gender is intended for this temporal life only and will not be reconstituted at the resurrection (Matt 22:30). However, to disregard the conditions of this present life by seeking to grasp the status of the resurrection here and now is to deny the not-yet dimension of the Christian life. This was precisely the problem Paul faced at Corinth and perhaps to some extent in Galatia. If Paul advised slaves to retain the place in life assigned to them by the Lord (1 Cor 7:17) and condemned those Jewish males who tried to remove the sign of circumcision from their bodies through surgery on their genitals, then *a fortiori* he had no sympathy for either men or women who sought to pervert their natural, God-given sexuality into a pattern of behavior or lifestyle at variance with that which God originally created and declared good.

Modern feminist theologians are not the first to interpret the "neither male nor female" formula of Gal 3:28 as a call for eliminating gender distinctions and the unique aspects of masculine and feminine personhood derived from them. In the second century this theme was picked up in a number of Gnostic documents and became a major feature in the teaching of this heretical movement. For example, the *Gospel of Thomas,* a Gnostic collection of Jesus-sayings discovered in Egypt in 1945, relates the following apocryphal dialogue between Jesus and his disciples:

---

[163] Longenecker correctly notes this change in construction but then declares, "It implies no real change in meaning" (*Galatians,* 157). For the contrary view, see S. B. Clark, *Man and Woman in Christ: An Examination of the Roles of Men and Women in Light of Scripture and the Social Sciences* (Ann Arbor: Servant, 1980), 155-72.

Jesus saw infants being suckled. He said to his disciples, "These infants being suckled are like those who enter the Kingdom." They said to him, "Shall we then, as children, enter the Kingdom?" Jesus said to them, "When you make the two one, and when you make the inside like the outside and the outside like the inside, and the above like the below, and when you make the male and the female one in the same, so that the male not be male nor the female female . . . then you will enter [the Kingdom]."[164]

In this saying the elimination of sexuality is a prerequisite for salvation. What circumcision was for the Judaizers of Galatia, gender reversal became for the Gnostic heretics of a later age. For the Gnostics, creation and the material world were inherently evil. Since sexuality was an obvious carrier of this fallenness, it had to be reversed or neutralized in order to achieve release from the constricting "prison house of matter." Over against this deviant disparagement of matter, orthodox Christians confessed, "I believe in God the Father Almighty, maker of heaven and earth." It is not surprising that contemporary radical feminists have reached back to the early Gnostics as a source for their own revisionist formulations of the Christian faith.[165]

Only by wrenching Gal 3:28 from its context and importing into it an ideology derived from somewhere else can this verse be turned into a manifesto for liberation theology. Moreover, the propriety of women leaders in the church must be decided through careful exegesis of those passages that touch on that issue. Galatians 3:28 cannot legitimately be used either as evidence or counterevidence in this debate. It is regrettable that recent discussions of this theme have obscured the amazing good news Paul set forth in this verse. There is a unity in the body of Christ and an equality of access to salvation through faith in Jesus. Paul's Galatian opponents had been saying that in order for Gentiles to become Christians they first had to become Jews, that circumcision was essential to salvation. Paul had shown that in the aeon, "the now age," inaugurated through the death and resurrection of Christ, a new reality had come to light. Although circumcision never saved anyone in the first place, as Paul demonstrated in the case of Abraham, there was a time when we were placed "under" the harsh tutelage of the law, subjected to the

---

[164] *The Nag Hammadi Library,* ed. J. M. Robinson (New York: Harper & Row, 1977), 121. On the provenance of *The Gospel of Thomas* see Hennecke-Schneemelcher, *New Testament Apocrypha,* 1:278-307.

[165] See, for example, how E. S. Fiorenza uses the *Gospel of Thomas* saying quoted above in her argument that "sexual dimorphism and strictly defined gender roles are products of the patriarchal culture, which maintain and legitimize structures of control and domination--the exploitation of women by men" (*In Memory of Her,* 212-13). See also W. A. Meeks, "The Image of the Androgyne: Some Uses of a Symbol in Earliest Christianity," *History of Religion* 13 (1974): 165-208.

demonic forces that hold sway in this present evil world. But, since Jesus Christ has shattered the bonds of death, hell, and the grave, this is no longer true. *Jesus is Victor*! He has perfectly fulfilled the law of God and emerged triumphant over all the hosts of hell. We witness to this triumphant victory in the death-burial-resurrection of baptism. Thus in respect to our standing before God, Jewish blood, free birth, and male sex count for nothing. The call of the gospel is radically egalitarian and completely universal: "Come, all you who are thirsty, come to the waters" (Isa 55:1); "Whoever wishes, let him take the free gift of the water of life" (Rev 22:17).

All those who have heard and received this good news are now called to a new pattern of life within the baptized community. The old distinctions have not been eradicated anymore than the soul of a new believer has been ripped out of his body. We still live in the tension between the "No Longer" and the "Not Yet." We still affirm the goodness of God's created order even while we recognize that it has been horribly marred by sin. But in Jesus Christ we have been called out of darkness into his marvelous light. This means that Christians have been liberated from the demonic forces of racism, materialism, and sexism. This has happened not through assimilation to the politically correct agenda of the world around us but rather through the inner transformation and liberation brought about through the sending of God's Holy Spirit into our hearts (4:6).

3:29 This verse serves both as a conclusion to the argument that began in 3:6 and as an introduction to a new train of thought to be developed in the following verses. Again the key phrase is "if you belong to Christ," a genitive construction in the Greek (lit., "if you are of Christ") but identical in meaning to the "in Christ Jesus" formula of the preceding verse. Paul was not teaching here the liberal Protestant doctrine of the fatherhood of God and the brotherhood of man. He did not say that all persons are by nature the children of God. He pointed instead to a decisive difference within the human family, the distinction between those who know God as Father through faith in Jesus Christ and others who remain under the curse of the law and in bondage to the demonic forces that prevail in the world at large. However, to be "in Christ" means that we are the "seed of Abraham." This is true regardless of whether we are male or female, slave or free, Jew or Gentile.

Earlier in this chapter Paul had shown how Jesus Christ alone is the true seed (singular) of Abraham (3:16). Through our union with Christ we have now inherited this privileged status. This has happened not through procreation but through regeneration, not by our goodness but by God's grace, not by works of the law but through faith alone. Paul would now show what it means for those who have been liberated from the curse of the law and the bondage of sin to enter into their new estate as "heirs according to the promise" (3:29).

(2) The Radical Change: From Slavery to Sonship (4:1-7)

¹What I am saying is that as long as the heir is a child, he is no different from a slave, although he owns the whole estate. ²He is subject to guardians and trustees until the time set by his father. ³So also, when we were children, we were in slavery under the basic principles of the world. ⁴But when the time had fully come, God sent his Son, born of a woman, born under law, ⁵to redeem those under law, that we might receive the full rights of sons. ⁶Because you are sons, God sent the Spirit of his Son into our hearts, the Spirit who calls out, "*Abba*, Father." ⁷So you are no longer a slave, but a son; and since you are a son, God has made you also an heir.

OUR PAST CONDITION (4:1-3). **4:1-2** In these verses Paul made explicit his shift of emphasis from the inheritance to the heir. Heretofore he had compared the law to a prison warden and a pedagogue. He now compared it to "guardians and trustees" whose role was to supervise and hold in check until the age of his legal minority was ended. As we have seen before, Paul was addressing both Jews and Gentiles throughout this section. However, just as in chap. 3 the situation of Jewish Christianity with its preoccupation with the law of Moses was foremost in Paul's mind, so here Paul reiterated and elaborated his former argument from the standpoint of Gentile Christians, many of whom had recently been converted from religious syncretism and pagan idolatry.[166]

Paul based his analogy on the legal practice of guardianship. As Longenecker describes it, "the picture he draws is of a boy in a home of wealth and standing who is legally the heir and so the 'young master' (*kurios*, literally 'lord' or 'owner') of the family estate, but who is still a minor (*nēpios*) and so lives under rules very much like a slave (*doulos*)."[167] It is difficult to reconstruct the precise legal background of the scenario Paul had in mind. Some have argued that he was thinking of an orphaned heir whose father had

---

[166] Paul opened this unit with a connecting expression, Λέγω δέ, "what I am saying" (NIV), "this is what I mean" (NEB). These verses are intended to clarify and extend the argument Paul had hitherto developed. They do not suggest that Paul was "not completely satisfied with his argument thus far" (Matera, *Galatians,* 154). On the contrary, he was now applying to the Gentile Christians of Galatia the same redemptive reality he had outlined in terms of Jewish history and OT precedence. Yet what he had to say applies to all Christians, regardless of their Gentile or Jewish background. This view is supported by Lightfoot, Burton, Betz, Schlier, among others. The contrary position has been argued vigorously by Bligh, *Galatians,* 330-33. He interprets the entire passage as a part of the discourse Paul addressed to the Jewish Christians at Antioch.

[167] Longenecker, *Galatians,* 162.

died, leaving his son under the care of a *tutor* until he came of age at fourteen, from which time he would be supervised by a *curator,* who would oversee his affairs until he reached the age of legal majority at twenty-five.

However, there are two arguments against locating Paul's analogy in this kind of legal context. First, there is no indication in Paul's example that the father is deceased. It stretches the bounds of credulity to imagine that Paul could have constructed an analogy where the father, representing God, was dead—the rantings of modern "death-of-God" theologians to the contrary notwithstanding. Just as important, in Paul's example the date for the heirs' entrance into his inheritance depends solely on the predetermined decision of the Father, not on a chronological age fixed by statute. The "young master" of the estate is subject to guardians and trustees "until the time set by his father." Paul was making a crucial theological point with these words. God is the primary actor in the drama of salvation. He alone determined the appropriate time for the sending of Christ (4:4). Similarly, he had foreordained the sending of the Holy Spirit into our hearts (4:6). In describing the movement of the Gentiles from slavery into freedom, from servanthood into sonship, Paul said that it is not only a matter of their coming to know God, the truth of salvation, but also their being known by God, the sovereign purpose of salvation in the grace of election (4:9).[168]

While the legal background of these opening verses may be difficult to reconstruct, Paul's general meaning is clear enough. Before a minor comes of age, he has no legal rights at all. He is a *nēpios,* literally an "infant," a word Paul used elsewhere (1 Cor 3:1) to describe spiritual immaturity but which here refers to the status of legal incompetence and dispossession. To be in this condition is no different from being a slave, Paul declared. The "guardians and trustees" who supervise the estate of the child during the time of his minority are comparable to the *paidagōgos* of 3:24, although their function is different in the life of their client. The *paidagōgos* was a harsh disciplinarian charged with supervising daily activities; the administrators and managers referred to here control the property and finances of the minor depriving him of all independent action so that in reality his liberty is

---

[168] Burton, *Galatians,* 213, has suggested that Paul may have had in mind the kind of situation described in 1 Macc 3:32-33; 6:17 and 2 Macc 10-14 where the Syrian king Antiochus IV (Epiphanes) appointed Lysias as the guardian of his son Antiochus V (Eupator) when he himself was away from the Seleucid kingdom. Should Antiochus IV have died in battle, Lysias was to become the protector and actual governor of the realm during the minority of Antiochus V, much as the Duke of Somerset did for Edward VI who in 1546 became the king of England at age nine, succeeding his father Henry VIII. On the legal background of Gal 4:1-2, see J. D. Hester, *Paul's Concept of Inheritance: A Contribution to the Understanding of Heilsgeschichte* (Edinburgh: Oliver and Boyd, 1968).

reduced to that of a slave. In itself this image is benign enough. Guardians can be wise and trustworthy stewards fulfilling a necessary role on behalf of someone else. However, a more sinister shadow falls across the page in the next verse, where Paul identified these custodians with the elemental spirits that hold sway in this present evil world.

4:3 This verse opens with the adverbial expression (literally) "likewise even we," or "so also in our case" (*houtōs kai hēmeis*), indicating that Paul was now ready to apply to the Galatian Christians the legal illustration of the minor deprived of his inheritance until the time appointed by his father. This application links Paul's earlier discussion of the Jewish tutelage under the law in 3:23-25 with the pre-Christian experience of the Galatian believers who were just as enslaved in their pagan idolatry as the Jews had been in their servitude to the law. The radical character of this bondage, which is the common lot of all the unsaved, Paul now expressed in terms of a universal subjection to a sinister coalition of evil powers he called *ta stoicheia tou kosmou.*

This expression, *ta stoicheia tou kosmou,* is found four times in Paul's writings, twice in this chapter (4:3,9), and twice in Col 2 (vv. 8,20). The ambiguity inherent in this term is seen in the various translations that have been suggested for it: "the elemental spirits of the universe" (RSV); "the elemental things of the world" (NASB); "the authority of basic moral principles" (Phillips); "the basic principles of the world" (NIV). Three central lines of interpretation have emerged concerning the meaning of this technical term in Paul's writings.[169]

1. *The Elements as Basic Principles.* Etymologically *ta stoicheia* (from the root word *stoichos,* a military term meaning "row," "rank") refers to things that belong together in a series, essential ingredients, basic components such as soldiers in a platoon, degrees on a sundial, or letters of the alphabet. It has been suggested that Paul was here referring to a basic set of philosophical or religious principles, the ABCs of faith one learns in an "elementary" school. Those scholars who advocate this interpretation (Lightfoot, Burton, Bandstra) point to the surrounding context in which Paul compared the believer to a young child subjected to the tutelage of a *paidagōgos* and an immature minor who has yet to come of age. On this view the

[169] In addition to the standard commentaries on Galatians and Colossians, the following studies are worthy of note: G. Delling, "στοιχεῖον," *TDNT* 7.670-83; D. G. Reid, "Elements/ Elemental Spirits of the World," *DPL,* 229-33; A. J. Bandstra, *The Law and the Elements of the World* (Kampen: Kok, 1964); B. Reicke, "The Law and the World according to Paul: Some Thoughts Concerning Gal 4:1-11," *JBL* 70 (1951): 259-76; E. Schweizer, "Slaves of the Elements and Worshippers of Angels: Gal 4:3,9 and Col 2:8,18,20," *JBL* 107 (1988): 455-68; C. E. Arnold, *Powers of Darkness: Principalities and Powers in Paul's Letters* (Downers Grove: InterVarsity, 1992).

law was a necessary form of rudimentary instruction, a kind of education in first principles, which has now been superseded by the fuller revelation given through the coming of Christ. For the Galatian Christians to revert to the ceremonies of Judaism would be like a university graduate student taking up kindergarten lessons all over again. After being liberated from the bondage of their former idolatry, they were once more subjecting themselves as slaves of another ceremonial law, one equally harsh and debilitating.

It is true that *ta stoicheia* can refer to the fundamental principles or rudimentary teachings of a given discipline or system of thought. For example, it is used precisely in this way in Heb 5:12, where wavering believers are described as slow learners needing "someone to teach you the elementary truths of God's Word all over again. You need milk, not solid food!" Drawing on this motif W. Ramsay connected Paul's statement about reversion to the rudiments of the world to his earlier depiction of the Galatians as "foolish," "senseless" (3:1). "Hence the address 'senseless Galatians,' already anticipates the longer expostulation (4:3-11), 'Galatians who are sinking from the educated standard to the ignorance and superstition of the native religion.'"[170]

This line of interpretation, however, presents several problems. In the first place, as we have seen already, the folly of the Galatians did not consist in their lack of intellectual prowess or academic acumen but rather in their spiritual blindness. Someone had bewitched them. Second, contrary to many interpreters, Paul nowhere presented the law as an earlier, undeveloped phase of a progressively unfolding revelation. In the context of his understanding of redemptive history, Paul portrayed the law both much more positively and much more negatively than that. As a God-given ordinance and reflection of the divine will, the law is holy, perfect, and spiritual (Rom 7:7,25). However, the primary function of the law (Luther's theological or spiritual use) was never to impart eternal life, nor even to provide a rudimentary revelation for those under its charge. The law was intended (by God) to restrain, condemn, and kill. By bearing the curse of the law in his own body on the cross, Jesus Christ has once and for all liberated true believers from the domineering bondage of the law. For the Galatian Christians now to revert back to the works of the law as a basis for salvation would be more than a retrogression from higher form of knowledge to rudimentary learning, from Ph.D.s to ABCs; no, such a reversion would be nothing less than backsliding into a cosmic captivity to the demon-lords and sham gods of their pagan past.

2. *The Elements as Material Components of the Universe.* Another

---

[170] Ramsay, *Galatians,* 396.

important understanding of *ta stoicheia tou kosmou* identifies them with the four elemental substances many ancients believed were the material components of the physical world, namely, earth, water, air, and fire. As E. Schweizer has pointed out, for more than a thousand years the Greek understanding of the cosmos was dominated by the idea of a "mighty strife" among these four elements.[171] Thus the Roman poet Ovid, writing around the time of Jesus' birth, described the chaotic conditions produced by the cosmic conflict among these four basic building blocks of the universe: "The air hung over all, which is as much heavier than fire as the weight of water is lighter than the weight of earth. There did the creator permit the mists and clouds to take their place, but they can scarce be prevented from tearing the world to pieces. So fiercely do these brothers strive together."[172]

This incessant warring among the elements, it was believed, would eventually lead to the destruction of the world in either a great deluge or a fiery conflagration. Turning to the New Testament, we find a similar description of "the day of the Lord" at the end of time in which "the heavens will disappear with a roar; the elements [*stoicheia*] will be destroyed by fire, and the earth and everything in it will be laid bare" (2 Pet 3:10).

In some circles the four elements were given proper names and regarded as personified deities: Hephaestus (earth), Hera (air), Poseidon (water), and Demeter (fire). It was widely believed that conflict among these elements produced the savage storms and violent contortions of nature—we still speak of being "buffeted by the elements"—as well as wars, tumults, and social upheaval among the peoples of the earth. In an effort to harmonize Jewish beliefs with popular Hellenistic philosophies, Philo surmised that the entrance of the Jewish high priest into the temple at Jerusalem during the Festival of the New Year had the effect of pacifying the warring elements and producing a temporary peace throughout the world.[173] In Col 2, however, Paul declared that what Philo believed the Jewish high priest to effect every year in this annual ritual, Jesus Christ has performed once and for all through his death on the cross. "And having disarmed the powers and authorities, he made a public spectacle of them, triumphing over them by the cross. . . . Since you died with Christ to the basic principles of this world, why, as though you still belong to it, do you submit to its rules?" (Col 2:15,20).

---

[171] Schweizer, "Slaves of the Elements," 456.

[172] Ibid., 458-59.

[173] "When the high priest enters to offer the ancestral prayers and sacrifices there may enter with him the whole universe, the long robe a copy of the heir, the pomegranate of water, the flower trimming of earth, the scarlet of fire . . . the twelve stones on the breast in four rows (στοιχεῖα) of threes of the zodiac, the reason-seat of the Reason (λόγος) which holds together and administers all things" (Philo, *Vita Moses* 2.125, 133).

Christ alone is the one through whom believers can escape the dominion of the elements of the world and thus find true deliverance and freedom from their enslaving power. The Galatian references to *ta stoicheia tou kosmou* are briefer and more cryptic than those in Colossians. But there is good reason to believe that the same demonic forces and fatalistic powers Paul condemned at Colosse were also endemic in the pagan religious culture of Galatia.

3. *The Elements as Spiritual Powers.* A third way of understanding "the elemental spirits of the universe" draws on the interpretation just presented but does not confine the reality of these spiritual powers to the four basic elements. Rather, a whole host of spiritual beings headed by Satan himself, whom Paul elsewhere called "the god of this age" (2 Cor 4:4), were regarded as exercising a temporal dominion in "this present evil age." This host of demonic beings is referred to variously in the New Testament as "principalities," "powers," "the enemies of God," and "the rulers of this age" (Rom 8:38; 1 Cor 2:6,8; 15:24,26). In the literature of Second Temple Judaism, these evil spiritual powers are also equated with the fallen angels who rebelled along with Satan and thus were expelled from heaven before the creation of the world. They are locked in a fierce cosmic conflict with the people of God in every age. Their goal is to separate believers from the love of Christ. To this end they will use trouble, hardship, persecution, famine, nakedness, danger, sword, destruction, hatred, and death.

We will encounter this theme again in v. 9, where Paul related these demonic slave holders to the idolatrous worship patterns of the Galatians prior to their receiving Christ. For the present it is important to note how the "elemental spirits of the universe" fit into Paul's overall understanding of God and the world. The following three points will be helpful in placing this teaching within the larger context.

First, we should not imagine that Paul had fallen prey to the kind of radical metaphysical dualism that earlier characterized the Persian religion of Zoroaster and found a later reincarnation in Manichaeism. The spiritual powers also belong to God's creation (Rom 8:39). There is no independent realm of devilish darkness existing apart from God's creative act and permissive will. Thus in the New Testament, as in the Old, God can make use of Satan in order to accomplish a greater good (2 Cor 12:7). As in the end time Satan will again be "loosed a little season" (Rev 20:3), so too in this present age his destructive capacity is limited by God's foreordained purpose: "The prince of darkness grim, we tremble not for him; his rage we can endure, for lo! his doom is sure, one little word shall fell him."[174]

---

[174] Martin Luther, "A Mighty Fortress Is Our God," *A New Hymnal for Colleges and Schools,* ed. J. Rowthorn and R. Schulz-Widmar (New Haven: Yale University Press, 1992), 460-61.

Second, the "elemental spirits" march under the orders of a personal devil and are themselves actual spiritual beings totally devoted to the victimizing energies of darkness and death. However, we should not imagine that these malevolent creatures always assume the forms attributed to them in medieval art or modern *Aliens* movies. The essence of the demonic is to twist, contort, and impersonate. Paul knew that Satan himself could masquerade as an angel of light (2 Cor 11:14). The early Christians saw demonic forces behind the astral deities represented by the zodiac, the pagan gods of Greece and Rome, as well as the national and tribal deities who were believed to superintend the political destiny of every distinctive ethnic group in the world. As we have seen, the three polarities of Gal 3:28 represent dimensions of human life—ethnicity, sexuality, and material blessing—that, though good in themselves, have been turned by demonic onslaught into arenas for violence, exploitation, and death. The shape of the demonic may change from age to age, but believers today, no less than in New Testament times, are called to spiritual warfare against "the unseen power that controls this dark world, and spiritual agents from the very headquarters of evil" (Eph 6:12, Phillips).[175]

Finally, while Jesus Christ has dethroned the powers of darkness through his triumphant death and resurrection so that true believers are no longer subjected to their tyrannical domination, Christians are nonetheless engaged in a continual, lifelong struggle against the evil designs of these elemental spirits. This is true because the Christian life even after conversion continues to be lived out on the conflicted plane of history. Thus the "powers" come upon the Christian "in the vicissitudes of his particular lot, that is, in his 'tribulation' and 'distresses,' etc. (Rom 8:35; cf. 1 Thess 2:18: 'Satan hindered us'). . . . They also come upon him in his temptations; Satan is the 'tempter' (1 Thess 3:5) against whom one must be on guard (1 Cor 7:5; 2 Cor 2:11)."[176] Galatians actually is a book about spiritual warfare. What Jesus said to Peter, Paul could have declared to the Galatians: "Satan has asked to sift you as wheat" (Luke 22:31). Paul, however, like a mother fighting for her threatened child (cf. 4:19), had entered the lists, attired in the full armor of God, to do battle against the powers of darkness on behalf of his spiritual progeny.

THE COMING OF CHRIST (4:4-5).   **4:4**   Verses 4-5 contain one of the

---

[175] For an insightful interpretation of the demonic in contemporary life, see A. C. McGill, *Suffering: A Test of Theological Method* (Philadelphia: Geneva, 1963). On Luther's development of this theme, see H. A. Oberman, *Luther: Man between God and the Devil* (New Haven: Yale University Press, 1989).

[176] R. Bultmann, *Theology of the New Testament* 1:258.

most compressed and highly charged passages in the entire letter because they present the objective basis, the Christological and soteriological foundation, for the doctrine of justification by faith. Many scholars believe that here, just as with the baptismal formula in 3:26-28, Paul reproduced, perhaps with some modifications, an early confession of faith drawn from the worship and proclamation of the first Christian churches.[177] The early incorporation of these verses into the traditional liturgy of Christmas also points to their appeal as a basic kerygmatic text.

When we analyze these verses in terms of their structure, we find four central ideas brought together within a single literary unit. To begin with, there is a temporal introduction, "but when the time had fully come," an expression that connects this passage to the illustration of the minor heir entering into his full inheritance at the father's preappointed time. Next there is the announcement of God's supernatural intervention in the mission of Jesus Christ, "God sent his Son." This sending formula is followed immediately by two parallel participial constructions describing the condition and status of the incarnate Son: He was "born of woman" and "born under the law." Finally, in v. 5, two purpose/result clauses, both introduced by *hina* ("in order that"), describe the reason for the coming of Christ and the great benefit believers receive through faith in him (literally): "in order that he might redeem those who are under law" and "in order that we might receive the adoption as sons." Thus in a remarkable way Paul brought into focus here both the person and work of Jesus Christ. Christology and soteriology can never be separated; where one is inadequate, the other will always be deficient. In this passage Paul united these twin peaks of evangelical doctrine under the controlling rubric of God's gracious initiative and divine purpose.

The expression "when the time had fully come," (Literally, "when the fullness of time had come"; JB "the appointed time"), is found only here in Paul's writings. In the analogy of the heir-in-waiting just developed by Paul, the time designated by the father for his son to enter into the inheritance corresponds to the time in human history fixed and appointed by God for the sending forth of his Son. So significant was the advent of Christ for the Christian understanding of time that believers of a later generation divided all the time there is by this seminal event into A.D. and B.C. Elsewhere Paul described Christians as those "on whom the fulfillment of the

---

[177] So Betz, Longenecker, Bruce. For a contrary view, see R. B. Hays: "I began this study under the assumption that Gal 4:4-5 was in fact a fragment of pre-Pauline tradition; this investigation has substantially undermined my confidence in this assumption, as most of the features which have been thought to market off from the 'grain' of Paul's thought have been shown to be capable of explanation in other ways" (*The Faith of Jesus Christ: An Investigation of the Narrative Substructure of Galatians 3:1-4:11* [Chico: Scholars Press, 1983], 135).

ages has come" (1 Cor 10:11).

What did Paul mean by the "fullness" of time? Early Christian apologists pointed to the fact that the birth of the Messiah occurred during the *Pax Romana*, a period of relative peace and stability. Others have pointed to the development of a common language, favorable means of travel, the emergence of an urban civilization that made possible the rapid spread of the Christian message, and so forth. Still others have pointed to the lapse of a definite period of time (cf. Dan 9:24) that had to occur before the appearance of the Messiah.[178] It is sufficient to say with Calvin that "the time which had been ordained by the providence of God was seasonable and fit. . . . Therefore the right time for the Son of God to be revealed to the world was for God alone to judge and determine."[179]

One could hardly find a more succinct summary of the Christian gospel than the expression "God sent his Son." Implicit in these words are two ideas, both of which are fundamental to a holistic Christological affirmation: divine intentionality and eternal deity. The coming of Jesus Christ into human history was not an accidental happening in late antiquity. Not only was the incarnation the fulfillment of myriads of Old Testament prophecies, but it also was the culmination of a plan devised within the eternal counsel of the triune God before the creation of the world. Thus the Epistle to the Hebrews places on the lips of Christ the words of Ps 40: "Then I said, 'Here I am—it is written about me in the scroll—I have come to do your will, O God'" (Heb 10:7). There can be no "christology from below" until first of all we acknowledge a prior "christology from above."[180]

Seen in the context of Paul's other statements concerning the preexistence of Christ (cf. 1 Cor 8:6; 10:4; Col 1:15-17; Rom 8:3; Phil 2:5-9), the confession "God sent his Son" can only mean that Jesus Christ is the eternally divine Son of God sent forth from heaven. This perspective was certainly not original or unique with Paul. Jesus himself described God as "he who sent me" (Mark 9:37).

Similarly, in the parable of the unworthy tenants (Mark 12:1-11) Jesus is the "beloved Son" who stands in a unique and unparalleled relationship to God on whose behalf he undertakes his dangerous mission. Fundamental to

---

[178] Burton, *Galatians*, 216.

[179] *CTNC* 11, 73. Calvin adds: "This ought to restrain all curiosity, if any man, not content with the secret purpose of God, should dare to dispute why Christ did not appear sooner."

[180] I realize, of course, that this thesis stands over against the preponderance of contemporary Christological models from J. Hick to W. Pannenberg. On the effort of Karl Barth to construct a theology of incarnation that takes seriously both the divine initiative and historical particularity of Jesus Christ, see B. Marshall, *Christology in Conflict* (Oxford: Basil Blackwell, 1987), 115-43.

this analogy is the fact that Christ was God's eternal Son prior to his being sent into the world. Christ did not begin to be the Son of God at Bethlehem, or the Jordan River, or at his resurrection or ascension. He is the "only-begotten God" resident in the "bosom of the Father" from all eternity (John 1:18; 17:1-10). As E. Schweizer has put it, "When we repeat the New Testament phrase 'God sent his Son' we are talking about God and at the same time narrating a story that happened in our worldly time and space. It is the story of the living God who decided to live in our world in Jesus of Nazareth."[181] God sent his Son not just from Galilee to Jerusalem, nor just from the manger to the cross, but all the way from heaven to earth. The full implications of this text can hardly be grasped in human language. In sending Jesus, God did not send a substitute or a surrogate. He came himself.

Having asserted so boldly the eternal deity of Jesus Christ, Paul now affirmed his true humanity and representative role as one "born of woman" and "born under the law." The phrase "born of woman" is used elsewhere in Scripture as a common Jewish expression denoting simply one's status as a human being—as, for example, Job 14:1, "For man born of woman is of few days and full of trouble" (cf. Matt 11:11). Paul was here affirming that during his earthly life Jesus experienced all of the finitude and fears, trials and temptations that are the common lot of every human being. As Heb 4:15 expresses it, Jesus was put to the test in every conceivable way that we can be put to the test—yet without sin.

Is Gal 4:4 an implicit reference to the virginal conception of Christ? This verse, along with Rom 1:3, has been taken to imply that Paul knew and taught what the Gospels of Matthew and Luke plainly declare, namely, that Jesus was conceived without the cooperation of a human father, "born of a woman" who was a virgin. On the other hand, many others point to the lack of an explicit mention of the virgin birth in Paul's writings in order to downplay or deny this supernaturalist teaching. For example, a liberal Baptist leader in Germany recently boasted that he believed about the virgin birth just what the apostle Paul did—nothing![182]

It is inconceivable that Paul, the travel companion of Luke, would not have known about the virginal conception of Jesus. The fact that he nowhere mentions the virgin birth in his letters could only mean that it was so universally accepted among the Christian churches to which he wrote that he

---

[181] E. Schweizer, "What do we really mean when we say 'God sent his Son . . .'?," in *Faith and History: Essays in Honor of Paul W. Meyer,* ed. J. T. Carroll, C. H. Cosgrove, and E. E. Johnson (Atlanta: Scholars Press, 1990), 310. On the controverted reading of μονογενὴς θεὸς in John 1:18, see B. Metzger, *A Textual Commentary,* 198.

[182] See J. Weiss, "Müssen Christen an die Jungfrauengeburt glauben?" *Frankfurter Rundschau,* 23 December 1985).

deemed no elaboration or defense of it necessary. As J. G. Machen noted, "The virgin birth does seem to be implied in the profoundest way in the entire view which Paul holds of the Lord Jesus Christ."[183]

Having said all this, it remains true that Paul's primary emphasis in Gal 4:4 is not the unique mode of the Savior's conception but rather his full participation in the human condition. While Jesus' conception was supernatural, his birth was perfectly normal, complete with a dingy manger, soiled swaddling clothes, and other unsanitary conditions attending the birth of a poor peasant in ancient Palestine. Only later in the history of the church did an exaggerated devotion to Mary lead to the doctrine of her perpetual virginity.[184] Certain Gnostic Christians further "demythologized" the birth narratives to say that Jesus was only born *through* Mary but not *of* (cf. the preposition Paul used, *ek*, "from" "out of," the virgin Mary). On this view Jesus brought with him a celestial body from heaven, passing through Mary as a drop of water goes through a pipe.[185] Still other heretics, called Docetists, denied outright that Jesus possessed a human body of any kind. He appeared or seemed to be human, but in reality he was a ghostlike phantom who floated through life, never becoming enmeshed in the evil realm of matter. Over against all of these ethereal Christologies, each of which has its contemporary counterpart, Paul declared that the eternal, divine Son of God was really and truly "born of woman."

In a parallel participial clause, Paul also asserted that Jesus was "born under the law." Not only was he a man, but he also was a Jewish man, circumcised on the eighth day as all Jewish males were. He grew up in a Jewish home reading the Torah, praying to his Heavenly Father, attending synagogue, faithfully fulfilling, as no one before or after him has ever done, all of the precepts and demands of the law. To some extent Jesus' life "under the law" was comparable to the heir of Gal 4:1-2. Of Jesus it was quintessentially true that he was "no different from a slave although he was the Lord of all." However, unlike the heir who was subject to custodians and trustees,

---

[183] Machen, *Virgin Birth,* 263.

[184] The earliest evidence of this teaching is found in *The Protoevangelium of James,* an apocryphal infancy narrative from the second century. In this story the midwife who delivered Jesus told Salome that a virgin had given birth. Whereupon Salome said, "As the Lord my God lives, unless I put forward my finger and test her condition, I will not believe that a virgin has brought forth." As soon as she had verified that Mary's virginity was intact, Salome's hands were burned off, only to be healed later as she sought forgiveness for her unbelief and bent down to touch the baby Jesus. See Hennecke-Schneemelcher, eds., *New Testament Apocrypha,* 1, 385.

[185] On the recrudescence of "celestial flesh" Christologies in the time of the Reformation, see George, *Theology of the Reformers,* 280-84. Menno Simons, though often accused of promulgating this heretical doctrine, sharply distinguished his own view from that of earlier condemned teachers such as Marcion.

that is, the elemental spirits of the universe, Jesus always acted in perfect freedom and filial obedience only to the Father. Jesus was not enslaved to the bondage of the elements but was victorious over them throughout his ministry—casting out demons, stilling the winds, cleansing the lepers, raising the dead. As F. F. Bruce has noted, while Jesus was "under the law," he was nevertheless not under sin (cf. 2 Cor 5:21). Thus "he himself had no need of slave-attendant, guardian or steward, and he came to bring his people to the point where they too could dispense with their services."[186]

4:5 In this verse Paul turned from Christology to soteriology, from the divine person and eternal deity of Jesus Christ to his saving work in redemption and regeneration. The Son of God became a human being and was put under the law in order (1) to redeem those who were under the law and (2) so that we might become God's sons. Some have thought the first aspect of Christ's work mentioned here, redemption, pertained only to the Jews while the other benefit, adoption, was meant exclusively for the Gentiles. However, as we have seen, Jews and Gentiles alike are under the bondage of the law including its curse; conversely, Jews who are outside of Christ, no less than Gentiles with their pagan past, can only be brought into God's family through personal faith in the Messiah. The whole purport of Gal 3 and 4 is to show that we are justified by faith, not through the flesh.

The word "redeem" recalls Paul's earlier statement (3:10-13) concerning the curse of the law Christ bore in his own body on the cross. The purpose and goal of Christ's incarnation and humiliation, his being made "in the likeness of sinful flesh," as Paul put it in Rom 8:3, was precisely so that God could condemn sin in the flesh and so receive as righteous all those who find in Jesus Christ the sole and sufficient substitute for the sin debt they owed but could not pay. As J. Denney expressed it: "Christ not only became *man,* bound to obedience . . . , but he became *curse* for us. He made our doom his own. He took on him not only the calling of a man, but our responsibility as sinful men; it is in this that his work as our Redeemer lies, for it is in this that the measure, or rather the immensity, of his love is seen."[187]

If redemption implies a basically negative background—we are redeemed *from* the curse of the law, *from* the slave market of sin, *from* the clutches of the hostile elemental spirits—Paul went on to show the positive purpose for Christ's sacrificial suffering and death. The Son of God was born of woman and put under the law in order to redeem us from the law so that we might receive "the full rights of sons." The Greek word translated "full rights of sons" in the NIV is *huiothesia,* literally "adoption."

---

[186] Bruce, *Galatians,* 196.

[187] J. Denney, *The Death of Christ* (New York: Armstrong, 1903), 156.

Within the body of Scripture, this word is uniquely Pauline and carries several distinct meanings. In Eph 1:5 adoption is rooted in God's sovereign election, for God has "predestined us to be adopted as his sons through Jesus Christ, in accordance with his pleasure and will." In Rom 8:23 adoption encompasses our future resurrection, "the redemption of our bodies" for which we eagerly wait. Elsewhere in Romans (9:4-5) adoption heads the list of the blessings given to the people of Israel because of their special relationship with God. Here in Gal 4:5 (cf. also Rom 8:15) adoption refers to the present status of sonship accorded to all believers who through the new birth have become heirs with Christ of the Abrahamic promise.

Adoption was a commonly known legal procedure in the Hellenistic world, the most famous example being Julius Caesar's adoption of his great-nephew Octavius, who later succeeded him as the emperor Caesar Augustus.[188] The Roman process of adoption would certainly have been known to Paul's Gentile converts in Galatia. They could well have identified with the idea of chosen and instated as new members of God's family given their own former life as idolaters and devotees of false gods.

More recently, however, J. M. Scott, among others, has argued for a specifically Old Testament/Jewish background for adoption in Pauline theology. The key text is 2 Sam 7:14, "I will be to him a father, and he will be to me a son," which is taken to be an adoption formula echoed elsewhere in the Old Testament (cf. Exod 2:10; Esth 2:7; Gen 48:5; Hos 11:1). According to this view, Gal 4:1-2 does not reflect the situation of a Roman heir held in legal infancy until the time of majority specified by his father but rather the situation of the nation of Israel awaiting deliverance from bondage prior to the exodus. "Just as Israel, as heir to the Abrahamic promise, was redeemed as sons of God from slavery in Egypt at the time appointed by the father, so also believers were redeemed to adoption as sons of God from slavery under the 'elements of the world' at the fullness of time and thereby became heirs to the Abrahamic promise. . . . In other words, believers who are thus baptized into the messianic Son of God and take up his very cry of 'Abba!' to the Father participate with him in the Davidic promise of divine adoption and in the Abrahamic promise of universal sovereignty."[189]

Whether the background of Paul's adoption language is Roman or Jewish, it speaks in a powerful way of the tremendous transformation in our relation-

---

[188] C. Roebuck, *The World of Ancient Times* (New York: Scribners, 1966), 560-61.

[189] J. M. Scott, "Adoption, Sonship," *DPL,* 15-18. See also F. Lyall, *Slaves, Citizens, Sons: Legal Metaphors in the Epistles* (Grand Rapids: Zondervan, 1984); W. M. Calder, "Adoption and Inheritance in Galatia, *JTS* 31 (1930): 372-74; J. I. Cook, "The Concept of Adoption in the Theology of Paul," in *Saved by Hope: Essays in Honor of R. C. Oudersluys,* ed. J. I. Cook (Grand Rapids: Zondervan, 1978), 133-44.

ship to God. Through God's gracious initiative we have been delivered out of slavery unto sonship, out of bondage to sin and the powers of destruction produced by it into the glorious liberty of the children of God. This radical change is further explained now in terms of the indwelling Spirit within.

THE SPIRIT WITHIN (4:6-7).   **4:6**   Paul now moved forward from Christology and soteriology to pneumatology. Just as God sent his Son into the world, so also he has sent the Spirit of his Son into our hearts. We should not imagine, of course, that the Holy Spirit was ever absent from the Father or the Son in the divine accomplishment of salvation. The Holy Spirit shared fully in the eternal decrees including the decision to create human beings in the divine image ("Let us make man," Gen 1:27). The Holy Spirit brooded over the primordial creation, bringing cosmos out of chaos (Gen 1:1-2). The Holy Spirit guided the nation of Israel and gave insight to the prophets of old. Likewise, the Spirit was sent to Nazareth to overshadow the virgin Mary, enabling her to give birth to the Messiah apart from the agency of a human father. Also the Holy Spirit was sent upon Christ at his baptism, giving visible manifestation and audible confirmation of his messianic destiny. In fulfillment of Jesus' prophecy, the Holy Spirit was sent to the early church on the Day of Pentecost, inaugurating a new era in redemptive history. The sending of the Spirit Paul referred to in this verse presupposes all of the others but moves beyond them in referring to "the successive bestowals of the Spirit on individuals."[190]

There has been a vigorous debate about whether the adoption to sonship precedes the sending of the Spirit or vice versa.[191] Paul began this section of his letter (3:1) by reminding the Galatians of their first experiences of the Spirit and then showed how the presence of the Spirit in their lives implied that they were true sons of Abraham, heirs of the promise, chosen and adopted by God. Here, however, Paul seems to have reversed that sequence by means of a causal construction: "Because [*hoti*] you are sons, God sent the Spirit." Clearly, the receiving of the Spirit is the sequel to the bestowal of sonship. When we realize that these two, God's sovereign adoption and

---

[190] Burton, *Galatians,* 223. W. F. Flemington, among others, associates the sending of the Spirit with the act of baptism. However, the latter presupposes the former: The coming of the Spirit "into our hearts" precedes our coming into the waters of baptism. Indeed, Paul could elsewhere speak of our baptism in or by the Holy Spirit (1 Cor 12:13), indicating the priority of the inner transformation to outward act of obedience which, to be sure, follows from it and is based upon it. See Flemington, *The New Testament Doctrine of Baptism* (London: Hodder & Stoughton, 1964), 58, and G. R. Beasley-Murray, "Baptism in the Epistles of Paul," in *Christian Baptism,* ed. A. Gilmore (London: Lutterworth, 1959), 128-49.

[191] See the extensive discussion of this issue in Betz, *Galatians,* 209-11; Longenecker, *Galatians,* 173; Bruce, *Galatians,* 198.

the regenerating ministry of the Spirit in our hearts, are both aspects of the same reality, then this dilemma appears less problematic than some have made it out to be. The best commentary on this text is Paul's parallel statement in Rom 8:15-16: "For you did not receive a spirit that makes you a slave again to fear, but you received the Spirit of sonship (*huiothesia*). And by him we cry '*Abba*, Father.' The Spirit himself testifies with our spirit that we are God's children."

The Holy Spirit is the sign and pledge of our adoption so that by his presence in our hearts we are truly convinced that God is for us, not against us, that indeed he is our Heavenly Father. The evidence Paul gave for this wonderful assurance is not that through the Spirit we are empowered to do miraculous works, receive ecstatic visions, speak in tongues, or any other kind of sensational phenomena. Rather, the first, most basic indication of our adoption is that we have a new form of address for God. The Spirit invites us to join in his invocation, crying "Abba, Father."

The word *Abba* is a term of familial intimacy that can still be heard through the Middle East as a word of address used by young children to greet their father. *Abba* is an Aramaic expression that may have derived originally from the first syllables uttered by an infant (cf. the corresponding *ʾimmā*, "mother"). However, we oversentimentalize this word when we refer to it as mere baby talk and translate it into English as "daddy." The word *Abba* appears in certain legal texts of the Mishna as a designation used by grown children in claiming the inheritance of their deceased father.[192] As a word of address *Abba* is not so much associated with infancy as it is with intimacy. It is a cry of the heart, not a word spoken calmly with personal detachment and reserve, but a word we "call" or "cry out" (*krazō*).

The fact that this word is given here, and also in Rom 8:15, in both Aramaic and Greek indicates the bilingual character of early Christian worship. Throughout the history of the church various Christian groups have attempted to canonize one particular language as the authorized sacred tongue of religious discourse. Some Orthodox Christians have done that with Greek, traditional Roman Catholics with Latin, and certain Protestants with the English of the *King James Version*. However, the fact that in Jesus Christ there is no longer Jew or Gentile does not mean that we must stop speaking Hebrew/Aramaic or Greek. The Spirit who cries out "Abba, Father" from our hearts enabled the gospel to be heard in many of the world's languages on the Day of Pentecost. The same Holy Spirit still

---

[192] Bligh, *Galatians*, 356. See also G. Kittel, "αββα," *TDNT* 1.5-6; J. Jeremias, *The Prayers of Jesus* (London: SCM, 1967), 11-65; W. Marchel, *Abba, Père! La prière du Christ et des chrétiens* (Rome: Biblical Institute Press, 1971).

blesses the translation of the Scriptures into the many diverse languages and dialects of the world today.

The word *Abba* directly links the Christian believer as an adopted heir and son of God to Jesus himself, the unique Son of God, for it was he who first dared to use this term of familial intimacy in his own prayers to the Father (cf. Mark 14:36). If J. Jeremias is right, this same word was originally used in the opening petition of the Lord's Prayer, "O *Abba,* our heavenly *Abba.*" Something of the shock implied in using this word as an address for God Almighty, the maker of heaven and earth, is seen in a vestige of the Latin liturgy in which the worship leader introduces the Lord's Prayer with the rubric *audemus dicere,* "we make bold to say." The idea is that it would be presumptuous and daring beyond all propriety to address God as *Abba* had Jesus himself not bidden us to do so.

The sense of awe and holy wonder that accompanied the praying of the Lord's Prayer in the early church was doubtless related to this fact. J. Bligh has reconstructed the atmosphere that might have prevailed in an early Christian congregation when the pastor would introduce the Lord's Prayer in this manner:

> "Bearing in mind the permission granted us by our Lord, we are so bold as to say"—here he takes a deep breath—"*Abba!*"—he pauses while everyone winces—"Thy kingdom come, Thy will be done!" This must have been a moment of climax and tension in the early liturgy—a moment when the believer *experienced* his sonship, feeling that God was drawing him into an almost frightening intimacy.[193]

Something of this kind of reverent ecstasy must have been experienced by the Gentile believers of Galatia when having been saved from religious superstition and the worship of idols they discovered through faith in Jesus Christ a welcome access into the very heart of God. The new relationship they had with God, evidenced by the *Abba* prayer, had been effected through the indwelling of the Holy Spirit. Already they were the children of God and heirs of the promise. All of this had happened through the grace of God, the God who sent his Son and who had now sent his Spirit into their hearts. Thus there was no need for them to be circumcised or to seek the favor of God by keeping the works of the law. With confident boldness they could approach the throne of God crying, "*Abba,* Father!"

4:7 This verse summarizes everything Paul had said from 3:6 onward. The opening "therefore" is linked directly to the preceding verses, which have outlined the plan of salvation in terms of a trinitarian confession very

---

[193] Bligh, *Galatians,* 355.

similar to that on which the Apostles' Creed was later modeled. I believe in God the Father, the God who planned from all eternity to redeem his people and who in the fullness of time sent his Son. I believe in Jesus Christ, the Son of God who became fully human and who "suffered under Pontius Pilate" the curse of the law. I believe in the Holy Spirit who effects the forgiveness of sins and a new relationship with the Father. "Therefore," because all of this is true, you are *no longer* a slave, but a son. You are no longer under subjection to the elemental spirits. No longer a minor heir with no rights to the inheritance. No longer is your relationship to God determined by your race, rank, or role. No longer are you under the harsh tutelage of the *paidagōgos*. No longer are you shut up in the prison house of sin. No longer are you under the curse of the law. The promise given to Abraham and fulfilled in his prophetic Seed, Jesus Christ, has now been extended to all of those who through faith in him have become sons, crying *"Abba!"* and heirs of the living God.

(3) The Danger of Turning Back (4:8-11)

[8]Formerly, when you did not know God, you were slaves to those who by nature are not gods. [9]But now that you know God—or rather are known by God—how is it that you are turning back to those weak and miserable principles? Do you wish to be enslaved by them all over again? [10]You are observing special days and months and seasons and years! [11] I fear for you, that somehow I have wasted my efforts on you.

From 3:6–4:7 Paul developed a tightly woven and carefully crafted argument for the doctrine of justification by faith. He offered an analysis of redemptive history centered on the true identity of the children of Abraham. Writing to largely Gentile congregations besieged by the false teaching of Jewish Christian missionaries, he argued primarily from the Old Testament Scriptures, drawing on texts from Genesis to Habakkuk, while also bringing in illustrations from Roman legal practice and Hellenistic culture (e.g., the pedagogue, the young heir awaiting legal instatement, adoption). At this point in the letter, Paul interrupted the *probatio* section of the epistle, his "proofs" from Scripture, to address the Galatians personally and directly.

The remainder of chap. 4 can be divided into three literary units. Verses 8-11 are an exhortation in which Paul reminded his Galatian converts of their former way of life, the great transformation that had happened to them through their adoption into God's family, and his deep concern that they were about to exchange their spiritual heritage for a mess of pottage. Verses 12-20 extend the theme of Paul's fear for the Galatians in the form of a personal expostulation. He recalled the endearing bonds of friendship and love he and the Galatians had enjoyed in days past and pleaded with them to remain faithful to the one and only gospel he had first preached among them. The final section, vv. 21-31, contain the allegory of Hagar and Sarah whose sons, Ishmael and Isaac, are taken as representative types of spiritual slavery and spiritual sonship.

Throughout this entire passage Paul was pouring out his soul in earnest entreaty to the Galatians. The urgency of the matter is reflected in the appeals he made: "I plead with you, brothers . . . I fear for you . . . I am again in the pains of childbirth for you . . . I am perplexed about you!" As in 3:1-5, Paul again used the rhetorical devise of the *interrogatio,* a series of pointed questions intended to force the Galatians to examine what was happening to them and return to their first love. In rapid-fire succession Paul asked them: "How is it that you are turning back to those weak and miserable principles? Do you wish to be enslaved all over again? What is happening to all your joy? Have I now become your enemy by telling you the truth? Don't you really know what the law says?"

Paul was frustrated and exasperated with the Galatians, and the tone of rebuke comes through loud and clear. At the same time, his love and affection for them was as strong as ever. Three times in this passage he called them brothers (4:12,28,31) and once, my dear children (v. 19). Paul had a right to speak so harshly to them because of his great love for them. His whole purpose was to win them back from the brink of apostasy. To this end he wrote not as an armchair theologian discussing abstruse points of philosophy but rather as an evangelist with a pastor's heart whose overriding concern is to protect his sheep from an imminent danger.

4:8 This verse opens with a strong adversative, *alla,* "however" or "but," followed by a temporal adverb, *tote,* "then," which sets up the contrast that will follow in v. 9. Paul was drawing a sharp distinction between the pre-Christian past of the Galatian believers and their present status as adopted sons in the family of God. Paul provided no details concerning the precise character of the Galatians' former religious commitments. Perhaps some of them were devotees of the various mystery religions that flourished in the Hellenistic cities of South Galatia. Others may have been devoted to the Roman Imperial cult or to the pagan deities of ancient Greece. Still others may have been caught up in the astrological lore and worship of the star gods, celestial bodies whose movement in the heavens were believed to control human life on earth. There was a temple to Zeus just outside the city of Lystra. After Paul and Barnabas had healed a crippled man in that city, the priest of Zeus brought bulls and wreaths to the city gates and attempted to offer sacrifices to them saying, "The gods have come down to us in human form!" In response Paul and Barnabas admonished them "to turn from these worthless things to the living God, who made heaven and earth" (Acts 14:11–15). At Iconium, another South Galatian city, an inscription has been found to the goddess Dindimene, also called Mother Zizimene, a goddess with four heads and ten breasts, a goddess similar to the Ephesian Artemis, the nursing mother of all life, who was worshiped in conjunction with her consort, the Greek wine god Dionysos.[194]

Conversion to Christ meant breaking completely with the idolatrous religion and false gods of the surrounding culture. The centrality and finality of Jesus Christ is at the heart of the Christian message. Modern liberal Protestantism, infatuated with the ideologies of pluralism and syncretism, has tended to forget this essential evangelical truth. For some, *evangelism* has become a dirty word not to be used in polite company, or, worse, it has been redefined as the effort to help the adherents of non-Christian religions to discover the best in their own traditions in hopes that a general fellowship of the various world religions will eventually emerge. Sadly, even some evangelicals have downplayed the doctrine of hell, the necessity of conversion, and the preaching of the cross in favor of the implicit universalism of many contemporary theologies. In many circles "sinners in the hands of an angry God" has been displaced by a truncated God in the hands of angry sinners. But Paul would have none of this. He knew, as Jonathan Edwards later wrote, that personal faith in Jesus Christ was "the only remedy which God has provided for the miserable, brutish blindness of mankind. . . . It is the only means that the true God has made successful in his providence, to give the nations of the world the knowledge of himself; and to bring them off from the worship of false gods."[195]

Whatever the exact provenance of the pre-Christian religion of the Galatian believers, Paul characterized their prior paganism as slavery to "those who in reality are not gods," or, as the NEB has it, "beings which in their nature are no gods." What was Paul saying about the status of these false gods? Scholars are divided about whether Paul held to the "atheistic" or

---

[194] Ramsay, *Galatians,* 219–20.
[195] *The Works of Jonathan Edwards* (Carlisle, Pa.: Banner of Truth, 1984), 2.253. See also T. A. Schafer, "Jonathan Edwards and Justification by Faith," *Church History* 20 (1951): 55–67. On the plurality of views among evangelicals concerning the destiny of the unevangelized, see J. Sanders, ed., *No Other Name* (Grand Rapids: Eerdmans, 1992). In 1993 the Southern Baptist Convention adopted a resolution on "The Finality of Jesus Christ as Sole and Sufficient Savior." This statement opposed "the false teaching that Christ is so evident in world religions, human consciousness or the natural process that one can encounter Him and find salvation without the direct means of the gospel, or that adherents of the nonchristian religions and world views can receive this salvation through any means other than personal repentance and faith in Jesus Christ, the only Savior" (*SBC Annual,* 1993, 94).

"demonological" interpretation of the nongods.[196] Long before Paul, the Old Testament prophets condemned idolatrous devotion to statues of wood or brass, deities who had eyes but could not see, ears but could not hear, hands but could not feel (cf. Ps 115:4-7). Elsewhere Paul too could describe an idol as "nothing at all in the world." There is only one God, the true God from whom all things came, the "jealous" God who brooks no competition. All other pretended deities are merely "so-called gods" (1 Cor 8:4-6). Significantly, one of the most damaging charges brought against Christians during the second century was that of atheism. By that time the majority of Christians were former Gentiles who had rejected the false gods of Greco-Roman religion. In response to this charge, the apologist Justin Martyr declared:

> We confess that we are atheists, as far as gods of this sort are concerned, but not with respect to the most true God, the Father of righteousness and temperance and other virtues, who is free from all impurity. But both him, and the Son who came forth from him and taught us these things, and the host of the other good angels who follow and are made like to him, and the prophetic Spirit we worship and adore, knowing them in reason and truth, and declaring without grudging to everyone who wishes to learn, as we have been taught.[197]

The Christians were persecuted for being atheists, that is, for repudiating and refusing to worship the false deities, the nongods, of the Roman Empire. This does not mean, however, that either Paul or Christians of Justin's generation believed that these false gods were merely projections of the human mind. Clearly, they understood them to be existent beings, fallen angels, demonic spirits, the *ta stoicheia tou kosmou* described earlier. These elemental spirits were indeed real enough: they could appear on earth in various guises, they could perform miracles, and wreak havoc in the world of nature. They trafficked in destruction and death and were especially violent in stimulating persecutions against the Christians.

On the cross, however, Jesus Christ had unmasked these pretentious deities—they were sham gods, nongods, who, though still active and powerful within the limitation of God's providential order, were nonetheless a part of "the fashion of this present world that is passing away." Compared to the one

---

[196] Betz cites the view that Paul may have been influenced by Euhemerism, an ancient theory of religion that distinguished between divine beings that existed merely by human convention and those who were so "in reality" (φύσει; *Galatians,* 213-15).

[197] Justin Martyr, *Apology* 1.6. See J. Stevenson, *A New Eusebius* (London: SPCK, 1957), 62-63. See also G. H. Williams, "Justin Glimpsed as a Martyr among Roman Contemporaries," in *The Context of Contemporary Theology: Essays in Honor of Paul Lehman,* ed. A. McKelway and E. D. Willis (Atlanta: John Knox, 1974), 99-126.

true God, these demonic beings were, to say the least, "weak and beggarly." Like a poisonous snake that has just been decapitated, these malignant forces were now writhing in their final death throes, lashing out at anyone who is "foolish" (3:1) enough to come within their reach. Why on earth, Paul asked, would someone who had been delivered from the grasping power of such evil entities choose to come once again within their malevolent control?[198]

4:9 Paul had just characterized the former life of the Galatian Christians in the bleakest of terms—not knowing God, they had been slaves to the evil sham gods. Verse 9 states the glorious reversal that happened through their conversion to Jesus Christ: "But now that you know God—or rather are known by God." The change from paganism to Christ is described in terms of knowledge (*gnosis*). To be "in the know," of course, was a dominant motif in the religious system known as Gnosticism, a dualistic worldview based on a stark opposition between the spiritual world and the evil world of created matter.[199] Later Gnostic exegetes seized on this passage as evidence that Christ had come to deliver humankind from the captivity and deception of the cosmic powers. For the Gnostics, Jesus was primarily a revealer; the object of salvation was to be released from this material world through the reception of a secret *gnosis,* a kind of esoteric gospel conveyed through passwords, magic formulas, and mantras.[200]

However, the kind of knowledge Paul was speaking of is neither intellectual acumen nor some kind of special information available only to an inner group of initiates. "To know" in the Pauline sense also goes beyond implied acknowledgment of monotheism and intellectual assent to Christian doctrines. This sort of knowledge is necessary but not sufficient for the kind of transformation Paul described as having taken place among the Galatians. Paul's concept of knowledge was more closely related to the Hebrew verb *yādaʿ*, which is frequently used in the Old Testament to refer to the kind of personal intimacy associated with sexual intercourse, as in Gen 4:1, "Now Adam *knew* Eve his wife, and she conceived and bore Cain." "To know" God in this kind of experiential intensity implies a divine-human encounter in which the total self, not merely the mind or thought processes, is claimed and transformed.

---

[198] Like Plutarch, Paul seems to have been able to combine both the atheistic and demonological versions of Euhemerism within the total framework of his thought. See Betz, *Galatians*, 215, n. 22. On Paul's identification of the nongods with the "elements of the world" (τα στοιχεῖα του κόσμου), see H. Koester, "φυσις," *TDNT* 9.272.

[199] See the article and bibliography cited by F. M. Yamauchi, "Gnosis, Gnosticism," *DPL*, 350-54.

[200] See, e.g., Heracleon's interpretation of Gal 4:8-11 in E. Pagels, *The Gnostic Paul: Gnostic Exegesis of the Pauline Letters* (Philadelphia: Fortress, 1975), 109.

But how docs this come about? As soon as Paul had declared that the Galatians who formerly knew not God had come to know God, he immediately inverted his statement and added a rhetorical correction—"or rather are known by God."[201] Paul was here clearly distinguishing the Christian understanding of salvation from the gnostic doctrine of revelation. Just as our adoption by the Father precedes his imparting of the Holy Spirit and our responsive cry, *"Abba!"* so also our knowing God is conditioned upon his prior knowledge of us. Nowhere is this scriptural truth more clearly stated than in the article on election in the *Abstract of Principles,* the first confession of faith adopted among Southern Baptists after the formation of the SBC in 1845.

> Election is God's eternal choice of some persons unto everlasting life—not because of foreseen merit in them, but of his mere mercy in Christ—*in consequence of which* choice they are called, justified, and glorified (italics added).[202]

Paul's insistence upon the divine initiative in salvation excludes both moralism and mysticism. We can neither keep God's commandments nor love him purely apart from his overcoming grace and prevenient favor toward us. "This is love: not that we loved God, but that he loved us and sent his Son as an atoning sacrifice for our sins" (1 John 4:10). Nor can human beings ever "find God" no matter what sort of religious techniques or spiritual exercises they may employ. We are like blinded rats lost in the labyrinth of sin until by God's amazing grace we who were all lost in the maze of self-justification are truly and everlastingly "found."

Following the expression *alla tote* "but then" that begins v. 8 in Greek, v. 9 begins "but now." Perhaps no one since Paul has grasped the meaning of this tremendous transition more completely than John Newton, the former slave trader whose remarkable conversion is reflected in his famous hymn, "Amazing Grace." As John Stott tells the story of Newton:

> He was an only child and lost his mother when he was seven years old. He went to sea at the tender age of eleven and later became involved, in the words of one of his biographers, "in the unspeakable atrocities of the African slave trade." He plumbed the depths of human sin and degradation. When he was twenty-three, on 10 March 1748, when his ship was in imminent peril of floundering in a terrific storm, he cried to God for mercy, and he found it. He was truly converted, and he never forgot how God had had mercy upon him,

[201] The term "rhetorical correction" is from Luther (cf. Latin: *castigatio rethorica*). *LW* 26, 401.

[202] "Abstract of Principles," in R. A. Baker, ed., *A Baptist Sourcebook* (Nashville: Broadman, 1966), 138.

a former blasphemer. He sought diligently to remember what he had previously been, and what God had done for him. In order to imprint it on his memory, he had written in bold letters and fastened across the wall over the mantelpiece of his study the words of Deut 15:15: "Thou shalt remember that thou wast a bondman in the land of Egypt, and the Lord thy God redeemed thee."[203]

All of this has happened to the Galatians by the grace of God, and yet they were in danger of subjecting themselves to a bondage similar to that from which they had been delivered. But how could this be? Had the Galatians actually renounced their Christian faith? Had they recanted their baptismal vows? Did they no longer believe that Jesus was the promised Messiah? Certainly not! The temptation they faced, prompted by the Judaizing false teachers, was to doubt that Jesus Christ *alone* was sufficient for salvation. They were being told that it was necessary to add to their faith in Christ circumcision and other outdated ceremonies of the Mosaic law. Yet to do this, Paul said, would be no different than succumbing to their former subservient obedience to the elemental spirits of the world.

Certainly Paul's opponents did not see it that way. Their purpose was to enhance the Christian faith, to improve upon it by bringing Gentile converts more into line with traditional Jewish observances. But Paul was unyielding on this point. Jesus Christ *and* circumcision, Jesus Christ *and* the Torah (understood as a requirement for salvation), Jesus Christ *and* anything else amounted to the same kind of syncretism and pagan slavery from which the Galatians had been delivered. As Longenecker has put it, "For Paul . . . whatever leads one away from sole reliance on Christ, whether based on good intentions or depraved desires, is sub-Christian and therefore to be condemned."[204]

---

[203] Stott, *Only One Way,* 110. Far from leading Newton to a life of quietism and inaction, the doctrine of sovereign grace propelled the former slave trader into one of the most remarkable ministries in the history of the Christian church. In his sermon on the "Sovereignty of God," Newton exclaimed: "Great and marvelous are thy works, Lord God almighty! Just and true are thy ways, thou King of saints! This is the God whom we adore. This is he who invites us to lean upon his almighty arm, and promises to guide us with his unerring eye. . . . Therefore, while in the path of duty and following his call, we may cheerfully pass on regardless of apparent difficulties, for the Lord, whose we are, and who has taught us to make his glory our highest end, will go before us. And at his word, crooked things become straight, light shines out of darkness, and mountains sink into plains. Faith may and must be exercised, experience must and will confirm what his word declares, that the heart is deceitful and that man in his best estate is vanity. But his promises to them that fear him shall be confirmed likewise, and they shall find him in all situations a son, a shield, and an exceedingly great reward" (*A Burning and a Shining Light: English Spirituality in the Age of Wesley,* ed. D. L. Jeffrey [Grand Rapids: Eerdmans, 1987], 438).

[204] Longenecker, *Galatians,* 181.

Was Paul saying that the Galatians could actually lose their salvation? Some have interpreted this passage, along with the famous text about "falling from grace" in 5:1, in this way. It is significant that the word Paul used for "turning back" (*epistrephō*) was a technical term for both religious conversion (cf. 1 Thess 1:9; Acts 9:35; 15:19) and religious apostasy (cf. 2 Pet 2:21-22).[205] However, real apostasy, as opposed to a temporary backsliding, is possible only for those who have never been genuinely converted. Paul had good reason to believe that this was not the case with his Galatian converts, whom he called "brothers" and "my dear children." At the same time, Paul did not claim to possess infallible knowledge of the spiritual status of his readers. He therefore had to entertain the possibility that at least some of them may have feigned repentance, received water baptism, and even "tasted the goodness of the word of God and the powers of the age to come" (Heb 6:5) without being savingly converted. Only thus can we make sense of his closing lamentation, "I fear for you, that somehow I have wasted my efforts on you" (Gal 4:11).[206]

4:10 This verse can be read either as a statement of fact (NIV), "You are observing special days," or as a question, "Are you beginning to pay atten-

---

[205] Ibid., 180. D. Moody makes apostasy the centerpiece of his systematic theology. See his *Word of Truth* (Grand Rapids: Eerdmans, 1981), 348-65. Concerning the present passage, Moody asks: "Why does [Paul] fear that those who come out of slavery into sonship will turn back to the weak, beggarly elemental spirits, if this is impossible?" The historic Baptist doctrine of the perseverance of the saints is nowhere better stated than in the Second London Confession of 1689: "Those whom God hath accepted in the beloved, effectually called and Sanctified by his *Spirit*, and given the precious faith of his Elect unto, can neither totally nor finally fall from the state of grace; but shall certainly persevere therein to the end and be eternally saved, seeing the gifts and callings of God are without Repentance (whence he still begets and nourisheth in them Faith, Repentance, Love, Joy, Hope, and all the graces of the Spirit unto immortality) and though many storms and floods arise and beat against them, yet they shall never be able to take them off that foundation and rock which by faith they are fastened upon: notwithstanding through unbelief and the temptations of Satan the sensible sight of the light and love of God, may for a time be clouded, and obscured from them, yet he is still the same, and they shall be sure to be kept by the power of God unto Salvation, where they shall enjoy their purchased possession, they being engraven upon the palms of his hands, and their name having been written in the book of life from all Eternity" (W. L. Lumpkin, ed., *Baptist Confessions of Faith* [Valley Forge: Judson, 1959], 272-73.

[206] Cf. the insightful comments of Betz on this controverted matter: "Paul reveals at this point that he considers it possible indeed to switch from Christianity back to paganism. But this possibility is in reality an impossibility! It is interesting to see what Paul has to say about a post-Christian religious life. The enlightenment gained by coming to the knowledge of the true God cannot be simply shaken off. Return to the worship of the pagan deities would include the knowledge that these deities are 'weak' and 'impotent' and they are not 'in nature' what they are said to be. Therefore, a return to paganism would be more than a taking up again of the 'old slavery.' Such an act would be irrational, an absurdity" (*Galatians*, 216).

tion to special days?" In either case, Paul probably was reacting to a report he had received concerning the inroads made by the agitators among the Galatian believers. It may be that the special observances mentioned in this verse were a first step in the "higher life" program of the Judaizers. Once they had persuaded the Galatians to submit themselves to such calendrical rituals, then the decisive step of circumcision could be imposed more readily. This interpretation is reinforced by the present tense of the verb *paratēreisthe* ("you are observing") together with the fact that Gal 5:2 indicates that the Galatians had not yet accepted circumcision.

Paul linked four measurements of time, each of which likely refers to certain aspects of the Jewish system of religious feasts. Thus *days* could refer to the weekly Sabbath observance as well as to other feasts celebrated for only a day; *months,* to the new moon rituals mentioned in Num 10:10; *seasons,* to the great annual feasts such as Passover, Pentecost, and Tabernacles (cf. 2 Chr 8:13; Zech 8:19); and *years,* to the Year of Jubilee, the Sabbatical Year, and the New Year celebrations. Burton probably is correct in claiming that the four terms without mutual exclusiveness cover all kinds of ritual celebrations and calendar dates the Jews observed at that time.[207]

Some Christians have found in this verse a general prohibition against any special observances or regular religious festivals including the annual celebrations of Christmas and Easter as well as other seasons of the Christian calendar. For example, when the Pilgrims came to America, they refused to celebrate Christmas in any special way, regarding it merely it as another workday of the year. However, for Paul, just as circumcision was neither good nor evil in itself, so too the observance of special feast days and holy seasons was neither mandatory nor inherently blameworthy. In Rom 14:5-6 he observed: "Some judge one day to be better than another, while others judge all days to be alike. Let all be fully convinced in their own minds. Those who observe the day, observe it in honor of the Lord."

Obviously Paul was concerned that the Galatian believers would be

---

[207] Burton, *Galatians,* 234. It is quite possible, of course, that the expression "days, months, seasons and years" was a kind of double entendre referring at once to Jewish calendar dates and pagan cultic observances. Thus Paul would be have been saying to the Galatians, "If you fall prey to the lure of the Judaizers, you will find yourselves just as captivated by the oppression of the astral deities as ever you were under the old paganism." W. Schmithals has put forth the view that Paul is here "employing a current familiar list which was not widespread in Jewish orthodoxy but which frequently occurs above all in the apocryphal or Gnostic or gnosticizing literature" (*Paul and the Gnostics* [Nashville: Abingdon, 1972], 44-46). G. Bertram also relates this listing of sacred times and seasons to the general astrological superstitions that were widely followed in the Hellenistic world ("ἐπιστρέφω," *TDNT,* 7, 726). He also discerns in this allusion a hint of the moral apostasy that apparently characterized some of the Galatians (cf. 2 Pet 2:21).

drawn into a religious system where adherence to certain cyclical celebrations was regarded as obtaining or maintaining a favorable standing with God. This is a recurring temptation for believers in all ages of church history. In medieval times Roman Catholics were taught that the ritual of annual confession and Easter communion was a minimal requirement for being a member of the church in good standing. Today in many evangelical churches thousands of "nonactive" members throng to worship services at Christmas and Easter assuming that such semiannual pilgrimages are all the Lord requires of them. Whatever the context, a religion of "days, months, seasons, and years" can never lead to liberation from the weak and beggarly elemental spirits whose grasp can only be escaped through faith in the one who came "in the fullness of time."

4:11 Paul concluded his rebuke of the Galatians with an expression of dismay. J. B. Phillips translates it, "You make me wonder if all my efforts over you have been wasted!" Obviously Paul was not afraid for himself. Here was a man who had suffered imprisonment, stoning, shipwreck, judicial thrashings, buffeting by the elements of nature ("I spent a night and a day in the open sea . . . I have known hunger and thirst . . . I have been cold and naked," 2 Cor 11:23-27), not to mention numerous other threats and dangers common to one "constantly on the move."

What could the heretical interlopers of Galatia possibly do to Paul that the Jews, the Romans, not to say other false brothers, had not already done? No, Paul was not afraid for himself, but he was deeply concerned for the Galatians. Could all of his ministry among them really have no continuing result? Had he indeed "wasted" his efforts on them? These questions must have haunted Paul in the long hours of the night as he thought and prayed for his beloved children in the Lord. We cannot lightly dismiss Paul's fears for the Galatians or the harsh possibility of their eventual loss that he here contemplated. Still, within the wider context of the entire letter, this bleak expression must be placed over against Paul's overall confidence and hope that the Galatians could still be won back from the confusion and danger that now beset them. In the following verses Paul would enter even more deeply into a personal, agonizing appeal as he laid bare his soul on behalf of his "dear children."

6. Paul's Personal Appeal (4:12-20)

This section of Galatians forms a personal parenthesis in Paul's overall argument for justification by faith, which he resumed and concluded in vv. 21-31 with one additional proof from Scripture. Commentators through the centuries have noted the gripping intimacy of these verses, which seem to

have been literally wrung from the apostle's heart. Chrysostom observed
that whereas Paul in the preceding verses had stretched out a hand to his tem-
pest-tossed disciples, he now brought himself into the very midst of the
storm.[208] In his 1519 Galatians commentary, Luther observed, "These words
breathe Paul's own tears."[209] When he revisited this text in his 1535 Galatians commentary, Luther sought to penetrate further into Paul's mind:

> Now that he has completed the more forceful part of his epistle, he begins to
> feel that he has handled the Galatians too severely. Being concerned that by
> his harshness he may have done more harm than good, he tells them that his
> severe rebuke proceeded from a fatherly and truly apostolic spirit. He
> becomes amazingly rhetorical and overflows with sweet and gentle words, so
> that if he had offended anyone with his sharp denunciation, as he had
> undoubtedly offended many, the gentleness of his language would set things
> right again. He also teaches by his example that pastors and bishops should
> take a fatherly and motherly attitude, not toward the ravenous wolves (Matt
> 7:15) but toward the miserable, misled, and erring sheep, patiently bearing
> their weakness and fall and handling them with the utmost gentleness.[210]

This passage, then, provides a window into the pastoral heart of Paul.
Although his language is compressed and allusive, we should not imagine
that in these verses he had been so overcome with emotion that he had produced here an "erratic train of thought," one totally disconnected from the
preceding doctrinal discussion.[211]

What we have in this personal aside is a poignant witness to the indissoluble linkage between theological content and pastoral concern. All true theology worthy of the name is pastoral theology.[212] As in the autobiographical
section of his letter, so here too Paul's concern for the truth of the gospel is

---

[208] NPNF 13.31.

[209] *LW* 27.299.

[210] *LW* 26.413.

[211] Schlier, *Galater,* 208. Burton notes the discontinuity between this section and its surrounding context: "Dropping argument . . . the apostle turns to appeal, begging the Galatians to
take his attitude toward the law" (*Galatians,* 235). Betz interprets Paul's "argument of the heart"
as an example of the "friendship" (περὶ φιλίας) motif that was a standard technique in the epistolary literature of the times (*Galatians,* 220-21). "A personal appeal to friendship is entirely in
conformity with Hellenistic style, which calls for change between heavy and light sections and
which would require an emotional and personal approach to offset the impression of mere
abstractions." Longenecker, also recognizing the passionate and emotional character of this passage, regards it as a forceful introduction to the *exhortatio* section of the epistle which according
to him includes all of the material from 4:12 to 6:10 (*Galatians,* 186-88): "Here Paul begins the
exhortation portion of his letter, principally by recalling his past relations with his converts and
contrasting their past and present attitudes to him."

[212] T. C. Oden, *Pastoral Theology* (San Francisco: Harper & Row, 1983).

bound up with his own apostolic vocation on the one hand and with his consuming burden for his "dear children" on the other.

In our own day these two essential aspects of balanced pastoral ministry are all too often torn asunder. It is possible, for example, for a pastor to be so preoccupied with theological ideas and doctrinal content that he appears insensitive and detached from the hurts and struggles of his people. More often, though, the imbalance goes the other way: pastors who spend most of their time trying to assuage the needs of their congregation through the techniques of self-help and secular psychology. Such a dichotomy is deadly for any ministry of pastoral care that seeks to be both biblically responsible and personally redemptive. What deeply agitated Paul in Galatians was not that certain people had misconstrued the doctrine of justification on a theoretical plane but rather that individual men and women whom he loved dearly were in spiritual jeopardy because of this doctrinal deviation. This concern, more than anything else, prompted Paul to leave "the lofty heights of theological argumentation" and address himself to the Galatians in this deeply personal and emotional appeal.

(1) His Labors among Them (4:12-16)

[12]I plead with you, brothers, become like me, for I became like you. You have done me no wrong. [13]As you know, it was because of an illness that I first preached the gospel to you. [14]Even though my illness was a trial to you, you did not treat me with contempt or scorn. Instead, you welcomed me as if I were an angel of God, as if I were Christ Jesus himself. [15]What has happened to all your joy? I can testify that, if you could have done so, you would have torn out your eyes and given them to me. [16]Have I now become your enemy by telling you the truth?

4:12 This verse presents us with the first imperative in Galatians: "Be as I am; for I am as ye are" (KJV). Paul's use of the imperative mood increases as he moves toward the conclusion of the letter.[213] In Gal 3 and 4 Paul set forth the heart of the Christian gospel. He then expected his Galatian readers to act on the truth they had received. The first command he gave is that they should become like him, just as he became like them. What did Paul mean?

---

[213] There are four other imperative verbs in chap. 4, all quotations from the Old Testament: "Be glad," "break forth," "cry aloud" from Isa 54:1, and the summary verse of the Hagar-Sarah analogy at 4:30, quoting Gen 21:10, "Get rid of the slave woman and her son!"

The *imitatio Pauli* theme recurs with some frequency in the writings of the apostle.[214] First Corinthians 4:14-16, for example, resonates with the language of Galatians. There Paul also warned his "dear children" who are said to have had ten thousand pedagogues but only one father in the Lord. In that context Paul urged the Corinthians to imitate him as worthy children should model themselves on their godly parents. Elsewhere Paul admonished his readers to imitate him as he in turn imitated Christ (1 Cor 11:1; Phil 3:17; 1 Thess 1:6).

In Gal 4:12, however, Paul was saying something rather different—not "become like me, for I have become like Christ" but instead "become like me, for I became *like you*" (italics added). Perhaps the closest parallel to this verse is the statement Paul made to King Agrippa in Acts 26:28-29. Upon hearing Paul's testimony, the king asked, "Do you think that in such a short time you can persuade me to be a Christian?" Paul replied, "Short time or long—I pray God that not only you but all who are listening to me today may become what I am, except for these chains." In effect Paul was saying to King Agrippa: "Even though you possess the power to judge and condemn, I, a fettered prisoner, am really much better off than you. Why? Because I have met the Lord of glory who has forgiven my sins, opened my eyes, and delivered me from the tyranny of Satan. In this respect, I wish that you could become what I am." Just so, Paul was saying to the Galatians: "Look at what has happened to me. I was once a zealous devotee of the Mosaic law, stricter than any of you in careful observance of its many requirements. But Christ has delivered me from bondage to the law. I now live by faith in him who loved me and gave himself for me (Gal 2:20). Now I long for you to become like me, living in the liberty of those who are truly the children of Abraham and of God through faith in Jesus Christ."

"For I became like you" (lit., "for I also like you) recalls 1 Cor 9:19-23, where Paul described his missionary strategy in terms of cultural accommodation without compromise of conviction for the sake of a wider gospel witness. Though he himself was a free citizen of Rome, he would forego his political prerogatives and live as a slave in order "to win over as many as possible." And to those without the law, for example, the Gentile inhabitants of Galatia, he became *anomos,* like one not having the law so as to win those who were aliens to the commonwealth of Israel.

Paul was a pioneer in what we call today contextualization, the need to communicate the gospel in such a way that it speaks to the total context of the people to whom it is addressed. Insofar as we are able to separate the

---

[214] See the definitive study by W. P. DeBoer, *The Imitation of Paul* (Kampen: Kok, 1962). See also Bruce, *Galatians,* 208.

heart of the gospel from its cultural cocoon, to contextualize the message of Christ without compromising its content, we too should become imitators of Paul. In the words of John Stott: "In seeking to win other people for Christ, our end is to make them like us, but the means to that end is to make ourselves like them. If they are to become one with us in Christian conviction and experience, we must first become one with them in Christian compassion."[215]

Paul's next phrase, "You have done me no wrong," has spawned numerous and divergent interpretations. Is he merely flattering his readers, playing out the theme of friendship to the point of mere hypocrisy? Or was he being sarcastic: "You have done me no wrong, have you? Really now!"[216] In fact, there is no way to read Galatians honestly without realizing that indeed Paul had been wronged, personally grieved and deeply hurt, by the defection of his followers. He was quite out of sorts with them and for good reason. Assuming that this expression is not merely a rhetorical flourish, we do better to interpret it as a retrospective glance at the warm reception Paul received when he and Barnabas first brought the gospel into Galatia. At that time they did him no wrong, as he would explain more fully in the next two verses, but how they had behaved since then was another story.

4:13   This verse has fascinated Pauline scholars primarily because of its tantalizing allusion to the undisclosed illness that occasioned Paul's first visit to Galatia. In the early church Jerome interpreted Paul's affliction to have been the temptation of sexual desire that he identified with the "thorn in the flesh" (Latin: *stimulus carnis*) of 2 Cor 12:7. During the Reformation Luther dismissed this interpretation entirely regarding the "weakness of the flesh" as a reference to the suffering and affliction Paul bore as the result of the persecutions he endured. "It is impossible for anyone afflicted with these profound trials to be troubled by sexual desire."[217] In recent years, however, most commentators have discarded both of these traditional interpretations in favor of the idea that Paul was referring here to some actual bodily illness that affected his missionary labors. Three major theories have emerged about what the nature of this illness may have been:

Malaria.   This theory was advanced by W. Ramsay, who surmised that Paul may have contracted malaria when he first came into the swampy region of Pamphylia in southern Asia Minor. This was the occasion when John Mark

---

[215] Stott, *Only One Way,* 113.

[216] Longenecker lists several other possible interpretations: You did not wrong me, but have wronged Christ or God (cf. 1:6); or, You did not wrong me, but have wronged yourselves; or even, Whatever you have said or done in my absence, I have not been personally wronged by what has gone on among Christians in Galatia (*Galatians,* 190).

[217] *LW* 26.420.

became disillusioned with missionary life and returned home to Paul's great consternation (Acts 13:13). It may have been that Paul's original plan was to travel westward toward Ephesus and Greece but that he was redirected because of his illness toward the higher terrain around Pisidian Antioch. There, high above sea level, he found a more congenial place to recuperate. On this theory Paul may still have been in the grips of a terrible fever when he first began his preaching mission in Galatia.

4:14 *Epilepsy.* The verb in v. 14 translated "you did not . . . scorn" literally means, "you did not spit out" (*ekptuō*). A common belief was that the evil demon that caused epilepsy could be exorcised or at least contained by spitting at the one thus possessed.[218] On this reading, Paul was commending the Galatians for receiving him with courtesy and favor even though they may have witnessed the unpleasant sight of his epileptic seizures.

Ophthalmia. In v. 15 Paul praised the Galatians for their willingness to tear out their own eyes and give them to him. This, together with Paul's reference in 6:11 concerning writing such "large letters" in his own hand, have led many scholars to believe that Paul's illness was some kind of serious eye disorder. But as F. F. Bruce has noted, "there can be no certain diagnosis" of Paul's ailment here, nor of his "thorn in the flesh," assuming the two are not to be identified.[219]

Whether Paul's illness was malaria, epilepsy, ophthalmia, or something quite different, it is important to see in this reference indirect evidence of the overriding providence of God in the mission of his church.[220] Paul did not say exactly how his illness became the occasion for his Galatian mission, but we can be sure that from his perspective this was no mere accidental happening. Just as the Son had come forth from the Father "when the time had fully come" (4:4), just so Paul, the apostle of Christ, had been sent to the Galatians in accordance with God's foreordained wisdom and plan. Paul's thorn in the flesh, though inflicted through the instrumentality of "a messenger of Satan," was intended to yield a redemptive purpose—Paul's realization of the sufficiency of grace (2 Cor 12:7-10). Time and again God has used the adversities of life—sickness, persecution, poverty, even natural disasters and inexplicable tragedies—as occasions to display his mercy and grace and as a means to

---

[218] See H. Schlier, "ἐκπτυω" *TDNT* 2.448-49. While the act of spitting had demonological associations in the Hellenistic era, by the time of Paul it was more commonly viewed merely as a gesture of disrespect, hence the derived meaning "despise." Galatians 4:13-14 is frequently cited as evidence by those who identified Paul's physical ailment with epilepsy (C. J. Klausner's, *From Jesus to Paul* [London: SCM, 1944], 325-30).

[219] Bruce, *Galatians,* 209.

[220] Cf. the comment of F. Mussner, *Galaterbrief,* 307: "For a man like Paul everything became a *kairos* ["favorable time"] when the gospel was to be proclaimed."

advance the gospel.[221]

Whatever the nature of Paul's physical affliction, it must have resulted in some kind of bodily disfigurement or obviously unpleasant symptoms so that his condition was a "trial" to the Galatians. In the culture of the times, such infirmity and weakness was commonly seen as a sign of divine displeasure and rejection. Paul would have stood in stark contrast to the strong, good-looking "superapostles" who boasted in their physical prowess, rhetorical eloquence, and academic achievements. The Galatians would have been tempted to reject scornfully one of whom it was said, quite apart from his physical malady, that "his actual presence is feeble and his speaking beneath contempt" (2 Cor 10:10, Phillips). But to their credit the Galatians had not yielded to this temptation. On the contrary, they had received Paul "as an angel of God, as . . . Christ Jesus." Some have seen in this expression a reference to the incident of Acts 14:8-18 when Paul and Barnabas were mistaken by the people of Lystra for the Greek gods Zeus and Hermes. On that occasion the two missionaries tore their garments and cried, "Men, why are you doing this?" However, here in Gal 4:14, Paul did not criticize the Galatians for their exaggerated devotion to a human preacher; rather, he commended them for their ability to recognize and receive him as a true apostle of the Lord Jesus Christ.

Three times in the Gospels Jesus had declared that those who welcomed his representatives also welcomed him (cf. Matt 10:40; Luke 10:16; John 13:20). Paul had come to Galatia representing not himself but Christ Jesus the Lord. What mattered, of course, was not the messenger but the message. With the blast of an anathema, Paul had already (Gal 1:6-9) placed under a curse anyone—even he himself or an angel from heaven—who dared to proclaim any gospel other than the one and only gospel of Jesus Christ. But the Galatians had heard the true gospel. They had welcomed Paul as though he were an angel from God or Christ Jesus himself. Despite the possibility of his contemptuous appearance and physical deformity, the Galatians had received him with joy and had heard him gladly.

When we read this text, we are left with a nagging question in our minds: What prompted the Galatians to respond so well to this fat little bald man with

---

[221] The expression εὐηγγελισάμην ὑμῖν τὸ πρότερον has been taken by some scholars to mean "when I preached the gospel to you on the former occasion" rather than when "I first preached the gospel to you," as the NIV has it. However, as Bruce has noted, "In Hellenistic Greek πρότερος has surrendered the meaning 'the first of two' to πρῶτος and now means 'earlier'" (*Galatians,* 209). Even if we insist on a literal translation, this does not rule out an early dating of the epistle, realizing that Paul and Barnabas first traveled eastward through the cities of South Galatia and then retraced their steps over the same terrain. See the discussion on the date of Galatians in the Introduction.

a crooked nose, this tent-making preacher at whom most people would be tempted to spit? Nothing in the character of the Galatians makes us think they were naturally disposed to receive with gracious hospitality the sort of figure Paul portrayed himself to have been. No, it was the simple preaching of the cross in the power of the Holy Spirit that softened the hearts of the Galatians and brought them to a saving knowledge of the Christ Paul proclaimed. In speaking on "the Holy Spirit in Connection with our Ministry, C. H. Spurgeon once remarked:

> To us, as ministers, the Holy Spirit is absolutely essential. Without him our office is a mere name. We claim no priesthood over and above that which belongs to every child of God; but we are the successors of those who, in olden times, were moved of God to declare his word, to testify against transgression, and to plead his cause. Unless we have the spirit of the prophets resting upon us, the mantle which we wear is nothing but a rough garment to deceive. We ought to be driven forth with abhorrence from the society of honest men for daring to speak in the name of the Lord if the Spirit of God rests not upon us. We believe ourselves to be spokesmen of Jesus Christ, appointed to continue his witness upon earth; but upon him and his testimony the Spirit of God always rested, and if it does not rest upon us, we are evidently not sent forth into the world as he was. . . . If we have not the Spirit which Jesus promised, we cannot perform the commission which Jesus gave.[222]

4:15-16 These verses indicate that a major change has occurred between his first bringing the gospel to the Galatians and the occasion for his writing of this letter. "Where, then, is that happiness of yours?" he asked. The Greek word for happiness, or "joy" as the NIV has it, is *makarismos,* a substantive form of the same word Jesus used in the Beatitudes, "*Blessed* are the poor in spirit, . . . *blessed* are the meek, . . . the merciful, . . . the pure in heart," and so on. This word connotes a state of well-being that results from being rightly related to God. In writing to the Corinthian Christians, Paul spoke of their "overflowing joy" that "welled up in rich generosity" (2 Cor 8:2).

The Galatians also responded to the gospel and its bearer Paul in this way, so much so that, had it been possible, they would have been willing to have their eyes transplanted and presented to Paul as an offering of love. Whether or not this near-hyperbole has any reference to Paul's presumed eye disorder, it clearly indicates the extravagant extremity and deep affection the Galatians felt toward their father in the Lord. But something had happened to dampen

---

[222] C. H. Spurgeon, *Lectures to My Students* (Grand Rapids: Associated Publishers, 1962), 3. On Spurgeon as a model of pastoral ministry, see the essays in T. Curnow et al., *A Marvelous Ministry* (Ligonier, Pa.: Soli Deo Gloria, 1993), and L. A. Drummond, *Spurgeon: Prince of Preachers* (Grand Rapids: Kregel, 1992), *passim.*

the ardor of their initial joy. Now they regarded Paul, their dearest friend in Christ, as an "enemy" simply because he persisted in telling them the truth.

"Speaking the truth in love" (Eph 4:15) is both an antidote to false teaching and a worthy means of building up the body of Christ. This was Paul's approach from the beginning of his ministry in Galatia, and it also marked his present intervention in the crisis that occasioned this letter. Had Paul not included the present paragraph, along with a few other references scattered throughout the letter (e.g., 1:11; 5:10; 6:9-10), we might suppose that his passion for truth had overshadowed his commitment to love. However, just as we cannot separate sound doctrine from holy living, so neither are we free to denigrate the truth of the gospel at the expense of the expression of love. In Galatians Paul was waging a fierce battle for the souls of people he loved dearly, a people who once at least felt the same kind of warm affection toward him.[223]

Although Paul was deeply troubled by the shifting loyalties of his erstwhile disciples in Galatia, he did not alter his message in order to curry their favor or win back their approval. He continued to practice tough love by speaking the unvarnished truth. Ministers of the gospel today have much to learn from Paul's constancy in dealing with the fickle Galatians. For a pastor to be held in the affection and esteem of his people is a blessing devoutly to be desired. As John Calvin wisely noted: "It is not enough that pastors be respected, if they are not also loved. Both are necessary; otherwise their teaching will not have a sweet taste."[224]

When pastors become estranged from their people for whatever reason, it is always appropriate for them to try to win back the former affection and goodwill of their flock, just as Paul was doing here with the Galatians. But we must remember that the pastor is not called to be popular but to be faithful. He has been commissioned by the Lord of heaven to preach the Word of God in season and out of season; he must not fail in this divine assignment whether he be applauded warmly or shunned as a leper. For the man of God there is an arena of approval infinitely superior to the opinion of his congregation, or the applause of his peers, or the approval of some denominational bureaucracy. As the Scottish preacher John Brown put it, "The hosannahs of the crowd are dearly purchased at the expense of one pang of conscience, one frown of the Savior."[225]

---

[223] It is significant that one of the fragments from the *Kerygmata Petrou*, an anti-Pauline writing from the postapostolic age, has Peter referring to Paul as "the man who is my enemy" (ἐχθρὸς ἄνθρωπος). Betz observes that this statement "no doubt reflects the knowledge of Paul and his gospel" (*Galatians,* 331, n. 9). It may well be that the polemic against "Paul the enemy" derived from an epithet originally hurled against the apostle by his Galatian opponents.

[224] CNTC 11.81.

[225] Brown, *Galatians,* 217-18.

(2) His Love for Them (4:17-20)

¹⁷Those people are zealous to win you over, but for no good. What they want
is to alienate you [from us], so that you may be zealous for them. ¹⁸It is fine to
be zealous, provided the purpose is good, and to be so always and not just when
I am with you. ¹⁹My dear children, for whom I am again in the pains of childbirth until Christ is formed in you, ²⁰how I wish I could be with you now and
change my tone, because I am perplexed about you!

4:17-18   Before declaring again (vv. 19-20) his enduring love and
anguished concern for the Galatians, Paul took a long sidewards glance at his
opponents, whose nefarious activities had precipitated the present crisis in
Paul's relationship with the Galatians. Neither here nor anywhere else in
Galatians did Paul name these troublesome agitators. The translation "those
people" is extrapolated from the third person plural form of the verb *zēlousin,*
a word that occurs three times in vv. 17-18. The English word "jealous"
comes from this same word (via the Late Latin *zelosus*) and usually means "to
be resentfully envious or suspicious of a rival or a rival's influence." In
English we seldom use the word "jealous" in anything but a negative sense.
In the Old Testament, however, God is described as a "jealous God" (Exod
20:5), meaning that he is watchful and solicitous in guarding that which
belongs to him. It is clear from the present context that Paul was using
zēlousthai in a morally neutral sense since he himself was possessed of "an
honest envy" (NEB) toward the Galatians. The problem with the agitators
was not the interest they had shown in the Galatians but rather their evil intentions and selfish motivation ("it is for their own ends," Phillips; "but for a dishonorable purpose," Knox). Thus some translators have preferred to render
this word in the language of courtship: "How keen these men are to win you
over" (Phillips); they are "courting your favor" (NAB). Perhaps Clarence Jordan's colloquial translation of vv. 17-20 comes closest to capturing Paul's real
meaning here:

> Now listen, those fellows who are giving you the rush are not on the level.
> They are trying to capture you so you can rush around for them. Now it's all
> right to make over somebody once in a while, provided it is done sincerely. I
> do it occasionally when I am not in the presence of you, my children, over
> whom I agonize again and again until Christ takes shape in you. I surely do
> wish I could be with you right now and change my tone of voice, because
> you've got me all befuddled. (Cotton Patch, 100)

What did these interlopers seek to accomplish by the fawning flattery and
self-interested attention they had foisted upon the Galatians? What they
wanted, Paul said, is to "shut you out," "to exclude you." But to exclude you
from what? Paul left this question open-ended, and various answers have

been supplied by the commentators. Perhaps the false teachers were envious of the newfound freedom and Christian liberty the Galatian believers enjoyed. In its place they wanted to impose again a burdensome "yoke of slavery" (5:1). Even though they would never have admitted it, was their real aim to exclude these Pauline congregations from Christ himself? This at least was the end result of their meddlesome intervention (5:2). However, Longenecker's interpretation best reflects the whole drift of the passage: "The context is entirely about whom the Galatians were going to follow and have fellowship with, Paul or the Judaizers. So it seems natural to interpret the desired exclusion as being one from Paul's leadership and fellowship ("from us"), which would also be, of course, at least in Paul's eyes, exclusion from Christ (cf. 5:4) and from God, 'who called' them (cf. 1:6)."[226]

The phrase "not just when I am with you" reflects the deep hurt Paul felt because of the fickle affection and shifting loyalties of his erstwhile disciples. Although he was not much to look at physically, Paul's actual presence and unique personality had no doubt contributed to the overwhelmingly favorable reception the Galatians granted to him during his first sojourn among them. But now all of that had changed. The Galatian Christians had been courted, seduced, and bewitched by false teachers whose true aim was to alienate their affection from Paul and to enlist them as devotees in their own campaign of self-aggrandizement. Like another Pauline congregation, the church at Ephesus, the Galatian Christians had forsaken their first love (Rev 2:4).

4:19 In the two preceding verses Paul's tone had been sharp and polemical as he brought within his sights the false teachers whose dishonorable wooing of the Galatians had led them so far astray. Now, however, there was a sudden change of mood as Paul turned to address himself with great tenderness to his misled flock. "Dear little children!" is the best translation of the Greek expression Paul used, *teknia*, a diminutive form of the ordinary Greek word for small child (cf. the Latin, *filioli*).[227] Although a term of endearment, *teknia* may also connote a lack of growth and maturity, spiritual babyhood, a stunted condition out of which Paul desired for the Galatian Christians to grow with all alacrity. To connect this language with two other metaphors Paul had already used in his letter, by allowing themselves to be wooed away from Paul's gospel by the blandishments of the Judaizers, the Galatians had in effect placed themselves once again under the harsh tutelage of the *paida-*

---

[226] Longenecker, *Galatians,* 194.

[227] The nondiminutive form, *tekna,* is well attested among the better witnesses and appears as the preferred reading in the most recent edition of the Nestle-Aland edition of the Greek New Testament. However, the vocative, *teknia,* makes more sense both syntactically and contextually. Diminutives in Greek are frequently used to express affection and familiarity. See H. W. Smyth, *Greek Grammar* (Cambridge: Harvard University Press, 1920), 235.

gōgos and the constricting supervision of "guardians and trustees" who keep
them in legal servitude.

Throughout the letter Paul had admonished the Galatians to move beyond
such infantile behavior and to claim the full inheritance that was theirs as the
children of God through faith in Jesus Christ. In the present context he
showed how deeply invested he himself was in their spiritual struggles. This
he did by comparing himself to a mother who must go again through the
pangs of childbirth for the sake of her children. This is a striking metaphor
without parallel in any other Pauline writing. A similar motif occurs in 1
Thess 2:7, where Paul likened himself to a nurse (*trophos*) caring for her little
children. More common still is the image of Paul as a father begetting sons
and daughters in Christ through the preaching of the gospel (cf. 1 Cor 4:15; 2
Tim 1:2; Phlm 10). Only here in Galatians does he appear in the role of a
mother, a mother who willingly undergoes the ordeal of pregnancy and deliv-
ery all over again in order to secure the well-being of her children. This image
bears witness to the deep personal anguish Paul was experiencing over the
defection of his spiritual offspring in Galatia.

Paul had endured the first round of labor pains during the initial evangelization of the Galatians. Later he would remind them that he still bore in his
body the "marks of Jesus" (Gal 6:17), a permanent vestige of the persecution
he endured as a consequence of his faithful proclamation of the gospel. But
the labor pains he was now experiencing were not the result of external pressures and attacks; they stemmed rather from the inner anguish and exasperation Paul felt because his Galatian converts had been careless with the truth
of the gospel.

The verb "to suffer the pains of childbirth" (*ōdinein*) occurs only two other
times in the New Testament, once again in this same chapter (4:27) and a final
time in Rev 12:2. In an insightful exegetical study of this concept, B. Gaventa
has observed that "*Odinein* . . . never refers to the mere *fact* of a birth, but
always to the accompanying anguish." With reference to Gal 4:19, she argues
that "Paul's anguish, his travail, is not simply a personal matter or a literary
convention . . . but reflects the anguish of the whole created order as it awaits
the fulfillment of God's action in Jesus Christ."[228] If this interpretation is correct, then Paul's distress over the Galatians was part of the eschatological
groaning referred to in Rom 8:18-28, the groaning of a broken creation awaiting the consummation of all things that will take place at the return of Christ

---

[228] B. R. Gaventa, "The Maternity of Paul: An Exegetical Study of Galatians 4:19," in *The
Conversation Continues: Studies in Paul and John in Honor of J. Louis Martyn*, ed. R. T.
Fortna and B. Gaventa (Nashville: Abingdon, 1990), 192-94. Also see the discussion in
Matera, *Galatians*, 161-62.

in glory. Paul's groanings, though unique to his own apostolic vocation, have been echoed again and again throughout the history of the church in the faithful witness of martyrs and missionaries, reformers and evangelists, pastors and prophets who have risked their lives for the sake of the gospel. Writing to the believers at Colosse, Paul described the divine commission of such Christians in terms of a theology of the cross: "I myself have been made a minister of the same gospel, and though it is true at this moment that I am suffering on behalf of you who have heard the gospel, yet I am far from sorry about it. Indeed, I am glad, because it gives me a chance to complete in my own sufferings something of the untold pains which Christ suffers on behalf of his body, the church" (Col 1:23-24, Phillips).

As he was wont to do in his letters, Paul now suddenly shifted his metaphor again, doubtless producing a note of jarring dissonance in the minds of his readers. Paul had just described himself as a pregnant mother determined to carry the Galatians to full term. The anguish of his labor over them had to continue, he said, "until Christ is formed in you." The Galatians who a moment ago were described as being formed in the womb were now spoken of as expectant mothers who themselves must wait for an embryonic Christ to be fully developed (*morphoō,* a medical term for the growth of the fetus into an infant) within them.[229]

Paul's language in this passage stretches our imagination to the limit, but his meaning is not in doubt. He was deeply anguished over the Galatians. He did not want them to suffer a spiritual miscarriage but desired instead that they make their calling and election sure. This can only happen through the birth of Christ in their hearts.[230] F. F. Bruce referred to the Puritan divine Henry Scougal's classic treatment of Christ being formed within the believer, *The Life of God in the Soul of Man,* originally published in London, 1672-73. This work had a decisive influence on the great evangelist George White-

---

[229] The NEB assumes a different interpretation: "I am in travail with you over again until you take the shape of Christ." The idea here is that Christ was being formed in the Galatians while they were still in the womb so that Paul's labor pains would cease at their birth when they received a new life from above. While this reading is smoother than the one given above, it lacks the dramatic impact of Paul's original wording.

[230] The theme of Christ's birth in the hearts of believers was well developed in patristic theology. See H. Rahner, "Die Gottesgeburt. Die Lehre der Kirchenväter von der Geburt Christi im Herzen des Gläubigen," *ZTK* 59 (1935): 335-418. Calvin also echoed this theme in his comment on this verse: "For [Paul] does not annihilate their former birth, but says that they must again be nourished in the womb, as if they were an immature and unformed embryo. But Christ being formed in us is the same as our being formed in Christ. For we are born that we may be new creatures in him. And he, on the other hand, is born in us so that we may live his life. Since the true image of Christ had been deformed through the superstitions introduced by the false apostles, Paul labors to restore it so that it might shine clearly and unhindered" (CNTC 11.82-83).

field, who wrote in his journal, "That they who know anything of religion know it is a vital union with the Son of God—Christ formed in the heart."[231]

4:20 Paul brought this section of the letter to a close by expressing his desire to be with the Galatians in their time of crisis. If, as we have suggested in the introduction, Galatians was written on the eve of the Jerusalem Council mentioned in Acts 15, then Paul would certainly have had ample reason for not being able to drop his other responsibilities and return immediately to Galatia. When he did visit the region again sometime later (cf. Acts 16:1-6), he would have been able to confirm the Galatians in their faith and receive a firsthand report on the effect of his letter to them. For the moment he wished he could be there in person and thus "exchange my voice [for this letter]."[232]

Finally, Paul confessed his bewilderment over the Galatians, crying out "I am so worried about you," or as the NEB has it, "I am at my wits' end about you."[233] Here Paul's true humanity is evident. This verse echoes his earlier unbearable thought of "wasted efforts" (4:11). He was exasperated, perplexed, and heartbroken. The situation was desperate, but defeat was not a foregone conclusion. The Galatians might still have been won back from the brink of disaster. The gleam of hope that later emerges in the letter (5:10) is based on the fact that the "all-surpassing power is from God and not from us." What Paul later wrote to the Corinthians he could also have said on this occasion to the Galatians: We are hard pressed . . . perplexed . . . persecuted . . . struck down. But we are not crushed . . . in despair . . . abandoned . . . or

---

[231] G. Whitefield, *Journals* (London: Banner of Truth, 1960), 46. Cited in Bruce, *Galatians,* 213. Whitefield described his own conversion in this way: "One day, perceiving an uncommon drought and a disagreeable clamminess in my mouth and using things to allay my thirst, but in vain, it was suggested to me, that when Jesus Christ cried out, 'I thirst,' his sufferings were near at an end. Upon which I cast myself down on the bed, crying out, 'I thirst!' Soon after this, I found and felt in myself that I was delivered from the burden that so heavily oppressed me. The spirit of mourning was taken from me, and I knew what it was truly to rejoice in God my Savior; and, for some time, could not avoid singing Psalms wherever I was; but my joy gradually became more settled, and, blessed be God, has abode and increased in my soul, saving a few casual intermissions, ever since. . . . Now did the Spirit of God take possession of my soul, and, as I humbly hope, seal me unto the day of redemption" (H. T. Kerr and J. M. Mulder, eds., *Conversions: The Christian Experience* [(Grand Rapids: Eerdmans, 1983], 66).

[232] So Longenecker, *Galatians,* 196. In context this reading makes more sense than two alternative interpretations: (1) Paul desired to change the tone of his speech, substituting the harsh language of rebuke for a more tender mode of address. (2) Paul wished to exchange his ordinary human speech for a heavenly language (cf. 1 Cor 13:1) in order "to dispel the magic charm that has taken possession of the congregation." The latter idea has been suggested by H. Schlier. See Betz, *Galatians,* 236, n. 183. Burton, *Galatians,* 250, and R. Y. K. Fung, *Galatians,* NICNT (Grand Rapids: Eerdmans, 1988), 203, among others, have understood Paul's change of voice as a reference to a modification of his tone.

[233] *Translators Handbook,* 107.

destroyed. Therefore we do not lose heart (2 Cor 4:7-9,16).

This entire passage has a great deal to say about ministerial ethics and the proper relationship between pastor and people. On one level it is a classic case of "sheep stealing." The Judaizers wormed their way into the congregations of Galatia by criticizing and attacking the apostle Paul. They tore him down in order to build themselves up. Their way of doing ministry was as perverted as their doctrine was corrupt. By contrast, Paul's missionary methodology was to preach the gospel to the unevangelized, "so that I will not be building on someone else's foundation" (Rom 15:20). False teachers today, no less than in apostolic times, frequently prey on the evangelical labors of others, bewitching God's people and leading many astray.

We cannot stress too much that Paul was not interested in developing a personality cult, a band of Pauline groupies, whose primary loyalty would be to him rather than to the gospel. No, his overriding interest was that Christ be formed in his "dear little children." For this reason alone he was in travail on their behalf. Calvin's words on this matter still ring true: "If ministers wish to do any good, let them labor to form Christ, not to form themselves, in their hearers."[234] Elsewhere Paul could rejoice when Christ was preached even out of envy and rivalry rather than goodwill (Phil 1:15). But in Galatia the false teachers were preaching "a different gospel—which is really no gospel at all" (1:6-7). They were guilty not only of sheep stealing but also of soul butchering. This is why Paul could not simply shrug his shoulders, shake the dust off his feet, and move on to some other venue where he would likely be more appreciated. Something eternal was at stake, and Paul had to contend earnestly for the faith once delivered. May God grant to the church today ministers of the gospel possessed of the constancy of Paul, ministers of God who will not turn and run at the first sound of opposition but who will lovingly stand their ground, weeping, pleading, praying until Christ be completely formed in the precious souls that have been given to their charge.

7. The Analogy of Hagar and Sarah (4:21-31)

Paul concluded this central theological section of Galatians by returning once more to the realm of biblical exegesis, picking up again the theme of Abraham and his descendants and applying it in a forceful way to the crisis that confronted his readers. Why does this passage occur where it does, rather far removed from the immediate context of the Abraham argument which Paul brought to a dramatic conclusion at the end of chap. 3? Is it, as Burton imagined, a supplementary argument that Paul added "as an afterthought" in

---

[234] CNTC 11.83.

order to make his train of thought clearer and more persuasive to the still-wavering Galatians?[235] Or is it, as Betz's rhetorical analysis of the letter has led him to conclude, the strongest argument in the entire *probatio* section (3:1–4:31), a deliberate ploy on the part of the apostle through which he "lets the Galatians find the truth for themselves" by means of a familiar analogy from the Old Testament?[236]

Longenecker, among others, has placed the Hagar-Sarah allegory with the closing appeals and exhortations that began with Paul's first imperative, "Become like me!" in 4:12.[237] This approach has also been supported by G. W. Hansen, who has connected this passage with the immediately preceding section in which Paul displayed the distress and pain he felt for his Galatian converts. On this view the appeal begun at 4:12, "I plead with you, brothers," continues into the story of Hagar and Sarah, coming to a crescendo with the command of 4:30, "Get rid of the slave woman and her son," in other words, expel the Judaizers and their false teaching from your midst.[238]

On balance it seems that the Hagar-Sarah example serves both as a concluding proof of Scripture, rounding out Paul's central concern for justification by faith, and also as a connecting link with the exhortatory section that follows in Gal 5:6. The theme of Christian freedom that is especially prominent in the last two chapters is anticipated here by the contrast between Hagar the slave and Sarah the free woman.

---

[235] Burton, *Galatians,* 251.

[236] Betz, *Galatians,* 240. Betz cites this quotation from Luther that seems to support his contention that Paul was here using picture language in order more readily to convince his readers of the truth he had earlier presented in didactic form: "The common people are deeply moved by allegories and parables; therefore Christ also used them often. They are like pictures of a sort, which show things to simple people as though before their very eyes and for this reason have a profound effect on the mind, especially of an uneducated person." On Luther's exegesis of the OT, see J. S. Preus, *From Shadow to Promise: Old Testament Interpretation from Augustine to the Young Luther* (Cambridge: Harvard University Press, 1969).

[237] Longenecker, *Galatians,* 199,

[238] G. W. Hansen, *Abraham and Galatians: Epistolary and Rhetorical Contexts* (Sheffield: JSNT, 1989), 141-54. See also Matera, *Galatians,* 172-73. J. L. Martyn's interpretation of this passage also connects it directly with the preceding personal appeal in 4:12-20. Paul had just lamented the labor pains he had to endure for the sake of his children (4:19). The word for "child" (τέκνον) occurs four times in the Hagar-Sarah allegory (4:25,27,28,31), where it is used to describe the offspring of both mothers, identified respectively as the children of the present Jerusalem and those of the heavenly Jerusalem. Martyn has argued that these two people groups are not to be equated with Judaism and Christianity per se but rather with followers of the law-observant mission of the Judaizers on the one hand and those of the circumcision-free apostolate of Paul on the other. See J. L. Martyn, "The Covenants of Hagar and Sarah," in *Faith and History: Essays in Honor of Paul W. Meyer*, J. T. Carroll et al. eds. (Atlanta: Scholars Press, 1990), 160-92.

The question still remains why Paul would choose to focus on these two women and their two sons in order to make his point in such a seemingly convoluted, roundabout way. The most plausible answer to this question has been provided by C. K. Barrett in his study "The Allegory of Abraham, Sarah, and Hagar in the Argument of Galatians."[239] Barrett supposes that Paul was here responding to an interpretation of the Hagar-Sarah story put forth by his Judaizing opponents. The story of Abraham's two sons, Ishmael and Isaac, was a well-worn text in rabbinic exegesis and would have lent itself to supporting the Judaizers' claim that only those who belonged physically to the family of Abraham had any share in the promise God made to him. To put it more starkly, the descendants of Isaac were the Jews; and those of Ishmael, the Gentiles. At Mount Sinai the Jews had received the enlightenment of the law while the Gentiles remained in the darkness of sin, alienated from the promises of God and the commonwealth of Israel. As Barrett puts it, "The seed of Abraham, understood physically, issued in legitimate and illegitimate children, the Galatians were urged to legitimize themselves. . . . Those who are not prepared to connect themselves to this community [the renewed people of God, that is, the church whose headquarters was at Jerusalem] by the approved means (circumcision) must be cast out; they cannot hope to inherit promises made to Abraham and his seed."[240] It is easy to see how this kind of argument would have carried considerable weight with the new believers of Galatia who were beginning to wonder whether simple faith in Jesus Christ was sufficient for inclusion in the true family of God. Paul, then, had to revisit the ancient story of Abraham's two sons in order to show that, properly understood, it supported not the program of the Judaizers but rather his own doctrine of justification by faith alone.

(1) The Historical Background (4:21-23)

[21]**Tell me, you who want to be under the law, are you not aware of what the law says? [22]For it is written that Abraham had two sons, one by the slave woman and the other by the free woman. [23]His son by the slave woman was born in the ordinary way; but his son by the free woman was born as the result of a promise.**

4:21 Paul introduced the analogy of Hagar and Sarah with a question, an interrogation similar to that he posed earlier in 4:9. There he wondered whether the Galatians wished to be enslaved all over again by the elemental spirits of the world. Here another kind of bondage, or better, another form of

---

[239] C. K. Barrett, *Essays on Paul* (Philadelphia: Westminster, 1982), 154-70.
[240] Barrett, "Allegory," 161-62.

the same bondage is in view, that which results from being "under the law." "Do you not hear what the law says?" Paul asked. The NIV translates the verb *akouō*, usually "hear," as "to be aware of," indicating full comprehension and realization of what was at stake. "Do you realize what you are getting into?" Paul asked. "Do you really know what is involved in what you are about to do? Then listen more carefully to what the law itself says."

In addressing himself to "those who want to be under the law," Paul indicated that complete apostasy to the Judaizing heresy had not yet occurred at the time of his writing. True, at least some of the Galatians had begun to observe the calendrical feasts and holy days of the Jewish year, and others were almost persuaded to undergo circumcision in keeping with the principles of the Judaizers. Erroneous ideas had been instilled into the minds of the Galatians, but on the whole Paul's converts had not yet been completely won over to the false teachings of his opponents. In order to win the Galatian believers back from a false allegiance to the law, Paul would set forth the true meaning of the law.

In one sentence Paul used the word "law" in two disparate senses. When he spoke of those desiring to be "under the law," he doubtless meant the law of Moses, the legislation given to the people of Israel at Mount Sinai along with the attendant regulations and prescriptions related thereto. But in his question, "Do you not hear the law?" Paul was referring to the Old Testament Scriptures, especially to the Pentateuch from which he would draw the principal argument concerning Abraham's two sons. This statement is similar to Paul's earlier declaration in Gal 2:19, "For through the law I died to the law so that I might live for God." In Galatians, no less than in Romans, the law is holy, righteous, and good; for it was given by a holy, righteous, and perfectly good God. But the law was never intended by God to serve as a means of justification. The law of Moses, properly understood, points beyond itself both backwards toward the Abrahamic covenant and forward toward its final fulfillment in Jesus Christ. To "hear" the law clearly, however, required more than traditional rabbinic exegesis as filtered through the lenses of the Judaizers' theology. Paul now offered his counterinterpretation of the Hagar-Sarah story.

4:22-23 Having invited his readers to "hear" the law, Paul here introduced the historical background of the Hagar-Sarah story by the well-known citation formula, "It is written." Paul frequently used these words when he was about to quote a specific text from the Old Testament.[241] In this instance, however, Paul did not provide a direct quotation but rather a succinct sum-

[241] See E. E. Ellis, *Paul's Use of the Old Testament* (Grand Rapids: Eerdmans, 1957), 48-49, 156-85.

mary of the Genesis narrative concerning the birth of Abraham's two sons. Paul drew on the Old Testament account as recorded in Gen 16– 17; 21. As given in Genesis this story is characterized by dramatic tension, personal poignancy, and fascinating historical detail. Paul did not concentrate on any of these features of the account but rather set forth three basic historical facts that are germane to the figurative meaning he would outline.

THE TWO SONS OF ABRAHAM.   As a matter of fact, Abraham had eight sons, six of them by Keturah (Gen 25:1-2), whom he married after Sarah's death. Paul did not mention Abraham's latter progeny because they were irrelevant to his present purpose. It does not follow, however, that Paul was not interested in giving "an historically accurate account of the Genesis narrative."[242] In retelling events of the past, it is possible to be accurate without being exhaustive. Unlike many contemporary biblical scholars and modern theologians who cavalierly dismiss the factual character and historical basis of many Old Testament events, Paul assumed that what the Bible declares to have happened in space and time really occurred just as the scriptural text indicates.[243] Biblical events that occurred in ages past can possess a meaning larger than their original setting but this does not argue against their historical reality.

The two sons of Abraham Paul was concerned with, of course, were Ishmael and Isaac, though neither of them is named at this point.[244] Ishmael and

---

[242] So Betz, *Galatians,* 241-42.

[243] Even an astute evangelical theologian such as C. H. Pinnock has written: "I do not think we should consider the historical value of the Samson or Elisha stories on the same level with the Exodus and the Resurrection of Jesus. We are not bound to deny the Bible the possibility of playful legend just because the central claim is historical, as if to admit a few mythical elements into the biblical story as a whole would automatically classify the Christian story itself as myth. Unquestionably, Jesus' Resurrection had to happen for the gospel story to be true; but the same does not hold for Elisha's ax head or the fate of Lot's wife. . . . Why is this such a delicate point for some people?" (*Tracking the Maze* [San Francisco: Harper & Row, 1990], 161). I applaud Pinnock's desire to move beyond modernism and fundamentalism to what he calls "a form of postmodern orthodoxy," and I certainly rejoice in his firm affirmation of the historicity of Jesus' resurrection. However, for many other theologians it is no more obvious that Jesus rose from the dead than that Lot's wife became a pillar of salt. For them neither event "had to happen for the gospel story to be true." See G. D. Kaufman, *Systematic Theology: A Historicist Perspective* (New York: Scribners, 1968), 411-34. Kaufman admits that the resurrection was an event of unparalleled importance, providing Christians with an insight into ultimate reality. At the same time, he also declares that "the Resurrection was nothing but (a) a series of hallucinations (b) interpreted by faith as God's act, both dimensions having their locus in the disciples' minds" (p. 426).

[244] Barrett, "Analogy," 161, considers the fact that Paul introduces this Old Testament example without naming any of the four principals as evidence for the prior interpretation of the story by the Judaizers. Likewise, Paul's summary of a rather large quantity of material from the Genesis narrative indicates that he is walking over familiar ground with his readers.

Isaac represent the two lines of descendants that sprang from Abraham. According to Gen 25:13-18, Ishmael begot twelve sons who became the ancestors of the Arab tribes, which occupied the territory "from Havilah to Shur," that is, the desert lands between Egypt and the Euphrates River.[245] In time the descendants of Ishmael became identified with the Gentiles in general, while the sons of Isaac were regarded as "a holy seed," the unique possession of God and cherished above all nations on the face of the earth.[246] Through what later theologians would call common grace, the Ishmaelites too enjoyed the uncovenanted mercies of God; but to the Jews alone belonged the law of Moses, the message of the prophets, and the promise of the Messiah. As the psalmist put it: "[God] has revealed his word to Jacob, his laws and decrees to Israel. He has done this for no other nation" (Ps 147:19-20).

THE STATUS OF THE TWO MOTHERS. Like the two sons, their mothers are not here referred to by name but instead are described with reference to their status. Hagar was an Egyptian slave attached to the household of Abraham whereas Sarah was a free woman, the lawful wife of Abraham. The contrast between freedom and slavery, suggested by the status of the two mothers, would play an important role in Paul's application of the example in the closing verses of this chapter. The natural barrenness of Sarah as opposed to the carnal fertility, if we may put it that way, of Hagar is also an important motif Paul would later use in his application of the prophecy of Isa 54.

THE CIRCUMSTANCES OF THE TWO BIRTHS. Not only did the two sons have different mothers, but they also were born in different ways. The son of the slave woman was born "according to the flesh," that is, by the normal means of human procreation; conversely, the son of the free woman was born "through the promise," that is, in direct fulfillment of God's word to Abraham. Luther correctly observed that the principal difference here was the absence of the word of God in the birth of Ishmael: "When Hagar conceived and gave birth to Ishmael, there was no voice or word of God that predicted this; but with Sarah's permission Abraham went into Hagar the slave, whom Sarah, because she was barren, gave him as his wife as Genesis testifies. . . . Therefore Ishmael was born without the word, solely at the request of Sarah herself. Here there was no word of God that commanded or promised Abraham a son; but everything happened by chance, as Sarah's words indicate: 'It may be,' she says, 'that I shall obtain children by her.'"[247]

---

[245] See F. F. Bruce, "'Abraham Had Two Sons': A Study in Pauline Hermeneutics," in *New Testament Studies: Essays in Honor of Ray Summers,* ed. H. L. Drumwright and C. Vaughan (Waco: Baylor University Press, 1975), 72.

[246] The diverse destinies of the sons of Ishmael and the sons of Isaac are set forth in the Book of Jubilees 16:17-25.

[247] *LW* 26.434-35.

The birth of Ishmael was the result of the outworking of the philosophy that God helps those who help themselves. Both Abraham and Sarah were childless in their old age, and it appeared that they would die that way. So they decided to "help God" fulfill his promise. The result was the birth of Ishmael, who was a source of contention and suffering for the rest of his life. Then fourteen years later God's promise was at last fulfilled in the birth of Isaac, so called because of the laughter, first of unbelief and then of joy, which greeted his birth. Ishmael was Abraham's son by proxy, according to the flesh; Isaac was his son by promise, a living witness to divine grace.

(2) The Figurative Meaning (4:24-27)

²⁴These things may be taken figuratively, for the women represent two covenants. One covenant is from Mount Sinai and bears children who are to be slaves: This is Hagar. ²⁵Now Hagar stands for Mount Sinai in Arabia and corresponds to the present city of Jerusalem, because she is in slavery with her children. ²⁶But the Jerusalem that is above is free, and she is our mother. ²⁷For it is written:

> **"Be glad, O barren woman,**
> **who bears no children;**
> **break forth and cry aloud,**
> **you who have no labor pains;**
> **because more are the children of the desolate woman**
> **than of her who has a husband."**

4:24 We now come to one of the most difficult and controversial words in the entire epistle. Referring to the historical summary he had just given in vv. 22-23, Paul here declared, "These things may be taken figuratively." The word translated "figuratively" in the NIV is a participial form of the verb *allegoreō*, which literally means "to speak in an allegory" or "to interpret allegorically." But what is an allegory? In its root meaning, to speak in an allegory means to "say something else." Allegorical interpretation seeks to discern a hidden meaning in a given story or text, a meaning that may be entirely divorced from the historical referent alluded to in the narrative itself.[248] A good example of an allegory in English literature is John Bunyan's *The Pilgrim's Progress*. This famous story is a Christian fantasy that Bunyan said came to him "under the similitude of a dream" and in which he depicted the various stages of the Christian life through a series of coded characters, events, and places—Pliable, Faithful, Hopeful, Giant Despair, Doubting-Cas-

---

[248] See the excellent study by D. S. Dockery, *Biblical Interpretation: Then and Now* (Grand Rapids: Baker, 1992), 27-41, 75-102. See also the article and literature cited in M. Silva, "Old Testament in Paul," *DPL*, 630-42.

tle, Hill Difficulty, City Beautiful, and so on. Allegorical exegesis was a common form of literary analysis in the Hellenistic world. The ancient stories of Homer had been allegorized by the Greeks just as the Old Testament texts were treated in a similar fashion by Jewish scholars of the diaspora, the most notable of whom was Philo of Alexandria. Significantly, Philo developed an allegorical interpretation of Sarah and Hagar. According to Philo, these two women represented two stages in the development of the mind, the one (Sarah) that reaches for the higher wisdom of philosophy and the other (Hagar) that is relegated to the lower learning of more basic studies.[249] Philo's allegorical methodology was "Christianized" by a school of exegetes based in Alexandria, the most prominent of whom was Origen.[250]

In contrast to allegorical interpretations, typological exegesis "seeks to discover a correspondence between people and events of the past and of the present or future. . . . [It is] based on the conviction that certain events in the history of Israel prefigure a future time when God's purposes will be revealed in their fullness.[251] In other words, a "type" is a kind of prophetic foreshadowing by one historical event of another yet to come. Thus there is a typological, but not an allegorical, correspondence between the brazen serpent Moses erected in the wilderness and the cross on which Jesus was impaled (Num 21:8-9; John 3:14). In the early church typological exegesis was championed by the biblical scholars associated with the school of Antioch who were wary of excessive allegorizing, which they found incompatible with the historical and grammatical meaning of the scriptural text.[252] Thus Chrysostom, who belonged to the Antiochene tradition, believed that Paul in Gal 4:24 had incorrectly described as allegory what was really a type.[253] Clearly Paul was not advocating the evaporation of biblical events or a departure from the basic

---

[249] See Bruce, *Galatians,* 215. On the contrast between Paul and Philo, see H. A. Wolfson, *The Philosophy of the Church Fathers* (Cambridge: Harvard University Press, 1955), 24-43. See also H. Chadwick, "St. Paul and Philo of Alexandria," *BJRL* 48 (1965-66): 286-307.

[250] See, for example, Origen's fascinating and fanciful allegorization of Leviticus in G. W. Barkley, "Origen's Homilies on Leviticus: An Annotated Translation," unpublished Ph.D. diss., The Southern Baptist Theological Seminary (1984). On the Philonic background of Origen's exegesis, see J. W. Trigg, *Origen: The Bible and Philosophy in the Third-Century Church* (Atlanta: John Knox, 1983).

[251] Dockery, *Biblical Interpretation,* 33.

[252] For example, Theodore of Mopsuestia, the greatest exegete of the Antiochene school, insisted that Gal 4:21-31 was grounded on historical fact. This has been lost sight of by the Alexandrian exegetes, he says, because they treat "all the history in the Bible as if it were no different from a succession of dreams in the night. They say that Adam was not Adam . . . and paradise was not paradise, and the snake was not the snake." Cited in Bligh, *Galatians,* 393, n. 39.

[253] NPNF 13.34: "Contrary to usage, he calls a type an allegory; this meaning is as follows; his history not only declares that which appears on the face of it, but announces somewhat farther, whence it is called an allegory."

meaning of Scripture as found in its natural and literal sense. What he here called allegory might be better termed typology: a narrative from Old Testament history interpreted in terms of new covenant realities.[254]

The entire analogy involves five sets of twos: two mothers, two sons, two covenants, two mountains (Mount Sinai versus Mount Zion, the latter being understood, but not expressed), and two cities (the present Jerusalem and the heavenly one). The two mothers, Hagar and Sarah, stand for two covenants, one derived from Mount Sinai and capable of bearing children destined only to be slaves; the other, the covenant of grace sealed in the blood of Christ, the only foundation for real freedom and release from sin and death.

The word "covenant" harks back to 3:15-16 where Paul used it in the primary legal sense of a last will and testament. Here, of course, covenant appears in a much broader and more distinctively theological sense meaning something like "a world order decreed by divine institution" that "contains God's definition of the basis and purpose of human life."[255] The best commentary on this passage is Paul's exposition of the glory of the new covenant in contrast to the fading splendor of the old Mosaic one in 2 Cor 3:7-16. Paul's meaning is clear: those who sought liberation through the Mosaic legislation were doomed to disappointment. The children of Hagar could never become the children of Sarah by observing the stipulations of that covenant, which was ratified at Sinai. And this applied to Jewish "Christians" (such as the Judaizers) and their Gentile followers no less than to unbelieving Jews who rejected Jesus as the Messiah altogether.[256]

4:25 In this verse Paul has extended his analogy further by declaring that Hagar stood for Mount Sinai in Arabia and also was a figure of the present city of Jerusalem, which, like the slave woman and her son Ishmael, suffered under the condition of slavery. It should be noted that some ancient and reliable manuscripts omit the word "Hagar" from this verse.[257] The omission is

---

[254] Bruce, *Galatians,* 217. Bruce does point out one example of a nontypological allegory in Paul. In 1 Cor 9:8-10 he cites the Pentateuchal command not to muzzle an ox when it is treading out the grain (Deut 25:4), which he interprets as an incentive to offer remuneration to those who preach the gospel.

[255] Betz, *Galatians,* 244; Longenecker, *Galatians,* 211. On the concept of διαθήκη see G. Quell and J. Behm, "διατίθημι, διαθήκη," *TDNT* 2.106-34; W. S. Campbell, "Covenant and New Covenant," *DPL,* 179-83.

[256] F. Thielman interprets Paul's comment about Mount Sinai bearing children for slavery as a reference to slavery to sin rather than slavery to the law itself. However, as we have seen, to be ὑπὸ νόμον means "to be subjected to the bondage of the law" that corresponds in Galatians to servitude to the στοιχεῖα τοῦ κόσμου. Still Thielman is correct in his observation that "it is not the law in its every aspect which Paul claims is annulled, but the law in its ability to perpetuate slavery to sin" (*From Plight to Solution,* 84).

[257] See Metzger, *A Textual Commentary,* 596. The twenty-sixth edition of the Nestle-Aland

reflected in the NEB translation of this verse: "Sinai is a mountain in Arabia and it represents the Jerusalem of today." The simplicity of the direct linkage between Sinai and Jerusalem is appealing, but the reference to "she and her children" in the concluding clause argues for the acceptance of the longer, more difficult reading that identifies Hagar with Mount Sinai. Hagar equals Mount Sinai, which corresponded to the present Jerusalem, because just as Hagar and Ishmael were both slaves so also were all those who sought to be made right with God on the basis of the law-observant system centered in Jerusalem in a state of spiritual servitude.

In this case the actual meaning of Paul's typology is more evident than the historical referent that lies behind it. On what basis could Paul equate Hagar with Mount Sinai, and why did he make the seemingly gratuitous allusion to Arabia? After all, Paul was not giving a geography lesson or writing a travel guide for visitors to the Holy Land. Some have pointed to the similarity in sound between the name Hagar and a similar Semitic word meaning "rock" or "crag." It is more likely, however, that Paul was here reflecting a certain geographical orientation acquired during his earlier sojourn in Arabia (cf. 1:17). According to Gen 25 (vv. 6,18), Hagar and Ishmael were expelled to "the land of the East," that is, to the region later known as Arabia. The name Hagar also appears in other Old Testament texts (cf. 1 Cor 5:10,19-20; Ps 83:6) to describe the geographical locality south of the Dead Sea and north of the Arabian peninsula. The word "Hagar" itself is still preserved in the name of the modern city of Chegra, located in what is today the extreme northwestern section of Saudi Arabia. According to certain ancient traditions, the mountain range near this vicinity was believed to be the site of Mount Sinai, where Moses received the law. Assuming that Paul had a certain local familiarity with this region and was cognizant of the popular traditions linking both the expulsion of Hagar and the giving of the law to this particular region, it is not surprising that he would have found a certain typological congruence in the identification of Hagar and Mount Sinai.[258] By emphasizing that Mount Sinai is in Arabia, the land of the Ishmaelites, Paul was preparing his readers for the dramatic reversal he was about to make in the received interpretation of the Sarah-Hagar analogy.

Greek NT prefers the longer reading as more genuine. Fung reviews the textual evidence and outlines various interpretations suggested by the variant readings (*Galatians,* 207-9).

[258] See the discussion in D. Lührmann, *Galatians* (Minneapolis: Fortress, 1992), 90-91. A subsidiary theme, pointed to by some commentators, relates to the fact that Arabia is outside the promised land, signifying that the law was given at a time when the people of Israel were still wandering in the wilderness prior to their entrance into the place of promise.

4:26   Paul concluded the preceding verse by claiming that Hagar/Sinai corresponds to "the present Jerusalem." The word translated "corresponds" in the NIV is *sustoicheō*, a term found nowhere else in the New Testament. It means literally to "stand in the same line" or "place in the same column."[259] Throughout this passage Paul was establishing two columns of implied correspondences and complementary antitheses:

HAGAR	SARAH
Ishmael, the son of slavery	Isaac, the son of freedom
Birth "according to the flesh"	Birth "through the promise"
Old Covenant	New Covenant
Mount Sinai	[Mount Zion]
Present Jerusalem	Heavenly Jerusalem

This lineup would have been very disturbing to any patriotic Jew just as it must have been to the Judaizers of Galatia. Everyone knew that the Jews were the sons of Isaac and the Gentiles were the descendants of Ishmael. Paul, however, had correlated the covenant of Sinai and the present religious system centered at Jerusalem with the offspring of the slave woman. They were those who sought to be justified before God "according to the flesh," that is, by observing the works of the law. Conversely, the children of the free woman were those who had embraced the promise of salvation through faith in Jesus Christ alone. They were the children of the covenant of grace. For Paul, it was completely irrelevant to their identification as the offspring of Sarah whether or not people were circumcised, of Jewish birth or Gentile background. No doubt much of the opposition that was mounted by the Judaizers related to the fact that the renewed people of God, the church of Jesus Christ, which began on the Day of Pentecost as an exclusively Jewish enclave, was coming increasingly to include a preponderance of Gentiles, many of them won to Christ through the efforts of Paul and his coworkers. Although the Judaizers may not have seen it in this light, efforts to make circumcision and observance of the law an entrance rite into the Christian faith was nothing less than a futile attempt to reverse the divinely ordained course of redemptive history.[260]

Paul mingled temporal and spatial imagery in contrasting the "present city

---

[259] This word is related etymologically to τα στοιχεῖα τοῦ κόσμου, a term Paul introduced earlier in the letter. See G. Delling, "συστοιχεω," *TDNT* 7.669; Burton, *Galatians,* 261-62.

[260] Betz reproduces H. Lietzmann's correlation of Paul's corresponding antitheses (*Galatians,* 245). See H. Lietzmann, *An die Galater* (Tübingen: Mohr, 1971), 253. For criticism of this reconstruction, see C. H. Cosgrove, "The Law Has Given Sarah No Children," *NovT* 29 (1987): 219-35.

of Jerusalem" with the "Jerusalem that is above." The concept of the heavenly Jerusalem, or the New Jerusalem, is deeply rooted in the Jewish apocalyptic tradition that forms the background of Paul's entire theological outlook. After the Babylonians had destroyed the first temple in 586 B.C., the prophet Ezekiel envisioned the building of a new temple on a grand scale in the renovated city of Jerusalem (cf. Ezek 40–48). The New Testament also looks forward to the coming age in which the New Jerusalem will come down out of heaven from God, "prepared as a bride beautifully dressed for her husband" (Rev 21:2). By contrasting the present Jerusalem with the one that is above, Paul here indicated that Christians have entered the last days. Even though they participate fully in the "groanings" of the fallen creation about them, they are really citizens of another commonwealth from which they await in hope the coming Lord of glory (Phil 3:21). As the writer of Hebrews said of faithful Abraham, "For he was looking forward to the city with foundations, whose architect and builder is God" (Heb 11:10).

The "Jerusalem that is above" is "our mother," Paul said, drawing perhaps on the statement of 4 Ezra 10:7, where Zion is called "the mother of us all."[261] The heavenly Jerusalem is the counterpart of Sarah, the freeborn wife of Abraham, just as the earthly, temporal Jerusalem corresponds to Hagar the bond woman. When Paul wrote these words to the churches of Galatia, the "present . . . Jerusalem" was indeed a city of servitude, held in bondage by the Roman occupation forces. In A.D. 70, just a few years after Paul's own death, the city of Jerusalem and its temple would be completely destroyed and the Jewish people deprived of a national identity for nearly two thousand years. Paul, however, looked beyond the transience of this present age toward the eschatological renewal God had promised for his people.

The dawn of God's new creation has broken already, and true believers share now in the "powers of the age to come." The advent of Christ and the coming of his Spirit have inaugurated the "last days." However, we must not collapse the future restoration God has promised into some kind of ethereal, realized eschatology. The heavenly Jerusalem is still *above;* it has not yet descended to earth. Only as we look forward in prayerful expectancy to the consummation of God's plan for the ages are we enabled to take our places on the front lines of the cosmic battle raging all around us in this "present evil age" (1:3). Paul reminded the Galatians that their true spiritual identity was to be found above, not below, forward, not behind, precisely because he knew

---

[261] In Ezra's vision the new, heavenly Jerusalem is compared to a mourning mother whose sorrow gives way to joy in the eschatological deliverance God brings to pass: "And I looked, and behold, the woman was no longer visible to me, but there was an established city, and a place of huge foundations showed itself (4 Ezra 10:27)" (see Thielman, *From Plight to Solution,* 84-86).

that believers who find their spiritual genesis in the old world are "like a company of soldiers who are armed with the wrong weapons, and who are fighting on the wrong front."[262]

4:27 Again Paul used the standard formula "It is written" to introduce a scriptural quotation, this one from Isa 54:1. This famous passage of Scripture likens the city of Jerusalem to a barren widow sitting at the gates of Jerusalem. She is covered in sackcloth and ashes because her husband has been carried away into captivity and she has no children to care for her in her old age. In the midst of this desperate situation, the voice of God breaks in: "Be happy, you childless woman! Shout and cry with joy, you who never felt the pains of childbirth! For the woman who was deserted will have more children than the woman whose children never left her."

How did Paul apply this famous text to the situation in Galatia? Several lines of interpretation have been put forth in response to this question. (1) Although the prophet Isaiah made no explicit reference to the Genesis narrative, the word "barren" suggests a possible linkage to the Sarah motif. Just as Sarah, who was formerly barren and childless, broke into hilarious laughter and shouts of joy at the birth of Isaac, so Christians have reason to rejoice because they are the true children of Abraham through faith in the one who was the antitype of Isaac, Jesus the Messiah. (2) The experience of the Christians to whom Paul wrote seemed to conform to the sullen image painted by Isaiah: a barren widow, bereft of her husband, with no offspring to give hope or cheer. Yet the prophet called for rejoicing, not lamentation; for celebration, not sorrow. The promise is this: God is about to restore the church, and his work will be extraordinary and wonderful. Many have seen this as a reference to the ingathering of Gentile believers through the worldwide missionary labors of the apostle Paul. The time would come when the children of the formerly barren woman, Sarah, that is, the Christian church, would outnumber the progeny of the one who was formerly so productive, Hagar, that is, Judaism. (3) A variation on the preceding view places the contrast not so much between Christianity and Judaism as between Paul's mission to the Gentiles and the competing activity of his Judaizing rivals.[263] (4) C. H. Cosgrove has pushed the analogy with Sarah even further, noting that, typologically, Sarah remained barren throughout history until the coming of her child, that is, Christ, the true "Seed" of Abraham, through whom many other children have been begotten. Thus, "if Isa 51:1, in speaking of Sarah-Jerusalem, implies that

[262] J. L. Martyn, "Apocalyptic Antinomies in Paul's Letter to the Galatians," *NTS* 31 (1985): 421.
[263] See J. L. Martyn, "A Law-Observant Mission: The Background of Galatians," *MQR* 22 (1983): 221-36.

her barrenness extends until the eschatological time of fulfillment, *then the law has given Sarah no children.* And with this point Paul reinforces in the strongest possible terms the repeated accent in Galatians that *life* (the Spirit, the realization of the promise, access to the inheritance, the blessing of Abraham) is not to be found in the Torah."[264]

Whatever the precise nuance intended by Paul in his citation of this Old Testament text, the burden of his message is clear. The great reversal envisaged by Isaiah—from barrenness to fruitfulness, from despair to joy, from desolation to blessing—can only be accomplished by the unilateral intervention of God himself. How dare anyone say to a person in such dire straits as the woman in this example that she should sing, rejoice, and shout for joy! The words ring hollow until we realize that it was the Lord himself who spoke thus to her. How could she not be afraid or fear disgrace when there was so much against her? Later in the same chapter (Isa 54:5) God himself provided the answer: "For your Maker is your husband—the Lord Almighty is his name—the Holy One of Israel is your Redeemer; he is called the God of all the earth." Again, Paul was pointing to God's gracious sovereignty and infinite love that is the foundation of our justification, freedom, and hope.

(3) The Personal Application (4:28-31)

28Now you, brothers, like Isaac, are children of promise. 29At that time the son born in the ordinary way persecuted the son born by the power of the Spirit. It is the same now. 30But what does the Scripture say? "Get rid of the slave woman and her son, for the slave woman's son will never share in the inheritance with the free woman's son." 31Therefore, brothers, we are not children of the slave woman, but of the free woman.

4:28-29 Paul here pointedly applied the analogy he had been developing to his readers, calling them again my "brothers," an indication of the common ties that linked them together in the family of faith. Paul had set forth his biblical argument, and now he drove it home with respect to the Galatians themselves. "You [emphatic] are the children of promise just as Isaac was." This is the only time in Galatians where Isaac is mentioned by name. Earlier in Paul's analogy he was referred to as the son of the free woman (4:22). Here Paul told the Galatians that they were "like Isaac" (*kata Isaak*, "after the order of Isaac") because they too had been born into Abraham's (and God's) family "as the result of a promise" (v. 23) and not by virtue of their biological lineage or human efforts. Against the claims of the Judaizers that the Gentile Christians were by nature Ishmaelites who could only become a part of the family

---

[264] Cosgrove, "The Law Has Given Sarah No Children," 231.

of Abraham through circumcision, Paul stressed the present reality of the salvation they had received. You are (by faith) *already* like Isaac, not Ishmael. Your connection to Abraham is not physical but spiritual. Your merit contributes nothing to your salvation, which is God's free gift.

Having just restated the central thesis of his letter in terms of the typology he had developed, Paul now spelled out the practical consequences of the believers' identification with Isaac. There was a negative correspondence between the two sons of Abraham in ancient times and their counterparts today. Just as Ishmael persecuted Isaac back then, so it is the same now. The polarities of flesh and promise in v. 23 are here transposed into the dualism of flesh and spirit, a pair of opposites Paul would exploit further in Gal 5–6. At this point, however, he was concerned not with the warring of two contradictory principles within the believer but rather with outward conflict between two types of people.

Most scholars believe that Paul was drawing on Jewish rabbinical traditions which attributed to Ishmael idolatry, wickedness, and overt hostility toward his younger brother Isaac.[265] The only biblical basis for this tradition stems from the statement in Gen 21:9 that Sarah saw Ishmael "playing with her son Isaac" during the festivities surrounding the weaning of the younger boy. The KJV gives a more sinister translation to Ishmael's activity, "Sarah saw the son of Hagar the Egyptian . . . mocking." Later traditions identified Ishmael's behavior as sexual immorality, the worship of false gods, and murderous sporting activities directed against his brother after the pattern of Cain and Abel.[266] However much Paul may have been influenced by these rabbinic interpretations, he clearly saw a corresponding historical parallel between the mistreatment of Isaac by Ishmael and the persecution being inflicted on Christians in his day.

Nowhere are Christians commanded to seek persecution or to cultivate a lust for martyrdom. Yet believers who are faithful to the gospel have no reason to believe that they will be exempted from such assaults. Jesus died on a rugged cross at thirty-three, not in a retirement center surrounded by the amenities of family and friends. Paul was hounded from one end of the Roman Empire to the other only to finish his course before an executioner's sword. Lest we be tempted to think that martyrdom was a possibility for Christians only in the days of the apostles, it is well to remember that literally thousands of believers are still executed every year because of their commit-

---

[265] Longenecker bring together a number of citations from Jewish writers who developed a stronger contrast between Isaac and Ishmael than is found in the text of the OT. See his helpful excursus, "The Hagar-Sarah Story in Jewish Writings and in Paul," in *Galatians,* 200-206.

[266] For example, one tradition interprets Ishmael's persecution of Isaac as his "shooting deadly arrows at him" during a presumed hunt for birds (ibid., 202).

ment to Jesus Christ.[267] Luther's comment on this text is very much to the point: "As soon as the word of God appears, the devil becomes angry; and in his anger he employs every power and wile to persecute it and wipe it out completely. Therefore it cannot be otherwise than that he should stir up endless sects and offenses, persecution and slaughter, for he is the father of lies and a murderer (John 8:44); he plants his lies in the world through false teachers, and he murders men through tyrants. . . . If someone does not want to endure persecution from Ishmael, let him not claim that he is Christian."[268]

4:30 This verse contains the punch line of the entire Hagar-Sarah analogy Paul had been working with since v. 21. Quoting again from the Genesis narrative (21:10), he adapted the words of Sarah concerning Ishmael to the conflicted situation in Galatia. "Cast out the slave woman and her son!" Paul was calling on his erstwhile disciples to free themselves from the grip of the Judaizers and to expel them from their midst. If C. K. Barrett's analysis of this passage is correct, then very likely Paul was here casting back in the teeth of his opponents the very same directive they had previously issued against him. This grim imperative, "Cast out!" raises the issue of the limits of tolerable diversity within the Christian community. It is clear from Paul's Corinthian correspondence that he was quite willing to tolerate considerable divergences of opinion and even irregularities in order to preserve unfractured the unity of the church. But the false teachers of Galatia had transgressed those bounds. What they were advocating was a denial of the gospel itself. When this kind of heresy invades the church, there can be no question of compromise or concessions for the sake of a superficial harmony. Thus as F. F. Bruce has put it, "Whatever moral or legal problems may have been raised by Sarah's demand in its historical setting, in Paul's application it becomes the statement of a basic gospel truth: legal bondage and gospel freedom cannot coexist."[269]

---

[267] See D. Barrett and T. Johnson, *Our Globe and How to Reach It* (Birmingham: New Hope, 1990), 62-63.

[268] *LW* 26.455, 451.

[269] Bruce, "Abraham Had Two Sons," 79. Longenecker rightly notes that Paul's directive in this verse is not "a broadside against all Jews or Judaism in general" (*Galatians*, 217). Paul was not advising the Christians of Galatia on how they should relate to unbelieving Jews; instead he was exhorting them to guard the spiritual integrity and doctrinal purity of their own congregations. Too often throughout the history of the church verses such as this have been wrenched out of context and used as a pretext for anti-Semitic sentiment and overt persecution of the Jewish people by Christians. Such tragic misinterpretations can only be deplored in light of Paul's own consuming passion for his kinsmen after the flesh: "Brothers, my heart's desire and prayer to God for the Israelites is that they may be saved" (Rom 10:1). No Gentile Christian who has truly grasped what Paul meant by grace will have any reason to boast or feel superior to the Jews. See K. Stendahl, "Judaism and Christianity I: Then and Now," in *Meanings: The Bible as Document and as Guide* (Philadelphia: Fortress, 1984), 213.

SUMMARY. **4:31**   This verse stands as a summary and conclusion not only of the Hagar-Sarah analogy but also of the entire theological argument Paul had developed from 3:1–4:30. The shift in pronouns from the second person plural *you* of v. 28 to the first person plural *we* signifies Paul's desire to identify himself with the Galatians whom he again addressed as "my brothers." This verse provides an answer to the central question of Gal 3–4: Who are the true members of the family of Abraham? Somehow the Galatians had become confused, "bewitched," about their own spiritual identity despite the fact that the Spirit had been abundantly poured out upon them when they were first converted to Christ (3:1-5). The false teachers who had led them astray were prolific Bible quoters and thus Paul announced a series of scriptural arguments in order to counter their heretical views.

He first pointed the Galatians back to Abraham, who was declared righteous before God by faith alone (3:6-9). Next he demonstrated by means of a long parenthesis the primary purpose and true function of the law (3:10-25). What was true of the Jews was no less true of the Gentiles, although their servitude was expressed as bondage to the elemental spirits rather than to the Mosaic covenant (3:26–4:11). On the basis of his personal love and intimacy toward them, Paul pleaded with the Galatians to "become like him" in their reliance on God's grace as the only basis for their salvation (4:12-20). Finally, he developed the analogy of Hagar and Sarah, doubtless an example familiar to the Galatians from the use already made of it by the false teachers. He had set forth two parallel lists of complementary items derived from this famous passage in Genesis. Sarah-Isaac-the New Covenant-Mount Zion-Jerusalem Above stand together over against Hagar-Ishmael-the Old Covenant-Mount Sinai-Jerusalem that Now Is. Paul's inversion of the traditional interpretation of the analogy shows that the true descendants of Isaac are those who are justified by grace through faith on the basis of God's unfailing promise, while the offspring of Ishmael are those, like the Judaizers, who seek to justify themselves "according to the flesh" (vv. 23,29, RSV).

There is a mutual incompatibility between these two systems of salvation, and thus Paul brought his entire theological argument to a climactic conclusion with an imperative command, "Get rid of the slave woman and her son!" (v. 30). With the concepts of slavery and freedom firmly fixed in the vocabulary of the Galatians, Paul was now ready to move on to the third major section of his letter in which he would set forth the goal of the gospel as God intended for it to be realized in the Spirit-controlled lives of the Galatian believers.

III. ETHICS: LIFE IN THE SPIRIT (5:1–6:18)

Commentators on Galatians historically have generally recognized that this Pauline letter contains three major sections of roughly two chapters each.[1] The three major divisions of Galatians are dubbed by various names: personal, doctrinal, hortatory; autobiographical, scriptural, exhortational, or, more expansively, the truth of the gospel, the children of the promise, and living by the Spirit. Following C. K. Barrett, I have called them simply history, theology, and ethics.[2] We have seen rather clearly how Gal 1–2 is related to Gal 3–4. Paul's apostolic calling and his doctrinal message were both under severe attack by the agitators in Galatia. Thus it was necessary for him to set the record straight, to rehearse the historical events related to his missionary labors, in order to secure a proper foundation for his theological exposition. But what is the relationship between the first two sections of Galatians and the final one in chaps. 5 and 6? Let us review several major theories that have been put forth in response to this question.[3]

At least one scholar, J. C. O'Neill, has claimed that a major part of the whole section (5:13–6:10) was an interpolation by a later editor of a disconnected collection of ethical instructions.[4] M. Dibelius, while not denying Pauline authorship, regarded Gal 5–6 as a form of epistolary parenesis that he defined as "a series of different and often unconnected exhortations with a common address."[5] The genre of parenesis, as Dibelius defined it, included general moral maxims and traditional listings of virtues and vices along with various ethical admonitions derived from certain philosophical schools of thought. On the whole Dibelius concluded that most of the material in Gal 5–6 had little connection either with the crisis that prompted Paul to write this

[1] I say roughly because many commentators place the beginning of the third section at 5:13, where the actual moral exhortation begins, rather than at 5:1. So R. N. Longenecker, *Galatians,* WBC (Dallas: Word, 1990), 235-37, and R. Y. K. Fung, *Galatians,* NICNT (Grand Rapids: Eerdmans, 1988), 221-42. Lightfoot, Burton, and Betz, among others, opt for 5:1 as the more natural beginning point of the final major section of the letter.
[2] C. K. Barrett, *Freedom and Obligation* (Philadelphia: Westminster, 1985), 3.
[3] I follow here the review of literature given by J. M. G. Barclay, *Obeying the Truth: A Study of Paul's Ethics in Galatians* (Edinburgh: T & T Clark, 1988), 9-26. See also C. Cousar, *Galatians,* IBC (Atlanta: John Knox, 1982), 121-25.
[4] "I can find nothing specifically Pauline in the collection, and nothing that would have had specific bearing on the situation facing the Galatians" (J. C. O'Neill, *The Recovery of Paul's Letter to the Galatians* [London: SPCK, 1972], 71). Barclay's quotation of the following comment by G. B. Caird is very much to the point: "The application of surgery to a biblical text is more often than not an admission on the part of the surgeon that he has failed to comprehend it as it stands" (quoted in Barclay, *Obeying the Truth,* 10, n. 26).
[5] See M. Dibelius, *Geschichte der urchristlichen Literatur* (Munich: Kaiser, 1975), 140. On parenesis as a standard feature in Paul's letters, see H. D. Betz, *Galatians,* Her (Philadelphia: Fortress, 1979), 253-55, and V. P. Furnish, *Theology and Ethics in Paul* (Nashville: Abingdon, 1968), especially chap. 2. W. G. Doty has argued that Paul's ethical teaching materials betray the influence of the Jewish sermonic tradition that was "always aimed at practical-paraenetic goals" (*Letters in Primitive Christianity,* 38).

letter or with the theological exposition he developed in the central section of the epistle.

A third major approach to this issue takes seriously the change of style and tone as well as content between the first four and the last two chapters of Galatians. To account for this apparent dichotomy, J. H. Ropes developed the "two-front theory" of Pauline opposition in Galatia (see p. 50). On this view Gal 3–4, the argument for justification by faith, was directed against Judaizing legalists who were trying to impose the law of Moses on Paul's Gentile converts. However, another set of opponents, spiritualists or libertines, exploited the evangelical freedom of the Galatian believers by encouraging them to throw off all moral restraints, resulting in a life of utter laxity and licentiousness. To counter these dangerous teachers, Paul drafted the ethical instructions found in the last two chapters of the letter.[6] Another novel solution has been propounded by W. Schmithals, who suggested that the heretics in Galatia were a group of Jewish-Christian Gnostics who practiced circumcision but were devoted to a libertine lifestyle (see p. 54).[7]

None of these theories, however, adequately explains the connection between Gal 5–6 and the earlier part of the letter. Still less convincing is the proposal of J. Bligh, who begins his exposition of this section of Galatians with these words:

> In the third main division, St. Paul turns his attention from the initial justification of the sinner by faith and baptism towards his final justification and admission to the Kingdom of God. The message of these last two chapters is that entry into the promised inheritance does not depend on faith alone but on works rendered possible by the Spirit of Christ given to believers in and through their faith.[8]

Yet this was precisely the doctrine Paul had labored so hard to counteract in the preceding two chapters. The Judaizers did not deny that the Spirit helped Christians do good works. Their point was that such works, notably circumcision and other requirements of the Jewish law, were necessary salvific supplements to simple faith in Christ. Nowhere did Paul distinguish "initial" and "final" justification. However well intentioned, this kind of soteriology inevitably tends toward a Pelagian doctrine of self-achieved salvation.

What Paul did in the closing chapters of Galatians was to draw out the implications of the doctrine of justification by faith alone and to describe

---

[6] J. H. Ropes, *The Singular Problem of the Epistle to the Galatians* (Cambridge: Harvard University Press, 1929).

[7] W. Schmithals, *Paul and the Gnostics* (Nashville: Abingdon, 1972), 13-64.

[8] Bligh, *Galatians*, 411.

what it meant for the believer who had "died to the law" now to "live for God" (2:19). The energizing principle of Christian ethics, then, is union with Christ and life in the Spirit. Justification by faith is not a morally barren doctrine. We are justified by faith, a faith that is active in love leading to holiness. Justification is the presupposition of the Christian life. As Luther put it so well: "Having been justified by grace, we then do good works, yes, Christ himself does all in us."[9]

1. Freedom in Christ (5:1-12)

(1) Stand Firm in Freedom (5:1)

> [1]It is for freedom that Christ has set us free. Stand firm, then, and do not let yourselves be burdened again by a yoke of slavery.

5:1   If Galatians is the Magna Carta of Christian liberty, then Gal 5:1 has reason to be considered one of the key verses of the epistle. With the language of freedom and slavery still ringing in their ears from the analogy of Hagar and Sarah, the Galatians are now told by Paul: "Plant your feet firmly therefore within the freedom that Christ has won for us, and do not let yourselves be caught again in the shackles of slavery" (Phillips).[10] This verse contains both an assertion, "For freedom . . . Christ has set us free," and a command based upon it, "Stand firm, then, and do not let yourselves be burdened again by a yoke of slavery."

The juxtaposition of an indicative followed by an imperative is a common grammatical feature in Paul's writings, as we see in the repetition of this pattern in 5:13. The imperative, "Stand firm," not only does not contradict the indicative, "Christ has set us free," but in fact results from it. Because of who God is and what he has done for believers in Jesus Christ, Christians are commanded to "become what they are," that is, to make visible in the earthly realm of their human existence what God has already declared and sealed in the divine verdict of justification. When this indissoluble connection is forgotten or downplayed, the temptation for the Christian to lapse into legalism on the one hand or into libertinism on the other

---

[9] *LW* 34.111. See the excellent exposition of this theme in P. Althaus, *The Ethics of Martin Luther* (Philadelphia: Fortress, 1972), 3-24.

[10] Many recent commentators, e.g., Bruce, Fung, Cole, follow Lightfoot in treating 5:1 as the proper conclusion to the Hagar-Sarah analogy rather than as the introduction to a new unit of material. It certainly provides a facile link to the preceding pericope; but, as Longenecker has noted, the lack of a transitional phrase or particle, together with the prominent placement of the watchword ἐλευθερία, suggests that this verse properly marks a new beginning in the epistle (*Galatians*, 223-24).

becomes a serious threat to Christian freedom.

The structure of the indicative/imperative formula in Paul also relates to the salvation-historical situation of the believer who must live out the Christian life in the eschatological tension between the No Longer and the Not Yet of this "present evil age" (1:4). We have seen Paul struggling with this tension throughout Galatians, and it continues to shape his ethical instructions in Gal 5–6. As W. Grundmann has put it: "The Christian stands in the tension of a double reality. Basically freed from sin, redeemed, and reconciled . . . he is actually at war with sin, threatened, attacked and placed in jeopardy by it."[11] The fact of justification propels the Christian into a world of struggle, an in-between time bounded by the great accomplishment of redemption in Christ's finished work on the cross on the one hand and the yet-to-be-realized consummation of God's salvific purposes at the second advent of Christ on the other. In this real world of struggle and temptation, the sham gods of this present evil world, *ta stoicheia tou kosmou*, war against the people of God, ever seeking to subject them "again" (*palin*) to the yoke of bondage.

By the power of the Holy Spirit, however, Christian believers are enabled to "stand firm" against the encroachment of such demonic forces. The indicative of their Christ-won freedom secures the imperative of their Spirit-led obedience and victory. In the words of Herman Ridderbos, "Indicative and imperative are both the object of faith, on the one hand in its receptivity, on the other in its activity. . . . The indicative represents the 'already' as well as the 'not yet.' The imperative is likewise focused on the one as well as the other."[12] On the basis of the No Longer, Paul could say to believers that all things are theirs, and they are Christ's, and Christ is God's (1 Cor 3:22-23). On the basis of the Not Yet, he could command, forbid, warn, and even threaten, as he did here in Gal 5–6. The object of Paul's ethical exhortations, then, is not a final justification, as if the first application did not quite take, but rather the Christians' growth in grace, their call to holiness, sanctification, and new life in Christ.[13]

Christian freedom is the precious birthright of every believer, "An inestimable blessing," Calvin called it, "for which we should fight even to the death. For we are not talking here about our hearths but about our altars."[14] Yet no word in the Christian vocabulary has been more misunderstood or

---

[11] W. Grundmann, "ἁμαρτάνω," *TDNT* 1.313. Grundmann also describes the believer's status in Christ as "sinless." However, as R. Fung has noted, this statement can only be applied to one's positional sanctification in Christ (*Galatians,* 283, n. 24). See 1 John 3:4-6.

[12] H. Ridderbos, *Paul,* 256-58.

[13] See R. Bultmann, *Theology,* 330-52; J. K. Chamblin, "Freedom/Liberty," *DPL,* 313-16; Barrett, *Freedom and Obligation, passim.*

[14] J. Calvin, CNTC 11.92.

abused than this one. What did Paul mean by *freedom?* First, he was not talking about political freedom. However much we Americans may believe on the basis of natural law that God has endowed all persons with certain inalienable rights, including that of political liberty, Paul provided no basis for the kind of philosophy articulated in our Declaration of Independence. Still less was Paul referring to freedom in a psychological sense. Emotional health is a desirable goal, and certain therapeutic techniques developed in the modern world may be quite compatible with New Testament Christianity. However, Christian freedom is not "an innate quality or state of being which the individual discovers (or recovers) by sorting out past experiences and relationships. It is a gift bestowed as a result of Good Friday and Easter."[15] Finally, Paul did not understand by Christian freedom the right to advocate theological anarchy within the confines of the believing community. A church that is unable to define and maintain the doctrinal boundaries of its own fellowship or, even worse, that no longer thinks this is a task worth doing, is a church that has lost its soul. The proclamation of the whole counsel of God involves identifying and saying no to those forms of teaching that, if carried out consistently, would threaten the truth of divine revelation itself.[16] This is one of the most serious issues facing the contemporary church today. We can err either by drawing the boundaries too tightly or by refusing to draw them at all. On the one hand, we lapse into legalism; on the other, into relativism.

We will not go astray if we remember that for Paul, Christian liberty was always grounded on the believer's relationship with Jesus Christ on the one hand and with the community of faith on the other. Outside of Jesus Christ, human existence is characterized as bondage—bondage to the law, bondage to the evil elements dominating the world, bondage to sin, the flesh, and the devil. God sent his Son into the world to shatter the dominion of these slaveholders. Now God has sent his Spirit into the hearts of believers to awaken them to new life and liberation in Christ.

When the Galatians first received the Spirit of God, they also received the gift of freedom, as Paul made clear in 2 Cor 3:17, "The Lord is the Spirit; and where the Spirit of the Lord is, there is freedom." When Paul listed the various graces included in the "fruit of the Spirit" (5:22-23), freedom was not included among these desirable virtues. This is because freedom is already presupposed in each one of them. Thus the fruit of the Spirit *is* freedom—

---

[15] Cousar, *Galatians,* 109.

[16] See T. George, "The Priesthood of All Believers and the Quest for Theological Integrity," in P. Basden and D. S. Dockery, eds., *The People of God: Essays on the Believers' Church* (Nashville: Broadman, 1991), 85-95.

freedom to love, to exude joy, to manifest peace, to display patience, and so on. It is *for freedom* that Christ has set us free. This means that Christian liberty is freedom for others, freedom that finds its true expression not in theological privatism ("I am free to believe anything I choose") or spiritual narcissism ("I am free to be myself no matter what") but rather freedom to love and serve one another in the context of the body of Christ.

Evidently one of the major problems among the churches of Galatia was that believers there did not know what to do with their Christ-won freedom. Some were using their liberty as a pretext for license, to the gratification of their sinful nature. Others were "Lone-Ranger" Christians, having forgotten the mandate to bear one another's burdens. Still others had fallen into discord and faction, backbiting and self-promotion. Thus in these closing two chapters Paul summoned the Galatians to a mature use of their spiritual birthright, reminding them that it is love, the love of Christ shed abroad in their hearts by the Holy Spirit, that brings liberty to its fullest expression.

(2) Falling from Grace (5:2-6)

[2]Mark my words! I, Paul, tell you that if you let yourselves be circumcised, Christ will be of no value to you at all. [3]Again I declare to every man who lets himself be circumcised that he is obligated to obey the whole law. [4]You who are trying to be justified by law have been alienated from Christ; you have fallen away from grace. [5]But by faith we eagerly await through the Spirit the righteousness for which we hope. [6]For in Christ Jesus neither circumcision nor uncircumcision has any value. The only thing that counts is faith expressing itself through love.

5:2 Having just instructed the Galatian believers a few verses earlier to expel the Judaizing false teachers, Paul now launched into a sustained harangue against the serious threat posed by these agitators. The passage ends with a bang in v. 12, where Paul expressed his wish that these trouble-makers go off and have themselves castrated. Doubtless this is one of the most strident passages in the entire letter, echoing the either/or language of Paul's opening blast in 1:6-9. The very way Paul introduced this section underscores the importance of what he was going to say. "Look! Listen! Mark my words! I, Paul, tell you." Paul was accenting his personal apostolic authority. He was putting himself on the line in this dramatic appeal to the Galatians. "I, Paul," not all the brothers who are with me (1:2), not even "I along with Barnabas" (whose defection at Antioch may still have been an embarrassment when Paul wrote these words), but I Paul, I myself, am telling you this. Paul was admonishing the Galatians to get the wax out of their ears, to sit up and listen well to what he was going to say.

Now for the first time in the letter the issue of circumcision is specifically mentioned with reference to the Galatians. Actually it had been in the background of Paul's polemic against the Judaizers all along. In chap. 2 Paul reminded the Galatians of his successful resistance against the efforts of certain "false brothers" to have the Gentile Titus circumcised during their visit to Jerusalem. Similarly, those who belonged to "the circumcision group" had provoked the incident which led to Paul's confrontation with Peter at Antioch. However, only here in chap. 5 does Paul engage the issue head on in terms of the crisis in Galatia. Now we know for sure what must have been perfectly clear to the original readers of the epistle all along, namely, that the Galatian agitators were demanding that Paul's converts should get circumcised.

According to Acts 15:1-2, the Judaizers believed that acceptance of this ancient Jewish ritual was absolutely necessary for salvation and incorporation into the people of God. But why should Paul's converts in Galatia have cared about that? Various answers have been given to this question. Some have suggested that circumcision was being touted as a kind of sacramental initiation rite similar to the initiatory rituals some of the Galatian Gentiles would have experienced in their pre-Christian devotion to the Hellenistic mystery religions. Others have suggested that circumcision may have been presented to the Galatians in a quasi-Gnostic sense as providing the key to perfection and spiritual advancement in the Christian life.[17]

J. Barclay has set forth another plausible theory concerning the willingness of the Galatians to entertain the appeal for circumcision. As Christian converts the Galatians would, of course, have broken all ties with the cult of the pagan deities to which they formerly had been devoted. Yet more was involved than a change in religion; conversion to Christ implied what A. D. Nock characterized as "the ever present loss of social amenities, club life and festivals."[18] Becoming a Christian involved the disruption of the whole pattern of one's life, including business relationships, social connections, and civic loyalties. Christians were frequently regarded as anarchists because they would not pay tribute to local urban deities. Into this situation of loss and social dislocation came the Judaizers offering a gospel of circumcision that would have at least put the Gentile Christians on a social par with adherents to the synagogue. By assuming the status of proselytes, then, the Gala-

---

[17] See W. Schmithals, *Paul and the Gnostics,* 38. See also N. J. McEleney, "Conversion, Circumcision and the Law," *NTS* 20 (1973-74): 319-41. Barclay has surveyed a number of proposals concerning the demand for circumcision made by Paul's Galatian opponents (*Obeying,* 45-60).

[18] A. D. Nock, *Conversion: The Old and New in Religion from Alexander the Great to Augustine of Hippo* (Oxford: Oxford University Press, 1933), 156.

tians could hope "to identify themselves with the local synagogues and thus hold at least a more understandable and recognizable place in society."[19] Beyond all of this, the Judaizers certainly had a theological rationale for their insistence upon circumcision, one based upon the LXX, to which Paul also appealed in his refutation of their ideas.

The conditional clause, "if you let yourselves be circumcised," uses a Greek construction indicating that when Paul wrote these words the Galatians had not yet taken this fatal step toward apostasy. Should they do so, however, he insisted that the consequences would be irretrievably dire: "Christ will be of no value to you at all." The issue, of course, was not circumcision per se but what circumcision represented. As Paul explained in v. 6, to be circumcised or not was neither here nor there. He himself was a circumcised Jew and rejected outright the efforts of certain Hellenizing males who reversed surgically the effects of circumcision through the procedure of *epispasm*.[20] On one occasion he himself had Timothy, whose mother was Jewish, circumcised in order to better facilitate his missionary work among the Jews. Yet Paul drew a line in the sand at the Judaizers' insistence that circumcision is necessary for salvation.

For the Galatians to accept this heretical theology and the practice derived from it would mean that they had rejected God's all-sufficient provision for salvation through faith in Jesus Christ and his finished work on the cross. This would be equivalent to their assuming "again" (*palin,* v. 1) the old yoke of bondage. In Gal 3–4 Paul drew a parallel between Jewish servitude under the Mosaic law and Gentile slavery to evil elements of the world. The same analogy still applies in the present context. For the Galatians to reject the cross of Christ by going "forward" into Judaism by accepting circumcision as a means of salvation would be the same as their sliding "backwards" into the paganism of their former life. For Paul, Jesus Christ was all or nothing. If you reject him now, he warned the Galatians, then he will be (future tense) of no use to you at all on the Day of Judgment.[21]

5:3 Paul now amplified what he had just said concerning the consequences of the Galatians' acceptance of circumcision. Not only would they lose Christ and all his benefits but they also would gain an intolerable burden

---

[19] Barclay, *Obeying the Truth,* 60.

[20] This practice is referred to with great contempt in 1 Macc 1:15. Circumcision was generally regarded with disdain in the Greco-Roman World and was later banned by the Emperor Hadrian.

[21] Longenecker denies that ὠφελήσει has any reference to the future eschaton, referring instead to the present alienation from Christ that a rejection of his redemptive work would imply (*Galatians,* 226). Betz (*Galatians,* 258-59), however, sees here a reference to the Parousia and Last Judgment. Cf. Rom 2:25-27.

they would not be able to bear. This was true because receiving the Jewish ritual of circumcision carried with it a further all-encompassing obligation: the necessity of observing the law in its every precept. This same point was made by Paul earlier in Gal 3:10 where he interpreted Deut 27:26 to mean that the curse of the law had fallen upon everyone since no one had been able "to do everything written in the Book of the Law."

Paul seems to have been apprising the Galatians of an implication of the position toward which they were drifting, one that had not been made clear to them by the appeals of the false teachers. It may be, as E. P. Sanders has suggested, that Paul's opponents had deliberately adopted "a policy of gradualism," introducing first Jewish calendar observances as a preliminary step toward circumcision with the idea that this decisive act would initiate the Galatians into a fuller observance of the law.[22] However Paul's opponents may have presented their demand for the Galatians to be circumcised, Paul clearly spelled out the comprehensive consequences of such an action. Later in the letter (6:13) he would observe that "not even those who are circumcised obey the law," again pointing to the utter futility involved in such an effort.[23]

Paul couched his warning in the language of a courtroom witness, "I bear witness," "I testify." He himself knew by personal experience what the law required and how utterly impossible it was to find peace with God through perfect obedience. For the Galatians then to accept circumcision and all that it implied was for them to throw away the precious gift of freedom and step back onto the unceasing treadmill of self-justification. If in urging circumcision on the Galatians the Judaizing teachers had claimed, "Paul has not explained to you the full demands of the gospel," for his part Paul replied,

---

[22] Sanders, *Paul, the Law,* 29. But it does not follow that "Paul may very well simply have been reminding his converts that, if they accept circumcision, the consequence would be that they would have to begin living their lives according to a new set of rules for daily living." Paul's point was rather that circumcision entailed keeping the law in its entirety, admittedly a strict view that may not have been shared by his adversaries. See Westerholm, *Israel's Law,* 205-9.

[23] Paul's rigorist understanding of the comprehensive obedience required by the law is reflected elsewhere in the NT (cf. Matt 5:17-20; Jas 2:10). As Sanders and others have shown, there was no uniformity of opinion among the rabbis of Second Temple Judaism concerning the extent to which faithfulness to the law of God required unerring obedience to its 613 prescriptions and prohibitions. It is not the case, however, that "no rabbi took the position that obedience must be perfect" (Sanders, *Paul, the Law,* 28). Betz has stated that "there can be little doubt that by the time of Paul this view [that strict obedience to the demands of the entire Torah were required for hope of salvation in the final judgment] was the generally accepted one in Judaism" (*Galatians,* 260). We may further cite the statement of Eleazar to the blasphemer Antiochus in 4 Macc 5:20-21: "The transgression of the law, be it in small things or in great, is equally heinous, for in either case equally the law is despised." See the literature cited in Bruce, *Galatians,* 229-31, and Longenecker, *Galatians,* 226-27.

"They have not explained to you the full demands of the law."[24]

5:4 Paul's whole purpose in writing this passage was to issue a wake-up call to those members of the Galatian churches who were being tempted to forsake the evangelical message Paul had proclaimed in favor of another gospel of that legal obedience. Paul here repeated and intensified his warning by pointing out that all those who seek to be justified by law are in reality (1) alienated from Christ and (2) fallen away from grace. The word for "alienated" (*katargein*) means literally "to cut off" or "make ineffective." Paul used the same word earlier in Gal 3:17 to indicate that the Mosaic law did not "set aside" or nullify the former covenant and promise God made with Abraham. Paul was saying that those who had renounced that way of justification God has established and, further, had become debtors to fulfill perfectly all of the commandments of the law had been "severed from Christ" (NASB), that is, removed from his sphere of operation and "hence completely cut off from relations with him."[25] Obviously, the Judaizers and their disciples did not for a moment believe that the imposition of circumcision involved their alienation from Christ. To the contrary, they saw it as an enhancement, a necessary additive required for the true possession of salvation. What they advocated was a Christianity by amalgamation, a mingling of the grace of Christ with the merit of works. Yet, as Calvin put it so well, "Whoever wants to have a half-Christ loses the whole."[26]

To be cut off from Christ in this sense is to have "fallen away from grace." Luther interpreted this expression to mean "You are no longer in the realm of grace" and illustrated it graphically in the following way:

> For just as someone on a ship is drowned regardless of the part of the ship from which he falls into the sea, so someone who falls away from grace cannot help perishing. The desire to be justified by the law, therefore, is shipwreck; it is exposure to the surest peril of eternal death. What can be more insane and wicked than to want to lose the grace and favor of God and to retain the law of Moses, whose retention makes it necessary for you to accumulate wrath and every other evil for yourself? Now if those who seek to be justified on the basis of the moral law fall away from grace, where, I ask, will those fall who, in their self-righteousness, seek to be justified on the basis of their traditions and vows? To the lowest depths of hell![27]

---

[24] Bligh, *Galatians,* 422.

[25] Fung, *Galatians,* 223. See also G. Delling, "καταργεω," *TDNT* 1.452-54. Two other suggestive uses of this word in the NT are 1 Cor 13:11 concerning the abandonment or putting away of childish things and Luke 13:7, where it is said of the fruitless fig tree, "Why cumbereth it the ground?" (KJV)

[26] Calvin, CNTC 11.93.

[27] *LW* 27.18.

Contrary to the Arminian interpretation of this text, Paul did not here contemplate the forfeiture of salvation by a truly regenerated believer. He was writing to Christian churches that were founded on the doctrines of grace but that were in danger of forsaking that sound doctrinal bedrock for a theology that can only lead to ruin.

5:5 Up to this point in Gal 5 Paul had spoken of the dire negative consequences of the Galatians' submission to the Judaizers demand for circumcision. If you do this, Paul warned, Christ will be of no value to you, you will place yourselves under the intolerable burden of obeying the whole law, you will cut yourselves off from Christ, and you will remove yourselves from the realm of grace. Now suddenly in v. 5 the apostle changed gears and, by means of the conjunction *gar,* "for," summarized the essence of the Christian gospel in a series of pithy slogans or "dogmatic abbreviations," as Betz prefers to call them.[28] The whole sentence fits together loosely in a grammatical sense and thus has proven difficult to translate smoothly. Literally the Greek reads: "For we by the Spirit through faith eagerly await the hope of righteousness." J. B. Phillips puts it like this: "For it is *by faith* that we await in his Spirit the righteousness we hope to see." The "we" (*hēmeis*) at the beginning of the sentence is deliberately emphatic, meaning "we who are true Christians" as opposed to the underhanded heretics who are Christians only in name.

"By the Spirit" and "through faith" recall two of the major emphases over which Paul had labored throughout the epistle. The Spirit was first introduced in 3:1-5 in the context of Paul's reminder to the Galatians of their conversion to Christ and the great difference it had made in their lives. In Gal 4:6 Paul further linked the sending of the Spirit into the hearts of God's children with the sending of the Son into the world to accomplish his redemptive mission. In Gal 4:29 Isaac, representing believers in Jesus Christ, was described as "the son born by the power of the Spirit." The mention of the Spirit in this present verse anticipates the increasingly prominent role Paul would assign to the Spirit in his depiction of the Christian life in the closing two chapters of the letter. Similarly, the catchword "by faith" has been close to the center of Paul's doctrinal exposition since its initial appearance in the summary definition of justification in 2:15-16. Paul's rehearsing of the Abraham story in particular focused on the patriarch's faith which God "credited to him as righteousness" (3:6). Faith is also directly connected with baptism and the unity of the church associated therewith (3:26-29). Here in Gal 5–6 faith is intimately connected with love, so much so that Paul could say, "The only thing that counts is faith expressing itself through love" (5:6).

---

[28] Betz, *Galatians,* 262.

In addition to the familiar themes of the Spirit and faith, we encounter here in 5:5 "the hope of righteousness" (*elpida dikaiosynēs*). Within the total context of Paul's thinking this expression indicates far more than a "slight eschatological flavor."[29] As we have seen, the church in Paul's letters was an eschatological community determined by the reality of a future already inaugurated through the ministry, death, and resurrection of Jesus and yet still awaiting in eager expectation the final consummation at the coming manifestation of Christ in glory. Although Galatians contains no lengthy chapter on the resurrection (cf. 1 Cor 15) nor a graphic description of the parousia (1 Thess 4:13-18), the entire letter is marked by what J. L. Martyn has called "apocalyptic antinomies," such as the Jerusalem above and the one here below mentioned in the Hagar-Sarah analogy (4:25-26). Both justification by faith and the bestowal of the Holy Spirit upon the church are eschatological events. The extension of the gospel to the Gentiles and Paul's unique mission therein are likewise end-time phenomena. They signal the shattering of the old broken-down structures of human existence and the breaking in of God's new aeon. In speaking of "the righteousness for which we hope," Paul was not saying, of course, that we must wait until the second coming of Christ either to receive justification or to be assured of it. The whole burden of Paul's doctrine of justification is that divine righteousness is imparted here and now through faith in Jesus Christ (cf. Rom 3:24; 5:1,9; 1 Cor 6:11; Gal 2:16; 3:22).[30] The "hope of righteousness" means instead "the hope to which the justification of believers points them forward."[31]

5:6 Here in v. 6 Paul picked up the theme with which he began his present exhortation to the Galatians. "For when we are in union with Christ Jesus" (GNB) neither circumcision nor the lack of it has any value. Paul would repeat this sentence almost verbatim near the end of the letter in 6:15. The question of whether or not one was circumcised has become, as it were, an adiaphorous issue, that is, a thing indifferent. In the old scheme of things physical circumcision had a distinctive religious meaning, but that had now been relegated to the realm of the No Longer. In the new creation "there is no Greek or Jew, circumcised or uncircumcised, barbarian, Scythian, slave or free, but Christ is all, and is in all" (Col 3:11).

The Colossian text along with Paul's relativization of the issue of circumcision in 5:6 and 6:15 recall his earlier description of the baptized community as the social sphere in which "there is neither Jew nor Greek" (Gal 3:28). In

[29] Cole, *Galatians,* 142.

[30] See Fung, *Galatians,* 225. See also P. S. Minear, *Christian Hope and the Second Coming* (Philadelphia: Westminster, 1954); K. H. Rengstorf and R. Bultmann, "ελπίς," *TDNT* 2.517-35.

[31] G. Vos, *The Pauline Eschatology* (Grand Rapids: Eerdmans, 1930), 30.

the new humanity brought about through faith in Jesus Christ, that is to say the church, these old realities and identities have been so transcended that they have lost all relevance as soteriological indicators. Thus in 1 Cor 9:20 we find Paul making this remarkable statement, "To the Jews I became *as if I were* a Jew." But of course Paul was a Jew, circumcised on the eighth day, of the tribe of Benjamin, and so on. Paul never renounced his distinctive ethnic background or sought to have himself uncircumcised. Yet his true identity was not defined by his being a Jew but rather by his being "in Christ." If the former identity markers have now become anachronistic, what really does matter for those who are "in Christ Jesus" is "faith expressing itself through love."

The faith that operates through love is nothing other than the faith by which we are justified before God. In medieval Catholic theology it was "faith formed by love" (*fides caritate formata*) that made one righteous, that is to say, faith built up through works of love and goodwill toward one's neighbor. Yet Paul never said that we are justified by love, either our love for God or our love for neighbor. We are justified by grace through faith, a faith that indeed is active in love leading to holiness. G. Bornkamm has pointed to the danger of interpreting these words in a synergistic sense that would undermine the gratuity of God's free initiative in salvation:

> We must guard against the misunderstanding current especially in Catholic theology (though Protestantism is far from exempt) that only faith made perfect in love leads to justification. This represents a serious distortion of the relationship between faith, love, and justification. In speaking of justification Paul never talks of faith *and* love, but *only* of faith as receiving. Love is not therefore an additional prerequisite for receiving salvation, nor is it properly an essential trade of faith; on the contrary, faith animates the love in which it works.[32]

Within the space of two verses Paul brought together the basic triad of Christian virtues—faith, hope, and love. None of these are self-generating qualities or mere human possibilities. They are gifts of God actualized in the lives of his children by the presence of his Spirit in their hearts.

(3) Circumcision or the Cross (5:7-12)

[7]You were running a good race. Who cut in on you and kept you from obeying the truth? [8]That kind of persuasion does not come from the one who calls you. [9]"A little yeast works through the whole batch of dough." [10]I am confident in the Lord that you will take no other view. The one who is throwing you into confusion will pay the penalty, whoever he may be. [11]Brothers, if I am still preaching circumcision, why am I still being persecuted? In that case the

---

[32] G. Bornkamm, *Paul*, 153.

offense of the cross has been abolished. [12]As for those agitators, I wish they
would go the whole way and emasculate themselves!

After sounding the clarion note of freedom in v. 1, Paul next turned to a
pointed description of the dangers of giving in to the Judaizing demand for
circumcision (vv. 2-4). He then gave a condensed statement of the Christian
alternative in which he summarized the major themes of the letter by bringing together a series of familiar Pauline concepts—faith, Spirit, righteousness, hope, and love. The closing expression of this section, "faith working
itself out through love," anticipates the fuller ethical discussion that would
occupy the apostle in the remainder of Gal 5–6. However, before he launched
into the final section of the epistle, he turned once more to remind the Galatians of the common history he had shared with them and to call them back
from their backsliding ways. Thus Gal 5:7-12 resembles in structure 4:12-20.
It is a personal parenthesis consisting of what Betz has called "a rambling
collection of pointed remarks, rhetorical questions, proverbial expressions,
threats, irony, and, climaxing it all, a joke of sarcasm."[33] In this section we
also feel the clash of turbulent and conflicting emotions, radical mood swings
as it were, as Paul vacillated between consolation and anger, exasperation
and hope.

5:7   Paul here compared the Christian life to the running of a race, an
athletic image found in many of his writings (cf. 1 Cor 9:24-27; Phil 3:14; 2
Tim 4:7). "Ye did run well," as the KJV puts it, refers to the auspicious beginning of the Christian movement in Galatia when Paul and Barnabas first
brought the gospel into that region. The image is of an Olympic athlete who
dashes from the starting line with great vigor, perhaps accelerating past his
competitors for a season, only to have someone from the stands surrepti-
tiously enter the race course and trip him up at an unexpected turn in the
road.[34] "Who cut in on you?" is a rhetorical question analogous to, "Who has
bewitched you?" in 3:1. Paul was not asking here for names and addresses,
nor did he have any lurid interest in ferreting out the identity of his opponents. Regardless of the instrumentality of his flesh-and-blood adversaries,
Paul knew that the prince of darkness was manipulating the situation in Gala-

---

[33] Betz, *Galatians,* 264.
[34] See O. Bauernfeind, "τρέχηω, δρόμος, προδρόμος," *TDNT* 8.226-35. See also C. E.
DeVries, "Paul's 'Cutting' Remarks about a Race: Galatians 5:1-12" in *Current Issues in Biblical and Patristic Interpretation,* ed. G. F. Hawthorne (Grand Rapids: Eerdmans, 1975), 115-20.
DeVries suggests quite plausibly that the interference in such a race would likely have come
from a fellow runner. This image would then apply to the rival missionaries whose malicious
efforts to "trip up" Paul and his Galatian converts occasioned this letter. Beyond the nefarious
activities of these agitators, however, was the sinister poise of Satan himself. Paul elsewhere
spoke of his being "hindered" by Satan (cf. 1 Thess 2:18).

tia. His "dear children" were besieged by a supernatural foe, one that only the power of the Holy Spirit can successfully resist.

The result of this sinister interference in the life race of the Galatians is that they had not continued to obey the truth. Earlier in the letter Paul had summarized his entire message under the rubric the "truth of the gospel" (2:5,14). This was precisely what the Galatians were on the verge of deserting through their dalliance with the unbelieving theology of the false teachers. Here Paul was calling them back from the brink of disaster.

Three important applications can be garnered from this verse: (1) The Christian life is marathon, not a hundred-yard dash. Paul wanted the Galatians who began so well also to finish well. Ministers have a special responsibility to disciple and nurture young believers so that they may stay the course and not be deterred by the hinderers who will surely come. (2) Paul did not give up on the Galatians even though many of them had shifted their loyalty from him to the usurpers and, to all outward appearances, appeared to be lost to the cause of God and truth. From God's omniscient perspective, of course, no person who has been genuinely regenerated will ever utterly or finally fall away from the faith (cf. John 10:28; Eph 1:4-6; Rom 8:29). From our limited point of view, however, persons who appear as bona fide Christians do abandon the truth of the gospel (cf. 1 John 2:19; Rom 11:22-23). Paul had "confidence" that the Galatians could be won back and thus labored strenuously to that end. So must every minister of the gospel who counsels with those who may be tempted to abandon the race they have begun. (3) The "truth of the gospel" is not only something to be believed but also something to be obeyed. Having forsaken the solid theological foundation Paul had laid for them, the Galatians soon found themselves awash in immorality and debauchery of all kinds. By undermining their confidence in sound doctrine, Satan seduced them into loose living. Nowhere do we see more clearly the correlation between theological integrity and spiritual vitality.

5:8-9 It is obvious that the circumcision-preaching agitators had exerted a powerful influence over Paul's converts. They had bewitched them and tripped them up in their race toward the finish line. What was the secret of their success? Paul answered this question by using a unique word, *peismonē*, "the persuasion," a term found nowhere else in earlier Greek literature.[35] Evidently the Judaizing missionaries had taken Galatia by storm. In

---

[35] See R. Bultmann, "πεισμονή," *TDNT* 6.9. Cf. the German translation: "*Solch Überreden ist nicht von dem, der euch beruft.*" Burton points out that πεισμονη may be taken in either an active or passive sense (*Galatians,* 283). "The passive sense involves the thought of a persuasion actually accomplished, the active an effort. It was, of course, the latter, but ἐνέκοψεν shows that in Paul's thought it was in a sense the former, also."

contrast to Paul, they must have been physically attractive, eloquent in speech, and able to put on a good show, so much so that the new Christian believers in the cities of South Galatia were persuaded to abandon the gospel of grace for their new theology of salvation by arduous achievement and human merit. Paul's methodology was very different. As he explained to the Corinthians, his message was not based on "wise and persuasive words," nor was it characterized by "eloquence or superior wisdom." Rather his proclamation of the gospel was done "in weakness and fear, and with much trembling" (1 Cor 2:1-5).

What was involved in these two distinct approaches, Paul said, was not merely a contrast of personalities but also divergent theologies. Because Paul did not seek to please men but God, he refused to engage in rhetorical gimmickry and other sinner-flattering techniques of persuasion. Thus when someone did respond to his message, he could be confident that this was a genuine moving of the Holy Spirit in their lives.[36] Behind the friendly persuasion of the false teachers stood, of course, the greatest flatterer of them all, Satan himself. Luther called the devil *ein Tausendkünstler,* a juggler with a thousand tricks, by means of which he is able "to impress such an obvious and shameful lie on the heart that you would swear a thousand times that it is the most certain truth."[37] Paul reminded his readers that such persuasiveness, no matter how effective, is not from the "one who called you," an expression always used in Paul with reference to God (cf. 1:6).

In v. 8 Paul was concerned with the methodology of the false teachers; in v. 9 he turned to consider the end result of their meddlesome interference. He did this by quoting a proverbial saying from the world of breadmaking: "It takes only a little yeast to make the whole batch of dough rise," as they say (GNB). This is a commonsense saying similar to our own English maxim, "Just one rotten apple spoils the whole barrel." Paul's point is clear: His opponents had not overturned the whole system of Christian teaching but were only making a seemingly minor adjustment to it—the imposition of the harmless rite of circumcision. But even a seemingly slight deviation on such a fundamental matter of the faith can bring total ruin to the Christian community. Just a little poison, if it is toxic enough, will destroy the entire body. Implicit in Paul's words is a warning to every church, denomination, and theological institution. Any community of faith that is unwilling to recognize and to reject perversions of the gospel when they crop up in its midst has lost

---

[36] Cf. the comment of Ignatius of Antioch (*Rom* 3,3): "Christianity is not the work of persuasiveness, but of greatness, when it is hated by the world" (*The Apostolic Fathers,* ed. K. Lake [Cambridge: Harvard University Press, 1912], 1.229).

[37] *LW* 26.196, n. 15.

its right to bear witness to the transforming message of Jesus Christ, who declared himself to be not only the Way and the Life but also the Truth, the only truth that leads to the Father (John 14:6).

Paul quoted the proverb of Gal 5:9 in 1 Cor 5:6, there in the context of his admonition to the Corinthians to exclude from their fellowship the recalcitrant member guilty of sexual immorality. In both letters the proverb speaks to the danger of an unguarded life or undisciplined church where evil is winked at or embraced under the pretext of moral relativism or doctrinal pluralism. The use of leaven or yeast as a symbol of festering corruption probably derives from the Old Testament prohibition against its use during the seven days of Passover (cf. Exod 12:14-20; Deut 16:3-8).[38] Paul's use of the same proverb in Galatians and 1 Corinthians indicates the interrelatedness of orthodoxy and orthopraxy. Just as in the churches of Galatia a compromise of the truth of the gospel led to licentious living, so in Corinth the easy toleration of open immorality within the church was followed by serious doctrinal deviation, in their case concerning the resurrection (cf. 1 Cor 15). Paul had begun the closing parenetic section of Galatians (5:1-2) with a strong warning against the major theological default that had preoccupied him throughout the letter because he knew that the ethical crisis he was about to address could not be divorced from the Galatians' prior departure from the truth of the gospel.

5:10 Verse 9 ended on a note of sourdough, a batch of bread thoroughly infested from a little morsel of yeast. As an analogy to the situation in the churches of Galatia, it was an example of ominous foreboding rather than hope. Now, suddenly, there is an abrupt change of mood as Paul declared his confidence that the Galatians would after all "take no other view," that is, that they would not ultimately capitulate to the false teaching and heretical ideas that were being presented to them with such persuasion. But how could Paul have been so confident when to all appearances it seemed the Galatians were nearly in the grips of apostasy already?

The answer to this question resides in the meaning of *en Kuriō*, "in the Lord," a phrase found forty-seven times in Paul's writings. Paul uttered a similar expression of confidence in the Lord in 2 Thess 3:4 to which he added this prayer, "May the Lord direct your hearts into God's love and Christ's perseverance" (2 Thess 3:5). Paul's confidence toward the Galatians was rooted in the same reality: the love of God and the faithfulness of Jesus Christ

---

[38] However, Jesus used the symbol of yeast in the double parable of the mustard seed and the leaven in Matt 13:31-35 in a positive sense to indicate that in the kingdom of heaven great things can come from small beginnings. See J. Jeremias, *The Parables of Jesus* (New York: Scribners, 1963), 147-49.

which in turn is the basis for the perseverance of the saints. Paul firmly believed that the Lord had truly saved at least some of the Galatians. He and Barnabas had preached to them the pure doctrine of the cross of Christ; they had repented, believed, and received the Holy Spirit with the evident demonstration of his power in their midst. This commitment had been further sealed in the experience of baptism and the gathering of local congregations in the several cities of South Galatia. What Paul later said of the Philippians he here intimated of the Galatians: The Lord who began his good work within them would keep right on developing it until it is brought to completion on that day when Jesus Christ returns (Phil 1:6). Thus Paul's expression of confidence here was neither a mere matter of tact nor a "conventional epistolary phrase"[39] but rather a robust assertion of reliance on the optimism of grace.

Paul's confidence was in the Lord, not in his own ability to reverse the situation. At the same time, he may have found some encouragement in the fact that the Galatians had not *yet* submitted to the demand for circumcision. The churches of Galatia were in turmoil. They were wavering and perhaps even tilting toward Paul's opponents, but they had not yet completely succumbed to their persuasive appeals. Doubtless Paul's primary purpose in writing his letter was to provide a counterweight to the false teachers. Paul's strategy not only reflected his genuine reading of the situation but it also made good pastoral sense. As J. Brown wisely observed, "The Christian teacher ought always to act under the influence of the charity which 'hopeth all things,' and when he stands in doubt of any of those whose souls are committed to his care, he must not conceal his hopes while he makes known his fears."[40]

While Paul expressed confidence in the perseverance of the true saints of Galatia, he was unsparing in his denunciation of those who had thrown them into such confusion. "But whoever it is who is worrying you will have a serious charge to answer one day!" (v. 10, Phillips). There has been much scholarly speculation concerning the identity of this unnamed troublemaker. Elsewhere Paul spoke of the Judaizers in the plural (1:7; 5:12). Still, they might well have had a ringleader whom Paul believed was principally to blame for the disturbances. Others have suggested that Paul was here taking a backhanded slap at James (cf. "the men from James" in 2:12 whose arrival in Antioch precipitated the incident there) or even Peter, who, according to F. C. Baur and his disciples, emerged as Paul's major rival and adversary in the early church.[41] The warning in this verse harks back to 1:7-9, where Paul

---

[39] Betz, *Galatians,* 266.
[40] Brown, *Galatians,* 274.
[41] See the extensive discussion of "St. Paul and the Three," in Lightfoot, *Galatians,* 292-374. See also Bligh, *Galatians,* 430-31.

hurled an anathema at anyone, whoever he may be, himself included, who dared to preach a gospel at variance with the one he had proclaimed by divine commission. Another parallel text is 2 Cor 11:15, where Paul declared of the false apostles who had deceitfully presented themselves as the servants of righteousness, "their end will be what their actions deserve." Earlier Paul admonished the Galatian believers to expel the false teachers from their midst (4:30, "Get rid of the slave woman and her son"). Here he spoke of the final eschatological judgment that will be meted out by God himself at the return of Christ. These are the only two sanctions the New Testament acknowledges for heresy: church discipline and divine judgment. The doctrine of religious liberty declares that the civil magistrate has no rightful authority to punish anyone because of religious beliefs or theological convictions.[42]

5:11 Evidently a part of the "confusion" referred to in v. 10 stemmed from a false accusation, a slanderous lie really, that Paul's opponents had circulated about him when they first came into contact with the Galatians. In urging circumcision upon the Gentile believers there, they apparently whispered, "Haven't you heard that Paul himself is an advocate of circumcision?" Perhaps they were saying that Paul preached circumcision when it suited him, when he was in the company of the Jerusalem church leaders, for example, but that he prudentially trimmed his message when speaking to Gentile audiences in order more easily to win them over to his version of Christianity. To us this seems like a preposterous charge, and Paul certainly thought it to be maliciously intended. Was there anything in Paul's life that would have made this charge appear at least plausible to the Galatians?

In the first place Paul did not wage an anticircumcision campaign. His basic rule of thumb was that a Christian should order his life according to his condition when God called him. "Was a man already circumcised when he was called? He should not become uncircumcised. Was a man uncircumcised when he was called? He should not be circumcised. Circumcision is nothing and uncircumcised is nothing" (1 Cor 7:18-19). Gentiles need not become Jews, nor Jews Gentiles, in order to belong to the family of God. True, it was rumored among the anti-Paulinist faction in Jerusalem that the apostle had taught "all the Jews who live among the Gentiles to turn away from Moses, telling them not to circumcise their children or live according to our cus-

---

[42] The early English Baptists advocated a universal religious toleration. As Thomas Helwys expressed it, "Let them be heretics, Turks, Jews, or whatsoever, it appertains not to the earthly power to punish them" (*A Short Declaration of the Mystery of Iniquity* [London: 1612], 69). See T. George, "Between Pacifism and Coercion: The English Baptist Doctrine of Religious Toleration," *MQR* 58 (1984): 30-49.

toms." But this was a trumped-up charge, as James and the elders of the church in Jerusalem knew (Acts 21:17-26). For Paul it was perfectly acceptable for Jewish believers in Jesus to have their infant sons circumcised so long as no salvific significance was attached to this ethnic ritual.

Some scholars have also seen in this verse a veiled reference to another incident in Paul's ministry, one that occurred in the South Galatian city of Lystra. When Timothy joined Paul and Silas on their missionary tour, Paul had his young friend circumcised so that he would have greater access to the Jewish communities on their evangelistic mission (Acts 16:3). Timothy's mother was Jewish, and Paul no doubt justified this act along the line of the principle of accommodation set forth in 1 Cor 9:20, "To the Jews I became like a Jew, to win the Jews."[43]

Still another interpretation of Gal 5:11 links the charge of Paul practicing circumcision to the incident related to Titus in 2:1-5. Certain Western witnesses omit the negative disclaimer "not" in 2:5, leaving the impression that Paul "did give in for a moment" to the pressures of the false brothers and had Titus circumcised. But this is clearly an inferior textual reading, and most scholars agree with B. Metzger that the resulting meaning ("because of the false brethren . . . I yielded for a brief time") seems "to be distinctly contrary both to the drift of the apostle's argument and to his temperament."[44] Still, the ambiguity of the textual tradition at this point may reflect a garbled version of this incident promulgated, among others, by Paul's opponents in Galatia.

Paul must have felt some sting in this accusation or else he would not have responded to it so abruptly. The adverb "still" (*eti*) may provide a helpful clue in our efforts to reconstruct this piece of the Judaizers' propaganda. "If I am *still* preaching circumcision," Paul asked, "why am I *still* being persecuted?" In Paul's preconversion days, when he was the persecutor rather than one of the persecuted, he himself had likely engaged in extensive missionary campaigns aimed at bringing Gentile proselytes and nonconforming Jews into line with the "traditions" of his fathers, that is, strict Pharisaic Judaism.

---

[43] J. Polhill gives the following account of the circumcision of Timothy: "Timothy would have been considered a Jew. His father, however, being a Greek, would not have had his son circumcised; and the local Jews were aware of this. Thus Paul had Timothy circumcised. Paul always worked through the Jewish synagogues where possible. To have had a member of his entourage be of Jewish lineage and yet uncircumcised would have hindered his effectiveness among the Jews. It was at the very least a matter of missionary strategy to circumcise Timothy (1 Cor 9:20). It may have been much more. Paul never abandoned his own Jewish heritage. He may well have wanted Timothy to be true to *his* (cf. Rom 3:1f.)" (*Acts,* NAC [Nashville: Broadman, 1992], 343). See also S. J. D. Cohen, "Was Timothy Jewish (Acts 16:1-3)? Patristic Exegesis, Rabbinic Law, and Matrilineal Descent," *JBL* 105 (1986): 251-68.

[44] Metzger, *Textual Commentary,* 591.

During those days Paul (Saul of Tarsus) would indeed have "preached circumcision" as an essential component of his own zealous Judaizing efforts. It was in the midst of such a campaign, of course, that Saul of Tarsus and Jesus of Nazareth came face to face on the road to Damascus. Although Paul's Letter to the Galatians was written some twenty years after that event, no doubt memories of Paul's preconversion activities still lingered in the minds of many people who must have known him at that time. But, Paul said, why dredge up my dastardly past when, to be sure, I persecuted the church of God and was an open enemy of the cross of Christ? Furthermore, why am I still being persecuted, hounded from pillar to post, if, as my opponents say, I am still preaching circumcision as I did in my pre-Christian past?

Later in Galatians (6:12) Paul would aver that one of the reasons the false teachers were so keen about circumcision was that their advocacy of it might allow them to dodge persecution themselves. But Paul had not taken this easy path. When he and Barnabas first brought the gospel to Galatia, they suffered ill-treatment at the hands of the synagogue authorities. The preaching of the cross was very much an "offense" (*skandalon*) to the Jews, and one could not at the same time preach Christ and circumcision too.[45]

Circumcision or the cross must now join the set of antitheses Paul had been developing throughout Galatians: the gospel of Christ versus a "different" gospel, faith versus works, grace versus merit, promise versus the law, Hagar-Ishmael-the present Jerusalem versus Sarah-Isaac-the heavenly Jerusalem, the Spirit versus the flesh, freedom versus bondage. The word *skandalon,* "offense," literally means "a trap, a source of embarrassment, a stumbling block that inevitably provokes a negative reaction."

In 1 Cor 1:18-31 Paul developed his understanding of the stumbling block of the cross with reference to both the received traditions of Judaism and the elitist culture of Greco-Roman civilization. The Jews, Paul said, demanded miraculous signs. They wanted to see a divine show-and-tell, something spectacular, something dazzling.[46] The cross is a scandal to this kind of

---

[45] This point is well made by C. K. Barrett: "You cannot preach both the cross and circumcision, for the cross is the enemy of all the rites and institutions to which men cling for salvation, in which they suppose they can make their salvation secure. It is circumcision as security, not as for example a national custom, that Paul opposes. And the cross is the denial of all security. It is only those who take up the cross and follow in the steps of Christ who find justification in him. The man who hangs on the cross has surrendered every kind of human security, and those who follow him must surrender it too. There is nothing so wounding as this to man's pride" (*Freedom and Obligation,* 69). G. Howard's thesis that Paul had only recently embraced a circumcision-free gospel and that Paul's opponents who were unaware of this change thought they were supporting rather than detracting from his mission is unconvincing (*Crisis in Galatia,* 39-44).

[46] This signs-and-wonders theology is represented by King Herod's challenge to Jesus in the musical *Jesus Christ Superstar* to prove himself by walking across a swimming pool.

signs-and-wonders theology because it is the prime example of God's using something weak and despicable, yea something shameful and cursed, to display his overcoming grace and redemptive victory. And the cross was no less scandalous to the Romans, with their love of power, and the Greeks, who were infatuated with intellectual achievement, *paideia,* that is, salvation through education. To this philosophy of life, even more pervasive in our own modern Enlightenment culture than in Paul's day, the cross is sheer folly. By trimming his message Paul could have removed the offense of a crucified Christ, but a crossless Christianity, then as now, leaves men and women helpless in the face of sin and death.

5:12 This verse contains what has been called "the crudest and rudest of all Paul's extant statements."[47] The rendering of the KJV is inadequate to express the force of the original, "I would they were even cut off who trouble you." The word for "cut off" is the future middle tense of *apokoptein.* The JB translates, "Tell those who are disturbing you I would like to see the knife slip." M. R. Vincent also captures the sense of Paul's startling statement in his paraphrastic translation of this verse: "These people are disturbing you by insisting on circumcision. I would that they would make thorough work of it in their own case, and instead of merely amputating the foreskin, would castrate themselves as heathen priests do. Perhaps this would be even more powerful help to salvation."[48]

The mention of heathen priests in Vincent's paraphrase refers to the ritual of sacral castration practiced by the priests of Cybele, a mother goddess (*Magna Mater*) and the focus of a thriving mystery cult in Asia Minor. The castration of the Cybeline priests was part of an annual ritual in which the dying and rising of Attis, the consort god of Cybele, was reenacted. Each year at the spring festival the worshipers of Cybele would fast, pray, and mourn the death of Attis. Then the priests would emasculate themselves, drink their own blood, and bear to his grave in solemn procession an image of the young god Attis.

> But on the morrow the streets would ring with exultant shouts as the people celebrated the resurrection of Attis and the renewal of the earth. "Take courage, O mystics," cried the priests, "the god is saved; and for you also will come salvation." On the last day of the feast the image of the Great Mother

---

[47] Longenecker, *Galatians,* 234.

[48] Cited in K. S. Wuest, *Word Studies in the Greek New Testament,* 1:146-47. Vincent's interpretive translation follows this earlier paraphrase by Theodore of Mopsuestia: "If they think that a frivolous excision of flesh is something good, let them cut off their genitals completely and gain still greater advantages!" See Bligh, *Galatians,* 433, n. 32.

would be carried in triumph through crowds that hailed her as *nostra domina,* "Our Lady."[49]

One of the major centers for the worship of Cybele was at Pessinus, a leading city in North Galatia. It is quite possible that some of Paul's readers may themselves have been devotees of the Cybeline cult in their pre-Christian days. In any event, they could not have missed the insinuation of Paul's allusion: the Judaizers who made so much of circumcision were really no better guides to the spiritual life than the pagan priests who castrated themselves in service to an idolatrous religion. In Gal 4:8-9 Paul had made the same point in another context. By submitting themselves to the law of Moses, the Gentile believers of Galatia would be sliding back into bondage to the very same elemental forces and demon gods they formerly had worshiped.

It is also possible to interpret Paul's remark with reference to this verse from the Pentateuch, "No one who has been emasculated by crushing or cutting may enter the assembly of the Lord" (Deut 23:1). In the Septuagint the words used to translate "the assembly of the Lord" are *ekklēsia Kuriou,* "the church of the Lord." By wishing that the Judaizers would emasculate themselves, Paul may have been intentionally weaving an ironic reversal. Just as the false teachers were urging the Galatian believers to have themselves circumcised in order to become a part of the true church or people of God, so Paul may have suggested that his opponents get themselves castrated and so, on the strength of Deut 23:1, be once and for all excluded from the church. But to be excluded from the church, that is, the invisible church of God's elect ones, was to be excluded from Christ, placed under a curse, and anathematized. Thus 5:12, harsh as it is, is really a reiteration of Paul's opening anathema against those who disturb the church through the promulgation of a false gospel (1:6-9).

After reading a verse like this we cannot help asking the question, Is it ever appropriate for a Christian minister to talk like this? Many have found Paul's language foul, offensive, even "disgusting," as W. M. Ramsay characterized it.[50] Some modern translations attempt to soften its impact (cf., e.g., Phillips: "I wish those who are so eager to cut your bodies would cut themselves off from you altogether!"; TLB: "I only wish these teachers who want you to cut yourselves by being circumcised would cut themselves off from you and leave you alone!"; Cotton Patch: "I wish to goodness that those who are unsettling you were themselves tarred and feathered"). However we translate the verse, we must not imagine that Paul meant any literal, physical

---

[49] W. Durant, *Caesar and Christ,* 523. See also F. Cumont, *Oriental Religions in Roman Paganism* (Chicago: University of Chicago Press, 1911).

[50] Ramsay, *Galatians,* 438.

harm to his opponents. He did not fight with carnal weapons but rather with "the sword of the Spirit, which is the word of God" (Eph 6:17). He also knew that vengeance belonged to the Lord and had just declared in v. 10 that there would be a day of reckoning for all evildoers. But that day, and that judgment, was in the hands of God not those of Paul or any other earthly church leaders.

We are tempted to read this verse through the lenses of modern psychoanalysis. Paul, after all, had been severely attacked by these people. His apostolicity had been denied, his ministry defamed, and his church field invaded. What would be more natural than for him to lash out in anger against the rabble-rousers? Perhaps this unseemly remark about castration was a cry for help, the howl of a wounded bear, or a fitful scowl masking inner fear and depression. But this line of interpretation, however amenable to modern sensitivities, totally misses the mark. What was at stake in the Galatian crisis was something much larger than Paul and the personal offense he must surely have felt at the ill-treatment he had received. What was at stake was the gospel itself. Paul had been commissioned by Jesus Christ to proclaim his good news especially among the Gentiles. Now that message was being systematically attacked and undermined by facile preachers in the service of the Evil One.

In this emergency situation Paul summoned the courage to utter a word of imprecation. It had to be said, and it was right for him to say it because a lesser rebuke would have signaled an unconscionable compromise and retreat. Let no one ever utter such words lightly, unadvisedly, or in a spirit of personal aggravation and revenge. Those kinds of statements are likely to return upon the one who pronounces them with all the reciprocal force of a boomerang. Luther's comment on Gal 5:12 spoke to this issue: "Here the question arises whether Christians are permitted to curse. Yes, they are permitted to do so, but not always and not for just any reason. But when things come to the point where the Word is about to be cursed or its teaching—and, as a consequence, God himself—blasphemed, then you must invert your sentence and say: 'Blessed be the Word and God! And cursed be anything apart from the Word and from God, whether it be an apostle or an angel from heaven!' "[51] Thus Peter answered Simon the sorcerer who thought to obtain spiritual power for money: "You and your money can go to hell!" (Acts 8:20, Cotton Patch). Karl Barth was surely right when he said: "If we do not have the confidence of *damnamus,* we ought to omit *credimus,* and go back to doing theology as usual."[52]

---

[51] *LW* 27.45.
[52] Barth, *Church Dogmatics* I/1.630.

2. Flesh and Spirit (5:13-26)

With the doctrinal foundations securely in place and the malicious maneu-verings of the trouble makers finally unmasked, Paul now turned his attention to specific ethical exhortations that we have grouped under two headings: flesh and spirit (5:13-26) and freedom in service to others (6:1-10). Galatians is not unusual in that it conforms to the typically Pauline pattern of theolog-ical, kerygmatic exposition followed by ethical instruction and guidance on practical Christian living (cf. Rom 12–15; Phil 4; Col 3–4; Eph 4–6).

Because this kind of parenetic instruction as a rule typically contains much traditional material such as a code of family behavior (a feature miss-ing from Galatians) and standardized lists of virtues and vices, many scholars have regarded the inclusion of such didactic instruction as a sort of pro forma appendix to the central theological concerns of Paul's letters. Thus, accord-ing to M. Dibelius, the parenetic material in Paul's letters "have nothing to do with the theoretical foundation of the ethics of the apostle, and very little with other ideas peculiar to him. . . . In particular they lack an immediate rela-tion with the circumstances of the letter. The rules and directions are not for-mulated for special churches and concrete cases, but for the general requirements of earliest Christendom. Their significance is not factual but actual—not the momentary need but the universal principle."[53]

It is quite true that much of the hortatory material found in Paul's letters, including Galatians, is by no means unique or peculiar to him. Similar instruction is found not only in other New Testament writings (e.g., James and 1 Peter) but also in postapostolic documents such as 1 Clement, the *Didache,* and the Shepherd of Hermas. In that sense we can agree that there is no specifically "Pauline ethics" but rather a pattern of Christian ethics set forth in a Pauline perspective. Even so, Paul knew nothing of Dibelius's "uni-versal principle." For Paul the gospel of grace and life in the Spirit that flowed from it were always contextually defined. This is true because the Christian faith itself is particularist, not general; the Word of God comes as an address to real men and women struggling with issues of life and death, caught in the tension between freedom and bondage, salvation and damnation, this present evil age and the inbreaking kingdom of God.

Up to this point in Galatians, Paul had set forth in no uncertain terms the doctrine of justification by faith alone. Through the redemption secured by Christ's death on the cross, believers have been liberated *from* the law and

---

[53] M. Dibelius, *From Tradition to Gospel* (New York: Scribners, 1934), 238-39. Dibelius also assumes that the ethical sections of Paul's letters arose from his preaching: "In his missionary work itself the apostle was accustomed to impress upon fresh converts the fundamentals of a new Christian life in the form of such directions."

have been accepted as righteous before God quite *apart* from the law. True, the law had an indispensable role to play in the history of salvation: it was our *paidagōgos* to point us to Christ. But we are "no longer" under its protective custody, having entered into our full inheritance as sons and daughters of God. We are not the children of Hagar but of Sarah, descendants not of Ishmael, the son of slavery, but of Isaac, the child of promise.

It is not hard to see how such a doctrine could be easily misunderstood and readily exploited to disastrous ends. There were in fact two distinctive temptations facing the Pauline congregations in Galatia. Most of Paul's converts there were Gentiles, former devotees of idolatrous cults and mystery religions. Their coming to Christ had brought an exhilarating freedom from such "slavery," but it also had produced a moral insecurity the Judaizers were eager to exploit. Their message was one of legalism: you must be circumcised in order to be saved; Jesus is the New Moses; the works of the law are as binding on Gentiles as they are on Jews.

But the Galatians also faced another temptation, equally dangerous—libertinism. This was an extreme form of antinomian teaching that held that freedom from the law meant release from all moral restraints. Paul wrote about and rejected this kind of perverted theology in Rom 6:1-2: "What shall we say, then? Shall we go on sinning so that grace may increase? By no means!" The logic of libertinism was appealing to many who had reduced the message of salvation to cheap grace. They must have argued something like this: "Why worry about moral rules and guidelines or even the Ten Commandments? We love to sin. God loves to forgive. Why not indulge our natural appetites so as to give God all the more occasions to display his grace?"

We know that this kind of distorted understanding of the Christian life was prevalent in the Corinthian church; it seems to have been present among the fickle believers in Galatia as well. The question of Gal 2:17, although set in the context of the Antioch discourse, also could have been whispered by Paul's opponents in Galatia: "If we seek to be justified by faith, doesn't that make Christ an agent of sin?" Paul's emphatic "God forbid!" shows how preposterous he considered this inference from his doctrine of justification to be. Nonetheless, the problem was a real one, and Paul found it necessary to counter the abuse of Christian freedom in libertinism as well as the squelching of it in legalism.

(1) The Law of Love (5:13-15)

[13]**You, my brothers, were called to be free. But do not use your freedom to indulge the sinful nature; rather, serve one another in love.** [14]**The entire law is summed up in a single command: "Love your neighbor as yourself."** [15]**If you keep on biting and devouring each other, watch out or you will be destroyed by each other.**

THE CALL TO LIBERTY (5:13a). **5:13a** Verse 13 marks an important transition from the theology of freedom, which Paul explicated in the previous two chapters, and the ethics of obligation, his primary concern in what follows. Our analysis will follow the natural division of the verse into three parts: the call to liberty, the temptation of license, and the service of love.

The conjunction *gar,* "for" (untranslated in the NIV), connects v. 13 with Paul's parting shot at the Judaizers in the preceding verse. Those agitators might as well have emasculated themselves, but *you* (emphatic pronoun), you are "my brothers." This affectionate word of address picks up on the note of confidence Paul had expressed just a few verses earlier concerning the eventual triumph of the gospel among the Galatians. The reason for that confidence is further explained in the characterization that follows: "For you, brethren, were called to freedom."

Several times in his letter Paul referred to the calling of the Galatians (1:6; 5:8). Paul did not think of himself as the one who called them, although he was the human instrument divinely chosen to extend the outward call to them through his faithful preaching of the gospel (cf. 3:1-3). But the one who called them was God himself. The freedom to which they had been called, then, was not the result of some natural right or the product of a human campaign for liberation. Christians are free because they have been called by God—affirmed and loved and elected by God. This means that Christians are known by God before they know him just as they are loved by God before they love him (4:9; 1 John 4:10). Thus Paul could say, "By the grace of God I am what I am" (1 Cor 15:10).

But you were called for a purpose—to be free! Paul's ringing declaration of freedom in this verse recalls his earlier statement in v. 1, "It is for freedom that Christ has set us free." Yet the disjunction between the two verses is also noticeable. In 5:1 freedom in Christ was threatened by a relapse into legalism, and so the apostle warned against assuming again the yoke of slavery. However, here in 5:13 Christian freedom is in danger of being undermined by presuming on the grace of God through licentious living resulting in moral chaos. Thus the Pauline indicative must be followed by another imperative, this time, however, a negative one.

THE TEMPTATION OF LICENSE (5:13b). **5:13b** "Only do not use your freedom as an opportunity for the flesh" (RSV). Here for the first time in Galatians we have a positive indication that the freedom for which Christ has set his people free can be horribly perverted and misused. Freedom can become a pretext or opportunity (Greek: *aphormē,* lit., a "springboard" or "base of operations") for throwing off all moral restraints and indulging the lusts of the flesh. When this has happened, freedom has been corrupted and liberty turned into license. The result is a fearful delusion, a "bewitching" every bit as spiritually paralyzing as a lapse into legalism. J. Brown's analogy is not too extreme: "The mad man who has mistaken his tattered garments for the flowing robes of majesty, and his manacles for golden bracelets studded with jewels, has not erred so widely as the man who has mistaken carnal license for Christian liberty."[54]

The word "flesh" (*sarx*) in Paul is a complex term meaning various things depending on the context in which it is used.[55] Elsewhere in Galatians Paul used the word "flesh" to refer to human life in its material dimension, our physical body, or to that which is merely human as opposed to spiritual or divine (2:20; 4:29). However, throughout Gal 5–6 flesh is used as an ethical term with a decidedly negative connotation. Flesh refers to fallen human nature, the center of human pride and self-willing. Flesh is the arena of indulgence and self-assertion, the locale in which "the ultimate sin reveals itself to be the false assumption of receiving life not as the gift of the Creator but procuring it by one's own power, of living from one's self rather than from God."[56] Thus we cannot restrict the term "flesh" to human physicality, although the "works of the flesh" Paul will shortly describe (5:19-21) seem to find their most lurid manifestations in connection with bodily life. It is God's intention for the believer in this present life to be "in the flesh" (*en sarki*: 2:20; 2:14; 6:7-10), but not "of" or "according to the flesh" (*kata sarka*: 2 Cor 1:17; 5:16). To live according to the flesh is to take the flesh as one's norm, that is, "to trust in one's self as being able to procure life by the use of the earthly and through one's own strength and accomplishment."[57]

---

[54] Brown, *Galatians,* 286. Antinomianism, no less than legalism, has been a persistent threat to evangelical Christianity throughout the history of the church. During the Reformation, Calvin wrote a treatise entitled *Against the Libertines* (1545) in which he described the particular form of this heretical teaching in his day: "They extend Christian liberty to include everything lawful for man, without any exceptions. In fact, since man has been changed into a beast, why shouldn't he be permitted to follow his sensual affection? Though we hold other beasts in check, or chain them up, or shut them up! But these feign give man full liberty so that nothing may hinder him or prevent him from having a good time. . . . These frantic people without any distinction abolish all the law, saying that it is no longer necessary to keep it, since we have been set free from it" (John Calvin, *Treatises against the Anabaptists and against the Libertines,* ed. B. W. Farley [Grand Rapids: Baker, 1982], 271).

[55] R. J. Erickson recognizes six distinct meanings for this Pauline term: physical matter, the human body, the human person or human race, a morally neutral sphere, a morally negative sphere, and rebellious human nature ("Flesh," *DPL,* 303-6). The discussion of R. Bultmann, *Theology of the New Testament,* 1, 232-46, is still helpful. On the concept of flesh in the Qumran community, see K. G. Kuhn, "New Light on Temptation, Sin and Flesh in the New Testament," in *The Scrolls and the New Testament,* ed. K. Stendahl (New York: Harper, 1957), 94-113.

[56] Bultmann, *Theology,* 232.

[57] Ibid. For a critique of the ἐν σαρκί/κάτα σαρκα distinction, see Barclay, *Obeying,* 191-202; R. Jewett, *Paul's Anthropolical Terms: A Study of Their Use in Conflict Settings* (Leiden: Brill 1971).

Paul warned the Galatians that they must not turn their freedom into license or use it as an occasion to gratify their fleshly desires.

THE SERVICE OF LOVE (5:13c).   **5:13c**   Paul's warning about not perverting the purpose of freedom is bracketed on the one side by his reference to the divine call of the Galatians and on the other by a reference to the positive alternative to license: "Instead, let love make you serve one another" (GNB). As C. K. Barrett has rightly observed, "The opposite of flesh is love . . . love that looks away from the self and its wishes, even its real needs, to the neighbor, and spends its resources on his needs."[58] Christian freedom is freedom to love and therefore freedom to serve.

Earlier in Galatians Paul introduced the concepts of freedom and love, but this is the first place he brought them together in a single thought. And, surprisingly, that which links freedom and love is the very thing Paul earlier said Christ has delivered us from: slavery. The English word "serve" does not adequately translate the Greek verb *douleuete* behind which stands the common Greek noun for slave, *doulos*. Through love, Paul said, you should make yourselves slaves to one another. Thus freedom and slavery are not simply mutually exclusive terms; they stand in the closest possible relationship to one another and can only be adequately defined in terms of object and goal: what we are slave *to* and what we are free *for*.

The glorious good news of justification by faith is that Christ has delivered us *from* servile bondage to the law and from captivity to the cosmic forces of evil. But the freedom we have received is not a static thing, something to be saved and admired and stroked like Silas Marner polishing his gold coins. No, true freedom is realized only in the slavery of love. Paul's admonition to mutual service is thus not a restriction on freedom but rather the very means of its actualization. No one has expressed the paradox of Christian freedom more succinctly than Luther in his famous maxim: "A Christian is free and independent in every respect, a bond servant to none. A Christian is a dutiful servant in every respect, owning a duty to everyone."[59]

---

[58] Barrett, *Freedom and Obligation,* 72-73.

[59] G. Ebeling, *Luther: An Introduction to His Thought* (Philadelphia: Fortress, 1972), 212. Luther insisted that a living faith expresses itself in works of love, in service to the neighbor. That such good works are done in freedom is a consequence of justification by faith. Believers who have been made right with God by faith no longer labor under the compulsion of the law or the self-centered need to serve others as a means of enhancing one's own status before God. In a sermon on 1 Cor 13 Luther asserted: "One does not love until he has become godly and righteous. Love does not make us godly, but when one has become godly love is the result. Faith, the Spirit, and justification have love as effect and fruitage, and not as a mere ornament and supplement" (quoted in G. W. Forell, *Faith Active in Love* [Minneapolis: Augsburg, 1954], 84, n. 27).

More than anywhere else the freedom that results in the slavery of love is exemplified in the passion and death of Jesus Christ. Already Paul had referred to this central fact of the gospel in 2:20, where he spoke of "the Son of God, who loved me and gave himself for me." Nowhere in his letters did Paul include an extensive description of Jesus' crucifixion, although this was a recurring theme in his preaching (cf. 1 Cor 2:2; Gal 3:1). Yet the example of Christ's self-sacrificing love was paramount in Paul's ethics of the Christian life. As he wrote to the Philippians (2:5, KJV), "Let this mind be in you which was also in Christ Jesus." Jesus was equal with the Father from all eternity yet freely chose to humble himself, becoming a slave (*doulos*) in his humiliation and death on the cross. For Paul true freedom and true theology were centered in the crucified Christ. In his description of the Christian life Paul never lost sight of this fact, which will surface again near the end of the letter as the only legitimate basis for Christian boasting (6:14).

5:14 Up to this point in Galatians, Paul had spoken of the law in decisively negative terms. All human beings are under the curse of the law and deserve the penalty of eternal damnation that it brings. Believers are no longer "under" the law, for Christ has redeemed them "from" its harsh tutelage. All who have been justified by faith have "died to the law," being the spiritual children of Sarah and citizens of the heavenly Jerusalem and not of the lineage of Hagar, who represents Mount Sinai and the religious system of self-salvation centered in the earthly Jerusalem. Christ has set us free from that "yoke of slavery." By no means were the Gentile Christians of Galatia to allow themselves to be circumcised lest, by placing themselves in bondage to the Mosaic legislation, they once again became pawns in the grip of those elemental spirits they formerly served.

Having said all of this, how could Paul then speak of the law in such a positive vein, invoking it in support of his own proposals for Christian ethics? Having shown so definitively that no one can be justified before God by doing the works of the law—to attempt such is to "fall away from grace"— why did Paul seemingly reverse himself and speak of the Christian as fulfilling the law of Christ? Was this just another way for legalism to creep in the back door? Had Paul taken away with one hand what he so generously gave with the other?

Various attempts have been made to resolve this dilemma, including the suggestion that Paul was an inconsistent thinker who flatly contradicted himself concerning the law, not only from letter to letter but even within the confines of a single epistle.[60] Another proposal has been set forth by H. Hübner,

---

[60] The most notable exponent of this view is H. Räisänen. See esp. his *Paul and the Law,* 199, and also his "Galatians 2:16 and Paul's Break with Judaism," 548-50. See also the discussion in F. Thielman, *From Plight to Solution* (Leiden; Brill, 1989), 50-54.

who argues that the whole law of Moses, which Paul summarized here in the commandment to love one's neighbor in Lev 19:18, is not identical with "the law as the whole," which holds good for Christians.[61] In other words, in Gal 5:14 Paul was using "the whole law" in a playful ironic sense as a polemical ploy against his Galatian opponents. E. P. Sanders has also offered a framework for correlating Paul's negative statements about the law in Gal 1–4 with his more positive appropriation of the law in 5:6. In the early part of Galatians Paul had denied that the law was a means for "getting in," that is, for obtaining a position of righteousness before God. "Getting in" was entirely a matter of grace, that is, justification by faith. However, "staying in" was based upon obedience to the law, and thus Paul's statement in 5:14 that it was incumbent on Christians to fulfill the whole law reflects his acceptance of "covenantal nomism" with its two-tiered soteriology.[62] Sanders' distinction between "getting in" by faith alone and "staying in" by faith plus works is strikingly similar to the later Roman Catholic distinction between first and final justification. For Paul to have adopted this position, however, would have meant that he was rejecting his confidence in the triumph of grace from first to last and adopting the posture of a semi-Judaizer himself.

Paul's ethical argument throughout this entire passage is based on the premise that the moral law of God, far from being abrogated by the coming of Christ, remains the divinely sanctioned standard for Christian conduct and growth in grace. Indeed, the believer is no longer "under law," as Paul would reiterate in this same context (5:18); rather believers are freed from the bondage of the law in order to fulfill the law in the power of the Spirit. The moral law of God is nothing less than the outward expression of God's holy character and will. The moral law of God thus antedates the Mosaic covenant. When in Rom 2:15 Paul said of the pagan Gentiles who had never heard of the law of Moses that the requirements of the law are written on their hearts and consciences, he was referring to that manifestation of the moral law that is present in the structure of creation itself, especially in the consciousness of God all humans have from being made in the divine image. Thus Cain committed murder and was held responsible for his sinful act, long before God had said in the Ten Commandments, "Thou shalt not kill." The Ten Commandments concretized the moral law of God, placing it center stage, so to say, in God's covenantal dealings with the people of Israel.

Still, Paul did not say that the entire law is summed up in the Ten Com-

---

[61] H. Hübner, *Law in Paul's Thought,* 37. See the fuller exposition of Hübner's views in his essay, "Das ganze und das eine Gesetz, zum Problem Paulus und die Stoa," *Kerygma und Dogma* 22 (1976): 250-76.

[62] Sanders, *Paul, the Law,* 93-114. See also the discussion in Longenecker, *Galatians,* 242.

mandments but rather in a single commandment (lit., "word," *logos*): "Love your neighbor as yourself." No doubt Paul was echoing here the words of Jesus, who quoted this same verse from Lev 19:18 in his own summation of the Law and the Prophets (Matt 5:43; 22:34-40). Not only here but also in Rom 13:8-10, Paul omitted the first great summation of the law mentioned by Jesus, "Love the Lord your God with all your heart." We should not imagine, however, that Paul was emphasizing the horizontal dimension of the Christian life to the exclusion of the vertical or that he was constructing an "ethics from below" as opposed to one "from above."

Why did Paul call the selfless love of neighbor the fulfilling of the whole law? Not because it is superior to the worship and adoration of God, but rather because it is the proof of it. As Calvin correctly noted, "God is invisible; but he represents himself to us in the brethren and in their persons demands what is due to himself. Love to men springs only from the fear and love of God."[63] Thus the commandment "Love your neighbor as yourself" sums up all the other commandments, including, as its basic presupposition, the first table of the Decalogue. The ceremonial and civil aspects of the Mosaic legislation are no longer binding on Christians today, but the moral law, expressed in the Ten Commandments, is indeed relevant for the New Testament believer who by divine grace has been incorporated into the people of God. This believer delights in the law of God in accordance with the new nature he has received and thus joins fervently in the exclamation of the Old Testament saint, "O how I love thy law! It is my meditation all the day" (Ps 119:97, KJV).[64]

Without relapsing into legalism, then, Paul was exhorting the Galatian believers to demonstrate their faith energized by love and leading to holiness. Having been justified by faith alone, they were no longer in bondage to the law, but the moral law had not been annulled. The Ten Commandments, summarized in the admonition to love one's neighbor, are still in force. Are there no appreciable differences, then, between believers who stand on this side of Good Friday and Easter and those who lived under the old economy of anticipation? With respect to the moral law we may note the following differences for believers on either side of the salvation-historical divide:

1. To the Old Testament saints who lived during the Mosaic dispensation

---

[63] Calvin, CNTC 11.101.

[64] The role of the law in the life of believers remains one of the most vexing issues in contemporary church life today. Among the more helpful guides in sorting through this issue are the following studies: J. Murray, *Principles of Conduct,* esp. 181-201; E. Kevan, *Moral Law* (Phillipsburg, N.J.: Presbyterian & Reformed, 1991); W. J. Chantry, *God's Righteous Kingdom: The Law's Connection with the Gospel* (Edinburgh: Banner of Truth, 1980). I am grateful to E. Reisinger for bringing to my attention the works by Kevan and Chantry.

the moral law was imbedded within a framework of ceremonies and rituals all of which were but images and shadows of the new covenant inaugurated by Christ.[65] The difference between the Old Testament and the New is the difference between the time of the night and the dawning of a new day (cf. 2 Pet 1:19). Even the prophets did not always understand the things of which they spoke, having only the confirmation of vague and shadowy types to sustain their faith. We now see, as no Old Testament saint ever did, the full and clear meaning of God's moral law as expounded by Jesus himself in the Sermon on the Mount.

2. Paul quoted Jesus' citation of the Pentateuchal command to "Love your neighbor as yourself." In rabbinic tradition also this Old Testament saying was interpreted as a basic summary principle for the whole law, although its characteristic form was the "Negative Golden Rule" attributed to Rabbi Hillel: "What is hateful to you, do not do to your neighbors; that is the whole Torah, while the rest is the commentary thereof. Go and learn it."[66] Jesus, of course, recast this principle in a positive—and much more difficult!—form. What is the difference? In the negative form of the Golden Rule we begin with ourselves: those things that are unpleasant to us, these we will not do to our neighbor. But in Jesus' version, which Paul followed, we begin with God before whom neither we nor our neighbors have any rights at all. In the freedom of grace, then, we are able to see and relate to others neither in terms of our own individual proclivities nor in terms of our neighbor's sin and greediness but in the way of Christ, who expended himself even for those who rejected him. D. M. Lloyd-Jones has given an unsurpassed exposition of what it means to fulfill the law of love in service to our neighbors:

> We see them now, no longer as hateful people who are trying to rob us of our rights, or trying to beat us in the race for money, or position or fame; we see them, as we see ourselves, as the victims of sin and of Satan, as the dupes of "the god of this world," as fellow-creatures who are under the wrath of God and hell-bound. We have an entirely new view of them. We see them to be exactly as we are ourselves, and we are both in a terrible predicament. And we can do nothing; but both of us together must run to Christ and avail our-

---

[65] Cf. Calvin's comment on this point: "Or, if you prefer, understand it thus: the Old Testament of the Lord was that covenant wrapped up in the shadowy and ineffectual observance of ceremonies and delivered to the Jews; it was temporary because it remained, as it were, in suspense until it might rest on a firm and substantial confirmation. It became new and eternal only after it was consecrated and established by the blood of Christ" (*Institutes* 2.11.4).

[66] See D. Daube, *The New Testament and Rabbinic Judaism* (London: Athlone, 1956), 65-72. Significantly, this negative form of the Golden Rule reappears in the postapostolic document the *Didache* (1:2): "Whatsoever thou wouldst not have done to thyself, do not thou to another" (*Apostolic Fathers* 1.309).

selves of his wonderful grace. We begin to enjoy it together and we want to share it together. That is how it works. It is the only way whereby we can ever do unto others as we would that they should do unto us. It is when we are really loving our neighbor as ourselves because we have been delivered from the thralldom of self, that we begin to enjoy "the glorious liberty of the children of God."[67]

Similarly, the question of the identity of one's neighbor takes a radically different form in light of Jesus' parable of the good Samaritan. No longer may our neighbors be defined exclusively as fellow Jews, fellow Baptists, fellow Americans, the families in my subdivision, the members of my race, or those who agree with me politically. Our neighbors include the loveless, the least, the unlikely. Indeed, as H. Greeven has said so well, "One cannot say in advance who the neighbor is . . . only the course of life will make this plain enough. One cannot define one's neighbor; one can only be a neighbor."[68]

3. The Christian is able to fulfill the law through the gift of love that is the result of the twofold sending Paul described earlier in Gal 4: God's sending of his Son into the world and his sending of the Holy Spirit into the hearts of believers. S. Westerholm has noted that Paul nowhere claimed that Christians "do" (*poiein*) the law; rather they are said to "fulfill" (*plēroun*) the law. In 5:3, for example, Paul spoke of the obligation for those who were "under the law" to obey its every precept, whereas in 5:14 the whole law is fulfilled or summed up in the commandment to love. In other words, "'doing' the law was what was *required* of those 'under the law'; 'fulfilling' the law, was, for Paul, the *result* of Christian living the norms of which are stated in quite different terms.[69] This is a helpful distinction so long as it does not obscure the fact that a Christian's fulfillment of the law will be operative in the keeping of God's commandments. As Jesus said to his disciples, "If you love me, you will keep my commandments" (John 14:15, RSV). And again, "If you keep my commandments, you shall abide in my love, even as I have kept my Father's commandments and abide in his love" (John 15:10, RSV).

"Keeping the commandments" of the Lord is a typically Johannine way of

---

[67] D. M. Lloyd-Jones, *Studies in the Sermon on the Mount* (Grand Rapids: Eerdmans, 1991), 2:214-15.

[68] H. Greeven, "πλησίον," *TNDT* 6.316-18.

[69] S. Westerholm, "On Fulfilling the Whole Law (Gal 5:14)," *Svensk Exegetisk Arsbok* 51-52 (1986-87): 235. See also Westerholm's essay "Letter and Spirit: The Foundation of Pauline Ethics," *NTS* 30 (1984): 229-48. The idea that Paul carefully distinguished between the "doing" and the "fulfilling" of the law was earlier set forth by Betz, *Galatians*, 274-76, and has since claimed support from Longenecker, *Galatians*, 242-44. For a critique of this construction, see Thielman, *From Plight to Solution*, 51-53.

speaking (cf. John 14:21; 1 John 3:21-24; 5:3). It does not connote the servile obedience of one who seeks to gain acceptance with God by observing the works of the law. It is rather the free and joyful obedience of one who has been liberated from the curse of the law and empowered by the Holy Spirit to fulfill that which formerly convicted and condemned him. In a versified sermon on "The Believer's Principles concerning the Law and the Gospel," the Scottish preacher Ralph Erskine affirmed both the evangelical freedom from the law and the Christian obedience to it.

> The law's a tutor much in vogue,
> To gospel-grace a pedagogue;
> The Gospel to the law no less
> Than its full end for righteousness.

> When once the fiery law of God
> Has chas'd me to the gospel-road;
> Then back unto the holy law
> Most kindly gospel-grace will draw.

> The law most perfect still remains,
> And ev'ry duty full contains:
> The Gospel its perfection speaks,
> And therefore give whate'er it seeks.

> A rigid master was the law,
> Demanding brick, denying straw;
> But when with gospel-tongue it sings,
> It bids me fly, and gives me wings.[70]

5:15 This verse is a window into the congregations of Galatia. In contrast to the law of selfless love, which Paul has just commended, they were engaged in a fierce, internecine struggle, the result of which could have led to the very dissolution of their communities of faith. All three verbs Paul used to describe their unholy uncivil war on one another—biting, devouring, being destroyed—were bywords commonly used in Hellenistic Greek to suggest wild animals engaged in deadly struggle.[71] The translation of the NEB suggests a catfight: "But if you go on fighting one another, tooth and nail, all you can expect is mutual destruction."

Obviously Paul was writing to churches caught in a serious theological conflict over the doctrines of the false teachers. It is possible that some of

---

[70] Kevan, *Moral Law,* 74-75.

[71] So Burton, *Galatians,* 297.

these churches may have divided into Paul-, James-, and Peter-parties much as the Corinthians did later. If that is true, it is worth noting that Paul, who had argued throughout the letter passionately and indignantly for the truth of the gospel, did not here promote the victory of his own partisan group. Paul spoke as a pastor to all of the believers in Galatia, warning them against continuing strife and mutual destruction. More likely, however, the intrusion of the Judaizers exacerbated an underlying conflict that was already present among these Christians. It is the works of the flesh that Paul would shortly enumerate, among which are dissensions and factions, that had produced the fractured fellowship and broken unity Paul here lamented.[72]

(2) Conflict and Victory (5:16-18)

[16]So I say, live by the Spirit, and you will not gratify the desires of the sinful nature. [17]For the sinful nature desires what is contrary to the Spirit, and the Spirit what is contrary to the sinful nature. They are in conflict with each other, so that you do not do what you want. [18]But if you are led by the Spirit, you are not under law.

5:16 Having just shuddered to contemplate the possible ruin and annihilation of the Galatian churches through their raucous attacks on one another, Paul now moved on to describe the divinely appointed remedy for this grave dilemma. "So I say," or "Here is my advice" (Phillips), is a common Pauline formula for introducing a new section of material as well as for alerting his readers to an emphatic point he was about to make. Just as Paul's declaration of freedom in 5:1 stated a thesis he subsequently developed against legalism (5:2-12) and libertinism (13-15), so here in v. 16 he set forth a general principle that would govern everything he had to say through 6:10.

Paul's diagnosis of the conflict that confronts every Christian begins with a command, "Walk in the Spirit," and a promise, "Ye shall not fulfil the lust of the flesh" (KJV). Both the command and the promise are conditioned upon Paul's earlier indicative in v. 13, "You, my brothers, were called to be free." Although the word "freedom" does not recur again in Galatians, Paul had by no means left this concept behind. But the freedom to which we have been called in Christ is always under attack. It can be subverted by legalism or dissipated through antinomianism. True Christian liberty avoids these dangerous extremes by expressing itself in loving service to the neighbor and joyful

---

[72] On the source of these quarrels Fung has observed that "it is difficult to conceive of Paul condemning disputes and controversy *related to the Galatian heresy* as 'fighting one another' since in this very letter (esp. chaps. 3 and 4; cf. 1:8f.) he is himself engaging in theological debate with the Judaizers" (*Galatians,* 247, n. 27).

fulfillment of the law of God.

But where does the believer acquire the resources for this kind of victorious Christian living? Modern religious pedagogy offers many answers: a winsome personality, one's innate abilities, advanced degrees in theological education, special seminars on the higher Christian life, social activism, spiritual psychotherapy, and others. Paul's answer is the Holy Spirit. Only the Spirit of God who has made us free from sin and given us new life in regeneration can keep us truly free as we experience through walking in him the power of sanctification.

Here in Gal 5 Paul used four distinct verbs to designate the Spirit-controlled life of the believer, all of which are roughly equivalent in meaning: to walk in the Spirit (v. 16), to be led by the Spirit (v. 18), to live by the Spirit (v. 25a), and to keep in step with the Spirit (v. 25b). Each of these verbs suggests a relationship of dynamic interaction, direction, and purpose. The present tense of the imperative *peripateite,* "walk," also indicates a present activity now in progress. Paul had earlier reminded the Galatians of how they received the Holy Spirit upon hearing him preach the message of Christ and his cross (3:1-3). Here he was exhorting them to continue the walk they had begun on that occasion. If they continued to walk in the Spirit, they would not be halted by the fleshly appeals of the Judaizers, their own libertine tendencies, or the debilitating disputes within their churches. Although this is the only place in Galatians where the word "walk" is used in this sense, it is a common Pauline designation for one's daily conduct or lifestyle. In its wider usage the Greek word means not only "to walk" in a general sense but "to walk around after someone or to walk in a particular direction." For example, the students of Aristotle were known as the *Peripatetics* because of their habit of following the philosopher around from place to place as he dispensed his teachings. In Paul's vocabulary, to walk in the Spirit or be led by the Spirit means to go where the Spirit is going, to listen to his voice, to discern his will, to follow his guidance.[73]

5:17 In this verse Paul set forth in the starkest terms possible the ethical dualism that rages in the world at large and from which no believer who must live in that real world can be exempt. Twice before in Galatians we have encountered an explicit antithesis between spirit and flesh. In Gal 3:3 Paul asked how the Galatians who had begun with the Spirit could possibly think

---

[73] The RSV incorrectly translates the second part of v. 16 as another imperative: "Do not gratify the desires of the flesh." However, as Burton observed, the aorist subjunctive with a double negative expresses a note of promise and assurance (*Galatians,* 299). Paul was making a strong assertion that once the Galatians allowed the Spirit to guide them, then they would "never satisfy the passions of the flesh" (Moffatt). See *Translator's Handbook,* 134.

that perfection in the things of God could come by means of the flesh, an obvious reference to the imposition of circumcision and the works of the law implied there from. Again in Gal 4:29 the births of Ishmael and Isaac are sharply contrasted in terms of their origin in the flesh, that is, human connivance and self-will as opposed to the Spirit, that is, promised and initiated by God. Here in 5:17 flesh and Spirit are portrayed as two warring forces locked in mortal conflict within the life of the believer. As we saw in v. 13, the word "flesh" in Paul's vocabulary cannot be reduced to the material or physical dimension of the human person. It is a far more encompassing term involving the mind, will, and emotions as well as the physical body. According to R. Jewett, the flesh was Paul's term for everything aside from God in which one placed his final trust.[74]

In contrast with most recent commentators, but in keeping with more classical expositions (not only Luther and Calvin but also Lightfoot), it seems best to interpret the conflict between flesh and Spirit that Paul referred to here in terms of the similar tension he described in Rom 7:7-25.[75] Much of the discussion hinges on how one interprets the closing phrase of this verse, "so that you do not do what you want." Were the desires in question the lusts of the flesh that war against the Spirit or, conversely, the holy and chaste yearnings for God that have come into conflict with the flesh? If the former, then Paul would have been saying: Since the Spirit opposes the flesh, and if you are really walking in the Spirit, then you are not free to do whatever you want to do, which is to gratify the desires of the flesh. Clarence Jordan captures this interpretation well: "That is why you cannot run wild, doing as you please" (Cotton Patch, 102). However, the more natural reading is to interpret "the things that ye would" (KJV) as those holy desires and affections given by God to believers in regeneration.

So long as we remain in this present life, we never outgrow or transcend the spiritual conflict Paul was describing in this passage. There is no spiritual

---

[74] R. Jewett, *Paul's Anthropological Terms,* 103. E. Käsemann has delineated the unique meaning of σάρχ in Pauline theology by contrasting it with other patterns of thought: "For in Greek, flesh is a substance which one can *have* but not *be,* let alone be possessed by; whereas in the Old Testament and pre-Philonic Judaism flesh denotes the creature that perishes, but it is not a hostile active power, opposed per se to the divine spirit and struggling against it for the mastery of the world. We meet this radicalization in Gal 5:16ff., however, and it determines the whole of Pauline anthropology" *(Perspectives on Paul* [Philadelphia: Fortress, 1971], 26).

[75] See the discussion in Betz, *Galatians,* 279-81; Burton, *Galatians,* 300-302; Fung, *Galatians,* 248-51. Ebeling admits that Gal 5:16-18 "[cries] out for comparison with Rom 7:15-23. In the latter passage, modern exegetes are nearly unanimous that Paul is speaking of humanity before Christ; it is indisputable, however, that here Paul has Christians in mind. . . . I would never suggest that in Rom 7 too, the so-called Christian interpretation has something to be said for it, just as here in Gal 5 there is also an element of universal anthropology" *(Truth,* 255).

technique or second blessing that can propel the believer onto a higher plane of Christian living where this battle must no longer be fought. In the early church Jerome, that hardy and stern disciplinarian, removed himself far from the lurid temptations of the city only to find that he had not escaped them at all. As he confessed:

> O how often I imagined that I was in the midst of the pleasures of Rome when I was stationed in the desert, in that solitary wasteland which is so burned up by the heat of the sun that it provides a dreadful habitation for the monks! I, who because of the fear of hell had condemned myself to such a hell and who had nothing but scorpions and wild animals for company, often thought that I was dancing in a chorus with girls. My face was pale from fasting, but my mind burned with passionate desires within my freezing body; and the fires of sex seethed, even though the flesh had already died in me as a man.[76]

The conflict between flesh and Spirit, and not only with reference to sexual temptations, is intense and unrelenting. One of the greatest dangers in the Christian life is complacency, the temptation to imagine oneself invulnerable, and hence impervious, to the allurement of the flesh. Yet Paul's words were addressed to the entire believing community. No Christians are so spiritually strong or mature that they need not heed his warning, but neither are any so weak or vacillating that they cannot be free from the tyranny of the flesh through the power of the Spirit. As Betz has put it, "In the battle between the forces of flesh and Spirit there is no stalemate, but the Spirit takes the lead, overwhelms, and thus defeats evil."[77]

5:18 Before enumerating the works of the flesh, Paul reiterated what he had just said in a conditional sentence that also brought back into view the central theological issue he had wrestled with throughout the letter, "But if you are led by the Spirit, you are not under law." Clearly, Paul still had his eyes on the Judaizers, and he wanted to give no one a pretext for saying that his ethical instructions were merely a form of watered-down legalism. Life in the Spirit stands in irreconcilable conflict with existence "under" the law. It is not that the moral law has been abrogated or that the Ten Commandments have become antiquated. Rather believers are now energized to fulfill the true intention of the law precisely because they have been set free from the law by the possession of the Spirit. Paul expressed the same thought later in Rom 8:3-4: "God has done what the law, weakened by the flesh, could not do: sending his own Son in the likeness of sinful flesh and for sin, he condemned sin in the flesh, *in order that* the just requirement of the law might

---

[76] *LW* 27.68-69.
[77] Betz, *Galatians*, 281.

be fulfilled in us, who walk not according to the flesh but according to the Spirit" (RSV; italics added).

(3) The Works of the Flesh (5:19-21)

[19]The acts of the sinful nature are obvious: sexual immorality, impurity and debauchery; [20]idolatry and witchcraft; hatred, discord, jealousy, fits of rage, selfish ambition, dissensions, factions [21]and envy; drunkenness, orgies, and the like. I warn you, as I did before, that those who live like this will not inherit the kingdom of God.

VIRTUES AND VICES? (5:19a)   **5:19a**   In 5:19-26 Paul developed further the antithesis between flesh and Spirit in terms of two distinctive listings of ethical qualities, the first a series of malevolent acts Paul described as "the works of the flesh"; the second, a somewhat shorter series of traits collectively described as "the fruit of the Spirit." These two lists bring to concrete expression Paul's earlier admonition that the Galatians should not use their Christian liberty as a base of operations for indulgence of the flesh (v. 13), as well as his exhortation for them to serve one another in love by walking and being led by the Spirit (vv. 16,18). At the conclusion of the two lists Paul appended two corresponding conclusions: first, the statement that belonging to Jesus Christ involves crucifixion of the flesh (cf. 2:20) and, second, the reminder that living by the Spirit means keeping in step with the Spirit so that the freedom for which Christ has set us free becomes neither a pretext for libertinism nor a step backward into legalism.

The final verse in chap. 5 harks back to the bitter conflict and infighting going on among the Christians in Galatia. Paul urged a cessation of pride, envy, and invidious provocation. Thus in delineating and contrasting the works of the flesh and fruit of the Spirit, Paul was not spinning out a general theory of ethics but rather addressing particular problems related to practical Christian living in the Galatian congregations.

Most commentators on Galatians have pointed out that Paul's two catalogs of sinful deeds and holy traits closely parallel similar listings of virtues and vices found frequently in the writings of such moral philosophers as Seneca, Cicero, and Epictetus as well as Hellenistic Jewish thinkers, such as Philo of Alexandria. It is certain that catalogs of virtues and vices were a common feature in the moral literature of the day, and some of the items in Paul's lists are duplicated in the systematic numeration of desirable and detestable qualities set forth by non-Christian thinkers. Aristotle, for example, included among the virtues of the soul justice, courage, self-control, and magnanimity.[78] In his *Nicomachean Ethics* Aristotle further defined a virtue

---

[78] Aristotle, *Rhetoric* 1.6.1362b, quoted in Longenecker, *Galatians,* 249.

as the observance of a mean or middle way between two extremes, either of which he considered a vice. The fact that in Gal 5–6 Paul was presenting Christian freedom as a kind of *via media* between the extremes of legalism on the one hand and libertinism on the other has been taken as further evidence that Paul had derived his catalogs of good and sinful acts from the standard catalogs of virtues and vices that were a common feature in the ethical teaching of the Greco-Roman and Hellenistic Jewish world.

Despite similarities in form and style, however, Paul's dual listing of so-called vices and virtues stands in marked contrast to those commonly reproduced by his contemporaries in the wider world of thought. As Ebeling has noted, Paul described throughout "human conduct that does not fit into the psychological schema of character and act but shines forth to fill the totality of life."[79] For Paul ethics could not be reduced to a branch of anthropology. The Aristotelian concept of "virtues of the soul" was totally foreign to his framework. For Paul flesh and Spirit were two powers, two modalities of existence, locked in conflict on the battlefield of every individual Christian. We have not properly understood the eschatological tension that characterizes the church of Jesus Christ in this present evil world nor the struggle between growth and decay, victory and defeat, which engages every believer until we have placed Paul's antithesis between flesh and Spirit in its broader cosmic context.

Before looking briefly at each one of the fifteen items Paul singled out in these two contrasting series, we do well to notice three important differences in the way the two lists were formulated. First, Paul did not contrast the *works* of the flesh with opposing *works* of the Spirit. The "works" of the flesh are the products of fallen human beings in their devising, conniving, and manufacturing (in the sense of "made with one's own hands") efforts at self-actualization. From the Tower of Babel to modern totalitarianism, from Aaron's golden calf to contemporary idols of money, sex, and power, the works of the flesh have littered the human landscape with misery, violence, and death. When Paul proceeded to describe the modality of the Spirit-led life, however, he deliberately shifted from the language of technology to that of nature—the *fruit* of the Spirit. Those who grow apples, oranges, and peaches know that however much they may seek to protect their orchards from bad weather or deadly insects at the end of the day the product yielded by a fruit tree is a gift, not the result of human ingenuity or agricultural prowess. Just so, that which the Holy Spirit effects in the lives of believers—the desirable traits of Paul's second list—is the result of his indwelling presence and the spiritual metamorphosis that dynamic reality brings about (cf. Rom 12:1-2).

---

[79] Ebeling, *Truth of the Gospel*, 256.

Second, there is an obvious and important difference in the way the two lists are structured. Paul's list of heinous sins is deliberately defined as plural in number, "works of the flesh." The fruit of the Spirit, however, is noticeably singular. There is one fruit of the Spirit that manifests itself in nine Christian graces nicely grouped into three well-balanced triplets: (1) love, joy, peace; (2) patience, kindness, goodness; (3) faithfulness, gentleness, self-control. By contrast, the works of the flesh roll topsy-turvy from Paul's stylus, a seemingly random assortment of terms with no inherent consistency or logical sequence. As Betz has noted, "The seemingly chaotic arrangement of these terms is reflective of the chaotic nature of evil; this chaos is to be contrasted with the oneness of the 'fruit of the Spirit' and its orderly arrangement (vv. 22-23)."[80]

Furthermore, the fifteen items Paul included in his catalog of evil were by no means intended to be exhaustive. And so when he came to the end of his enumeration he added a postscript, "and the like." It is as though Paul were saying: "You know, I could go on forever like this! No one can name all the works of the flesh, for there are multitudinous ways for the principle of evil to manifest itself in human perversions, depravities, enmities, excesses, obsessions—and the like!" Only God himself can bring definitive closure to this cycle of wickedness, and this he surely would do in the judgment that is to come (v. 21). Thus the pluriformity and interminability of the works of the flesh stand in marked contrast to the singularity and organic harmony of the fruit of the Spirit.

Finally, the works of the flesh inevitably recall Paul's earlier polemic against the works of the law. This, despite the fact that the law clearly condemns the immoral, idolatrous, and intemperate lifestyle epitomized by the deeds listed here, all of which would have been formally repudiated by the Judaizers as well as by Paul. But to live *kata sarka,* "according to the flesh," is to invite precisely these kinds of abominable corruptions and faults to take root in one's life whether that happens through an antinomian aloofness to the moral law of God or a nomistic distortion of that law as an end in itself. Thus Paul's concluding comment concerning the components of the fruit of the Spirit, "against such things there is no law" (v. 23), is not merely "an understatement given for rhetorical effect."[81] Rather it is another way of expressing what Paul later stated in Rom 8:1: "There is therefore now no condemnation to them who are in Christ Jesus, who walk not after the flesh, but after the Spirit" (KJV). Only those redeemed by grace can bear the fruit of the Spirit, and the law of God will not bring them into condemnation,

[80] Betz, *Galatians,* 283.
[81] Longenecker, *Galatians,* 263.

although neither will it spare them from accountability, at the second coming of Christ. The contrast with those who dissipate their lives in the works of the flesh is jarring: "Those who live like this will not inherit the kingdom of God" (v. 21).

A CATALOG OF EVIL (5:19b-21a).   **5:19b-21a**   Our analysis of the fifteen items in Paul's catalog of evil corresponds to the traditional grouping first suggested by Lightfoot, who divided these sinful acts into four classes: (1) sensual passions, (2) unlawful dealings in things spiritual, (3) violations of brotherly love, (4) intemperate excesses.[82] Let us glance briefly at Paul's exposé of the sins of immorality, idolatry, animosity, and intemperance.

Sins of immorality:

Sexual Immorality (porneia).   It is significant that the first three acts in Paul's list of sins have to do with loose sexual relations. This typically Pauline feature characterizes his listing of evil offenses in other writings as well (cf. 1 Cor 6:9; 6:18; Eph 5:5; 1 Thess 4:3). It resonates with Jesus' own categorizing of unclean acts that come out of the heart and defile the whole person. In Jesus' list evil thoughts and sexual immorality precede theft, murder, adultery, greed, malice, deceit, lewdness, envy, slander, arrogance, and folly (Mark 7:20-22). Why this prioritizing of sexual immorality? It is not because these sins are more intrinsically heinous than the others but rather because they display more graphically the self-centeredness and rebellion against God's norm that mark all of the others as well. For believers to be caught up (whether or not they are "caught") in sexual misconduct deeply grieves the Holy Spirit, whose presence within their lives has made of their bodies temples unto the Lord (cf. 1 Cor 6:18-20). The word *porneia* originally meant "prostitution" (cf. the Greek *pornē*, "prostitute," from the verb *pernēmi*, "to sell slaves," since prostitutes were frequently bought and sold on the slave market), although by the time of Paul it had gained the more general meaning of sexual immorality or irregularity. *Porneia* is invariably translated "fornication" in the KJV although it denotes any unlawful sexual intercourse, including adultery and incest (cf. 1 Cor 5:1). Acts of sexual immorality, although often done in the name of love, are really the antithesis

---

[82] Lightfoot, *Galatians,* 210. We may ignore Lightfoot's comment to the effect that the third class of sins would be especially enticing to "the excitable temperament of a Celtic people," as well as his jibe that the mention of orgies and drunkenness was "not unfitly addressed to a nation whose Gallic descent perhaps disposed them too easily to these excesses." Later commentators have tended to follow, with some modifications, Lightfoot's fourfold division of Paul's catalog of vices. See Burton, *Galatians,* 304-10; Fung, *Galatians,* 253-61; Matera, *Galatians,* 208-9. See also C. G. Kruse, "Virtues and Vices," *DPL,* 962-63; E. Schweizer, "Traditional Ethical Patterns in the Pauline and Post-Pauline Letters and their Development," in *Text and Interpretation,* ed. E. Best and R. McL. Wilson (Cambridge: Cambridge University Press, 1979), 195-209.

of love, which is the foremost fruit of the Spirit.

Impurity (akatharsia). This word literally means "uncleanness" and has both a medical and ceremonial connotation. Even today doctors speak of cleaning a wound before they apply medication to it. Under the Mosaic law ceremonial impurity barred one from participation in the worship rituals of the temple until the impediment was removed. Thus lepers cried "Unclean!" whenever anyone approached them. Even after Jesus had healed or "cleansed" a leper, he required him to complete the ritual of purification in accordance with the Old Testament provision (cf. Matt 8:1-4). Uncleanness, then, speaks of the defilement of sexual sin and the separation from God that it brings.[83] The remedy for such sins is confession and repentance. If we confess and repent, the promise of God's Word is that Christ is faithful and just to forgive and purify (*katharisē*) from all unrighteousness (1 John 1:9).

Debauchery (aselgeia). W. Barclay defines this particular vice as "a love of sin so reckless and so audacious that a man has ceased to care what God or man thinks of his actions."[84] In speaking of the unbridled wantonness of the children of Israel in his day, the prophet Jeremiah asked: "Are they ashamed of their loathsome conduct? No, they have no shame at all; they do not even know how to blush" (Jer 6:15). Debauchery, then, speaks of the total loss of limits, the lack of restraint, decency, and self-respect. Paul was not saying that all of the Galatians were guilty of such extreme licentiousness, but he was warning against a loose disregard for standards of sexual purity, a liberal lifestyle that in the end would lead them to the very pit.[85]

---

[83] See Eph 5:3, where in typical fashion Paul linked impurity and sexual immorality: Πορ-νεία δὲ καί ἀκαθαρσία πᾶσα. See also F. Hauck, "ακαθαρτος, ἀκαθαρσία," *TDNT* 3.427-29.

[84] W. Barclay, *Flesh and Spirit: An Examination of Galatians 5:19-23* (London: SCM, 1962), 31.

[85] Longenecker quotes three examples of the use of ἀσέλγεια in the *Jewish War* of Josephus: once in reporting a false accusation against Mariamne that she recklessly "exhibited herself" before another man, so inflaming Herod with murderous jealousy (*J.W.* 1.439); once describing the Essenes' asceticism in keeping themselves from "women's wantonness" (*J.W.* 2.121); and once in portraying the actions of the Zealot soldiers within Jerusalem in the last days of the city's siege, who in their drunkenness imitated both the dress and the passions of women, "devising in their excess of lasciviousness unlawful pleasures and wallowing as in a brothel in the city which they polluted from end to end with their foul deeds" (*J.W.* 4.562; (Longenecker, *Galatians,* 254-55). Elsewhere in the NT (cf. Eph 4:19) ἀσέλγεια carries a more general meaning of total abandonment to evil. However, by grouping it with πορνεία and ακαθαρσία in this context, Paul seems to have restricted its meaning to illicit sexual activities in their grossest manifestations. In a parallel text Paul brought the same three words together in 2 Cor 12:21, where he expressed his grief over the lapse of the Corinthians, many of whom "have sinned earlier and have not repented of the impurity, sexual sin and debauchery in which they have indulged." See also O. Bauernfeind, "ἀσέλγεια" *TDNT* 1.490.

Sins of idolatry:

Idolatry (eidōlolatria). Paul moved from deeds of impurity to consider two items associated with the heathen worship of false gods. It is significant that the word "idolatry" is not found in the texts of the classical writers but belongs to the unique Christian vocabulary of the New Testament. From the ancient fertility cult of Baal to the sacral prostitution at the Temple of Aphrodite in Corinth, the homage paid to false gods was often accompanied by shameful displays of sensuality. The abuse of the gift of sex inevitably leads to the elevation of the creature to the level of the Creator. In our day the form of idolatry has changed, but the reality is as pervasive now as in the time of Paul. Clarence Jordan's translation of this term as "worshiping gadgets" is especially relevant in an age of computers, MTV, and F-16s!

Witchcraft (pharmakeia). At the root of this word is *pharmakon,* literally "drug," from which we derive our English word "pharmacy." In classical Greek *pharmakeia* referred to the use of drugs whether for medicinal or more sinister purposes, e.g., poisoning. In the New Testament, however, it is invariably associated with the occult, both here in Galatians and in Revelation, where it occurs twice (Rev 9:21; 18:23). English translations usually render *pharmakeia* as "witchcraft" (KJV, NIV) or "sorcery" (RSV, NEB). These words correctly convey the idea of black magic and demonic control, but they miss the more basic meaning of drug use. In New Testament times *pharmakeia* in fact denoted the use of drugs with occult properties for a variety of purposes including, especially, abortion. As J. T. Noonan has written, "Paul's usage here cannot be restricted to abortion, but the term he chose is comprehensive enough to include the use of *abortifacient* drugs."[86] In the early church both infanticide, often effected through the exposure of newborn babies to the harsh elements, and abortion, commonly brought about by the use of drugs, were regarded as murderous acts. Both are flagrant violations of Jesus' command to "love your neighbor as yourself."

Sins of animosity:

Hatred (echthrai). This is the first of eight nouns Paul would mention,

---

[86] J. T. Noonan, Jr., "An Almost Absolute Value in History," in *The Morality of Abortion: Legal and Historical Perspectives* (Cambridge: Harvard University Press, 1970), 9. That φαρμακεία was a common term for abortion-inducing drugs is borne out by its recurrence in other early Christian writings. Thus the *Didache* includes the following list of negative imperatives Christians were expected to obey: "You shall not kill. You shall not commit adultery. You shall not corrupt boys. You shall not fornicate. You shall not steal. You shall not make magic. You shall not practice medicine (φαρμακεία). You shall not slay the child by abortions (φθορα). You shall not kill what is generated. You shall not desire your neighbors wife" (*Did.* 2.2). See further T. George, "Southern Baptist Heritage of Life" (Nashville: Christian Life Commission of the SBC, 1993).

all of which refer to the breakdown of interpersonal relationships. Hatred or enmity (cf. "quarrels," NEB) is the opposite of love. In Rom 8:7 Paul used this same word to describe the hostility of the sinful mind to God. Here, however, its destructive force is played out on the plane of human relationships. The specific forms this hatred can take in tearing down community life Paul would enumerate in the following words:

Discord (eris).   In the New Testament this word is unique to Paul, who used it nine times to characterize the strife and discord that beset so many of his congregations. The NEB translation "contentious temper" points to the source of so much wrangling and ill will among Christian brothers and sisters. Paul was aware of some who even preached Christ "out of envy and rivalry" (Phil 1:15). This shows that it is possible for the Lord to use even unworthy motives and selfish means to accomplish the greatest good. But what damage is done to the body of Christ when ministers of the gospel do not walk in the Spirit but rather are pulled aside by petty bickering and pride!

Jealousy (zēlos).   As we have seen, jealousy can be used in the Bible in a good sense to describe even God himself. But here a negative connotation is meant. A jealous person is someone who wants what other people have. A jealous pastor looks with envious eyes on the more prosperous church field of a neighboring minister. Jealousy often leads to bitterness and sometimes erupts into violence, as when Joseph's brothers seized him in anger and sold him into slavery (cf. Gen 37:12-36). At the root of all sentiments of jealousy is the basic posture of ingratitude to God, a failure to accept one's life as a gift from God. To envy what someone else has is to fling one's own gifts before God in unthankful rebellion and spite.

Fits of Rage (thymoi).   Here is another word with various shades of meaning depending upon the context in which it is used. For example, this same word is used in Revelation to refer both to God's wrath (14:10; 19:15) and Satan's rage (12:12). Here in Galatians it means a passionate outburst of anger or hostile feeling. Such displays of uncontrollable verbal violence should not be excused as the product of "an Irish temper" or a natural propensity to "fly off the handle." Such fits of rage are a form of conduct unbecoming to a Christian. They drag us away from God and the promptings of his Spirit and further enmesh us in the works of the flesh.

Selfish Ambition (eritheiai).   This is a term that derived from the political culture of ancient Greece, where it meant "office seeking" or "canvassing for office."[87] Although many godly men and women have been called to live out their Christian vocation in political life, it is also true that politics attracts those persons given to self-promotion and self-service rather than the service

---

[87] Aristotle, *Politics* 5.2.9.

of others. For such "political animals," climbing the ladder of success or manipulating the process for personal gain is all a part of self-seeking lifestyle. While such characteristics are bad enough in secular politics, they are especially corrupting to the community of faith whose Lord and Savior modeled the opposite of this vice—he came not to be served but to serve and to give his life as a ransom for many.

Dissensions (dichostasiai).   Paul used this same word only on one other occasion, in Rom 16:17: "I urge you, brothers, to watch out for those who cause *divisions* and put obstacles in your way that are contrary to the teaching you have learned. Keep away from them." Like the preceding word, "dissensions" carries political overtones suggesting the cultivation of a party spirit or exclusive elite within the church. Whenever this happens, the unity and fellowship of the body of Christ is fractured. Soon the backbiting, badmouthing, and mutual destruction Paul warned the Galatians of earlier (5:15) manifest themselves to the detriment of the life and witness of God's people.

Factions (haireseis).   This word too finds only one other occurrence in the Pauline corpus, in 1 Cor 11:19, where Paul spoke of the various factions in the church at Corinth. The basic meaning of this word derives from the verb "to choose" (from which we also get our English word "heresy," a deliberately chosen doctrine at variance with the rule of faith). This verse reminds us the divisive tendency so evident in many congregations is the result of intentional choices to walk in the way of selfish pride, envy, and bickering rather than the royal road of love, forgiveness, and magnanimity.[88]

Envy (phthonoi).   This is another classical word similar in meaning to the trait of jealousy listed earlier, except that *zēlos* is singular and *phthonoi*, "envyings," is plural, suggesting the multitudinous expressions of envious desire. This word is invariably used in a negative sense except in the highly exceptional case of Jas 4:5, where this same word is used of the Holy Spirit in an almost shocking way: "Do ye think that the scriptures saith in vain, The spirit that dwelleth in us lusteth to envy?" (KJV). The paraphrase of *The Living Bible* is much closer to the mark at this point: "Or what do you think the Scripture means when it says that the Holy Spirit, whom God has placed within us, watches over us with tender jealousy?" But in Gal 5:21 it is not the tender jealousy of the Holy Spirit who indwells and protects the believer that Paul had in mind. Rather it is the evil conduct and unacceptable rivalry that had sprung from the malice and ill will of the Galatians toward one another.[89]

---

[88] See H. Schlier, "αἱρεσις," *TDNT* 1.180-83.

[89] After "envyings" the KJV includes another work of the flesh, "murders," reflecting a strong textual tradition represented by a wide range of witnesses who read at this point φθόνοι φόνοι. Metzger surmises that the insertion of φονοι may have been made by copyists in recollection of Rom 1:29. See Metzger, *Textual Commentary,* 597-98.

Sins of intemperance:

Drunkenness (methai).   We come now to the fourth group of sinful deeds Paul included in his catalog of the works of the flesh. There is no place for drunkenness in a Spirit-directed lifestyle. Alcohol abuse was a common feature of urban life in the Roman Empire, but Paul expected a different, higher standard of conduct among those who belonged to Christ. He later wrote to the Ephesians in this same vein: "Do not get drunk on wine, which leads to debauchery. Instead, be filled with the Spirit" (Eph 5:18).[90] In addition to the common abuse of alcohol, Paul may also have had in mind the cultic inebriation practiced by the mystery religion of Dionysos, the wine god. Some of those who were in the habit of getting drunk before participating in the Lord's Supper at Corinth may have been influenced by this pagan ritual (cf. 1 Cor 11:21). Before they became Christians the Gentile believers of Galatia may have been addicted to their own bacchanalia. If some of them had now been convinced by the libertines in their midst to turn their Christian liberty into moral license, it is possible that they may have returned to their former habits of tippling without realizing how damaging this kind of behavior was to their new life in the Spirit. In any event, Paul portrayed excessive drinking as incompatible with real Christian commitment.

Orgies (kōmoi). This word is variously translated "revelings" (KJV), "carousing" (RSV), "wild parties" (TLB), "horsing around" (Cotton Patch). It occurs three times in the New Testament (here and in Rom 13:13 and 1 Pet 4:3). In each case it is linked to the sin of drunkenness. In New Testament times, as in our own day, the abuse of alcohol contributed to marital infidelity, child and spouse abuse, the erosion of family life, and moral chaos in society. Throughout these verses Paul has led us down fifteen steps into the pit of depravity. He has shown us the ugly reality of the flesh. He could have gone on and on as he indicates by his closing tag "and the like." Only the interposition of divine grace made operative by the transforming power of the Spirit can rescue one from the snare of such a loveless life.

SIN'S FINAL END.   **5:21b**   Paul now lets us in on the fact that what he had just said to the Galatians concerning the works of the flesh should have come as no surprise to them, for he had simply repeated the warning he gave to them before. This is the only way to understand his expression, "I warn you, even as I did before," that is, unless we search the first part of the letter for some enigmatic allusion to the exhortations of Gal 5 or, even more farfetched, project an earlier correspondence between Paul and the Galatians that is no longer extant.[91] The warning Paul reiterated in this verse must have

---

[90] See the commentary by M. Barth, *Ephesians 4–6* (New York: Doubleday, 1974), 580-82.

[91] Cole, *Galatians,* 164.

been given during his first preaching of the gospel in Galatia so that he was here recalling his readers to an earlier instruction they had been tempted to forget or ignore.

In this verse Paul looked forward to the personal, visible return of Jesus Christ in glory. This is the blessed hope of the Christian, but it is also an event of great foreboding for those outside of Christ because Jesus is coming again to judge the living and the dead (Acts 10:42). After this graphic, though not exhaustive catalog of evil, Paul said that those who "behave in such ways" (NEB), that is, those who habitually indulge in such immoral, idolatrous, impure, unjust, or intemperate acts, will be excluded from the celestial blessedness of the kingdom of God. This is not an idle threat but a solemn warning from the pen of a divinely inspired apostle of Jesus Christ.

But had not Paul himself forgotten what he wrote in Gal 1–4? Had he now ceased to teach that we are justified by faith alone apart from the works of the law? There is nothing in this passage that suggests the slightest hint of compromise on this cardinal doctrine of the Christian faith. As R. A. Cole has correctly noted, "Paul's whole point is that *they which do such things* thereby show themselves to be without the transforming gift of faith . . . [the Christian] shows the reality of the 'faith that justifies,' and the reality of the 'new life in Christ' that is within him, by a clear break with all these 'works of darkness,' familiar though they may have been to him in the past."[92] Those who are slaves to the works of the flesh show themselves to be no heirs of the kingdom of God; and, as Jesus said, unless they repent and turn from their wicked ways, they will all likewise perish.

Yet where is the Christian who can stand and boast that he has achieved perfect victory over the flesh and must no longer struggle with it? Such a person would surely be guilty of thinking more highly of himself than he should. Paul did not sound his warning in order to instill despair in struggling Christians. Rather he wanted us to see the heinous character of sin and so be led by the Spirit to repentance and mortification of the flesh. Calvin's comment on this verse expresses well Paul's evangelical intention:

> For who is there who does not labor under one or other of these sins? I reply: Paul does not threaten that there shall be excluded from the Kingdom of God all who have sinned, but all who remain impenitent. The saints themselves are heavily burdened, but they return to the way. Because they do not surrender, they are not included in this catalog. All the threatenings of God's judgments call us to repentance, for which pardon is always ready with God; but if we continue obstinate, they will be a testimony against us.[93]

---

[92] Ibid.
[93] Calvin, CNTC 11.104-5.

(4) The Fruit of the Spirit (5:22-26)

²²**But the fruit of the Spirit is love, joy, peace, patience, kindness, goodness, faithfulness, ²³gentleness and self-control. Against such things there is no law. ²⁴Those who belong to Christ Jesus have crucified the sinful nature with its passions and desires. ²⁵Since we live by the Spirit, let us keep in step with the Spirit. ²⁶Let us not become conceited, provoking and envying each other.**

A CATALOG OF GRACE (5:22-23). **5:22-23** After listing fifteen specific misdeeds, fifteen one-word illustrations of the works of the flesh, Paul turned to consider the contrasting graces of the Spirit-controlled life. The listing of the sinful acts in the catalog of evil was disorderly, chaotic, and incomplete, corresponding to the random and compulsive character of sin itself. In stark contrast now, the character traits contained in the catalog of grace appear in beautiful harmony, balanced and symmetrical, corresponding to the purposeful design and equilibrium of a life filled with the Spirit and lived out in the beauty of holiness. Paul grouped these nine graces into three triads that give a sense of order and completion, although here too there is no attempt to provide an exhaustive list of the Christian virtues:

> Love, joy, peace
> Patience, kindness, goodness
> Faithfulness, gentleness, self-control.

Various interpretations have been given about the meaning of this three-fold structure of threes. Three, of course, is the number of the divine Trinity, signifying in this case the perfect unity and loving reciprocity that has existed from all eternity among Father, Son, and Holy Spirit. Lightfoot suggested the following categorization of the nine graces: the first three comprising habits of the Christian mind, the second reflecting social intercourse and neighborly concern, and the third exhibiting the principles that guide a Christian's conduct. More simply still, J. Stott has described this list as a cluster of nine Christian graces that portray the believer's attitude to God, to other people, and to himself.[94] While these are all helpful ways of analyzing this description of the kind of ethical character produced in those who walk according to the Spirit, we should not press any of these subdivisions too far. Each of the nine qualities flows into one another, mutually enriching and reinforcing the process of sanctification in the life of the believer.

The concept of fruitfulness is well attested in Paul's other writings as well as throughout the Old Testament. Israel, for example, is frequently referred

---

[94] Lightfoot, *Galatians,* 212; Stott, *Only One Way,* 148. See also the excellent article and literature cited in D. S. Dockery, "Fruit of the Spirit," *DPL,* 316-19.

to as the "vineyard" of the Lord (cf. Isa 5:2-4; Hos 14:6). Likewise the man who delights in the law of the Lord and walks in his way is compared to "a tree planted by streams of water, which yields its fruit in season" (Ps 1:3). As we saw earlier, Paul deliberately contrasted the fruit (singular) of the Spirit with the works (plural) of the flesh. The former results from God's supernatural reshaping and transforming of human life, whereas the latter are contrived and manufactured out of the old sinful nature. Again, we should sit back and contemplate the beauty of this image rather than overinterpreting and analyzing it to death as W. Perkins came close to doing in his allegorical reading of this passage: "And by this, much is signified: namely, that the church is the garden of God, that teachers are planters and setters, that believers are trees of righteousness, but the Spirit of God is the sap and life of them, and good works and virtues are the fruits which they bear."[95] Here, then, are the evidences of a Spirit-filled life.

Love (agapē). "Love" is one of the most frequently used words in Paul's vocabulary, the noun *agapē* occurring seventy-five times, and the verb *agapaō*, "to show love," thirty-four times in his writings. It is significant that love heads the list of these nine graces of the Christian life. Paul might well have placed a period after love and moved on into the conclusion of his letter, for love is not merely "first among equals" in this listing but rather the source and fountain from which all of the other graces flow.[96] Before love is the fruit of the Spirit in the life of the believer, it is the underlying disposition and motivating force in election, creation, incarnation and atonement. As C. S. Lewis put it so well, "God, who needs nothing, loves into existence holy superfluous creatures in order that he may love and perfect them. He creates the universe, already foreseen—or should we say 'seeing'? there are no tenses in God—the buzzing cloud of flies about the cross, the flayed back pressed against the uneven stake, the nails driven through the mesial nerves, the repeated incipient suffocation as the body droops, the repeated torture of back and arms as it is time after time, for breath's sake hitched up. . . . This is the diagram of love Himself, the inventor of all loves."[97]

Love as a characteristic of the Christian life is consequent upon God's unfathomable love and infinite mercy toward us. For Paul this was founda-

---

[95] Perkins, *Galatians,* 391. Perkins correctly notes, however, that there are no true virtues or good affections without the prior grace of regeneration. "The virtues of the heathen, how excellent so ever they seemed to be, were but shadows of virtue, and served only to restrain the outward man, and no further."

[96] So Luther: "It would have sufficed to list only love, for this expands into all of the fruit of the Spirit" (*LW* 27.93). See R. Mohrlang, "Love," *DPL,* 575-78; E. Stauffer, "ἀγάπαω," *TDNT* 1.21-55; C. Spicq, *Agapē in the New Testament* (London: Herder, 1965).

[97] C. S. Lewis, *The Four Loves* (New York: Harcourt, Brace & World, 1960), 176.

tional to everything he had said and would yet say in Galatians—"I live by
faith in the Son of God, who loved me and gave himself for me" (2:20). The
result of the transforming, sanctifying ministry of the Holy Spirit in our lives
is just this: that we are enabled to love one another with the same kind of love
that God loves us. Paul profiled this kind of love in 1 Cor 13; it is a love that
"seeks not its own."

Only twice in Paul's letters did he speak explicitly of the believer's love
for God (Rom 8:28; 2 Thess 3:5), although everything he said about the call
to devotion, worship, and service presupposes the upward movement of such
love. However, Paul's emphasis here in Galatians as elsewhere was on the
Christian's love for his fellow human beings. While the horizon of the love
of neighbor is by no means restricted to fellow believers, it is supremely
important that Christians learn to live together in love. When Christians forget this, then two horrible consequences invariably follow: the worship of the
church is disrupted as the gifts of the Spirit are placed in invidious competition with the fruit of the Spirit, as happened at Corinth; the witness of the
church is damaged as unbelievers stumble and fall over the obvious lack of
love within the body of Christ.[98]

Joy (chara). Paul repeatedly stressed the divine origin of joy, encouraging believers to rejoice "in the Lord" (Phil 3:1; 4:4), "rejoice in God" (Rom
5:11), and to realize that the kingdom of God is not "a matter of eating and
drinking, but of righteousness, peace and joy in the Holy Spirit" (Rom
14:17).[99] The Greek root for joy (*char-*) is the same as that for "grace,"
charis. Obviously, there is a close connection between the two concepts.
"Those who have come to experience God's grace, as Paul had done, know
that, by standing firm in their faith (2 Cor 1:24), they can continue to celebrate the Christian life as a festival of joy (1 Cor 5:8), in perfect freedom
from all anxious worries and fears."[100] Joy is also closely related to hope, a
word Paul did not list in his catalog of the Spirit's fruit. Hope is that element
of Christian joy that differentiates it from secular happiness. In the Aristotelian morphology of human virtues, joy was defined as finding the ideal mean
between the excesses of pleasure (satiety) and pain (suffering). Joy in this
sense depends upon an environment of pleasant circumstances. Christian joy,
however, is lived out in the midst of suffering. Christian joy is marked by celebration and expectation of God's ultimate victory over the powers of sin and
darkness, a victory actualized already in the death and resurrection of Jesus
Christ, who "for the joy set before him endured the cross" (Heb 12:2) but

[98] See K. S. Hemphill, *Spiritual Gifts* (Nashville: Broadman, 1988), esp. 75-91.
[99] See W. G. Morrice, "Joy," *DPL,* 511-12; H. Conzelmann, "χαίρω," *TDNT* 9.359-72.
[100] Morrice, "Joy," 512.

now has been exalted to the right hand of the Father whence he will come in power and great glory. The joyful cry of the believer is *"Maranatha!"* "Lord, come quickly!"

Peace (eirēnē). Just as true joy cannot be gauged by the absence of unpleasant circumstances, so neither can peace be defined in terms of the cessation of violence, war, and strife. The Hebrew concept of *shalom* is much more positive than that, referring to a condition of wholeness and well-being that includes both a right relationship with God and loving harmony with one's fellow human beings. Paul spoke both of "peace with God," the consequence of being justified by faith, and the "peace of God," which transcends human understanding (Rom 5:1; Phil 4:7). Christians are called to be peacemakers both within the family of faith and throughout the broader human community. Paul admonished believers to make every effort to do what leads to peace and to mutual edification (Rom 15:19). *The Baptist Faith and Message* contains an article on "Peace and War" that speaks of the peacemaking, not just peace keeping, responsibilities of every believer:

> It is the duty of Christians to seek peace with all men on principles of righteousness. In accordance with the Spirit and teachings of Christ, they should do all in their power to put an end to war. The true remedy for the war spirit is the gospel of our Lord. The supreme need of the world is the acceptance of his teachings in all the affairs of men and nations, and the practical application of his law of love.[101]

It may be, as some have suggested, that the Pauline triad love-joy-peace was a familiar watchword among the early Christians comparable to faith, hope, love. Clearly these three graces cover the whole range of Christian existence. "The fabric is built up, story upon story. Love is the foundation, joy the superstructure, peace the crown of all."[102]

Patience (makrothymia).   Patience refers to that quality of mind that disposes us "to take everything in good part and not to be easily offended."[103] It is the ability to put up with other people even when that is not an easy thing to do.[104] Patience in this sense, of course, is preeminently a characteristic of God, who is "long-suffering" with his rebellious creatures. He is the loving Lord who in the face of obstinate infidelity and repeated rejection still says of his people, "How can I give you up, Ephraim? How can I hand you over, Israel?" (Hos 11:8). Paul's point is clear: if God has been so long-suffering

---

[101] R. A. Baker, *A Baptist Source Book* (Nashville: Broadman, 1966), 210.
[102] Lightfoot, *Galatians,* 212.
[103] Calvin, CNTC 11.105
[104] Cole, *Galatians,* 167.

with us, should we not display this same grace in our relationships with one another? This quality should characterize the life of every believer, but it has a special relevance for those who are called to teach and preach the Word of God. As Paul instructed Timothy, "Preach the Word; be prepared in season and out of season; correct, rebuke and encourage—with great patience and careful instruction" (2 Tim 4:2).

Kindness (chrēstotēs). Like patience, kindness is a characteristic of God intended to be reproduced by the Spirit in God's people. God is forbearing and kind toward sinners in his wooing of them to salvation (Rom 2:4). Kindness is not sentimentality, and Paul admonished believers to observe both "the kindness and the sternness of God" (Rom 11:22). Paul frequently appealed to Christians to "be kind to one another" and to clothe themselves with kindness (Eph 4:32; Col 3:12). Where was this Christian grace to be seen among the Galatians who were biting, devouring, and consuming one another?

Goodness (agathōsynē). "Goodness" is a rare word found only four times in the New Testament (and only in Paul). It conveys the idea of benevolence and generosity toward someone else, a going the second mile when such magnanimity is not required. We sometimes speak of a deed done "out of the goodness of one's heart," which comes close to the meaning here except that, as with all nine items in the list, we are dealing with ethical characteristics produced in the believer by the Holy Spirit, not with natural qualities or personality traits cultivated apart from this supernatural dynamic.

Faithfulness (pistis). The word *pistis* bears several distinct meanings in the New Testament, three of which are represented in Galatians. First, there is faith in the sense of the basic content of the Christian message, *the* faith once delivered to the saints. Paul used *pistis* in this sense in Gal 1:23, where he spoke of the report that circulated about him following his dramatic conversion: "The man who formerly persecuted us is now preaching *the* faith he once tried to destroy." More commonly, *pistis* refers to one's acceptance of this gospel message and the committal of oneself to Christ as Savior and Lord. Throughout Galatians Paul had spoken repeatedly of being justified by faith in this sense of the word. As an aspect of the fruit of the Spirit, *pistis* has yet a further meaning: faithfulness, fidelity, that is, the quality of being true, trustworthy, and reliable in all one's dealings with others. In its adjectival form Paul used this word in his instructions to Timothy concerning the appointment of church leaders: "And the things that thou hast heard of me among many witnesses, the same commit thou to faithful men, who shall be able to teach others also" (2 Tim 2:2, KJV). For those who are called to serve as leaders of God's people, now as then, faithfulness should be a far more coveted mark of ministry than temporal success, ecclesiastical recognition, or popular acclaim. After having served in India for eight years with few visible results to show for his efforts, William Carey wrote to his friend John Williams, "Pray for us that we may be faithful to the end."[105]

Gentleness (prätēs). This word connotes a submissive and teachable spirit toward God that manifests itself in genuine humility and consideration toward others. It is regrettable that the English word "gentleness" has come to have the popular connotation of a wimpish weakness and nonassertive lack of vigor. As an expression of the fruit of the Spirit, gentleness is strength under control, power harnessed in loving service and respectful actions. One who is gentle in this sense will not attempt to push others around or arrogantly impose one's own will on subordinates or peers. But gentleness is not incompatible with decisive action and firm convictions. It was after all "gentle Jesus meek and mild" who expelled the mercenaries from the temple with a scourge because of their obstinate defilement of his Father's house.

Self-control (enkrateia). This word refers to the mastery over one's desires and passions. In 1 Cor 7:9 Paul used this expression in a context related to the control of sexual impulses and desires. That idea is certainly included here as well, although self-control as a Christian virtue cannot be restricted to matters of sexuality. Paul's athletic imagery for the Christian life helps us to interpret this word. In 1 Cor 9:24-27 he compared Christians to athletes who must undergo strict training in order to compete as a runner or boxer. A Christian without self-control, he intimates, is like a racer who runs aimlessly from one side of the course to the other or a boxer who merely pummels the air, never landing a blow. In contrast, Paul said, "I discipline and subdue my own body so that, after I have preached to others, I myself will not be disqualified for the prize." The fact that self-control appears last in Paul's list may indicate its importance as a summation of the preceding virtues. It would also have particular relevance for the Galatian setting: Antinomians veering out of control desperately needing the discipline of self-control reinforced by a new respect for God's moral law.

DEAD OR ALIVE (5:24-26). **5:24** This verse and the one that follows it serve as a dual conclusion to Paul's two catalogs of vices and virtues. If the Christian life is a continuous tug-of-war between the flesh and the Spirit, are not believers consigned to a spiritually meager existence of perpetual defeat and minimal growth? In these verses Paul asserted the sufficiency of the Spirit to deal with the flesh by pointing the way to Christian victory. That way is the path of sanctification Paul described here in terms of the dual process of mortification, daily dying to the flesh, and vivification, continuous growth

---

[105] T. George, *Faithful Witness: The Life and Mission of William Carey* (Birmingham: New Hope, 1991), 154.

in grace through the new life of the Spirit.

Many commentators interpret these verses in terms of Paul's earlier testimony of having been crucified with Christ and made alive through faith (2:20). The language in these two passages is strikingly similar, but there is a noticeable difference in meaning. In Gal 2:20 the verb is passive, "I *have been crucified* with Christ." This refers to a past act, a *fait accompli*, something done to the Christian and for the Christian by someone else. We have been crucified with Christ in that he died in our place on the cross and on the basis of which we are declared righteous by God through faith. In 5:24, however, the passive voice has given way to an active construction. Crucifixion of the flesh is described here not as something done to us but rather something done by us. Believers themselves are the agents of this crucifixion. Paul was here describing the process of mortification, the daily putting to death of the flesh through the disciplines of prayer, fasting, repentance, and self-control.

The basic demand of Christian discipleship is that we take up our cross daily and follow Christ (Luke 9:23). Paul stretched this metaphor further by saying that "we must not only take up our cross and walk with it, but actually see that the execution takes place."[106] The mortifying work of self-crucifixion is a continuous, lifelong process, for this side of heaven we dwell in mortal bodies and are bound by inordinate desires. J. Brown describes the continual putting to death of the flesh with all its sinful passions and desires in this way: "Crucifixion . . . produced death not suddenly but gradually. . . . True Christians do not succeed in completely destroying it (that is the flesh) while here below; but they have fixed it to the cross and they are determined to keep it there till it expires."[107] This verse tells us that there is no shortcut to spiritual victory in the life of the Christian. No second blessing, or rededication, or spiritual quick-fix can take the place of consistent, obedient, vigilant renunciation of the world and mortification of the flesh. The very first and the last two of Luther's *Ninety-Five Theses* points to the significance of this fact for us:

1. When our Lord and Master Jesus Christ said, "Repent" (Matt 4:17), he willed the entire life of believers to be one of repentance.
94. Christians should be exhorted to be diligent in following Christ, their

---

[106] J. Stott, *Only One Way,* 150. Lührmann draws a parallel between the crucifixion of the flesh mentioned there and Paul's reference to his dying to the law in 2:19-20. "This verse refers back to 2:20 in the crucifixion of the self through the law. It is therefore only logical that in the context of Rom 7 (where Paul characterizes the law more positively than he does in Galatians), Paul connects the law with flesh, desires, and sin. In 6:14 he will summarize this connection once more in his personal postscript as the crucifixion of the world" (*Galatians,* 112-13).

[107] Brown, *Galatians,* 309.

head, through penalties, death, and hell;

95. And thus be confident of entering into heaven through many tribulations rather than through the false security of peace (Acts 14:22).[108]

5:25 In this verse Paul repeated the indicative/imperative structure we saw at the beginning of the chapter. "Since we live by the Spirit," an accomplished fact, "let us keep in step with the Spirit," an exhortation to obedience. As before, the imperative rests on and appeals to the indicative precisely because we live by the Spirit, or, as Paul said elsewhere, "Christ is in you, the hope of glory" (Col 1:27). Having been engrafted into his body by faith, we are to walk in the Spirit, be led by the Spirit, and keep in step with the Spirit every day of our lives. The verb translated "keep in step with" is a military term meaning to "be drawn up in line," to "stand in a row."[109] In Hellenistic philosophical circles, this word was used to mean "follow someone's philosophical principles." It suggests, therefore, the basic idea of discipleship: conformity to Christ under the leadership of the Spirit. Therefore, just as we put to death the old existence of the flesh in mortification, so too we move forward in the life of faith by keeping in step with the Spirit in our attitudes, conduct, and lifestyle.

5:26 This is an important transitional verse connecting Paul's discussion of the Christian life with the specific situation in the churches of Galatia. Grammatically it is linked with the preceding verse as the negative counterpart to Paul's exhortation concerning the work of the Spirit in the life of the believer. "Let us keep in step with the Spirit . . . let us not become conceited." This verse harkens back to the fractious conditions Paul alluded to in v. 15, and it anticipates his instructions of 6:1-10, where he would deal with specific attitudes and behaviors among the Galatians that, to judge by their fruit, belong not to the Spirit but to the realm of the flesh.

As J. Stott has noted, "This is a very instructive verse because it shows that our conduct to others is determined by our opinion of ourselves."[110] The Greek adjective *kenodoxos,* "conceited," refers to the attitude of being puffed up with pride, arrogant, boastful, "setting value on things not really valuable," or "glorying in vain things."[111] The translation of the KJV, "Let us not

---

[108] *LW* 31.25, 33. The ἐσταύρωσαν is correctly translated as a perfect, "They have crucified," in that it refers to a past event with continuing results and implications for the present. The beginning of sanctification is coterminous with regeneration, but it continues throughout the whole course of the Christian life. In the words of Calvin, "We must strive toward repentance itself, devote ourselves to it throughout life, and pursue it to the very end if we would abide in Christ" (*Institutes* 3.3.20).

[109] Betz, *Galatians,* 294, n. 13; Longenecker, *Galatians,* 265-66.

[110] Stott, *Only One Way,* 156.

[111] Burton, *Galatians,* 324.

be desirous of vainglory," suggests that some of the Galatians were preoccupied with seeking popular acclaim and the high esteem of others. Such an attitude belongs to the world of the flesh, not to the life of the Spirit. In any event, this lust for the limelight led to disastrous results for the fellowship of the Galatian churches: they began to provoke and envy one another. Perhaps one party among the Galatians boasted of their recent submission to the law of Moses and their new status as the "true sons of Abraham." Another party, the Libertines, may have been equally offensive in parading their newfound freedom from all the restraints of the moral law, thus provoking additional wranglings and disputes over the great theological debate between Paul and his opponents.

There is another implication of this verse that has particular relevance for us today. Galatians was written as a circular letter addressed to several congregations within a particular geographical region. Some of the provocation and envy Paul condemned in v. 26 may have taken place not only *within* local churches but also *among* them. Today how much pride-filled glorying and invidious competition there is among ministers, churches, seminaries, and denominations. How we love to glory in our distinctions even, nay especially, when they are about such trivial, nonessential matters as personality, style, and social standing. How all of this must blunt our witness, harden the lost, and grieve the Holy Spirit! May God deliver us all from such vainglory and cause us to only glory in the cross of our Lord Jesus Christ (6:14).

3. Freedom in Service to Others (6:1-10)

Thus far in his moral exhortation Paul had presented the case for Christian ethics not in terms of a general theory of human behavior but as the unfolding of the principle of evangelical freedom in the life of the individual believer and that of the community of faith to which the believer belongs. Following Paul's opening thesis statement on Christian liberty—"For freedom Christ has set us free"—Paul proceeded to show how the wonderful gift of freedom could be, and obviously had been, corrupted from two diametrically opposite extremes.

In 5:2-12 Paul reviewed the danger to Christian living from the error of legalism. Paul condemned the influence of the Judaizers in no uncertain terms and summed up the normal Christian life in two terms that presuppose the doctrine of justification he had set forth so clearly in Gal 1:4, "obeying the truth" and "faith expressing itself through love." Then in 5:13-15 Paul turned to address the opposite but equally destructive distortion of grace known as libertinism or antinomianism. This error arises when believers presume on the grace of God and misuse their freedom in Christ as a pretext for self-indulgence, immorality, and disregard for the moral law of God. The antidote to the pernicious abuse is the law of loving service to one's neighbor. The remainder of chap. 5 centers around Paul's description of the works of the flesh and his elaboration of the counterveiling fruit of the Spirit. Believers are exhorted to walk according to, to be led by, to keep in step with, and to live in the Spirit. To do so is to fulfill the commandment of love and to stifle the passions and desires of the flesh. Thus Christian life in this present evil world is inevitably one of conflict and tension, but by no means does this necessarily mean defeat. By God's grace every believer has been transferred from the realm of slavery and alienation into the position of freedom and sonship.

However, "these benefits of Christ" are not gifts to be taken for granted; they are rather realities to be owned and proved in the daily spheres of obedience and testing. For this reason Paul turned now in 6:1-10 to apply the principles he had outlined in the preceding verses to specific cases in the life of the Galatian churches.[112]

(1) Bearing One Another's Burdens (6:1-3)

[1]Brothers, if someone is caught in a sin, you who are spiritual should restore him gently. But watch yourself, or you also may be tempted. [2]Carry each oth-

---

[112] Various theories have been put forth concerning the form, structure, and function of this unit within the larger context of Galatians. H. D. Betz identifies 5:25–6:10 as a collection of *sententiae,* individual opinions or maxims, demonstrating Paul's ability as "a gnomic poet . . . in the Cynic-Stoic diatribe tradition" (*Galatians,* Her [Philadelphia: Fortress, 1979], 291-93). B. H. Brinsmead regards the ethical instructions of Gal 6 as a specific refutation of the moral teachings and traditions of Paul's Galatian opponents. See his *Galatians as Dialogical Response to Opponents* (Chico, Cal.: Scholars, 1982). J. M. G. Barclay has criticized Brinsmead's technique of "mirror-reading" the epistle, seeing instead the logical sequence in this unit determined by the themes of responsibility and accountability, i.e., the Galatians' corporate responsibilities to one another and the individual's accountability before God (*Obeying the Truth: A Study of Paul's Ethics in Galatians* [Edinburgh: T & T Clark, 1988], 146-77). All scholars recognize the similarity between Paul's parenetic materials in this section of Galatians and general, aphoristic moral statements both in Jewish writings and in Hellenistic philosophical literature. Failing to see anything specifically Pauline in this material, J. C. O'Neill has suggested that the entire unit was interpolated back into Galatians by a postapostolic writer, thus incorporating traditional material into Paul's original epistle to the Galatians, which, on this theory, probably ended at the close of chap. 4. See his *Recovery of Paul's Letter to the Galatians* (London: SPCK, 1972). R. N. Longenecker reviews all of these reconstructions and concludes that in this new epistolary subsection Paul "gives a series of exhortations that have to do with both personal and corporate responsibilities within the Galatian churches. The exhortations are expressed in somewhat general terms, without details regarding the specific circumstances they have in mind, though, it must be assumed, Paul thought he knew the circumstances to which he spoke and, furthermore, believed that his converts knew them as well. . . . We must not treat them as only addenda to Paul's previous exhortations of 5:1-26 that were drawn for the ethical wisdom of the day and simply tacked on to what has preceded" (*Galatians,* WBC [Dallas: Word, 1990], 268-72).

er's burdens, and in this way you will fulfill the law of Christ. ³If anyone thinks he is something when he is nothing, he deceives himself.

6:1 This is an extremely important verse in understanding the character of congregational discipline in the life of the early church. Paul returned to his favorite word of address for the Galatians, the vocative *adelphoi*, "brothers," indicating not only a new topic to be discussed but reiterating his affectionate regard for his readers. He thus reinforced his earlier expression of confidence that they would "take no other view" (5:10), that is, because they were after all true believers, they would not utterly or finally fall away from the truth of the gospel.

Much speculation has been devoted to the exact meaning of Paul's next comment, "if someone is caught in a sin." The word for "caught" means literally to be "detected, overtaken, surprised."¹¹³ Because this word appears in the passive voice in this context, it may connote the idea of surprise: someone suddenly entrapped or discovered in an unseemly situation or heinous act. What this particular transgression was we do not know, nor can we be sure whether Paul was here referring to an actual "case study" that had come to his attention or whether, as seems more likely, he was providing a general guideline for dealing with serious moral lapses that were occurring with some frequency among the Galatians. Clearly Paul was responding to a real life situation in which concrete acts of wrongdoing such as those he had just listed among the works of the flesh were disrupting both the Galatians' relationship to God and their fellowship with one another.¹¹⁴ What were the believers to do in such a situation?

Paul addressed his advice to "those who are spiritual," the *pneumatikoi*. Again, there has been much scholarly debate about who these "spirituals" were. W. Schmithals, among others, has argued on the basis of this word that Paul was addressing here an incipient party of Gnostics whose disruptive activities among the Galatians had occasioned Paul's letter in the first place.¹¹⁵ Although later Gnostics did use the word *pneumatikoi* as a term of

---

¹¹³ G. Delling, "προλαμβάνω," *TDNT* 4.14-15. Given Paul's depiction of the serious nature of this offense and the necessity for disciplinary procedures to deal with it, it is unlikely that the sin in question was merely "a fault into which the brother is betrayed 'unawares,' so that it is not intentionally wrong."

¹¹⁴ The word for sin in this verse is παράπτωμα, "transgression," a term found with some frequency in Paul (cf. Rom 4:25; 5:15-18; 2 Cor 5:19). See W. Michaelis, "παραπίπτω, παράπτωμα, περιπίπτω," *TDNT* 6.170-73. See also L. Morris, "Sin, Guilt," *DPL,* 877-81.

¹¹⁵ See W. Schmithals, *Paul and the Gnostics* (Nashville: Abingdon, 1972), 46-51. E. Pagels indicates how later Gnostics actually interpreted Gal 6:1: "Paul directs the pneumatics specifically to restore the psychics who are caught in sin and need (6:1-2). In doing this 'fulfill the law of Christ,' the only law the pneumatics recognized, the 'law of love' (5:14)" (*Gnostic Paul* [Philadelphia: Fortress, 1975], 111).

self-designation, there is no reason to believe that Paul was here addressing such a self-conscious heretical group. Another, more plausible interpretation has been set forth by those who detect a note of irony and sarcasm in Paul's use of this term in the Galatian context. Given the picture that has already emerged of a group of fractious Christians consumed by arrogance, conceit, and selfish ambition, we can well imagine that a group of "Holy Joes" and "Pious Pollys" had formed themselves into a cadre of moral watchdogs and were self-righteously lording it over their less "advanced" brothers and sisters. If we accept this interpretation, then Paul would, in effect, have been saying: "Listen to me, those of you who think you're so 'spiritual.' You talk as though you've swallowed the Holy Ghost, feathers and all! If you're so 'spiritual,' then demonstrate your spirituality by acting responsibly and lovingly with your fallen brothers and sisters."[116]

It seems best, however, to understand the "spirituals" in the same kind of positive sense Paul used it in 1 Cor 2:15–3:4. There the apostle contrasted the "spiritual" believers at Corinth with those who were *sarkikoi,* "fleshly," worldly minded, that is, those who had to be fed on milk instead of meat because they were spiritually immature. They were, so to say, baby Christians more concerned with status and self-gratification than with the mind of Christ or service toward others.[117]

In Gal 6:1, then, "those who are spiritual" are identical with those Christians who walk in the Spirit, are led by the Spirit, and keep in step with the Spirit. Some early Methodist church registers contained three columns for listing those persons who attended services of worship: the seekers, the saved, and the sanctified. Paul was not here dividing the body of Christ into a two- or three-tiered society. However, he was acknowledging the fact that believers can and do sin and fall. While all sin is detestable before God and should be resisted as the plague, certain transgressions are especially hurtful to the fellowship of the church and must be dealt with according to the canons of Christian discipline. Those who are spiritually minded, that is, those whose lives give evidence of the fruit of the Spirit, have a special responsibility to take the initiative in seeking restoration and reconciliation with those who have been caught in such an error.

---

[116] The ironic interpretation has been favored by H. Schlier, *Der Breif an der Galater,* KEK 7, 10th ed. (Göttingen: Vandenhoeck & Ruprecht, 1899), 270, and R. A. Cole, *The Epistle of Paul to the Galatians,* TNTC (Grand Rapids: Eerdmans, 1965), 172.

[117] See C. H. Talbert, *Reading Corinthians* (New York: Crossroad, 1989), 4-11. See also B. Pearson, *The Pneumatikos-Psychikos Terminology in 1 Corinthians* (Missoula: Scholars Press, 1973).

But how is this to be done? The lapsed brother or sister should be "restored gently." The word for "restore" is *katartizō,* literally "to put in order," "to restore to its former condition." Elsewhere in the New Testament (cf. Matt 4:21; Mark 1:19) this same word is used for the mending or overhauling of fishnets. It was also a part of the medical vocabulary of ancient Greece, where it meant "to set a fractured or dislocated bone." In 1 Cor 1:10 Paul used the same word in an ethical sense exhorting the strife-torn Corinthian believers to put aside their dissensions so that they may be "restored" to unity in thought and purpose.

Here in Galatians Paul did not outline a specific procedure of church discipline, but he likely knew and presupposed the one given by Jesus in Matt 18:15-17.[118] That process incorporates several levels of appeal beginning with personal admonition in a one-on-one encounter, moving to a small group discussion involving two or three others, and culminating with a congregational conference ("tell it to the church") and, if necessary, formal excommunication, that is, withdrawal from the fellowship of the Lord's Table and expulsion from participation in the governance of the church body. From Paul's perspective the purpose of such disciplinary procedures was always remedial and never punitive, even in the drastic case of the immoral brother at Corinth who was to be handed over to Satan "for the destruction of the flesh, that his spirit may be saved in the day of the Lord Jesus" (1 Cor 5:5, KJV).

However, Paul clearly hoped that matters would not deteriorate to that level among the Galatians. For this reason he not only reminded the spiritually minded among them of their responsibility to restore a sinning brother, but he further instructed them in how it should be done. This delicate ministry is to be carried out in all wisdom, humility, and "gentleness." Contrary to some interpretations of the word "gentleness," Paul was not here calling for the kind of leniency that overlooks the transgression committed or precludes any kind of penitential act on the part of the transgressor.[119] But he was saying that the work of restoration should be done with sensitivity and consideration and with no hint of self-righteous superiority.

---

[118] C. H. Dodd has argued convincingly that Paul had access to the tradition of the words of Jesus contained in the gospels and that the command of Christ concerning the discipline of an erring brother constituted "the solid, historical and creative nucleus" of Paul's own exhortation on this matter. See his *"Ennomos Christou," More New Testament Studies* (Grand Rapids: Eerdmans, 1968), 148.

[119] So Betz, *Galatians,* 297-98, following Chrysostom.

Gentleness is an aspect of the fruit of the Spirit and cannot coexist with a harsh and censorious spirit. Furthermore, vigilance and self-examination are prerequisites for the would-be restorer lest he or she fall prey to the same temptation. What Paul later wrote to the Corinthians applies here as well, "Let any one who thinks that he stands take heed lest he fall" (1 Cor 10:12, RSV). Thus while Paul was deeply grieved over the loose living and immoral behavior of the Galatian believers, he was equally anxious that the process of corrective church discipline remain free from the kind of conceited cocksureness that is so contrary to the law of love and the fruit of the Spirit.[120] Restoration cannot be accomplished without confrontation, and this may require firm words and a stern rebuke. Yet even—especially!—in these cases, Luther's advice to a pastor charged with setting a lapsed brother back on the right path should be heeded: "Run unto him, and reaching out your hand, raise him up again, comfort him with sweet words, and embrace him with motherly arms."[121]

It is a sign of the spiritual stupor that has befallen the body of Christ that church discipline is seldom if ever raised as a viable concern in evangelical churches today. Historically, the practice of discipline served a twofold function in the Free Church tradition: it aimed at restoring the lapsed brother or sister to full fellowship if possible, and it marked off clearly the boundaries between the church and its environing culture. In both of these ways, discipline helped preserve the purity of the church's witness in the world. The loss of this historic distinctive has resulted in the crisis of spirituality that pervades so much of our church life today. Can we recover a structure of accountability in our congregational life without relapsing into narrow judgmentalism? What are the standards of personal holiness that ought to distinguish a man or woman of God? What are the ethical implications of our corporate decisions? We will not find answers to these questions until we recover that pattern of personal striving and self-examination by which serious Christians endeavor, in the words of the Puritan Richard Rogers, "to keep our lives and hearts in good order."[122] When this happens in our individual lives, then we are ready to recover the biblical practice of congregational discipline and to recognize it, along with God-centered worship and the preaching of the Word, as an essential mark of a true visible church.

---

[120] Cf. Longenecker's comment on this verse: "While Paul was always against sin in whatever form, for him pride, aloofness, and conceit were also sinful, being often, in fact, far more damaging to the community of believers and the gospel message than overt moral lapses" (*Galatians,* 274).

[121] *LW* 27.110-11.

[122] *Two Elizabethan Puritan Diaries,* ed. M. M. Knappan (Chicago: University of Chicago Press, 1933), 72.

6:2-3   The church of Jesus Christ is not a charitable organization like the Red Cross or a civic club such as the Rotary or Kiwanis. It is rather a family of born-again brothers and sisters supernaturally knit together by the Holy Spirit in a common fellowship of mutual edification and love. In this context Paul admonished his readers to bear one another's burdens and so fulfill the law of Christ. The immediate context refers back to the preceding verse and conveys the idea of the spiritually mature bearing with and helping to restore those who have fallen into sin. But burden bearing cannot be restricted to that one situation alone. The word for "burden" (*baros*) means literally "a heavy weight or stone" someone is required to carry for a long distance. Figuratively it came to mean any oppressive ordeal or hardship that was difficult to bear, as in Matt 20:12, where Jesus spoke of the workers in the vineyard "who have borne the burden of the work and the heat of the day." The old-fashioned English word "tote" conveys something of this idea in our language. To tote something is not simply to pick it up and put it back down again. It is rather to carry or haul a heavy load, usually on one's arms or back, for a great distance, perhaps many miles. We may gather four important truths about practical Christian living from Paul's injunction to bear one another's burdens.

The Reality of Burdens.   All Christians have burdens. Our burdens may differ in size and shape and will vary in kind depending on the providential ordering of our lives. For some it is the burden of temptation and the consequences of a moral lapse, as in v. 1 here. For others it may be a physical ailment, or mental disorder, or family crisis, or lack of employment, or demonic oppression, or a host of other things; but no Christian is exempt from burdens. Creation itself is broken and groaning, and believers groan with it waiting for the final deliverance that will come only with the return of our Redeemer in glory (Rom 8:18-28). Prosperity gospels of easy believism and quick-fix recovery belong more to the spirit of this age than to the Spirit of Christ, who "Son though he was, had to prove the meaning of obedience through all that he suffered" (Heb 5:9).

The Myth of Self-sufficiency.   We all have burdens, and God does not intend for us to carry them by ourselves in isolation from our brothers and sisters. The ancient philosophy of Stoicism taught that the goal of the happy life was *apatheia,* a studied aloofness from pleasure and pain, and self-sufficiency, the ability to brave the harsh elements of life without dependence upon others. As the Roman philosopher Seneca put it, "The primary sign of a well-ordered mind is a man's ability to remain in one place and linger in his own company."[123] But there is a vast difference between Stoic equanimity and Christian courage. The myth of self-sufficiency is not a mark of bravery but rather

---

[123] Seneca, *Epistulae Morales,* 2; quoted in W. Durant, *Caesar and Christ,* 306.

a sign of pride. Paul's maxim in v. 3 is aimed at this perverted understanding of the self. "If a man thinks he is 'somebody,' he is deceiving himself, for that very thought proves that he is nobody" (Phillips). Such an attitude of conceited self-importance leads to two fundamental failures in relationship: one, the refusal to bear the burdens of others, for that would be a task too menial and deprecating for a person who "thinks he is something"; the other, the refusal to allow anyone else to help shoulder one's own burdens since that would be an admission of weakness and need. To live this way, however, is to practice the art of self-deception, for "no man is an island entire to itself."[124]

The Imperative of Mutuality.   Because all Christians have burdens and since none are sufficient unto themselves to bear their burdens alone, God has so tempered the body of Christ that its members are to be priests to one another, bearing one another's burdens and so fulfilling the law of Christ. Paul's most extensive elaboration on the theme of Christian mutuality is in his discourse on the body of Christ in 1 Cor 12. There in the context of a fractured fellowship beset with rival parties and self-serving leaders, Paul declared that God has so brought the members of the congregation into mutual relationship "that there should be no division in the body, but that its parts should have equal concern for each other. If one part suffers, every part suffers with it; if one part is honored, every part rejoices with it" (1 Cor 12:25-26). Luther said that a Christian must have "broad shoulders and husky bones" in order to carry the burdens of his brothers and sisters.[125] The command to bear one another's burdens in no way mitigates against the other New Testament imperative to cast all our cares upon Christ, since he cares for us (1 Pet 5:7). The apostle Paul knew a great deal about burdens. On one occasion he was severely oppressed by afflictions at every turn—fightings without and fears within. In this moment of crisis, he later wrote, "But God, who comforts the downcast, comforted us by the coming of Titus" (2 Cor 7:5-6). J. Stott comments on this text:

---

[124] Most scholars recognize 6:3 as a traditional maxim of the Greco-Roman world that Paul here adduced in support of his appeal for Christian ethics. So Longenecker, *Galatians,* 276. However, C. K. Barrett has seen in Paul's use of the verb δόκειν a possible linkage with his earlier reference to Peter, James, and John as "those who were reputed to be something," and "those reputed to be pillars" (2:6,9). Thus Paul, near the end of his epistle, would have been taking a final slap at the Jerusalem authorities whose backing his Galatian opponents had claimed. Certainly what Paul said in this verse would apply to the Jerusalem church leaders as well as to all other Christians. However, it is stretching the evidence to suggest that Paul singled out any particular group in setting forth this general principle of Christian conduct. See Barrett, *Freedom and Obligation,* 80-82. The word φρεναπάτᾶ, "deceives, hoodwinks," is a hapax legomenon, although the cognate noun φρεναπάτες, "deceiver," occurs in Titus 1:10. See Burton, *Galatians,* 331-32.

[125] *LW* 27.113.

God's comfort was not given to Paul through his private prayer and waiting upon the Lord, but through the companionship of a friend and through the good news which he brought. Human friendship, in which we bear one another's burdens, is part of the purpose of God for his people. So we should not keep our burdens to ourselves, but rather seek a Christian friend who will help to bear them with us.[126]

The duty of bearing one another's burdens is stated in the imperative mood; it is not an option but a command. One of the much-neglected features of contemporary Baptist church life is the congregational covenant, an expression of communal commitment in responsibility, setting forth the ethical standards and obligations incumbent upon all members. Historically, Baptist church covenants have encouraged not only public worship, personal devotion, and congregational discipline but also a caring and pastoral attitude on the part of each church member toward every other member. In this context Gal 6:2 has been frequently paraphrased in these historic documents. On November 4, 1790, an English Baptist church meeting in the Horse Fair, Stony Stratford, Buckinghamshire, set forth as a part of its congregational covenant the following statement, agreeing:

To walk in love toward those with whom we stand connected in the bonds of Christian fellowship. As the effect of this, we will pray much for one another. As we have opportunity, we will associate together for religious purposes. Those of us who are in more comfortable situations in life than some of our brethren, with regard to the good things of Providence, will administer as we have ability and see occasion, to their necessities. We will bear one another's burdens, sympathize with the afflicted in body and mind, so far as we know their case, under their trials; and as we see occasion, advise, caution, and encourage one another. We will watch over one another for good. We will studiously avoid giving or taking offenses. Thus we will make it our study to fulfill the law of Christ. . . . These things, and whatever else may appear enjoined by the Word of God, we promise in the strength of divine grace to observe and practice. But knowing our insufficiency for anything that is spiritually good, in and of ourselves, we look up to him who giveth power to the faint, rejoicing that in the Lord we have not only righteousness but strength. Hold thou us up, O Lord, and we shall be safe! Amen![127]

---

[126] Stott, *Only One Way,* 158. Again, Paul's expression of gratitude to the Philippians for sending him a financial gift indicates how often his apostolic labors were furthered through the loving prayers and cooperative support of God's people: "Yet it was good of you to share in my troubles. . . . I am amply supplied, now that I have received Epaphroditus the gifts you sent. They are a fragrant offering, an acceptable sacrifice, pleasing to God" (Phil 4:14,18).

[127] "The Church Covenant of the Particular Baptist Church, meeting in the Horse Fair, Stony Stratford, Bucks," *The Baptist Quarterly* 3 (1926): 41-44; reprinted in C. W. DeWeese, *Baptist Church Covenants* (Nashville: Broadman, 1990), 129-30.

Living by the Law of Christ. Bear one another's burdens, Paul said, *and in this way* you will fulfill the law of Christ. Nowhere else did Paul use the expression "the law of Christ" (*nomos Christou*), although 1 Cor 9:21 contains a similar phrase, "though I am not free from God's law but am under Christ's law (*ennomos Christou*)." Throughout the earlier part of Galatians, Paul frequently pictured Christ and grace opposed to law and works, showing conclusively that justification can never be achieved by observing the requirements of the Mosaic legislation, which no one can do perfectly in any event, but only through faith in Jesus Christ, who in his atoning death on the cross bore the curse of the law and now freely offers salvation for all who believe. This is the heart of the gospel and Paul is not here backtracking or sidestepping from this fundamental doctrinal commitment. However, as Paul has shown already in Gal 5–6, the moral law of God has never been abrogated or annulled, although the civil and ceremonial aspects of the Mosaic legislation have been made obsolete by the coming of Christ. The moral law of God, epitomized in the Ten Commandments and summarized in Jesus' restatement of the "new commandment" given to his disciples (John 13:34; 15:12; 1 John 3:23), continues to play an important role in the life of the justified believer. In sum, the "law of Christ" is for Paul "the whole tradition of Jesus' ethical teaching, confirmed by his character and conduct and reproduced within his people by the power of the Spirit" (cf. Rom 8:2).[128]

(2) Carrying One's Own Load (6:4-5)

⁴Each one should test his own actions. Then he can take pride in himself, without comparing himself to somebody else, ⁵for each one should carry his own load.

6:4 This verse and the one that follows it must be read in tandem, for they present two diverse aspects of the Christian's scrutiny and examination before God: the first, the serious self-examination Paul enjoined upon all believers regarding their Christian walk in this present life; the second, the evaluation that will be disclosed by Christ himself when every believer

---

[128] Bruce, *Galatians,* 261. As J. Wesley observed, as far as justification is concerned, the law has done its work for one who has been truly converted. "Yet in another sense, we have not done with this law: for it is still of unspeakable use, first, in convincing us of the sin that yet remains both in our hearts and lives, and thereby keeping us close to Christ, that his blood may cleanse us every moment; secondly, in deriving strength from our head into his living members, whereby he empowers them to do what his law commands; and, thirdly, in confirming our hope of whatsoever it commands and we have not yet attained—of receiving grace upon grace, till we are in actual possession of the fullness of his promises" (*Christian Theology,* 176; quoted in E. F. Kevan, *The Law of God in Christian Experience,* 71).

appears before his judgment seat to give an account of the stewardship of his life. The word for "test" is *dokimazō,* which is the word used for the fiery testing of gold so as to determine its purity. This verse has important implications for Christian spirituality, and we do well to heed its message in our own individual lives.

First, there is a great difference between introspection and self-examination. The former can easily devolve into a kind of narcissistic, spiritual navel-gazing that has more in common with types of Eastern mysticism than with classic models of the devotional life in historic Christianity. True self-examination is not merely taking one's spiritual pulse beat on a regular basis but rather submitting one's thoughts, attitudes, and actions to the will of God and the mind of Christ revealed in Holy Scripture. To "test" or "prove" something presupposes that there is some external standard or criterion by which the quality or purity of the object under scrutiny can be measured with accuracy. No higher or better standard can be found for this important exercise than the law of Christ Paul had just extolled. This does not mean, of course, that we should not seek the assistance of fellow believers in the process of self-examination. An important part of bearing one another's burdens is to offer spiritual guidance and friendship to one another, holding each other accountable to the high calling of God in our lives.

A second dimension of self-examination has to do with competition and boasting in the Christian life. If the churches of Galatia were anything like the one in Corinth, and there are parallels as well as differences, we may assume they were overloaded with spiritual gifts. We know there had been a display of miracles in their midst (3:5). Did they also speak in tongues, heal the sick, cast out demons, receive visions and revelations? Perhaps, like the Corinthians, they used such gifts not to edify the body but rather to flatter themselves, seeking ever greater spiritual highs until they became critical of others who were less advanced in such high-tech pneumatics. Instead of serving one another in love, they became puffed up with pride and boastful of their exalted status in spiritual matters. They whispered in small circles about those other members who were "not one of us." At church meetings they compared the scores on their Spiritual Aptitude Tests and snubbed those who did not measure up. As a corrective to this kind of destructive attitude, Paul said bluntly, "Test yourself!" God will not hold you accountable for the gifts he gave to someone else. Don't compare yourself with Pastor Jim or Deacon Smith or Sister Jones. God wants you to bring your own life before the open pages of his Holy Word. Are you more loving and patient than you were this time last year? How do you gauge your gentleness and self-control, your kindness and faithfulness? No one who honestly brings his or her life before God in this kind of way is going to have any interest in "comparing himself to somebody else." This kind of honest scrutiny will issue in confession, not competition, in humility, not in vainglory.

6:5   On first blush it seems that Paul had flatly contradicted himself within the space of three short verses. In 6:2 he instructed the Galatians to "carry each other's burdens." Now in 6:5 he said that each one "should carry his own load." This apparent discrepancy is easily resolved when we realize that Paul was using two different words to refer to two disparate situations. The word translated "burdens" in v. 2 (*barē*) refers, as we have seen, to a heavy load, an oppressive weight, which one is expected to carry for a long distance. But the word for "load" in v. 5 is *phortion,* which is used elsewhere to refer to a ship's cargo (cf. Acts 27:10), a soldier's knapsack, or a pilgrim's backpack.[129] J. Stott correctly delineates the difference between the two "loads" in Gal 6: "So we are to bear one another's 'burdens' which are too heavy for a man to bear alone, but there is one burden which we cannot share—indeed do not need to because it is a pack light enough for every man to carry himself—and that is our responsibility to God on the day of judgment. On that day you cannot carry my pack and I cannot carry yours."[130]

On several occasions throughout this commentary we have had occasion to note that Galatians, while not laden with apocalyptic imagery or extensive discourses on last things, nonetheless presupposes a strong eschatological orientation. Here in v. 5 Paul placed the verb in the future tense (*bastasei*) to indicate that he was thinking not merely of an individual's carrying his own weight or bearing his own responsibility here in this life but more particularly the future reckoning that every Christian must make before the judgment seat of Christ.

First Corinthians 3:10-15 teaches that the second coming of Christ will usher in a distinctive judgment for believers. The purpose of this judgment seat of Christ is not to determine the salvation or damnation of anyone. That matter will have been settled before this great event occurs. On this occasion the Lord of the church will review what every Christian has done with the gift of salvation from the moment of salvation to the end of life. If we have built our lives and ministries out of shoddy materials, this will be made known, and we will "suffer loss," though not the loss of eternal salvation. On

---

[129] Moffatt translates this verse, "Everyone will have to bear his own load of responsibility." Burton correctly notes that no sharp distinction can be drawn between these two words as such (*Galatians,* 334). However, the context in Gal 6 clearly shows that Paul had two distinct meanings in mind.

[130] Stott, *Only One Way,* 159-60. Cole has suggested that Paul may be here taking one final glance toward the Judaizers, reminding them that they should be less concerned with "counting scalps" than with their own standing before God on the coming day of judgment (*Galatians,* 175).

the other hand, if our life's work has been erected on the solid foundation of Jesus Christ, we will receive a reward, a "crown of righteousness" that we may cast at the feet of our Savior along with the rewards of all the saints who have come before us (2 Tim 4:8). On that examination day every believer will have to bear his own load.[131]

(3) Sharing with Teachers (6:6)

⁶Anyone who receives instruction in the word must share all good things with his instructor.

6:6 This verse has been more than a little puzzling to most commentators appearing as it does as "an independent piece of advice"[132] with no clear connection to the preceding passage or the one that comes after it. Apparently Paul was again adapting a well-known maxim with various parallels in both Hellenistic and Jewish writings. However, Jesus himself said that "the worker is worth his keep" (Matt 10:10), and Paul appears simply to have been drawing out the implications of that dominical saying. It is well known that Paul himself did not receive a regular stipend from his churches (although he did receive with gratitude a personal gift of money from the Philippians) but rather used his skills as a leather worker to make and sell tents for a living. However, he never held himself up as an example to others in this regard. To the contrary, he persistently encouraged the churches he had founded to provide material support for the pastors and teachers in their midst (cf. 1 Cor 9; 2 Cor 11:7-11; 1 Thess 2:7-10). It may well be, as some-

---

[131] Betz has argued that "the future tense is gnomic . . . not eschatological" (*Galatians,* 304). But an eschatological inference is supported by Schlier, Mussner, and Bruce, among others. Bruce comments: "In the 'day of Christ' Paul would not be asked how his achievement compared with Peter's: his *kauchēma* would be the quality of those who had been won to Christ through his own ministry (Phil 2:16). At that tribunal 'each of us will give an account of himself to God' (Rom 14:1; cf. 2 Cor 5:10)" (*Galatians,* 263). The theme of self-examination in Gal 6:4-5 should be compared with the same motif in 1 Cor 11:27-32. In this latter passage Paul admonished the Corinthians to examine themselves as a prerequisite to participation in the Lord's Supper. There careless living and casual conduct around the table of the Lord had apparently resulted in God's preemptory judgment in the immediate death of some of their members. In this context Paul said, "If we were closely to examine ourselves beforehand, we should avoid [this] judgment of God" (11:31, Phillips). In the same vein, Paul had intimated to the Galatians that the serious scrutiny and self-examination of their lives and ministries before God there and then would prevent their shame and embarrassment at the judgment seat of Christ when there will be no passing of the buck or shifting of responsibilities. On the question of whether degrees of reward pertain only to the millennial interim or to heaven itself, see H. Hunt, *Redeemed!: Eschatological Redemption in the Kingdom of God* (Nashville: Broadman & Holman, 1993), 358-60.
[132] R. Y. K. Fung, *The Epistle to the Galatians*, NICNT (Grand Rapids: Eerdmans, 1988).

one has suggested, that Paul had "a gentlemanly dislike for talking about money."[133] Still, he fully recognized that financial stewardship was an indispensable element of faithful service to Christ and his church. Repeatedly he exhorted believers to give regularly, generously, and joyfully both to his special collection for the poor saints in Jerusalem and to the regular maintenance of godly teachers in their midst.[134]

This verse speaks of a relationship between the "teacher" and the "one receiving instruction," *katēchoumenos,* from which we derive the word "catechumen." We know from the history of the early church in the second and third centuries that a well-developed system of catechetical instruction did emerge as a standard feature of church life with teachers (who were often opposed by the bishops!) playing a major role in the formation of Christian doctrine. Origen, for example, began his ecclesiastical career as a teacher in the catechetical school at Alexandria. While we should not read these later structures back into apostolic times, it probably is correct to say with C. K. Barrett that Gal 6:6 "may be the earliest reference to any kind of paid Christian ministry."[135]

It is interesting to speculate about why Paul felt it necessary to impart this particular word of instruction to the Galatian churches. We know that after the initial wave of evangelization in this region, Paul and Barnabas had appointed elders in every church, some of whom were perhaps singled out as the first pastors and teachers of these fledgling congregations. It could be that the Judaizing agitators had attacked the ministry of these men, who were far less able than Paul to defend the truth of the gospel against such interlopers. In turn, many of the Galatians may well have withdrawn material support from these church leaders in their infatuation with the new theology advanced by Paul's opponents. In any event, Paul reminded them here, in the broader context of his command for them to bear one another's burdens, of the importance of sustaining a faithful gospel ministry through generous financial support. Such teachers, of course, must prove themselves worthy of such support by their offering "instruction in the word." Paul was not merely concerned to maintain the principle of "paying the preacher." His burden was for the furtherance of the gospel, and he knew that the God-

---

[133] Bligh, *Galatians,* 483.

[134] J. G. Strelan has interpreted the entire motif of burden bearing in this passage in terms of Paul's appeal for the Galatians to support his collection for the Jerusalem Christians. See his "Burden-Bearing and the Law of Christ: A Re-examination of Galatians 6:2," *JBL* 94 (1975): 266-76. On the whole question of the collection, see K. F. Nickle, *The Collection: A Study in Pauline Strategy* (Naperville: Allenson, 1967), and D. Georgi, *Die Geschichte der Kollekte des Paulus für Jerusalem* (Hamburg-Bergstedt: H. Reich, 1965).

[135] Barrett, *Freedom and Obligation,* 82.

ordained means for accomplishing this was the steady proclamation of the Word of God by faithful men of God.

Does a verse like this have anything to say to us today? Much in every way! First, the *primary* responsibility of pastors is to teach and preach the Word of God. All other aspects of the ministry, however worthy, must be subordinate to this fundamental task, for God has chosen "the foolishness of preaching to save them that believe" (1 Cor 1:21, KJV). Second, there is a special relationship between those who dispense instruction in the Word of God and those who hear and receive it. A workman is still worthy of his keep, and faithful pastors should not be taken for granted but rather recognized as a special gift from the Lord, one worthy of unstinted and generous support. Finally, in receiving such support from their people, pastors should guard against two temptations. On the one hand pastors who are richly blessed with material goods can forget the basic purpose of their ministry and become seduced by "the love of money [which] is the root of all evil" (1 Tim 6:10, KJV). On the other hand, it is possible for a pastor to become so inured to a comfortable living that he functions as a mere hireling, forgetting that one day he must stand before Christ to give an account of the ministry to which he was called and the message he was privileged to preach.[136]

(4) Sowing and Reaping (6:7-8)

[7]Do not be deceived: God cannot be mocked. A man reaps what he sows. [8]The one who sows to please his sinful nature, from that nature will reap destruction; the one who sows to please the Spirit, from the Spirit will reap eternal life.

6:7-8 In 6:1-6 Paul provided a series of specific instructions illustrating the two-sided character of Christian freedom he had set forth earlier in 5:13-

---

[136] There is considerable discussion about whether the "all good things" those receiving instruction are to share with their teachers includes spiritual blessings as well as material benefits. Most commentaries follow the interpretation set forth in the translation of the *Jerusalem Bible:* "People under instruction should always contribute something to the support of the man who is instructing them." While this seems to be the purport of Paul's meaning here, the command to provide material support for ministers of the Word does not preclude a wider sharing of spiritual blessings, especially those related to the fruit of the Spirit. W. Perkins held that Paul added this word of instruction because the churches of Galatia were especially neglectful of caring for their ministers, a situation he saw replicated in his own day: "There are so many needy, poor wandering Levites, which would gladly serve for a morsel of bread, or a suit of raiment, it is a pregnant proof that there is very small devotion in men for the maintenance of religion; especially in those which are so straightlaced and short-sleeved in bestowing anything for the good of the ministry, and yet in keeping of hounds and hawks, and worse matters, in maintaining players, jesters, fools, and such like, are very lavish and profuse, to their great cost" (*Galatians,* 479).

26. Now with these concrete examples clearly in mind, he returned, as it were, to the broader theme represented by the antithesis between the works of the flesh and the fruit of the Spirit. Verses 7 and 8 are again general principles drawn from the Old Testament as well as the world of philosophical wisdom. Paul applied them, however, in a specifically Christian context with a view toward the impending eschatological judgment. Verses 9 and 10 will conclude the main body of the letter with two further appeals summarizing the theme of personal accountability and mutual responsibility.

Verse 7 contains three aphoristic statements presented in the Greek text one after the other in staccato-like fashion: "Be not deceived . . . God's not mocked . . . you'll reap what you sow!" Earlier Paul referred to the Galatians as "senseless" Christians who had been "bewitched" by some evil deceiver. Now he instructed them by means of a negative imperative that they were not to be misled in such a dangerous way. This is a strong expression that Paul used twice in 1 Corinthians, in both cases as an introductory formula to a severe warning concerning the consequences of immoral behavior. In 1 Cor 6:9 he warned against a kind of situation ethics that would make such sins as idolatry, adultery, and homosexuality compatible with the kingdom of God. Again in 1 Cor 15:33 he warned against worldly living. Don't be misled, he said, into thinking you can keep yourself unspotted from the world while you wallow in dens of iniquity, for "bad company corrupts good character."

Here in Gal 6:7 the deception into which the Galatians had fallen, or were in danger of falling, was even worse. Make no mistake, Paul pleaded, for God is not about to be mocked. As Clarence Jordan puts it so well, "Don't let anybody pull the wool over your eyes—you can't turn up your nose at God!" (Cotton Patch, 103). The Greek verb *myktērizein* is found nowhere else in the New Testament, although it is well attested in the Septuagint. It means literally to "turn up the nose in mockery or contempt." The Old Testament references are mostly to the mocking of God's prophets; only once is this graphic word applied to a blasphemous mocking of God himself. In Ezek 8:17 the Lord asked the prophet a series of questions: "Have you seen this, son of man? Is it a trivial matter for the house of Judah to do the detestable things they are doing here? Must they also fill the land with violence and continually provoke me to anger? Look at them putting the branch to their nose!" By this foul gesture the children of Israel were showing contempt for the Almighty, actually mocking the Maker of heaven and earth. Yet on the other side of such arrogance and blasphemy the tables were turned, and it was God himself who suddenly appeared as the divine Mocker: "The One enthroned in heaven laughs; the Lord scoffs at them . . . I in turn will laugh at your disaster; I will mock when calamity overtakes you—when calamity overtakes you like a storm, when disaster sweeps over you like a whirlwind, when distress and trouble overwhelm you" (Ps 2:4; Prov 1:26-27).

Paul's point was the same: God *cannot* be mocked! There will be a payday someday because "a man reaps what he sows." You cannot outwit God; the crop you plant in the soil in the spring will inevitably sprout forth into the harvest of the fall. This is a commonsense saying, a prudential maxim found in ancient writers as diverse as Demosthones, "For he that furnished the seed is responsible for what grows," and the prophet Hosea, "They sow the wind and reap the whirlwind" (Hos 8:7).[137]

In v. 8 Paul moved on from his general statements about the impossibility of cheating God and the indelible law of sowing and reaping to apply these truths to the Galatian situation in terms of his earlier antithesis between flesh and Spirit. In a perfectly balanced construction, he claimed that "he that soweth to his flesh shall of the flesh reap corruption; but he that soweth to the Spirit shall of the Spirit reap life everlasting" (KJV). We see here drawn out on a canvas of eternity a scenario of the end results of the two catalogs of virtues and vices Paul enumerated in 5:19-23. If we continue to indulge in the works of the flesh, moving deeper and deeper into the pit of depravity, then we can be certain of the harvest we will receive—corruption.

The word *phthora,* "destruction," "decay," "corruption," conveys the idea of a putrid corpse in the process of decomposition. As we saw in our earlier discussion of the works of the flesh, *sarx* as an ethical principle involves far more than the physical or material aspect of the human. Nonetheless, the consequences of sin are nowhere more vividly seen than in the ravaging of the human body through disease, decay, and death. As Burton correctly observes, "Paul here affirms that devotion of one's self to the material, bodily side of life, brings physical death unrelieved by the Christian hope of resurrection which rests upon the indwelling of the Spirit of him that raised up Jesus from the dead."[138] However, we should not be misled by this graphic depiction of utter decay and desolation into thinking that the final destiny of those who sow to the flesh is annihilation or nonexistence. Hell is both final and eternal. In Rev 21:8 the role call of those who will find their place in the fiery lake of burning sulphur is remarkably similar to Paul's category of evil in Gal 5: the cowardly, the unbelieving, the vile, the murderers, the sexually immoral, those who practice magic arts, the idolaters, and all liars. Apart from eternal separation from God, the most horrible thing about hell is the incorrigibility of those who go there. "He that is unjust, let him be unjust *still;* and he which is filthy, let him be filthy *still"* (Rev 22:11, KJV;

---

[137] Cited in Burton, *Galatians,* 341.
[138] Ibid., 342.

italics added). This is the "corruption" of the second death.

Like a chalk artist, Paul painted a vivid portrait of the dark side of reality—the certainty of judgment, the harvest of destruction and death, the inescapable and eternal outcome of sowing to the flesh. But the counterdestiny of those who sow to the Spirit is just as glorious as that of unrepentant sinners is horrible. If the works of the flesh issue in corruption and death, the fruit of the Spirit yields the harvest of eternal life. Although "eternal life" as a theological motif is more typically associated with the Johannine writings, it does occur at a number of strategic points in Paul's letters as well (cf. Rom 2:7; 5:21; 6:22-23; 1 Tim 1:16; Titus 1:3; 3:7).

Eternal life, of course, is not merely life that lasts eternally. It is rather God's very own life, the life of the Father, the Son, and the Holy Spirit, graciously bestowed upon the children of God through faith in the Redeemer. Eternal life is the present possession of all who truly trust in Christ as Savior and Lord (John 3:36; 11:25-26). But Paul had in mind here the final consummation of salvation that will be ushered in by the return of Christ and the resurrection of the dead. Paul was using "eternal life" in the same sense Jesus did when he responded to Peter's complaint, "We have left all we had to follow you!" to which the Master replied, "I tell you truth, . . . no one who has left home or wife or brothers or parents or children for the sake of the kingdom of God will fail to receive many times as much in this age and, *in the age to come,* eternal life" (Luke 18:29-30; italics added). The splendor of the age to come and the glory of heaven beckons us forward just as the lights of the Celestial City summoned Bunyan's Christian toward the final goal of his pilgrim travels. In the *Institutes of the Christian Religion* Calvin devoted an entire chapter to "Meditation on the Future Life." He concluded that discussion with these words: "If believers' eyes are turned to the power of the Resurrection, in their hearts the cross of Christ will at last triumph over the devil, flesh, sin, and wicked men."[139]

(5) Don't Quit! (6:9-10)

[9]Let us not become weary in doing good, for at the proper time we will reap a harvest if we do not give up. [10]Therefore, as we have opportunity, let us do good to all people, especially to those who belong to the family of believers.

6:9 Still trading on the agricultural imagery of seedtime and harvest, Paul here admonished his readers to persevere in the faith, knowing that at the proper time God will fulfill his promise and bring to pass the consummation of all things in accordance with the good pleasure of his own divine will.

---

[139] Calvin, *Institutes* 3.9.6.

Throughout Gal 5–6 Paul had instructed the Christians of Galatia to do a number of specific things: expel the agitators, love your neighbor as yourself, keep in step with the Spirit by manifesting the fruit of the Spirit in your lives, practice church discipline by restoring those who have fallen, bear one another's burdens, examine yourself in light of the judgment seat of Christ, and provide material support for those who instruct you in the faith. In this verse Paul summarized all of these duties under the general rubric of "doing good."[140] Doing the good in this sense is the same thing as fulfilling the law of Christ. Why did Paul feel it necessary to persist in reminding the Galatian believers to practice the plain duties of the Christian faith? Calvin offers several answers to this question:

> This precept is especially necessary because we are naturally lazy in the duties of love, and many little stumbling-blocks hinder and put off even the well-disposed. We meet with many unworthy, many ungrateful people. The vast number of the needy overwhelms us; we are drained by paying out on every side. Our warmth is damped by the coldness of others. Finally, the whole world is full of hindrances which turn us aside from the right path. Therefore Paul does well to confirm our efforts, so that we do not faint through weariness.[141]

Paul's message to the Galatians is quite simply, "Don't quit!" Faced with the temptation of legalism on the one hand and libertinism on the other, many of Paul's converts in Galatia were beginning to lose heart. Having begun well in the life of the Spirit, they were in danger of losing their first love, being diverted from witness and service into petty bickering and greedy self-concern. To these fatigued and spiritually exhausted Christians, Paul made his appeal: "Let us not become weary in doing good."

In the last part of v. 9 Paul added a word of motivation to this urgent reminder: "For at the proper time we will reap a harvest if we do not give up." The word for "the proper time" is *kairos,* the same word Paul used in 4:4 to describe the opportune moment, the fullness of time, in which God sent his Son into the world. The same expression is used in 1 Tim 6:15 to describe the *parousia* or second advent of Christ—"which God will bring about in his own time." At this point Paul's metaphor of the spiritual life as a process of sowing and reaping breaks down. When a farmer plants a crop in the springtime, he can calculate with reasonable accuracy the time of the harvest. Of course, there are always variables to be taken into consideration, matters such as changing weather patterns, a swarm of destructive insects,

---

[140] So Betz: "The phrase το καλὸν ποιεῖν ('do the good') includes everything the Christian is responsible for doing. Thus, it is identical with the concepts of the 'fruit of the Spirit' (5:22-23) and of 'following the Spirit' (5:25; cf. 5:16)" (*Galatians,* 309).

[141] Calvin, CNTC 11.114.

and the like. Still, with the aid of the *Farmer's Almanac* or more scientific agricultural techniques, the wise farmer can usually depend on the expected timetables of seedtime and harvest. Not so in the spiritual life. One of the greatest frustrations in the Christian ministry, and a principal cause for "weariness in well doing," is the inability to calculate the spiritual outcome of faithful labors in the work of the Lord. For this reason we must be cautious in putting too much stock in what we often call "visible results." We serve a Sovereign God who has promised that his Word will not return void. The ultimate harvest is assured, but it will only come "at the proper time," that is, in God's own good time.

William Carey arrived in India in 1793 with a burden to preach the gospel of Jesus Christ to those who had never heard the name. For seven years he proclaimed the gospel message faithfully week after week, month after month, with not a single native of India converted to Christ. Through years of struggle and doubt, Carey was often discouraged but never defeated. To his sisters back home in England he wrote:

> I feel as a farmer does about his crop: sometimes I think the seed is springing, and thus I hope; a little blasts all, and my hopes are gone like a cloud. They were only weeds which appeared; or if a little corn sprung up, it quickly dies, being either chocked with weeds, or parched up by the sun of persecution. Yet I still hope in God, and will go forth in his strength, and make mention of his righteousness, even of his only.[142]

On December 28, 1800, Carey baptized in the Ganges River his first Hindu convert, a carpenter named Krishna Pal. William Ward, who witnessed the dramatic deliverance of this man from the grip of paganism into the glorious truth of the gospel, wrote in his diary: "Ye gods of stone and clay, did ye not tremble, when in the Triune Name one soul shook you from his feet as dust?"[143] This was the beginning of a mighty harvest of souls that God granted to Carey and his coworkers at the Serampore Mission in India.

Although Paul's reference here to the harvest that will be reaped in "due time" can properly bear a this-worldly application, its larger fulfillment points to the eschatological consummation at the return of Christ.[144] Paul could not let go of the fact that there is coming a day in which all persons will be brought to see themselves as God sees them, a time when God's perfect love and perfect justice will prevail in heaven, on earth, and even under

---

[142] George, *Faithful Witness,* 116.

[143] Ibid., 132.

[144] Cf. Longenecker's comment concerning the future tense of θερίσομεν: "[It] is a promise with a future, but again without any specification as to whether that time is to be a this-worldly existential future or an other-worldly eschatological future, or both" (*Galatians,* 282).

the earth. However ambiguous the present course of human history, however imperceptible the mysterious workings of divine providence in the midst of time, Christians look forward to the day when every knee shall bow and every tongue confess that Jesus Christ is Lord to the glory of God the Father. This is the blessed hope of the believer and the greatest motivating force for Christian ethics and Christian missions in the church today.[145]

6:10 The two particles that open this verse, the inferential *ara* ("then") followed by the transitional *oun* ("therefore"), signal that Paul was about to bring to a conclusion the ethical exhortations he had presented in his letter. There is a direct logical connection between this verse and Paul's preceding comment concerning the eschatological harvest that is yet to come. The word *kairos* is used in both verses, and the connection between them may be understood as follows: Just as the time of reaping will come "at the proper time," so now we must make good use of the present "opportunity" to sow to the Spirit rather than to the flesh. Paul's words should certainly not be understood as an endorsement for a lackadaisical approach to ethical living, as if he were saying: "Let us do good to others from time to time as the occasion may present itself." No, the *kairos* Paul spoke of in this verse is the divinely given opportunity for fulfilling the law of Christ, the unique dispensation of service granted to every born-again believer through the providential ordering of God. Paul here bore witness to the limitations of human life. The freedom of the Christian is a freedom of service in the moment of opportunity. The life of every person rushes toward its appointed end (Heb 9:27). The time for harvest is irretrievably set in the divine date book. Because this is true, consequently, therefore as we have opportunity (cf. "as opportunity offers," NEB), let us faithfully fulfill the ministry God has given us to do.

As Paul summarized it in this verse, Christian ethics has a dual focus: one is universal and all-embracing, "Let us do good to all people"; the other is particular and specific, "especially to those who belong to the family of believers." Paul's universalistic appeal was based on the fact that all persons everywhere are created in the image of God and are thus infinitely precious

---

[145] Earlier in this century R. Niebuhr warned against the prevalence of a domesticated theology that proclaimed "a God without wrath who brings men without sin into a kingdom without judgment through the ministrations of a Christ without a cross." Precisely this kind of attenuated eschatology is seen in B. Hebblethwaite's restatement of the last judgment: "We shall do well to play down the picture of God or Christ as Judge. A range of alternative models, the healer, the therapist, the patient lover, the counselor, all seem more appropriate for bringing out the primary interest of divine judgment, namely, the restoration of the creature to integrity and the winning of his love, despite what he has done or made of himself in the past" *(The Christian Hope* [Grand Rapids: Eerdmans, 1984], 215). Such a perspective is utterly incompatible with the Pauline view of the God who is not mocked.

in his sight. Whenever Christians have forgotten this primary *datum* of biblical revelation, they have inevitably fallen victim to the blinding sins of racism, sexism, tribalism, classism, and a thousand other bigotries that have blighted the human community from Adam and Eve to the present day.[146]

Believers are duty bound to do good to all persons whether or not they are Christians. However, in addition to this unrestricted ethical imperative, there is a further, particular obligation for the Christian to do good *especially* to those who belong to the family of faith. Luther and Calvin, following Jerome, saw a linkage between this verse and Paul's earlier admonition in v. 6 concerning the liberal support of the ministers of the churches.[147] Others have interpreted the adverb "especially" (*malista*) as an oblique reference to Paul's collection of funds for the poor saints in Jerusalem.[148] The language Paul used can allow for either of these interpretations, but it is more likely that he was here simply pointing to the special responsibility all Christians have to help alleviate the suffering of their needy brothers and sisters in Christ. This is not merely a recognition of the general maxim that "charity begins at home" but rather an affirmation of the supernatural bond that obtains among all those who belong to the household of faith. In commenting on this verse, J. Brown offered the following interpretation of this important principle:

> Every poor and distressed man had a claim on me for pity, and, if I can afford it, for active exertion and pecuniary relief. But a poor Christian has a far stronger claim on my feelings, my labors, and my property. He is my brother, equally interested as myself in the blood and love of the Redeemer. I expect to spend an eternity with him in heaven. He is the representative of my unseen Savior, and he considers everything done to his poor afflicted as done to himself. For a Christian to be unkind to a Christian is not only wrong, it is monstrous.[149]

4. The Apostolic Seal (6:11-16)

We come now to the subscription or final paragraph of Paul's letter to the Galatians. Just as the introduction of this epistle differed from the usual Pauline pattern in that it contained no thanksgiving section and began with an immediate polemical punch, so too this concluding subscription varies

---

[146] Cf. Betz's comment on this verse: "Since before God there is no partiality, there cannot be partiality in the Christian's attitude toward his fellowman" (*Galatians,* 311).

[147] *LW* 27.128-29; Calvin, CNTC 11.114.

[148] A connection between Gal 6:6-10 and the Jerusalem collection was first proposed by Lightfoot, *Galatians,* 55, and H. Lietzmann, *An die Galater,* 39-42. This thesis has been further elaborated by L. W. Hurtado, "The Jerusalem Collection and the Book of Galatians," *JSNT* 5 (1979): 46-62. For a thorough critique of this view, see Bruce, *Galatians,* 265-66.

[149] Brown, *Galatians,* 348.

from Paul's usual epistolary practice in several ways. For one thing, it is longer than most, containing a summary recapitulation of the main themes Paul had pursued throughout the letter. There are no expressed greetings from Paul or anyone else; not even the unnamed "brothers with me" of 1:2 reappear in these final words of farewell. Nor did Paul offer a doxological confession of praise, nor reiterate his desire to see the Galatians soon, nor request their prayers on his behalf.

Many commentators attribute this lack of a personal touch to the strained relations and distant feelings between Paul and the Galatians that characterize the tone of the letter throughout.[150] This point, however, should not be pressed too far. The closing word of the letter, before the final "Amen," is the vocative *adelphoi,* "brothers," Paul's favorite word of address to his readers throughout the body of the letter. Likewise, the "peace benediction" of v. 16 and the more typical "grace benediction" of v. 18 should not be read as mere stylistic devices at the close of a letter. They express the heart and soul of the apostle Paul summarizing in two majestic words the essence of the gospel he labored so valiantly to set forth in this brief but powerful letter.

Thus, despite the lack of personal greetings and intimate disclosures, Paul did not lose sight of his primary reason in writing this letter to the Galatians: to win them back from the brink of apostasy to a full-orbed faith in the one and only gospel of Jesus Christ, his Lord and theirs. To this end he reviewed in what Lightfoot called "terse eager disjointed sentences" the principal themes of the letter.[151]

In these verses history, theology, and ethics are interwoven in a convincing summary of the key points Paul had been trying to make in all that went before. The personal, autobiographical, historical dimension is there in the large letters Paul used to autograph this subscription, as well as in his near sardonic warning in v. 17, "Let no one cause me trouble." The antithesis between the cross and circumcision also recalls the great struggle between Paul and his Judaizing opponents. And just as Paul had placarded Christ crucified to the Galatians during his first preaching mission among them (cf. Gal 3:1-3), so it is still the centerpiece in the final conclusion of this letter. Here the cross is not only the place where the Son of God suffered to redeem fallen sinners from the curse of the law; it is also the line of demarcation between the believer and the world—the world understood as the realm of the flesh, of defeat, and finally of death.

Paul's entire theology of justification is reflected in the way he used the word "boast" in this context (vv. 13-14). On this side of forgiveness and new

---

[150] So Longenecker, *Galatians,* 288-89.
[151] Lightfoot, *Galatians,* 220.

life, the only boasting permitted is that of the justified sinner who has surrendered the autonomy of the self to the lordship of Christ, the hymnic boast of redemption: "In my hands no price I bring, Simply to thy cross I cling." In the body of the letter history and theology led with an irresistible and evangelical logic to the theme of ethics, an ethics of freedom and obligation rooted in a life filled and controlled by the Holy Spirit. The "new creation" of v. 15 and the "rule" of v. 16 recall the ethical exhortations, the imperatives based on indicatives, which occupied Paul's attention in Gal 5:6. Erasmus once remarked that in this closing paragraph Paul talked "pure flame."[152] In the light of that incandescent flame we see again the message of grace and truth, freedom and faith pressed home to the "brothers" who share with Paul a participation in the life, death, and resurrection of Jesus Christ.

(1) Paul's Autograph (6:11)

11See what large letters I use as I write to you with my own hand!

6:11   The NEB translates this verse: "You see these big letters? I am now writing to you in my own hand." It was a common convention of Hellenistic letter writing that a secretary or amanuensis would prepare the main body of the letter while the sender would append his signature and perhaps a few closing words of benediction as a way of attesting the contents of the letter and assuring the reader of his full endorsement. We follow much the same practice today when an attorney or legal secretary draws up an official document that requires the signature of a client for validation. We gather from other comments in Paul's letters that it was customary for him to dictate his letters orally to an amanuensis and then add a personal postscript and signature in his own hand at the end of the epistle (cf. 1 Cor 16:21; 2 Cor 10:1; 2 Thess 3:17; Col 4:18). Thus most commentators believe that 6:11 is the place in Galatians where Paul took the stylus from the hand of his secretary and finished off the letter in his own handwriting using, for some reason, unusually large letters to which he drew attention in this verse.[153]

---

[152] Barrett, *Freedom and Obligation*, 84.

[153] See Longenecker, *Galatians,* lix-lxi; Fung, *Galatians,* 300-302; W. P. Doty, *Letters in Primitive Christianity,* 40-41. Despite the strong internal evidence for Paul's use of an amanuensis, we should not imagine that these helpers were given such great freedom and leeway as actually to compose the materials found in the Pauline Epistles. It is much more likely that he dictated to a secretary word by word. His signature at the end was his "apostolic seal" verifying that the foregoing content was precisely what he had intended to convey to his readers. For two different assessments of this feature of Paul's epistolary practice, see G. H. Bahr, "The Subscriptions in the Pauline Letters," *JBL* 87 (1968): 27-41, and R. N. Longenecker, "Ancient Amanuenses and the Pauline Epistles," in *New Dimensions in New Testament Study,* ed. R. N. Longenecker and M. C. Tenney (Grand Rapids: Zondervan, 1974), 281-97.

Some commentators, going back to John Chrysostom, have argued on the basis of the aorist tense of the verb *egrapsa,* "I have written," that Paul meant to say that he had written the entire Letter to the Galatians in his own hand and with abnormally large characters.[154] It is better, however, to read this verb as an epistolary aorist (cf. 1 Cor 5:11; Phlm 19,21) which should be translated, "I am now writing" (cf. RSV, NASB). Thus the autographed portion of the letter would include 6:11-18 and not the entire epistle.[155] Assuming that Paul did employ a secretary to do the actual writing of the bulk of Galatians, we have no idea who that person may have been. Paul frequently used his traveling companions and assistants to write out the major portions of his letters. It is quite likely that these persons are to be identified among the names Paul included in the salutations of his letters—Silas and Timothy (2 Thess 1:1; Phil 1:1; Phlm 1), Sosthenes (cf. 1 Cor 1:1), Tertius (cf. Rom 16:22), or his beloved Luke, who remained Paul's faithful companion during his final imprisonment at Rome (cf. 2 Tim 4:11). It is a reasonable conjecture that the scribe of Galatians was one of the unnamed brothers to whom Paul alluded in 1:2.

But why did Paul write in such large letters, that is, in Greek uncials rather than in the smaller cursive script?[156] Much speculation has been given to this question. Was it Paul's poor eyesight (cf. 4:15) that required him to write in this unusual manner? Or was his writing hand twisted or defective as a result of some harsh persecution he had received?[157] Was Paul simply

---

[154] Burton's comment on this hypothesis is difficult to refute: "The improbability that the apostle should have thought at the outset to use the pen himself and to write in a noticeably large hand, and that he should have kept up this strained and difficult method of emphasis through all the pages of the letter, only now at the end calling attention to it, is so great, especially in the case of a letter written to groups of people and intended to be read aloud to them, as to amount to practical impossibility" (*Galatians,* 349).

[155] For the contrary view, see Bligh, *Galatians,* 489, citing Chrysostom (*PG* 61.678A). Calvin gives an interesting twist to this interpretation: "To convince the Galatians more fully of his anxiety and at the same time to make them read it more carefully, he mentions that this long letter had been written by his own hand. The greater the toil he had undertaken for them, the stronger their inducement to read it, not carelessly, but with the closest attention" (*Galatians,* 115).

[156] Some have interpreted the "large letters" as a reference to the length of the epistle rather than to Paul's peculiar handwriting. So Luther, *LW* 27.129-30. However, Paul invariably used the word ἐπιστολῇ for a "letter" in the sense of an epistle (cf. 1 Cor 5:9; 16:3; 2 Cor 3:1; 2 Thess 2:5). Although γράμματα can sometimes mean "an epistle" (cf. Acts 28:21), Paul consistently used this term to refer to the individual, and in this sense handwritten, characters of the alphabet. See F. Stagg, "Freedom and Moral Responsibility," *RevExp* 69 (1972): 492-93.

[157] N. Turner has surmised that Paul sustained permanent damage to his hand from undergoing an actual crucifixion at Perga in Pamphylia. See his *Grammatical Insights in the New Testament* (Edinburgh: T & T Clark, 1965), 94. This view has been discounted by subsequent scholars such as Bruce, *Galatians,* 268, and Longenecker, *Galatians,* 290.

reflecting the fact that he wrote not as a professional scribe but as a workman whose hands were more accustomed to shaping leather and making tents than to cultivating the kind of precise penmanship many of his readers would perhaps expect from a religious teacher? Do the "large letters" signify that Paul was "a Hebrew of the Hebrews" more familiar with the large Semitic characters of his mother tongue than with the congested traffic of a Greek sentence? All of these are intriguing possibilities, but none of them can be set forth with certainty. It is more likely, as Lightfoot said, that "the boldness of the handwriting answers to the force of the apostle's convictions. The size of the characters will arrest the attention of his readers in spite of themselves."[158] So, in addition to authenticating the letter as genuine and attesting that he had "meant what he said," Paul wanted to underscore and reemphasize both the central message of the letter and his own personal investment in it.[159]

(2) Boasting in the Cross (6:12-16)

[12]**Those who want to make a good impression outwardly are trying to compel you to be circumcised. The only reason they do this is to avoid being persecuted for the cross of Christ.** [13]**Not even those who are circumcised obey the law, yet they want you to be circumcised that they may boast about your flesh.** [14]**May I never boast except in the cross of our Lord Jesus Christ, through which the world has been crucified to me, and I to the world.** [15]**Neither circumcision nor uncircumcision means anything; what counts is a new creation.** [16]**Peace and mercy to all who follow this rule, even to the Israel of God.**

A PARTING BLOW (6:12-12). **6:12-13** Throughout Galatians Paul waged a steady campaign against a group of false teachers, commonly known as Judaizers, who had sown great confusion among the apostle's recent converts by teaching that becoming Jewish was necessary for salvation. As we learn from 5:2-4, a major plank in the platform of the agitators related to the ancient rite of circumcision. They insisted that Gentile believers submit themselves to circumcision as a necessary prerequisite for belonging to the covenant people of God. As Paul had said before and would reiterate again in this closing passage (6:15), the issue at stake was not circumcision per se but rather the salvific significance the false teachers attached to this ceremony. Paul again revisited this debate and issued a final

---

[158] Lightfoot, *Galatians,* 221.

[159] Burton points out that "the size of the letters would have somewhat the effect of boldface type in a modern book, or double underlining in a manuscript, and since the apostle himself called attention to it, it would impress not only the one person who might be reading the letter to a congregation, but the listening congregation, also" (*Galatians,* 348).

blistering attack against the agitators who were trying to compel the Galatians to accept circumcision.

In these two verses Paul leveled a dual charge against his opponents, accusing them not only of dangerous doctrinal deviation but also of unscrupulous and unworthy motivation. Why had they sought so vigorously to "compel" (not by physical force, to be sure, but by such underhanded maneuvers as the denigration of Paul's ministry and illicit appeals to apostolic authorities in Jerusalem) Paul's Gentile converts to undergo circumcision? Paul answered this question by claiming that their basic motive was spiritual self-aggrandizement: they wanted "to make a good impression outwardly"; "they want you to be circumcised that they may boast about your flesh."

Paul's opponents evidently were Jewish Christian missionaries who were waging an aggressive evangelistic campaign of their own. It is not far-fetched to imagine that they had strong ties to the "Mother Church" at Jerusalem, especially to the ultralegalistic wing in it—the same group that gave Paul such a hassle upon his subsequent return to the city of his early adulthood (cf. Acts 21–22). This party was well represented at the Jerusalem Council, where they argued (unsuccessfully) for the adoption of their policy toward Gentiles who wanted to become Christians: "Unless you are circumcised, according to the custom taught by Moses, you cannot be saved" (Acts 15:1). There is no doubt that this view was deeply and sincerely held by many Jewish Christians who were alarmed at the large number of Gentiles being brought into the church through the ministry of Paul and his coworkers. Paul did not deny that there was an element of sincere conviction among his opponents, but he did claim that there was a more sinister and self-serving motivation at work as well. They wanted to boast and brag about how many Gentile Christians they had converted into Jewish proselytes.

The word translated in the NIV "to make a good impression outwardly," is *euprosōpein,* a term found nowhere else in the New Testament and only attested elsewhere among recently discovered papyri documents.[160] Paul's opponents wanted "to present a pleasing front to the world" (Phillips). "Paul's point was that the Jews wanted 'ecclesiastical statistics'; so many circumcisions in a given year was certainly something to boast about."[161] When they returned to Jerusalem, they wanted to be able to stand up at the missionaries' meeting and declare that they had traveled far and wide and had a good many scalps to show for their efforts.

A gruesome story from the Old Testament provides an analogy for the

---

[160] See E. Lohse, "Εὐπροσωπέω, προσωπολῆμψια," *TDNT* 6.779.
[161] Cole, *Galatians,* 181.

Judaizers' activity. In 1 Sam 18 we read of David's negotiations with Saul concerning Michal, Saul's daughter, whom David desired to marry. The "price" Saul proposed for this marital dispensation was "a hundred Philistine foreskins." Thus "David and his men went out and killed two hundred Philistines. He brought their foreskins and presented the full number to the king so that he might become the king's son-in-law. Then Saul gave him his daughter Michal in marriage" (1 Sam 18:27). Figuratively, Paul's opponents were doing the same thing David and his soldiers had done of old: presenting Gentile "foreskins" as a mark of their own success and ingenuity as representatives of the Jewish Christian establishment.

What a great warning this verse holds for Christian ministers today, a challenge not only for our message to be sound but also for our motives to be pure. How many pastors' conferences turn into Monday morning brag sessions where we tout our own "ecclesiastical statistics," tipping our hat to the Good Lord, to be sure, but craving the luster of the limelight for ourselves? No one can escape this temptation fully, for the tinderbox of pride flares up in every believer who is not yet perfectly conformed to the image of Christ, which is to say, every Christian who lives and ministers on this side of heaven. The only antidote to the poison of pride is the daily self-crucifixion of the flesh with its passions and desires (cf. 5:24).

Paul suggested one additional motivation for the insistence of his Jewish Christian opponents that the Gentile Christians of Galatia undergo circumcision. They did this, he said, in order to "avoid being persecuted for the cause of Christ." But how could the circumcision of Gentile believers in Galatia result in the nonpersecution of these itinerant missionaries? The most natural interpretation is to assume that Paul was here simply applying his own experience of persecution to the agitators. In other words, he was saying in effect: Sure, I could have avoided persecution too had I been willing to compromise the message of salvation by grace alone. By insisting on the circumcision of Gentile believers, the Judaizers could cast themselves in a favorable light with the local synagogue authorities: they were simply recruiting more Jewish proselytes for the nation of Israel, thereby mitigating, to some extent at least, the scandal of the cross with its particularistic emphasis on salvation through Jesus Christ alone.

The verb *diōkomai,* "persecuted," is one Paul used earlier in his rhetorical question of 5:11: "If I am still preaching circumcision, why am I still being persecuted?" However, in an important article entitled "The Agitators and the Galatian Congregation," R. Jewett has suggested a more concrete historical context for Paul's allusion to the avoidance of persecution in 6:12. He has argued "that Jewish Christians in Judea were stimulated by Zealotic pressure into a nomistic campaign against their fellow Christians in the late forties and early fifties. Their goal was to avert the suspicion that they were in communion with lawless Gentiles."[162] But by circumcising the converts of the renegade missionary Paul, they could thus show to the fanatical Zealots back home that belief in Jesus as Messiah involved no breach of the Mosaic law or the sacred ceremonies of the Jewish people. This theory makes good historical sense in terms of the increasing tension between the Christian community in Jerusalem and the hostile Jewish authorities there, a conflict that eventually issued in the martyrdom of James in A.D. 62. Other scholars have wondered, however, whether Jewish Christian missionaries would have been motivated to travel hundreds of miles in order to circumcise Gentile converts so as to avoid persecution of Zealots in far away Judea.[163] Whatever the exact historical referent Paul had in mind, the theological meaning of his statement is clear: to follow Jesus Christ faithfully and to proclaim his gospel unflinchingly is to invite persecution. The Galatian Christians knew this from their own experience (cf. 3:4). By using the motivation of the Judaizers as a foil, Paul was here reminding them of how much they had already suffered for the cause of Christ and encouraging them to remain steadfast in their discipleship.

THE CROSS AND THE NEW CREATION (6:14). **6:14** In contrast to the false teachers, who boasted and bragged about their own accomplishments and who were especially proud of their success in winning over Gentile believers to the requirement of circumcision, Paul declared in the strongest possible terms—"God forbid" (KJV)—that the only possible ground and object of his own boasting was the cross of the Lord Jesus Christ. Paul developed the theme of boasting more than any other New Testament writer, for the kind of self-confident assertion it conveyed stood in marked contrast to the attitudes of humility and receptivity called forth by divine grace. Thus in Rom 3:21-27, immediately following his exposition of the righteousness of God which is apart from the law, Paul posed the question, "Where, then, is boasting?" His answer was dogmatic and definitive, "It is excluded!" When confronted with the infinitely amazing grace of God, the very thought of self-glorification, spiritual ego-stroking, vanishes away.

Yet it is not exactly true to say that Paul disavowed the possibility of Christian boasting altogether. There was a kind of boasting that not only was permitted but held up to the Galatians as desirable and worthy of imitation: it was boasting in the cross or, as Paul put it elsewhere, "Let him who boasts boast in the Lord" (1 Cor 1:31; 2 Cor 10:17). The common anthropological assumptions of Greek philosophy and Hellenistic culture, not unlike those of

---

[162] Jewett, "The Agitators," 205.

[163] See the discussion in Matera, *Galatians*, 230-31; Bruce, *Galatians*, 269.

the modern cult of self-esteem, greatly valued all forms of human assertiveness as badges of excellence, strength, and virtue (from the Latin *virtus,* meaning "manliness" or "worth"). Physical prowess (cf. Augustine's recollection of how his pagan father Patricius used to take pride in showing off his well-formed adolescent son in the public baths), military feats, oratorical abilities, intellectual acumen, political power, monetary success, social status—all these were things to be proud of and to glory in.

Paul, however, chose something utterly despicable, contemptible, and valueless as the basis of his own boasting—the cross of Christ. For two thousand years the cross has been so variously and beautifully represented in Christian iconography and symbolism that it is almost impossible for us to appreciate the sense of horror and shock that must have greeted the apostolic proclamation of a crucified Redeemer. Clarence Jordan helps a little when he paraphrases this verse: "God forbid that I should ever take pride in anything, except in the lynching of our Lord Jesus Christ" (Cotton Patch). Actually the Latin word *crux* was regarded as an expression so crude no polite Roman would utter it in public. In order to get around this difficulty, the Romans devised a euphemistic circumlocution, "Hang him on the unlucky tree" *(arbori infelici suspendito).*[164] But what the world regards as too shameful to whisper in polite company, a detestable object used for the brutal execution of the dregs of society, Paul declared to be the proper basis for exultation. In this and in this alone he would make his boast, in life and death, for all time and eternity.[165]

> When false foundations all are gone,
> Each lying refuge blown to air,
> The Cross remains our boast alone:
> The righteousness of God is there.[166]

The false teachers Paul confronted in Galatia, not unlike many contemporary theologians today, found the cross a matter of severe embarrassment. They could not deny that the Messiah had in fact been impaled on a Roman cross. That was too palpable and public an event for anyone to try to hide. But if they could not deny the cross, they would certainly de-emphasize it. They would conceal the full meaning of atonement by arrogating unto sinful human beings a share in their own salvation. Their argument might have run

---

[164] Bruce, *Galatians,* 271, quoting Cicero, *Pro Rabirio,* 13.

[165] On the theme of boasting in Paul see R. Bultmann, "καυχᾶομαι," *TDNT* 3.645-54. On the repugnance and horror with which the cross was perceived in Hellenistic culture, see M. Hengel, *Crucifixion in the Ancient World and the Folly of the Message of the Cross* (London: SCM, 1977).

[166] "Glassite Hymn," quoted in Brown, *Galatians,* 370.

something like this: "Yes, of course, Jesus died on the cross, and that is a great example of God's love. But if you want to be saved and really belong to the true Israel, then you must do something more than merely rely on that past event. Yes, Jesus was the Messiah, and he did a lot for us. But now it is up to you to complete what he began."

Over against this kind of truncated gospel, Paul declared that what happened on the cross was more than a prolegomenon to salvation. "God was reconciling the world to himself in Christ," for "God made him who had no sin to be sin for us, so that in him we might become the righteousness of God" (2 Cor 5:19,21). What was true in Paul's day is no less true in ours: where the doctrine of the cross is not received, Jesus Christ is not received. It has been well said that a person might preach with great knowledge and zeal upon everything in the Bible except the cross, and his preaching will have been in vain, for the message of the cross is the power of God unto salvation to all who believe (1 Cor 1:18).

In the latter part of v. 14, Paul developed further his understanding of the cross of Christ by declaring that through it the world had been crucified to him and he to the world. In reality there is a triple crucifixion to be considered in this text: the crucified Christ, the crucified world, and the crucified Christian.[167] What happened to Jesus outside the gates of Jerusalem is, of course, the decisive and controlling event of redemptive history. But something also happened to the cosmos, the created realm, on the day Christ died. The creation itself, cracked and groaning under the weight of sin, is yet to be redeemed on the basis of the cross of Christ. When Jesus died, the earth quaked, the sun refused to shine, and cemeteries were disturbed. In these events God was giving notice to Satan and his pomp that their lease on Planet Earth was about to run out. The devil is still the "God of this cosmos," but his kingdom is doomed. Jesus is *Christos Pantokrator,* Christ the All-Powerful!

But there is more: the cosmological significance of Jesus' death has ethical implications for every believer. Not only is the world crucified to believers through their identification with Jesus' once-for-all victory on the cross, but through the ongoing process of mortification and self-denial, believers also are crucified to the world. The "world" in this sense, of course, means not so much the physical world of space and time (lest we lapse into a kind of docetic dualism) but rather the world-system that in its basic values and orientation is alienated from God. To be crucified to the world, then, means to walk in the light, to bear the fruit of the Spirit, and to live in the freedom

---

[167] See the fascinating study by P. S. Minear, "The Crucified World: The Enigma of Galatians 6:14," in *Theologia Crucis—Signum Crucis* (Tübingen: Mohr, 1979), 395-407.

with which Christ has set us free.

6:15 Paul then applied the principle of v. 14 to the concrete situation that had prompted him to write this Letter to the Galatians. This verse has an earlier parallel in the letter at 5:6, where Paul declared that neither circumcision nor uncircumcision had any value but only "faith expressing itself through love." Here the irrelevance of circumcision/uncircumcision is contrasted with a more comprehensive expression of the life of faith effected through the cross of Christ, "a new creation." J. B. Phillips translates this last phrase as "the power of new birth," and certainly the fact of regeneration is essential to Paul's meaning here. But the "new creation" includes far more than the spiritual beginnings of the Christian life. In 2 Cor 5:17 Paul expressed this idea in fuller terms: "Therefore, if anyone is in Christ, he is a new creation; the old has gone, the new has come!" The new creation, then, involves the whole process of conversion: the regenerating work of the Holy Spirit leading to repentance and faith, the daily process of mortification and vivification, continual growth in holiness leading to eventual conformity to the image of Christ. The new creation implies a new nature with a new system of desires, affections, and habits, all wrought through the supernatural ministry of the Holy Spirit in the life of the believer. No spiritual gymnastics, no twelve-step program on the deeper life, no quick-fix "How-to-Be-a-Better-Christian" seminar can produce this kind of transformation. Paul's emphasis was on the act of God in effecting a new thing. This is the result of faith working by love leading to holiness culminating in a life filled with the Spirit. As Paul had done throughout the letter, so too here in these closing lines he reiterated the central thesis he had developed from numerous perspectives: no one is made right with God on the basis of external ceremonies or human efforts of any kind but only through the unilateral action of God in the cross and resurrection of Jesus Christ, the object of the believer's trust and the One whose Spirit liberates and empowers all those whose sins are forgiven. Put otherwise, justification by faith is not a legal fiction but a living reality that manifests itself in the new creation.

6:16 Nearing the end of his letter, Paul appended here a conditional benediction: "Peace and mercy to all who follow this rule." Here we find no large-hearted "greet all the saints in Christ Jesus," as we have at the conclusion of Philippians. Nor are there any holy kisses to be passed around on the order of Paul's instructions to the Corinthians and Thessalonians. This is a formal and restricted benediction, sincerely meant no doubt but clearly targeted to a specific group—those who follow Paul's rule. The Greek word for rule is *kanōn,* which literally meant "cane," or "measuring rod," and which later assumed the technical meaning of "canon" or "rule of faith."

Most scholars believe that Paul was here referring to the principle of justification by faith that he had just summarized in the preceding verse under the general rubric of the "new creation." Thus he invoked the peace and mercy of God upon those members of the congregations of Galatia who remained faithful to the truth of the gospel Paul had originally preached among them. This conditional blessing at the end of the letter stands in marked contrast to the conditional curse with which Paul opened his epistle (1:6-9). This conditional blessing "applies a threat against those who, after having read the letter, do not intend to conform to Paul's rule and, consequently, fall under the curse."[168] Paul knew very well that he was writing to churches caught up in intense conflict over a serious theological matter. Rather than smoothing over the difficulty in the interest of a superficial harmony, Paul did the opposite: he emphasized the sharp differences between him and his opponents and forced the Galatians to make a choice. On the one side of that choice was the apostolic curse; on the other, the apostolic blessing.

Who were the "Israel of God" for whom Paul also invoked divine mercy? This expression is found only here in the New Testament, and it has baffled Pauline scholars considerably. It is tempting to follow the majority of commentators in interpreting this expression as a general appellation for the Christian church. On this reading the "Israel of God" would stand in apposition with "all those who follow this rule." The NIV assumes that this is the case and thus translates the *kai* ("and") as "even." As we have seen throughout this commentary Paul convincingly argued that the true children of Abraham were not to be identified simply with the physical descendants of the twelve sons of Jacob. As Paul would put it elsewhere, "For not all who are descended from Israel are Israel" (Rom 9:6). Furthermore, the worldly distinctions of role, race, and rank have been transcended by the "new creation" in which there is "neither Jew nor Gentile," "neither circumcision nor uncircumcision." God has one plan of salvation for all peoples everywhere, and that plan involves a personal act of trust in Jesus Christ, the promised Messiah, who bore the penalty for sin and endured the curse of the law in his substitutionary, atoning death on the cross. Jesus is the true seed of Abraham, and all who belong to God through faith in him are children of the promise. Given all this, why can we not simply equate Israel and the church, especially now that we stand on this side of Good Friday and Easter and can see with evangelical clarity what was only foreshadowed in the old dispensation? Despite the allure of this interpretation, there are several reasons why it may not be the most exegetically satisfying solution to the identity of the "Israel of God."

---

[168] Betz, *Galatians,* 321.

First, while the grammatical structure of the verse is not entirely clear, reflecting perhaps the Hebraism of an earlier formula Paul may have been adapting here, it seems best to give the particle *kai* its full connective sense ("and" or "also") rather than translating it as an intensive link ("even") with the preceding phrase. P. Richardson has suggested the following translation, which seems to represent better Paul's meaning: "May God give peace to all who will walk according to this criterion, and mercy also to his faithful people Israel."[169] Second, it is strange that if Paul intended simply to equate the Gentile believers with the people of Israel that he would make this crucial identification here at the end of his letter and not in the main body where he developed at length his argument for justification by faith. Stranger still, Paul did not put this potent expression to use in his magisterial exposition on the role of Israel in salvation history in Rom 9–11. As W. D. Davies has observed, "If this proposal were correct one would have expected to find support for it in Rom 9:11, where Paul extensively deals with 'Israel.'"[170] Third, although the New Testament elsewhere (1 Pet 2:9-10) refers to the Christian church as a chosen race, a royal priesthood, a holy nation, and a people belonging to God, there is no explicit identification of the church as the "New Israel" anywhere in early Christian literature until about A.D. 160, when Justin Martyr used this language for the first time.[171]

It is best, then, to see the "Israel of God" as an eschatological reference to the whole people of God, who will find mercy through the Messiah, including both converted Gentiles (the wild olive shoots who have been grafted in) and completed Jews (the natural branches God will yet redeem). In the mysterious providence of God, the temporal hardening of national Israel has opened the door for the evangelization of the Gentiles. Paul himself was the harbinger of this great missionary movement that continues down to the present moment in the history of redemption. However, when the "full number of the Gentiles has come in," then the elect remnant of the Jewish people will also confess Jesus as Messiah and "so all Israel will be saved" (Rom 11:25-26). In the meantime, God has not abandoned his ancient people but continues to deal with them in the context of his eschatological ordering of world events. Indeed, one of the most remarkable facts of world history is the survival of the Jewish people. No other group or nation has withstood so many attempted genocides—from Haman to Hitler

---

[169] P. Richardson, *Israel and the Apostolic Church* (Cambridge: Cambridge University Press, 1969), 84. For discussion of Richardson's rendering, see Betz, *Galatians,* 322-23; Longenecker, *Galatians,* 296, 99.
[170] W. D. Davies, "Paul and the People of Israel," *NTS* 24 (1977): 10-11, n. 2.
[171] See W. S. Campbell, "Israel," *DPL,* 441.

and Hussein. As W. S. Campbell has aptly noted, "It would be naive to suggest that it is merely an accident of history that the historical people of God, the Jewish race, should continue to exist alongside Christianity."[172] Throughout this torturous history there has always been a remnant of believing Jews who have accepted Jesus as Messiah and look forward to his coming again in glory. Just as Paul preached the gospel "to the Jew first," so too Christians today have a special warrant to share the good news of Jesus Christ with Jewish people, among whom God is still calling to faith those who repent and believe in the Messiah.

(3) Brand Marks of Jesus (6:17)

[17]**Finally, let no one cause me trouble, for I bear on my body the marks of Jesus.**

6:17 The Greek word for brand marks is *stigmata*. Some have interpreted this word to mean that Paul actually bore in his hands, feet, and side the imprinted marks of Jesus' passion and death. The most famous historical example of this phenomenon is Francis of Assisi, who was believed to have had the scars of Christ's passion supernaturally imposed upon his body near the end of his life, on September 17, 1224.[173] In all, more than three hundred claims to such stigmatization have been put forth across the centuries. Whether or not we regard these accounts as bona fide reports of actual events, or as attestations of neuropathic bleedings, or, as Luther put it bluntly, "a pure fiction and a joke," they have little to do with Paul's use of this word near the end of his Letter to the Galatians.[174]

When Paul said that he carried around in his body the death of Jesus (cf. 2 Cor 4:10) and that he constantly bore the Lord's brand marks, he was referring to the actual scars of persecution and marks of physical suffering he

---

[172] Campbell, "Israel," *DPL,* 446.

[173] According to Bonaventura, Francis received his stigmatization following a prolonged fast and a divinely given vision of the crucifixion of Christ: "As the vision disappeared, it left his heart ablaze with eagerness and impressed upon his body a miraculous likeness. There and then the marks of nails began to appear in his hand and his feet, just as he had seen them in his vision of the Man nailed to the cross. His hands and feet appeared pierced through the center with nails, the heads of which were in the palms of his hands and on the instep of each foot, while the points stuck out on the opposite side. The heads were black and round, but the points were long and bent back, as if they had been struck with a hammer; they rose above the surrounding flesh and stood out from it. His right side seemed as if it had been pierced with a lance and was marked with a livid scar which often bled, so that his habit and trousers were stained" (*Saint Francis of Assisi: Omnibus of Sources,* ed. M. A. Habig (Chicago: Franciscan Herald Press, 1983), 731.

[174] See Stott, *Only One Way,* 181-82; *LW* 27.142.

received throughout his apostolic ministry because of his unflinching witness for the gospel. As several commentators have noted, there may well be
a veiled reference here to the effects of the brutal stoning Paul received outside the city of Lystra during his first preaching mission there (cf. Acts
14:19-20). In this case at least some of the Galatians to whom Paul was writing would have had good reason to know firsthand about the "marks" to
which he referred in this verse.

Why did Paul mention the brand marks here at the very end of his letter,
as a kind of climactic conclusion to all that he had written? He did so for two
reasons at least. First, Paul's readers immediately would have identified the
branding of the flesh with slavery, for slaves in the ancient world frequently
were marked with the insignia of their master as a badge of identification. In
addition, certain devotees of the mystery religions also tattooed themselves
as a way of showing their devotion and loyalty to a particular cult or deity.
So, in effect, Paul would have been saying: Look, I too have been branded!
I am a slave of my faithful Savior Jesus Christ. If you care to look for yourselves, here is his insignia imprinted in my very flesh. I am no fair-weather
Christian but one who has come to know his Lord in the fellowship of his
sufferings as well as the power of his resurrection.

Paul's reference to the brand marks also recalls his bitter opposition to the
false teachers and their penchant for "boasting" in the flesh. Paul already had
said that he would boast only in the cross of the Lord Jesus Christ (v. 14).
The Judaizers, on the other hand, had their own distinctive brand mark of
which they boasted and bragged—the mark of circumcision. Their entire
theological program was tied up not only with their own physical circumcision but also with their ability to persuade Gentile believers to accept this
religious rite, a means of salvation and identification with the true people of
God. Paul blew the whistle on this kind of "theology of glory" by pointing
to the "theology of the cross" and its outworking in his own sufferings as a
Christian. "Let no one cause me trouble," Paul said to the Galatians; that is,
stop harassing me and trying to undermine my ministry because my apostolic labor has already been validated by Christ—not only on the Damascus
Road but also in my suffering and affliction, the signs of which are evident
for all to see. In this sense the brand marks are a seal and sure evidence of
true doctrine and faith.

Finally, the brand marks of Jesus recall the fact of Christian baptism to
which Paul referred in the heart of his letter (3:26-28). We cannot and should
not try to duplicate Paul's sufferings, for they were unique to his own apostolic mission. But every believer who has been baptized "into the death of
Christ" has become identified with Jesus in the *koinonia* of his sufferings no
less than in the triumph of his resurrection. Baptism betokens a breach with

the world, a passage from the realm of Satan into the ownership of Christ. As D. Bonhoeffer expressed it:

> The baptized Christian has ceased to belong to the world and is no longer its slave. He belongs to Christ alone, and his relationship with the world is mediated through him. . . . The old man and his sin are judged and condemned, but out of this judgment a new man arises, who has died to the world and to sin. Thus this death is not the act of an angry Creator finally rejecting his creation and his wrath, but the gracious death which had been won for us by the death of Christ; the gracious assumption of the creature by his creator. It is death in the power and fellowship of the cross of Christ. He who becomes Christ's own possession must submit to his cross, and suffer and die with him. . . . It is a death full of grace. The cross to which we are called is a daily dying in the power of the death which Christ died once and for all. In this way baptism means sharing in the cross of Christ.[175]

5. Benediction (6:18)

[18]The grace of our Lord Jesus Christ be with your spirit, brothers. Amen.

6:18 Paul already had provided a "benediction of peace" in v. 16. Here he concluded his letter with a second benediction, this one a prayer for the grace of the Lord Jesus Christ to be with the Galatians, whom he again called his brothers. Paul began his letter with a customary salutation of grace (1:3), and he closed it with this final formula again, pointing to the central theme that had been his primary concern throughout the epistle. This is a fitting conclusion to such a tumultuous letter. It is as though Paul were saying to the Galatians: Dear brothers, in writing to you in this way I have put it all on the line. Now you know exactly the burden of my heart. I will end the letter as I began it, commending to you the awesome and marvelous grace of our Lord Jesus Christ. The only thing left for me to do is to pray from my heart that Christ will confirm my labors among you, restoring you to the truth of the gospel and granting you the gift of perseverance unto life eternal. So may it be. Amen!

---

[175] D. Bonhoeffer, *The Cost of Discipleship* (New York: Macmillan, 1968), 257-58.

Selected Subject Index

Person Index

Scripture Index

Selected Bibliography

Books

Arichea, D. C. and E. A. Nida. *A Translator's Handbook on Paul's Letter to the Galatians.* London: UBS, 1976.

Arnold, C. E. *Powers of Darkness: Principalities and Powers in Paul's Letters.* Downers Grove: InterVarsity, 1992.

Barclay, J. M. G. *Obeying the Truth: A Study of Paul's Ethics in Galatians.* Edinburgh: T & T Clark, 1988.

Barrett, C. K. *Freedom and Obligation.* Philadelphia: Westminster, 1985.

————. *Paul: An Introduction to His Thought.* Louisville: Westminster John Knox, 1994.

Beker, J. C. *Paul the Apostle.* Philadelphia: Fortress, 1980.

Betz, H. D. *Galatians.* Her. Philadelphia: Fortress, 1979.

Bornkamm, G. *Paul.* New York: Harper & Row, 1971.

Brown, J. *An Exposition of the Epistle to the Galatians.* Marshallton, Del.: Sovereign Grace, 1970.

Bruce, F. F. *The Epistle to the Galatians.* NIGTC. Grand Rapids: Eerdmans, 1982.

Burton, E. deW. *A Critical and Exegetical Commentary on the Epistle to the Galatians.* ICC. Edinburgh: T & T Clark, 1921.

————. *Spirit, Soul and Flesh.* Chicago: University of Chicago Press, 1918.

Calvin, J. *The Epistles of Paul the Apostle to the Galatians, Ephesians, Philippians, and Colossians.* Trans. T. H. L. Parker. CNTC. Vol. 11. Grand Rapids: Eerdmans, 1965.

Chantry, W. J. *God's Righteous Kingdom: The Law's Connection with the Gospel.* Edinburgh: Banner of Truth, 1980.

Cole, R. A. *The Epistle of Paul to the Galatians.* Grand Rapids: Eerdmans, 1965.

Cosgrove, C. H. *The Cross and the Spirit: A Study in the Argument and Theology of Galatians.* Macon, Ga.: Mercer University Press, 1989.

Cousar, C. B. *Galatians.* Interpretation. Atlanta: John Knox, 1982.

DeBoer, W. P. *The Imitation of Paul.* Kampen: Kok, 1962.

DeVries, C. E. "Paul's 'Cutting' Remarks about a Race: Galatians 5:1–12." In *Current Issues in Biblical and Patristic Interpretation.* Grand Rapids: Eerdmans, 1975.

Duncan, G. S. *The Epistle of Paul to the Galatians.* MNTC. London: Hodder & Stoughton, 1934.

Dunn, J. D. G. *The Epistle to the Galatians.* Peabody, Mass.: Hendrickson, 1993.

————. *The Theology of Paul the Apostle.* Grand Rapids: Eerdmans, 1998.

Ebeling, G. *The Truth of the Gospel: An Exposition of Galatians.* Philadelphia: Fortress, 1984.

Ellis, E. E. *Paul's Use of the Old Testament.* Edinburgh: Oliver & Boyd, 1957.

Fee, G. D. *God's Empowering Presence: The Holy Spirit in the Letters of Paul.* Peabody, Mass.: Hendrickson, 1994.

Fung, R. Y. *The Epistle to the Galatians.* NICNT. Grand Rapids: Eerdmans, 1988.

Guthrie, D. *Galatians.* NCB. Grand Rapids: Eerdmans, 1973.

Hansen, G. W. *Abraham in Galatians: Epistolary and Rhetorical Contexts.* Sheffield: JSOT, 1989.

————. *Galatians.* Downers Grove: InterVarsity, 1994.

Hawthorne, G. F. et al. *Dictionary of Paul and His Letters.* Downers Grove: Inter-Varsity, 1993.

Hays, R. B. *Echoes of Scriptures in the Letters of Paul.* New Haven: Yale University Press, 1989.

————. *The Faith of Jesus Christ: An Investigation of the Narrative Substructure of Galatians 3:1–4:11.* SBLDS 56. Chico, Cal.: Scholars Press, 1983.

Hemer, C. J. *The Book of Acts in the Setting of the Hellenistic History.* Tübingen: Mohr, 1989.

Hengel, M. *Crucifixion in the Ancient World and the Folly of the Message of the Cross.* London: SCM, 1977.

————. *The Pre-Christian Paul.* London: SCM, 1991.

Howard, G. *Paul: Crisis in Galatia.* Cambridge: Cambridge University Press, 1979.

Jewett, R. *Paul's Anthropological Terms: A Study of Their Use in Conflict Settings.* Leiden: Brill, 1971.

Kevan, E. F. *The Law of God and Christian Experience.* London: Pickering & Inglis, 1955.

————. *Moral Law.* Phillipsburg, N.J.: Presbyterian & Reformed, 1991.

Lightfoot, J. B. *Saint Paul's Epistle to the Galatians.* London: Macmillan, 1986.

Longenecker, R. *Galatians.* WBC. Dallas: Word, 1990.

————. *Paul: Apostle of Liberty.* New York: Harper & Row, 1964.

Lührmann, D. *Galatians.* Minneapolis: Fortress, 1992.

Lull, D. J. *The Spirit in Galatia: Paul's Interpretation of the Promise of Divine Power.* SBLDS 49. Chico, Cal.: Scholars Press, 1980.

Luther, M. *Luther's Works,* Vols. 26 and 27. St. Louis: Concordia, 1963–64.

Lyall, F. *Slaves, Citizens, Sons: Legal Metaphors in the Epistles.* Grand Rapids: Zondervan, 1984.

Machen, J. G. *Machen's Notes on Galatians.* Phillipsburg, N.J.: Presbyterian & Reformed, 1977.

McKnight, S. *Galatians.* Grand Rapids: Zondervan, 1995.

Martin, B. L. *Christ and the Law in Paul.* Leiden: Brill, 1989.

Matera, F. *Galatians.* Sacra Pagina. Collegeville: Liturgical, 1993.

Morris, L. *The Apostolic Preaching of the Cross.* Grand Rapids: Eerdmans, 1965.

————. *Galatians: Paul's Charter of Freedom.* Downers Grove: InterVarsity, 1996.

Munck, J. *Paul and the Salvation of Mankind.* Richmond: John Knox, 1959.

Murray, J. *Principles of Conduct.* Grand Rapids: Eerdmans, 1957.

Perkins, W. *A Commentary on Galatians.* New York: Pilgrim, 1989.

Polhill, J. *Paul and His Letters.* Nashville: Broadman & Holman, 1999.

Ramsey, W. M. *The Cities of St. Paul: Their Influence on His Life and Thought.* Grand Rapids: Baker, 1960.

————. *A Historical Commentary on Saint Paul's Commentary to the Galatians.* Grand Rapids: Baker, 1965.

————. *St. Paul the Traveller and Roman Citizen.* London: Hodder & Stoughton, 1897.

Richardson, P. *Israel and the Apostolic Church.* Cambridge: Cambridge University Press, 1969.

Sanders, E. P. *Paul and Palestinian Judaism.* Philadelphia: Fortress, 1977.

————. *Paul, the Law, and the Jewish People.* Philadelphia: Fortress, 1983.

Schlier, H. *Der Brief an der Galater.* KEK 7. 10th ed. Göttingen: Vandenhoeck & Ruprecht, 1949.

Schreiner, T. R. *Interpreting the Pauline Epistles.* Grand Rapids: Baker, 1990.

———. *The Law and Its Fulfillment.* Grand Rapids: Baker, 1993.

Seifrid, M. *Justification by Faith: The Origin and Development of a Central Pauline Theme.* Leiden: Brill, 1992.

Stendahl, K. *Paul among Jews and Gentiles.* Philadelphia: Fortress, 1976.

Stott, J. R. W. *The Cross of Christ.* Downers Grove: InterVarsity, 1986.

———. *Only One Way: The Message of Galatians.* Downers Grove: InterVarsity, 1968.

Strickland, W. G., ed. *The Law, the Gospel, and the Modern Christian: Five Views.* Grand Rapids: Zondervan, 1993.

Stuhlmacher, P. *Gerechtigkeit Gottes bei Paulus.* Göttingen: Vandenhoeck & Ruprecht, 1966.

Thielman, F. *From Plight to Solution.* Leiden: Brill, 1989.

———. *Paul and the Law: A Contextual Approach.* Downers Grove: InterVarsity, 1994.

Westerholm, *Israel's Law and the Church's Faith: Paul and His Recent Interpreters.* Grand Rapids: Eerdmans, 1988.

Williams, S. K. *Galatians.* Nashville: Abingdon, 1997.

Witherington, B. III. *Grace in Galatia: A Commentary on St. Paul's Letter to the Galatians.* Grand Rapids: Eerdmans, 1998.

Wright, N. T. *The Climax of the Covenant: Christ and the Law in Pauline Theology.* Minneapolis: Fortress, 1991.

Articles

Bammel, E. "Gottes *Diathēke* (Gal 3:15–17) und das jüdische Rechtsdenken." *NTS* 6 (1959–60): 313–19.

Banks, R. "The Eschatological Role of Law in Pre- and Post-Christian Jewish Thought." In *Reconciliation and Hope: New Testament Essays on Atonement and Eschatology.* Grand Rapids: Eerdmans, 1974.

Belleville, L. L. "'Under Law': Structural Analysis and Pauline Concept of Law in Galatians 3:21–4:11." *JSNT* 26 (1986): 53–78.

Bruce, F. F. "Abraham Had Two Sons': A Study in Pauline Hermeneutics." In *New Testament Studies: Essays in Honor of Ray Summers.* Waco: Baylor University Press, 1975.

———. "The Conference in Jerusalem—Galatians 2:1–10." In *God Who Is Rich in Mercy.* Homebush West, NSW: Anzea, 1986.

———. "The Curse of the Law." In *Paul and Paulinism: Essays in Honor of C. K. Barrett.* London: SPCK, 1982.

Cavallin, H. C. C. "'The Righteous Shall Live By Faith': A Decisive Argument for the Traditional Interpretation." *ST* 32 (1978): 33–43.

Cook, J. I. "The Concept of Adoption in the Theology of Paul." In *Saved by Hope: Essays in Honor of R. C. Oudersluys.* Grand Rapids: Zondervan, 1978.

Cosgrove, C. H. "The Law Has Given Sarah No Children (Gal. 4:21–30)." *NovT* 29 (1987): 219–35.

Cranfield, C. E. B. "St. Paul and the Law." *SJT* 17 (1964): 43–68.

Davies, W. D. "Paul and the People of Israel." *NTS* 24 (1977): 4–39.

Dunn, J. D. G. "The New Perspective on Paul." *BJRL* 65 (1983): 95–122.

———. "The Relationship Between Paul and Jerusalem According to Galatians 1 and 2." *NTS* 28 (1981–82): 461–78.

————. "Works of the Law and Curse of the Law." *NTS* 31 (1984–85): 523–42.

Dupont, J. "The Conversion of Paul and Its Influence on His Understanding of Salvation by Faith." In *Apostolic History and the Gospel: Biblical and Historical Essays Presented to F. F. Bruce on His Sixtieth Birthday.* "Paul and His Opponents: Trends in the Research." In *Christianity, Judaism, and Other Greco-Roman Cults.* Leiden: Brill, 1975.

Fuller, D. P. "Paul and 'The Works of the Law,'" *WTJ* 38 (1975–76): 28–42.

Hays, R. B. "Christology and Ethics in Galatians: The Law of Christ." *CBQ* 49 (1987): 268–90.

Hemer, C. J. "Acts and Galatians Reconsidered." *Themelios* 2 (1976–77): 81– 88.

Hester, J. D. "The Rhetorical Structure of Galatians 1:11–2:14." *JBL* 103 (1984): 223–33.

Jones, P. R. "Exegesis of Galatians 3 and 4." *RevExp* 69 (1972).

Kaiser, W. C. Jr. "Leviticus 18:5 and Paul: 'Do This and You Shall Live' (Eternally?)." *JETS* 14 (1971): 19–28.

Longenecker, R. N. "The Pedagogical Nature of the Law in Galatians 3:19– 4:7." *JETS* 25 (1982): 53–61.

Lull, D. J. "'The Law Was Our Pedagogue': A Study in Galatians 3:19–25." *JBL* 105 (1986): 481–98.

MacGorman, J. W. "Problem Passages in Galatians." *SWJT* 15 (1972): 35–51.

Martyn, J. L. "Apocalyptic Antinomies in Paul's Letter to the Galatians." *NTS* 31 (1985).

————. "A Law-Observant Mission: The Background of Galatians." *MQR* 22 (1983): 221–36.

Minear, P. S. "The Crucified World: The Enigma of Galatians 6:14." In *Theologia Crucis—Signum Crucis.* Tübingen: Mohr, 1979.

Moo, D. J. "'Law,' 'Works of the Law,' and Legalism in Paul." *WTJ* 45 (1983): 73–100.

Polhill, J. "Galatia Revisited: The Life-setting of the Epistle." *RevExp* 69 (1972).

Reicke, B. "The Law and the World according to Paul: some Thoughts Concerning Gal 4:1–11." *JBL* 70 (1951): 259–76.

Schreiner, T. R. "Is Perfect Obedience to the Law Possible? A Re-examination of Galatians 3:10." *JETS* 27 (1984): 151–60.

————. "Paul and Perfect Obedience to the Law: An Evaluation of the View of E. P. Sanders." *WTJ* 47 (1985): 245–78.

Warfield, B. B. "The New Testament Terminology of 'Redemption.'" In *Biblical Doctrines.* New York: Oxford University Press, 1929, 327–72.

Westerholm, S. "Letter and Spirit: The Foundation of Pauline Ethics." *NTS* 30 (1984): 229–48.

Wilcox, M. "The Promise of the 'Seed' in the New Testament and the Targumim." *JSNT* 5 (1979): 2–20.

Williams, S. K. "The Hearing of Faith: ΑΚΟΗ ΠΙΣΤΕΩΣ." *NTS* 35 (1989): 82– 93.

————. "Justification and the Spirit in Galatians." *JSNT* 29 (1987): 91–100.

Wright, N. T. "Justification: The Biblical Basis and Its Relevance for Contemporary Evangelicalism." In *The Great Acquittal: Justification by Faith and Current Christian Thought.* London: Collins.

Young, N. H. "PAIDAGOGOS: The Social Setting of a Pauline Metaphor." *NovT* 29 (1987): 150–76.

————. "Who's Cursed—and Why? (Galatians 3:10–14)." *JBL* 117 (1998): 79–92.